HISTORY OF CANADIAN AIRPORTS—SECOND EDITION

LUGUS PUBLICATIONS

HISTORY OF CANADIAN AIRPORTS

by

T.M. McGrath

LUGUS

Published by Lugus Publications
in co-ooperation with Transport Canada
and the Canadian Government Publishing Centre,
Supply and Services Canada.

Catalogue No. T52-64/1990-1E

Canadian Cataloguing in Publication Data

McGrath, T. M.
    History of Canadian Airports

Includes bibliographical references and index.

ISBN: 0-921633-11-4

1. Airports - Canada - History.   I. Title.

TL726.4.C2M3   1991   387.7'36'0971   C91-095584-0

© Minister of Supply and Services, Canada 1992
Translated into French by: Secretary of State Canada.

CONTENTS

FOREWORD

The twentieth century has witnessed the birth and maturity of a major world wide industry—air transportation. This industry and its components—the air navigation system, aircraft and airports—have had and will continue to have significant impacts on the economic, social and cultural fabric of Canada and its neighbours in our global community.

This second edition of the History of Canadian Airports has been updated from its April 1984 edition and is presented in two distinct parts. The first part summarizes the growth and development of the Canadian airport system from its humble beginnings to its present stage as the country's dominant passenger transportation mode. The second part, arranged alphabetically, contains individual histories of many of Canada's airports.

This history documents the development of the airports industry and its achievements over time and is dedicated to the many men and women who have given of themselves in service to the Canadian public and travelling community.

The airport industry has a rich heritage and a future filled with challenges and opportunities to continue our tradition of service to the travelling public. This history endeavours to capture and record the growth and development. I encourage both the professional historian and others to assist us in the maintenance and updating of information contained herein. Documentation should be sent to Transport Canada—Airports Group—Ottawa— K1A 0N8.

Victor Barbeau
Assistant Deputy Minister
Airports Group
Transport Canada

PREFACE

When I retired from the Airports and Construction Directorate of Transport Canada in 1978, the Air Administration invited me to undertake the task of writing a history of Canadian airports. This was something that had never been done, despite the fact that aviation in Canada was then over seventy years old. I feel honoured to have been entrusted with this important task.

The purpose of the project was to record the history of Canada's airports and to try to recapture some of the background of airport development from the end of the First World War, which was also the real beginning of civil aviation in this country. It was never intended that this work would add much original history to the record. The aim, rather, was to provide a basic source book for Transport Canada that would also serve as a research tool for the aviation community and others interested in particular airports. Although a considerable body of information existed, it was scattered, fragmented, and not readily available. Much airport history had been lost already, but it was hoped that in the preparation of the book some of it would be rediscovered. It was hoped too that the book would provide an up-to-date record of existing airports to which airport managers and others could add in future.

I have been associated with aviation for about forty-five years. Much of this time was spent in airport operation and administration, both on-site and in the headquarters of Transport Canada. Because of this, I was able to bring to the task a background of personal knowledge that was of value in assessing aviation archives and other material. In addition, I had the assistance of my own notes and diaries extending back for many years. To my surprise, some of this material I found to be of significant historical value, and I am glad to be able to share it with the readers of this book.

As I began the project, I soon found the scope of the task to be enormous; it became necessary to reduce it to manageable proportions. I therefore decided to deal with the subject in two parts. The first part begins with the first airplane flight in Canada (McCurdy in 1909) and traces the growth of the airport, from the construction of the first one in 1915 to the RFC aerodromes of 1917 to 1919 and the earlier flying fields of 1910 to 1920. I follow the development of government air policy and the aerodromes, airharbours, and airports through the years 1920 to 1930. Then comes the big leap forward with the construction of the Trans-Canada Airway in the 1930s and the Trans-Atlantic Air Route between 1937 and 1945. Next come the airports of the war years, 1940 to 1946, and then the post-war developments. Having thus dealt with the evolution of the airport, I go on to present the histories of 143 airports in Part II. Admittedly, these are not all dealt with in the same depth. There is some deliberate repetition of material in the individual histories. Since it was felt that few would read all the histories but would select only those of particular interest to themselves, it was decided to make each history complete in itself. I decided to limit the discussion to land airports because the number of seaplane bases and anchorages was endless, but I made an exception in the case of the flying boat bases connected with the establishment of the Trans-Atlantic Air Service in 1937 because of the significance of that enterprise to Canada. I also decided to deal only with civil airports, except where a military airport had a particular historical significance in civil aviation.

During my research, I discovered much interesting background material that had never been published. While some of it touches on airports, some goes beyond and deals with the development of civil aviation. Even if some of the material is slightly outside my terms of reference, I nevertheless feel that it is important enough to publish here in appendix form. The selection of the material has obviously been a random one.

In preparing this book, I have done most of the research myself using material available from the Directorate of History, Department of National Defence (principally minutes of the Air Board and Reports on Civil Aviation); the Public Archives of Canada; Transport Canada (files and documents); the J.A. Wilson Papers; the Archives of Newfoundland and Labrador; Memorial University of Newfoundland; the "Airport Notes" of R.L. Clarke; various histories of Canadian aviation; other aviation literature; and contributions from airport managers. All of these sources are identified and acknowledged in the book.

In conclusion, I wish to acknowledge with thanks the valuable assistance I have received from the personnel of the Public Archives of Canada (Document and Photography departments), the Department of National Defence (Directorate of History and Photo Centre), the Transport Canada Library, the National Aviation Museum, the Royal Canadian Flying Club Association, Air Canada (Historical Services), Pan American World Airways (Research and History Department), the Archives of Newfoundland and Labrador, and the Directorate of Airports and Construction Services of Transport Canada, especially the word processing and administration branch staffs. I would also like to thank the airport managers and regional managers of airports, and my wife, for her assistance in editing and proofreading the text through its many drafts.

T.M. McGrath
Ottawa

February 9, 1983

PREFACE TO THE SECOND EDITION

The first edition of the History of Canadian Airports was printed in limited numbers only and treated as a Transport Canada document for internal use. Some copies were given out on request to members of the aviation community with a special interest in airport history. This outside interest indicated the book had a potentially wider audience than anticipated and so, in late 1988, it was decided to update and publish it as a second edition, to be made available for sale to the public.

I agreed to undertake the task. This has been done, using material received from regional offices of the Airports Group of Transport Canada. I have taken the opportunity to expand some of the information on early airports in Part I and to correct errors discovered in the text. Additional photographs have also been included.

During the project I received, and gratefully acknowledge, the continued co-operation and assistance of the sources mentioned in the first preface. I wish to thank K.M. Molson, well-known aviation historian, for his help in recommending new sources for my research. I also thank Mr. Molson, Fred Hotson, and Ray Crone for the use of photographs from their private collections.

I owe special thanks to members of the Airports Group at Transport Canada headquarters in Ottawa for their unfailing support and assistance, and, in particular: Paul White, the project manager, for facilitating my task; Tim McCarthy and Walt King of the Graphic Services and Photographic Reproduction section, for professional services rendered for both the first and second editions; and Murray McDougall, for transcribing my illegible writing into a very acceptable text.

I want to thank Maureen van Dreumel, the initial project co-ordinator, for her invaluable assistance in providing liaison assistance at Transport Canada headquarters in Ottawa, and I am particularly grateful to her for the outstanding job she did in editing the text.

I also want to thank the second project co-ordinator, Donna MacKinnon, for the many tasks she performed in assembling the text and photographs of the final manuscript, and for acting as liaison with Supply and Services Canada and the publisher, Lugus Productions Limited.

Finally, I must thank all of those who provided site information and answers to my endless questions and to the Airports Group Community Relations Officers who co-ordinated the updating of the first edition.

T.M. McGrath
Ottawa

CHAPTER 1

First Airplane Flight in Canada: 1909

Although this book is about airports and their development, it begins with mention of the first flight of a "flying machine" in Canada.

On February 23, 1909, Canadian J.A.D. McCurdy made this historic first flight at Bras d'Or Lake, Baddeck Bay, Nova Scotia.[1] He took off and landed on the ice and flew a distance of a half mile [almost one kilometre]. The aircraft, named Silver Dart, was a pusher biplane equipped with wheels. It had been designed and built by McCurdy at Hammondsport, New York, under the auspices of Dr. Alexander Graham Bell's Aerial Experiment Association.

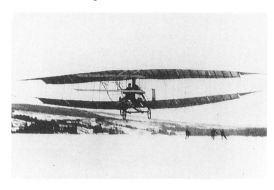

1. McCurdy's Silver Dart Drome No. 4
Braddock Bay, Nova Scotia, February 24, 1909.

Bell, the inventor of the telephone, had been interested in the possibilities of flight for some time and conducted experiments with kites near Baddeck. In 1907, he formed the Aerial Experiment Association in Baddeck for the purpose of constructing "a practical aerodrome or flying machine driven through the air by its own power and carrying a man."[2] The other members of the

2. McCurdy and the Silver Dart, Baddeck Bay, Nova Scotia. March 22, 1909.

association were Glen Curtiss, an American well-known as a designer of light and efficient internal combustion engines; Lieutenant Thomas Selfridge, on leave from the United States Army; and two Canadians, J.A.D. McCurdy (whose home was in Baddeck) and F.W. (Casey) Baldwin, both graduates of the University of Toronto's School of Practical Science. The group worked at Baddeck and in Hammondsport, New York, where Curtiss had a machine shop.

3. Silver Dart being towed across ice.
December 9, 1908.

The association developed, designed, and built a number of aircraft during its two years of existence—the Silver Dart being the most successful. Two hundred flights were made from the ice at Bras d'Or Lake during operations of the Aerial Experiment Association.

Incidentally, Baldwin became the first British subject to fly a heavier-than-air machine.[3] He made that flight in the Red Wing on March 19, 1908, at Lake Keuka, near Hammondsport, New York. McCurdy, the first Canadian to pilot a flying machine in Canada, was also the first British subject to fly a heavier-than-air machine in the British Empire.[4]

4. The Aerial Experiment Association of Baddeck, 1909.

As the base for Bell's Aerial Experiment Association and the site of the first airplane flight in Canada, Bras d'Or Lake has some claim to being Canada's first airfield. That title, however, has been given to Long Branch, near Toronto, and is dealt with in Chapter 2.

It is interesting to note that in 1909 "aerodrome" meant a "flying machine." *Webster's Practical Dictionary* defines aerodrome as "a name proposed by Langley for a flying machine and used for his first model." Samuel Langley of the Smithsonian Institution, and a good friend of Bell, had been experimenting with gliders and flying machines for some time before the Wright brothers began their work. K.M. Molson and H.A. Taylor also discuss the word "aerodrome" in Canadian Aircraft Since 1909: "aerodrome was the term adopted for his aircraft by Dr. Alexander Graham Bell from Samuel P. Langley in the belief that it meant the complete aircraft while aeroplane meant only the wing."[5]

Footnotes to Chapter 1

[1] F.H. Ellis, *Canada's Flying Heritage* (Toronto: University of Toronto Press, 1961), p.9.
[2] J.A. Wilson, *Development of Aviation in Canada 1879-1948* (Ottawa: King's Printer), p.11.
[3] Ellis, p.5.
[4] Ellis p.9.
[5] K.M. Molson and H.A. Taylor, *Canada's Aircraft Since 1909* (Stittsville: Canada's Wings Ltd., 1982), p.22.

CHAPTER 2

First Airfield: 1915

Long Branch, Toronto, was the first airfield in Canada,[1] and the first flight took place there on May 20, 1915. It had three hangars and was operated by the Curtiss Flying School, part of Curtiss Aeroplanes and Motors Ltd., an offshoot of the Curtiss Company in Hammondsport, New York. Long Branch was also the site of Canada's first flying school; training began there on June 22, 1915, using Curtiss JN-3 biplanes.

In the spring of 1915, the Curtiss Company opened a branch factory on Strachan Avenue, Toronto, to manufacture the JN-3 for the British Admiralty. The factory and the school were managed by McCurdy.

Prior to 1915, Canadians wishing to join the Royal Flying Corps (RFC) or Royal Naval Air Service (RNAS) had to learn to fly at their own expense before they could apply. This was especially difficult and costly because Canada had no flying schools of its own. Hence, the Curtiss Company decided to establish one in Toronto to fill the need. The school also operated flying boats at Hanlan's Point, on one of the islands in Toronto Harbour, and close to the present Toronto Island Airport. This was the first

seaplane base in Canada, and two hangars were located there[2]. Pupils took their initial training on flying boats and then graduated to landplanes at Long Branch before going solo. In 1916, fly-

5. View of hangar and aeroplanes at Long Branch, Toronto, 1915.

ing boat training ceased; and Long Branch closed in December 1916. In 1917, it was taken over for a short time by the Royal Flying Corps Brigade from England, which set up flying schools at several places in the area. But flying training at Long Branch ended in July 1917 when Camp Borden and other more suitable airfields were ready. After that, Long Branch was used for cadet training and as a ground school.

The airfield, originally a rifle range, located on Lakeshore Road on the fringes of metropolitan

6. The first ten students at Long Branch, Toronto, Ontario. June 28, 1915.

Toronto is now the site of the Ontario Hydro Steam Generating Plant. In September 1969 an historic plaque was unveiled, marking the site as Canada's first aerodrome.

Footnotes to Chapter 2

[1] F.H. Ellis, *Canada's Flying Heritage* (Toronto: University of Toronto Press, 1961), pp.109-113; see also Ronald Dodds, "Long Branch—Canada's first flying school," *Canadian Geographical Journal*, (April, 1974), pp.22-29.
[2] Ellis, p.109.

CHAPTER 3

First Air Stations: 1918

In 1918, at the request of the British Admiralty, the Canadian government agreed to establish two air stations in Nova Scotia—one at Halifax (Dartmouth-Baker's Point) and the other at Sydney (Kelly Beach)—for anti-submarine operations. These were the first air stations in Canada.[1]

On June 5, 1918, the government approved the building of the two stations, and the Department of Marine Service began to plan the organization

7. Seaplane base at Baker's Point, Dartmouth, Nova Scotia, 1921.

of an Air Arm. The new service was officially created by Order in Council PC 2154 of September 5, 1918, which stipulated that the proposed organization be regarded as temporary for the purpose of meeting the needs of the war and that it be called the Royal Canadian Naval Air Service (RCNAS). It was to have a strength of eighty aircraft cadets, twelve airship cadets, and up to 1000 ratings.[2] The RCNAS thus became the first Canadian military air unit. The thousands of Canadians already serving in the air were members of the Royal Flying Corps or the Royal Naval Air Service and were therefore in British, rather than Canadian service. It was not until November 1918, that two squadrons of Canadians, already serving in the Royal Air Force, were assigned to the Canadian Air Force (CAF) while officially remaining under the RAF. These squadrons were formed "for the purpose of the present war," and the Air Ministry bore the cost of the Canadian organization until June 1919. Soon after, the CAF ceased to exist.[3]

RCNAS recruits were sent to Britain and the United States for training in airship and airplane operations. Until the Canadian cadets could be trained, the U.S. Naval Air Force equipped and operated the two air stations beginning in August 1918. When the war ended in November 1918, eighty-two RCNAS personnel were still in training. The RCNAS was soon disbanded and the stations closed. The U.S. donated all flying material to Canada, including a number of Curtiss HS-2L flying boats and some kite balloons. These flying boats later played an important role in Canadian aviation for a number of years.

The Dartmouth station was used to store the surplus war equipment and, in 1920, it served the Operations Branch of the Air Board as a base for the repair and maintenance of flying boats. The Halifax Aero Club used the hangar for its two Moth seaplanes from 1928 to 1930. The base

8. Air Board Station Personnnel, Dartmouth, Nova Scotia, 1920.

was used again by RCAF Stranraer flying boats on coastal patrol in 1939 and is now part of the larger Shearwater establishment.

Footnotes to Chapter 3
[1] The term "air station" was a civil appellation that continued in use until 1932 when it was replaced by "RCAF station."
[2] S.F. Wise, *Canadian Airmen in the First World War* (Toronto: University of Toronto Press, 1980), pp.605, 607.
[3] Wise, pp.600, 602, 610, 619.

CHAPTER 4

Royal Flying Corps Aerodromes, 1917- 1918.

In 1917, five aerodromes were constructed in Ontario for the Royal Flying Corps (RFC) pilot training scheme. Apart from the one built by Curtiss Aeroplanes and Motors Ltd. at Long Branch in 1915, these were the first aerodromes to be built in Canada. This activity marked the beginning of serious flying in Canada, although it was for military purposes.

The established success of Canadian pilots overseas and the presence in Canada of an almost untapped reservoir of future strength drew the attention of the British War Office to Canada.[1] In 1916, with the consent and co-operation of Canada, it was decided that a brigade of the RFC would be established in Canada to recruit and train pilots. The Imperial Munitions Board was responsible for the erection of buildings and the preparation of aerodromes and supplies. Airplanes were purchased from the Curtiss Company in the United States and in Canada. The board eventually took over the Curtiss Company in Canada and established Canadian Aeroplanes Ltd.

The RFC in Canada was an Imperial unit, paid for by the Imperial Treasury, and wholly independent of Canadian military command. There was no military service act in Canada at the time (January 1917) and a special Order in Council was passed to authorize the activities of the RFC in Canada. The Imperial Munitions Board was granted an initial credit of £4 million by the British government.

The advance group of the RFC arrived in Toronto in January 1917, established headquarters there, and immediately dispatched recruiting officers across Canada and to major cities in the United States.[2] Airfield construction began on January 27 at Borden under a contract let and supervised by the Imperial Munitions Board. After autumn 1917, all work was done by the construction section of the board's aviation department, and by the end of the war, six aerodromes and four hundred buildings had been constructed. The first commanding officer of the RFC in Canada was Lieutenant Colonel C.G. Hoare, who remained for the duration of the war and rose to the rank of brigadier general.

The following aerodromes were constructed for the RFC:

Long Branch

Long Branch was built in 1915 by Curtiss

Aeroplanes and Motors Ltd. on Department of Militia and Defence land on Lakeshore Road, Toronto. It was taken over by the RFC in 1917, which began its flying activities there in early April. It thus became the first flying unit of the RFC in Canada. Long Branch, only one hundred acres [forty-one hectares] in area, soon proved to be too small and muddy for the amount of flying activity, and the school was moved to Armour Heights, one of the new aerodromes. After that, Long Branch was used for cadet training and as a ground school.

Armour Heights

Located eight kilometres north of Toronto, Armour Heights opened in July 1917 and replaced Long Branch for flying training. It was about 180 acres [seventy-three hectares] in area and situated north of Wilson Avenue. Colonel F.R. Robins loaned the property to the training establishment. The aerodrome continued in operation after the war and was granted a Public Customs airharbour licence in 1920. The site is now covered by Interchange 52 of Highway 401.[3]

Camp Borden

Camp Borden was opened in 1916 as an infantry training camp for the Canadian Expeditionary

9. Royal Flying Corps Canada, hangars and aerodrome, Camp Borden, Ontario, 1917.

Force. In 1917, the Department of Militia and Defence placed one thousand acres [405 hectares] at the disposal of the RFC. Work began on the aerodrome at the end of January 1917, and flying began in April. Borden eventually had eighteen hangars, each capable of storing ten aircraft. It was thought to be the finest flying camp in North America.

Shortly after Armistice Day on November 11, 1918, Royal Air Force training operations ceased and its establishments were dismantled. The RFC and RNAS became the Royal Air Force on April 1, 1918. Camp Borden reverted to Canada and was placed on a caretaker basis. It became a storage facility for aircraft and equipment donated to Canada by Great Britain in June 1919. Borden was reactivated in 1920 and became the school of aviation of the new Canadian Air Force. (Its later history is dealt with in Chapter 7.)

Leaside

10. Royal Flying Corps Canada, Camp Leaside, Ontario, 1917. Curtiss JN-4S fitted with skis.

Leaside, eight kilometres northeast of Toronto, was a site of 222 acres [ninety hectares]. It was a good airfield and had nine hangars housing three squadrons, each with eighteen aircraft. All work, including the construction of buildings, was completed in seven weeks. When the United States entered the war on April 6, 1917, it sent

men to Canada for training with the Royal Flying Corps. Some of these trainees were assigned to Leaside.

During the winter of 1917-18, flying training at Camp Borden and Mohawk was suspended and the personnel were sent to Texas to continue operations, returning to Canada in the spring of 1918. At Leaside, experiments were carried out in 1917-18 to see if winter flying was feasible. Skis were designed and fitted to many aircraft, and, while cold weather operations were difficult for everybody, flying training was continued, and the personnel "established themselves as pioneers of cold weather flying in Canada".[4]

Leaside also earned a place in Canadian aviation history as the termination point of the first official air-mail flight.[5] On June 24, 1918, Captain Brian Peck of the RAF training school at Leaside flew a bag of mail from Montréal (Bois Franc Polo Grounds) to Toronto in a JN-4 biplane and landed at Leaside after refuelling at Kingston. Peck had flown to Montréal to see his family and to do some demonstration and recruiting flights. Officials of the Montréal branch of the Aerial League of the British Empire had the idea of carrying a bag of mail and made arrangements with Post Office officials and the RAF. Other RAF officers made further air-mail flights between Leaside and Ottawa on August 15, 17, 26 and September 4, 1918.

11. Royal Flying Corps Canada, School of Aerial Gunnery, Beamsville, Ontario, 1918.

Leaside was used as an airport after the war until its closure in 1931.

Beamsville

Beamsville, one and a half kilometres east of the village of that name, just off Highway 8 (which runs from Hamilton to Niagara Falls), was first the RFC School of Aerial Training and later the School of Aerial Fighting. The airfield consisted of 282 acres [114 hectares] and had twelve hangars. The first flight took place on March 30, 1918. The camp comprised four squadrons, fifty-four aircraft, and a population of approximately 1,000. It closed down in March 1919, but one hangar still stands and is used to house road maintenance equipment.[6]

"[During] the late 1920s and 1930s although Beamsville was not an official airport, private planes used this strip."[7] The old site was surveyed for the British Commonwealth Air Training Plan in 1942 as a possible satellite for St. Catharines Elementary Flying Training School, but it was not used.

Desoronto

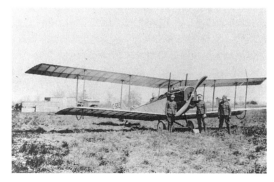

12. Curtiss JN-4A at Camp Rathbun, Desoronto, Ontario, 1917.

Desoronto, 209 kilometres east of Toronto, was also chosen as a site for an RFC aerodrome. Since it was impossible to obtain a large enough piece of land at Desoronto, the camp was split between two sites: the resulting aerodromes were named Mohawk and Rathbun. Wing headquarters was located in Desoronto.

Rathbun

Rathbun, a site of 315 acres [128 hectares], located half a kilometre northeast of Desoronto, was leased from the Rathbun family. The aerodrome housed two squadrons and thirty-six airplanes. Part of one hangar still remains: it has been reduced in size and converted into a residence.

Mohawk

Mohawk aerodrome was three kilometres southwest of Desoronto. It was an unusually level site with fairly open country around it, was approximately 350 acres [142 hectares] in area and had twelve "flight sheds." Mohawk had three squadrons and fifty-four airplanes, and was occupied in the early spring of 1917. One of the instructors in the summer of 1918 was Captain Robert Dodds,[8] who became director of civil aviation in the Department of Transport and retired in 1958.

After the First World War, the Mohawk aerodrome was used as a public airharbour (the term for an airport at that time) and was licensed as such under the name of Desoronto in 1922. It had Customs service. (See Chapter 7.)

Mohawk was rebuilt, enlarged to 628 acres [254 hectares], and used as an aerodrome again in the Second World War when it became an Instrument Flying School in the British Commonwealth Air Training Plan. It served as No. 1 Relief Aerodrome for the Central Flying School

13. 82 Squadron Royal Flying Corps at Camp Mohawk, Ontario, 1918.

at Trenton. The site was used in 1952 and 1953 by the RCAF for a drone target evaluation program, testing and flying the OQ 19-A drone aircraft. Mohawk (or Desoronto) was used as a civil aerodrome until the 1960s. The Prince Edward Flying Club carried out some of its flying operations there. A few of the hangars still remain.[9]

Footnotes to Chapter 4

[1] Lieutenant Alan Sullivan, *Aviation in Canada 1917-18* (Toronto: Rous and Mann Ltd., 1919), p. 15ff.

[2] F.H. Ellis, *Canada's Flying Heritage* (Toronto: University of Toronto Press, 1961, p. 120ff.

[3] C.D. Long, "Toronto Airports, Before Malton," *CAHS Journal* (Winter 1965), p. 94.

[4] R.V. Dodds, "Canada's First Air Training Plan," *The Roundel* Vol.15, No.1, p. 19.

[5] Ellis, p. 137ff.

[6] Hugh Halliday, "Beamsville Story," *CAHS Journal* (Fall 1969), p. 75.

[7] W.E. Chajkowsky, *Royal Flying Corps*, (Cheltenham: the Boston Mills Press, 1979), p. 117.

[8] S.F. Wise, *Canadian Airmen and the First World War* (Toronto: University of Toronto Press, 1980), unpaged photograph.

[9] Chajkowsky, pp. 33, 34. More information on Mohawk and Desoronto was provided by Murray Clapp of Milford, Ont., and J. Allan Smith of Trenton, Ont.

CHAPTER 5

Early Flying Fields: 1910 to 1920

A. The Pioneers

A "flying field" is defined in this context as a field or area, such as a frozen lake, used for early experimental, exhibition, or passenger flying during the ten years following McCurdy's first flight at Baddeck in 1909. To mention all the fields used during these early days is impossible, but an attempt has been made here to cover the more significant ones. Lack of historical data has been a problem in the research for this and other histories. As F.H. Ellis comments in Canada's Flying Heritage: "One reason for the dearth of historical data on the pioneer period of Canadian Aviation is that until 1915 there were no flying fields in the country where organizations could be formed whose records would furnish the historical data".[1]

Flying fields fall into four main groups: cow pastures (often with cows!), race tracks, polo parks, and exhibition grounds. Much of the information that follows has been gleaned from Ellis' Canada's Flying Heritage and other identified sources.

Bras d'Or Lake

The first flying field was Bras d'Or Lake, Baddeck. Here, J.A.D. McCurdy, of Alexander Graham Bell's Aerial Experiment Association, made the first flight of an airplane in Canada on February 23, 1909, from the frozen surface of the lake. Two hundred flights were made from the ice of Bras d'Or Lake during the operation of Bell's Association.

On March 31, 1909, after the Aerial Experiment Association dissolved, McCurdy and Baldwin formed a company to manufacture airplanes: the Canadian Aerodrome Company of Baddeck. This was the first airplane manufacturing organization in Canada. The men built three airplanes (calling them aerodromes) and flew them from a field at Baddeck, thus making that site an historic airfield.[2]

14. Baddeck I
at Baddeck, Nova Scotia, 1909.

Petawawa

Another field of some historic significance, if only for its negative impact on aviation, was Petawawa military camp, located northwest of Ottawa. Here, McCurdy and Baldwin hoped to prove the military value of the airplane to officials of the Department of Militia and Defence. Successful flights were made in the Silver Dart on August 2, 1909, a week after Bleriot flew across the English Channel. On the fifth flight of

15. Baddeck I aircraft of the Canadian Aerodrome Company during trials at Petawawa, Ontario, 1909.

the day, the airplane was wrecked when landing on the rough ground. McCurdy and Baldwin tried again on August 12 and 13 in their second aircraft, Baddeck I, and after several successful flights, this machine, too, was wrecked during a landing, and the trials ceased. These events are commemorated by an historic plaque on the site.

Writing of this event thirty years later, J.A. Wilson, Director of Air Services, Department of Transport, commented:

Unfortunately the trials were carried out under the most adverse conditions. These aircraft which had flown brilliantly in 200 flights from the smooth ice of Baddeck Bay were expected to perform equally well on the rough moorlands of Petawawa Camp without any preparation in the way of a made field. So, though flights were made, all ended with damaged undercarriages. The Colonel Blimps of these days shrugged their shoulders and said "I told you so" and resumed their customary somnolence refusing to be disturbed by any newfangled notions. Had a fair trial been given there is little doubt that it would have resulted in the formation of a small section of the Canadian Army, manned by enthusiastic volunteers, to carry on the development under Government auspices and a certain amount of financial support.[3]

McCurdy tried again to get the government interested. In August 1914, he had an interview with the minister of Militia and National Defence, General Sam Hughes. McCurdy wanted to start a Canadian air service, but Hughes was adamant. He spoke for his age when he crushed McCurdy with the retort, "The aeroplane is an invention of the devil and will never play any part in such a serious business as the defence of a nation, my boy."[4]

An aerodrome was built at Petawawa Camp in 1936 and named the Silver Dart Aerodrome.

Lakeside

Lakeside, sixteen kilometres west of Montréal, between Valois and Pointe Claire, was the scene of the great Montréal Air Meet of June/July 1910.[5] The field was made up of five adjoining farms with fences removed, ditches filled, and bumps levelled. The site is notable for the amount of work done to improve the field in contrast to the ususal "use as is" philosophy. The meet lasted eight days and was described as the largest held in North America up to that time. On one day, twenty thousand people attended. A large number of airplanes from the United States and Europe took part, including Wright biplanes and Bleriot monoplanes. As many as three airplanes were in the air at one time! Two airships also took part in the meet. The most famous participant in the flying events was the well-known French airman, Count de Lesseps, the second man to fly the English channel. During the meet, on July 2, 1910, de Lesseps flew over the city of Montréal, a flight claimed to be the first over any Canadian city.[6] McCurdy also took part in the meet and flew Baddeck I.[7]

Tretheway Farm—de Lesseps Field

Tretheway Farm, at Weston (near Toronto), was the scene of a similar air meet the following week (July 9 to 15), with many of the same aircraft and airmen participating, including de Lesseps. This field was later named after de Lesseps. The site of 110 acres [forty-five hectares] was in Mount Dennis, northeast of Jane Street and Tretheway Drive.[8] It was used by De Havilland in 1928 and Canadian Airways in 1929. C.D. Long notes that "it was later used by the RCAF and closed to flying in 1940. One of the hangars owned by Aircraft Ltd. still remained in 1965 at 708 Tretheway Drive." In the Table of Licensed Airports, 1929 (Appendix 20), it is shown under the ownership of "Toronto Airport Ltd., Weston, Ont".

Dean's Farm

Dean's Farm, near Mount Tolmie, Victoria, was the scene of a flight of two hundred feet [sixty-one metres] made by W.W. Gibson on September 8, 1910. According to Ellis, this was the "first free flight to be made by a built in Canada airplane."[9] The engine, also built by Gibson, is credited by Ellis as being "the first successful aero engine fabricated in Canada."[10] It is now on display in the National Aviation Museum in Ottawa. The meadow later became part of the Lansdowne Aerodrome.

Minoru Park Race Track

Minoru Park Race Track, at Lulu Island near Vancouver, was the site of the first airplane flight in Western Canada when, on March 25, 1910, Charles Hamilton, an American, landed in his Curtiss biplane. He remained several days doing exhibition flights.

In April 1911, William Templeton and his cousin William McMullen test-hopped their home-built biplane. Templeton later became the first manager of the Vancouver Municipal Airport.

In 1912, Minoru Park was again used as a flying field when William M. Stark flew his Curtiss biplane on exhibition flights. He also carried passengers.

On December 15, 1915, the Aero Club of B.C. was formed with William Stark as instructor, to train pilots for the RFC and RNAS.[11] Two pilots graduated in November 1915. It was the first flying club in Canada, and, for a short time, flights were made from a site near the Minoru Park race track. The operation moved to a farm at Pitt Meadows in 1916. The Department of Transport built an airport in this area in 1963, and the club moved there once more, this time from the Vancouver International Airport.

On August 7, 1919, Captain Ernst Hoy took off from Minoru Park in his Curtiss JN-4 on the first flight over and through the Rockies, landing at Vernon, Grand Forks, Cranbrook, Lethbridge, and finally Calgary (Bowness Park).

Cartierville (Montréal)

Percy Hall Reid of Montréal began making aircraft in 1909 and learned to fly in New York in 1912. He used the polo grounds at Cartierville, the site of the present Cartierville Airport, for his experiments. This makes the Cartierville Airport the oldest continuously used airfield in Canada.[12] (See also Part II and Appendix 4)

Slattery's Field

On October 8, 1913, an American named William C. Robinson flew a Lillie biplane from Snowdon Junction, Montréal, to Slattery's Field, Ottawa, with four stops en route (three scheduled and one unscheduled). He carried copies of the *Daily Mail* for delivery to Prime Minister Borden, and Mayor Ellis. He was supposed to

16. First Airplane flight in Ottawa, September 11, 1911.

land at Lansdowne Park football field but found it swarming with people who had come to see him, so he landed at nearby Slattery's Field where the mayor and the crowd rushed over to meet him. This flight was of much historical importance in that it was the first between two cities in Canada. The same field was used by Len Hammond who, flying a biplane, performed before crowds at the Central Canada Exhibition at nearby Lansdowne Park on September 11 and 14, 1911. The site is marked by a bronze plaque erected by the Canadian Aviation Historical Society at 35 Riverdale Avenue, Ottawa:

In this area, once a cow pasture, the first aeroplane flights occurred in the Ottawa Region. Between September 11 and 14, 1911, Len Hammond flying a biplane performed before crowds attending the Central Canada Exhibition. On October 8, 1913, William C. Robinson landed at Slattery's Field after flying from Montréal, the first flight between two Canadian cities. Both pilots had to contend with cows and horses, which shared this crude airfield.

The original field was bounded by Clegg Street on the North, Main Street on the East, Echo Drive on the West, and Riverdale Avenue and Mount Pleasant Drive on the South.[13]

34. Curtiss Flying Boat, Hanlan's Point, Toronto, 1915.

Bowness and Shouldice Parks

During 1914 and 1915, F.H. Ellis, the aviation historian, and Tom Blakely flew their West Wind airplane, first at Bowness and later at Shouldice, near Calgary. The airplane was a Curtiss biplane that they had rebuilt themselves after it crashed some time earlier at Moose Jaw; it was flown previously by an American barnstormer.

Bowness Park was used by Captain Ernest Hoy in August 1919 on the first flight over the Rockies, and by the Canadian Air Force trans-Canada flight[14] when, on October 11, 1920, a DH-9 landed there from Regina. A fresh DH-9 waiting at Bowness continued the journey through the Kicking Horse Pass to Vancouver on October 13.

Long Branch Airfield

This was the first airfield in Canada and was established in Toronto in 1915 by Curtiss Aeroplanes and Motors Ltd. It was used as Canada's first flying school. For details, see Chapter 2.

Hanlan's Point

Canada's first seaplane base was located at Hanlan's Point on Toronto Island, near the present Toronto Island Airport. It was established by Curtiss Aeroplanes and Motors Ltd. in 1915 and used in connection with its flying school at Long Branch. For more details, see Chapter 2.

Armour Heights Aerodrome

This was one of the Royal Flying Corps training fields opened at Toronto in 1917 (see Chapter 4), replacing Long Branch for flight training. After the war, it was operated by Bishop-Barker Aeroplanes Ltd. and was granted Airharbour Licence No. 10 in May 1920.

Leaside Aerodrome

Another Royal Flying Corps airfield was constructed in 1917, near Toronto for use as a flying training school (see Chapter 4). Leaside was the termination point of the first official airmail flight, which was carried out by Captain Brian Peck, Royal Air Force, between Montréal (Bois Franc Polo Grounds, Cartierville) and Toronto on June 24, 1918. The event is commemorated by a plaque erected at 970 Eglinton Avenue East by the Ontario Archaeological and Historic Sites Board. Leaside was used by aircraft on the New York-Toronto-New York Air Race of September 1919.

Leaside remained in use after the war, and Airharbour Licence No. 24 was issued to the Ericson Aircraft Ltd. on July 25, 1920. The Air Board lent a Bessoneau hangar to the Aero Club of Canada at the airport. In 1929 the licence was held in the name of the Toronto Flying Club, and the city of Toronto paid the club "$3,000 per year to cover their operation of the municipal airport."[15] The facility was the most active one in the Toronto area until it closed in 1931. In July 1927, the first Ford tri-motor airplane landed there.

Canadian Airways began the first scheduled air mail service from the airport to Montréal on May 5, 1928, and moved to Mount Dennis (de Lesseps Field) in May 1929. National Air Transport used the airport from mid-1928 to early 1930, when they moved to Barker Field. Canadian Flying Service, a subsidiary of Colonial Western Airways, carried air mail from Leaside to Buffalo from September 1929, until the following August.

Crystal Beach

Crystal Beach, which is situated on Lake Erie, eighty-one kilometres south of Toronto, deserves mention because it was the landing place of the first fare-paying passenger to make an aerial trip across the U.S.—Canadian border. He was carried from Buffalo, New York, in a Curtiss Jenny owned by Allied Airplanes Ltd. of Brantford on July 23, 1919. Crystal Beach was used that summer as a base of operations by the company for exhibtion flying, carriage of passengers at one dollar per minute, and trips over Niagara Falls. It was also the scene of the first parachute jump from an airplane by a Canadian in Canada. The feat was performed by F.H. Ellis on July 5, 1919.[16]

McClelland Field

McClelland Field, near Saskatoon, was established at 22nd Street West and Dundonald Avenue in April 1919, by W. Stan McClelland, ex-RAF, who set up a commercial flying operation there, building a hangar for his Curtiss JN-4 biplane. The field was used by the U.S. Army Air Services flight of four DH-4B airplanes on July 25, 1920, on their way from New York to Nome, Alaska.

At the same time as McClelland was setting up at his site, another field was established four kilometres away on the northern outskirts of Saskatoon near the Hudson Bay Slough. It was operated by Keng Wah Aviation and, until it closed in 1922, was used to train young Chinese from the United States, Canada, and China for Dr. Shun Yat-Sen's revolutionary army.[17]

In the List of Airharbours of 1922 (Chapter 7), Saskatoon is shown as having two public-commercial airharbours, one 600 by 800 yards [549 by 732 metres] and the other, 300 by 400 yards [274 by 366 metres] in area.

St. Charles Field

St. Charles Field, ten kilometres west of Winnipeg, was established in 1919 by the British Canadian Aircraft Company, which became Canadian Aircraft Limited in 1920. The company purchased seven AVRO aircraft in England for barnstorming in Western Canada. The field was used by landplanes of the Canadian Air Force on their trans-Canada flight in 1920. One of the De Havilland DH-9 landplanes took off from St. Charles on October 11, 1920.[18]

In 1928, Western Canada Airways transferred some operations from its base at Brandon Avenue, Winnipeg, to Kirkland Park at St. Charles.[19]

The List of Airharbours of 1922 also shows Winnipeg as having two private-commercial airharbours, one under 300 yards square [84 metres square], and the other, 300 by 500 yards [274 by 457 metres].

Virden

Virden Aerodrome in Manitoba was in operation in 1920 when the Air Board lent the town a Bessoneau hangar.[20] The aerodrome, listed in the Table of Airharbours as public and licensed for Customs, was located on a quarter section of land owned by the town less than one kilometre to the south. The site remained in use as an airport until the opening of No. 19 Elementary Flying Training School under the British Commonwealth Air Training Plan in May 1941, when the town then closed its airport and sold the land. The new airport, one and a half kilometres north of Virden, was leased by the town from the Department of Transport at the end of the war. The municipality later purchased the facility, which is still in use.[21]

Note: No attempt has been made here to identify the many fields used by the barnstormers and exhibition flyers who criss-crossed Canada between 1910 and 1914. For the most part, they operated from farmers's fields and exhibition grounds. Many were hired as the main attraction at the local fair and, in many areas, flew the first airplanes to be seen by local residents. During the war, there was very little civil flying. In fact, it was prohibited except with special permission from the Department of Militia and Defence. The evolving story of early aerodromes and airports is continued in Chapter 7.

B. Airfields and seaplane bases associated with early Atlantic flights.

The Atlantic Ocean was conquered by the airplane in the year 1919. The crew of the successful flight, John Alcock and Arthur Whitten Brown, won the £10,000 prize offered by Lord Northcliffe, owner of the London Daily Mail. All flights, successful and unsuccessful, started from Newfoundland and therefore served to focus a great deal of public interest on that country and its geographic position as the nearest point of land to Europe. Later, in 1937, Botwood became the base for commercial transatlantic flying boat service, and in 1940, Gander became the main base for the RAF Ferry Command's operations for the delivery of bombers to Britain. For these reasons, the fields and bases used by the 1919 pioneers of ocean flying are part of this history.

Glendenning's Farm

17. Sopwith Atlantic aircraft beginning attempted transatlantic flight, Glendenning's Farm, Nfld., May 18, 1919.

The first airmen to come to Newfoundland were Harry Hawker and MacKenzie-Grieve with their Sopwith Atlantic biplane. They arrived from England on March 30, 1919 and set up their hangar and workshop at Glendenning's Farm, Mount Pearl, ten kilometres west of St. John's. It is now part of the Brookfield Road Agricultural Research Station. It was a difficult site for an airfield but the best the advance party could find. The area around St. John's is very hilly, there were few level fields and, to make matters worse, the area was still covered with snow . The longest dimension of the field was 400 yards [366 metres].

18. Undercarriage jettisoned by Sopwith, start of attempted transatlantic flight, May 18, 1919.

In spite of the difficulties and hazards the airplane made its first flight on April 10—the first flight of an airplane in Newfoundland. It was not until May 18 that conditions were favourable for the Atlantic flight and Hawker and MacKenzie-Grieve could take off in their overloaded airplane from the rough field. A cross-wind of about 20 m.p.h. [32 km/h] made it, in Hawkers' own words, "A ticklish job; it meant going diagonally across the L-shaped runway and avoiding a slight hill and deep drainage ditch".[22] To reduce weight and drag they dropped their undercarriage when crossing the coast. It was later recovered and

placed in the St. John's Museum. About halfway across the ocean the engine overheated, and approximately 1,130 kilometres west of Ireland, they were forced to land beside a small ship that had no wireless. They were given up for lost until the ship reached land a week later and reported them safe on board. By chance, the aircraft with its mail bag still on board, was discovered floating in the Atlantic five days later and was picked up.

Glendenning's Farm was used again on November 19, 1930 when two Newfoundland airmen, Douglas Fraser and Arthur Sullivan, landed there in a Gypsy Moth carrying the first air mail from Canada (Sydney) to Newfoundland.

Pleasantville (Quidi Vidi Lake)

Major F.P. Raynham and Major C.W.F. Morgan were the next crew to reach St. John's. They arrived by ship on April 11 with a Martinsyde biplane, called the Raymor, and set up their base, including a canvas hangar, at Pleasantville, a small level field at the edge of Quidi Vidi Lake. In the early 1930s, Douglas C. Fraser, a St. John's pilot, built a hangar for his seaplane-skiplane operation near the same spot. In 1941, the nearby area became Fort Pepperell, the U.S. Army headquarters in Newfoundland. Raynham and Morgan made their first flight on April 16,

19. Fuelling Martinsyde aircraft, Quidi Vidi Lake, Nfld., May 18, 1919.

and were preparing for the Atlantic flight on May 18 when Hawker and MacKenzie-Grieve flew overhead and headed out to sea. Two hours

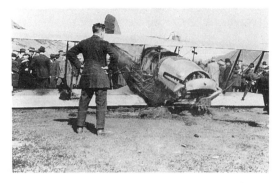

20. Matinsyde "Raymor" crashed on second transatlantic attempt, July 17, 1919.

21. Quidi Vidi Lake, St. John's, Nfld., 1933.

22. U.S. Navy Dirigible C-5 arriving at Pleasantville, St. John's, Nfld., May 15, 1919.

later they attempted to take off. Barely airborne, the aircraft began to drift sideways in a cross-wind, the undercarriage collapsed, and the airplane was damaged. It was repaired, but the undercarriage collapsed once more when Raynham tried again on July 17.

Pleasantville was also used as a base for the U.S. Navy "blimp" C-5, which arrived in St. John's from New York on May 15, 1919, in charge of Lieutenant Commander Coil and a crew of five. They were to attempt to cross the Atlantic, but that same afternoon the blimp broke away from its moorings in a gale. Two men on board at the time jumped clear as the airship rose into the air and was blown out to sea. It was never seen again.

Harbour Grace

While preparations were under way in St. John's, Vice-Admiral Sir Mark Kerr with Major Brackley, Major Gran, and crew arrived in Harbour Grace (Conception Bay) by train with a fourteen-ton, four-engined Handley Page bomber in 105 crates. They had despaired of finding a suitable field in St. John's, the best areas having been taken over already by their competitors, but were able to set up operations at Bishop's Field, near the present St. Francis High School. However,

23. Handley Page V/1500 aircraft Atlantic landing after test flight, Harbour Grace, Nfld., June 10, 1919.

before their airplane was ready, Alcock and Brown had flown the ocean, and Kerr abandoned his flight. He decided to take his airplane to New York, but it was damaged in a forced landing at Parrsboro, Nova Scotia, on July 5.

A new Harbour Grace airfield was built at a different site in 1927 after Lindberg's successful flight to Paris that year and was used extensively by aircraft attempting to fly the Atlantic (see Chapter 7).

Lester's Field

Alcock and Brown were the last of the competing airmen to reach Newfoundland. They arrived in St. John's on May 14, 1919, five days before

24. Alcock, Montague & Brown with Vickers Vimy during its erection at Pleasantville, St. John's, Nfld., June 1919.

Hawker and MacKenzie-Grieve took off on their unsuccessful flight. Their aircraft, a twin engined Vickers Vimy bomber, arrived by ship from England May 26. Alcock had not by then found a suitable field, but Raynham, whose airplane was still being repaired after his unsuccessful take-off attempt on May 18, generously offered him the use of his field at Pleasantville. Alcock accepted, and the Vickers Vimy was assembled there and test flown on June 9. The field, however, was too small for a full load take-off by the larger Vimy, so the plane was flown to Lester's Field at the west end of St. John's. Alcock had found this field on June 4.

It was a rolling field 400 by 600 yards [366 by 549 metres] with trees, stumps, and a drainage ditch across the middle—far from ideal for his purpose, but with willing work by many people,

25. Alcock & Brown taking off on their transatlantic flight from Lester's Field, St. John's, Nfld., June 14, 1919.

stumps were removed, the ditch filled, and the worst bumps levelled, all in four days. Alcock and Brown took off after noon on June 14, 1919, and after a difficult flight landed at Clifden, Ireland, 16 hours and 28 minutes later.[23] The time coast to coast was 15 hours, 57 minutes.

Monuments mark the take-off at Lester's Field and the landing spot in a bog at Clifden. These monuments were erected by the Newfoundland and Irish Historical Societies respectively, and the former may be found on Blackmarsh Road, St. John's. This was the first non-stop flight across the North Atlantic by an airplane.

Trepassey Bay

While the preceding events were taking place in St. John's and Harbour Grace, history was also in the making at Trepassey Bay, ninety-seven kilometres south of St. John's. Here the U.S. Navy flying boats NC-1, NC-3, and NC-4 were preparing to fly to Plymouth, England, by way of the Azores and Lisbon. Sixty U.S. destroyers were stationed at intervals along the route. The three aircraft took off on May 16, 1919. The NC-

4 arrived at the Azores 15 hours and 18 minutes after leaving Trepassey. NC-1 came down in the sea short of the Azores where the crew was picked up, but the aircraft was lost. NC-3 also came down at sea but managed to taxi to the island of Porto Delgada three days later. The NC-4 reached Lisbon on May 27, thus completing the Atlantic crossing.

Trepassey was used again in later years as a refuelling point on transatlantic flights. De Pinedo, on his flight from New York to Rome, left Trepassey for the Azores on May 23, 1927, (the day after Lindberg's flight to Paris). He ran out of fuel 483 kilometres short of the Azores, landed on the sea, and was towed in. He reached Rome on June 16. Amelia Earhart and crew flew from Trepassey to Burry Point, Wales, in the seaplane *Friendship* on June 17-18, 1928.

Footnotes To Chapter 5

[1] F.H. Ellis, *Canada's Flying Heritage* (Toronto: University of Toronto Press, 1961), p. 109.

[2] Alice Gibson Sutherland, *Canada's Aviation Pioneers* (Toronto: McGraw-Hill Ryerson, 1978), p. 257. By permission of the publisher.

[3] J.A. Wilson, *Development of Aviation in Canada 1879-1948* (Ottawa: King's Printer), p. 11.

[4] Material on Petawawa has been taken from Ellis, pp. 10-11, 375; and from J.R.K. Main, *Voyageurs of the Air* (Ottawa: Queen's Printer, 1968), p.10, 11.

[5] Ellis, pp. 59, 68-73.

[6] Ellis, p. 71.

[7] Sutherland, p. 257.

[8] C.D. Long, "Toronto's airports before Malton," *CAHS Journal* (Winter 1965), p. 93.

[9] Ellis, p. 28.

[10] Ellis, p.25.

[11] Rudy Morin, "The Aero Club of B.C.", unpublished article.

[12] K.M. Molson, *Pioneering in Canadian Air Transport* (Winnipeg:James M Richardson and Sons Ltd., 1947), p. 1.

[13] Geoff Rowe, "Early Flying In Ottawa," *CAHS Journal* (Spring, 1969), p. 21.

[14] This was the first flight across Canada and was made by aircraft of the CAF between October 7 and 17, 1920. Several aircraft and crews were used. Aircraft for the western portion had been shipped ahead by train. HS-2L flying boats were used from Halifax to Winnipeg and DH-9 landplanes for the rest of the way. The flight of 3, 262 miles (5,254 kilometres) took forty-five hours flying time.

[15] C.D. Long, "Toronto airports before Malton," *CAHS Journal* (Winter 1965), p. 93.

[16] Ellis, pp. 147-148.

[17] "Airports '79, 50 Years in Flight," *Saskatoon Star-Phoenix*, (May 31, 1979) supplement.

[18] Ellis, pp. 152, 159, 182.

[19] Molson, p. 38.

[20] Canada, Air Board, *Report of the Air Board* (Ottaw: King's Printer, 1920), p. 7.

[21] Recent information was supplied by the town of Virden (C.S. Coleman), January 24, 1980.

[22] Ellis, p. 173.

[23] These times are taken from Brown's own flight log. See John Alcock and Arthur Whitten Brown, *Our Transatlantic Flight* (London: Wm. Kimber, 1969), pp. 80, 101.

CHAPTER 6

Development of Government Airport Policy

A. 1918 to 1945

At this point, it is useful to examine the evolution of government policy on aviation from 1918, particularly as it relates to airports, and to look at the changes in government organization that affected the development of civil aviation.

In the immediate post-World War I era, the dominion government was oblivious to the importance of aviation and the role it could play in Canada. J.R.K. Main notes that "the Minister of Reconstruction in December 1918, after listening patiently to an enthusiastic description of the possibilities of aviation in the Canadian north...remarked that he did not think Canada would ever have need for an air service."[1] Fortunately, the government's attitude changed from that negative view, and aerodromes and airports began to develop slowly in the 1920s and 1930s and more rapidly during the Second World War.

Aviation was not sufficiently developed to require any form of control before the First World War; during the conflict, the need for concentration on military efforts prevented any civil development. The contribution of Canadians to the war in the air was a notable one, but the government itself did not take any direct part in this until the summer of 1918. All the active service units overseas were under the jurisdiction of the British authorities, and pilot training, carried out in Canada during 1917 and 1918, was given by the Royal Flying Corps under British direction and control. The extension of enemy submarine attacks to the Atlantic coast of Canada and the torpedoing of an oil tanker within sixteen kilometres of Halifax harbour led to the establishment of coastal air patrols there and at Sydney and to the organization of the Royal Canadian Naval Air Service. This service was still in the early stages of organization at the time of the armistice, when it was then disbanded, as were the two distinctively Canadian squadrons of the Royal Air Force that had been formed overseas. Canada thus entered the post-war period without any air organization or legislation on aeronautics.

The successful use of aircraft during the war raised the possibility of air transport in the more remote parts of Canada where other modern means of transport were entirely lacking. Recommendations made immediately after the armistice called for some form of legislation to be established to control flying in the Dominion and to provide an organization for the development of air transport. Pilots were returning from overseas, and surplus aircraft left in Canada by the Royal Air Force were coming on the market at low prices. No action was taken in the matter, however, until an application was received in February 1919 from the Canadian Pacific Railway for legislation to extend its charter to include the operation of aircraft. The government then decided that legislation was needed, and, the Air Board Act was passed by parliament. The United Kingdom Air Navigation Acts of 1911 and 1913 were the only precedents available, and the Canadian act was largely based on anticipated requirements and the trend of development.

The prime purpose of the Air Board Act was the administration and control of civil aviation. (An Air Board in the United Kingdom controlled aviation there, including the RFC, until 1918, when the Air Ministry was established.) Members of the board were appointed from the Departments of Militia and Defence, Naval Services, Customs, and the Post Office. A civil organization, suitable for the establishment of air regulations, civil air operations, and technical and administrative services, was drawn up by the Civil Service Commission and a staff appointed by the Commission during 1919 and 1920.

The Air Board Act became law on June 6, 1919, and the board was required to:
(a) supervise all matters connected with aeronautics;
(b) construct and maintain all government aerodromes and air stations;
(c) control and manage all aircraft and equipment necessary for the conduct of any of His Majesty's Services;
(d) operate such services as the governor in council may approve;
(e) prescribe aerial routes;
(f) co-operate with the offices of the Department of Militia and Defence and Naval Services on all questions relating to the air defence of Canada.

The board was given the power to "regulate and control aerial navigation" and to make regulations with respect to:
(g) the licensing, inspection, and regulation of all aerodromes and airstations;
(h) the use and control of aerial routes.

The board's small staff produced the Air Regulations in 1920. These were based on British air regulations passed in April 1919, with minor changes made to adapt them to Canada. Both the British and Canadian regulations conformed to the provisions of the International Convention on Air Navigation of 1919. The board began the control of civil aviation and formulated the government's policy towards this new mode of transportation.

In November 1919, a remarkable paper was prepared by the Air Board for publication in a special aviation issue of a number of leading Canadian newspapers. It was entitled "Air Administration in Canada" [2] and clearly set out the aims of the board as well as the aviation policy the government would follow. The paper was remarkable for its foresight, and the policy set out in it governed the development of civil aviation from its post-war rebirth. It set the path the

government planned to follow (and, in fact, did follow) in aerodrome development.

The government established and operated only those aerodromes required for government use. The federal government had little money and was well aware that it could not meet the demands from every municipality that wanted an aerodrome. It felt local initiative could be counted on to meet local aspirations. However, the government accepted the responsibility of providing emergency landing fields on air routes that might be established to connect terminal aerodromes provided by municipalities. It also assumed the role of regulating commercial air traffic, mapping defined air routes, and developing weather and communication services. Further, it undertook to establish aerial survey and forest protection services and to experiment with air transportation in the north.

That was the framework in which civil aviation began to develop during the first few years after the war. J.A. Wilson, then controller of aviation, summarized the activities:

In 1920, we tried to explore the whole situation with a view to determining our best line of progress. As in other countries, the possibilities of air mail were thoroughly canvassed. We came to the conclusion then that owing to the expense we could not touch this phase but must leave it until public opinion was riper, more suitable aircraft were available and the experimental work had been done in other countries. We resolutely turned our backs on air mail development then and turned to the North country, where there was an urgent need for better means of transport and aviation could play an immediately useful part...the foresters, surveyors, mining men and northern traders welcomed our advent in the North and a tremendous amount of really useful and sound work has been the result. To start this off and show the possibilities, the Air Board, which had a lot of H.S. and F.3 boats and other surplus war aircraft at its disposal, felt they must do the experimental work, and we, therefore, formed a Civil Government Air Operations Branch for this purpose. It was our intention to retire from each field the moment the case had been proved and when the organizations for whom we worked, such as the foresters, surveyors, and mining companies, were prepared to take over their own service, by contract or direct operation. All the officers and men in the C.G.A.O. Branch were then civilians and were licensed in the ordinary way as commercial pilots, air engineers, etc.[3]

Under the Air Board Act of 1919, one of the duties given the board was "to construct and maintain all *government* aerodromes and air stations...to operate such services as the Governor in Council may approve..." [emphasis added]. To support its Civil Government Air Operations, the board constructed the required seaplane bases at Vancouver (Jerico Beach) and Roberval, and aerodromes at Morley and Ottawa (Rockcliffe). The latter was also for use by seaplanes, and was the only combined land-sea base in Canada. Dartmouth, the former RCNAS Station, was reactivated as a base for the erection and repair of seaplanes and flying boats for the Air Operations Branch.

Aerodromes and seaplane bases for civil use were the responsibility of the communities or aviation companies concerned, since it was argued that the users, as beneficiaries, should provide their own aerodrome or base.

The formation of a Canadian Air Force received consideration at the time of the drafting of the Air Board Act, and again after the appointment of the board. The first report of the Air Board (1920) contained a paragraph stating that "a final decision on this point was, however, postponed until the general policy with regard to Canada's future sea, land and air forces were determined." It was then expected that the necessary reorganization of the defence forces would be undertaken immediately and that a defence department would be formed to include air as well as naval and military forces. Pressure for continued participation in air force activities from ex-air force officers in all parts of the country, and the delay in the formation of the defence department, impelled the Air Board to take action on June 30, 1920, to institute the Canadian Air Force (see Appendix 5) and establish a base where air force training could be continued. The air force was organized on a wholly nonpermanent basis and was regarded as a stop-gap measure pending a decision on the post-war reorganization of the defence forces.

Until 1924, flying in Canada was "used principally as an improved method of observation. Straight transportation work [was] subsidiary to this and [was] undertaken only when other modern facilities were lacking..."[4] There was no assistance or subsidy to civil aviation, which "had to fly by itself in Canada, as perhaps in no other country."[5]

The result of the government's policy was the development throughout northern Canada of efficient commercial air services that were self-sustaining, required no subsidy and gave access to the remotest districts of the country. More was learned of northern Canada during the first ten years of this air service than in the preceding three hundred. Foresters, surveyors, geologists, prospectors, mining engineers, the clergy, doctors, nurses, the police—in fact, all participants in activities in northern Canada, found their tasks greatly lightened, their range of action extended, and their efficiency increased, by the use of aircraft. Journeys that a few years earlier had meant weeks or months and sometimes even years of strenuous toil and hardship were now undertaken with relative ease and comfort in a few hours. The expansion of Canada's mining industry, which helped greatly to sustain Canada through the days of the depression, was immensely assisted and hastened by aviation; and new mining fields owed their discovery and development entirely to aircraft.[6]

As to the establishment of air-mail service, this could await further developments. Aircraft available were war types not specifically suited for public transport, either of passengers or mail. Little was known about winter flying at that time, and there were practically no aerodromes or bases available from which to operate. In addition, the transport system of Canada was considered to be overdeveloped and it was felt that it would not be possible, in the circumstances of the time, to contemplate the establishment of another expensive system of inter-city transport. Until public opinion was riper and experience had been gained in other countries, the operation of such services would be costly and premature. It was not, in fact, until 1927 that inter-city mails again received active consideration.[7]

Although the federal government encouraged the establishment of municipal aerodromes at municipal expense, it did little to develop its own aerodromes. In 1920, the only ones in existence were Camp Borden (inherited from the RAF at the end of the war), Morley (Alberta), and Rockcliffe, near Ottawa. The last two were operated by the Air Operations Branch of the Air Board and staffed by civilians. Morley was used for the improved fire protection of the Dominion Government's Forest Reserve on the eastern slope of the Rocky Mountains, and Rockcliffe was maintained largely for experimental work. Borden was operated by the CAF as the training station for the small air force. The reason given for this dearth of federally funded aerodromes was that their expense could be avoided by the use of seaplanes and flying boats, taking advantage of Canada's lakes and rivers. This, in fact, is what happened in both civil and government flying. Another reason for this approach, as far as the Air Board was concerned, was the large number of flying boats Canada inherited from the U.S. Navy and the RAF at the end of the war.

On January 1, 1923, the Department of National Defence Act came into effect. The Air Board was abolished and all of its functions were taken over by the minister of National Defence. In the reorganization of the Air Services under the new department, practically all civil positions were abolished. Aviation was treated as if it were wholly military, whereas, under the Air Board, the organization had been mainly a civil one, with its work divided into three functions: (a) the control of civil aviation; (b) the conduct of flying for other government departments (Government Civil Air Operations); and (c) the organization of the CAF. Under the new act, the chief of general staff and the director of the CAF were made responsible for the direction of all activities, civil and military, and no recognition was given to the obvious fact that a large part of the administration of aeronautics dealt with purely civil functions that had little relation to the air force.

The assumption of responsibility for all civil aviation by the new Department of National Defence created some difficulties for the civil group of the former Air Board, although these difficulties were attenuated to some extent by the fact that J.A. Wilson, the secretary of the board, became secretary of the Canadian Air Force. The initiative for the change had come from the military group of the Air Board, which felt that civil aviation was getting too much attention and too large a share of the budget. They wanted to see the fledgling CAF develop into a full air force under military auspices. This ambition was far beyond the original intent in founding the CAF,

which had been to provide a non-permanent force for the training of ex-RAF pilots and others as a reserve air force for use in case of war. The military way of thinking was influenced in part by the strong feeling in England that civil aviation there should be under the Air Ministry, which controlled the Royal Air Force. The feelings of the civil group of the Air Board were further hurt by the fact that they were not consulted in the drafting of the National Defence Act, whereas the military had a direct input. The secretary of the board set out his fears and concerns in a strong letter to the deputy minister designate of the new department on November 2, 1922. This letter is a valuable historical paper and is reproduced in full in Appendix 6.

Despite these internal government problems, civil aviation and aerodromes began to develop. In 1922, while there were three government aerodromes there were twenty-three civil ones, of which six were "public" (see Table 2, Chapter 7). There were twenty-four airharbours in 1924, (for definition, see Appendix 18), thirty-four in 1926, and thirty-three in 1928. The government, through the Department of National Defence, introduced a scheme to assist in the establishment of light aeroplane clubs in 1927 (see Chapter 7). Sixteen clubs were formed in 1928, each with its own aerodrome. There were additional clubs and aerodromes in 1929, by which time there were forty-five licensed civil airharbours. The term 'airport' was used for the first time in the 1927 Report on Civil Aviation. By 1928, there were thirty-three licensed airports.

In 1927, there was a further structural change in the government's administration of aviation when four directorates were set up in National Defence:

(a) Royal Canadian Air Force (the CAF became the RCAF on April 1, 1924);
(b) Government Civil Air Operations;
(c) Control of Civil Aviation;

(d) Aeronautical Engineering.

The RCAF continued as part of the branch of the chief of staff. The others, which in large measure dealt with civil matters, were placed directly under the deputy minister, as civil head of the department. In 1930, when responsibility for natural resources was transferred to the provinces, the Government Civil Air Operations directorate was greatly reduced and that branch, together with Aeronautical Engineering, was again absorbed by the RCAF. Civil aviation, under the controller of civil aviation, remained a separate branch under the deputy minister until its transfer to the Department of Transport, which was formed in 1936.

In 1928, when it was decided to construct the Trans-Canada Airway, the Civil Aviation Branch was divided into two separate divisions: Air Regulations, and Airways. The latter was "charged with airway and airport surveys, the location and construction of aids to navigation on the airways, including intermediate aerodromes, lighting, the co-ordination of the radio and meteorological services and the licensing of airports and seaplane bases."[8] Airways division was also responsible for the operation and maintenance of the governnment's only two civil airports, St. Hubert and Rimouski. The growing importance of the airport activity was finally recognized in the organization.

The construction of St Hubert and Rimouski airports began in 1927. This major departure from the policy outlined in the early part of this chapter came about as the result of circumstances rather than planning. At the Imperial Conference of 1926 in London, Prime Minister MacKenzie King promised the support of Canada in the development of a system of Empire air communications by airship through the construction of an airship base in eastern Canada. St. Hubert was the site selected. Land was purchased by the government, and a mooring tower and a gas-generating plant were built. (See Appendix 7 for the press release of 1927, which carefully explains the project.)

Before going ahead, the Department of National Defence (Air Service) had consulted the City of Montréal to see if it would participate in the scheme by building a municipal airport at or near the site. The deputy minister's letter of April 21, 1927, stated that "if the municipal authorities in Montréal are interested in this project and have any suitable location for an airship base in view, arrangements can be made to inspect it. It might be possible to combine the airship site with a municipal aerodrome, as the characteristics required for both services do not differ materially... ." The department had already written to the city in January, asking if it were considering a municipal aerodrome, as other Canadian municipalities had already done. (See Appendix 8 for a copy of this correspondence. The same letter was sent to Vancouver and set out the government's hopes of municipal co-operation.) Montréal declined, and the department proceeded on its own, purchasing the land and paying the full cost of construction. Later, when Quebec City tried to use the St. Hubert case as a precedent, the mayor was told that "the Montréal field had been purchased solely to help the development of long distance travel by airship and if it had not been for the airship scheme, the St. Hubert property would not have been purchased... ."[9] There was a second reason for the St. Hubert aerodrome: the establishment of an experimental airmail service between Montréal and Rimouski, where mail was to be transferred to and from ocean liners plying between England and Montréal. The Post Office looked to the Department of National Defence to provide the aerodromes required.

It is interesting to speculate about what would have happened if the airship base had not already been a commitment of the government. The controller of Civil Aviation remarked:

As regards Rimouski, the locality there would expect little benefit from the field, as little or no local mail service would be provided. The industrial and commercial communities of Quebec, Montréal, Ottawa, Toronto, Winnipeg and the West would benefit from the speeding up of the mail service in a way that Rimouski would not and the terminal field there was, on this account, considered as in the direct interest of the Dominion as a whole and, therefore, had been provided by the Dominion authorities...[10]

The precedent of St. Hubert undoubtedly caused problems for the department, and, in a memorandum of September 18, 1931 to the deputy minister, the controller of Civil Aviation commented:

St. Hubert has been developed as a national airport like Croydon, near London, Le Bourget, near Paris, and Tempelhof in Berlin. Whether, in view of the benefit the City of Montréal had derived from its establishment, relieving the City authorities of the necessity of furnishing their own airport, an endeavour should be made to obtain from them a yearly grant towards its maintenance, should be considered. The City undoubtedly gains by the location of such a fine establishment at its door. It should be clearly understood, however, that St. Hubert has a national interest, as well as a local one, as the airport of Montréal. It was built by the Dominion Government following a decision on national policy, into which purely local considerations did not enter.

The federal government continued to operate St. Hubert as a civil airport until August 1941, when operations were transferred to the new airport at Dorval. St. Hubert was the principal government airport and, as such, was used for testing and developing airport equipment and opera-

tions. While it had the first paved runways, airfield lighting, and snow removal (as distinct from snow dragging and compaction). It never served its original purpose as the terminal airship harbour. The airship R-100 did make one successful trip to Montréal on August 1, 1930, but the crash of the sister ship R-101 in France on October 5, 1930, brought an end to the projected transatlantic air service.[11]

In 1927, there was a significant change in government policy—one that was to have a great impact on airport development. In that year, the Department of National Defence announced a scheme to assist the establishment of light aeroplane clubs, similar to that which the British government had operated so successfully for the previous two years. Under the scheme, if a local group could provide a suitable aerodrome, a hangar, an instructor, an air engineer, and thirty members wishing to learn to fly, the department would issue two airplanes and pay a grant of one hundred dollars for each member obtaining a licence (see Appendix 9 for details). The aim of the scheme was to provide, at no expense to the government, aerodromes in principal cities. It would also provide a pool of trained pilots to meet the increasing demands of expanding civil aviation. Until this time, pilots had been hired from England and elsewhere.

The flying club policy was an instant success, and sixteen clubs were formed in 1928. Eight more were formed in 1929. The policy to assist clubs was one of the most imaginative and successful steps taken by government to assist civil aviation. Its objectives were fully realized: pilots were trained, and good aerodromes were established across Canada, which in turn facilitated the establishment of inter-city air-mail services. During World War II, twenty-five of these clubs took part in the British Commonwealth Air Training Plan and operated twenty-two elementary flying training schools, which trained over

41,000 pilots for Canadian, British, and Commonwealth air forces.

Air mail played an important role in the development of civil aviation and here the Post Office was a very progressive partner. For many years, mail had been carried to isolated areas by seaplanes (using skis in winter); to provide inter-city service on a regular, scheduled basis required intermediate aerodromes, airway lighting, etc., and the attendant expenditures. By 1927 the time had come to review the situation (see Appendix 10). St. Hubert and Rimouski airports were built, and the Montréal-to-Rimouski mail service began. Inter-city service in Europe was successful, and the United States airway system was growing. Wilson notes:

the cost of establishing a trans Canada airway was estimated at between $5 million and $6 million, but revenues were buoyant and it was felt it would become an essential part of Canada's transportation system before many years had passed. Canada, as a great trading nation could not afford to ignore the new form of fast travel and transport but must move with the times. Signs were evident of the desire of the United States air transport companies to tap traffic in the main centres of population and industry in Canada, all of which lie adjacent to the international boundary, and to feed it into the United States airway system. In 1928, permission was given to begin the survey for a Canadian trans-continental airway.[12]

This was the beginning of massive intervention by the government (the Civil Aviation Branch of the Department of National Defence) in the development of commercial civil aviation, and, from that time on, government played an active role in airports. Because of the activities of the flying clubs and the support these clubs received from their communities, a chain of airports was being established from coast to coast.

The foundation for the Trans-Canada Airway was hereby provided by the municipalities the airway would serve.

Wilson notes that the government agreed to provide "intermediate aerodromes to fill the gap between these major airports, the lighting required for night flying, without which the project would not be efficient, and radio and weather services" and that it would "also pay for the carriage of mails by contract with the Post Office Department which stoutly backed the project."[13] By assisting in the provision of aerodromes, radio aids, lighting, and meteorological services, the government was following the precedent already set in marine navigation that had aided in the construction of Canadian seaports by lighting the coasts and providing wireless communication and direction finding facilities.

The survey, facilities design, and construction constituted an enormous undertaking for the Civil Aviation Branch and, for the next ten years, was their major occupation. It was an undertaking that changed and influenced the development of commercial aviation and had major social and economic effects on the country. From the scheduled inter-city air-mail services came passenger services and finally the transcontinental service of Trans-Canada Air Lines connecting Halifax (and later St. John's) to Victoria.

The story of the Trans-Canada Airway is told in Chapter 8, but in the context of airport policy, there is a special significance: the undertaking to construct the airway led the government into a radical change in its relationship with municipal airports.

In 1929, the government made its first cautious entry into financial assistance to airports on the Trans-Canada Airway. Order in Council PC 322 of February 22, 1929, authorized the Department of National Defence to:

make a contribution towards the proper

lighting of such aerodromes of 50% of the cost of lighting equipment furnished by the owners and lessees, including flood, boundary and obstruction lights required within the limits of the aerodrome, but not including the cost of the installation of such lights; such grants, however, not to exceed $10,000 for any one aerodrome.

The department would also supply, free of charge, one flashing beacon.

As the country struggled out of the depression in the mid-1930s, the development of municipal airports was seen to have fallen far behind the standards set by the government. Many of the fields were not equipped to meet the needs of the latest types of aircraft; where the municipality was unable to pay for required improvements, the government had to help finance the airports and assume responsibility for special services. This, the second step in providing financial assistance, was introduced in 1937 (PC 3166 of December 14, 1936). The Department of Transport agreed to contribute one-third of the cost of developing the "terminal" airports, while provinces and municipalities were to undertake the rest (see Appendices 12 and 14). This program continued until the outbreak of World War II. Trans-Canada Air Lines, however, had begun operations in the meantime, even though a number of municipalities declined to participate, notably Montréal, Ottawa, North Bay, and London. Consequently for these and other cities, the Department of Transport, under its mandate from the Trans-Canada Air Lines Act, undertook the whole cost of airport development.

With the formation of the Department of Transport on November 1, 1936, came the complete separation of civil and military aviation. The goal of those dedicated individuals who, through the Air Board and various reorganizations of National Defence, had striven over the years to foster and develop civil aviation, was realized at last. They, and especially J.A. Wilson, first secretary of the Air Board, had always argued that military and civil aviation should be separate. Civil aviation, which by now had become so important a part of the transportation system of the country, could now be administered by the same organization that dealt with railway, canal, marine, and highway services, to which it is complementary. Civil aviation, together with radio and meteorology on which it so clearly depends, now formed a group in the new department under the chief of Air Services.

In 1937, the government made another significant policy move when it introduced an act to establish Trans-Canada Air Lines to operate the airway. The Trans-Canada Air Lines Act was passed on April 6, 1937, and, among other things, it provided:

15 (2) (f)—for the operation and maintenance by the government of Canada, without charge to the corporation, of emergency landing fields, lights and radio beams, necessary for the operation of the said Trans-Canada Lines and for the supply to the corporation, free of charge, of weather reports; but when the revenues of the Corporation, in the opinion of the Minister, will permit, charges may be imposed for landing, lighting and weather reports such as are charged for other similar competing coast-to-coast services in North America;

Thereafter, the Department of Transport, in support of Trans-Canada Air Lines, "the instrument of the Government in maintaining all transcontinental air transport services,"[14] played an increasing role in improving municipal airports, building new airports and facilities and, finally, engaging in the direct operation of main airports.

The Department of Transport, through the Air Services Branch, took on another large commitment early in World War II, namely, the construction of aerodromes for the British Commonwealth Air Training Plan (BCATP). Responsibility for selecting and building these aerodromes was given to the Department of Transport in recognition of the experience of Civil Aviation staff in building the Trans-Canada Airway before the war. More on the BCATP in Chapter 10, but mention must be made here of the effect it had on civil airport policy.

Where the location was suitable, the airports and aerodromes already forming part of the Trans-Canada Airway were brought into the BCATP. All suitable municipal airports were leased by the government for the duration of the war and enlarged and modified to meet BCATP requirements. The heavy aircraft traffic called for hard-surface runways and taxi-strips at all main service training school aerodromes and at some relief aerodromes. New aerodrome sites were selected, so far as military requirements would permit, with a view to serving the future commercial needs of the areas in which they were located. When hostilities ended, 149 new aerodromes had been built and seventy-three existing facilities were vastly expanded for the BCATP.

In meeting the requirements of the Air Force, "the aim of the Department of Transport had been to ensure that when the time came to return to normal peace conditions, as much as possible of the war effort and expenditure [could] be adapted to increasing the facilities for civil air transport in the Dominion".[15] The civil airport situation was greatly improved through that policy. The size of all main airports on the Trans-Canada Airway and its principal feeder lines were increased, new hard surfaces added, and many large hangars built.

B. Post-War Policies—1946 to 1979

Before World War II, the main airports along the Trans-Canada Airway were owned and operated by the municipalities except for St. Hubert, Ottawa, and North Bay, which were operated by the Department of Transport. At the beginning of the war, the municipal airports were taken over by the government under lease for the duration of hostilities.

During the war, twenty municipal airports were improved under the BCATP. Some were operated by the RCAF, but airports where there was a large proportion of civil air traffic were managed by the Department of Transport. At the end of the war, the department owned and operated sixty-two airports, aerodromes and emergency landing fields, and the government owned or leased 252 airfields of all classes.

As the end of the war approached, the Department of Transport began to give serious thought to future airport policy. The controller of Civil Aviation wrote to the acting deputy minister on May 12 and 14, 1945 (see Appendix 13), with recommendations. He pointed out that the greater the number of airports that could be kept in operation, the greater would be the demand for aircraft, leading to more employment in aircraft manufacture and maintenance. He felt the federal government should take the lead in co-ordinating the interests and activities of provinces, municipalities, and others in establishing airports. Standards of airport operations and maintenance would be required to ensure the efficiency of the scheduled airlines, and while this could be more easily attained if all airports were owned and operated by the government, it would be less costly under municipal operation. In this case, however, municipalities would require financial assistance from the government for operation and maintenance costs, and to facilitate future improvements and expansion. If municipalities would not take over airports they should be expected to transfer their airport investment to the federal government at no cost.

Policies along these lines were in fact adopted, and municipal airports were returned to the municipalities. Some, however, refused to get back into the airport business and, where these airports were served by Trans-Canada Air Lines, the Department of Transport took over. In later years, as both operating and capital costs increased, more and more municipalities dropped out and sold their facilities to Transport so that today the department operates all main line and international airports in Canada.

To foster civil aviation, the government adopted the policy of leasing surplus aerodromes, for a nominal sum, to interested municipalities or other responsible public bodies on certain conditions, which included an undertaking to operate a public airport.[16]

In 1945 and 1946, a special committee of two (J.P.R. Vachon of the Air Transport Board and W.F. Hilchie of the Department of Transport) set up by the minister of Transport reviewed the situation to determine what might be done to encourage and assist municipalities. As a result of their recommendations, and, effective November 1, 1946, the department offered to pay municipal airports an operating subsidy of five cents per square yard of paved surface. Separate agreements were to be entered into with each municipality. The first subsidy was granted to Edmonton on November 1, 1946. Where the Department of National Defence had large operations at a municipal airport, it paid a grant in lieu of landing fees. This was also based on the paved area and amounted to one cent per square yard at Vancouver and Edmonton, two cents at Calgary, and five cents at Sudbury.

This simple system of assistance was remarkably successful for a number of years until rising operating and maintenance costs made assistance beyond five cents per square yard necessary. (See Appendix 16 for a list of airports receiving a subsidy by December 1, 1956.) A new subsidy program was therefore developed and introduced effective July 1, 1957 (Order in Council PC 1958-48/955 of July 10, 1958), under which the department was authorized to pay a portion of the operating loss based on a formula that took into account the airport's operating revenue. Incentives to increase revenue were also offered. The scheme was originally to be for a period of five years, but was renewed every five years up to 1972. Under the authority of TB 712 467 of July 13, 1972, the current operating assistance policy came into force under which the department was authorized to pay the full operating deficit at national airports serving scheduled air carriers where airport traffic reached a specified minimum level.

In 1948, the minister of Transport described to parliament the main principles followed by the department in establishing airports and airways:
a) The progressive development of main line airports to permit the utilization of the most modern types of aircraft at the minimum capital outlay consistent with safety and economy of operation.
b) The development of a minimum number of international airports, consistent with Canada's position in the international civil aviation field and our obligations under international air agreements.
c) The encouragement of and assistance to municipalities for the development of airports throughout Canada where it seems desirable that such airports should be developed, maintained, and operated by municipalities to standards set by the Dominion Government.
d) Assistance in the establishment of airstrips at air bases feeding remote areas for the purpose of stimulating the development of Canada's natural resources.
e) The assumption of the costs of maintenance and operation of those airports which are under the control of the Department of Transport, and to assist municipalities in the maintenance and operation of essential airports where the cost strains municipal resources.
f) The provision and maintenance of aerial aids to navigation, such as radio ranges, instrument landing systems where necessary, meteorological services and air traffic control as necessary, to ensure the regularity and safety of air navigation.[17]

With the evolution of the airport subsidy policy, a capital assistance policy was developed. An earlier subsidy, cautiously entered into in 1929 and 1936, was discontinued at the outbreak of World War II, when the federal government took over complete control of the municipal airports. It was reinstated in 1946 when capital grants of up to $25,000 were made available for projects undertaken by municipalities which qualified for the operating subsidy. In addition to assistance to airports on main air routes, the government also provided aid by direct grants, or undertook construction of airports, on secondary or feeder routes, where this was in the public interest. The grants in aid were on a fifty-fifty cost-sharing basis, up to a maximum of $25,000 per item. (Some airports received more than one $25,000 grant.) Although these grants were small, from 1948 to 1957 an estimated $1,665,000 was expended on capital grants to municipalities, and $2.3 million on operating subsidies. During that same period, a further $18.7 million was spent for construction work undertaken by the Department of Transport at terminal or intermediate municipal airports served by scheduled air carriers.

By 1953, it became evident that grants-in-aid of $25,000 were insufficient for Trans Canada Air Lines' airport requirements, and therefore some cost-sharing grants of 50 per cent were additionally made. During the period 1952 to 1958, ad hoc capital grants of 75 per cent of the cost of providing public space in air terminal buildings were made. Other space was considered to be revenue-producing and hence self-supporting.

In comparison to the time prior to 1939, the government, through the Department of Transport, was becoming heavily involved in airport development and operation while still trying to continue municipal participation. In October 1958, after two years of study, a new policy was adopted which, it was felt, would better meet the growing needs of both scheduled air services and general aviation.[18] Under the policy, airports were categorized as main line, satellite, local, remote, or development. The Department of Transport accepted direct responsibility for satellite airports and for facilities at main line airports, i.e. those served by scheduled or regular service carriers using DC-3 or larger aircraft. It would make a contribution in capital development funds of up to $100,000 for local airports and up to $50,000 for remote airports. The operating subsidy introduced in 1957, under which the department paid a portion of the operating loss, continued for main line airports operated by municipalities.

In 1965, further policy rationalization met the demands for better facilities and more airports of the smaller category: the Department of Transport was to pay the full cost of local airports, not including land, and for remote airports it was to pay up to $100,000. The grant for terminal and equipment buildings was increased to 85 per cent. and the stipulation that main line airports be served by DC-3 or larger aircraft was dropped. Total capital contributions in any one year were limited to $1 million, not including air terminal and equipment buildings at main line airports. The operating subsidy payable to municipal main line airports was continued: municipalities were reimbursed for the operating costs in an amount equal to their earned revenue, but not exceeding the operating loss.

Effective January 1, 1972 (under authority of TB 712 467 of July 13, 1972), there was a further change in the airport assistance policy. Airports were reclassified into two basic groups—national and community—according to an Air Traffic Demand Index, T.D.I., (a formula taking into account local passengers, mail, freight and aircraft movements). The Department of Transport took responsibility for developing, operating, and maintaining national airports that supported commercial air services operating on a regular basis. The policy enabled government to build satellite airports to relieve congestion at major airports. Where national airports were operated by a municipality, the department agreed to provide financial assistance of up to 100 per cent of approved capital expenditures, as well as 100 per cent of operating deficits.

In the community category, financial assistance for the construction of the new airports (especially in isolated regions) or for the improvement of existing ones, could be granted up to established percentages and ceilings for the subcategories of feeder, local industrial, intermediate local, small local, and remote. These varied from 80 to 100 per cent of cost to fixed sums of from $100,000 to $250,000. In some situations, an operating subsidy could be paid to an airport in the feeder group.

The assistance policy of 1972 was the final rationalization of the need for financial assistance to municipalities and other local groups that required airports or help in development or expansion. The government had made great progress since 1919, when it had decreed that communities should provide their own airports. And even by the beginning of World War II, the Department of Transport had operated only two major airports on the Trans-Canada Airway. After the war, municipalities were encouraged to take back their airports and were given capital and operating grants and subsidies. By 1970, there were

416 licensed airports in Canada: eighty were operated by the Department of Transport, and 336 were run by others—municipalities, corporations, and the Department of National Defence. —of which thirty-one received operating subsidies. The following table provides a breakdown of the airports by category:[19]

Category	No.	Transport	Others	Subsidy
National	65	42	23	12
Feeder	22	8	14	6
Local	253	10	243	7
Remote	30	-	30	4
Development	5	-	5	-
Satellite	4	4	-	-
Arctic	36	16	20	2
Special Case	1	-	1	-
Totals	416	80	336	31

Table 1. Licensed Airports 1970

The department's heavy involvement is evident from the table

While the policy of 1972 recognized the need to assist community airports, the capital grant ceiling of $2 million per year became inadequate. Each year, construction costs increased, a smaller number of projects could be assisted. Because of variations in air carrier traffic, the T.D.I. was no longer a suitable index to use in establishing eligibility for operating subsidies. Therefore the Treasury Board asked that a new financial policy be developed.

Until the establishment of such a policy, the government froze all subsidy funds. Finally, on March 31, 1979, much capital funding was eliminated by discounting all capital assistance to community airports, leaving only the national airports group eligible for support.

Ever since the introduction of capital assistance for the construction of local airports in

1958, funding by the Department of Transport has been a problem. Because there was never enough money to meet requests from interested communities, some provincial governments, notably Manitoba, Alberta, and Ontario, had participated in assistance to local airports. As the Table of Licensed Airports shows, there were 243 local airports owned by others, many of which were originally funded by the provinces.

Manitoba had a program of capital grants up to $4,000, loans up to $20,000, and operating and maintenance grants of $600. Alberta offered 100 per cent capital cost assistance. British Columbia provided cost-sharing with municipalities, districts, and commissions up to 100 per cent. Saskatchewan had a program of capital grants representing 50 to 60 per cent and contributions of $1,000 to $2,000 for operations. Ontario's program provided capital assistance up to 80 per cent and operating assistance up to 50 per cent.

Alberta was particularly active and, in 1977, the province began to participate where delays in federal funding postponed the construction of terminals in which the province had a particular interest—at Grande Prairie and Lethbridge, for example. In these cases, the province advanced the money for immediate construction and entered into agreements with Transport Canada under which Transport, the operator of the airport, would pay back the capital costs over a number of years and eventually become the owner of the buildings.

Ontario entered into local airport construction as part of its development of intra-Ontario air services by Norontair.

Such provincial participation has resulted in the more timely development of vital aviation facilities, and has relieved the federal government of an obligation it assumed in earlier days.

In 1955, there was an important and far-reaching change in government policy concerning land leases at airports. Prior to that time, leases to hangar sites could be granted, but were subject to cancellation on short notice "for a public purpose" by the government and without any compensation to the lessee. From 1955 land leases could be granted for long terms (i.e., twenty years). While the government retained the right to cancel on proper notice, it undertook to compensate for the lessee's capital investment on the land, less the depreciation of the asset. The rate of depreciation was set out in the lease and was normally 5 per cent per annum.

The first of the new leases was granted to Timmins Aviation Ltd., which built its own hangar at Dorval in September 1955. The new policy allowed the aviation industry to raise mortgage money to build hangars, air cargo terminals, flight kitchens, etc., on Department of Transport airports. The flying clubs benefited, too, because they could now have tenure for the hangar and other buildings they bought from the government. The policy was subsequently modified by removing the stipulated rate of depreciation, and requiring full compensation.

C. Policies for the 1980s

Financial Assistance

While the cost of construction increased over the years, government funding did not. Fewer projects could be assisted, and the revised financial assistance policy of 1972 could not be fully implemented. Further problems arose during the late 1970s, when the Canadian Transport Commission (CTC) no longer demanded flight statistics based on aircraft and passenger movements. The Air Traffic Demand Index, therefore, became obsolete and the classification of airports was increasingly difficult.

The 1978 freeze on the Financial Assistance to the Construction and Operations of Municipal Airports policy is still in effect, pending a comprehensive review. Transport Canada is now dealing with regional, local, and local-commercial airports on an interim basis, without a revised policy.

Community airports which were eligible for operating subsidies at the time of the freeze continue to receive help under a sort of "grandfather" right. By 1986, the number of subsidized airports had risen to thirty-seven; the operating subsidy budget had increased to approximately $21 million. Owing to financial restraints, the minister announced in August 1986 that this budget would be capped at $17 million. (See Appendix 34 for a list of subsidized airports, 1989.)

In 1982, after four years of austerity, capital assistance funding was once again made available to community airports under the control of the minister, who had received a $5 million annual budget. To meet the increasing needs created by deregulation and to refurbish deteriorating assets, the annual budget for capital contributions in 1988 was increased from $7.1 million to $20 million per year.

Requests for capital project assistance among airports not operated by Transport Canada are now handled on a more pragmatic basis, linked to government regional development plans and the role community airports can (and do) play in economic growth of communities. For example, if a capital project, such as the expansion of a runway to accommodate jet traffic, will generate industrial expansion within an area, the minister will consider financing it.

The primary objective of a new financial assistance policy would continue to be the operation of a basic national network of airports necessary to support the federal role in air transportation. Assistance may continue to consist of both capital and operating subsidies.

The following are three examples of programs in which Transport Canada's capital assistance has had a role:

Special Recovery Programme (1983-1985)

This involved the initiation or acceleration of a number of capital projects selected for their potential contribution to Canada's economic and regional development. The objective of the programme was to put infrastructure in place in advance of economic recovery by accelerating labour intensive projects.

Labrador Coast Airstrip Programme (1981-1988)

This covered the provision of airstrips in fourteen communities in coastal Labrador, thus facilitating service by wheel-equipped Twin Otter type aircraft on a regular year-round basis. The programme is a joint federal/provincial initiative and is under the aegis of the Newfoundland Transportation Plan.

Nouveau Quebec Airports Development Plan 1983-1990

This is a joint Federal/Provincial plan for the development of air transportation infrastructure in the territory covered by "The James Bay and Northern Quebec Agreement." It will provide facilities at three Cree and eleven Inuit communities.

Airport Operation

The early part of this chapter outlined the government's policy in the provision and operation of airports. Civil aviation began to develop in Canada in the early part of 1920 and, with it, the need for airports. The government took the position that it was the responsibility of each community wishing to have an aerodrome or airharbour (airport) to provide its own. By 1927, the government operated only two airports—St. Hubert and Rimouski—and each was constructed for a reason which the government stoutly defended as not setting any precedent. St. Hubert was built to fulfill the prime minister's commitment to the London Imperial Conference in 1926 to provide the Canadian terminal for the proposed airship service that was to connect the Empire countries. St. Hubert and Rimouski became the terminals for the government's experimental ship-to-shore air-mail service to Montréal. The creation of the Trans-Canada Airway system in 1929 changed the picture of the provision and operation of airports and the federal government accepted the responsibility for intermediate aerodromes. Later, the government built facilities in some major cities where the municipal governments refused to provide airports for the airway, e.g. Ottawa, where the government argued there would be no real Trans-Canada Airway if the nation's capital was not served. At the end of the war in 1946, many cities refused to take back the airports the federal government had leased from them for the duration of the war for the use of the British Commonwealth Air Training Plan. Where these airports were on the Trans-Canada Airway, the government, through the Department of Transport, had no option but to take them over and operate them. The government was now in the airport business in a big way and, as time went by, the involvement grew until by 1986-87, Transport owned 138 airports valued at $8 billion. It operated ninety-one, including all nine international airports. In that year, Transport spent $735 million on airports and collected $718 million in revenue.

Recognizing the need for more responsiveness to local concerns within a context of rising costs, the government reviewed its involvement in civil airport activities. This followed the 1985 Nielson Task Force on government operations, which had suggested a fundamental change in airport policy, aimed at a new approach of non-federal ownership and operation. A ministerial task force was appointed and extensive studies were undertaken to determine whether a self-sustaining system of airports could be provided which would allow for independent operation of local airports. Four options emerged from the studies:

   Private sector operation
   Local airport authorities
   Transport Canada Airport Authority Model
   Crown Corporations

Under any of these options, Transport would retain responsibility for safety and security, air navigation, air regulations and certification of airports.

In April 1987, the Minister of Transport announced the decision to move forward in two parallel yet distinct thrusts:

1. Discussions regarding ownership of operations by "others," where there is local interest, i.e. the local airport authority option;

2. A new approach towards managing airports retained by Transport that would emphasize commercial orientation, potential contribution to economic development and responsiveness to local interests and concerns, i.e. the Transport Canada Airports Authority Model.

While the government is interested in divestiture, there would be no intention to pressure municipalities or provinces.

During 1989, more detailed studies continued. Negotiating principles for divestiture were developed, feasibility studies for takeover were undertaken, and discussions began regarding four major federal airports. An Airport Transfer Advisory Board appointed from the private sector, nationwide, was formed in July 1988 to advise the minister. Airport Transfer Task Force working groups have also been set up to study policy and strategic issues, and operational implications. The first airport transfer is expected in 1990. The second thrust towards a more commercial approach to the management of airports retained by Transport is also progressing with an emphasis on more efficient operation and maximum development of airport revenue from non-aviation sources.

Footnotes to Chapter 6.

[1] J.R.K. Main, *Voyageurs of the Air* (Ottawa: Queen's Printer, 1968), p. 28.

[2] Public Archives Canada (PAC), Records of the Air Board, J.A. Wilson Papers, file 3564-1011-1-5, "Air Administration in Canada," November, 1919. (The paper is reproduced in full in Appendix 3).

[3] Public Archives Canada (PAC), Records of the Department of National Defence, MG 30 E243, vol. 2, personal letter from J.A. Wilson, controller of civil aviation, to E.P. Warner, editor of Aviation, dated 26, March 1932. (Warner became the first president of the International Civil Aviation Organization in 1964.)

[4] Canada, Department of National Defence, Report on Civil Aviation (Ottawa, King's Printer, 1924), p. 12.

[5] Ibid.

[6] Public Archives Canada (PAC), Records of the Department of National Defence, MG 30 E243, vol 17, radio address by the Honourable D.M. Sutherland, Minister of National Defence, February 1934.

[7] J.A. Wilson, "Aviation in Canada," *Development of Aviation in Canada 1897-1948* (Ottawa: King's Printer), p.11.

[8] Ibid.

[9] Public Archives Canada (PAC) MG 30 E243, vol. 6, memorandum from the controller of Civil Aviation to the deputy minister of National Defence concerning the aerodrome for Qubec City, 15 May 1928.

[10] Ibid.

[11] When the R-100 was dismantled, one of the two steering wheels was presented to J.A. Wilson, controller of Civil Aviation. It is now on display at the Museum of Science and Technology, Ottawa.

[12] Public Archives Canada (PAC), records of the Department of National Defence, MG 30 E243, vol. 7, a paper on air transport policy, which explains the thinking that led to the constrruction of the airway. It also sheds light on government air policy in general, 17 March, 1933. See appendix 11.

[13] Ibid

[14] The Prime Minister to the House of Commons on 2 April 1943, as reported in J.A. Wilson, "The influence of civil aviation in the development of Canada's air power," *Development of Aviation in Canada 1879-1948* (Ottawa: King's Printer, p. 37.

[15] J.A. Wilson, "Aerodrome Construction for the British Commonwealth Air Training Plan 1940," *Development of Aviation in Canada 1879-1948* (Ottawa: King's Pinter), p. 37.

[16] Canada, Department of Transport, Annual Report, (Ottawa: King's Printer, 1945-46), p. 149.

[17] Department of Transport, Document AAP 508, of October 18, 1950. Interdepartmental Committee on Airways and Airport Policy—reproduced in full in Appendix 17

[18] Canada, Department of Transport, file 5161-2-0, vol. 1, TB 536 635, dated 6 October, 1958, was supplemented by TB614 722, dated 6 January 1964, in order to permit grants (for air terminal buildings) of 75% of the cost of public space and 100% of government space.

[19] Canada, department of Transport, file 5161-1vol. 3, "A Proposed Policy for Sharing Airport Costs," 30 June 1970.

CHAPTER 7

Aerodromes, Airharbours, and Airports: 1920 to 1930

Pursuant to the Air Board Act of June 6, 1919, the Air Board was appointed to control aeronautics by Order in Council, June 23, 1919. A.K. Maclean, Minister without Portfolio, introduced the Bill in the House of Commons, and said that government thought that an interim board should be set up to to deal with the new subject of aviation as a form of transportation. Air regulations under the Act came into force on January 17, 1920. By these steps, the government established legislation and machinery whereby aviation was to be controlled in Canada. The new term, airharbour, came into use and was defined; so was the older term, aerodrome. Airharbours were required to be licensed. (See Appendix 18 for definitions.)

Lac à la Tortue: Canada's First Airharbour, 1919

Canada's air transportation industry began in 1919, with flying operations at Lac à la Tortue in the valley of the St. Maurice River, Quebec.

Ellwood Wilson, chief forester, Laurentide Co., had been interested in the possibility of using airships (or dirigibles) for forestry purposes since 1908, and in 1919, he got the agreement of the St. Maurice Forest Protective Association to use airplanes for his operations. The association, made up of six pulp and paper companies, loaned two Curtiss HS-2L flying boats from the Dominion government. These aircraft were among the twelve flying boats presented to Canada by the United States at the end of the war. (See Chapter 3.) Stuart Graham, a former RNAS and RAF pilot, and Walter (Bill) Kehoe, an air engineer, were hired to fly the two aircraft from Halifax to Lac à la Tortue, June 5 to 8, and June 21 to 23—the longest cross-country flights in Canada up to that time. The aircraft were based on Lac à la Tortue, five kilometres southeast of Grand Mère, Quebec.

Operations began immediately. The men lived in tents until the living quarters, workshops, and a 125-foot launching track (to bring the flying boats on shore for servicing) were completed at the end of July. On July 7, one of the association pilots spotted a fire bordering on the River Croche, about sixty-five kilometres away. This was the first time that an airplane was used to detect forest fires.

The operation was also to determine whether or not aerial photography was of value to the pulp and paper industry. Although early results were disappointing, by autumn the association had found a more suitable aerial camera and the improved photographs exceeded all expectations. During 1919, fifty-seven flights and eighty hours were completed for the association.

However, some members were dissatisfied with the results and the costs, and the organization was dissolved. But one member, the Laurentide Co., carried on the operation during 1920. The aircraft was transferred to the company and Graham and Kehoe were retained. And when, at the end of that year, Graham and Kehoe resigned, they had completed seventy flights and 150 hours for the season. During that time, they spotted thirty-four fires, plotted forest surveys using their sketching and aerial photography skills, and carried passengers.

Roy Maxwell replaced Graham in 1921. At the end of the season's work (ninety-five flights and ninety-two hours flying time), the Laurentide Co. decided to buy flying services rather than run its own operation. It persuaded Maxwell to form a new company. In 1922, Laurentide Air Service Ltd. was established, and the Laurentide Co. turned over without charge all of its facilities, including workshops, launching track, and housing for personnel at Lac à la Tortue.

The new company performed forestry work and general transportation services for the Laurentide Co., the Ontario government, and others. In 1922, they flew 688 hours and carried 659 passengers, 310 of whom paid fares. In 1923, the company expanded its operations and carried freight and passengers into uninhabited and unmapped territory. It now had twelve aircraft, ten pilots, and ten engineers. In that year, it flew 1,480 hours and carried 550 passengers. In November 1923, the company moved all its operations from Lac à La Tortue to Three Rivers because the maintenance facilities had become inadequate, and Lac à la Tortue remained frozen until late spring, which delayed the start of operations. At Three Rivers there was early open water, and Maxwell moved into the base formerly occupied by the Three Rivers Shipbuilding Co. Laurentide Air Services Ltd. continued to operate until it went out of business at the end of 1925: while the company was a great success operationally, it didn't make money.

In 1922, a new company, Fairchild Aerial Surveys (of Canada) Ltd. was formed, with headquarters in Grand Mère, to carry out aerial survey work. It was a subsidiary of Fairchild Aerial Surveys of the United States, the foremost aerial survey company in North America. The formation of the Canadian company was influenced by Ellwood Wilson, who had been so impressed by the results of the operations of the Laurentide Co. and Laurentide Air Services Ltd. in the previous three years. Initially, the Fairchild Aerial Surveys company had two aircraft: a Curtiss Seagull flying boat, and a Standard JL. The latter was operated on skis during the winter of 1923-24, "thereby constituting what is believed to be the first record of a commercial aviation company operating successfully throughout the year on floats, wheels and skis."[1]

The company established an airfield at Lac à la Tortue, with three runways, each 1,600 feet [488 metres] long, on a field 600 feet [183 metres] wide. In 1924, a hangar was built from the crates of HS-2L flying boats. An all-metal hangar was built in 1927, followed by a second in 1929. Fairchild entered the air transportation business in 1926, initially as part of Elliot-Fairchild Air Service. Later that year, Fairchild split with Elliot, and the company became Fairchild Air Transportation Ltd. In 1927, the company expanded from three to seven aircraft and entered into the air-mail business in the fall of that year. The company eventually became part of Canadian Airways, which succeeded to the property at Lac à la Tortue in 1929, and the base became the main repair depot for Canadian Airways Ltd. (Eastern Lines). It was an ideal site for air operations in that it was one of the few combined seaplane and landplane bases in Canada.

The Department of National Defence *Report on Civil Aviation for 1923* discussed the early operations at Lac à la Tortue in 1919 and commented: "the first Civil Airharbour was thus established and the first practical use made of Civil

26. Curtiss Seagull and Curtiss HS-2L aircraft at Lac à la Tortue, Québec, 1920.

27. Lac à la Torture, c. 1921.

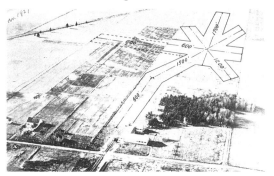

28. Lac à la Torture, c. 1928.

29. Lac à la Tortue, 1929.

Aviation in Canada."[2] Air regulations came into force in January 1920, and all existing civil air activities were slowly brought under regulation. Laurentide Co.'s aerial operations at Lac à la Tortue were licensed as follows: the two HS-2L flying boats were registered as G-CAAC and G-CAAD; Graham was granted a pilot licence; and Kehoe and his engineers, licences. An airharbour licence for a seaplane base at Lac à la Tortue was issued to Laurentide Co., on June 2, 1920, location 46 36 N and 72 40 W, three miles [five kilometres] southeast of Grand Mère.[3] In the 1929 List of Airports (see Appendix 20), Lac à la Tortue is shown as a seaplane base, at the same location, in the name of Fairchild Aviation Co., Grand Mère. In the Department of National Defence Airways Bulletin No. 1 of March 1, 1932, Lac à la Tortue is shown as having two licences, both in the name of Canadian Airways Ltd., Grand Mère. One is for the seaplane port, having the same geographical coordinates as above. The other is for aerodrome "two miles [three kilometres] east of Grand Mère on the west shore of Lac à la Tortue" at 46 36 30 N and 72 40 W.[4] In the 1989 issue of the Canada Flight Supplement, Lac à la Tortue is shown as a public airport, operated by Bel Air Laurentian Aviation Inc. at 46 37 N and 72 38 W, with a note, "seaplane traffic on adjacent lake."[5]

First Licensed Airharbour

Airharbour licence No. 1 was issued on April 22, 1920, to Aerial Service Co. at Regina. The airharbour was classed as "commercial" and was located southwest of the city near the parliament buildings. The licence was issued under the first Canadian Air Regulations, which came into force on January 17, 1920. (See Appendix 4 for a list of the licences issued in 1920 and 1921.)

Rockcliffe

In 1920, the Department of Militia and Defence agreed that the vacant land near the gun range at Rockcliffe, Ottawa, could be used as an aerodrome. The Air Board had selected the site as the most suitable one for an aerodrome within a radius of fifteen miles [twenty-four kilometres] of Ottawa. There was already a Civil Government Air Operations (CGAO) seaplane base nearby on the Ottawa River, and the addition of the aerodrome presented a combined land-water unit, the only one in the CGAO. It was opened in the fall of 1920, and its major activities for the next forty years included aerial photography for mapping much of Canada, air transportation (including "Mailcan," the RCAF's wartime Overseas Mail Service), and aeronautical experimentation. Operations were transferred to Shirley's Bay seaplane base in 1925 but returned to Rockcliffe early in 1929. At that time, the aerodrome was increased by twenty-two acres [nine hectares].

The aviation history of Rockcliffe goes back to late 1918 when the Royal Air Force training organization in Canada carried out a number of experimental air-mail flights between Toronto (Leaside) and Ottawa in August and September, using the area behind the Rockcliffe rifle butts as a landing ground. Rockcliffe aerodrome remains in use to this day. It is now operated by the Rockcliffe Flying Club and is restricted to club use.

30. Canadian Air Board Station, Rockliffe, Ontario, May 26, 1921.

A steep take-off and landing (STOL) port was constructed at Rockcliffe by the Department of Transport in 1974 and was used from July 24 of that year to April 30, 1976, for the experimental STOL service between Montréal (the Expo '67 parking lot) and Ottawa.

Camp Borden

Built by the Royal Flying Corps in 1917, Camp Borden aerodrome was reactivated in 1920 on January 8 and is thus the oldest air force land station. At that time, RAF aircraft were withdrawn from storage, assembled, and flown.[6] When the formation of the Canadian Air Force was authorized on February 18, 1920, Borden became its school of aviation, and was then the only aerodrome in the CAF. Borden is not only the birthplace of Canada's air force; because of the wartime activities of the RFC/RAF, it is also the first important centre for military flying in Canada. As late as the spring of 1927, J.A. Wilson, then head of the Civil Aviation Branch of Department of National Defence, considered that Camp Borden was the only "real airport" in Canada and that the other private and municipal aerodromes could in no way be termed airports in the contemporary sense of the word.

In 1931, many of Borden's activities were transferred to a new permanent training centre at Trenton. But when World War II began, Borden was reactivated. It became No. 1 Service Flying Training School in 1940 and began training pilots for the British Commonwealth Air Training Plan. In 1946 it was disbanded, and No. 2 Technical Training School was re-established there. Today, it is the major centre for training skilled tradesmen for the Canadian Forces Air Element. The airfield is maintained as an "emergency satellite airfield" and is used primarily to support military transients and base training requirements. It is also home for a flying club and a gliding club.

Morley

Morley aerodrome was established for Government Civil Air Operations in 1920 on an Indian reserve in the Bow Valley, and a Bessoneau hangar (see Appendix 1) was erected there in August. The aerodrome was one of the air bases built following recommendations of an interdepartmental conference held in January 1920 to consider proposals for the institution of government air services. Morley was established to provide better fire protection for the Dominion Government Forest Reserve on the eastern slopes of the Rocky Mountains. DH-9A landplanes were used. The site eventually became too limited and in 1921 the station was moved to High River, sixty-four kilometres south of Calgary.

Hanna

There was an airharbour in Hanna, Alberta, in 1921, licensed in the name of C.M. Holbrook and E.L. McLeod, who had purchased a JN4 airplane from Stan McClelland in Saskatchewan and had flown it to Hanna on April 28, 1920. Their licence, No. 7, was issued on May 10, 1921. Maximum dimensions for landing were less than three hundred yards [274 metres]. There were facilities for minor repairs to Curtiss JN-4 aircraft, and a hangar with accommodation for one machine.[7] McLeod and Holbrook's company closed down in 1923.[8] As of 1989, the town of Hanna operates a public airport not far from the original site.

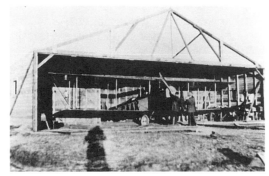

31. McLeod and Holbrook's Curtiss JN-4 Canuck G:CAAK in hanger on Hanna airfield, Alberta, 1920.

The 1922 Report of the Air Board contains the first published list of airharbours available for use.[9]

Place	Type	A/S*	Size	Customs
Vancouver	Govt	Sea	+4 mls sq	-
Vancouver	P/C*	Sea	±2 mls sq	-
Esquimault	P/C	Sea	+800 yds sq	-
Comox	P/C	Sea	+800 yds sq	-
Hazelton	P/C	Both	200 x 600 yds	-
High River	Govt	Aero	600 x 800 yds	-
Calgary	P/C	Aero	300 yds sq	-
Banff	P/C	Sea	1000 yd x 5 mls	-
Edmonton	P/C	Aero	-300 yds sq.	-
Hanna	P/C	Aero	-300 yds sq	-
Lethbridge	P/C	Aero	600 x 800 yds	-
Saskatoon	P/C	Aero	300 x 400 yds	-
Moose Jaw	Public	Aero	400 x 700 yds	Customs
Regina	P/C	Aero	+800 yds sq	-
Wapella	P/C	Aero	-300 yds sq	-
Yorkton	P/C	Aero	-300 yds sq	-
Victoria Beach	Govt	Sea	+800 yds sq	-
Winnipeg	P/C	Aero	-300 yds sq	-
Winnipeg	PC	Aero	300 x 500 yds	-
Brandon	P/C	Aero	400 x 600 yds	-
Virden	Public	Aero	800 yds sq	Customs
Ottawa	Govt	Both	400 x 700 yds	-
Camp Borden	Govt	Aero	1 x 2 mls	-
Deseronto	Public	Aero	400 x 700 yds	Customs
Toronto	Public	Aero	400 yds cir dm	-
Toronto	Public	Aero	400 x 700 yds	-
Brantford	P/C	Aero	300 x 400 yds	-
Sault SteMarie	P/C	Sea	+800 yds sq	-
Roberval	Govt	Sea	+800 yds sq	-
Chicoutimi	P/C	Sea	+800 yds sq	-
Grand Mere	P/C	Sea	+800 yds sq	-
Montreal	Public	Aero	400 x 750 yds	Customs
Montreal	P/C	Aero	-300 yds sq	-
St. Jovite	P/C	Aero	300 x 500 yds	-
Fredericton	Public	Sea	+800 yds sq	Customs
Halifax	Govt	Sea	+800 yds sq	-

*P/C - Private-Commercial
*A/S - Aeroplane/Seaplane

There were, then, twenty-three airharbours for landplanes, twelve for seaplanes, and only two for both. Seven airharbours were government, while only another seven were public.

Air Board policy encouraged the establishment of municipal aerodromes and its 1920 Report records the loan of spare Bessoneau hangars to the town of Virden and the Canadian division of the Air League of the British Empire in Montréal (at Cartierville).

When, on January 1, 1923, the Air Board ceased to exist as a separate department of the government, responsibility for civil aviation was placed under the Department of National Defence, which issued the annual reports on Civil Aviation thereafter. The 1924 report explains the application of air regulations to airharbours:

Airharbours

As no aircraft may be operated except from a licensed airharbour, the company leases or buys a site for its airharbour, and applies for its licence. An inspector visits the site and reports on its suitability. The points given special attention are the wind conditions and, in the case of a seaplane station, its exposure to heavy seas; the area available for taking off and alighting; whether it is surrounded by buildings or natural objects likely to obstruct the taking off of aircraft; the surface of the ground and the nature of the soil. If the site is found satisfactory a licence is issued. Airharbours have been divided into the following classes:-

I. Airship harbours (i.e. for lighter-than-air machines).

II. Aerodromes and seaplane stations, subdivided as follows:-

(a) Public airharbours open by day and night.

(b) Public airharbours open by day only.

(c) Public customs airharbours open by day and night.

(d) Public customs airharbours open by day only. (Airharbours licensed under classes (c) and (d) are recognized by the Customs and Immigration authorities as ports of entry from foreign countries. Classes (a) to (d) are open to all traffic on payment of approved landing and storage charges.)

(e) Commercial airharbours.

(f) Commercial customs airharbours (Airharbours licensed under (e) and (f) are for the use of the licensee only.)[10]

In the same report, the term "civil" is used for the first time in relation to licensed airharbours. The term "airports" was first used in the 1927 Report.

The following table shows licensed civil airharbours by province and year:

Province	1924	1925	1926	1927	1928	1929
British Columbia				2	2	5
Alberta	1	1		4	4	5
Saskatchewan	4	4		4	6	3
Manitoba	3	3		2	4	3
Ontario	6	16		9	12	19
Quebec	9	9		4	3	7
New Brunswick	1	1		1	1	1
Nova Scotia					1	2
Totals	24	34	34	26	33	45

Light Aeroplane Clubs

In 1927, the Department of National Defence announced a plan encouraging the formation of flying clubs similar to the one used successfully by the British government from 1924. The flying club plan turned out to be of great importance in the development of aerodromes, because one of the conditions of a grant was that the association or club must provide "a flying field or seaplane station which fills the requirements of the Air Regulations, 1920."[11] The light aeroplane club proposal was well received and, in 1928, fifteen clubs were organized and granted assistance by the government under the standard conditions (see Appendix 9). Clubs were formed at:

Halifax	(seaplanes)
Granby	
Montréal	(St. Hubert airport)
Ottawa	(Uplands airport)
Toronto	
Hamilton	(municipal airport—the first club to join)
London	(municipal airport)
Border Cities	(Windsor-Walker airport)
Winnipeg	(municipal airport)
Regina	
Moose Jaw	
Saskatoon	(municipal airport)
Calgary	(municipal airport)
Edmonton	(municipal airport)
Victoria [12]	

In 1929, there were eight new clubs, operating at:

Sydney
Saint John   (municipal airport)
Kingston
St. Catharines
Brant and Norfolk
Fort William
Brandon
Aero Club of B.C. (Vancouver—municipal airport)[13]

St. Hubert

The circumstances surrounding St. Hubert's development have already been described. The 1928 Report on Civil Aviation stated: "St. Hubert is also being developed to form a great public air terminal aerodrome, which may be used on equitable terms by all desiring to do so."[14] In November 1927, the demand for an aerodrome became urgent, and a temporary facility adjacent to the mooring tower was cleared and graded for use and a wooden hangar was built while the permanent aerodrome was under construction. The aerodrome was first used in November 1927 by a Fairchild owned by the Post Office and operated by (government) Air Services in connection with the experimental airmail flights from Rimouski. In 1928, a permanent hangar was erected, and aerodrome lighting and a beacon installed, "so that night flying is now possible from this field. A radio station has been erected and weather reports are being received regularly...The airport, when complete, will rank as one of the most efficiently equipped airports in the world."[15] The first scale of user fees was also introduced (see Appendix 19). St. Hubert was the first civil aerodrome to be built and operated by the government of Canada. Prior to this, municipalities were required to provide their own.

Rimouski

Rimouski was the second civil aerodrome to be owned by the government. It was constructed in 1927 near to the government wharf for use on the experimental air-mail service between Montréal and Rimouski, and was first used in November. Mail was transferred to and from ocean liners as part of a Canada-U.K. scheme to speed delivery between the two countries. Rimouski was chosen because of its proximity to Father Point, where the ships picked up or dropped off St. Lawrence River pilots. Initially, flying boats and seaplanes were used, but they were found unreliable because of rough water.

32. Curtiss HS-2L flying boat of Canadian Airways Ltd. inaugurating the air-mail service between Rimouski and Montréal, Québec, 1927.

Toronto and Montréal Airports

In the late 1920s, several aerodromes and airports were established in the Toronto and Montréal areas.

Toronto Area

In the Winter edition of the CAHS Journal of 1965, C.D. Lang gives short descriptions of twelve airports. Some of these have been referred to in Chapters 2, 4, and 5. The remaining seven are mentioned below, with credit to Long.[16] [Toronto Map, page 266]

Barker Field

This field of about 220 acres [eighty-nine hectares] was located on the west side of Dufferin Street, north of St. Lawrence Avenue, Toronto. First operations took place in 1927. Training, sightseeing, and aircraft sales were carried out by Toronto Airways, Century Airways Ltd., C.L. Murray, Manning Bros., and others. National Air

33. Barker Field, Toronto, 1939.

Transport built a combined hangar and office building in the northeast corner of the site, which was officially opened as Barker Field on June 6, 1931. Leavens Brothers Air Services moved to this field in the spring of 1937 and built several hangars and workshops. Flying here ceased in 1953 and urban expansion claimed the site.

Willowdale

The field was located on the west side of Yonge Street, south of the present Park Home Avenue, Toronto. It was used during 1927 by Howard Watt, and in 1928 by Landau Air Transport for sightseeing and charter flying. It had no buildings. The field was licensed until January 17, 1929.

Canadian Air Express Airport

This site, on the east side of Dufferin Street,

south of Sheppard Avenue, comprised about 220 acres [eighty-nine hectares]. It was opened by Canadian Air Express in 1928. Two hangars were built on the north side of the field, and were used by Fitton Air Service, International Airways, Latcham Airways, and Air-Lac Ltd. for training, sightseeing, and charter flying from 1928 to 1936. Canadian Airways and Canadian Flying Service used the field for their air-mail operations from August 1930 until the cancellation of the air-mail service in April 1932. Today, this property forms the northeastern portion of RCAF Station at Downsview.

Newtonbrook

This was a field of about 140 acres [fifty-seven hectares] on the east side of Yonge Street, between Bishop and Cummer Avenues, Toronto. It was used from May to September 1928 by Elliot Air Services Ltd. as a base for training, sightseeing, and charter flying and had no buildings. The area is now covered by Ontario Hydro transmission lines, just south of the Algonquin Hotel.

195. Temporary Airharbour, Toronto September 2, 1930.

Toronto Airharbour

Opened by the Toronto Harbour Commission in May, 1929, this was a seaplane base on the bay, east of Yonge Street. It had a Customs office, waiting room, timber bleaching ramp, fuelling dock, crane, and moorings. It was used by Colonial Western Airways in 1929 for scheduled twice-daily service to Buffalo, flying Sikorsky S-38 amphibians. During that year, it was also used by Dominion Air Transport for the demonstration and charter of Savoia-Marchetti flying boats. Until the fall of 1938, it was used regularly by de Havilland Aircraft as a base for the installation of seaplane floats, and by Austin Airways for charter flying. A seaplane base was opened at the new Toronto Island Airport in 1939.

Downsview Airport

Originally a field of seventy acres [twenty-eight hectares] on the south side of Sheppard Avenue between Dufferin and Keele Streets, this airport was opened by de Havilland in August 1929, with a new brick and steel building on a siding just east of the CNR, and with some of the bigger buildings from Mount Dennis re-erected to the east. Between 1936 to 1938 a paint shop and a hangar were added to the south, and the main building was extended.

During World War II, the aerodrome was expanded and factory and flight-test buildings were added. Following the war, this became the property of the Department of National Defence, with

35. Downsview Airport in 1944, showing wartime growth.

the exception of a ninety-five acre [thirty-nine hectare] area at the south end of the field, where the present de Havilland offices and factory were erected in 1953.

Toronto Flying Club

This 220 acre [eighty-nine hectare] field on the north side of Wilson Avenue, just east of Dufferin Street, was officially opened on June 27, 1931, by the Toronto Flying Club. The Imperial Oil office moved there from Leaside, and an existing farm house was converted into a comfortable club house and restaurant on the south side of the field, about three hundred yards [274 metres] from Dufferin Street.

36. Leaside, Toronto
Toronto Flying Club, 1929.

37. Capreol and Austin hangar, Toronto Flying Club Airport, 1936.

The club was used for flying, training and recreation until it moved to Malton in 1942; and it was the principal Customs entry point for visiting aircraft until Malton opened in 1939. Austin Airways Limited (originally Capreol and Austin Air Services) carried out their landplane operations here, using a hangar leased to them by the club from 1934 until 1938. The property now forms the south-eastern portion of RCAF Station Downsview.

38. de Haviland Aircraft of Canada Ltd. at De Lessep's Field, Mt. Dennis, Toronto, 1929.

39. de Lessep's Field, Mt. Dennis, Toronto, 1932.

Montréal Area

The 1929 List of Licensed Airports, Appendix 20, shows the following:

Vickers Airport was a seaplane base on the St. Lawrence River described as a "private seaplane port" owned by Canadian Vickers Ltd.

Pointe aux Trembles was also on the St. Lawrence River. In 1929 it was a "seaplane anchorage-private" owned by Compagnie Aerienne Franco Canadienne.

Curtiss Reid Seaplane Port: also on the St. Lawrence; licensed in 1929 as "public" and owned by Curtiss Reid Aircraft Company. [Montreal Map, see page 267]

LaSalle Airport: owned by Dominion Aircraft Co. Ltd., and in 1929 licensed as a "public airport" of 1,800 square feet [167 square metres].

St. Hubert was a "public airport" with Customs. (See also Part II.)

Reid Airport (Cartierville): a "public airport"

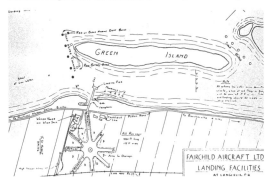

40. Fairchild's Airport and seaplane base, Longueuil, 1929.

owned by Curtiss Reid Aircraft Co. The site has been in use as an airport since 1912. (See also Part II.)

Longueuil Airport and Seaplane Port: located on the St. Lawrence River thirteen kilometres from Montréal at Longueuil, owned and operated by Fairchild Aircraft Ltd. of Montréal. The port was listed in 1929 as having two licences, one as a "public seaplane port," and the other as a "private airport." The latter had four runways, each 1,800 feet [549 metres] long. Imperial Airways (later British Overseas Airways Corporation) used the seaplane facility as the Montréal base for its fly-ing boats on the transatlantic air service, from 1937 to 1945. (See Map p.267.)

Air Mail

In 1927, the Post Office inaugurated regular air-mail service and granted contracts for four winter routes. Before this time, there had been many *ad hoc* air-mail flights authorized by the Post Office as special exhibition or experimental flights, exploratory flights to remote areas, or supply flights to mining camps. However, in the United States and in Europe, air-mail service was established; and the Post Office in Canada realized that a regular service was needed. While flights by float-equipped or ski-equipped airplanes had been successful, they were neither satisfactory nor reliable—as the early flights between Montréal and Rimouski had shown. Aerodromes and routes facilities would be necessary if a regular service, like that in the United States, was to be provided. The Post Office realized that time and money would be needed to provide aerodromes, especially in those parts of Canada where the terrain was uncompromising. The government, however, decided to first carry out surveys across Canada to determine where and in what manner a service could be operated.

A start was made on this long-term project in 1928; and it was hoped that the light aeroplane club plan would help to provide good aerodromes in each city.

In 1928, the Post Office awarded contracts for services between a number of major cities: in May, Canadian Airways Ltd. won the contract to carry mail between Montréal and Toronto, on flights that were scheduled to connect with the Montréal to Rimouski flights made by Trans-Continental—which carried mail for transatlantic ships. And in October, Colonial Airways began to carry mail between Montréal and Albany, New York. The Post Office awarded Western Canada Airways a contract in December 1928 for an experimental mail service connecting Winnipeg, Regina, Calgary, Saskatoon, and Edmonton.

41. First transatlantic mail by air to Ottawa, ex S.S. Mont Royal, October 27, 1927.

Aerodrome Development

The light aeroplane club scheme prospered and in 1928 sixteen clubs were operating at private or municipal aerodromes. The 1929 Report on Civil Aviation notes that "the club movement has been instrumental in establishing splendid aerodromes throughout the country."[17] The table in Appendix 20 lists all of the licensed public airports and intermediate and private aerodromes for the year 1929 and provides a status report on these facilities. The ownership column is of particular significance, since it identifies the local sponsor of aviation. Comparison with the Table of Airharbours for 1922 (Table 2) shows the progress made in the seven-year period.

Harbour Grace

Before closing the record of the 1920s, one more airfield, Harbour Grace, must be mentioned, even though Newfoundland was not then a part of Canada. Harbour Grace had figured in the 1919 Atlantic flights when it became the base for Vice-Admiral Kerr's Handley Page airplane.

The year 1927 opened a new era of transatlantic flights, beginning with Lindberg, Chamberlain, and Byrd. Early that year, a representative of the Stinson Aircraft Company of Detroit came to Newfoundland to find a suitable "hopping off" location for one of its customers. He chose Harbour Grace, and the citizens of that town constructed a suitable air strip, supplying both the money and the labour required. The strip, 4,000 by 200 feet [1,220 by 61 metres], running east-to-west, was built near Lady Lake on a plateau northwest of the town. The field was used for transatlantic flights between 1927 and 1936, and a listing of aircraft and crews may be found in Appendix 21. It is still serviceable and it is in use today.

42. Harbour Grace Airfield, Newfoundland, 1933.

Sources:

Brandt, Anthony S. "The First Canadian Fairchild Company, 1922-29). CAHS Journal vol. 9, no. 2. (Summer 1971).

Canada. Department of National Defence. Report on Civil Aviation. Ottawa: King's Printer, 1923.

Canada. Department of National Defence. Report on Civil Aviation. Ottawa: King's Printer, 1926.

Gallop, M.W. "Air Bases: Grand Mère, Quebec". The Bulletin [published by Canadian

43. Stinson SMI, "Pride of Detroit", first airplane on Harbour Grace airstrip.

44. "Green Mountain Boy" at Harbour Grace, August, 1932.

45. Amelia Earhart at Harbour Grace, May 20, 1932, during the re-fuelling of her Lookheed Vega.

Airways Ltd.] vol. 3, no. 5. (November 1931).

Molson, K.M. "Laurentide Air Service",

46. Jim Mollison and his Bellanca 28-40 Flash, "Miss Dorothy," enroute from New York to London England, October 1936 at Harbour Grace.

CAHS Journal, Vol 21, No.3 (Fall 1983), p.68-85.

Molson, K.M. Pioneering in Canadian Air Transport. Winnipeg: James Richardson and Sons Ltd., 1974.

United States. Department of Commerce. "Airports in Canada and Newfoundland". Trade Information Bulletin no.716. Washington: U.S. Government Printing Office, 1930.

Footnotes to Chapter 7.

[1] M.W. Gallop, "Our Air Bases: Grand Mère, Quebec," *The Bulletin*, vol. 3, no. 5 (Canadian Airways Ltd., November 15, 1931), p.2.

[2] Canada, Department of National Defence, *Report on Civil Aviation, 1923*, (Ottawa, King's Printer), p. 13.

[3] See appendix 4.

[4] Canada, Department of National Defence, Civil Aviation Branch, *Airways Bulletin No. 1* (1 March, 1932). p. 108.

[5] Canada, Department of Energy, Mines and Resources, Canada Centre for Mapping, *Canada Flight Supplement, 1989*, p. B324.

[6] These aircraft were left in Canada at the end of the war and donated to Canada by Britain. The Air Board, at its fifth meeting on July 28, 1919, decided that of the fifty aircraft stored at Borden, forty with spares were to be disposed of and ten with spares should be retained.

[7] "Canadian Airharbours," *Aviation and Aircraft*

Journal vol. XI, no. 17, (October 24, 1921), p.449.

[8] Ray Crone of Regina, in a personal letter to the author, April 2, 1990.

[9] Canada, Air Board, *Report of the Air Board* (Ottawa, King's Printer, 1922), p.17.

[10] Canada, Department of National Defence, *Report on Civil Aviation* (Ottawa: King's Printer, 1924), p. 21.

[11] See appendix 9, paragraph 1 (a).

[12] Canada, Department of National Defence, *Report on Civil Aviation* (Ottawa: King's Printer, 1928), p. 41

[13] Canada, Department of National Defence, *Report on Civil Aviation* (Ottawa: King's Printer, 1929).

[14] Canada, Department of National Defence, *Report on Civil Aviation* (Ottawa: King's Printer, 1928), p.73.

[15] Canada, Department of National Defence, *Report on Civil Aviation* (Ottawa: King's Printer, 1928), p. 74.

[16] C.D. Long, "Toronto Airports—Before Malton," *CAHS Journal*, (Winter, 1965), pp. 94, 96. The sections on Downsview and the Toronto Flying Club are copied directly.

[17] Canada, Department of National Defence, *Report on Civil Aviation* (Ottawa: King's Printer, 1929), p. 37.

CHAPTER 8

Airports of the 1930s: The Trans-Canada Airway

Despite the economic depression, the 1930s saw dramatic advances in both civil aviation and the construction and improvement of airports. This progress was marked by the completion of the Trans-Canada Airway, the establishment of the Department of Transport in November 1936, the creation of Trans-Canada Air Lines (TCA) in April 1937, and the inauguration of TCA's transcontinental passenger and mail scheduled services on April 1, 1939.

The Trans-Canada Airway was founded on the airports provided by municipalities across Canada, many of which came into being as part of the flying club movement. The government's role was to provide intermediate aerodromes between major airports as well as radio and weather services and lighting for night flying—an element crucial to the project's success.

Surveys began in 1928, and construction started in 1929. The prairie section—the easiest—was completed first. In March 1930, a contract was granted to Western Canada Airways for nightly service between Winnipeg and Edmonton via Calgary. At the same time, the Post Office awarded a contract to Canadian Airways for a daily air-mail service from Moncton to Montréal, Kingston, Toronto, Hamilton, Brantford, London, Windsor, and Detroit; and, by U.S. air mail, to Pembina, south of Winnipeg. There was, therefore, a through connection by air between Moncton and Edmonton by the spring of 1930.

Surveys were continued through the Rocky Mountains to find the best route to Vancouver. Unfortunately, at that time the effects of the depression began to be felt, and on March 31, 1932, the government discontinued the inter-city air-mail service. However, those sections of the airway that had been constructed were maintained and surveys for its completion were continued.

In 1933, the government established construction camps as unemployment relief projects (see Appendix 23). Airway construction work was especially suitable, and authority was given to begin construction of the intermediate aerodromes in British Columbia, Ontario, Quebec, and the Maritime provinces. Much valuable work was done on forty-three aerodrome sites through this scheme during 1934 and 1935. On July 1, 1936, the government closed the camps, and the Civil Aviation Branch continued the work by tendering contracts.

In 1937, the government stepped up the tempo of construction on the airway, which had been intermittent for ten years, and took measures to hasten completion from coast to coast (see Appendix 22). For the first time, adequate funds for a project of this magnitude were provided. By the end of January 1938, the construction of the aerodromes, radio ranges, and field lighting, and the installation of other necessary facilities between Winnipeg and Vancouver were sufficiently advanced to permit Trans-Canada Air Lines to begin its training program. TCA inaugurated regular air-mail service over this section on March 6, 1938. (See Airways Map, p.268.)

Meanwhile, the government pressed for the completion of the airway facilities on the long section between Winnipeg, Toronto, and Montréal through the rough and unsettled terrain of northern Ontario so that a regular service connecting eastern and western Canada by air might finally be possible. Training and familiarization flights over this section began on September 7, 1938. These were followed by mail and express services, and on April 1, 1939, passenger service over the whole system west of Montréal began regular operation.

On the section east of Montréal, TCA mail and passenger service between Montréal and Moncton began on February 15, 1940. It was extended to Halifax on April 16, 1941, and to St. John's, Newfoundland, on May 1, 1942.

The Trans-Canada Airway construction program involved the enlargement, paving, and lighting of all the principal airports. On the airway there were nineteen main airports at which regular stops were made, twenty-four intermediate fields with radio ranges, and forty-two emergency fields.

The construction of the Trans-Canada Airway merits a book of its own, but here we are interested mainly in the airports and aerodromes it produced.

Reports on Civil Aviation for the years 1931 to 1940 describe in detail the progress of the airway:

1931

During the year, the following facilities were provided:

Lighted public airports	12
Lighted intermediate aerodromes	30
Beacon (lights)	99
Radio beacon station	5
Lighted Routes	miles
Eastern Airways	226
Western Airways	994.5
Total distance lighted	1220.5

The establishment of lighted airways and the provision of other aids to air navigation were closely associated with the development of terminal and intermediate airports by municipal and private interests. Until December 31, 1931, the department contributed half the cost of field lighting equipment at such airports. All other expenditures were met by civic or private funds.

Major improvements were made to the following airports during 1931: Vancouver, Vernon, Cranbrook, Fernie, Edmonton, Calgary, Lethbridge, Regina, and Hamilton. Hamilton was lighted for night flying, the entire cost of which was borne by the city.[1]

1935

The construction of intermediate aerodromes and landing fields, hangars, buildings, and radio stations on the Trans-Canada Airway progressed during 1935. Crews continued work on forty-eight locations. Some locations permitted winter construction, while others could only be worked during the summer. Of the total, twenty became usable within that year, and on nine other sites construction was sufficiently advanced for emergency use.

By December 31, 1935, twenty municipal and public airports formed part of the Trans-Canada Airway; altogether, thirty intermediate aerodromes had been completed before 1930.[2]

1938

Fully equipped airports and aerodromes were completed at approximately every hundred mile interval from Vancouver to Montréal by 1938. The short feeder airways from Lethbridge to Calgary and Edmonton, from Regina to Saskatoon, Prince Albert, and North Battleford, and from North Bay to Toronto, were similarly equipped, and all had the following facilities:

a) one to four landing strips, 500 by a minimum of 3,000 feet [153 metres by a minimum of 915 metres], sea-level basis;
b) field lighting, including boundary and obstruction lighting, a rotating beacon, and a code light;
c) buildings, including offices for the radio and meteorological staffs; housing for employees in remote locations; equipment garages; and, where no commercial power was obtainable, a diesel power plant for the radio and lighting services and an emergency power plant for the radio range;
d) a meteorological observing and reporting station;
e) radio range station, approximately four miles [six kilometres] from the site and remotely controlled from the airport office;
f) a teletype station.

Two hard-surfaced runways had been constructed at the municipal airports at Vancouver, Lethbridge, and Edmonton, and three at Winnipeg. These fields were also fully lighted. At Calgary, two landing strips 500 by 4,000 feet [153 by 1,219 metres] were completed with stabilized base runways 150 feet [46 metres] wide. During 1938, the Department of Transport improved the airport facilities at Cranbrook and Medicine Hat and developed the sites at Cowley, Penhold, and Broadview as hundred-mile airports. Transport also built two runways and an administration building at North Bay; salt-stablized runways at Earlton and Pagwa; and two hard-surfaced runways at Kapuskasing. Further improvements were carried out at Kenora, Sioux Lookout, Wagaming, Nakina, Pagwa, Porquis, Muskoka, and Killaloe.

Three other major airport facilities were completed in 1938. The Toronto Harbour Commission finished construction at both Malton and Toronto Island municipal airports. Malton Airport was equipped with two hard-surfaced runways, one grass landing strip, full lighting, weather reporting capability, and radio range equipment; Port George VI Airport, as the island airport was first known, offered both land and sea facilities, complemented by a municipal hangar and an administration building. Work at Ottawa (Uplands) Airport was wrapped up with the completion of two hard-surfaced runways, a government hangar, and a radio range station.

The government also constructed a new north-south runway at St. Hubert, demolished the mooring mast that had been built to accommodate the Airship R 100, and built a new radio range station and a transmitter building, the latter offering two-way communication for the transatlantic service (routes flown by flying boats from Montréal to Southampton via Botwood, Newfoundland, and Foynes, Ireland).

Plans for the completion of the eastern section from Montréal to Moncton were under way. At Moncton, a major airport with full facilities was laid out, and construction started. At Megantic and Blissville, hundred-mile airports were under construction, and improvements to the airports at Saint John and Halifax began.

The installation of radio range stations at all hundred-mile airports from Vancouver to Montréal—thirty in all—was completed. Meteorological and teletype services based on the hundred-mile aerodromes equipped with radio range facilities were provided on a twenty-four hour basis over the whole airway system from Vancouver to Montréal.[3]

1939

By now fully equipped airports and aerodromes located at approximately hundred-mile intervals across Canada from Vancouver to Moncton had been completed at the following points, either by direct government provision or by assistance to municipalities: Vancouver, Princeton, Grand Forks, Cranbrook, Lethbridge, Medicine Hat, Swift Current, Regina, Broadview, Rivers, Winnipeg, Kenora, Sioux Lookout, Armstrong, Nakina, Pagwa, Kapuskasing, Porquis, Earlton, North Bay, Muskoka, Toronto (Island and Malton), Killaloe, Ottawa, Montréal, Megantic, Blissville, and Moncton.

These airports, providing as they did a continuous line of fields equipped with servicing facilities and aids to navigation from coast to coast, were of immense value to both military and civil services alike. In addition the intermediate aerodromes, spaced at approximately thirty-five-mile intervals between the one hundred-mile airports, were proving necessary to the ferrying of short range aircraft.

Western Section

The Lethbridge-Edmonton service was completed by the addition of Penhold to the airports already established at Calgary and Edmonton.

Canadian Airways Company Limited was running a daily service on floats from Vancouver to Victoria pending the completion of the airport at Patricia Bay.

Prairie Airways Limited was operating a daily service with twin-engine Beechcraft from Regina to Moose Jaw, Saskatoon, Prince Albert, and North Battleford. Full airport lighting was installed at the latter three sites.

Northern Section

Assistance was given to municipalities at Kamloops, Williams Lake, Prince George, Peace River, and Grande Prairie. The construction by the Department of Transport an airport at Fort St. John was undertaken but could not be completed because early frost. This site would be of considerable future importance since it formed a junction point on the Vancouver—Whitehorse and Edmonton—Whitehorse routes. Additionally, a survey was made over the section from Fort St. John to Whitehorse, possible sites selected, and preliminary surveys made of fields at approximately one hundred-mile intervals.

Central Section

Steps were being taken to extend Trans-Canada Air Line services between Toronto and New York, Toronto and Buffalo, as well as Toronto and Windsor, where airport construction began, with a summer, 1940 completion target.

The airport at Fort William, complete with lighting, was finished in the autumn. An intermediate aerodrome at Graham, approximately halfway between Fort William and Sioux Lookout, was also nearing completion.

Eastern Section

The municipal airport at Charlottetown was almost finished when Canadian Airways began operating a daily service from Moncton to Halifax and Charlottetown.

Administration Buildings

The Department of Transport constructed administration buildings at Regina, Calgary, North Bay and Malton, the latter being undertaken by Toronto with financial assistance from Transport. Buildings completed by March 31, 1940 were:[4]

Radio range buildings	41
Radio-meteorological buildings	19
Caretakers' cottages	10
Power houses	21
Radio staff living quarters	44
Terminal buildings	3
Hangars	8

The Trans-Canada Airway was a tremendous undertaking, and its completion was a great credit to all those involved in its planning and construction. The introduction of regular scheduled coast-to-coast air-mail and passenger services transformed aviation in Canada and contributed enormously to the country's social and economic wellbeing.

Early Airport Traffic Control

By 1939, the volume of air traffic at major airports necessitated the formation of the Airport Traffic Control service of the Department of Transport . The 1939-1940 Report states:

Airport Traffic Control—The increase in traffic on and around many of the larger airports in Canada has made it necessary, in the interests of public safety, to institute a system of control of traffic in the vicinity of such airports, both on the ground and in the air. An assistant inspector who had had previous experience in this work was sent to the United States to study airport control systems in that country and regulations were drawn up embodying the best accepted practice on this continent. These regulations, among other things, require that an officer in charge of the control of traffic at an airport must be licensed by the department.

It was decided to install control on all the larger departmental airports and applications for the position of Airport Traffic Control Officer were invited by the Civil Service Commission. The selection of a group of 10 candidates was made from this list, and this initial group is being given a course of training on the St. Hubert airport, after which licences will be granted to the successful candidate.

Consideration is also being given to the purchase of the necessary physical equipment, including ground-to-air radio, visual signalling apparatus, and the construction of control towers.[5]

For more information on air traffic control, see Appendix 24.

During my research, I found an unsigned document entitled "Airport Construction in Canada" dated February 21, 1940 in the J.A. Wilson papers. It gives a complete account of airport construction to that time, and, while it covers more than the Trans-Canada Airway, its inclusion in this chapter is appropriate, even at the risk of some repetition. The latter part of the paper serves as a link between the Trans-Canada Airway and the airport program of the war years, dealt with in Chapter 10.

Airport Construction In Canada

The efficiency of any airway system depends largely on the quality of its ground services. As motor transport is dependent on a good highway system, air transport requires a good airway system. With this in view, the Air Services Branch of the Department of Transport, since its formation on November 2, 1936, has devoted its energies to the building up of a modern airway system.

A chain of good airports is a first essential. These are spaced along the airway at intervals of approximately 100 miles and are 'all weather' fields, i.e., surfaces are prepared so that they are usable at all seasons of the year. The length of clear landing runway in two or more directions is 3,000 ft. at sea level, with an added length of 150 ft. [914 metres] for every 1,000 ft. [305 metre] increase in the altitude of the aerodrome above the sea level. The approaches to the flightways are cleared of all obstructions in a ratio of 1 in 50 for safe approaches in conditions of poor visibility. These '100-mile' aerodromes are fully lighted for night flying with a 1,000,000 candle power rotating airway beacon, boundary and obstruction lights, and flush contact lights outlining hard surfaced runways.

A radio range station is installed about three miles from each of these aerodromes. The directional signals or beams from these range stations overlap the beams from the two adjoining ranges to give a continuous indication to the pilot in flight of his correct course along the airway. The pilot flying along the airway above an overcast can determine his exact position from the cone of silence directly above the range and fix his position relative to the aerodrome, should he wish to land. The radio range stations are controlled from the Radio—Meterological Station in which continuous watch is kept and the weather observations are taken hourly. These are relayed to the principal forecasting stations on the route and from them are compiled the weather maps and forecasts necessary for the operation of the route.

Thirty-eight such airports have already been built on the trans-Canada airway. These are of two classes:

(a) The stopping places or terminals for traffic or refuelling stations; and

(b) The secondary airports necessary to fill the gaps between the main airports but normally not used as stopping places.

At the principal airports, in addition to the weather, lighting and radio services outlined above, terminal facilities for the handling of passengers, mail and express traffic; hangars and workshops for the maintenance and shelter of Trans-Canada Air Lines' planes; and gasoline storage for refuelling have been constructed.

The principal airports are naturally located in good traffic centres. In this class are the airports at Vancouver, the Western terminal; Lethbridge, the junction for Calgary and Edmonton, Regina, Winnipeg, North Bay, Toronto, Ottawa, Montréal and Moncton. To bridge the long gap in Northern Ontario, similar facilities have been provided at Kapuskasing and Armstrong. Early next summer the trans-Canada system will be extended into Western Ontario and up-to-date airports are now nearing completion at Windsor and London.

All these airports, with the exception of four—at Wagaming and Kapuskasing, where there is no municipality capable of supplying this need; and at Ottawa and Montréal (St. Hubert), where the Department of Transport has built airports to meet its own requirements, have been provided by the municipalities. The Department of Transport during the last four years, by grants in aid for the development of municipal airports, has constructed the improvements necessary to bring them up to the standard required by the trans-Canada airway system. All the intermediate '100-mile' aerodromes have been constructed by the Department of Transport with the exception of that at Medicine Hat, which is a municipal airport improved by a grant in aid.

Once the main line system was completed, attention was given to the need for establishing feeder line services to give ready access to communities not on the main line. Assistance has been given to municipalities on such feeder lines to improve their airports to the required standard. Services of this nature are now established in Saskatchewan, serving Moose Jaw, Saskatoon, Prince Arthur and North Battleford, and connecting with the main airway at Regina. These cities have had generous assistance in improving their aerodromes during the past two years. A similar connection to the Lake Head cities of Prince Albert and Fort William is now being arranged. A modern airport complete with radio range on a site provided by the city of Fort William has been built and an intermediate field at Graham, Ontario, half way between Fort William and Sioux Lookout on the main airway.

In the Province of Quebec, plans are under consideration for assistance in building airports to serve the principal centres of population and industry. The Cap de la Madeleine airport has already been improved by a grant and a new airport site near Quebec City has been selected and its improvement will be undertaken during the summer of 1940. Sherbrooke is temporarily served by the intermediate aerodrome near Windsor Mills.

In the Maritime Provinces, assistance has been granted to the municipalities of Halifax, Saint John, Charlottetown, Summerside

and New Glasgow to improve their airports so as to increase the efficiency of the local services which now join the trans-Canada system at Moncton, N.B., the eastern terminal of Trans-Canada Air Lines.

In British Columbia a chain of aerodromes connecting with the trans-Canada airway at Oliver is being constructed to give access to the interior. Airport sites have been purchased by the municipalities of Kamloops, Williams Lake, Prince George, Vanderhoof and Fort Saint John, and grants have been made for their improvement. The municipalities of Vernon, Kelowna and Quesnel have also selected sites and their improvement will be undertaken when funds are made available. In the Peace River district airports have been built with assistance from the Department of Transport at Fort St. John, Grande Prairie and Peace River, and other projects have been considered for similar work at McLennan and Dawson Creek.

Activity in the location and improvement of airports has not been confined to the settled parts of the country. During the past few years, through the co-operation of the Department of Mines and Resources, a system of airports and inter-mediate aerodromes has been constructed in the Yukon Territory with main bases at Whitehorse, Dawson and Mayo. Surveys were made with a view to linking up the Yukon system with the Peace River district by an airway from Fort St. John to Whitehorse and five sites have been located at approximately 100-mile intervals, which will be developed as soon as funds are made available. Airports are necessary in this area as it is a comparatively dry country and lacks suitable rivers and lakes for the use of seaplanes. The Department of Mines and Resources has also co-operated with the Department of

Transport in the improvement of the seaplane and winter landing facilities in the McKenzie Basin at Fort Smith, Resolution, Providence, Simpson and Aklavik.

In all, the Department of Transport has built or improved, directly or through grants in aid to municipalities, 109 aerodromes. These include 15 principal airports, 23 secondary airports and 50 emergency landing fields on the Trans-Canada System and 21 airports to branch lines. Grants have been made to 32 municipalities to improve their airport under this comprehensive programme for the development of a modern airway system serving all parts of the Dominion.

These airports, built wholly for peacetime uses, were of great value in the existing national emergency, and without the transcontinental airway Canada's defence effort would have been seriously handicapped. In the early stages of the war it was necessary for the R.C.A.F. to transfer many units from their peacetime bases and to concentrate the available aircraft on either coast. The existence of a chain of modern airports from coast to coast made this possible and has increased the mobility of the Canadian Air Force many times. In addition, the fine municipal airports in our principal cities made possible immediate expansion of the pilot training programme to meet the wartime needs of the R.C.A.F.

The existence of good aerodromes throughout the Dominion will reduce the cost of the Empire air training scheme very greatly and what is more important will lessen the time taken to inaugurate training. At least 80 aerodromes will be required when the scheme is in full operation. Many of these will require to be specially built as use cannot be made, for various reasons, of all existing facilities. Many of these are in remote localities where the amenities necessary for training under favourable conditions are entirely lacking. Others cannot be used because of physical and climatic difficulties. At least 30 schools will be accommodated on existing civil aerodromes. These were built to meet the needs of a transport system and some of them will need modification to suit them for training purposes. The cost of making these modifications, however, is comparatively small as compared with the cost of building new aerodromes and the time required to complete the modifications to make them ready for training purposes is comparatively short.

Agreements are being negotiated with the municipalities of Vancouver, Lethbridge, Calgary, Edmonton, Medicine Hat, North Battleford, Prince Albert, Saskatoon, Moose Jaw, Regina and Winnipeg in Western Canada and with the municipalities of Fort William, Toronto, London, Windsor, St. Catharines and Moncton in Eastern Canada for their aerodromes to be taken over by the Department of Transport for the duration of the war. This is necessary as these airports will continue to be used by commercial air services. This will necessitate a complete airport control system and calls for uniformity in management and direction at all points so that the Air Force training programme and commercial air services may both function efficiently. In addition, the present programme calls for the utilization of many of the department's secondary and emergency landing fields in the programme.

The provision of all aerodromes required for the Empire Training Scheme is the responsibility of the Department of Transport. In October, 1939, the knowledge and experience of the Civil Aviation Branch in airport construction was placed at the disposal of the Department of National Defence and since that time its staff has been working in close co-operation with the R.C.A.F. in the selection of suitable aerodrome sites. Some 1500 individual sites have been examined. Survey reports on 163 aerodromes have been prepared and detailed contour and property surveys have been made of 82 sites. Based on these surveys, engineering plans and specifications are now being drawn up so that tenders for the preparation of the aerodromes may be called for. The work included grading, drainage, surfacing and lighting of the aerodromes as necessary for the training plan. Options on sites approved for development are being obtained rapidly so that the properties may be purchased, contracts let for the development, and the work finished on all sites required for the fall of 1940.[6]

Footnotes to Chapter 8

[1] Canada, Department of National Defence, *Report On Civil Aviation* (Ottawa: King's Printer, 1931), p. 15.
[2] Canada, Department of National Defence, *Report On Civil Aviation* (Ottawa: King's Printer, 1936), p. 98.
[3] Canada, Department of Transport, *Annual Report*, (Ottawa: King's Printer, 1938-39), pp. 20-21.
[4] Canada, Department of Transport, *Annual Report,* (Ottawa: King's Printer, 1938-39), pp. 21-23.
[5] Canada, Department of Transport, *Annual Report*, 1939-40, (Ottawa: King's Printer), pp. 23-24.
[6] "Airport Construction in Canada," unsigned document in J.A. Wilson papers, date February 21, 1940. (PAC, MG30 E243, Vol. 9). [for Airport Map see page 268]

CHAPTER 9

The Transatlantic Air Route: 1937 to 1945

The late 1930s saw plans for the establishment of a new air route and a regular transatlantic air service between Canada and England.

At the earliest planning stages of civil aviation in Canada, the government foresaw the need for an airway between Vancouver and Halifax, to be extended later to England, and finally from Vancouver across the Pacific to the Orient (see Appendices 25 and 26). The Trans-Canada Airway was regarded as the first part of this global plan.

The airship service operated between England and Canada in 1930 (with its Canadian base at St. Hubert) was to have been the beginning of the Atlantic air route, but it failed after one return trip. Before that, in 1927, the Montréal-to-Rimouski experimental air-mail was established to speed up mail carried by ocean liners between Canada and England. This was a small first step made towards developing the Atlantic air route. Other countries were also becoming interested in routing air-mail across the ocean. Seaplanes carrying mail destined for New York were catapulted from French liners off the Halifax coast during the summer of 1930. In 1931, Lufthansa aircraft made similar flights from the German liners, Bremen and Europa, reducing the normal sea crossing time by about twenty-four hours.

In the fall of 1930, representations were made to Canada on behalf of the American airline, Pan American Airways. In 1931, on the basis of a U.S. Post Office contract, the airline began to operate a summer daily service from Boston and Portland to Saint John and Halifax, with the option of extending the service to Sydney and St. John's.[1] The Montréal-Moncton air-mail service had been cancelled in June 1931 for economic reasons, thus making the American "intrusion" into Canadian air service a matter of great concern. (See Appendix 10 for a full background of the position as seen in 1931.)

Another issue was Newfoundland, which was not part of Canada at that time and was therefore in a position to grant traffic and landing rights to foreign airlines. Imperial Airways, with the approval of the British government, was negotiating with Pan American Airways, with the knowledge of the U.S. government, to set up an experimental transatlantic air service using flying boats. Newfoundland had agreed to grant Imperial Airways "full right and permission to operate air services between Newfoundland and other countries and... the right to operate air service within the territory of Newfoundland for the transport of passengers, mail and/or freight."[2]

Meetings were held in St. John's in July 1933 with representatives of Newfoundland, Canada, and the United Kingdom, and later, with officials of Imperial Airways and Pan American Airways, to discuss the proposed Atlantic service and route. The three governments agreed to co-operate fully with one another. Control of the ground organization, including air bases, wireless stations, and meteorological services, would remain wholly in British hands; Newfoundland would grant traffic rights to Imperial Airways, and similar rights would be available to a Canadian company, if desired; Pan American Airways would operate in Newfoundland by agreement with Imperial Airways. Imperial also agreed that any transatlantic service would include Montréal, and that any United States-to-Newfoundland service would stop at a Canadian airport designated by Canada. (See Appendix 27 for the press notice on the meetings.)

The United Kingdom's plans for the Atlantic Service were set out in a Dominions Office Dispatch of August 9, 1933. Essentially, it emphasized four major steps:

(a) the completion of two short "Empire" flying boats equipped with special tanks by the spring of 1936 so that experimental flights could commence the following summer;

(b) the development of larger and more powerful flying boats for the inauguration of regular mail and passenger services in 1937;

(c) the construction of two British experimental long-range landplanes for service in 1937 as an alternative to flying boats; and

(d) research into short-wave wireless direction finding in order to install experimental equipment at the Bermuda base, for testing with aircraft on the Bermuda-to-New York air service, once established.[3]

In November 1935, the governments of the United Kingdom, Canada, the Irish Free State, and Newfoundland met in Ottawa and agreed to co-operate in a programme of transatlantic air service development. This agreement, signed in Ottawa on December 2, 1935, set out two stages of development: (a) survey and experimental flights, and (b) regular service.[4] Imperial Airways would carry out the first, while a joint operating company would be set up for the second stage, which was expected to come about by 1938. During the experimental stage, the United Kingdom would finance flying operations. The Joint Operating Company, when established, would be financed by the participating governments. Each government was to arrange for the provision, in its own territory, of airports, radio and meteorological services, and other aids to air navigation. The government of Canada was to provide radio and meteorological services within Newfoundland although, in fact, radio services in Newfoundland were provided by the United Kingdom. Canada provided radio facilities on the route between Montréal and Botwood. Appendix 29 gives details of the requirements for the bases and communications at Montréal and Botwood.

Pan American Airways had been working closely with Imperial Airways, and planned to operate jointly on the North Atlantic route through Newfoundland and Bermuda. Approvals for the survey flights were granted by the governments of the United Kingdom and Newfoundland. Traffic rights were also granted for the future regular services. Canada granted similar rights, but insisted that both airlines land in Canada on the service between England and the United States. Imperial Airways readily

agreed to a regular stop in Montréal, but Pan American Airways considered Montréal too far off the route and, as a compromise, agreed to make its regular stops at Shediac, New Brunswick. (See Appendices 30 and 31 for copies of the permits.)

The bases selected for the survey flights in Newfoundland and Canada were Botwood, Shediac, and Montréal:

Botwood

47. Botwood wireless station, 1937.

Botwood, Bay of Exploits, Newfoundland (thirty-two kilometres from Grand Falls and fifty-six kilometres by air from Gander) was a seaport for the shipment of newsprint and ore. It offered a large sheltered water area but was closed because of ice for four months of the year. In 1937, Newfoundland and the United Kingdom provided the moorings, dock, shipway, and a temporary staff house (known locally as The Folly), while the U.K. provided a large temporary wireless station (for ground-to-air and point-to-point services, and for radio direction-finding). The base was controlled by Newfoundland. Canada provided meteorological services which, developed a world-wide reputation for weather forecasting on the North Atlantic route.

Botwood's connection with aviation goes back to 1921, when F.S. Cotton built a hangar there and began flying operations in Newfoundland. His radio operator, W.H. Heath, subsequently became officer-in-charge of the Air Radio Station at Gander. Botwood became an RCAF "Canso" station for anti-submarine patrol in 1941, and

48. Flying boat base staff house, Botwood, Nfld. 1937.

Canada built a large air force station at the old base, complete with hangars, slipway, and personnel accommodation buildings including quarters for army anti-aircraft batteries. In 1943, by agreement between Canada and Newfoundland, Canada handed over some of the A.A. Battery buildings to provide accommodation and a restaurant for passengers and crews on the transatlantic service. The buildings were operated by BOAC (Imperial Airways became the British Overseas Airways Corporation in 1940)

49. Shell Oil's refuelling barge, Oscar, at Botwood, Nfld., July 25, 1938.

50. Aerial shot, Botwood, Nfld., 1944.

and became known as the Caledonia Camp, named for the Imperial Airways' flying boat that made the first experimental crossing of the Atlantic in 1937. BOAC accepted the buildings as they were and the Department of National Defence charged no rent. The camp was jointly financed by the U.K. and Newfoundland.

Botwood was used by commercial flying boats from 1937 to 1945, when the North Atlantic service came to an end and landplane services began through Gander. As a matter of interest, no landing fees were charged at Botwood because the service was deemed experimental. The old "Boat House" and slipway still exist, and the site is marked by an historic plaque. Gander Lake was the alternate to Botwood, and moorings, a staff house, etc. were provided near Gleneagles. The buildings were used as a rest and recreation centre for the RCAF at Gander during the World War II.

Shediac

Shediac, twenty-four kilometres northeast of Moncton, is on the Northumberland Strait. Pan American Airways who made a temporary base there in 1937 with the approval of Canada, leased part of the government pier at Point du Chêne, laid moorings in sheltered water, constructed a floating dock with a gangway to the

pier, and put up an administration building. Canada provided a wireless station, while the company purchased and installed short—and long-wave direction finding equipment. Shediac was a regular stop for Pan American Airlines on its transatlantic service from New York to Southampton via Botwood in 1937 and 1939 and in 1942 to 1945. Air France did a survey flight into Shediac in 1939 but did not enter the transatlantic service. Imperial Airways chose Shediac as its alternate to Montréal.

51. Pan American Airways base, Shediac, New Brunswick, July 1939.

Shediac had been used as a base for an RCAF seaplane detachment from 1932 to 1934 to carry out "anti-rumrunning" patrols. It was also used on July 14, 1933, by General Balbo and his Italian air armada of twenty-four flying boats en route from Rome to the Chicago World's Fair, and for their return flight on July 25th. Shediac had also figured in 1932 plans for extending the ship-to-shore air-mail service to carry mail from ships in the Cabot Straits to Shediac by seaplane, transfer it by road to Moncton, and then send it by regular air mail to Montréal.[5] Money for a hangar and slipway was included in the estimates for several years, but the plans were never implemented. The service via Rimouski to Montréal was continued until November 1938.

Montréal

The Montréal base at Longueuil, on the St. Lawrence River, thirteen kilometres below the city of Montréal, served as the Fairchild Company's seaplane base and was chosen as the best landing area in the district; it was located thirteen kilometres from St. Hubert Airport. Moorings were provided, the channel marked, and a scow moored adjacent to the shore to serve as a landing platform. During World War II RAF Ferry Command had used Boucherville, about nineteen kilometres northeast of Longueuil, as its flying boat base.

The other bases on the transatlantic route used during the years of the flying boat service were Port Washington in New York, Foynes (on the Shannon River) in the Irish Free State, and Hythe, Southampton, England.

52. Imperial Airways' Caribou at Longueuil, Québec, 1939, after inagural transatlantic weekly service from Southampton.

1937

The Atlantic Service began in 1937 on July 5, Imperial Airways' Short C class *Caledonia* (under Captain A.S. Wilcockson) left Foynes, and Pan American Airways' Sikorsky S-42 *Clipper III* (under Captain H.E. Gray, who later became president of Pan American) left Botwood. They passed each other in mid-Atlantic and made the crossing without incident. *Clipper*'s time was 12 hours, 40 minutes; the *Caledonia*'s time was 15 hours, 28 minutes. The *Caledonia* went on to Montréal on July 8 and to New York, on July 9, then back to Botwood before leaving for Foynes on July 15. The *Clipper III* went on to Southampton from Foynes and returned via Foynes, Botwood, and Shediac, July 14 to 18.

Imperial Airways' flying boat *Cambria* (under Captain G.J. Powell) made the second trip from Southampton to New York via Foynes, Botwood, and Montréal from July 27 to August 2, and returned August 6 to August 9.

53. Pan American Airways' Sikorsky S-42 *Clipper III*, July 1937.

During 1937, Imperial Airways made ten flights across the Atlantic, six by the *Caledonia* and four by the *Cambria*. The *Cambria* also made courtesy visits to Ottawa, Toronto, Windsor, and Hamilton in September.

Pan American made another trip July 28 to 31: New York-Shediac-Botwood-Foynes-Southampton. The return trip by the same route was made August 4 to 7. Between August 16 and 29, Pan American made a survey flight, New York-Bermuda-Horta(Azores)-Lisbon-Marseilles-Southampton, and returned to New York by the same route August 29 to September 3. This flight concluded Pan American's survey flights for 1937.

54. Short Empire class flying boat G-ADMH *Caledonia* of Imperial Airways at Botwood, Nfld., July 6, 1937.

From June 18 to November 14, 1937, Pan American and Imperial Airways each carried out a weekly round trip commercial flying boat service between New York (Port Washington) and Bermuda. Between November 14, 1937, and April 6, 1938, Baltimore was used as the winter base instead of Port Washington, and each airline operated two weekly round trips. The service was continued by Pan American and Imperial Airlines in 1939. Imperial had only one aircraft, *Cavalier*, on the route; and when this was lost at sea due to carburetor ice on January 21, 1939 (three lives were lost and ten survivors were picked up by ship), Imperial Airlines was unable to replace it, and abandoned the New York-Bermuda route until 1946. In that year, Imperial Airways, renamed the British Overseas Airways Corporation, put three Boeing-314 *Clippers* on the route at the end of the North Atlantic season.[6]

1938

In 1938, Imperial Airways made one return transatlantic flight using the four-engine seaplane, *Mercury*, which was the upper component of the Short-Mayo composite aircraft. The lower component, *Maia*, a modified Empire flying boat, took off with *Mercury* on its back; the two aircraft would then separate in the air. By this unusual method, Mercury could be launched at cruising altitude with a load it could not lift off unaided.

On July 20-21, 1938, *Mercury* (under Captain Bennett) flew non-stop from Foynes to Montréal in 20 hours, 20 minutes, carrying a payload of 1,000 pounds [454 kilograms], making what is claimed to be the first commercial transatlantic flight by an airplane. The crossing from Foynes to the coast of Newfoundland took 13 hours, 29 minutes. The aircraft flew to New York from Montréal on July 22. Mercury made the return flight from New York via Botwood, Horta, and Lisbon to Southampton on July 25 to 27. The airplane took off under its own power on the return

55. Imperial Airways short *Mercury* at Botwood, July 1938, en route to the U.K. via the Azores.

trip, but because it could not lift enough fuel without the help of Maia, it was unable to make the direct crossing from Botwood to Foynes.

Mercury's was the only North Atlantic flight in 1938. Pan American made no transatlantic flights that year, apart from its New York-to-Bermuda service.

In December 1938, the Botwood radio station and meteorological office moved to permanent facilities in Gander. Each summer thereafter a small staff was sent to Botwood for the flying boat season.

56. Short Empire class flying boat G-ADHK *Maia* with Short seaplane G-ADHJ *Mercury* used for experimental airmail flights by Imperial Airways, England, 1939.

1939

The year 1939 was a busy one on the North Atlantic route. On June 24 to 28, Pan American Airways inaugurated transatlantic air-mail service on the northern route via New York-Shediac-Botwood-Foynes-Southampton in the

57. Pan American Airways Yankee Clipper at Botwood, Nfld., June 27, 1939.

Boeing 314 Yankee Clipper, NC 18603, with Captain H.E. Gray in command. He returned over the same route, June 30 to July 2.

On July 8 to 9, Pan American operated the first passenger service on the northern route, carrying seventeen passengers and a crew of twelve. Nineteen passengers were carried on the return westbound trip, July 12 and 13.

58. Imperial Airways' Cabot at Botwood, Nfld., 1939.

Pan American Airways continued to offer weekly return flights until the outbreak of World War II in September, when Pan American flights terminated at Foynes rather than Southampton.

59. Handley Page *Harrow* aircraft G-AFRL refuelling Short Empire flying boat G-AFCU *Cabot* of Imperial Airways, 1939.

Its last flight for the season was made through Botwood on October 10. In total, 540 passengers were carried through Botwood, including the first fare-paying passenger from New York to Botwood and the first from Botwood to England.

During 1939, Pan American also inaugurated air-mail (May 20) and passenger service (June 28) on the southern route, New York-Horta-Lisbon-Marseilles.

Although Imperial Airways had planned to begin North Atlantic air-mail service in June, it was

60. American Export Airlines' PBY at Botwood, Nfld., 1939.

delayed because aircraft were unavailable. However, it made sixteen flights between August 5 and September 29 on the New York-Montréal-Botwood-Foynes-Southampton route using Short modified C class flying boats G-AFCV *Caribou* (under Captain Kelly-Rogers) and *Cabot* (under Captain Bennett). On August 5-6, *Caribou* inaugurated the first British North Atlantic air mail to Canada and the United States.

Caribou and *Cabot* were refuelled in the air over both Botwood and Foynes by Handley Page *Harrow* air tankers operating from Gander and Shannon airports, respectively. In this way, the payload could be increased. Nevertheless, on *Caribou*'s first flight from Botwood, it had to take off without flight refuelling because the weather prevented the *Harrow* from making contact.

Cabot made the first night landing at Botwood on September 24. Both the *Cabot* and the *Caribou* were lost to enemy action in Norway in May 1940—at that time they were attached to the Royal Air Force.

Air France made three survey flights in 1939 through Botwood and Azores in flying boats F-ARAP(2) and F-NORD(1) and also visited Shediac.

American Export Airlines, a new U.S. airline, made a number of survey flights through Botwood and Foynes using a PBY.

1940

In 1940, BOAC made eleven Atlantic crossings between August 4 and October 10 using two aircraft, G-AFCZ *Clare* and G-AFCX *Clyde* (the same type of aircraft as those used during the previous year), but without using in-flight refuelling. These aircraft carried mail and a small number of official passengers. Pan American did not operate the North Atlantic route in 1940 nor in 1941, because of the United States Neutrality Act.

1941

Between May 18 and November 7, 1941, BOAC made eleven flights through Botwood to Baltimore, with its terminal at Foynes. It did not include Montréal, which, since May 4, 1941, had been served by the Return Ferry Service operated by BOAC between Prestwick and Montréal using converted Liberators. BOAC flew Boeing 314A *Clippers*, G-AGCA, *Berwick* GAGCB *Bangor* and G-AGBZ *Bristol* on the North Atlantic, carrying passengers and mail.

Note: In 1941, a large RCAF seaplane station and an army base were built at Botwood next to the civil flying boat base, which was manned by RAF Transport Command personnel from Gander, who looked after operations for the civil flying boat service.

1942

The North Atlantic route was busier in 1942 and saw the return of Pan American to the New York-Shediac-Botwood—Southampton route.

BOAC again used Boeing 314 *Clippers*. On June 26, Captain Kelly-Rogers flew Prime Minister Winston Churchill to Britain via Botwood in the *Bristol,* having earlier flown him non-stop from Britain to Washington. The last flight for the season was eastbound on October 28.

American Export Airlines operated under contract to the U.S. Navy. It flew Sikorsky VS-44A flying boats, carrying sixteen passengers, making some stops at Botwood, and several non-stop flights from New York to Foynes. One of its flying boats, the *Excalibur*, NC 41880, crashed during take-off at Botwood on October 3, 1942, killing eleven people.

1943

Pan American flew via Shediac and Botwood again in 1943; American Export Airlines and BOAC continued their operations through Botwood. On May 26, Captain Gordon Store took Prime Minister Winston Churchill and party non-stop from Botwood to Gibraltar in the *Bristol*. Churchill was returning from a visit to Washington. The last flight for the season was eastbound on October 28.

1944

Pan American, BOAC, and American Export Airlines operated through Botwood until it closed for the season on October 22. Pan American also continued to use Shediac.

1945

BOAC used Baltimore instead of Port Washington as its American terminal, and in October, at the end of the season, BOAC's Boeing-314 flying boats were transferred from the North Atlantic to the New York-Bermuda route.

Pan American continued to use Botwood and Shediac. On October 24, 1945, the *Atlantic Clipper* made Pan America's 455th and last transit of Botwood since service began in 1937; the airline had made 277 round trips in five years of summer operations, and 6,400 passengers had been carried through Botwood.

Landplane Service

1945 was the last year of commercial flying boat service through Botwood, and following the end of the war in Europe, commercial landplane service began through Gander Airport. American Overseas Airlines (successor of American Export Airlines) carried its first passengers through Gander using DC-4s on October 23, 1945; Pan American Airlines used DC-4 landplane *Clippers* on October 30; and Trans World Airlines used *Constellations* on November 25. BOAC was already operating *Liberators*, and Trans-Canada Air Lines used *Lancastrians*.

Atlantic Air Service Airports

Gander Airport, then known as Newfoundland Airport, and built by the United Kingdom and Newfoundland to serve the North American air route, had been completed in 1939.

The Newfoundland Airport was designed and built on massive lines and at the time was the largest airport in the world. It had four paved runways: one was 4,800 by 1,200 feet [1,463 by 366 metres], and three were 4,500 by 600 feet [7,242 by 183 metres]. The runways were built to that scale so that an airplane could land in any weather, for there was no alternate airport in Newfoundland, and the mainland of Canada was beyond aircraft range on a westbound flight from Ireland. The airport was equipped with the latest long- and short-wave radio direction-finding equipment. The main, and widest, runway had a Lorenz blind landing installation complete with inner and outer marker beacons and a directional beam down the runway. The Lorenz was a German system licensed to the English Marconi Wireless Telegraph Company and was the forerunner of the later Instrument Landing System (ILS). The runways were equipped with in-pavement lights; the instrument landing runway had sodium vapour lights for fog penetration.

The Newfoundland Airport did not serve its intended role for several years. The airplane for which it had been constructed, the de Havilland 91 *Albatross*, was built in England and first flew in May 1937 but was plagued with problems from the start. Atlantic flights were planned to begin in September 1937. Albatross I was to make two return flights from England to Montréal and New York via Dublin and Newfoundland airports; Albatross II was to fly out and stay in Newfoundland for winter experience. Following initial delays, the aircraft were expected to be ready by the spring of 1938; but after many modifications, one of the aircraft suffered structural failure on the ground and, while it was repaired, the aircraft was deemed unsuitable for its intended transatlantic role. The two original *Albatross*, re-named *Faraday* and *Franklin*, served in 271 Squadron of the RAF. Five more aircraft of the same sort were built under the class name *Frobisher* for passenger transport, and were used from 1938 to 1943 on several Imperial Airways' routes, including London to Paris. The *Frobisher* was a four-engine low wing monoplane; it carried twenty-two passengers and a crew of four, and had a cruising speed of 210 m.p.h [338 km/h]. It was of wood construction, similar to that of the very successful D.H. *Mosquito* used in World War II.[7]

The transatlantic flying boat service continued each summer until the end of the war, when suitable long range landplanes became available, and began service at Gander toward the end of 1945.

Although Gander did not fulfil its original objective in the development of a commercial landplane service across the Atlantic, it played a most important military role during World War II. It was first used as the farthest east base for the RCAF's anti-submarine aircraft patrols and became the home of 10 BR Squadron in 1940, and also it became the principal staging base for the RAF Ferry Command in delivering military aircraft to England. In 1942, the U.S. Air Force established a large base at Gander to ferry its aircraft direct to operational roles in Europe. Thousands of aircraft were delivered to England through Gander during the war years.

More about Gander's history may be found in Part II.

Footnotes to Chapter 9.

[1] The permission granted to Pan American to operate in Canada did not give them the right to carry mail or passengers between Canadian points. The people of Halifax and Saint John protested this, as they felt they should be allowed to use the service.

[2] Newfoundland Archives, file 229/33, extract from the draft act "For the Encouragement of Aerial Enterprise" of the Newfoundland Legislature, 14 July 1933.

[3] Public Archives Canada, MG 30E243, vol. 8, "Dominion's Office Dispatch Regarding Plans for Transatlantic Air Service," 9 August 1935. See appendix 28.

[4] Newfoundland Archives, file 570/35 Transatlantic Air Service Agreement, 2 December 1935.

[5] Dr. Fred Hatch, "Ship to Shore Air Mail Service of the 1920's," *Canadian Geographic* (August/September 19780, p. 56.

[6] Robin Higham, *Britain's Imperial Air Routes 1918-39* (London: G.T. Foulis & Co. Ltd., 1960) pp.199, 202.

[7] Higham, p. 294; and John Stroud, *Annals of British and Commonwealth Air Tansport* (London: Putnam, 1962) p. 151.

Chapter 10

Airports and Air Projects of the War Years: 1940 to 1946

The years between 1940 and 1946 were significant in the construction and improvement of airports. Although the impetus came from war requirements, the needs of civil aviation were always in the minds of Department of Transport officials. Improvements to the airports on the Trans-Canada Airway were of immediate benefit to both military and civil aviation, and as far as military requirements permitted, new airports for the Royal Canadian Air Force (British Commonwealth Air Training Plan (BCATP) and other activities) were sited so as to have a post-war use for civil purposes. Municipal airports taken over for the BCATP were enlarged and improved, and many were provided with paved runways.

The main wartime programs were the BCATP 1939-1944; the Northwest Staging Route, 1941-1944; the Crimson Route, 1942; and major projects in connection with the Home War Establishment and the Atlantic Ferry Service. While all of this was going on, the needs of the Trans-Canada Airway were not neglected, and new terminal buildings and control towers were built at major airports in the early 1940s.

The British Commonwealth Air Training Plan[1]

During World War I, Britain had set up flying training schools in Canada, (see Chapter 4). Immediately following the outbreak of World War II, Britain again approached Canada for assistance in training pilots. With the rapid expansion of the RAF, air space in the United Kingdom was crowded, and Canada offered the best prospect as a flying training centre, not only for Britain, but for the Commonwealth. Delegates from the United Kingdom, Australia, and New Zealand gathered in Ottawa in September 1939; the scope of the plan was determined in early October, and a cost-sharing agreement was signed on December 17, 1939. Britain, Australia and New Zealand were to send

their recruits to Canada for training, and Canada agreed to provide the necessary airport facilities and flight training. The cost was about $2 billion.

The original scheme called for sixty-four flying training schools, twenty of which were to open in June 1940, thirty-six in 1941, and the remaining eight during the first half of 1942. The requirements were later increased to seventy-five schools. Sixty-five of these centres were completed in 1940 and the remaining ten in 1941. This tells of prodigious organizational activity which ensured the success of the plan, especially since some of the bigger schools required two relief aerodromes to reduce congestion .

Immediately after the establishment of the air training plan in 1939, the Civil Aviation division of Transport became responsible for the selection of suitable aerodrome sites. As this branch was just completing a ten-year airport development program for the Trans-Canada Airway, its staff had acquired the necessary expertise. (See Appendix 32 for a list of the principal officials concerned.)

The construction season was already over, and it was only possible to select and survey the aerodrome sites during the autumn of 1939 before snowfall. Survey parties were organized across Canada and arrangements were made with provincial governments for detailed engineering surveys of each site as soon as its selection had been tentatively accepted by the Department of National Defence. This task was pursued with energy and, before the end of the year, suitable sites had been designated and surveys put in hand for about 80 per cent of the program.

The RCAF, hampered for years by a lack of funds for aerodrome construction, had only five aerodromes ready for use at the outbreak of the war, and six others were under construction.

The government arranged for the Department of Transport to take over practically all the larger

municipal airports in Canada for war-training purposes.[2] In a few instances, the Department of National Defence for Air took over the administration of these airports.

Where there was a considerable amount of civil flying, Transport retained control of the airport and provided the necessary staff for operation and maintenance, taking care that training schools and RCAF units were interfered with as little as possible by civil flying. This situation existed at airports in Vancouver, Edmonton, Windsor,[3] North Battleford, Lethbridge, Regina, London, Charlottetown, Calgary, Winnipeg, Malton (Toronto), and Fort William.

Municipal facilities were acquired by Transport and administered by the RCAF at Medicine Hat, Saskatoon, Prince Albert, Cap de la Madeleine, and Grande Prairie.

In addition, the following airports, built and owned by the Department of Transport, and forming part of the Trans-Canada Airway system, were used for air training purposes: Penhold, Swift Current, Rivers, Ottawa, St. Hubert, and Moncton (Ottawa and Moncton remained under Transport control).

New staff were hired and trained at most of these airports, with the exceptions of Vancouver and Edmonton where personnel had long been employed by the municipalities concerned.

As wartime air traffic increased at St. Hubert (due in part to BCATP and Atlantic Ferry Service operations), the federal government built another airport in the Montréal area, at Dorval, which was to be Montréal's civil airport. Facilities at St. Hubert were dedicated to RCAF air training, while the ferry service went to Dorval, where construction began in 1940 and was completed in September 1941.

The provision of training facilities under the BCATP had, for the most part, been completed by the end of 1942 and, during 1943 and 1944, construction was mainly for enlargement or improvement. (See Appendix 33 for a list of BCATP aerodromes.) The final period of operation for the training plan was 1944-45. Several schools closed before March 31, 1944, and many of the aerodromes became surplus to RCAF requirements. Later in the spring of 1944, an agreement was reached whereby such aerodromes would be passed to to the Department of Transport through the Crown Assets Allocation Committee. The department would retain those fields necessary for post-war operation, and the remainder would be disposed of through the War Assets Corporation. On August 1, 1944, the first such aerodrome went to the Department of Transport, and by March 31, 1945, eight hard-surfaced fields and twenty-three grass aerodromes had gone to the department. Of these, four hard-surfaced fields, comprising one municipal airport and three grass aerodromes, were recommended for retention.

Northwest Staging Route

The Department of Transport became involved in the construction of another airway in 1940. As a result of surveys begun in 1935, a recommendation was made to the government for an airway between Edmonton and Whitehorse via Fort St. John, Fort Nelson, and Watson Lake. Aerodrome sites were selected at Whitehorse, Watson Lake, Fort Nelson, Fort St. John, and Grande Prairie. Intermediate emergency landing fields were also to be provided. Despite the preoccupation of the Air Services Branch of the department with the urgent British Commonwealth Air Training Plan, it was decided to go ahead with the northwest airway, later known as the Northwest Staging Route. The joint Canada-United States Board on Defence strongly recommended the project in November 1940 because of its great strategic value. When the United States entered the war in December 1941, Canada was able to offer the use of an airway remote from the Pacific Coast, equipped with modern aids to air navigation, and connecting the airway systems of Canada and the United States at Edmonton and Vancouver, leading into the heart of Alaska at Fairbanks.

Canada bore the entire expense of developing the airway from Edmonton to the Yukon-Alaska boundary. Work began in February 1941, and, by early September 1941, the airway between Edmonton and Whitehorse was usable in fine weather and daylight. By the close of 1941, the radio ranges were in operation.[4]

Following the initial development of aerodromes at Grande Prairie, Fort St. John, Fort Nelson, Watson Lake, and Whitehorse during the summer of 1941, a much larger program was undertaken in the spring of 1942 to connect the existing fields with the Alaska Highway and to provide additional emergency landing strips and navigational aids between Edmonton and Northway, Alaska. This involved the establishment of a large-scale construction program to provide facilities for the American forces at Calgary, Edmonton, Grande Prairie, Fort St. John, Fort Nelson, Watson Lake, and Whitehorse, and to development of five landing strips at intermediate points between Fort St. John and the Yukon-Alaska boundary, with their associated buildings and radio range facilities.[5] This undertaking was well advanced by the close of the 1942 construction season.[6]

By the end of June 1943, the original project was almost completed. Additional buildings and facilities required by the United States and the Royal Canadian Air Force were built at four of the main airports on the system.

By July 1943, American contractors assumed responsibility for the completion of their original program at Grande Prairie, Fort St. John, Fort Nelson, Watson Lake, and Whitehorse, in addition to an extensive building program and the provision of supplementary field facilities, including taxi-strips and increased parking areas. The Department of Transport had responsibility for completion of the five emergency landing strips between Fort St. John and the Yukon-Alaska boundary, and for the additional field development at Calgary and Edmonton.

The large volume of traffic throughout the system since construction was completed in 1942 led to the need for a substantial runway rehabilitation program for the main staging aerodromes. The prevailing wind runways at Fort Nelson and Watson Lake were entirely reconstructed, while in 1944, the Department of Transport took over and completed the development begun by U.S. forces at Fort St. John in 1943. Additional concrete aircraft parking areas were also constructed at Edmonton Airport.[7]

The Northwest Staging Route leading to Fairbanks from Edmonton had been planned in pre-war days as a future extension of the Trans-Canada Airway, giving the shortest and most economical route to the Orient. Its completion in late 1941 simplified the huge construction task on the Alaska Highway and made possible the immediate augmentation of the U.S. air forces in Alaska and the delivery of thousands of U.S. built fighters, bombers, and transports to Russia via a safe and practical route.

West Coast—Defence

Following the entry of Japan into the war in December 1941, there was an immediate need to increase defence facilities on the West Coast. Work began in 1942 and was completed a year later; by that time, fifteen new aerodrome sites had been developed and longer, wider runways provided at twenty-three existing sites.

The Canol Project

The Canol Project, undertaken in 1942-43, is

worthy of brief mention, although it turned out to be of little value. As long as Japan dominated the Pacific, there was a possibility that American communications with Alaska might be cut off. Large military units were moved in to protect the peninsula, but the effectiveness of these forces could have been seriously hampered through lack of fuel. It was decided, therefore, to use the oil reserves at Norman Wells to meet the possible deficiency. This plan entailed building an oil pipeline from Norman Wells through the Rocky Mountains to the watershed of the Yukon and thence to Whitehorse—some of the roughest country over which an oil pipeline had ever been built.

The project could not have been completed in the time allowed but for the use of aircraft to move construction crews to selected points along the pipeline route. The airplane placed crews and their equipment on the ground, kept them supplied, and maintained communications over the route. To achieve this, the U.S. forces, with the approval and assistance of the Canadian government, built an air route to connect with the rail heads at Peace River and Waterways. Norman Wells was the northern terminus of the route. Aerodromes were constructed at Fort McMurray, Embarras, Fort Smith, Fort Resolution, Hay River, Fort Providence, Fort Simpson, and Wrigley for the winter movement of supplies during the long period of the year when water transportation on the Mackenzie River system was impossible.

The pipeline was built between Norman Wells and Whitehorse, where the refinery was also constructed. Oil was refined and gasoline and other products were manufactured, but when the U.S. Navy gained control of the eastern Pacific, the whole Canol project was rendered unnecessary. The refinery was closed and the pipeline abandoned.[8]

The Crimson Route

One further project must be mentioned in the airport program; the so-called Crimson Route[9] proposed by the U.S. Air Staff to provide a direct staging route from California to Northern Europe via a new transatlantic route using the Arctic Islands, Greenland, and Iceland as bases. Its advantage was that it called for shorter hops than were possible on the existing routes via Newfoundland and Labrador. In the opinion of the Canadian government, this project was not essential, and the difficulties involved would require men, money, and material that could be better used elsewhere. An airport at The Pas was built by Canada as part of the route, and permission was given to American authorities (who insisted that this was a necessary war measure) to construct the Arctic bases with their own forces. They built airports at Churchill, Coral Harbour on Southampton Island, Fort Chimo in Northern Labrador, and Frobisher on Baffin Island.

The route was never used for ferrying during the war, which proved the soundness of the Canadian decision[10], but in the post-war settlement of accounts between the two countries, Canada paid the U.S. in full for the construction costs and took over the airports. These airports gave access to the Arctic Islands and to the meteorological and scientific bases that were being established in the far North to help in the development of this hitherto remote region.[11]

Transatlantic Ferry Service and the Northeast Staging Route

In the history of the wartime development of airports, these two programs are interrelated.

The British Air Ferry Operation, initially managed by CP Air Services, began in 1940 at St. Hubert and Gander (which was then Newfoundland Airport). In September 1941, the Royal Air Force Ferry Command ((RAFFC), the new name of the Atlantic ferry organization) moved to Dorval Airport, which the Department of Transport had built as the new civil airport for Montréal and the main base for transatlantic ferry operations. St. Hubert was then transferred to the RCAF, and Newfoundland transferred Gander Airport on a temporary basis to Canada on April 1, 1941, so that it could be developed as a major air force establishment for use by the RCAF, the RAFFC, and the U.S. Air Force.

To improve air communications across the Atlantic, the Department of Transport was authorized in 1941-42 to construct new bases at Mont Joli, Saguenay, Seven Islands, Moncton, Sydney, Torbay, and Goose Bay (the latter with the approval of Newfoundland). At this time, Gander was greatly expanded. The United States, with Canadian consent, built a large intermediate airport at Mingan, Quebec, to assist the movement of aircraft from Montréal to Goose Bay along the northern route.[12] These new bases substantially improved the efficiency and safety of the transatlantic ferry system and of the anti-submarine patrols off the Atlantic and Gulf of St. Lawrence coasts. They also serve the important purpose of providing staging aerodromes to service other bases built by the United States in Greenland and Iceland.[13]

So far in this chapter, airport development during the Second World War has been dealt with under a series of headings to identify the project or program under which it was built. Vast as these projects were, other airport construction and development was going on at the same time, and this is my next subject.

Home Establishment and the Trans-Canada Airway

Since some of the projects under this dual heading are interrelated, no attempt is made to deal with them separately.

During the period 1940 to 1945, the Department of Transport constructed combined administration-terminal buildings at Windsor, London, Charlottetown, Dorval, and Whitehorse, and built and operated control towers at Winnipeg, Regina, Ottawa, Vancouver, Edmonton, Lethbridge, Calgary, Moncton, Windsor, London, Malton, North Bay, and Montréal. Dorval Airport was constructed as a civil aviation facility. Following this, a new airport was constructed at Ancienne Lorette to serve the RCAF, BCATP, and Quebec City. Improvements to airports in eastern Canada and Newfoundland were carried out at Torbay, Sydney, Dartmouth, Seven Islands, Moncton, and Gander.

As the huge airport development program began to wind down towards the end of 1943, J.A. Wilson, director of Air Services in the Department of Transport, stated:

The construction programme has been continuously expanded during the past four years until it now comprises not only the aerodromes required for the Training Plan but those required for all defence services, including those required by the U.S. Army Air Service for their special purposes. It now stretches from the Labrador and Newfoundland Coasts to the Pacific Coast and the Yukon-Alaska Boundary, and from the International Boundary to the Arctic Circle. It comprises 324 separate projects and funds exceeding $180,000,000 have been made available to the Air Services Branch by the Defence Services for this purpose. Military and civil services have worked in closest harmony and cooperation in its execution. The Aerodrome Development Committee of the RCAF meets each week and is attended by representatives of the Civil Aviation

Branch. In this Committee final recommendations as to the choice of sites, development plans and other matters are discussed between the services before approval of expenditures is given. This immense task has thrown a great strain on the small Airway Staff of the Civil Aviation Branch, who have spared no effort to meet all requirements of the R.C.A.F.

The construction programme is virtually complete, though as we all know, no aerodrome is ever finished, and extensions and modifications to meet new conditions continually arise. Every effort has been made in choosing the new aerodrome sites to place them where they will be of some advantage in the post war world, but no ulterior motive of this nature has been allowed to interfere with the main objective of providing airports which would in the first place be entirely suitable for training purposes.[14]

The time had now come for the government to prepare for the return to peace and, by the end of the fiscal year 1944-45, much thought was being given to the revival of peacetime aviation and the airports that would be required to serve it.

Transition to Peacetime Aviation

In his 1944-45 annual report to Minister of Transport C.D. Howe, Deputy Minister C.P. Edwards reported on some first steps:

With completion of the period of operation for the British Commonwealth Air Training Plan, and in anticipation of an early conclusion of hostilities, necessary steps have been taken by the Department of Transport to acquire facilities no longer necessary for defence or training purposes in order to meet requirements of the possible expansion of aviation as a transportation media in the post-war period. An agreement was reached whereby all aerodromes built for the Royal

Canadian Air Force under the British Commonwealth Air Training Plan would revert to the Department of Transport through the Crown Assets Allocation Committee and such fields as are necessary for post-war operations will be retained. Similarly, negotiations were successfully concluded whereby the United States was reimbursed by Canada for any aerodrome improvements or facilities constructed by them in northern Canada during the critical days of the Pacific campaign. These airports and facilities will eventually be turned over to the department for use in civil aviation, wherever possible. It has been noted that there has already come a marked revival in northern development in prospecting, mining and trapping as a result of the relaxation of military requirements in relation to civilian services.[15]

The same report of the Department of Transport provides more detail on Canada's purchase of American facilities—a most significant event in the preservation of Canada's sovereignty:

During the critical days of the Pacific campaign, the United States Army authorities were given permission to assist in the improvement of airports and ancillary facilities on the Northwest Staging Route, construct landing strips down the Mackenzie River, construct airports and ancillary facilities at Churchill, Southampton Island, Frobisher and Chimo on the proposed route from The Pas to the northeast, and at Mingan on the north shore of the St. Lawrence River. The aerodrome at The Pas was built by the Department of Transport. During the year negotiations were successfully concluded whereby the United States was reimbursed by Canada for all improvements made by it on these airports. On completion of their use for war purposes, these airports and facilities will be turned over to the Department of Transport where arrangements will be made for their use in civil flying wherever possible.[16]

A Downpayment On Canadian Sovereignty

In discussing the acquisition of the American assets in Canada, J.R.K. Main stated:

The Prime Minister, Mackenzie King, had made up his mind that no loophole would be left for American legislators to claim property or any other special rights in Canada after the conclusion of hostilities, and rightly judged that the few millions involved would be a low price to pay for the avoidance of any misunderstanding on this score.

This was no bargain counter. Costs are rarely considered in wartime, and these were probably three times higher than they would have been in other circumstances. However, the Permanent Joint Board on Defence, in whose hands the negotiations rested, made an assessment on the basis of the amount to be allowed as compensation for war extravagances.

Main went on to provide details of the sums paid to the United States which are as follows:

North-West Staging Route	$31,311,196
Flight strips along the Alaska highway	3,262,687
Flight strips along the Mackenzie River	1,264,150
Hudson Bay air route (Crimson Route)	27,460,330
Mingan Airport, P.Q.	3,627,980
Goose Bay Airport	543,000
Telephone Line from Edmonton-Alaska boundary	9,392,208
Total	$76,811,551

The actual costs incurred by the United States ran to $90,683,571, from which a sum of $13,872,020 was deducted on the assumption that this represented the value of the facilities in excess of their permanent usefulness.

The costs incurred by the Canadian government on American government accounts were:

North-West Staging Route	$18,359,953
North-West Canada	1,290,010
Goose Bay Airport, Labrador	9,950,000
Total	$29,599,963

In addition, the Canadian government paid $5,161,000 for improvements underway on the North-West Staging Route.

To preserve the Canadian peace of mind and keep Canadian sovereignty unblemished, some $111,000,000 was paid out for assets, some of which were of doubtful value.[17]

To conclude the story of airports of the war years, the following two tables, taken from the Department of Transport Report for 1945-46, sum up, in cold and concise form, the results of the many wartime construction programs:[18]

The airports built or improved for war purposes are detailed as follows:

New airports and aerodromes constructed for British Commonwealth Air Training Plan and Western Hemisphere Operations -	148
Municipal airports extended and improved for B.C.A.T.P. and W.H.O. and War -	20
Department of Transport Airports and Intermediate Aerodromes extended and improved for B.C.A.T.P. and W.H.O. -	25
R.C.A.F. and other aerodromes constructed, extended and improved for B.C.A.T.P. and W.H.O. and War	14
Total number of airports and aerodromes on which the construction for B.C.A.T.P.,	

W.H.O. and War was done by the Department of Transport - 207

Airports, Aerodromes and Emerency Landing Fields owned and operated by Department of Transport number 62 of which 17 are included under War total, leaving additional 45

Total of all Airports, Aerodromes and Emergency Landing Fields owned or leased by the Government 252

The tremendous needs of wartime aviation produced many fine airports across the land, and, at the end of 1940-46 period, Canada was well placed to meet the needs of civil aviation. There were now 587 airports, airfields, and anchorages, and the following table shows the distribution by province, the type of facility, and the operators.

See Table overleaf

In 1945 the Government introduced a new policy: "As a measure of fostering civil aviation, the policy was adopted of leasing surplus aerodromes for a nominal sum to interested municipalities or other responsible public bodies, on certain conditions which included an undertaking to operate a public airport and place insurance on any buildings which were retained for airport use."[20]

Footnotes to Chapter 10

[1] Some of the material in this section is from J.R.K. Main, *Voyageurs of the Air* (Ottawa: Queen's Printer, 1968), pp. 166-167; and J.A. Wilson, "Aerodrome Construction for the British Commonwealth Air Training Plan 1940," "Northwest Passage by Air," "Aviation in Canada," all found in *Development of Aviation in Canada 1878-1948* (Ottawa: Department of Transport), p.27ff.

[2] The airports were leased at a nominal rent of one

SUMMARY OF AIRPORTS, AIRFIELDS, AND ANCHORAGES — MARCH 1946[19]

	P.E.I.	N.S.	N.B.	P.Q.	ON	MB	SK	AB	B.C.	N.W.T.	Y.T.	TOTAL
Airports (Land and Water) Airfields and Anchorages												
Airports (Land) and Airfields	3	10	9	35	80	26	24	38	56	12	25	318
Airports (Water) and Anchorages	1	12	5	34	53	27	15	10	75	31	6	269
Landing Areas (Total)	4	22	14	69	133	53	39	48	131	43	31	587
Airports (Land and Water) Airfields and Anchorages by Licenceees or Operators and Provinces												
Canadian Pacific Airlines' Airports (Land) and Airfields				12	1	1		1			5	20
Canadian Pacific Airlines' Airports (Water) and Anchorages				10	10	9	5	2	4		1	41
Department of Mines and Resources Airports (Land) and Airfields								3		1	7	11
Department of Mines and Resources Airports (Water) and Anchorages								2		9		11
Department of Transort Airports (Land) and Airfields		4	5	10	45	19	17	21	23	10		154
Municipal Airports (Land) and Airfields	1	3	1	2	10	1	5	7	8			38
Municipal Airports (Water) and Anchorages			1		4	1		1		2		9
Ontario Provincial Air Services' Airports (Water) and Anchorages					14							14
Royal Canadian Air Force Airports (Land) and Airfields	2	2	2	3	17	4	3	6	9		5	53
Royal Canadian Air Force Airports (Water) and Anchorages		2	1	1	2				10			16
United States Army Air Forces (Land) and Airfields				2						1		3
Misc. Airports (Land) and Airfields		1	1	6	7	1			16		8	40
Misc. Airports (Water) and Anchorages	1	10	3	23	23	17	9	5	59	22	5	177
												587

Note:—Included in the above figures are a number of Department of Transport Airports eligible for license and for which licencees are not issued.

"Airport" is defined as any aerodrome at which facilities available to the public are provided for shelter, servicing or repair of aircraft, and for receiving or discharging passengers or cargo.

"Airfield" is defined as any aerodrome other than an airport.

dollar per year for war purposes. The leases provided, among other things, that the government could salvage buildings and other structures erected on the airports at any time during the three years after the cessation of hostilities. Also, in the event of sale, the municipality first, and then the province concerned, had the right of first refusal. (Canada, Department of Transport, *Annual Report* (Ottawa: Queen's Printer, 1945-46, p. 149).

3 In 1942-43, Windsor was acquired outright by the Department of Transport on the understanding that the city could repossess it in ten years' time.

4 J.A. Wilson, "Northwest Passage by Air," *Development of Aviation in Canada 1878-1948* (Ottawa: King's Printer), p. 43 ff.

5 At Grande Prairie and Fort St. John, the old aerodrome sites continued in use until the fall of 1942, when all services moved over to the better sites built as part of the program. (Wilson, p. 47)

6 Canada, Department of Transport, *Annual Report*, (Ottawa: King's Printer, 1942-43), p. 127.

7 Canada, Department of Transport, *Annual Report* (Ottawa: King's Printer, 1943-44), p. 144.

8 Main, pp. 177-78.

9 According to Main, p. 178, the use of the word 'Crimson' arose from the fact that hospital cases were to be flown over the route from Europe to America in easy stages under the direction of the Red Cross.

10 Instead, the route via Goose Bay, Greenland, and Iceland was used heavily by short-range aircraft.

11 Wilson, pp. 91, 99-100.

12 The U.S. also built major airports and military bases at Stephenville and Argentia, Newfoundland, in 1941 under the "U.S. Bases" agreement with the U.K. and Newfoundland.

13 Canada, Department of Transport, *Annual Report*, (Ottawa: King's Printer,) 1940-41, 1941-42, 1942-43, 1943-44.

14 Wilson, P. 63.

15 Canada, Department of Transport, *Annual Report* (Ottawa: King's Printer, 1944-45), P. 135.

16 Ibid, p. 148.

17 Main, pp. 179-180.

18 Canada, Department of Transport, *Annual Report* (Ottawa: King's Printer, 1945-46), p. 149.

19 Canada, Department of Transport, *Annual Report*, (Ottawa: King's Printer, 1945-46), p. 148.

20 Canada, Department of Transport, *Annual Report* (Ottawa: King's Printer, 1945-46), p. 147

Chapter 11

Post-War Developments: 1946 to 1989

In 1936, the federal government established the Department of Transport, which took over responsibility for civil aviation from the Department of National Defence. The new department also became responsible for radio and meteorological services. The honourable C.D. Howe was the first minister of Transport and played a leading role in the completion of the Trans-Canada Airway; the establishment of Trans-Canada Air Lines; the creation of the Air Transport Board (to regulate commercial air carriers); the organization of air services; and the general development of the aviation industry. When Howe became minister of Munitions and Supply in 1940, he took ministerial responsibility for the Air Services Branch of the Department of Transport with him. The administrative side of all aviation matters remained in the department, and the deputy minister of Transport, C.P. Edwards, reported to Howe on Air Services. This arrangement continued when Howe became minister of Reconstruction and Supply in 1947. Finally, May 4, 1948, ministerial responsibility for Air Services was returned to the minister of Transport, then the honourable Lionel Chevrier. C.D. Howe, therefore, had ministerial responsibility for Air Services from 1936 to 1948, twelve momentous years for civil aviation in Canada.

At the end of World War II, all airports surplus to needs of the Department of National Defence were handed over to the Department of Transport, which selected those required for civil use. The rest were sold by War Assets Disposal Corporation. Airports that had been leased for the duration of the war were returned to municipal owners, complete with improvements made during the war. The Department of Transport retained some sites because the cities would not accept them: this situation arose in Lethbridge, Windsor, London, Malton, Winnipeg, and Moncton. As mentioned before, capital assistance and operating subsidy schemes were later introduced to help municipalities finance their airport operations. During 1946-47, a strong revival of the flying club movement took place. At the end of March 1946, clubs were in operation at Edmonton, Toronto and Ottawa: one year later, there were twenty-nine active clubs across Canada.

Commercial and private aircraft flew a total of 28.2 million miles [45.4 million kilometres] in 1946, and this increased to 34.7 million miles [55.9 million kilometres] in 1947. That year, 940,029 passengers, 34.2 million [15.5 million kilograms] pounds of freight and express, and 6.9 million pounds [3.2 million kilograms] of mail were carried. In 1948, 307.9 million passenger miles [495.5 million kilometres] were flown. Civil flying was obviously off to a good post-war start.

Runway Construction

Although much airport construction had been carried out during the war, it did not end with the cessation of hostilities and, in the annual report of the Department of Transport for the fiscal year 1946-47, it was noted that runway extensions were completed at Windsor, Malton, North Bay, and Montéeal. Runway work was also in progress at Lethbridge, Kimberly, Penticton, Calgary, Churchill, Kenora, Armstrong, Sioux Lookout, London, Ottawa, Moncton, St. John's (Torbay), Yellowknife, Saskatoon, Winnipeg, and Graham. Surveys were made for proposed sites: Sarnia, Kitchener, Hanas Lake (Hollinger), Rivière du Loup, and Fredericton, and on behalf of the Department of Mines and Resources at Mayo, Selkirk, Minto, Braeburn, Dawson, North Fork Beach, Yukon Crossing, McQueston, Freegold, and Carimacks in the Yukon District. Alterations and extensions were completed at Lethbridge and London airports to provide for international passenger traffic. At Montréal, extensions were made to the former RAF Ferry Command administration building to accommodate passengers travelling by transatlantic air services.

The work of extending runways and improving airport facilities went on year after year to meet growing passenger traffic, larger aircraft, and finally, the demands of revolutionary jet aircraft: first, the De Havilland Comet, then the Boeing 707, the Douglas DC-8, and finally, today's Boeing 747, DC-10, and L-1011. With the introduction of the DC-4M North Star aircraft into domestic service in 1947, a new program of lengthening and strengthening runways at major airports was started.

When Trans-Canada Air Lines introduced the DC-3 in 1945, runways were upgraded to provide 4,500 feet [1,372 metres] at sea level. The North Stars required 6,000 feet [1,829 metres]. In 1946, the International Civil Aviation Organization (ICAO) recommended 8,000-foot [2,438-metre] runways for first-class international airports, with pavement strength for 150,000 pounds [68,040 kilograms] gross weight aircraft. Super-Constellations, introduced in Canada in 1954, required 7,000 to 7,500 feet [2,134 to 2,286 metres] of runway. Trans-Canada Air Lines introduced its first jet aircraft, the DC-8, in

1960. Other foreign air carriers had already been using the Boeing 707. Runways were now required to be 9,000 feet [2,743 metres] long and, by 1961, Dorval had one 7,000 feet [2,134 metres], one 9,600 feet [2,926 metres], and one 11,000 feet [3,353 metres] long.

Takeover of Gander Airport

In April 1949, when Newfoundland joined Canada, the Department of Transport became responsible for the international airport at Gander. It was the largest of the department's airport operations. At the time, in addition to the heavy transatlantic passenger air traffic, Gander was a community of 4000 people who drew their livelihood from the airport and for whom the airport provided municipal services and utilities, fire protection and housing, as well as a hotel, restaurant, 24-hour bar, and other commercial enterprises. Gander had a revenue of $3.2 million, compared to total revenues from all other transport airports of $1.4 million in the previous year.

The Air Terminal Building Program

In the first ten post-war years, the Department of Transport devoted its efforts and financial resources mainly to the improvement of airports to accommodate large four-engine aircraft and to update safety and navigational aids (lighting, ILS, radar).

During that period, passenger traffic was increasing—it had more than doubled every five years since 1945—and air terminal buildings (ATB's) at all the major airports were becoming seriously overcrowded. Consequently, a massive program of air terminal construction was begun in the mid-1950s, with buildings being erected at Gander, Montréal, Toronto, Winnipeg, Edmonton, Halifax, and Ottawa. These were all

large buildings of the latest design, incorporating features from the leading airports in the world. The program attracted much attention in the airport world and established a high reputation for Canadian airports.

Gander was the first to be completed and was opened by Her Majesty Queen Elizabeth on June 2, 1959. Prime Minister Diefenbaker opened Ottawa's new ATB on June 30, 1960. Other major sites which opened new terminal facilities were Halifax (1960); Regina (October 12, 1960); Montréal--Dorval (December 15, 1960—the orginal had been opened in December, 1941); Winnipeg (January 17, 1964); Edmonton (February 15, 1964); Toronto's Aeroquay No. 1 (February 28, 1964); and Vancouver (1965). Others opened during the 1960s were Kamloops, Victoria, Yellowknife, the Moncton extension, Lakehead, North Bay, Sault Ste. Marie, Fredericton, and London.

Early Warning Radar for Defence

Between 1951 and 1958, three systems of early warning radar were built across Canada for the continental defence of North America: Pine Tree, Mid-Canada, and the DEW (Distinct Early Warning) Line.[1] While Pine Tree was located in generally accessible areas, the DEW Line and Mid-Canada were in the most isolated areas of Canada. The inhospitable terrain called for a heavy dependence on air freighting.

Pine Tree

This was the first radar detection line established, and it was truly a joint enterprise undertaken by Canada and the United States. The line had stations on both sides of the American-Canadian border and generally ran through settled areas, but in Newfoundland and Labrador supplies and equipment had to be flown into sites that were inaccessible by either land or sea. Aircraft were also used to supplement sea supply in winter. Eastern Provincial Airways was one of the major carriers.

Pine Tree was financed mainly by the United States with a substantial Canadian contribution. Stations were manned by the U.S. Air Force and the Royal Canadian Air Force. Eventually, the RCAF took over all stations in Canada. The first installation was ready in 1952, and the line was in full operation in 1954.

Mid-Canada Line

Before the basic Pine Tree network was finished, proposals were made to fill the gaps in the line and to extend the coverage beyond the main target areas. Accordingly, in February 1953, Canada ordered the construction of a second radar line, the Mid-Canada Line, along the 55th parallel. It was 2,600 miles [4,184 kilometres] long and extended from Hopedale, Labrador to Dawson Creek, British Columbia. This line, an exclusively Canadian undertaking, was staffed by civilian personnel and a few RCAF officers at the main centres.[2] Most of the proposed sites were isolated and, consequently, the helicopter became vital to the completion of the project. At this time, however, civil operators in Canada had too few heavy-lift helicopters for the task, so the RCAF did much of the work with its own helicopters of the 108 Communications flight from Bagotville and Knob Lake, Great Whale, Moosonee, Winisk, and The Pas. Larry Milberry notes that "eventually, No. 108 had 25 S-55s, H-21s and H-34s working on the mid Canada Line...For 1956, No. 108 logged 10,000 hours and moved 9,000 tons [9.2 million kilograms] of cargo and 14,000 passengers... its helicopters [were eventually] turned over to a civilian contractor—initially to Okanagan in the west and to Spartan in the east. These assumed the task of transportation for the re-supply and maintenance of the remote and manned stations along the line."[3] About fifty-five airplanes provided the airlift from main centres of supply to the helicopter bases in support of the helicopter operations. The following airlines took part: Wheeler, Northern Wings, Eastern Provincial, Quebecair, Mont Laurier, Dorval Air Transport, Central Northern (Transair),[4] Austin, and Arctic Wings (Transair). The Mid-Canada Line came into operation in 1957 and, with the installation of stronger radar along Pine Tree, was closed down in 1965.

DEW Line

In 1955, the minister of National Defence announced that a third radar line, the Distant Early Warning (DEW) Line, would be built. Although it was conceived and planned jointly by the United States and Canada, it was financed solely by the U.S. It was built north of the Arctic Circle and extended along the 68th parallel from the Alaska-Yukon border to Cape Dorset, Baffin Island. Forty-one surveillance stations were built. The line was considered an urgent project and was technically ready in July 1957. All sections of the line were working by January 1, 1958.

Because many of the sites were accessible only by air, the DEW Line could not have been constructed without air transportation. The airlift developed for the DEW Line was probably the largest ever undertaken in Canada, and certainly in the Arctic. It is estimated that 106,000 tons of freight were flown in one year, over an average distance of 1,500 miles [2,414 kilometres]. Seventy per cent of the tonnage was transported by air, and 90 per cent of that was lifted by Canadian carriers. The two main contractors were Pacific Western Airlines at Edmonton for the west, and Maritime Central Airways at Moncton for the east. In total, eleven Canadian air carriers participated using nineteen DC-4s, three DC-3s, five Yorks, one Bristol Freighter, thirty-five C-46s, three PBYs, and one B-17: sixty-seven aircraft in all.

The main supporting airports were Norman Wells, Sawmill Bay, Yellowknife, Coral Harbour (Southampton Island), Fort Chimo (Kuujjuaq), Frobisher Bay (Iqaluit—where the Americans had a large base), Coppermine, Cambridge Bay, and Churchill. Smaller aircraft were used from these airports to reach individual sites.

Three of the four main bases—Cape Perry, Cambridge Bay, and Hall Lake—were on the sea, so it was feasible to build winter landing strips on the ice.

The eastern line of communications led from Mont Joli or Moncton to Goose Bay, Fort Chimo, and Frobisher Bay, with lateral distribution from there.

The central sector was fed from Churchill through Coral Harbour to Hall Lake, a distance of about 850 miles [1,368 kilometres], and thence by lateral distribution.

In the west, there were two lines from Edmonton: one touched at Yellowknife and Contwoyto Lake en route to Cambridge Bay; the other followed the Mackenzie River from Fort Simpson and Norman Wells to Cape Perry. There was an auxiliary base at Tuktoyaktuk.

The Department of Transport provided weather and radio services and radio navigation aids.

By the end of the summer of 1956, twenty-one bases had gravel strips 3,000 to 5,000 feet [915 to 1,524 metres] long, and sixteen had strips of 750 to 900 feet [229 to 274 metres]. Four had to be serviced by helicopters. Steep take off and landing (STOL) aircraft were used extensively for lateral supply operations.

Some regional air carriers now fly route patterns that were first established in support of the Mid-Canada and DEW Line projects.

Airport Subsidization

The Department of Transport *Report* for 1950-51 states there were then 13,600 miles [21,887 kilometres] of designated airways and routes, of which 10,091 miles [16,240 kilometres] were controlled. There were 296 airports, of which thirty-nine terminal, thirty-four secondary, and forty-three other airports were operated by Transport. There were eighteen control towers and seven area control centres.

As of December 1, 1956, the following municipal airports had been receiving operating subsidies from the dates shown:

Edmonton	November 1, 1946
Medicine Hat	April 1, 1947
Prince Albert	April 1, 1947
Vancouver	November 1, 1947
Brandon	June 1, 1948
Calgary	July 1, 1949
Fredericton	April 1, 1951
Saint John	January 1, 1952
Sudbury	February 1, 1954
Trenton	April 1, 1955
Regina	July 1, 1955
Timmins	June 1, 1956

The following airports were still operated by municipalities and received operating subsidies during 1965-66:

Trenton	Lynn Lake	Peace River
Saint John	Dauphin	Kelowna
Rouyn	Brandon	Dawson Creek
Riviére du Loup	Flin Flon	Campbell River
Forestville	Prince Albert	Castlegar
Charlevoix	Beaverlodge	

Although operating subsidies were improved from time to time to meet rising operating costs, many municipalities gave up. One of the main problems was the cost of providing new air terminal buildings to meet increasing passenger traffic. The municipalities were unwilling to undertake the expenditures, and considered the Department of Transport capital grants to be insufficient. As these crises came to a head, the department took over the airports and purchased the municipalities' capital assets in them. Transport took over the following principal airports during the years given:

Fredericton	1959	Calgary	1967
Timmins	1961	Saint John	1968
Kamloops	1961	Regina	1972
Vancouver	1962		

Transport opened two completely new airports at Halifax and Edmonton in 1959. Civilian traffic was moved to the Halifax International Airport from the RCAF's Dartmouth Airport, and Edmonton International became the city's principal airport. The city of Edmonton continues to operate the old airport as the Edmonton Municipal Airport, but without an operating subsidy.

The following municipal airports received operating subsidies in 1979-80.[5] (They are grouped according to Transport Regions.)

Atlantic	Central	Québec
Charlo	Brandon	Blanc Sablon
Churchill Falls	Dauphin	Charlevoix
Chatham	Dryden	Chevery
	Flin Flon	Gagnon
Western	Gillam	Gaspé
Dawson Creek	Lynn Lake	Mingan
Fort Chipewyan	Norway House	Natashquan
Peace River	Prince Albert	Rouyn
Rainbow Lake	Thompson	
	Uranium City	
Ontario	Pacific	
Hamilton	Campbell River	
Moosonee	Cranbrook	
Pembroke	Grank Forks	
Sarnia	Kelowna	
Sudbury	Powell River	

Airport Security

In 1968, there was a rapid increase in the number of aircraft hijackings throughout the world and particularly in the United States, where there were twenty-two attempts. In Canada, there was one, occurring in 1968 on Air Canada, between Saint John and Toronto. In 1969, two members of the Front de libération du Quebec (FLQ) hijacked an Eastern Airlines flight between New York and Miami.

As a matter of interest, possibly the first case in the world of a bomb destroying an aircraft in flight, occurred in Canada in September 1949. A bomb placed on board a Quebec Airways flight destroyed the plane in the air, killing twenty-three persons on board. The motive in this case was to collect insurance on one of the victims. Three people were convicted of the crime and subsequently executed. There was a second case in August 1965 when a bomb exploded on a Canadian Pacific Airlines aircraft, killing fifty-two persons. It was suspected that a passenger had taken a bomb on board to commit suicide and ensure payment of insurance to next of kin.

In 1969, there were forty hijackings of American aircraft, thirty-seven of which were attempts to reach Cuba. In 1970, there were twenty-seven incidents in the United States. Because of the alarming increase in terrorist activities, the Canadian Airline Pilots' Association pressed for legislation to make hijacking a criminal offence. Two significant events led to the establishment of airport security measures in Canada: (a) an extraordinary meeting of the International Civil Aviation Organization, which drew up international standards for airport security; and (b) the FLQ crisis and the proclamation on October 16 of the War Measures Act, requiring immediate activation of security measures at all Canadian international airports. Joint action was taken by the government (the Department of Transport and the RCMP) and the airlines to accelerate the introduction of these measures at airports. Air Canada (the new name of Trans-Canada Air Lines as of 1965) and Canadian Pacific Airlines screened their passengers in order to prevent the carriage of explosives and weapons on international and transborder flights. Transport Canada began to provide X-ray and metal detection equipment to check all carry-on luggage. Increased numbers of RCMP were posted at strategic points. In 1972, explosive detecting equipment and specially trained dogs were provided; security measures were also extended to major domestic airports.

Hijacking threats peaked in Canada in 1972-1973. During these two years, Canada was involved in ten incidents: six with Canadian registered aircraft and four with American. During the period 1968 to 1979, there were nine attempted hijackings of Canadian aircraft, of which only only two were successful. During the same period, seven American aircraft that had been hijacked in the United States landed at Canadian airports.

Hijackings continued in the U.S. In 1977, there were five unsuccessful attempts; in 1978, there were eight; and, in 1979, ten.

The situation overseas was even worse as violent attacks against aircraft were made by terrorists. In May 1972, the Japanese Red Army terrorists attacked the Lod airport, when twenty-eight people were killed and an equal number were wounded. Following this incident, El Al Airlines and Canadian Pacific Airlines overseas flights were given special protection at Canadian airports. In December 1973, terrorists attacked Rome's International Airport and hijacked a Lufthansa aircraft. The Japanese Red Army issued a warning in 1975 that it might make Canada its target, and in 1976, Montréal airports took special security measures during the Olympic Games. Also that year, an Air France plane was hijacked and held at Entebbe Airport, where a rescue operation was carried out by Israeli commandos. A Lufthansa aircraft was hijacked at Magadishu Airport in 1977 and rescued by German commandos. Terrorists fired on an El Al Israel Airlines aircraft at Orly Airport, France in 1978.

Between 1969 and 1979, there were 1,206 threats made against Canadian aircraft: bomb threats, hijacking, extortion threats, and "joke" threats all had to be taken seriously.

In the early 1980s, the terrorist threat shifted from hijacking to in-flight bombings and frontal attacks on air terminals. Tragedies included the Trans World Airlines and Egyptair incidents and the frontal attacks on the Rome and Vienna airports. In December 1988, the bombing of Pan American Flight 103 over Locherbie, Scotland focused attention on the scale of in-flight bombings and the ingenuity of the terrorist in using cassette radios as the containers for explosive devices. Overall, response to the Air India incident[6] was upgraded training of passenger pre-board screening staff, RCMP enhancements, an access clearance program, and a multi-level threat response system. The future includes development of new equipment capable of detecting plastic and other explosives.

Crash - Fire Services

In 1930-31, funds were provided for a fire engine and firehall at St. Hubert—the first airport to have fire services. Fully-manned Airport Crash-Fire Protection Services began in Canada as military establishments: the first one to come under Department of Transport operation was at Montréal (Dorval), when, in 1946, the department took over the crash-fire service formerly operated by the RAF Ferry Command. In 1949, the Department of Transport assumed control of the crash-fire service at Gander, which had been operated by the Newfoundland authorities. Gander Airport began operations in 1939, with a crash-truck and one full-time fireman. When the Department of Transport took over Goose Bay Airport in 1949, it inherited the military crash-fire establishment. By 1950, the Department of Transport owned a total of thirty-eight crash trucks, twenty-nine of which were at airports

where Transport provided the vehicles, while airport and airline employee volunteers manned them. There were forty-nine full-time firefighters at Montréal and Gander in that year. According to the Department of Transport Report for 1951-52, Montréal (Dorval) and Gander were the only airports where the department had full-time firefighters. The A.V. Roe aircraft factory provided crash-fire service at Toronto's Malton Airport, and the Canadair plant supplied a similar service at Cartierville Airport. Elsewhere, the RCAF provided crash-fire facilities and staff at many Department of Transport sites where the forces were based. The Department of National Defence continues to provide this service at Ottawa International Airport.

The department's subsequent heavy involvement in crash-fire protection followed from the International Civil Aviation Organization's (ICAO) adoption of minimum standards of protection for international airports. The same standards were applied by Transport at its major domestic airports. The department gradually withdrew its firefighting capacity for buildings in favour of protection from the adjoining municipality to which it was already contributing grants in lieu of taxes and paying capital grants for the expansion of municipal water services.

Airport Emergency Services (AES) was created as a division of the Airports Branch of Transport in 1960 to provide crash services at its airports, and was made responsible for the development of standards. In the 1970s and 1980s, AES worked with ICAO to develop world-wide standards for international airports.

In 1982, the department established the Transport Canada Crash Firefighting and Rescue Standards and adopted the policy that Airport Emergency Services were to be provided at all airports operated by Transport Canada that are used by commercial air carriers on a regularly established basis. Seventy-five crash vehicles were ordered, additional personnel hired, and funds provided for operations.

Airport Emergency Services (AES) was renamed Crash Firefighting and Rescue Services (CFR) in 1983 because of the division's expanded field of activity.

As of 1990, the CFR programme is under review. The department is studying its existing levels of service, general rescue requirements, and regulatory relationship with airports not owned by Transport Canada.

Currently, the department employs 617 professional firefighters at fifty-eight Transport Canada operated airports. At Calgary International Airport, CFR services are provided by the city of Calgary (municipal) fire department. The Department of National Defence provides CFR services at North Bay, Ottawa International, and Goose Bay Airports. Overall, the department funds CFR services at 121 airports, which includes subsidized sites.

Pre-clearance

Pre-clearance is a process whereby passengers bound for a foreign country are examined by the Customs and Immigration country of destination before leaving the country of departure. Pre-clearance in Canada began at Toronto (Malton) Airport in 1952, when passengers going to the United States were processed by American authorities at Toronto airport and so cleared into the United States without the need for further inspection on arrival at American destinations. Airport pre-clearance was established at Montréal (Dorval) in 1954, Winnipeg in 1959, Vancouver in 1960, Calgary in 1978, and Edmonton in 1979. At the present time, only the United States provides pre-clearance services in Canada.

Improved Aircraft and Passenger Facilities

1. Landing Aids

After the war, navigation aids were also updated to meet the challenges of advancing aviation technology. The use of the Instrument Landing System (ILS), a set of components including a localizer, a glide path indicator, and ground markers, was slowly adopted across the country. During 1948-49, twelve ILS were installed at seven airports. The first installation to be completed in Canada was at Montréal (Dorval) on April 24, 1948. Installations were also completed that year at Toronto (Malton), Winnipeg, Vancouver, Saskatoon, Calgary, and Lethbridge. Each ILS was supported by a high-intensity approach lighting system. By 1967, there were forty ILS, six precision approach radar (PAR), sixteen airport and airways surveillance radars (AARS), seventy-seven low-frequency radio ranges (still in use), and forty-six visual omni ranges (VOR) in Canada.[7] The advanced category two (CAT2) ILS was commissioned at Dorval in the spring of 1973.

One of the latest developments is the use of microwave landing systems (MLS). Here a microwave beam allows aircraft to access a wider variety of approach paths, and to take steeper approach angles than were previously accessible with ILS, because the transmission of the microwave signal is not affected by the terrain in front of the aerial. MLS is therefore valuable in congested areas. However the expense of introducing this new system has been a deterrent.

2. Aircraft Hydrant Refuelling

The first aircraft hydrant refuelling systems in Canada were installed at Gander in 1959, separately by Shell Oil and Imperial Oil . The Department of Transport opened its own system at Montréal (Dorval) in July 1961, which it later sold to a consortium of airlines. A group of airlines installed a hydrant system at Toronto in 1964.

3. Air Bridges

Air bridges are currently used at many airports in Canada to provide a safe and convenient means for passengers to transfer between aircraft and the air terminal building. The first air bridge in Canada was installed by Air Canada at Montréal (Dorval) airport on December 1, 1966. Later, Air Canada installed bridges at Edmonton and Winnipeg. Other airlines also provided air bridges at major airports to improve service. The Department of Transport introduced a policy in 1979 which formally recognized that the airlines could install and manage such facilities. Later revisions to the policy enabled the Department of Transport to provide air bridges (based on passenger traffic) and to improve its control over the number and location of such facilities. The policy is subject to periodic review so that it responds to the needs of the air industry and departmental objectives.

3. Noise

In the late 1950s, noise began to be a problem in the vicinity of Canada's major airports where jet aircraft traffic was increasing. In 1959, noise abatement studies were undertaken by the Department of Transport, and special flight procedures were introduced at Montréal, Toronto, and Winnipeg the following year. In 1960, airline operations at Montréal were restricted between 11:59 p.m. and 7:00 a.m. Noise studies at other airports followed with the subsequent introduction of night flight restrictions at Canadian airports that were close to the cities they serve. The first fixed Noise Monitoring System was installed at Toronto in 1979 and at Calgary and Vancouver in 1985 and 1986 respectively. Edmonton Municiapl Airport embarked on a vigorous noise management program in the early 1980's.

4. STOLports

In 1974, there was a new airport development in Canada: the construction of the first short take off and landing (STOL) port.

The Department of Transport built two STOLports, one at Ottawa (Rockcliffe) and another at Montréal (Victoria Car Park, formerly used by Expo '67). Each new airport, had a single runway 2,000 feet [610 metres] long and 100 feet [30 metres] wide, terminal building, control tower, garage, hangar, and microwave landing system for precision approach.

The ports were provided as part of the STOL Demonstration Service financed by the government to determine the feasibility of a commercial STOL passenger service between Ottawa and Montréal. Airtransit Ltd., a subsidiary of Air Canada formed solely for the purpose of the STOL demonstration operated the service. There were twenty-two flights per sixteen-hour day. Six DH Twin Otter aircraft (modified) were used.

61. Rockliffe Airport, 1975, showing the STOL runway.

The Department of Transport operated both STOLports for the duration of the demonstration from July 24, 1974, to April 30, 1976, after which both were closed. Rockcliffe, which was part of the old RCAF airport, is still in use for limited general aviation.

Some Airport Statistics

As a conclusion to this summary of post-war developments, the following statistics of airports and airport activity are provided, showing the status of airports in Canada in December 1979 and at the end of 1988.[8]

LAND AIRPORTS

Region	A	B	C	D	E	F
Pacific	15	11	35	61	73	134
Western	21	8	75	104	63	167
Central	15	10	102	127	106	233
Ontario	12	10	92	114	128	242
Québec	12	17	87	116	109	225
Atlantic	13	2	24	39	18	57
Totals	88	58	415	561	497	1,058

A: Owned and Operated by Transport Canada
B: Owned by Transport Canada; Operated by Others
C: Owned and Operated by Others
D: Total Land Airports
E: Total Helicopters and Water Airports
F: Line Total

The ten busiest airports (1988) for passenger traffic were:[9]

TRAFFIC VOLUMES, 1988

Airports Ranked By Passenger Volumes
Enplaned & Deplaned Revenue Passengers (000s)
Itinerant Aircraft Movement (000s)

1.	Toronto	20,267.4	347.7
2.	Vancouver	8,840.1	325.2
3.	Dorval	6,536.2	203.1
4.	Calgary	4,549.8	206.2
5.	Ottawa	2,711.4	176.9
6.	Winnipeg	2,459.8	153.3
7.	Halifax	2,308.8	100.1
8.	Mirabel	2,221.3	68.8
9.	Edmonton International	2,072.4	84.0
10.	Edmonton Municipal	965.1	117.7

For a list of airports supsidized in 1989, see Appendix 34.

Footnotes to Chapter 11.

[1] The Mid-Canada Line was also known as the McGill Fence. For more information on these three systems, see J.A.R. Main, *Voyageurs of the Air* (Ottawa: Queen's Printer, 1968), pp. 225-230, 235 ff., 246; and Lieutenant Colonel D. J. Goodspeed, *Armed Force of Canada 1867 to 1967* (Ottawa: Canadian Forces Headquarters, Directorate of History, 1967), pp. 225-227.

[2] Goodspeed, pp. 225-227.

[3] Larry Milberry, *Aviation In Canada*, (Toronto: McGraw-Hill Ryerson Ltd., 1979), pp. 251-252. By permission of the publisher.

[4] Alice Gibson Sutherland, *Canada's Aviation Pioneers* (Toronto: McGraw-Hill Ryerson Ld., 1979), p. 238. By permission of the publisher.

[5] Director Airport Planning, Airports and Construction Services Directorate, Air Administration, Transport Canada.

[6] On June 23, 1985, an Air India 747 en route from Montréal to London crashed off the coast of Ireland killing all 329 people on board. Sabotage is considered to be the probable cause of the tragedy. (Security Policy & Planning, Airports Group, Transport Canada).

[7] J.R.K. Main, *Voyageurs of the Air* (Ottawa: Queen's Printer, 1968) p. 328.

[8] Transport Canada, Report of Task Force on Airport Management, 1979. Vol. 2, Appendix 3, p. 12.

[9] Transport Canada.

PART II
AIRPORT HISTORIES

Introduction

Airports were not always the major operations they are today. They evolved over the years to meet the ever-increasing demands of the developing airplane. Early airplanes operated from cow pastures—often in competition with the cows. The first airfields were grass fields. Then came gravel runways, and then paved surfaces. The Wright brothers' requirements of 1903 were met by a small wooden track that provided a catapult, or launching rail, 60 feet long. Today, 12,000 feet (3657 metres) paved runways are not uncommon.

The evolution of the airport has been covered in Part I. Now it is time to look at the histories of the many airports in Canada.

This part contains the histories of 167 airports, arranged alphabetically. The large number of airports to be covered and the resources available made in-depth research impossible in many cases. The history of some airports, therefore, is covered only in outline. The history of each site is, however, complete in itself, making cross-references unnecessary.

The source of the material is identified and credited in each history. Frequent use has been made of airport notes by the late Robert L. Clarke, who was a long time employee of the Civil Aviation and Airport Branches of Transport Canada. Before his retirement he compiled notes on many airports from departmental files.

Abbotsford Airport
(British Columbia)

Abbotsford Airport is located in the district of Matsqui in the central Fraser valley, sixty-one kilometres southeast of Vancouver. The area served by the airport for general aviation ranges from Mission City in the north to Sumas in the south, and from Yarrow in the east to Aldergrove in the west.

In 1940, preliminary investigations were made into the purchase of land for a Royal Canadian Air Force airport near Abbotsford. A first proposal was rejected because the site was too close to the American border; but in June 1942, approval was given for the construction of an airport based on a triangular layout. Initially, there were three runways 5,000 by 150 feet [1,524 by 46 metres], but these were enlarged to 5,271 by 200 feet [1,606 by 61 metres].

Construction was completed in 1944, and No. 24 Elementary Flying Training School was set up at the airport under the British Commonwealth Air Training Plan. An Operational Training Unit flying Liberators was based there later.

In 1945, Abbotsford Airport became the weather alternate for Vancouver International Airport.

The RCAF station at Abbotsford Airport closed in 1946, but the airport was maintained by the RCAF on a caretaker basis. Although it was closed from 1952 to 1958, air carriers listed it unofficially as an alternate to Vancouver; and in 1956-57, the RCAF permitted automobile drag racing on the site. From December 1956 to March 1957, accommodations and facilities at the airport were used by the Department of Citizenship and Immigration for housing Hungarian refugees.

On April 1, 1958, the airport was officially transferred to the Department of Transport. Hangar no. 2 was converted into an administration and terminal building with a large waiting room, Customs and Immigration facilities, and accommodation for air carriers. Runway 06-24 was extended by 1,500 feet [457 metres] to 6,770 feet [2,063 metres] in length.

In 1960, the airport zoning was registered under the *Aeronautics Act*.

A control tower began part-time operations in January 1960 to handle IFR traffic diverted to Abbotsford whenever Vancouver International Airport was closed because of fog. Then with the increase in traffic, the tower began full-time operation in December 1961.

The first Abbotsford Air Show was held in 1962, sponsored by the Abbotsford Rotary Club and the Abbotsford Flying Club: it is now an annual event, and the 1987 exhibition was the largest in the show's history. Airshow Canada, a bi-annual aerospace trade show, was combined with the annual event in 1989. Exhibits from around the world, including the United States, Russia, and Great Britain, were featured.

Runway 06-24 was extended to 8,000 feet [2,438 metres] in 1963, and major runway repairs were carried out in 1973.

In 1966, Skyway Air Services was granted permission to use the airport for a gliding school. Conair Aviation Ltd., which is the largest fire-bombing and aerial application operation in North America was established in 1969, and it is the most important general aviation tenant in the airport.

The airport was again officially designated a weather diversion alternate for Vancouver International Airport in 1974, and permission was granted to allow Boeing 747 landings.

In 1975, modifications were made to the Customs and Immigration areas of the terminal. Abbotsford Air Services opened a restaurant in 1976, and a new control tower was commissioned in 1981.

Abbotsford Airport was temporarily transformed to accommodate the historic visit of Pope John Paul in September 1984, when more than 100,000 people attended the ceremonies held on the airport grounds.

Today, the airport has two runways: 07-25 at 2,438 metres, and 19-01 at 1,607 metres.

The airport had 4,100 passengers and 153,625 aircraft movements in 1988.

The following have served as airport managers:

H. Luesley	1954 to 1977
C. Fraser	1977 to 1978
D. Reid	1978 to 1980
F. J. Rowe	1980 to 1982
James Logan	1982

Source:
Transport Canada, Pacific Region.

Alert Airstrip
(Northwest Territories)

The Joint Arctic Weather Station (Canada-United States) at Alert, on the northern tip of Ellesmere Island in the Northwest Territories, 1,110 kilometres northeast of Resolute by air, was established in 1950. It is the northernmost permanent human habitation in the world— only 805 kilometres from the North Pole. There is no permanent population at Alert. The Departments of National Defence, Environment, and Transport, totalling about three hundred personnel, post staff for a period of six months (Defence) to two years (Environment and Transport) at the base.

The single runway, of gravel, is 1,676 by 46 metres, and although intended only for use when frozen, is serviceable for most of the summer. There are no hangar or aircraft servicing facilities. In 1975, a complete lighting system was installed at the airfield, and the electrical system was improved in 1976. The Department of

National Defence owns and operates the airstrip.

Scientific projects at Alert include snow surveys, ice movement during the ship navigation season, ice thickness and rate of growth, snow density, permafrost temperatures, and direct and reflected solar radiation.

The northern, ice-bound location of Alert prevents ships routinely from reaching the station. All supplies must be flown in by Hercules aircraft, and large quantities of fuels, construction materials, and provisions are brought in three times a year during Operation Boxtop, when temporary radar facilities and navigation aids are installed. The round-the-clock deliveries are routed through Thule Air Base, Greenland.

On July 31, 1950, an RCAF Lancaster crashed at Alert while making an air drop of supplies. The crew of seven, and two observers, died and were buried at Alert on Cape Belknap, overlooking the Arctic Ocean. The RCAF, next of kin, and the Arctic Institute of North America jointly erected a memorial.

Sources:
1. Transport Canada, Central Region.
2. Lieutenant D.M. McCutcheon, "Project Trelar - Year Two and Beyond", The Canadian Military Engineer (Summer 1977).
3. Department of National Defence, History Directorate, Operation Boxtop, CFB Edmonton, Op Plan 150.

62. Canadian Forces Hercules aircraft on an oil supply flight at Alert airport, N.W.T.

Armstrong Airport
(Ontario)

Armstrong Airport is located thirteen kilometres east of the town of Armstrong and has two asphalt runways: 30-12 at 1,341 metres (extended from 1,155 metres in 1987), and 36-18 at 914 metres. Both are 46 metres wide.

The Armstrong Airport was one of the intermediate airports built one hundred miles apart on the Trans-Canada Airway and was originally named Wagaming Airport. It was constructed as part of an unemployment relief project that began in November 1932.

By January 1933, a north-south landing strip, 3,000 by 500 feet [914 by 152 metres], had been cleared, and, by September 1934, all clearing and most of the grading had been completed. On May 18, 1935, a pilot of Consolidated Mining Company of Trail, British Columbia, made the first private aircraft landing, while on a transcontinental flight. In May 1936, grading of the third runway began. The relief camp closed on June 30, 1936, and the Civil Aviation branch of National Defence took over responsibility for completing construction. (The Department of Transport was established on November 1, 1936.) The four landing strips were completed in October 1936, as were the hangar and other buildings; a caretaker was put in charge of the airport on December 16, 1936.

Trans-Canada Air Lines began scheduled service through Armstrong on May 3, 1939, and, under a lease from the Department of Transport, assumed responsibility for the operation and maintenance of the airport.

On July 4, 1939, the name of the airport was changed from Wagaming to Armstrong Airport.

During the war, the Department of National Defence built another hangar to provide facilities for winter experiments, which continued until 1950. The hangar was later transferred to the Department of Transport.

On July 1, 1947, Trans-Canada Air Lines withdrew from Armstrong when the Great Lakes Airway via Lakehead (now Thunder Bay) was commissioned. The Department of Transport took over the operation and maintenance of the airport on August 10, 1947.

The airport is now operated by the Ontario Ministry of Transportation and is used primarily by tourist aircraft during the summer months.

Awood Air Ltd. offers daily scheduled service Monday to Friday at this site.

There is a weather station at the airport.

Sources:
1. Transport Canada, Central Region.
2. Clark, R.L. "Airport Notes." (Ottawa: Transport Canada, undated)[unpublished collection].
3. Glen Bates, Airport Operations Officer, Ontario Ministry of Transportation.

Baie Comeau Airport
(Quebec)

The Quebec North Shore Company built the original Baie Comeau airport at Hauterive before 1943. The town of Baie Comeau bought this site in 1950-51 and agreed to operate the facility. Baie Comeau Air Service began operating at the airport in 1959 and was the first flying school on the North Shore.

In 1957, the town approached the Department of Transport, requesting a site upon which a new airport could be built: population and industry had grown considerably, but the Hauterive site was unsuitable for expansion.

A study made in 1960 resulted in the choice of Pointe Lebel as the location for a new Baie Comeau airport, but construction did not begin until 1964. The new airport was completed in 1966, with the Department of Transport contributing $212,000 towards the cost.

The airport opened on April 17, 1967, and the town of Baie Comeau agreed to operate it for four years. The licence for the Hauterive airport was cancelled in June 1971.

In 1970, the Club Aéronautique des Satellites (flying school) was established.

On November 1, 1970, the Department of Transport took over the airport from the town and continues to operate it. There is one paved runway, 10-28, at 1,832 metres long.

In 1971, construction of the access road and taxiway towards the commercial aviation zone began, and in October of that year, a start was made on a new air terminal and control tower: the buildings were opened in Ꭺgust 1972.

A new instrument landing system was installed in 1973.

Technicair Inc. began operations in September 1989.

In 1988, the airport had 58,600 passengers and 22,994 aircraft movements.

Inter-Canadian, Air Alliance, Air Satellite Inc. (formerly Golfair, Baie Comeau Air Services and the Aeronautique Club Inc., Les Satellites) and Technicair Inc. provide services to the airport.

Source:
Transport Canada, Quebec Region.

Baker Lake Airport
(Northwest Territories)

Baker Lake Airport is located on the northwest tip of Baker Lake, approximately 644 kilometres northwest of Churchill, Manitoba.

The history of Baker Lake began in 1761 when Captain William Christopher of the Hudson's Bay Company sailed his ship into Hudson Bay, through the inlet, and onto the lake. He named the inlet after Sir William Baker, then governor of the Hudson's Bay Company. The North West Mounted Police had a base at the end of the lake in 1915.

Aviation activity began at Baker Lake when C.H. "Punch" Dickins made his historic flight in 1928 from Winnipeg through the Northwest Territories and back again—a trip of 4,000 miles [6,437 kilometres], in twelve days, forty flying hours. In 1929, Northern Aerial Mineral Explorations (NAME) became the first company to establish a base at Baker Lake. The well-known T.M. "Pat" Reid was one of their pilots. Colonel and Mrs. Lindberg landed at Baker Lake in August 1931 en route from New York to the Orient via the Arctic while conducting a feasibility study of world airline routes.

The Department of National Defence established the airfield in 1946, and the RCAF maintained it until 1949. It was built in support of "Operation Muskox," a Canadian expedition that involved a trek across the Arctic by military personnel from Churchill through Baker Lake and Yellowknife to Edmonton. The expedition, to test men and equipment operating under Arctic conditions, was carried out in 1946 and 1947. The Canadian Army Signals Corps set up radio communications and weather observations in support.

The Department of Transport took over the site on June 8, 1950.

The gravel landing strip, built in 1945-46, is 1,280 by 46 metres. It is located five kilometres southwest of the settlement of Baker Lake.

In 1988, there were 3,125 itinerant aircraft movements (compared to 1,996 in 1974) and the airport handled 6,300 passengers.

Baker Lake has a population of 1,009.

Transportation into Baker Lake consists of the annual sea-lift and scheduled service by both Calm Air (on a tri-weekly basis) and Nunasi Central Airlines Ltd. (on a twice-daily basis).

Ron Bodner is currently the airport manager. The following have previously filled this position: Ron Bedard, Tom Kabloona, Doug Fahlgren, George Elliot, Jack Nicholson, Martti Raito, and Sid Denby.

Sources:

1. Transport Canada, Central Region.
2. Clark, R.L. "Airport Notes" (Ottawa: Transport Canada, undated) [unpublished collection].

Boston Bar Airstrip
(British Columbia)

Boston Bar is an unlicensed aerodrome owned by Transport Canada, built to serve as a supplementary airfield on the Trans-Canada Airway. It has a gravel runway, 762 by 91 metres.

The site was chosen in 1930, but work did not begin until October 1933 as an unemployment relief project. Although the field was usable by August 1935, the first aircraft landed on May 15, 1936. The relief camp closed in August 1936, and the airfield came under the control of the Civil Aviation branch of the Department of National Defence. The airport manager at Abbotsford is responsible for maintaining the aerodrome.

Because of its strategic location on the Fraser Canyon VFR route, the field is frequently used by aircraft encountering weather problems.

Sources:

1. Transport Canada, Pacific Region.
2. Clark, R.L. "Airport Notes" (Ottawa: Transport Canada, undated) [unpublished collection].

Boundary Bay Airport
(British Columbia)

Boundary Bay Airport reopened on June 11, 1983, after having been closed since 1946.

The airport is sixteen kilometres southeast of Vancouver International Airport and is bordered by Boundary Bay on the south. The surrounding land use is primarily agricultural, with industrial and urban land development west of the airport.

The original airport was constructed for the RCAF and opened in 1941. No. 18 Elementary Flying Training School (EFTS) of the British Commonwealth Air Training Plan (operated by Boundary Bay Flying Training School Ltd.) was located at the airport from April 10, 1941, until May 25, 1942. At that time, No. 18 EFTS moved inland, and Boundary Bay became a "Home War Aerodrome" under Western Air Command, with a fighter training squadron—No. 5 Operational Training Unit (OTU)—based there from April 1, 1944, to October 31, 1945. No. 5 OTU was under RCAF Command, but operated for RAF purposes as a heavy bomber unit equipped with four-engined Liberators, the largest aircraft used in the BCATP. The unit added a control tower, bombing range, maintenance hangar, and drill hall to the station.

The airport had three runways: 07-25 and 12-30, 5,900 by 200 feet [1,798 by 61 metres], and 01-19, 5,000 by 200 feet [1,524 by 61 metres], in a triangular configuration. There were three hangars and forty support buildings.

The RCAF closed the airport in 1945, but in 1946 the army took over the site and established a Department of National Defence Communications Centre, including an extensive antenna system erected between runways 01-19 and 12-30. The runways were closed, and one hangar and a large number of buildings were declared surplus and removed from the site. The communications centre was closed in 1968. Transport Canada took over administration in 1972, and acquired title to the 498 hectares from the Department of National Defence in 1977.

Between 1972 and 1983, the airport site was leased (in various parcels) to a wide selection of users, including a car racing club, driver training organizations, radio-controlled model airplane enthusiasts, dog show/trial associations, wildlife research groups, agriculturalists, and construction firms.

During the late 1970s, the congested airspace over Vancouver was becoming a problem; and the inadequate runway system for the traffic mix of jets and light aircraft at Vancouver International Airport was causing one of the heaviest air traffic control workloads in the country. At peak periods air traffic control restrictions had to be placed on light aircraft.

Consequently, Transport Canada decided to shift a substantial percentage of light aircraft operators to another location; and in 1976, released the Lower Mainland Area Master Plan, which presented six alternatives. Unfortunately, each specific option had its drawbacks.

Pitt Meadows Airport, thirty-five kilometres east of Vancouver on the north shore of the Fraser River was already the second busiest airport in Canada. Langley, just to the south, was operating near capacity and was located in a noise-sensitive area near a hospital, a school, and residential areas. While Abbotsford still had some runway capacity available, it was sixty-eight kilometres from Vancouver Airport, and, worse was the site of airline jet training.

All alternatives were rejected as being too expensive, too close to high terrain, a poor choice for environmental reasons or, most important, unable to offer uncrowded airspace. The solution was to reactivate the ex-RCAF base at Boundary Bay: airfield facilities already existed and could be made operational in comparatively little time for an estimated cost of $10 million.

In late 1976, Transport Canada referred the Boundary Bay Airport Reactivation Project to the Federal Environmental Assessment Review Office. A review panel of six specialists was formed with expertise in relevant areas such as aviation and ecology. Following a series of public hearings in 1979, the Environmental Assessment Review Panel concurred with Transport Canada's proposal to reactivate the Boundary Bay Airport.

The reactivation project, completed at an actual cost of $7.3 million, included the construction of new access roads for the support area and control tower, and the rehabilitation of taxiways and two of the existing runways. A temporary trailer was used as a control tower on the site until the construction of the new tower could be completed.

On June 11, 1983, Boundary Bay Airport was officially reopened, marking the end of a thirty-five-year absence of aviation and a six-year struggle by Transport Canada to reactivate the airfield. The new facility was available for use by helicopters and single or multi-engine piston and turbo prop aircraft under 12,500 pounds (5670 kilograms). Jet aircraft were prohibited.

The airport is licensed in the name of the Aztec Aviation Group which, under a lease agreement with Transport Canada, is responsible for the operation, maintenance, and further development of the airport. Aztec also provides service, hangar space, maintenance, et cetera, for general aviation. This is the first time Transport Canada has turned over the operation, maintenance, and development of one of its airports to the private sector. The agreement is for forty-nine years and provides for rental payments of one dollar per year plus a percentage of gross revenue.

Boundary Bay Airport is open sixteen hours a day, seven days a week, for visual flight rules (VFR) operations for general aviation. The two 1,067-metre runways are equipped with autolight for night landings.

A new $1.5 million air traffic control tower opened on July 4, 1984. The tower has a number of special features developed in the Pacific region, of which the most important concerns the tower's cab: it has no mullions (vertical bars that normally divide windows in a tower cab) to obscure a controller's view. The tower, Transport Canada's only presence on the airport, is manned by eight air traffic controllers and the tower chief.

In 1988, the airport had 155,608 aircraft movements.

Source:
Transport Canada, Pacific Region
(newspaper research conducted by Sharon Johnson).

Brandon Airport
(Manitoba)

In 1930, the public airport at Brandon was located west of the city and owned by Brandon Aero Association Ltd. It was used as a stop on the airmail service.

The present Brandon Airport is now located eight kilometres north of the city centre. It was constructed in 1940 as No. 12 Service Flying Training School under the British Commonwealth Air Training Plan[1] and opened in early 1941. The establishment consisted of five hangars and approximately forty-two frame buildings: only two hangars and three buildings remain today. Roughly one hundred Type T-50 Cessna Cranes were used as the principal trainer aircraft at the school, while standard Beam Approach training used about eight Anson Mark II airplanes.

Six paved runways were constructed for the school in two triangular configurations comprising inner and outer runways. In 1959, the three inner runways were removed, and one outer runway, 08-26, completely rebuilt, black-topped, and lengthened to 5,700 feet [1,737 metres] to handle larger transport aircraft. At the same time, the ramp, and taxiways were reconstructed. Threshold and approach lighting were installed on runway 08-26.

After the end of the war in 1945, the airport was declared surplus, and a number of buildings were demolished. The material from the buildings was used to construct homes. Following negotiations with the Department of Transport, the airport was leased to the city of Brandon in 1946 for use as a future municipal airport and to serve as the new site for the Brandon Flying Club. This club, known before the war as the Brandon-Virden Flying Club, was located on Brandon's north hill, approximately three kilometres south of the present airport. Brandon city council initially appointed a commission to run the newly inaugurated airport, but in April 1952, the Brandon Flying Club assumed operational responsibility. On July 1, 1970, the city reclaimed its managerial role.

Scheduled air service was introduced into Brandon with the inauguration of daily Trans-Canada Airlines flights on June 1, 1948, using DC-3 aircraft. This coincided with the official opening of the Brandon Municipal Airport, when the RCAF, Army Airborne and Paratrooper Units, and Trans-Canada Airlines put on the most spectacular airshow ever seen in Brandon. In the spring of 1963, Trans Air Ltd acquired the passenger route from Trans-Canada Airlines and serviced it with DC-3 aircraft.

On June 1, 1981, Pacific Western Airlines began daily flights between Calgary, Brandon, and Toronto. Canadian Airlines pulled B-737 service out of Brandon in 1988; it was replaced for a brief stint by Calm Air HS-748s. Currently, Perimeter and Ontario Express are flying out of Brandon using Queen Air and J-31 Jetstream aircraft, respectively, with forty-four scheduled movements per week.

A Department of Transport operations building for air traffic control and telecommunications was finished in 1969, and a new terminal building (connected to the operations building) was completed in 1970.

The Brandon Flying Club and Maple Leaf Aviation Ltd. occupy two wartime hangars.

There is also a small private hangar used as an airport maintenance garage. The Canadian Air Training Museum shares Hangar no. 1 with Maple Leaf Aviation.

The city receives an airport operating subsidy from Transport Canada.

The airport is used by Ontario Express, Perimeter Airlines Inland Ltd., the Brandon Flying Club, Maple Leaf Aviation Ltd., the Canadian Air Training Plan Museum, and the Canadian Armed Forces.

Brandon has three runways: 08-26, extended to 1,981 metres in 1986, 02-20 at 852 metres, and 14-12 at 914 metres long.

In 1988, there were 30,262 aircraft movements and 19,000 passenger movements.

The following have served as airport managers:

Howard Chase	1949 to 1952
E.R. McGill	1952 to 1970
R.T. Isleifson	1970

Sources:

1. Transport Canada, Central Region.
2. United States. Department of Commerce. "Airports in Canada and Newfoundland." Trade Information Bulletin No. 716. Washington: U.S. Government Printing Office, 1930.

Footnotes: Brandon Airport

[1]Chater, Manitoba, was Relief Station No. 1 for No. 12 SFTS.

Buchans Aerodrome
(Newfoundland)

Buchans Aerodrome was completed in July 1944, after the Department of Transport had leased the 992-acre [402 hectare] site from the Anglo Newfoundland Development Company (ANDCO) of Grand Falls for thirty years, renewable from January 12, 1943.

The gravel strip, 4,000 by 500 feet [1,219 by 152 metres] was located about one and a half kilometres northeast of the town.

The aerodrome, which had a radio range, was constructed as an emergency landing field for the Trans-Canada Airlines (TCA) route Moncton-Sydney-Gander-St. John's, which began service to Gander and St. John's on May 1, 1942. In June 1943, the commanding officer, RCAF Gander (Wing Commander Annis), recommended that the aerodrome, then under construction, be extended and paved as an alternate to Gander, because of the better weather at Buchans, but the Department of National Defence turned down the proposal.

In 1958, the Department of Transport decided to discontinue maintenance of the site because of its limited use (a new airport had been constructed at Deer Lake, forty-eight kilometres from Buchans, in 1955); high costs of reconstructing the runway (large boulders were working their way up through the gravel surface). The department transferred maintenance equipment and supplies to Gander in September 1958 and withdrew the airport's licence on October 28, 1958.

After the lapse of the original lease between the Department of Transport and ANDCO, the land and the aerodrome on it reverted back to the owners. By this time, ANDCO had been bought by Abitibi-Price Incorporated, which, in turn, contracted responsibility for mining operations in Buchans—and thus, the aerodrome—to the American Smelting and Refining Company. (ASARCO).

The site is now an emergency landing strip which remains unmaintained and can be used only at the pilot's own risk.

The Buchans mine closed in 1984.

Runway 06-24 is now 1,219 by 30 metres. It is used eight to ten times yearly by light aircraft.

Source:

1. George Neary, Manager-Consultant, ASARCO Incorporated.

Calgary International Airport
(Alberta)

Calgary's first airfield was near Bowness Park, ten kilometres west of the city. It was there, in 1914, that Frank Ellis, the aviation historian, and Tom Blakely flew their West Wind biplane, which they had built from parts salvaged from a Curtiss biplane that had crashed near Moose Jaw. In 1915, Ellis and Blakely continued their flying near Shouldice Park until the plane was badly damaged in a crash. The pilot, Ellis, was not hurt. Bowness Park was also used in August 1919 by Captain Ernest Hoy as the termination point of the first flight over the Rockies, and on October 7 to 17, 1920 by a Canadian Forces DH-9 airplane during the first trans-Canada flight.[1]

An aviation show featuring "Passenger-Carrying Aeroplanes and Aviation Stunts" was presented at the Calgary Exhibition Grounds, July 28 to July 15, 1919, by Captains Fred McCall DSO, MC and Bar, DFC, and W. May, DFC. (Calgary airport was later named after McCall.)

63. Captain Ernest Hoy's JN-4 aircraft taking off from Bowness Park on his attempted return trip to Vancouver, 1919.

64. Captain Ernest Hoy in his aeroplane at Calgary, Alberta, 1919.

In 1922, when the Air Board published its first list of airharbours available for use, Calgary was shown as having a private-commercial airharbour at Bowness, 300 yards [84 metres] square and licensed for Customs. The field was used by ex-war pilots—such as Fred McCall and Jack Palmer—embarking on peacetime aviation. The field, owned by the city of Calgary, had no facilities, and was operated privately by the pilots involved.

City land was chosen for a new airfield—the Banff Coach Road Airport—southwest Calgary, located on the bluff overlooking the Bow River. The airfield was privately operated. The Calgary Aero Club started flying there in September 1928 and held its first air show on September 15, with

65. Curtiss JN-4 aircraft No. 34210 at Bowness, Alberta, 1919.

W.L. Rutledge, Captain McCall, and J.E. Palmer participating in Moth aircraft. An official government report of September 1928 stated: "Calgary Aero Club have erected their first 'Moth'; temporary license issued to temporary airport for one month; one runway excellent, other not so good."[2]

In 1929, the city finally built the Calgary Municipal airport at Renfrew in the northeast section of the municipality, to replace the Banff Coach Road Airport, which had too much turbulence for small aircraft. The Calgary Aero Club moved to the Renfrew field in 1929 and staged its second air show on September 29 at the official opening. The airport was operated by the City Electrical System, whose superintendent, Robert MacKay, became in effect the first airport manager. The Renfrew field operated until 1940.

In 1929, Great Western Airways Ltd. and Rutledge Air Service Ltd. were based at the Renfrew Airport. The latter had a hangar 100 by 80 feet [30 by 24 metres]. One of the airport's original hangars still stands at 12th Avenue and 6th Street NE. During 1929, surveys were under way to extend air-mail service from Calgary to Vancouver.

Concern over the condition of the Calgary airport led the controller of Civil Aviation to write to the chief of Air Services on September 16, 1937:

On September 3rd the Minister wrote the Minister of National Defence asking whether the military aerodrome recently constructed at Calgary could be made available temporarily for commercial operations pending the establishment of adequate municipal airport facilities in Calgary.[3] This action was taken because on August 13th the City Council decided that it could not see its way clear to proceed with the construction of an airport as it was impossible for the city to raise $156,000, which would be its share of

66. Captain F.R. McCall in Curtiss JN-4 aircraft G-CAAH of McCall Aero Corporation, Calgary, Alberta, 1920.

the proposed development on Section 10, Township 23, Range 1, West of the 5th Meridian. Nothing further has transpired but from information received informally yesterday, there is a probability that there may be a change of heart in the Calgary Council.[4]

Despite the city's initial reluctance the controller was able to report dated October 6, 1938:

3. Calgary has also been active in aviation. The city built its own airport in 1929 and it has always been considered an important traffic point on the trans-Canada system. It has not the same opportunities of traffic as Edmonton has, as it has not great hinterland to the north, but local companies have been active and run passenger and express ser-

67. Calgary Airport looking west, 1931.

68. Calgary Municipal Airport, Alberta, 1937.

vices to the Turner Valley and other points in the vicinity, where traffic has justified the development of air services. The Calgary Aero Club has been successful and has trained 103 private pilots and 22 commercial pilots.

4. In 1931, when a final decision was made that the trans-Canada airway should pass by the Crow's Nest Pass route to Vancouver through the Mountains, Lethbridge was included in the trans-Canada line, which formerly passed direct from Medicine Hat to Calgary.[5]

From 1928 to 1938, the federal government gave $96,000 in assistance to the Calgary Airport, plus $50,000 for a radio range.

The fourth site—the present international airport—was chosen in 1938. The city purchased 640 acres [259 hectares] of land in the northeast sector of Calgary for the proposed Trans-Canada Air Lines (TCA) air service planned for development in 1938-39.

The main line for TCA was through Lethbridge, 209 kilometres to the south of Calgary; Edmonton and Calgary were to be serviced three times daily by a feeder line from Lethbridge. The decision to place Lethbridge rather than Calgary on the main line was made because the mountainous terrain west of Lethbridge was not nearly as formidable for TCA's Lockheed 10-A aircraft as the mountains west of Calgary.

Construction of the new airport started in 1938 with a single runway (02-20) and a combined hangar and administration building. (This hangar still stands on the east side of the airport and is occupied by Munro Aero Engine.) The facilities were ready for use by TCA when they began their proving flights in 1938. Robert MacKay, who had managed the Renfrew airport for the city, assumed operational responsibility at the new site.

During the Second World War, the Department of Transport took over the airport; but although the site had a great deal of military traffic, including flying training for the British Commonwealth Air Training Plan (BCATP), it was operated as a civil airport. The city continued to collect the rent from its hangar, which has also served as the TCA terminal and airport offices. TCA had three daily return services on the Lethbridge-Calgary-Edmonton route.

Calgary was the home of No. 2 Wireless School and No. 37 Service Flying Training School of the Royal Air Force. High River Training School Ltd., a subsidiary of the Calgary Aero Club, operated No. 5 Elementary Flying Training School at High River under the BCATP. (Frank Lake was Relief Station for No. 5 EFTS.)

During the war, the airport underwent expansion and development to runways and buildings to accommodate the RCAF the RAF, and the United States Air Force (USAF). After the United States entered the war in December 1941, the USAF became very active along the northwest airway to Alaska, and when the Alaska Highway was built, many of the airports along the airway were expanded or rebuilt. In Calgary, the USAF built hangars and other facilities and used the site as a refuelling service stop for aircraft being ferried to Russia via Alaska. The USAF developed the west side of the site and constructed the large concrete ramp that was influential in the decision to locate the city's air terminal building there in 1948.

The airport was returned to the city of Calgary in July 1949, and G.E.C. Craig became airport manager. At that time, the airport consisted of a four-runway configuration (the longest runway being 4,500 feet [1,372 metres]), and five large hangars that had been used by the RAF. The original city-built hangar on the east side continued to function as a terminal building housing all Department of Transport and TCA services.

From July 1, 1949, the airport began to receive an operating subsidy of five cents per square yard of paved aircraft manoeuvring area (500,000 square yards) from the Department of Transport.

Following the war, TCA, Chinook Flying Service, and Kepler Aviation Ltd. provided the only commercial traffic, the latter two companies having recently begun operations, using war surplus Cessna T-50 aircraft. Kepler aviation was forced to close after a short period because of a lack of business.

In 1948, TCA relocated its main line from Lethbridge to Calgary, because the acquisition of the more powerful Lodestar and North Star aircraft enabled the airline to overcome the chal-

69. Calgary's second terminal building, 1948.

70. Hangar in which Calgary's first terminal was locate, 1938.

lenges of the mountain ranges west of Calgary. But the relocation of the main line through Calgary coincided with severe flooding of the Fraser River in British Columbia, and Calgary Airport became the base for Operation Sandbag. All types of military aircraft, from DC-3s to Lancasters, were used to fly sandbags to Vancouver to stem the flood, and as a result the main runway 16-34 at Calgary was completely broken up. Consequently, after only one Trans-Canada North Star landing, the main line reverted to Lethbridge.

While runway 16-34 was being rebuilt and extended to 6,440 feet (1963 metres), the terminal facilities were moved out of the original hangar and relocated on the west side of the airport, to take advantage of the concrete ramp built by the USAF. Two existing buildings were renovated and adapted as an airport terminal. TCA then moved its main line operations back through Calgary, giving area residents direct main line service to Vancouver, Winnipeg, and Toronto for the first time.

In 1949, an Instrument Landing System (ILS) was installed on runway 16-34, and runway 07-25 was rebuilt and extended to 6,200 feet [1,890 metres]. Calgary had finally come of age in the national air transportation system as part of the

main line of TCA: it had two new runways, an ILS, and a 'new' terminal.

Canadian Pacific Air Lines (CPAL) started flying between Calgary, Cranbrook, Castlegar, and Penticton in 1950, providing Calgary with direct air service to the interior of British Columbia for the first time. This, together with the steadily increasing traffic at Calgary Airport, created a need for a more modern terminal building. Accordingly, in 1951, the city agreed to plan a new terminal adjacent to the west ramp. A by-law was passed to provide the necessary money, and, in late 1951, an architectural firm was retained. The terminal opened in 1956 and was to serve Calgary for twenty-one years, (during which time five major extensions were added). But when jets arrived in Calgary in 1961, the new terminal—opened five years earlier—became obsolete. Temporary measures were taken until 1977, when the terminal built by Transport Canada opened.

In 1959, Western Airlines (an American carrier) moved its Canadian terminus from Lethbridge to Calgary and, in 1960, Air West (now Hughes Air West) began offering service from Calgary to Spokane, and from that point to Seattle and Portland. Scheduled jet service into Calgary began on January 15, 1961, with TCA providing transcontinental service between Toronto, Montreal, and Vancouver. CPAL, in 1962, inaugurated non-stop Calgary to Amsterdam service: and thus Calgary, in the space of less than two years, became a truly international airport.

In 1962 Calgary city council named the airport 'Calgary International Airport—McCall Field.' Earlier it has been officially named 'McCall Field' in honour of Calgary flying ace Captain Fred McCall, who had been instrumental in starting commercial operations in Calgary following World War I; but the name McCall Field is rarely used today.

In 1961, a new runway, 10-28, was built at a total length of 8,000 feet [2,438 metres], and in 1963, runway 10-34 was extended to 12,675 feet [3,863 metres]. In 1963, Pacific Western Airlines began operations out of Calgary with their famous 'Airbus' service between Calgary and Edmonton, which continues today. In 1966, Lethbridge Air Services (now Time Air) began operations, linking Lethbridge and Medicine Hat to Calgary. Time Air subsequently extended its service to Edmonton and Grande Prairie.

These additional services strained the Calgary terminal beyond its limits. In spite of additions to the building, a new terminal would have to be built if the needs of the citizens of Calgary and airport users were to be met.

Therefore in April 1967, the airport was turned over to Transport Canada for $2 million and the promise of a new terminal. Before planning a new facility, however, the first priority was the addition of a major extension to the existing building. Completed in 1968, this provided ten gates and their respective holding rooms, so permitting operations during the planning and construction stage of the new facility.

The new terminal opened in 1977. It is a beautiful, modern structure and, with its 'incremental planning' concept, should serve Calgary until at least the turn of the century. Part of the old terminal is used as an operations building and houses weather services, telecommunications, and the civil aviation office of Transport Canada.

The history of general aviation in Calgary has been as exciting and progressive as the development of airline transportation. In 1945, the airport started with the establishment of two small companies and today is one of the busiest general aviation airports with the finest facilities in the country. It is used by what is probably the largest fleet of corporate aircraft in Canada.

Of the five hangars taken over by the Department of Transport in 1967, only one is still owned by the airport; hangar no. 10 (a former drill hall) leased to Kenting Helicopters. The rest were sold to the aviation industry and now function as sales, service, repair, and overhaul facilities.

Coincident with the development of the new air terminal complex, Air Canada (the new name of TCA) built an air cargo terminal in the northeast section of the airport. In the same area, south of the terminal building, International Aviation Terminal Ltd. built an air cargo centre, and Cara Operations Ltd. opened a new flight kitchen. Canadian Pacific Hotels Ltd. constructed an airport hotel near the terminal building and car parking structure.

Pacific Western Airlines constructed the first hangar (11,705 square metres) to house a major scheduled commercial air carrier in 1982; and during that year, the third-phase development of the Executive Flight Centre hangar complex, in the corporate and general aviation area of the first airport, opened, providing an additional 11,269 square metres to the first two phases of 11,705 square metres.

71. The third air terminal at Calgary International Airport, 1956.

In 1983, fire destroyed hangar no. 2 (an original hangar from the 1940's) and several small aircraft. Losses were over $1 million.

The following new facilities have been constructed by airport tenants during the last decade: a Shell Aero Centre hangar in 1982; an Air Canada Commissary building in 1984; an Avis Rent-A-Car service centre in 1985; a Tilden Rent-A-Car service centre in 1986; and a Purolator Courier office/warehouse in 1986.

Transport Canada also expanded its airport facilities; and in 1986, because of increasing international traffic, the Canada Customs facility was increased from 2,000 square metres to 3,000 square metres and included new baggage conveyor systems, an additional baggage carousel, and the expansion of the existing carousel.

In 1987, Transport Canada relocated the airport concessions from the mezzanine to the departures level, thereby strategically placing stores within the main stream of traffic. This has resulted in significant increases in revenue; and the number of concession operators has doubled since this move was made.

A new traffic control tower was built in 1988 because the existing air tower had reached its capacity and was unable to accommodate future radar system requirements. It will be in full operation 1990, when the installation of new radar equipment is completed.

Expansion of the international finger at the air terminal building began in 1989, adding two bridges and providing better washroom facilities.

Since 1983, the following airlines have begun to offer scheduled service at Calgary: United Airlines (1983), America West (1984), Continental Airlines (1985), KLM (1986), and Air BC (1988). Big Sky and Republic Airlines ceased operations (the latter in 1983); American Airlines and Lufthansa German Airlines spent brief periods of time (1984 to 1985 and 1983 to 1989 respectively) at this site. Canadian Airlines International was formed by a merger of Pacific Western Airlines and Canadian Pacific Airlines on January 1, 1988. Western Airlines merged

72. The latest terminal building, Calgary International Airport, opened in 1977.

with Delta Airlines in 1986 and now operates at Calgary as Delta Airlines.

Airlines Serving Calgary in 1989:

Domestic	Transborder	International
Air Canada	Air Canada	Air Canada
Can. Airlines	Can. Airlines	Can. Airlines
Wardair	Delta	Wardair
Time Air	Continental	KLM
Air BC	American West	
	United Airlines	

To relieve the amount of small aircraft traffic at Calgary International, the Department of Transport constructed a satellite airport at Springbank, about thirteen kilometres west of Calgary. It opened in February 1969 and provides facilities for small aircraft and *ab initio* flying training.

In February 1988, when Calgary hosted the XV Winter Olympic Games, its international airport dealt with 85 per cent of all Olympic-related travellers; and a total of 156 Olympic-related charters and extra sections passed through the terminal. In all, there were 400,000 passengers during February 1987. The most substantial increase was in international travel—150 per cent more passengers; and general aviation increased up to hundred aircraft daily.

Calgary International Airport celebrated its fiftieth anniversary on June 10, 1989, drawing 30,000 people to the airport general aviation area at the south end to view commercial, corporate, and general aviation static aircraft displays on Apron IV, and Canadian Armed Forces, U.S. Air Force, and RAF aircraft static displays on Apron VI. The celebration also included a mini-airshow with the Western Warbirds, a CAF CF18, the Airdrie Modellers Aircraft Association, and Bill Carter with the Pit Special.

The following are brief biographies of the managers who have served at the Calgary Airport since 1940:

Cyril Huntley (1940 - 1945)
Huntley was appointed airport manager in 1940 by the Department of Transport, immediately following takeover of the airport from the city. He retired in December 1945.

G.E.G. Craig (1946 - 1959)
Craig, who succeeded Huntley in January 1946 and retired in 1959, served in the Royal Flying Corps during the First World War as a pilot and, for many years, flew in the Canadian North, prior to his appointment as airport manager at Calgary.

During his term of office, the airport made the transition to a full civil airport from a largely military field in 1946. There was little traffic at first. When he retired in 1959, the airport was preparing to enter the jet age. One of Mr. Craig's notable achievements was the development of what was then the most modern terminal in Canada. It was opened in 1956.

Between 1948 and 1958, revenue grew from $105,581 to $272,628, expenditures from $61,221 to $199,861, and passengers handled from 46,558 to 294,331.

W.J. Watts (1959 - 1979)
Watts served in the RCAF during the Second World War as a pilot. He worked as Craig's assistant from 1946 until 1951, when he resigned to go into commercial aviation as a corporate pilot. Upon the retirement of Craig in 1959, Watts was appointed airport manager. He was retained in this position by the Department of Transport in 1967, when the department bought the airport from the city.

Between 1959 and 1979, revenue increased from $308,341 to $10,500,000, expenditures from $230,000 to $6,500,000, and passengers handled from 313,077 to 3,000,000.

Larry V. Le Gros (1979 - 1988)
Le Gros was appointed airport manager in 1979. He moved to Calgary from Vancouver, where he had served with the Department of Transport in the Pacific regional office since 1974 within the Civil Aviation and Airports branches. He was a navigator in the RCAF from 1959 to 1964.

Richard Paquette (1988 -)
Paquette assumed the position of airport general manager in August 1988. He worked for Transport Canada for sixteen years in various positions in the Pacific region (Vancouver) and as airport general manager at Edmonton International prior to his move to Calgary.

The following statistics illustrate the growth of Calgary International Airport:

	Aircraft Movements	Enplaned/Deplaned Passengers
1981	188,467	4,254,128
1982	157,857	3,797,335
1983	147,760	3,533,476
1984	151,132	3,633,446
1985	157,296	3,683,017
1986	147,759	3,814,607
1987	195,000	3,944,427
1988	206,704	4,600,000 est.

Sources:
1. W.J. Watts, former airport manager, Calgary International Airport.
2. R. Paquette, Airport General Manager, Calgary International Airport.

Footnotes: Calgary International Airport

[1] F.H. Ellis, *Canada's Flying Heritage* (Toronto: University of Toronto Press, 1961), pp. 38-46, 178, 180.

[2] Public Archives Canada, MG 24-3577, file 866. 1-53, vol. 2, September 1928.

[3] At Currie Barracks in the southwest end of Calgary. During the war, it was used by No. 3 Service Training School of the British Commonwealth Air Training Plan, and later, by No. 10 Repair Depot. A small hanger still stands, even though the airport no longer exists.

[4] Public Archives Canada, MG 30 E243, vol. 9.

[5] Ibid.

Cambridge Bay Airport
(Northwest Territories)

The explorer Roald Amundsen, in his ship, the *Gjoa*, visited Cambridge Bay in 1905 during his voyage through the Northwest Passage. The ship, *Maud*, in which he later drifted through the passage, is still partially visible where it was sunk in the bay near the hamlet of Cambridge Bay. It was bought by the Hudson Bay Company in 1927 for use as a supply vessel, and was subsequently moored in the harbour, as a warehouse, machine shop, and wireless station. It was from the *Baymaud* that the first weather reports from the Canadian Arctic were transmitted and relayed south through Royal Canadian Signal Corps Stations.

73. Cambridge Bay Airport terminal N.W.T.,1975.

The hamlet of Cambridge Bay is an incorporated municipality administered by an elected body of mayor and eight councillors. A full-time chief administrative officer handles the day-to-day business of the community with funding from the Municipal and Community Affairs Department of the government of the Northwest Territories

The airport, located approximately 1,931 kilometres northeast of Edmonton at 69°6'N and 105°8'W, has a single runway, 1,524 by 46 metres, which is surfaced with a clay and crushed gravel mixture. This location, 322 kilometres north of the Arctic Circle, has a nine-month winter, and, because it is above the treeline, experiences fierce blizzards, when there is no visibility. The average annual temperature in Cambridge Bay is -14.6°C. The only alternative to air travel and freight is possible during the short shipping season.

Although the first aircraft is reported to have landed in the Cambridge Bay area in 1929, the present airport site was not officially in use until late in World War II with the establishment of Operation *Beetle*, a joint RCAF/USAF venture into a world-wide navigation system. The 632 foot [193 metre] LORAN (Low Frequency Radio Range) tower and buildings were erected in the late 1940s, but as *Beetle* lost its promise and

funding ran out, the site was turned over to the Department of Transport in 1951. A radio communications centre and weather station were established permanently at that time. A few years later, when the construction of the DEW Line, began, Cambridge Bay was to become a major site. The airport (which is about five kilometres from the tower) was upgraded as part of the radar installation and became the transportation hub for the Central Arctic communities, now called the Kitikmeot region (an Inuit word meaning 'in the middle'). The airport still serves this purpose for the communities of Gjoa Haven, Spence Bay, and Pelley Bay.

The Department of Transport took control of the airport on November 16, 1960, and control of associated land was transferred by Order in Council from the Department of Indian and Northern Affairs in March 1974. The airport is licensed for day and night Instrument Flight Rules (IFR) operations, is operated under a comprehensive contract with a local company, Fred H. Ross and Associates, but is managed by Transport Canada through an airport manager. Other departmental staff include six flight service specialists, who provide domestic and international air/ground radio services, and an electronics technician for communications and navigational equipment. The Atmospheric Environment Canada Weather Service also maintains a staff of five surface and aerological weather technicians, who support civil aviation, the general public, and the North Warning Radar System (the new name for the upgraded DEW Line System).

The Arctic being what it is—barren and frozen—the utilities normally associated with an airport are somewhat improvised. Water and sewage are handled by municipal service trucks, which fill or empty (as the case may be) the airport building tanks three times per week. The GNWT Power Corp. provides electricity via a

diesel operated and wind-power supplemented electrical power system. Heating fuel is delivered by local contractor truck, as is vehicle fuel, when required. Northwestel has telephone services, both local and to the outside world. The ANIK satellite relays CBC television and CBC-FM radio from the northern network, and Arctic Cablevision transits its services via the CAN-COM Satellite.

The hamlet of Cambridge Bay, through the airport, is served by three scheduled carriers: Canadian Airlines International Ltd. (jet service twice a week); Northwest Territorial (jet service two times and Lockheed Electra 1 service once a week); and First Air (HS-748 service six times a week). NWTAir also bases a DC-3 at Cambridge Bay which serves Coppermine, Gjoa Haven, Spence Bay, and Pelley Bay three times a week each way. A single local charter aircraft operator, Adlair Aviation, uses Beaver, Single Otter, Twin Otter, and KingAir equipment to provide business, government, and tourist travel services. Canadian Airlines (with B-737s) and Bradley Air Services (with HS-748s) provide transportation for the North Warning Radar Station and lateral support sites.

In 1988, the airport had over 12,900 passengers and 4,900 aircraft movements.

The following is a list of Cambridge Bay airport managers:

R. Manderfield	1963 to 1967
A.L. Hendrick	1967 to 1968
K.H. Howard	1968 to 1973
J. McKay	1974 to 1976
D.B. Funston	1976 to 1978
R.C. Miller	1978 to 1980
J.V. Logan	1980 to 1982
R.P. Proulx	1982 to 1984
R.L. Proulx	1984 to 1987
S.F. Sutherland	1987 to 1989

Source:
Transport Canada, Western Region.

Campbell River Airport
(British Columbia)

This airport, seven kilometres south of the community, is currently owned by Transport Canada and operated on a subsidized basis by the District of Campbell River.

Following a survey in 1955, the municipality acquired 259 acres [105 hectares] in 1959 and constructed an airport—for $34,000. The first licence was issued on September 4, 1959, and Pacific Western Airlines began a scheduled passenger service with DC-3 aircraft the following year. Five years later, the 4,200 foot [1,280 metre] runway was paved.

The Crown purchased the airport (worth $128,045) for one dollar in 1967, and the District of Campbell River resumed operational responsibility for the site through a lease arrangement. During that year, the runway was extended to 5,000 feet [1,524 metres], and lighting was installed to permit night operation. Instrument Landind System (ILS) was added in 1980.

A new terminal building was opened in 1968 and enlarged during two renovations in 1980 and 1988.

Three scheduled airlines are based at Campbell River: Time Air offers four daily flights with Short 360, Dash 7, and Dash 8 aircraft; Air BC has five daily flights, operating Dash 7, and Dash 8 aircraft; and Skylink Airlines provides six scheduled flights per day (if required) using Cessna 402 and Metro-liner aircraft.

Comox Flying Club, Weldwood of Canada, Vancouver Island Helicopters Ltd., M.C.B. Industries, Falcon Airways, I & J Logging Ltd., the Campbell River Air Youth Association, and the B.C. Forestry Service (through contract with Conair Aviation) are based at the airport.

In 1988, there were 88,100 passengers, and 44,668 aircraft movements.

Ernest Dreger is airport manager.

Source:
Transport Canada, Pacific Region.

Carp Airport
(Ontario)

The Department of National Defence originally built Carp Aerodrome in 1942 as an RCAF base on a site of 630 acres [255 hectares]. The Department of Transport began to assume responsibility for the site when they licensed it for the Air Cadet League of Canada on November 1, 1946, for daytime operations by light- and medium-weight aircraft. The three original runways, laid in a triangular configuration, were classified as serviceable—the east-west runway was the longest at 2,973 by 148 feet [906 by 45 metres].

In May, 1946, the Crown leased the airport to Huntley Township, which took responsibility for management and maintenance, and subsequently subleased to Bradley Air Services Ltd., the principal tenant at the airport. A rotating beacon and flare path lighting, added in the mid-1950s, permitted night flying.

An airport licence (No. 284) was granted to Carp as a public airport in 1954, with general aviation listed as the major activity. Suggestions to develop an airport facility at Carp to relieve congestion at Ottawa (Uplands) Airport, were rejected because its distance—thirty-five kilometres—was too great for the Ottawa Flying Club and other general aviation activities. During the 1960s and 1970s, the airport served as a local general aviation airport with Bradley Air Services and G.F. Field Air Service (now Mylight Aircraft Ltd.) undertaking commercial aviation activities. In 1974, with the amalgama-

tion of the townships of Huntley, Fitzroy, and Torbolton, and the creation of the township of West Carleton, responsibility for management and maintenance of the Carp Airport was transferred to the new municipality and again sub-leased to a management company formed by Bradley Air Services. This arrangement continues. The Electronics Systems Training Centre at Carp Airport, established by Transport Canada as a telecommunications training centre, was transferred to Cornwall in 1978.

Although two planning reports concluded that a reliever site should be located at Carp, and land was bought to increase the airport to 966 acres (391 hectares), no further action was taken, and Carp remains a local commercial airport. It is used primarily as a base for Westair Aviation flying school and charter activities, and as a maintenance centre for Bradley Air Services. Nipissing Helicopter, Campeau Corporation, the Canadian Aerosport Technical Committee, and Transport Canada are also located at the airport.

The existing runway, an asphalt surface with a gravel overshoot, (10-28), is 1,028 metres long and 45 metres wide.

Approximately 150 people work on the site, largely employed in the administrative offices of Bradley Air Service. Since 1982, maintenance facilities have been expanded and an instrument shop has been established.

Sources:
1. Canada. Department of Transport. Carp Airport Master Plan.
2. Ted Lennox, Bradley Air Services.
3. Maureen Goodyear, Bradley Air Services.
4. Rod Macdonald, Westair Aviation.

Cartierville Airport
(Montreal, Quebec)

Cartierville Airport is the oldest airfield in

Canada. The site—then the polo grounds—was first used by Percy Hall Reid in 1911 for experiments with aircraft he built between 1911 and 1914; and he built the first hangar there in 1912.

74. Fairchild FC-2 aircraft 4012 of Canadian Colonial Airways Inc., at Cartierville, Québec, May 5, 1928.

RAF Captain Brian Peck carried the first official air mail from the polo grounds at Cartierville to the Royal Air Force field at Leaside, Toronto, on June 24, 1918, flying a JN-4 airplane. (The Montreal branch of the Aerial League of the British Empire made the arrangements with the Post Office and the RAF to deliver the mail by air on this occasion.)

In a letter of May 14, 1920, the Air Board[1] advised the president of the Aerial League at Montreal that the field could be turned into a public Customs aerodrome after some improvements were made—at the time, it was used by Raymond and Wiltshire as a commercial aerodrome. To achieve this goal, the board agreed to lend the league a Bessoneau hangar[2] large enough to house six aircraft; and the league entered into an agreement with Raymond and Wiltshire "to provide the services of an engineer as called for."[3]

The aerodrome was located at the intersection of the CNR (running east-west) and the Cartierville Road (running north-south), and the site was described as "the only field that can be

obtained for the present, to be used as a Customs Aerodrome for the City of Montréal and vicinity."[4] Customs agreed to the licence on June 24, 1920, and it was issued to the Aerial League. The aerodrome was described under different names as the Montreal Aviation Field, the airharbour at St. Laurent, the aerodrome at the polo grounds, St. Laurent, the airharbour at Cartierville, or the Bois Franc Aerodrome of the Aerial League of the British Empire. In March 1922, the Air Board renewed the loan of the Bessoneau hangar to the league for another year, but in a letter of May 27, 1921, the league complained that if one waited for "our municipal government to become interested in the aerodrome, you would have to wait a long time and, quite possibly, they wouldn't be interested at all."[6]

An argument developed between the federal government and the Air League concerning the definition of a public aerodrome and the conditions of its use; the terms and means of paying for its maintenance when airport revenues proved insufficient to cover costs; and, in particular, the circumstances dictating the provision of engineering services at the Cartierville aerodrome. That dispute centred on the licensing requirement that an air engineer be available on the site. While Raymond and Wiltshire had agreed to supply the engineer "in consideration

75. Cartierville Airport, inauguration of airmail, Montréal to Rimouski., May 5, 1928.

of the use of the aerodrome, to the exclusion of any other commcercial aviation company, but not to the exclusion of its use as a general airport,"[7] their definition of available service seemed to indicate that an engineer would only be made available to the extent revenues covered the cost of his services. Finally (and probably as a result of this on-going dispute), the Air Service branch of the Department of National Defence wrote to the Air League on May 17, 1923: "the licence for the Montréal Public Customs Aerodrome has this day been cancelled, as this aerodrome is no longer available for use as such."[8]

On June 1, 1923, the Deputy Minister of National Defence asked the Montréal Harbour Commissioners to consider establishing an airharbour within the same general area as the Cartierville aerodrom, and referred to a contract with Canadian Vickers Ltd. to construct flying boats at their works in Maisonneuve. The airharbour was established, and over 2,600 square feet [242 square metres] of the harbour of Montreal just below the Dry Dock basin was licensed as a public Customs airharbour in the name of Canadian Vickers Ltd.

Further development occurred in the region when the Department of National Defence built the St. Hubert Airport in 1927, which served as Montréal's airport until the construction of Dorval in 1941, and is referred to elsewhere.

In 1928, the Reid Aircraft Co. Ltd. was incorporated and became established at the Cartierville Aerodrome. It purchased 242 acres [98 hectares] of land, obtained an airport licence issued under the name of Reid Aircraft, and erected two small hangars on the east side of the airport. Although the aerodrome had been in use since 1911, its development began with Reid's purchase. The company had been set up to manufacture the Reid Rambler airplane, which W.T. Reid had designed. Then in 1929, the company was purchased by the Curtiss Aeroplane and Motors

Co. of New York and became the Curtiss-Reid Aircraft Ltd. J.A.D. McCurdy, the first man to fly an airplane in Canada, was president of the company from 1929 to 1932. Curtiss-Reid did a lot of levelling and drainage work at the airport, erected a brick aircraft factory on the north side of the airport and built a third hangar. When the company failed in 1932, some of its assets were taken over by Montréal Aircraft Industries Ltd.

In 1935, Noorduyn Aircraft Ltd. established itself at Cartierville Airport in space leased in the Curtiss-Reid factory, manufactured the Norseman (which became famous as a bush aircraft in Canada), and later bought the Curtiss-Reid factory. During the war, Noorduyn produced Harvard training planes and large numbers of Norsemen for the Canadian and American air forces. When the company went out of business at the end of the war, its plant was purchased by Canadair Ltd.

In 1938, Cartierville was the home of the Montreal Light Aeroplane Club, which had been formed at St. Hubert in 1928, and resumed operations at Cartierville after the war.

In 1939—when Cartierville had two landing strips 2000 feet (610 metres) long—the Department of Transport was looking for a site for a new airport to replace St. Hubert, and one of these was the Cartierville Airport. (The owner, Curtiss-Reid Aircraft Co., was anxious to sell the land which it had retained after its aircraft business had failed). However, Cartierville was rejected because the site was too small and hemmed in by obstructions.

In 1940, the Department of Munitions and Supply began to acquire land at the Cartierville Airport to establish an aircraft production centre. Included in the land purchased was the parcel owned by Montreal Aircraft Industries Ltd. (formerly Curtiss-Reid Flying Services Ltd.) Munitions and Supply took over the airfield and constructed a hard-surfaced runway northeast-southwest in late 1941; but the airport licence remained in the name of Montreal Aircraft Industries Ltd., and Noorduyn Aircraft Company looked after airport maintenance until late 1944. At that time, Federal Aircraft Ltd. (the Crown corporation formed to take over aircraft production from Munitions and Supply) assumed responsibility for the airport. The Department of Transport assumed ownership on December 17, 1945.

During the war, there were four aircraft factories at Cartierville: Noorduyn Aircraft Ltd.,

76. Cartierville Airport, Québec, 1929.

Canadian Vickers Ltd., Canadian Car and Foundry Ltd., and Canadair Ltd.

Canadian Vickers Ltd. began business in Montréal as a builder of ships and heavy machinery and entered aircraft manufacture in 1923. By the beginning of World War II, it had produced the Vickers Viking, Vedette, Vancouver, Fairchild FC-2, Fokker, and Bellanca. The company also made Stranraers and Northrop Deltas for the RCAF, and components for the H.P. Hampden. In 1941, Canadian Vickers received a contract for the Canso and initially began assembly at St. Hubert. Then, it moved, in December 1942, to a large new factory built by the government at Cartierville, where assembly of the Canso began in July 1943.

Canadian Vickers gave up aircraft manufacturing in 1944—by which time it had produced 312 Cansos. It was then taken over by the newly formed Canadair Ltd.

Canadian Car and Foundry Ltd. had two factories in Montréal that made aircraft component, and opened a plant at Cartierville Airport in 1943, (on the Bois Franc Road near Noorduyen's facility) to work on the Anson conversion program and make aircraft components. The company bought the rights to the Norseman airplane in 1945 and was involved in the development of the prototype Burnelli airplane—which never went into production.

The Canadian government formed Canadair Ltd. in 1944 to take over the aircraft manufacturing business of Canadian Vickers, which included the government factory at Cartierville. Canadair assumed control on November 11, 1944, when Canadian Vickers had two contracts, one to produce Cansos—and the other to develop a new version of the Douglas DC-4. The DC-4 prototype, later known as the DC-4M, flew in 1946 and was later sold to TCA, the RCAF, CP Air, and BOAC. The company also converted the military C-47 airplane to the civil DC-3 and manufactured spares for both planes for worldwide sales. At the end of the war, Canadair purchased the Noorduyn plant on the north side of the airport.

Cartierville Airport was closed to civil air traffic on October 1, 1968, because its proximity to Dorval endangered aircraft using the international airport. Most of the general aviation and flying school operations moved to St. Hubert, which was taken over by the Department of Transport from National Defence on October 1, 1968, for operation as a satellite airport for Montréal. At the time it closed, Cartierville handled the largest volume of aircraft movement in Canada—most of it flight training.

And history should record that in an early

planning study for Dorval in 1968, one of the options considered—but rejected—was the enlargement of Dorval by incorporating the Cartierville Airport.

The government sold Canadair to the Electric Boat Co., an American corporation (later taken over by General Dynamics), but in January 1976, bought back control. It again sold Canadair Ltd., in August 1986, to Bombardier Inc.; and in December of the same year, it also sold the Cartierville airport to Bombardier.

Canadair facilities at Cartierville consist of the plant originally occupied by Canadian Vickers, the Noorduyn buildings, and the plant formerly occupied by Canadian Car and Foundry. The airport is now licensed in the name of Canadair and is closed to all traffic except Canadair and military flights. There is one paved runway, 10-28 at 2,680 by 46 metres.

Since World War II Canadair has built the following types of aircraft: DC-4M North Star, Argus, Cosmopolitan, CL-44 (Swing-Tail freighter), CL-215 Water Bomber, Sabre, T-33, Tutor, F-104, and CF-5. It remains in business at Cartierville today and is now producing the Challenger executive jet.

Sources:

1. Clarke, R.L. *Airport Notes*. (Ottawa: Transport Canada, undated) [unpublished collection].
2. Molson, K.M. and H.A. Taylor. *Canadian Aircraft Since 1909*.(Stittsville: Canada's Wings Inc.), 1982.
3. Fuller, G.A., J.A. Griffin and K.M. Molson. *125 Years of Canadian Aeronautics*. (Willowdale: Canadian Aviation Historical Society,) 1983.

Footnotes—Cartierville Airport

[1] The Air Board was then the federal government's authority in charge of civil aviation in Canada.
[2] For more information on Bessoneau's hangars, see Appendix 1.
[3] Public Archives Canada, RG 24, vol. 3533, letter from the Aerial League of the British Empire to the Air Board, 21 May, 1920.
[4] Public Archives Canada, RG 24, vol. 3533, letter from J.A. Wilson, secretary of the Air Board, to the Minister of Customs, 7 June, 1920.
[5] Ibid.
[6] Public Archives Canada, RG 24, vol. 3533, letter from the Air League to the Air Board, 27 May 1921.
[7] Public Archives Canada, RG 24, vol 3533, letter from J.A. Wilson, secretary of the Air Board, to the Minister of Customs, 7 June, 1920.
[8] Public Archives Canada, RG 24, vol. 3533, letter signed by the Contoller of Civil Aviation, 17 May, 1923.

Castlegar Airport (British Columbia)
Formerly Ralph West Airfield

Castlegar Airport is owned by Transport Canada and operated under contract by Pacific Building Maintenance Ltd. Until December 1976, it was run by an airport committee representing the local municipalities of Nelson, Castlegar, Kinnaird, and Trail; the city of Castlegar later assumed full responsibility for the site in 1977 until March 1979.

The airfield was built in 1945 at Ootechenia as an emergency field for the Trans-Canada Airway. The city of Nelson bought the site in 1946, and the grass field was given a temporary licence in 1947, when the site was served by Canadian Pacific Airlines.

In 1948, the local municipalities of Nelson, Castlegar, and Kinnaird took over the airport and named it Ralph West Airfield. West was the first chairman of the Castlegar Airport Committee, to whom the airport licence was transferred 1961. The title to the airport lands was transferred to the Department of Transport in 1965.

The runway, 4,800 feet [1,463 metres] long, was paved in 1954, resurfaced in 1965, and reconstructed between April 3 and May 19, 1978, when the aorport had to be closed. Runway 13-31 is now 914 by 23 metres.

The first air terminal building was opened in 1963, and a new one built in 1971. A new control tower was opened in 1976. The terminal building was completely renovated and enlarged to three times its original size in a $3 million project in 1987 and reopened officially in July 1988. The main aircraft operating apron was also resurfaced at this time.

In 1969, B.C. Airlines took over scheduled services from CP Air, and, in 1971, Pacific Western Airlines assumed the service. Today, Time Air and Air BC offer scheduled service at the airport.

Adastra Aviation Ltd., Highland Helicopters Ltd., Selair Pilot's Association, and B.C. Forest Services are based atCastlegar.

In 1988, the airport had 95,000 passengers and 27,000 aircraft movements.

John Michelson was airport manager from March 1967 to June 1989. John Perry is the present airport manager.

Source:
Transport Canada, Pacific Region.

Charlevoix Airport
(Quebec)

In October 1955, the federal government made grants to Charlevoix East and Charlevoix West to develop a public airport, which theses counties would thereafter operate and maintain. Additional funds were granted in 1956.

In October 1958 the two municipalities asked the federal government to complete the work so that an air service for the Malbaie (St Irénée) area could begin. Construction using gravel from two adjacent pits began in April 1959 and a non-directional navigational beacon was approved.

Although not completed, the airport had limited use in the fall of 1961, when it was known as either St. Irénée or la Malbaie Airport. The airport was officially opened on June 16, 1962, with 10,000 people in attendance.

When construction was completed in January 1963, at a total cost to the federal government of $555,705, the airport was leased to the counties of Charlevoix East and West for $1.00 per year.

The airport has one paved runway, 15-33, at 1,372 by 46 metres and is still operated, with a federal subsidy by the municipality.

Source:
Canada, Transport Canada, file 5151-1439, 9 February 1972.

Charlo Municipal Airport (New Brunswick)
(also known as Campbellton-Dalhousie Airport)

Charlo Municipal Airport, eight kilometres from the port of Dalhousie and twenty-seven kilometres south of Campbellton, serves the northeastern part of New Brunswick and the southern Gaspé area of Quebec. 70,000 people live within an eighty kilometre radius of the airport.

The Department of Transport first surveyed the location in 1947 as a possible RCAF air station, but it was rejected in favour of Chatham. No progress was made until 1960, when, following the recommendations of the Restigouche Joint Airport Committee, Transport agreed to offer a grant towards the construction of the airport. (The federal government's final contribution was $53,176 of the total cost of $121,189). In anticipation of the new facility, Maritime Central Airways promised to operate a service between Moncton, Charlo, and Sept-Iles when the airport was in operation.

Restigouche Municipal Airport was officially opened before a large crowd on June 15, 1963—a day which had been declared a county holiday in honour of the occasion. The site had a small terminal building, one crushed gravel runway 5,000 by 350 feet [1,341 by 107 metres], and a 600 foot [183 metre] taxiway. Maritime Central Airways made their first commercial flight from the airport two days after its inauguration. Management was provided by an airport committee of the Restigouche County Council.

By 1965, Eastern Provincial Airways had replaced Maritime as the scheduled carrier, two flying clubs were based at the airport with their own hangars, and the runway had been paved.

On November 21, 1967, the airport operation was reorganized, and under new management the site became known as the Dalhousie-Campbellton Municipal Airport. A company was established to run the airport, and shares in the new business were held by the directors, the town of Dalhousie, and the city of Campbellton. During the following year, Eastern Provincial began offering daily service to Montreal with Dart Herald aircraft.

The Department of Transport announced in 1973 that the airport would be expanded to permit the entry of jets, a decision which led to the extension of the runway to 6,000 feet [1,829 metres] and the introduction of Boeing 737s on Eastern Provincial Airway routes.

In 1975, airport management, in co-operation with the Department of Transport, launched a modernization programme: a new terminal building, garage, fire hall, communications services and weather office building, taxiway, and ramp, as well as the installation of new navigation aids, including an ILS. The new facilities, to which the federal government had contributed $8 million, opened on September 20, 1980. The name of the airport was changed to Charlo Municipal Airport in 1981; and the site is currently administered by a twelve-member board of directors from both Charlo and Dalhousie.

The airport has fourteen full-time employees, a flight services station, and a weather station.

Names of the airlines servicing Charlo Airport have changed over the years. First, Maritime Central became Eastern Provincial, which was taken over by Canadian Pacific. It later became Canadian Airlines International, which was in turn replaced by Inter-Canadian (operating daily Fokker 100 service to Montreal). In April 1989, Air Atlantic began service with the Dash 8.

In 1988, there were 4,006 aircraft movements, and 24,300 passengers.

Two airport managers have served at the site since its inception:
Francis Bernard 1967-75; Hebert Arsenault 1976-.

Source:
1.   June Hickey, Transport Canada, Atlantic Region.

Charlottetown Airport
(Prince Edward Island)

The present airport site on the Brackley Point Road was not Charlottetown's first airfield. Flying was, in fact, introduced to Charlottetown as early as 1912 when an aircraft landed at the city exhibition grounds; but it was not until 1931 that an airport became a reality: it was known as Upton Field, located on land owned by Dr. J.S. Jenkins, chief physician at the Charlottetown Hospital.

In 1927, Fairchild FC-2 aircraft ran an air-mail between Moncton and Prince Edward Island. When the federal government introduced its plan to assist light aeroplane clubs in Canada in 1927, the Prince Edward Flying Club was formed and, in May 1929, its members selected an airport site, which was subsequently recommended for licence provided the land was acquired by the club—but no action was taken. In April 1930, the Charlottetown Flying Club, which was being organized at the time, asked the Civil Aviation branch of National Defence to survey the area for an aerodrome in the area. Again, there was no action.

In a report of November 24, 1931, the superintendent of Airways dealing with airport inspections in the Maritime provinces, wrote:

an aerodrome provided by Dr. J.S. Jenkins is part of his farm, two miles north of the City; Province and City to provide machinery and Dr. Jenkins to pay the cost of labour; it will be an excellent aerodrome; Canadian Airways will use it for daily service between Charlottetown and Moncton; Mrs. Jenkins is a pilot; he [Dr. Jenkins] is taking instruction and may buy an aircraft.[1]

The site, called Upton Airport, was licensed on January 16, 1932. It had two turf landing strips, 2,800 and 1,600 feet [853 and 588 metres] long, and was leased to Canadian Airways Ltd. from October 9, 1932 to October 9, 1938. The licence remained in force until June 30, 1938.

When the city of Charlottetown asked the Department of Transport for assistance to develop a municipal airport in June 1938, two sites were considered: Upton Airport, and a three hundred acre [121.5 hectare] property at Sherwood Station on the Brackley Point Road. The federal government accepted the Brackley Point Road site because the Upton site lacked space for future expansion, and the city purchased it for $30,000. Charlottetown also negotiated with the provincial government to bear half the cost of the site, and the province agreed to do so on condition that it receive half the profits of airport revenue. The city was to operate the airport.

The city not only wanted the airport for reasons of transportation, but to alleviate unemployment. All workers were to come from the city's relief lists. On September 2, 1938, the Department of Transport let a contract for clearing; and, in July 1939, work began on three landing strips.

In December 1939, city council wrote to the deputy minister of Transport, V.I. Smart, and offered free use of the airport to the Canadian government for defence purposes until the conclusion of the war. The government accepted, and on May 1, 1940, the Department of National Defence announced the establishment of No. 5 Bombing and Gunnery School at the Charlottetown Airport under the British Commonwealth Air Training Plan (BCATP). A miniature town rapidly took shape at the airport: forty-three buildings were erected, including six hangars.

The field was officially handed over to the Royal Air Force on June 15, 1941, by which time three hard-surfaced runways had been constructed. Early in 1941 the airport became the base of No. 31 General Reconnaissance School—the Bombing and Gunnery School originally planned. This was a response to the local lobster fishermen, because the bombing range would close valuable lobster grounds on the north shore between Covehead and St. Peters.

Under the BCATP, three more aerodromes were built on Prince Edward Island: No. 9 Service Training Flying School (SFTS) at Summerside (the airport is still operated by the Department of National Defence; however, plans to close the airbase in 1990 have been announced); two other aerodromes to relieve pressures at No. 9 SFTS Summerside - No. 1 station at Mount Pleasant (now operated by Mount Pleasant Flying Services Ltd.), and No. 2 school at Wellington.

Commercial air services from the Charlottetown Airport under the management of Canadian Airways Limited linked Charlottetown and Moncton. In April 1941, TCA inaugurated a feeder service, with a Lockheed Electra ten-place plane, linking Charlottetown and Summerside with the mainland flight to Moncton. In mid-October the air service was taken over by a new company organized by Carl Burke, known as

Maritime Central Airways, which flew out of the Charlottetown Airport until 1963, when Eastern Provincial Airways was formed.

Under the BCATP, the Royal Air Force operated Charlottetown Airport, until February 1944, when the Royal Canadian Air Force took over, and the station became known as No. 2 Air Navigational School.

When, in late January 1945, local politicians were told that the RCAF Navigation School at Charlottetown was to be transferred to Summerside, they were afraid that they they would also lose the civil airport. However, after much discussion with Defence authorities in Ottawa, Charlottetown had the order rescinded.

When, after a little more than four years, the BCATP School at the Charlottetown Airport offically closed on July 7, 1945, 1,200 students from Canada, England, France, Norway, Poland, Australia, New Zealand, and the United States had graduated. Training was in twin-engined Anson aircraft; two to three hundred air force personnel and about one hundred civilian workers were on staff at the time of the closure.

The Department of Transport took over Charlottetown Airport from the RCAF on February 1, 1946; William "Bill" Gillespie was appointed as airport maintenance foreman.

When negotiations with the city failed, the department accepted full responsibility for the operation and further development of the airport in July 1947.

The Department of National Defence turned over sixty-five BCATP buildings to the War Assets Corporation, and many went to the city of Charlottetown. In 1946, when veterans returning from overseas caused an acute housing shortage, the city converted the buildings into an emergency housing project, known as Maple Hills. But the project proved to be too expensive for the city, which turned it over for the provincial Department of Reconstruction to operate. In late

77. Charlottetown (Uptown) Airport, P.E.I.,
February, 1932.

1948 many units were purchased at minimal cost and torn down or moved to sites where veterans had purchased land. The buildings that remained (mainly the larger ones) went to the Department of Transport to administer; others were rented or sold, and the site was leased. It was well into the 1950s before the government had completely disposed of the buildings but none remain today. A hangar bought by the city was demolished in the early 1970's, and the last remaining hangar, no. 4, which housed the maintenance garage and fire hall for the Department of Transport, was demolished in 1979 to make way for expansion.

The first frame construction terminal building was built in 1941. It was never an air force building, but housed the terminal and the radio range station; George Champion was officer-in-charge of the latter. Champion came to the Charlottetown Airport at the beginning of 1939 and first operated the radio in an old farm house near the future site of the terminal building. The terminal accommodated Canadian Airways, TCA, Maritime Central Airways, and Eastern Provincial Airways.

Bill Gillespie retired on March 31, 1959, after fourteen years as the airport maintenance foreman. Hiram Noel became the first airport manager and remained in that position until 1963. He was followed by Charlie Matheson, who was formerly an airport mechanic, in 1964 and who remained until late in 1969. Les Clarke became the next manager in 1970, remaining until July 31, 1972. He was followed by Donald MacMillan, who had been employed at Ottawa headquarters. MacMillan completed his tour in October 1975. L.L. Campbell followed in 1975-76 and was replaced by R.E. Howard. Following Howard's sudden death in April 1982, Michael D. Campbell, a native of Charlottetown, became manager.

No major work was done at the Charlottetown Airport until 1960, even though city council and local politicians had tried to implement plans for expansion. The opening of the new 03-21, 7,000 foot [2,134 metre] runway at the airport on September 29, 1960, was described as a "tremendous boon" to the province. To Islanders, the runway meant easier access to and from the mainland. Runways 09-27 and 18-36 were also upgraded. Runway 03-21 was used by Air Canada and Eastern Provincial Airways' jet aircraft.

The local newspaper, the Guardian, "gratefully attributed the awarding of a contract for aircraft maintenance on the Island and the prospect of some 200 new jobs for Islanders directly to the new facility." The contract to which the newspaper referred was the establishment of the Enamel and Heating Products Ltd. maintenance shop at the airport, which opened in hangar no. 4. in March 1960 and ended operations in late 1963. It repaired and did routine maintenance on the Sabre jet, better known as the F-86, including some work for the RCAF's Golden Hawks. Some modifications were also done to Lancaster bombers. The operation ended when the Sabre jets were removed from active service, and the hangar was subsequently used by the Department of Transport until late in 1979 as the airport maintenance garage. It was later disposed of through the Crown Assets Disposal Corporation.

In 1960, Maritime Central Airways operated DC-3 and C-46 aircraft at the airport. The airline purchased the Dart Herald in 1962, to replace the DC-3 on many of the scheduled runs. When Eastern Provincial Airways bought MCA in 1963, it continued to operate these aircraft from Charlottetown. In 1969, EPA operated the first jet aircraft through the airport, the Boeing 737.

The next major expansion to the airport was enlargement and improvement of the terminal building in 1970. The original terminal building was designed to accommodate twenty-five to thirty people. With the new jet aircraft, ninety to one hundred people were embarking and disembarking at any one time. The terminal building was enlarged by eighty-two square feet [eight square metres] and included new washrooms, airline offices, ticket counter areas, and a waiting room. Two additional extensions of thirty-two square feet [three square metres] each were made to the terminal building in 1971 and 1973, and a further extension was built in 1974, comprising new and enlarged washroom facilities attached to the westside, and a passenger lounge on the east side of the building. Yet another extension in 1980 provided more space for baggage handling and a 'racetrack' baggage conveyor system. During the early 1970s, the ramp as well as the parking lots were enlarged and repaved.

78. View showing Charlottetown air terminal, equipment garage and firehall.

In early 1975, Air Canada began service from Toronto to Ottawa to Charlottetown. Since the airline traffic had increased significantly, upgrading of the air traffic control facilities became necessary. A temporary steel tower was installed and began operation on June 4, 1975.

A master plan for the future of the airport was prepared in 1974 which recommended that the current facility be developed rather than moved to a new location. It also recommended the construction of a new terminal building and runways and the acquisition of additional land. In effect, it meant rebuilding the whole airport at an estimated cost of $21 million (a figure which later rose to $30 million).

The plan met with much local opposition regarding its cost, necessity, and impact on land development. However, beginning in 1979, a combined services building, terminal ramp, and taxiways were built, and utilities updated. The combined-services building comprised 1,950 square metres and featured both active and passive solar collectors. This building now houses the fire hall and maintenance sections.

Improvements to the airport parking lot helped eliminate parking on the highway.

The airport closed for two months in 1983 in order to resurface runway 03-21. Air Canada and Eastern Provincial Airlines operated out of CFB Summerside during this period, and passengers were bused to and from Summerside for each flight.

A new control tower and operations building, and a 1,524 metre crosswind runway were completed in 1984. The construction of the runway, designated 10-20, necessitated the acquisition and appropriation of land and the re-routing of the Union Road.

In March 1986, the new airport terminal building and complex became operational, marking the completion after nearly ten years of the $30 million project. The new complex consists of the expanded air terminal building, the new control tower (officially called the Air Navigation Services Operations Building), a combined services building, runway 03-21 (2,134 metres), runway 10-28 (1,524 metres), a ramp, a parking lot, an access road, fencing, and landscaping. The air terminal building which cost $5.8 million accommodates Air Canada and its partner, Air Nova, and Canadian Airlines International, with its partners, Air Atlantic and Inter-Canadian. It features extensive seating areas, modern baggage handling equipment, a restaurant, lounge and gift shop, a lobster outlet, and the airport administration offices. The control tower is a seven floor structure, housing air traffic control, a flight service station, and the technical services branch.

A recent addition in the air terminal building consists of a permanent exhibit of artifacts, documents, and photographs depicting the history of the airport and local aviation from the date of the first recorded flight at the Charlottetown Exhibition Grounds on September 24, 1912.

In 1988, 205,700 passengers passed through Charlottetown Airport, and 28,398 aircraft movements were handled.

Sources:

1. Bob Romkey, Transport Canada, Atlantic Region.
2. Clarke, R.L. *Airport Notes*. (Ottawa: Transport Canada, undated) [unpublished collection].
3. L.L. Campbell, former airport manager, Charlottetown Airport.
4. M.E. FitzGerald, Transport Canada, Atlantic Region.

Footnote to Charlottetwon Airport

[1] Department of National Defence, Civil Aviation Branch, 1931.

Chesterfield Inlet Airstrip
(Northwest Territories)

Chesterfield Inlet is located 483 kilometres northeast of Churchill on the western shore of Hudson Bay, 63°20'N and 90°42'W. It was established as a marine-radio station in 1931, became a marine-aeradio facility in 1962, and changed again, on March 1, 1968, to an aeradio facility. Among the first to make aviation history in this area was "Punch" Dickens. In August 1928, he made his aerial survey of the Northwest Territories by flying about 4,000 miles [6,437 kilometres] in forty hours, over a period of twelve days. His route took him from Winnipeg over Chesterfield Inlet on a great loop through the Territories and back to Winnipeg. Chesterfield Inlet was also used as an air support base in 1928 by Northern Arctic Mineral Explorations, Dominion Explorations, and the MacAlpine Exploration party.

In 1969, the Department of Indian and Northern Affairs constructed a landing strip of 600 by 75 feet [488 by 23 metres]. The first aircraft to use the strip was Lambair's Islander CF-XYK, which landed there on October 2, 1969. During the summer, the aeradio station was modernized.

The airstrip, now 914 by 30 metres, is operated by the settlement of Chesterfield Inlet, and the community is served by Calm Air and Nunasi Northland scheduled services.

In 1988, there were 571 aircraft movements and 2,600 passengers.

Source:

Transport Canada, Central Region.

Chevery Airport
Formerly Harrington Harbour
(Quebec)

The initial decision to construct a runway at

Harrington Harbour was made in 1956, but the actual winter runway, 2,500 feet [762 metres] long, was not opened until 1963.

Two years later, Harrington Harbour municpality established a new airport site, thirteen kilometres from town, with a runway of 6,000 feet [1,829 metres]. This sole runway was paved in 1969.

In December 1970, the Department of Transport assumed responsibility for the Harrington Harbour Airport from the Quebec government. During the early years of the decade, the municipality built an air terminal building with the aid of grants provided by the federal government. The site became known as the Chevery Airport in October 1973 in order to more accurately represent the geographical location of the facility, which is now positioned on the mainland closer to Chevery than to the island of Harrington Harbour.

Many further improvements were made during the early seventies: a new gravel runway, 08-26, 5,000 feet [1,524 metres] was built in 1973; a radio beacon was installed in 1974; and the weather station was transferred from Harrington Harbour island in 1976.

During the following decade, a maintenance garage was built in 1981, and runway 08-26 was paved in 1984.

The airport is operated currently by the municipalité de la Basse Côté-Nord-du-St. Laurent and receives an operating subsidy from Transport Canada. Airline service is provided by Intair and Transcote, and the only operator based at the site is Helilittorel. The airport reported 2,917 aircraft movements for 1988.

Source:
1. Transport Canada, Quebec Region.
2. Harris Robbit, Airport Manager, Chevery Airport.

Churchill Airport
(Manitoba)

The community of Churchill is located at the estuary of the Churchill River, 965 kilometres northeast of Winnipeg on the southwestern shore of Hudson Bay. Its history goes back to 1619, when a Danish navigator, Jans Munck, discovered the mouth of the Churchill River. In 1717, the Hudson's Bay Company established a trading post there. The Hudson Bay Railway terminated in Churchill in 1929 and established the seaport for grain shipments to Europe.

Churchill's aviation history began when the first aircraft arrived from Winnipeg in 1927. By 1928, it was a regular port of call for many pioneer airmen such as "Punch" Dickins, Pat Reid, Duke Schiller, Leigh Britnell. Dominion Explorations, Northern Aerial Mineral Explorations and Western Canada Airways (later amalgamated with Canadian Airways, which became Canadian Pacific Airlines) all operated in Churchill and beyond. Arctic Wings was another well-known area operation that merged with Central Northern Airways of Winnipeg in 1955 and eventually formed TransAir.

Churchill Airport was constructed in 1942 by the United States Air Force, which chose the site because of its strategic position on their intercontinental air routes. The route, sometimes known as the Crimson Route,[1] ran from the rich industrial areas of northern California across Hudson's Bay, southern Baffin Island, Greenland, and Iceland to the United Kingdom. Even the longest flight leg would be relatively short using the great circle route. Canada displayed little enthusiasm for the project because of doubts that the route would ever be used as proposed; however, it was built nevertheless with some Canadian aid. While Canada constructed the airport at The Pas, the Americans (with Canadian approval) built the airports at Churchill, Coral Harbour, Fort Chimo, and Frobisher.

Nothing came of this venture from a purely military point of view, but the airports built in Canada played an important part during the construction of the DEW Line in 1955 and in the subsequent development of the Arctic. Despite its lack of enthusiasm for the route, Canada did not want to leave any loopholes for the American legislators to claim property or any other special rights in Canada after the war, and therefore decided at an early date to pay the U.S. for its Canadian installations. It cost over $27 million to buy the Crimson Route facilities, but this was a comparatively small price paid to ensure Canadian sovereignty and avoid any future misunderstanding.

The U.S. Air Force operated and maintained the airport until the end of the war. At that time, the Americans turned the base over to the Department of National Defence, which operated it until April 1, 1964 when it was taken over by the Department of Transport. After that, the airport was used for some time by the USAF Strategic Air Command. It is an excellent all-weather airport, capable of handling the largest aircraft, with good refuelling and communication facilities. The airport handled its heaviest traffic during the construction of the DEW Line, 1955-58.

A rocket range, known as the Churchill Research Range, was constructed 16 kilometres south of Churchill Airport in 1957, and is operated under a joint Canada-United States intergovernmental agreement. Until October 1978, the range was operated by Pan American World Airways under a lease with the two countries with each sharing responsibilities and command duties. Many Canadian and international scientific organizations, such as the National Research Council (NRC), the National Aeronautics and Space Administration (NASA) and several universities have conducted experimental lauches from the site.

On August 4, 1958, the airport had an unusual visitor: the U.S. Navy Airship ZPG-2, which arrived from Akron, Ohio. The airship moored at a temporary mast erected for the occasion and was handled by a crew from the U.S. Army Test Centre at Churchill. It was en route from Weymouth, Massachusetts to Ice Island T-3 (79°N 121°W) to visit a group of scientists on an International Geophysical Year project. The airship left for Resolute on August 7 and arrived there twenty-four hours later. It left Resolute on August 9 but was unable to land at T-3, so it returned to Resolute and, on finding it still had thirty-six hours of fuel, continued to Churchill without stopping. It arrived at Churchill on August 10, forty-four hours after the original departure from Resolute, refuelled immediately and departed from Churchill at 22:30 hours on August 10 for South Weymouth, where it arrived August 12, thirty-two hours after departure.

Transportation into Churchill is by rail, sea, and air, but transportation by sea is limited to the ice-free summer months. Tri-weekly air service south to Winnipeg is provided by Canadian Airlines. Calm Air and Nunasi Northland provide scheduled flights to Rankin Inlet, Eskimo Point, Baker Lake, Coral Harbour, Repulse Bay, and Chesterfield Inlet. Charter services are offered by several operators such as Calm Air, Nunasi Northland, and Keewatin. There is a seaplane base located at Farnsworth Lake, (or, as the local inhabitants prefer to call it, Landing Lake), five kilometres south of the Churchill Airport. Besides Nunasi Northland and Calm Air, a number of privately owned aircraft utilise the facility.

In April 1979, the National Research Council, which is currently responsible for the operation of the rocket range, moved its headquarters to Gimli, Manitoba, and a skeleton crew was left in Churchill to oversee the reduced operation.

The role of Transport Canada at Churchill Airport has broadened considerably since the original takeover of the airport facilities from the Department of National Defence in 1964. Churchill Airport is the centre of a complex consisting of airports at Baker Lake, Chesterfield Inlet, Coral Harbour, Eskimo Point, Rankin Inlet, Hall Beach, and Whale Cove. Tradesmen are dispatched to these sites to make the necessary repairs to the facilities as required.

The original radio range and communications equipment was installed in 1942 by the USAF and operated by Canadian radio operators employed by the Department of Transport. When the United States withdrew their personnel, the Department took over the complete operation of the station and all its facilities. In February 1949, the telecommunications operations building was completely destroyed by fire, making it necessary to move to the radio range site until new facilities could be provided.

The present telecommunications establishment is a combined flight service station and Coast Guard radio station, which includes three operating positions for domestic aviation, international aviation, and marine operations facilities. The low-frequency range was converted to a non-directional beacon in 1966. At the present time, Churchill is well served by various navigational and approach aids: an Instrument Landing System (ILS), for runway 33, commisioned in 1968; VHF omni-directional Range (VOR); Distance Measuring Equipment (D.M.E.); Visual Approach Slope Indicator System (VASIS); Runway Visual Range (RVR), the Yankees' Beacon ("Y") and the Quebec Beacon ("Q"), which also serve as marine navigation beacons.

The U.S. Air Force established the first aviation weather office at Churchill in 1942, which was turned over to the RCAF at the end of the war. The RCAF operated it with Department of Transport forecasters supplemented by air force personnel. When the department took over the operation in 1964, the Meteorological Branch assumed all the weather office duties providing services which included hourly, special and synoptic surface weather reports and upper air observations and forecasts. In 1970, the forecasters left Churchill and were replaced by weather briefers.

The aircraft manoeuvring surfaces of Churchill Airport consist of runways 15-33 and 07-25, taxiways A, B and F, which are presently in use, and aprons one and four. Runway 15-33 has an asphalt surface and is 2,804 by 49 metres with a 305 metre overshoot at the southeast end. This runway is lighted by high-intensity runway, threshold and approach lights, as well as VASIS and strobe lights. Runway 07-25 is 1,524 by 61 metres. Runway and threshold lighting is medium-intensity with two bar VASIS on both ends, and strobe lighting. The taxiway is lit with blue marker lights with side lights on apron 4.

A combined terminal-hangar building is the main airport facility. A large hangar area provides storage and aircraft maintenance space. Two-storey lean-tos run the full length of the building on both the north and south sides. The upper level on the north side houses the telecommunication offices, while the lower level includes the mechanical room, store-rooms, Shell Oil dispatch and general offices and Calm Air mechanical room. On the south side, the upper level houses the atmospheric environment offices, Calm Air offices, flights services station, and the airport management offices. On the lower level are the cafeteria, public waiting room, Canadian Airlines and Calm Air ticket offices and baggage room.

Since the Department of Transport took over the airport in 1964, traffic has grown from 3,682 movements to 9,357 in 1988. In 1988, the airport had 34,100 passengers.

The present airport manager is Tony Van Eindhoven. Doug Walsh, Ron Nair, and Phil Nicholas were previous managers.

Sources:
1. Transport Canada, Central Region.
2 Greenway, K.R., W/C, RCAF, senior navigator. "To the Top of the World by Airship", *CAHS Journal*, 18 (Fall 1980), No. 3.

Footnotes—Churchill Airport

[1]See also Chapter 10 for information about the Crimson Route.

Churchill Falls Airport
(Labrador)

The original airport was located at Twin Falls, forty kilometres from the present Churchill Falls site. The airstrip was built in 1960 to support the construction of the Twin Falls power project, which was to supply electrical energy to the Labrador City and Wabush mining operations. The airstrip was used during initial construction at Churchill Falls, but it was abandoned in 1969.

As construction at Churchill advanced, it became evident that an airport was required in the immediate vicinity; and the present airport was built seven kilometres from the town, serving a population of 1,300. The airport is owned and operated by Churchill Falls

79. Churchill Falls Airport Terminal, Labrador, 1978.

(Labrador) Corporation Ltd. with a subsidy from Transport Canada.

The runway is 1,524 metres long and cost approximately $1.5 million to construct. Transport gave a grant for the runway, and later contributed $100,000 towards the construction of an air terminal building.

The first aircraft landed on the gravel strip on October 31, 1968, and one year later, the first commercial jet flight landed on the paved runway.

Aviation activities at the airport were largely related to the hydro-electric plant. Eastern Provincial Airways was the main commercial carrier to operate into Churchill Falls. During the 1970s and early 1980s, it operated six flights a week into the airport. This frequency was reduced to two flights a week after the construction period was over. The airport serves the needs of the local population, the hydro company, government, tourism, and development agencies. It is the only means of travel for eight months of the year.

The following served as airport managers:

H. Swiggum	1968 to 1974
R. Rouleau	1974 to 1981
J. Murphy	1981

In 1988, the airport handled 5,600 passengers and 3,383 aircraft movements.

Source:
Transport Canada, Atlantic Region.

Comox Airport
(British Columbia)

Comox Airport opened in 1942 and was operated by the Royal Canadian Air Force. During the war, No. 6 and No. 32 Operational Training Units were based at the site. The Royal Air Force staffed the latter unit.

In 1947, the airport was handed over to the Department of Transport for operation, but in 1951, it was returned to the RCAF and rehabilitation started. It is still operated by the Department of National Defence.

In 1957, a new air terminal was built for civil operation, and in 1988 48,000 passengers were recorded.

The airport has two paved runways, 11-29, 3,048 metres, and 18-36, 1,524 metres long, and it is served by Air BC and Time Air.

Source:
Transport Canada, Pacific Region.

Coral Harbour Airport
(Northwest Territories)

In 1942-43, Coral Harbour on Southampton Island consisted of two main settlements, one at Southampton Settlement and the other at the Coral Harbour Airport (north camp). In addition, there is a small Inuit settlement located at Snafu Beach, an area named by American army personnel during the construction of the airport. The beach is used for unloading supplies and materials from ships during the resupply season in August and September.

The airport is fifteen kilometres northwest of the main settlement and 804 kilometres northeast of Churchill.

Coral Harbour Airport was constructed by the United States in 1942-43 as part of the Crimson Route from the U.S. to Europe by way of Canada, Greenland, and Iceland. The route included The Pas (built by Canada), Churchill, Coral Harbour, Fort Chimo, and Frobisher, the latter four airports being provided by the U.S. with Canada's permission. The airports never did

79

play their intended military role, but they had an important part in the subsequent development of the Arctic. At the end of the war, Canada bought the American-built airports from the U.S. in order to avoid any future problems over sovereignty.

From five hundred to one thousand men were employed to construct the runways, build a hospital, communications and operational buildings, and living quarters.

Coral Harbour was also a staging point during the DEW Line construction from 1955 to 1958 and saw considerable activity for a brief period.

The airport has two widely separated gravel runways: 15-33 is 1,524 by 30 metres, and 06-24 is 1,584 by 43 metres. The latter, located approximately five kilometres south of runway 15-33, is considered to be an emergency strip and is not maintained in winter.

In spring 1989, Coral Harbour Airport was transferred from Transport Canada to the government of the Northwest Territories, which manages the site in conjunction with the local community.

In 1962, there were only 262 aircraft movements but by 1988, there were 1,086. There is no hangar at the airport.

The airport is served by First Air, Calm Air, and Nunasi Northland using Beach Kingair HS-0748, Twin Otter, and C-130 aircraft. All airport operational services are located on property (North Camp) 14 kilometres from the settlement of Coral Harbour.

Robert D. Harron has been the airport manager since October 18, 1982. Former airport managers were Berry Smith, Tony Van Eindhoven, George Elliott and Ted Kess.

Source:
Transport Canada, Central Region.

Cranbrook Airport
(British Columbia)

Cranbrook Airport opened in its present location in 1968 and was constructed to serve Cranbrook, Kimberly, and the East Kootenay area.

Prior to 1968, the city was served by another airport, located in downtown Cranbrook, which had a scheduled service offered by Canadian Pacific Airlines. There was also an emergency field at Kimberly associated with the low frequency range system, established for the commencement of the trans-Canada airway.

Transport Canada owns the airport, and the city of Cranbrook operates the facility on a subsidized basis. A terminal building was built in 1974. The site has one paved runway, 16-34, which is 1,829 metres long. Cranbrook airport is an official Customs port of entry.

The airport is served by Air BC and Time Air. Adastra Aviation Ltd. (a medivac unit), Star Aviation (a maintenance outfit), Horizon Air 1986 Ltd. (a charter and flight training business), and the B.C. Forestry Service are operators based at the Cranbrook Airport.

The airport had 90,400 passengers and 21,193 aircraft movements in 1988.

The following have served as airport managers at the Cranbrook Airport:

D. Dakin	1968 to 1971
C.W. Purdy	1971 to 1985
C. Kaldestad	1985

Source:
Transport Canada, Public Affairs, Pacific Region.

Dauphin Airport
(Manitoba)

The Dauphin Municipal Airport is owned by Transport Canada and operated by the Town of Dauphin. It is located five kilometres south of the community, which is the commercial hub of a large agricultural area bounded on the south and southwest by the Riding Mountains, and on the north and east by Lakes Winnipegosis and Manitoba. The airport serves the parkland region of communities such as Gilbert Plains, Grandview, St. Rose du Lac, McCreary, and Roblin.

Before the war, the only aviation facilities near Dauphin were the local farmers' fields. The Department of National Defence constructed Dauphin Airport in 1940 as an RCAF flying training school under the British Commonwealth Air Training Plan. It became No. 10 Service Flying Training School and was supported by Relief Stations No. 1 at North Junction and No. 2 at Valley River.

In 1947, when Dauphin took over the airport, it had three asphalt runways 2,800 by 100 feet [834 by 30 metres], which formed a triangular configuration. A meteorological building, sewage disposal plant, and several hangars were located on the site.

During the 1950s, further improvements were made: in 1953, medium intensity runway lighting was installed; in 1957, runway 14-32 was extended to 5,000 by 150 feet [1,524 by 46 metres] and a taxiway and approach lights added; a concrete parking area was built.

Four of the original buildings (hangars 2 and 5, the drill hall, and air traffic control building) are still in use.

Transport Canada currently owns all of the maintenance equipment and buildings with the exception of two hangars and the drill hall, which are privately owned. The municipality of Dauphin continues to manage the site with the aid of operating subsidies provided by Transport.

At the present time, the Dauphin Municipal Airport has two active runways, 14-32 and 08-

26—runway 02-20 was removed from service in the early 1980s. A new terminal building and air traffic control centre are planned, though actual construction has not begun. Although only two full-time staff are employed by the town to maintain the airport, between twenty and thirty people at the site work for private companies and government agencies. Military, RCMP, and air ambulance aircraft all land at Dauphin while serving the surrounding communities. In 1962, when the Neepawa Airadio Station closed, staff and equipment moved to Dauphin, and are now located in the Met building with Perimeter Airlines (Inland) Ltd. and Keystone Air Service.

Keystone Air Service provides scheduled service six days a week with as many as four flights per day. Perimeter Airlines operates a scheduled air service for Winnipeg, Dauphin, and Brandon five days a week. Dauphin Air Service offers flying training, crop spraying, and charter services. Freeman's (aircraft maintenance), A.G. Air Services (crop spraying), and Timber-Fab (rafter manufacturers located in the drill hall) are also based at the site. Manitoba Hydro and Manitoba Telephone System rent space at the airport.

In 1988, Dauphin Municipal Airport had 14,950 aircraft movements and 1,100 passengers.

Source:
Transport Canada, Central Region.

Debert Airport
(Nova Scotia)

Debert Aerodrome, built for the RCAF, and completed in April 1941, was used as an Operational Training Unit in the British Commonwealth Air Training Plan by the RCAF and the RAF.

The Department of National Defence (DND) established an army camp adjacent to the aerodrome in 1941 as an overseas staging area for troops, capable of accommodating a division of 20,000 fully equipped recruits.

Until 1954 the aerodrome supported active flying operations as a refuelling, maintenance, and flying training practice centre. The aerodrome was transferred to the Royal Canadian Navy in 1960 and was used as a Flight Carrier Landing Practice Centre until 1969, when the aerodrome was closed.

In 1964, a Regional Emergency Government Headquarters (REGHQ) was established at Debert to house Emergency Government Offices, the Provincial Warning Centre, the alternate HQ for the Atlantic Region Military Command, and 720 Communication Squadron.

In 1971, Camp Debert, consisting of 4,804 acres [1,944 hectares], was declared surplus by the Department of National Defence and purchased from Crown Assets Disposal Corporation by the Province of Nova Scotia in 1972. The airfield was included in the purchase.

The Department of Transport licensed the airport for public use as a Visual Flight Rules (VFR) day operation on June 19, 1973. There were three 5,000 by 150 foot [1,524 by 46 metre] runways.

The province transferred the lands of the Debert Air Industrial Park, including the airport, to Industrial Estates Ltd., a provincial Crown corporation, on March 31, 1978.

Since December 1, 1974, the Truro Flying Club has operated the airport under a management contract.

There are four privately owned hangars at the airport.

The following are based at the airport: Truro Flying Club which offers charter services, recreational flying, and flying training; Webber Aircraft Maintenance Limited which provides aircraft servicing; Arnold Carter which operates a private buy/sell/fix-up operation; the Atlantic Regional Glider Training School, which teaches cadets from the Atlantic provinces the fundamentals of gliding under the direction of DND.

Source:
Nova Scotia Business Corporation, via Airports Authority Group, Atlantic Region.

Deer Lake Airport
(Newfoundland)

Deer Lake Airport was built in an area formerly known as Junction Brook just east of the town of Deer Lake, between the Trans-Canada Highway and the Humber River.

The Department of Transport made a site survey in 1953, and preliminary construction began in 1954 as a joint venture between the town of Deer Lake and the Bowater Organization of Corner Brook and Deer Lake. By the fall of 1955, a gravel strip 4,000 by 200 feet [1,219 by 61 metres] was being used by small aircraft. The airport was operated by the town.

In 1956, Eastern Provincial Airways (EPA) began to serve the airport using Lockheed 10-A aircraft, with flights to Buchans, Frenchman's Cove, and St. John's.

The gravel runway was lengthened to 5,000 feet [1,524 metres] in 1959 and it was used to accommodate the arrival of Queen Elizabeth, on tour of Canada, in an RCAF North Star aircraft.

In 1961, EPA used DC-3 and C-46 aircraft and, later in 1963, Dart Heralds. During the development of Wabush, Labrador City, and Churchill Falls from 1967 to 1969, it used Convairs (converted DC-4s), and in 1969, it began to use Boeing 737 jet aircraft on its service to northern and mainland points.

An air terminal building was constructed in 1963 and enlarged in 1975. The Department of Transport paved the runway in 1963 and extended it to 6,000 feet [1,829 metres] in 1973. Queen Elizabeth revisited Corner Brook via Deer Lake Airport during her 1978 tour of Canada.

The Department of Transport took over the airport in 1961, and EPA managed the site for Transport under a contract arrangement until 1973, when International Telephone and Telegraph Company (IT&T) took over until 1976.

In 1981, an application by EPA, Deer Lake's lone carrier, to move its base to Stephenville, Newfoundland, signalled bad news for the airport's future. The Canadian Transport Commission, now the National Transportation Agency, rejected EPA's application, but the airport's business future was still cast into doubt by a lack of demand for air travel.

In 1985—Freedom to Move year—air traffic amounted to approximately forty flights a week. But in 1985-86, economic regulatory reform of the air industry began, and Deer Lake Airport was rejuvenated. Canadian Airlines International bought EPA in February 1986 and moved into Deer Lake; six months later, Air Nova, a new regional carrier, moved to the site.

Transport Minister John Crosbie announced plans in the fall of 1986 to modernize the airport. A new $6.7 million terminal, adjacent to the existing facility, features space for three airlines, four car-rental outlets, a bar-restaurant, a sixty-seat security area, a carpark for 167 vehicles, as well as metred and employee parking. The administrative and air traffic services offices, previously housed in trailers behind the terminal, will be relocated into the new building. The old terminal building will be demolished, and the land made available for additional parking.

The airport serves about 120,000 people in a catchment area that includes the city of Corner Brook, the nearby town of Pasadena, and communities along the Northern Peninsula and White Bay.

The airport is served by Canadian Airlines, Air Atlantic, Air Nova, and Atlantic Airways to points in Labrador, Newfoundland, Nova Scotia, New Brunswick and Quebec. In addition, the airport is used by a number of smaller operators, such as Labrador Air Transport and several couriers.

Frank Le Drew was airport manager under EPA and IT&T from 1969 until he retired in September 1976, when Transport Canada assumed management.

The following have served as airport managers under Transport:

Paul Muise	1976
Frederick C. Smith	1976 to 1978
Alphonsus Hawco	1978 to 1980
David Bussey	1981 to 1983
Patrick Kenney	1983

The airport handled 158,800 passengers and 20,744 aircraft movements in 1988.

Source:
Transport Canada, Atlantic Region.

Dog Creek Airport
(British Columbia)

The Department of National Defence built an aerodrome at Dog Creek during World War II as a supplementary field on the Vancouver-Prince George-Prince Rupert route. It was transferred to the Department of Transport in July 1946 as an emergency field, and maintained as a supplementary facility on Blue Route 2.

A temporary licence was issued on August 1, 1946. J.E. Eve, a pioneer aviator in British Columbia, was appointed aerodrome maintenance foreman. A permanent licence was issued on July 19, 1947.

In April 1950, the village of Williams Lake, eighty-seven kilometers to the northeast, requested that the staff and equipment of Dog Creek be moved to their municipal airport as Dog Creek was serving only as an emergency landing field. The Department of Transport agreed, but proposed to develop a new airport at Williams Lake since the existing municipal field had limitations. This plan was executed in due course, and staff and facilities were moved from Dog Creek to the new airport at Williams Lake in 1960.

Dog Creek aerodrome was not closed, but was kept in operation on a limited basis. A gravel strip 1,938 metres long is maintained, while two other runways remain closed.

The airport was purchased by Circle "S" Cattle Company on May 16, 1962, and is used by hunters and fishermen.

J.E. Eve (1946) and E. Wilson (1952) have managed the airport for the Department of Transport.

Sources:
1. Transport Canada, Pacific Region.
2. R.L. Clarke, "Airport Notes" (Ottawa: Transport Canada) [unpublished collection].

Dryden Airport
(Ontario)

Dryden Municipal Airport was constructed by the Department of Transport (with some funding by the Ontario government) and opened in July 1969. The land was supplied by the town.

The airport was built in response to a request from Dryden's airport committee, and replaced that owned by the Dryden Flying Club, located three miles [five kilometres] southwest of the town. The latter was subsequently abandoned.

Transport Canada leases the airport to the

town, whose airport commission operates the site with the aid of federal government subsidies.

80. Dryden air terminal, 1972 . Boeing 737.

The airport has two runways: 11-29 is paved, lighted and 1,829 metres in length; 05-23 is 610 metres in length with a sand and grass surface. Float equipped aircraft are accommodated on nearby Lake Wabigoon.

In 1984, a new air terminal building was constructed, replacing the original ATCO trailer units. The new building, providing some 1,100 square metres of space, was a most welcome improvement to travel in the area and indicated that the airport has been successful in serving as a hub for travel to northwest Ontario. Transair started offering passenger service to Dryden in 1969 with a DC-3. The service was later assumed by Nordair, which operates four B737 flights per day.

The airport has served as a regional transportation centre, with B-737 aircraft connecting to Winnipeg in the west and Thunder Bay, Sault Ste. Marie, and Toronto in the east. With the advent of deregulation, the 737s were withdrawn by Canadian Airlines International and replaced by Dash 8 service, offered by Air Ontario, and Jet Stream 31 aircraft, operated by Canadian Partner.

Dryden Airport is home to the Ministry of

Natural Resources Fire Base, a large complex providing fire detection and attack, warehousing, and administration.

A based operator provides fixed wing and helicopter services. Esso refuelling services are available.

In 1988, there were 35,800 passengers and 14,565 aircraft movements.

The first airport manager was Bill Morrison. He resigned in February 1970 and was succeeded by the present manager, Peter Louttit.

Sources:
1. Transport Canada, Central Region.
2. P.A. Louttit, Airport Manager, Dryden Airport.

Earlton Airport
(Ontario)

Earlton Airport is located just outside the village of Earlton in the district of Temiskaming. The land was acquired in 1937, and between 1937 and 1940 it was developed as an emergency field on the Trans-Canada Airway. A temporary airport licence was issued on January 21, 1949. The permanent licence was not issued until 1954.

To meet the requirements of the Department of National Defence, a new runway, 07-25, 6,000

81. Earlton Air Terminal, Ontario built in 1952.

by 150 feet [1,829 by 46 metres], was built in 1952-53 to serve as an emergency fighter strip for Air Defence Command. The airport also has a gravel runway, 16-34, of 920 metres.

In November 1952, Canadian Pacific Airlines began a scheduled service from Montreal to Toronto by way of Val d'Or with a stop at Earlton. The route was later taken over by Trans-Canada Air Lines and operated until December 1973, when the service ended. Since that time, the airport has been served by Norontair with four daily flights, connecting with Air Canada at North Bay and Sudbury. Voyageur Airways provides flights to Toronto, Kirkland Lake, and Rouyn.

The airport has a terminal building, which was erected in 1952. Since 1986, the building has been extensively altered to accommodate passengers with disabilities.

The airport was originally classified as a remote site because there was no accommodation available in the vicinity, and Transport Canada had to provide residences for airport employees. However, Transport no longer maintains a twenty-four-hour presence on the site, and steps were taken in 1986 to sell and remove the residences.

Tenants and concessionaires at the airport include Ontario Northland Transportation, Tilden Rent-A-Car, Earlton Airways Ltd, Imperial Oil Limited, and Ross MacDuff Ltd.

In 1988, Earlton Airport reported 4,500 passengers and 12,513 aircraft movements.

The following have been airport managers:

Cliff Lalond	1938 to 1940
Slim Wilson	1940 to 1941
Mark Cahill	1941 to 1956
Wilfred Martinson	1956 to 1961
Robert Laberge	1961 to 1965
James Albeartie	1965 to 1973
Benoit Dupuis	1973 to 1975
Wilfred Martinson	1975

Sources:
1. Transport Canada, Ontario Region.
2. R.L. Clarke, *Airport Notes* (Ottawa: Transport Canada) [unpublished collection].

Edmonton International Airport
(Alberta)

Edmonton International Airport is twenty-four kilometres south of the city in the Nisku-Leduc area. It began operating on November 15, 1960.

The international airport was constructed by the Department of Transport with the agreement of the city of Edmonton, to alleviate congestion at Edmonton Municipal Airport, which in 1957 had 208,421 aircraft movements. As it was surrounded by residential and industrial areas, there was no inexpensive way the airport could be enlarged to cope with increasing traffic and the larger airline aircraft being introduced. Therefore, it was agreed that the Department of Transport would build a new airport for continued domestic air service and, at a later date, for the introduction of international air services to Edmonton.

The new airport was expected to replace the municipal one, which would be sold for industrial development. As the construction of the new airport progressed, however, the closure of the municipal airport was protested by the aviation industry located there which did not want to move from the municipal centre. The city hired a respected American aviation consultant, Leigh Fisher Ltd., whose recommendation was accepted by the city on November 21, 1960, shortly after the international airport opened. The municipal airport should remain in its present city location, and be developed as an industrial and commercial airport.

In 1967, the Department of Transport again raised the question of closing the municipal airport (then called Edmonton Industrial Airport), because it believed that the city's aviation needs could be better served at the international airport. The matter was still unresolved in 1971, when by agreement between the city and the department, an Edmonton area aviation system master plan was undertaken. In 1973, this study led to an agreement between the two parties, stipulating that: (a) the industrial airport would continue in use as a special purpose airport to serve business and commercially oriented aviation; (b) the Department of Transport would provide a satellite airport to serve recreational and training flying more efficiently and reduce congestion at Edmonton Industrial Airport;[1] (c) specific future traffic assignment be delineated for both airports; (d) commuter scheduled operations (PWA's "Airbus") would remain at the industrial airport. This arrangement remains essentially the same today, but controversy continues to arise occasionally because of suggestions about the municipal airport's position in the Edmonton Airports System. Basically, all international, transborder, and long-haul domestic traffic operate out of the international airport, while the municipal airport handles general aviation traffic, corporate business traffic, and the air bus traffic to and from Calgary and some other provincial destinations.

The site for the new airport was chosen in 1955 and land assembly began: 47.5 quarter sections (7,600 acres, [3,078 hectares]) were purchased for $1,469,657. It was all good farmland, and some of the land not required for runways and other operational purposes continued to be farmed by the original owners under lease arrangements with the Department of Transport.

Construction of the airport began in 1957, and two runways, 11-29 at 10,200 feet [3,109 metres], and 01-19 at 11,000 feet [3,353 metres], were completed by November 1960. The Department of Transport's DC-3, CF-CUE, was the first airplane to use the airport officially when it landed there on November 14. The airport licence was issued in the name of the Department of Transport on the same day. Then Trans-Canada Air Lines, Western, and Northwest Airlines began providing service at the Edmonton International Airport on November 15, having moved operations from Edmonton Municipal Airport. The Honourable Leon Balcer, Minister of Transport, officially opened the airport on December 3, 1960.

When the airport opened, its temporary terminal was located in a new hangar owned by Northwest Industries Ltd, and operated by them under contract with the Department of Transport. The $10 million air terminal building was placed in service on December 3, 1963, and opened by the Honourable J.W. Pickersgill, Minister of Transport, and the Honourable E.C. Manning, Premier of Alberta, on February 15, 1964.

The building, made of steel and glass, provided 370,000 square feet [34,373 square metres] of commercial and administrative space for airlines, the Department of Transport, and the travelling public, including restaurants and shops. It features several works of art, the most noteworthy of which are the large mural dedicated to pioneer aviation in the northland, and the "Gas Beacon." Painted by Jack Shadbolt of Vancouver, the mural dominates the waiting room at the arrivals level. It is a mosaic of the two-dimensional patterns so familiar to those who flew over the northern areas. The artist spent some time flying over the north in the cockpit of the Department of Transport's DC-3 and tried to capture in his painting something of the vastness and loneliness of the land as it might have appeared to the early bush pilots.

The "Gas Beacon," a tribute to the gas and oil resources in Alberta, was created by sculptor Norman Slater of Montreal. It is a stainless steel shaft, eighteen metres high, designed to have an array of gas flames spiralling upward. It stands in front of the land side of the terminal building and can be seen by motorists approaching the airport.

The beacon's appearance and behaviour was altered by changes in the weather—temperature, humidity, and precipitation—and often roared in the wind. Because natural gas that fuelled the beacon cost $35,000 per year, harsh economies soon overtook art appreciation, and, before long, the gas was turned off. For a few years after, it was lighted up at Christmas; but today—although it is still in place—it is no longer lit and it cannot rotate.

Meteorological services and telecommunications moved from the municipal airport to the administrative wing of the terminal in December 1963. Air traffic services moved its area control centre from the municipal airport to the eighth floor on February 4, 1963.

When Edmonton International Airport opened in 1960, Trans-Canada Air Lines became established at the site with Super Constellations, North Stars, and Viscounts—replacing these aircraft with DC-8's and Vanguards during 1961. Canadian Pacific Airlines covered the staging route of Grande Prairie, Fort St. John, and Whitehorse using Convairs, and offered charter services on DC-6s and Super Constellations. Western Airlines also operated DC-6s (until withdrawing from Edmonton in 1961), and Northwest Orient Airlines used DC-7s (until ceasing operations in August 1962). Alaska Airlines was based there until 1962. The latter three American airlines were premature in serving this location, and they failed to establish viable operations at Edmonton until twelve years later.

When operations moved to the new terminal building in December 1963, only two airlines occupied ticket counters: TCA and CP Air. Pacific Western Airlines remained at the municipal airport, as its basic operations involved flights into the Northwest Territories and Airbus service between Edmonton and Calgary. PWA opened its ticket counter in the International terminal on March 1, 1974.

Having been designed to serve a twenty-year period, both the terminal building and the airport were under-utilized during the early years and were the target of much public criticism. From 1962 to 1964, airline traffic at the airport decreased from 394,000 passengers to 300,400, due, in part, to the exodus of the three American airlines and to the decline in economic activity. As this table shows, traffic began to grow at a steady pace after 1964.

	Airline Flights	Total Passengers
1962	10,800	394,000
1964	10,064	300,400
1966	11,526	392,800
1968	14,030	522,100
1970	15,110	585,040
1972	14,670	754,615
1974	26,780	1,190,432
1976	30,877	1,520,040
1978	30,337	1,844,903
1980		2,476,021

By the early 1970s, the terminal building began to show signs of overcrowding in some areas, particularly in 1974, when three American airlines began service to Edmonton. In that year, airport revenues increased by 57 per cent.

Loading bridges were added to the terminal building in 1969, two owned by Air Canada and one by CP Air. Currently, there are eight loading bridges, four of which are owned by Air Canada, two by Canadian Airlines International, and two by Transport Canada. Transport will add an additional bridge to the south end of the terminal building.

As the result of the bilateral air agreement between the United States and Canada, three American air carriers were given traffic rights at Edmonton, and in 1974, the following airlines began service: Hughes Air West (Republic), Northwest Orient, and Western Airlines.

Wardair began charter operations at Edmonton International in May 1962 with DC-6 aircraft, and in May 1966 began using a Boeing 727 and leased space in the terminal building. In 1968, it introduced the Boeing 727, and in 1973, the Boeing 747, while operating from the Northwest Industries hangar. CP Air ground-handled the aircraft. On March 1, 1974, Wardair leased ticket counter space in the terminal building.

Preclearance service for U.S. Customs and Immigration was introduced in 1979, allowing passengers to be 'cleared into the United States' before leaving Canada, thus permitting them to disembark without going through the usual formalities.

The industrial area of the airport has grown significantly since 1960:

1960: the Northwest Industries hangar—the temporary terminal—was left empty with a caretaker in charge for many years after the department moved to the new building. Although some aircraft were stored there from time to time, it found little aviation use until 1970, when it was leased in total until 1976 by Wardair Ltd, and since enjoyed full use.

The first secondary aviation entrepreneur was National Aviation Services Ltd., which supplied aviation support service from a millwright building in February 1961. Although the proprietor, Carl Peterson, was a respected aircraft engineer, there was only limited demand for the service, and the building soon stood empty until 1966, when Peterson sold it to the Avis and Hertz rental companies as a service garage.

At the outset, three fuel companies established tank farms offering tender service to aircraft: Imperial Oil Ltd.; British American Oil Company (now Gulf); and Texaco, operated by Timmins Aviation Ltd. Shell Oil joined these companies a year later. This was at the time the American carriers were leaving, and Shell closed its operation in 1963. The Timmins Aviation agency was the largest operator, and sold out to Atlantic Aviation in January 1967. When Texaco lost its big Air Canada contract, it closed in April 1971. By 1982, there were only Imperial Oil Ltd. and Gulf Oil. The latter was operated by Consolidated Aviation, which took over the agency on January 1, 1979. In 1986, the airlines and Consolidated Aviation joined to form a consortium known as the Edmonton Fuel Facilities Corporation, and, since that time, both of the tank farms that originally belonged to Imperial Oil and Texaco have been shut down and the land returned to agricultural use. A new fuel facility with direct airside access has been built north of the main apron between the terminal building and the firehall. In addition, hydrant refuelling has been installed along the front of the air terminal building to feed all bridge positions, and in 1989, an extension was added to the hydrant refuelling system to accommodate future bridges.

1964: Air Canada constructed the first air cargo building, providing space for its own use and for lease to other carriers.

1970: Camston Ltd. began development of the Cara flight kitchen. Prior to this, Cara had operated its flight kitchen out of the air terminal, but had expanded to the point where it needed its own building.

1971: Imperial Oil Ltd. (now Esso Resources) constructed an air freight and passenger terminal, put into operation early in 1972, and in steady use since that date for resupplying and staffing the company's northern operations. The Esso Resources air freight and passenger terminal is still used by Echo Bay Mines and Wescan as a freight terminal servicing Northwest Territorial Airlines.

1972: On October 15, 1972, construction on the Wescan terminal, designed for passenger and air freight and catering to oil exploration companies in the far north. It was a custom service, leasing to any company requiring that type of accommodation. The principal tenant over the years has been Panarctic Oil Company. The terminal has been a most successful operation and is still in use. In 1988, it was purchased by Echo Bay Mines and is now operated as a part of their complex. Echo Bay Mines later built a hangar, opened in January, 1988, for their aviation operations and for their corporate aviation offices. The company is also leasing the old Imperial Oil air freight terminal.

The Wescan terminal is still used to service flights to and from the north—less than it was, because of the slowdown in oil and gas exploration. Recently, however, Cargolux was granted the right to operate to and from the international airport, and now serves the site once a week with a Boeing 747 pure freighter, operated and handled by Echo Bay/Wescan.

1973: International Aviation Ltd. constructed a 10,000 foot [929 square metres] air freight building for lease to CP Air. It is currently occupied by Canadian Airlines International.

1974: Air Canada constructed an equipment building and moved much of its ground support equipment out of the air terminal.

1976: Wardair Canada (1975) Ltd. built a hangar, occupying a 9 acre (3.6 hectare) site, to accommodate its new Boeing 747. The hangar is currently owned by Northwest Industries.

Pacific Western Airlines constructed a freight building, and a flight kitchen, which is currently leased by Cara Flight Kitchens.

1978: Paul Gervais of A.M.E. Aeroworks Ltd. constructed a hangar for private and executive-jet aircraft. Gervais and Gunther Moellenbeck, the co-owners of AME Aeroworks/Sky Harbor, are located at the Ramp No. 2 facility where they

service both corporate and general aviation requirements, in addition to supplying fuel for these aircraft on behalf of Shell Canada Ltd.

Marathon Air Terminals began work on a major air cargo building, completed in 1979, and designed as a shared facility for all airlines. The requirements had been collated by the Airlines Consultative Committee, which reviewed proposals from various developers and chose Marathon. In those years, air freight movements were rising steeply, and all the space was leased out within a year of the opening. The building is still in operation.

1979: Tilden Rent-A-Car constructed a car service centre, which is still being used by the company.

Air Canada began a new air cargo building, completed in the following year, with aircraft docking facilities.

1980: Budget Rent-A-Car built a car rental service centre next to Tilden. Later that year, Monks Compact Rent-A-Car also established a service garage, bringing the number of car rental garages to five. The Monks Compact Rent-A-Car Service garage has since changed hands and is now operated by Hertz and Avis Rent-A-Car agencies as their airport service centre.

1981: International Aviation added a new building, which is currently occupied by airlines, customs brokers, and Canada Customs.

Transport Canada extended its taxiway to give oil-related industries greater access to airport development land.

The airport manager's office was established in the regional headquarters early in 1960, several months before the airport opened. By October 1960, key personnel were on staff, and the office was moved to the airport to prepare for the opening. Most of the initial staff had transferred from northern airports within the western region.

When the airport opened, the personnel of airfield operations encountered many problems and

82. Edmonton International air terminal, Alberta.

hardships. The equipment and garage building, known as the combined operations building, had not been finished; during the winter of 1960-61, the employees worked out of a farmer's barn—a shell of a building that could not be adequately heated. And it was a bitter winter with heavy snow and long periods of great cold! Mechanics wearing parkas and gloves had to work outside, and heavy equipment engines had to be kept running twenty-four hours a day, or else they could not be started. But the following summer, the new combined operations building was completed, and operations moved inside, anticipating a less rigorous winter!

In 1979, runway 11-29 was overlayed with asphalt to level it, and, in 1982, runway 01-19 was similarly rejuvenated. The taxiways have also been overlayed.

The air terminal building, having served the twenty years for which it was designed, handled 2,476,021 passengers in 1980. A $21 million expansion was completed in 1983-84 resulting in greatly improved Canadian Customs and Immigration areas and United States preclearance facilities. Additional space was created for airline passenger check-in, restaurants, bars, gift shops, and other outlets. Since that time, renovations and modernization have continued, and recently, the departures level retail areas were re-

built. Currently, two escalators and a central core passenger elevator are being installed.

A new firehall was built in 1983, and the space formerly occupied in the combined operations building was turned over to airside maintenance.

Edmonton International Airport is currently served by Air Canada, Canadian Airlines International, Northwest Airlines, Wardair, American Airlines, America West, Northwest Territorial Air, and Air BC. The general aviation operator is Sky Harbour. Other industrial operators are Northwest Industries and Echo Bay Mines.

Of the hangars on the airport, Northwest Industries owns two, and Echo Bay Mines and Skyharbour each own one as well as other buildings.

Over the past five years, Edmonton International stopped using passenger transfer vehicles (PTVs)—which carry passengers between the terminal and remotely parked aircraft. The last of five PTVs was shipped out during the summer of 1989; three to Pearson International in Toronto, and two to Mirabel in Montreal.

In 1988, the airport reecorded 2,072,400 passengers and 84,020 aircraft movements.

During the first twenty-two years of the airport, there have been only three airport managers: Ian S. Macaskill, W.A. (Wilf) Morley, and G.R. (Geoff) Hutchison.

Macaskill, who joined the Department of Transport at Frobisher Bay Airport, was the first manager, from 1960 to 1966. He worked at Ottawa headquarters before coming to the Edmonton International Airport.

Morley operated an aircraft servicing facility as a maintenance engineer before joining the Department of Transport in 1950. He served as airport manager at Swift Current, The Pas, and Whitehorse. Following a period as Regional Superintendent of Airports at Moncton, he was appointed airport manager at the Edmonton International Airport in September 1967, and served until December 1978.

Hutchison took over in January 1979. He joined the Department of Transport in 1960 as a radio operator in Inuvik, N.W.T. and later became an electronics technician before moving to management positions—all in the Western region, except for a one-year posting to Toronto in the early 1970s. He was superintendent of community airports in Edmonton Regional Headquarters.

Sources:

1. J. Harvey Freeman, *Edmonton International Airport - The First Two Decades*, [unpublished historical sketch] Edmonton International Airport.
2. G.R. Hutchison, Airport General Manager, Edmonton International Airport.

Footnotes—Edmonton International Airport

[1]This satellite airport is located at Villeneuve and opened in October 1976.

Edmonton Municipal Airport
Formerly Blatchford Field
(Alberta)

Edmonton was involved with aviation from the beginning of flying in Canada. In 1916, Katherine Stinson, an American flyer, made exhibition

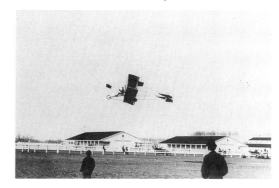

83. Hugh Robinson, Edmonton Exhibition Grounds, April 29, 1911.

84. Curtiss JN-4 Jenny aircraft,
May Airplanes Ltd., 1919.

flights at Edmonton. On a return appearance on July 9, 1918, she carried the first air mail from Calgary to Edmonton[1]—the first mail carried by air in the west and only the second in Canada. The exhibition grounds were used for those early flights.

There was also much early aviation activity based in Edmonton itself. May Airplanes Ltd., one of the first aviation companies in Canada, was incorporated in Edmonton on May 19, 1919. Its pilots were "Wop" May and George Gorman. On January 28, 1920, the Edmonton Airplane Company was established with Jack McNeill as principal owner and Captain Keith Tailyour as pilot. May and Gorman set up operations on a piece of farmland leased from Walter Sprole in 1919 on the old St. Albert Trail near the northwestern limits of Edmonton, and a hangar was built on the field. McNeill and Tailyour also found a location at the northwestern corner of the city and leased a part of the Hagmann farm which adjoined Portage Avenue, a two-mile stretch of concrete highway built in an unsettled part of the city. They, too, built a small hangar. Edmonton now had two aerodromes.

On July 27, 1920, four DH-4B airplanes of the U.S. Army Air Service landed in Edmonton en route from New York to Alaska, and again on October 8 during the return flight, using the May-Gorman aerodrome on the St. Albert Trail.

Imperial Oil Company's two Junkers airplanes were based at the May-Gorman aerodrome in 1921 and were later christened Rene and Vic. Both airplanes became well known throughout the north. In May 1921, Tailyour was killed in a crash at Camp Borden, where he was temporarily acting as a flying instructor for the new Canadian Air Force. In autumn of 1921, when the leases of both fields were coming to an end, Imperial Oil took over the Edmonton Airplane Company's lease of the Hagmann aerodrome. In April 1920, a delegation from the Air Board, the federal authority for aviation, visited the Mayor of Edmonton and requested that the city set aside land for a municipal aerodrome, indicating that 8,000 square yards [6,690 square metres] would be needed. It further stated that, since the new Air Regulations came into force on January 17, 1920, municipal aerodromes would have to be approved and licensed by the Air Board.

The 1922 Report of the Air Board lists 37 airharbours available for use in Canada (twenty three for landplanes and twelve for seaplanes).[2] Among those listed was one at Edmonton, identified as a private-commercial site under 300 yards (275 metres) square. This was Edmonton's first officially recognized airfield, and was located on the St. Albert Trail, northwest of the present airport.

In 1924, Mayor Blatchford became convinced of the need for a city aerodrome and had council agree to reserve the former Hagmann farm (then owned by the city) for this purpose. On October 13, 1924, the city engineer, assisted by "Wop" May, the well-known bush pilot, submitted a plan for the proposed airfield. Council approved it and, on May 10, 1926, authorized expenditures of $400 for preliminary work. Ottawa approved the Hagmann site, and an airharbour licence was issued on June 16, 1926.

The airport, called Blatchford Field, was offi-

85. De Havilland 4-B aircraft, First Alaska Air Expedition, US Army Air Service, Edmonton, AB.

cially opened on January 8, 1927, when Flying Officer C.H. "Punch" Dickins and Flight Lieutenant R. Collins of the RCAF landed their two ski-equipped Siskin airplanes on the snow-covered field, having flown from RCAF Station High River. Each officer was given an engraved silver cigarette box to commemorate the occasion.

The Edmonton and Northern Alberta Aero Club was formed on August 27, 1927, with Jimmy Bell, (who was to become the long-time manager of the Edmonton Municipal Airport), became its vice-president. The club operated from the airport and began flight instruction in June 1928 with May as instructor. In 1930, the club trained more pilots and completed more flying hours than any other in Canada.

In 1929, the city authorized the expenditure of $35,000 on airport improvements, including work on the runways and the construction of hangar no. 1. During the same year, to prepare for the air mail program, the federal government made a grant of $5,000 for airport lighting. Hangars No. 2 and 3 were built by the city in 1938. In April 1939, the federal government gave the city a grant of $69,000 for improvements already completed at the airport.

With the increasing activity at the airport, the city decided that the flying club could no longer be expected to carry the heavy burden of operating the airport for the city. It therefore decided to take over the administration of the airport, and Bell, a well-known supporter of aviation in Edmonton and former wartime pilot, was appointed airport manager in February 1930. He remained in the position until he retired in 1962.

On June 30, 1931, Wiley Post and Harold Gatty landed at Blatchford Field on their around-the-world flight. They were unable to take off from the field because the ground was soft from heavy rain, so Bell had the overhead wires removed from a two-mile stretch of the 100-foot wide paved Portage Avenue adjacent to the airport, so that Post and Gatty could take off from there. Post also used Blatchford Field and Portage Avenue on his solo around-the-world flight in 1933.

In 1938, the Controller of Civil Aviation wrote:

Edmonton has always been regarded as a key point and one of the principal bases of operations in commercial flying. It is the base of supplies for the whole Mackenzie and Peace River areas and an important terminal point on the trans-Canada airway. Air mail services between Winnipeg and Calgary and Edmonton were the first to be inaugurated on the trans-Canada system in 1930, after a period of survey and construc-

86. Hangar, Blatchford Field, Edmonton, 1927.

tion in 1928 and 1929. The Edmonton airport has always been one of the busiest in the country. It is not only an important point on the trans-Canada airway, but the point of departure for the air mail services extending as far as Aklavik, Bear Lake and, later, a base for the important service covering the Peace and Liard Rivers, making connection with the Yukon at Whitehorse. The City of Edmonton was one of the first cities to take an active interest in airport construction, and its airport has proved to be a profitable venture for the City, as it has been self-sustaining from the outset. The Flying Club of Edmonton has been one of the most successful in the country and has trained 171 private pilots and 34 commercial pilots...[3]

At the outbreak of World War II, this airport, like all the large municipal airports, was taken over by the federal government for the duration, under lease, for one dollar a year. The Department of Transport managed and operated any airport having a large amount of civil flying—as there was at Edmonton—and the existing municipal staff were taken over by the department. Edmonton was used for flying training under the British Commonwealth Air Training Plan and, in August 1940, became the base for No. 2 Air Observers School operated by Canadian Airways (Training) Ltd., and in Novemver 1940 for No. 16 Elementary Flying Training School (EFTS), which was run by the Edmonton Flying Training School Ltd., a subsidiary of Edmonton and Northern Alberta Aero Club. For these activities, a number of hangars and other buildings were erected and the airport was expanded and developed. The government also erected an aircraft repair depot on the north side of the airport, which was operated by Aircraft Repair Limited. These buildings were occupied for many years by Northwest Industries Ltd. which subsequently re-

87. Edmonton Airport, Alberta, c. 1938.

moved to Edmonton International Airport; and since then, several manufacturers have occupied the premises.

The City constructed a new $92,834 administration building in 1942, housing a control tower, passenger waiting room, and offices for weather, radio, and general airport staff. The building also accommodated Trans-Canada Air Lines and Canadian Pacific Airlines. In the same year, the Department of Transport increased the airport area from 160 to 750 acres [65 to 304 hectares] and constructed paved runways.

In 1943, the U.S. Air Force, which had extensive operations through Edmonton on the Northwest Staging Route to Alaska and ferried aircraft to Russia, built hangars and other facilities on the east side of the airport.

Traffic increased; and Airport Manager Bell claimed that on one day, September 29, 1943, it handled 860 aircraft. To relieve congestion, some air training was moved to Penhold and Claresholm; and the Americans decided to build a new airport for their operations at Namao, eleven kilometres north of Edmonton. Some sixteen months later, in 1945, their new airport, on a six-kilometre-square site, was completed, with two 7,000 foot [2,134-metre] runways, and the ferry to Russia moved there. At the end of the war, this airport was taken over by the department of

National Defence (RCAF) and in 1954 Blatchford Field's military operations were transferred there.

The city of Edmonton resumed control and operation of the airport in 1945. On November 1, 1946, it began to receive an operating subsidy from the Department of Transport under the new policy which paid five cents per square yard of pavement. Edmonton was the first city to receive an airport operating subsidy, and it continued to do so until 1957, when the airport became completely self-supporting.

During the period—in 1951—the city extended the administration building at a cost of $86,000.

In 1957, the airport made a profit of $61,192 for the city, and between 1958 and 1960 made $444,958 as well as accumulating a plant extension reserve fund. It was truly a self-supporting enterprise, and in this respect it was unique in Canada.

In 1957, the Department of Transport began the construction of a major new airport, whose history is already given above. By that time, the municipal airport was becoming crowded: in 1957, it had 208,421 aircraft movements. Buildings and houses were encroaching on the airport area, and there was no acceptable way of extending the runways to accommodate larger airline aircraft. The Department of Transport and the city therefore agreed that the Department should build a new airport. This would ensure that the city would continue to be served by the major airlines using the new and larger aircraft, and that the international air services could be brought to Edmonton. As construction of the new airport progressed, some controversy developed over the future of the municipal airport. Some people were becoming concerned over the possibility of aircraft crashing in the built-up area. Others, aware of the high property value of the airport site, felt the airport should be closed

and the land used for industrial development. The aviation industry already located at the municipal airport wanted to remain, rather than moving twenty-four kilometres outside Edmonton. So, city council hired a well-known American airport consulting company, Leigh Fisher Ltd., to study the future of the airport. On November 21, 1960, council accepted the Fisher Report and its major recommendation that the municipal airport be retained in its present location and developed as an industrial and commercial airport.

It opened in November 1960, and all major air carriers moved their operations there from the municipal airport. Pacific Western Airlines, then a small regional carrier, remained at Blatchford Field.

88. Edmonton Municipal Airport, terminal building, c.1944.

Jimmy Bell retired as manager of the municipal airport in 1962 and was succeeded by D. Jacox, who resigned in 1964 to join Pacific Western Airlines. Les Marchant succeeded him, and when he retired in 1984, was follwed by the present airport manager, Barry Temple.

Between 1961 and 1963, $625,129 was spent on runway paving and purchase of wartime buildings from the Crown Assets Disposal Corporation. This included hangars No. 2, 3, 6, 9, and 11. These capital projects were financed

from the plant extension reserve fund and debenture borrowing.

City Council changed the name of the airport to Edmonton Industrial Airport on November 13, 1963.

Pacific Western Airlines, now Canadian Airlines, inaugurated its highly successful Edmonton-Calgary airbus service from the industrial airport in 1963 using DC-4 aircraft; this service is still operating from the airport. In 1968, the airline began using Boeing 737 aircraft. On April 7, 1971, PWA carried its one-millionth passenger on this service; 233,000 were carried during the year. Today, Air BC also offers airbus service out of Edmonton.

In 1967, the Department of Transport again raised the question of closing the industrial airport, because it beleived the city's aviation needs could be served better at the international airport. It also argued that airport traffic control and related costs at the industrial airport should be paid by the city if the airport continued to operate.

In the same year the club, now known as the Edmonton Flying Club, leased land from the airport on which it constructed a new facility to replace the one destroyed by fire earlier that year.

New airport policies and changes were introduced in 1968 that eliminated the chronic financial losses suffered during the years 1961 to 1967 and put the airport operation in the black once more.[4]

The terminal building was renovated again in 1969, with additional public areas provided, including an airbus departure lounge. In the same year, the provincial government agreed to cooperate with the Cooking Lake seaplane base, thus freeing the industrial airport of the responsibility.

In June 1971, Transport decided that, with the existing control tower and equipment, it was not possible to operate an adequate level of control over the traffic then using the industrial airport. (There were 175,836 aircraft movements in 1971.) Restrictions, were placed on the airport to reduce the volume and mix of traffic, and a new control tower was built. It opened on May 2, 1972, and traffic restrictions were removed the same day. By 1974, the airport was the fourth busiest in Canada, with 236,778 aircraft movements.

But the future of the industrial airport and the overall air service to Edmonton remained a matter of concern because of the proximity of the two airports. An Edmonton area aviation system master plan study was undertaken in 1971, with results that have been described in the previous chapter, following discussions between the Department of Transport and the city. Department, city and private consultants participated in the study, which was completed in June 1972. By 1973, a formal agreement had been reached between Transport and the city which provided that: (a) the industrial airport would continue in use as a special purpose airport to serve business and commercially oriented aviation; (b) the Department of Transport would provide a satellite airport to serve recreational and flying training more efficiently and reduce congestion at Edmonton Industrial Airport;[5] (c) future traffic

89. Old terminal building, Edmonton Municipal Airport.

would be specifically assigned for both the industrial and international airports; and (d) commuter scheduled operations (PWA's airbus) would remain at the industrial airport.

The City proceeded with major capital improvements now that the future of the industrial airport was settled. A new terminal building was designed to replace the thirty years-old facility, and plans were made for a 100,000-square-foot [9,290 square metre] hangar for long-term lease to PWA. This was occupied in November 1974.

On May 15, 1975, the city changed back the airport's name from Edmonton Industrial to Edmonton Municipal Airport—and this solved two important problems. First, the airport was not a true industrial airport and could not acquire the land necessary to become one; second, there was some confusion between the abbreviations normally used for the industrial (IND) and international (INT) airports.

The new $4 million terminal building was officially opened on November 24, 1975. The old terminal was demolished and the site used for car parking and road access. Hangars no. 12 and 13, built in 1929 and 1938, were demolished in May 1975. The old hangar doors were salvaged and sections used in the tables and decoration of the *Air Harbour* lounge and restaurant in the new terminal and in the coffee shop of the main floor.

The airport celebrated its fiftieth anniversary in 1976. August 22 to 28 was proclaimed Aviation Week in Edmonton. On August 28, 1976, Mayor Cavanagh unveiled a statue of "The Bush Pilot" in the new air terminal building, dedicated to all pioneer bush pilots and to pay tribute to the airport as the cradle of northern aviation and development.[6] The airport was also honoured by Canada's Aviation Hall of Fame on November 19, 1976, by the presentation of the Orders of Icarus and Polaris. On December 31,

1976, the Edmonton Historical Board mounted a plaque on the arrival level of the terminal building designating Edmonton Municipal Airport (Blatchford Field) a historical site.

The city began to make payments to Transport for air traffic control services at the municipal airport from October 15, 1978.

The airport's new car parking structure, which cost $6.3 million, was officially opened on October 10, 1980. It has seven levels and can accommodate 1,046 cars.

The City of Edmonton's land use by-law, passed in July 1980, included legal height zoning protection for the municipal airport and its flight paths, and thus resolved a persistent problem.

In 1986, Hangar 9, a World War II structure, was demolished to make way for a $2 million general aviation terminal, built by Hamilton Aviation Ltd., and officially opened in May 1987.

Also in 1986, the airport installed a comprehensive airport noise monitoring system and introduced stringent rules to help reduce noise from the airport.

A new hangar to the west of the terminal building was completed for Luscar in 1989; another to the south is under construction for Hamilton Aviation. Shell is planning to build a hangar next to the control tower in the near future.

The airport has two runways: 11-29, 1,788 metres long, and 16-34, 1,737 metres long.

It is served by the following scheduled airlines: Canadian Airlines, Time Air, Wapiti, Air BC, and Northwest Territorial Air.

In addition, the following non-scheduled operators are based there: Aero Aviation Centre Ltd., Airspray Ltd., Angus Aviation Ltd., Brooker Wheaton Aviation Ltd., Centennial Flying Service Ltd., Edmonton Flying Club, Interprovincial Pipelines, Alberta Government Services, Faith Aviation, General Systems Ltd, Esso, PetroCanada, Shell, the RCMP and Transport

Canada (the hangar is owned by Transport, the land leased from the city).

In 1988, Edmonton Municipal Airport reported 848,900 passengers with 117,718 aircraft movements, and was the tenth-busiest airport in Canada, averaging 317 arrivals and departures per day.

Sources:

1. Marchant, L.W., former Airport Manager, Edmonton Municipal Airport.
2. Main, J.R.K., *Voyageurs of the Air* (Ottawa: Queen's Printer, 1967).
3. Myles, Eugenie Louise, *Airborne from Edmonton* (Toronto: The Ryerson Press, 1959).
4. Milberry, Larry. *Aviation in Canada* (Toronto: McGraw Hill Ryerson Ltd., 1979) [by permission of McGraw--Hill Ryerson Ltd.].
5. Harry Matties, Duty Manager, Edmonton Municipal Airport.

Footnotes to Edmonton Municipal Airport

[1] J.K.R. Main, *Voyageurs of the Air* (Ottawa: Queen's Printer, 1967), p. 18.

[2] This table is shown in Chapter 7.

[3] Extract from Public Archives Canada, MG 30 E243, vol. 9, J.A. Wilson. "Civil Aviation in Alberta," 6 October 1938.

[4] Included was a user fee levied on each disembarking or embarking passenger. In 1968, the fee amounted to $298,639: today, this continues to be the largest airp'ort revenue item—in 1988 it represented 44 per cent of the airport`s revenue.

[5] Villeneuve Airport was opened in October 1976

[6] Edmonton has a proud record of bush pilot achievement. Many Edmonton-based pilots won the McKee Trophy in its early days, including "Punch" Dickins, "Wop" May, Moss Burbidge, Elmer Fullerton, Walter Gilbert, Matt Berry, and Grant McConachie.

Eskimo Point
(Northwest Territories)

Although Eskimo Point has appeared on maps of Hudson Bay for centuries, it remained a summer camp for the inland Pallirmuit Inuit of south Keewatin until comparatively recently. Eskimo Point began to acquire the status of a permanent settlement when the Hudson's Bay Company post was established in 1921. In 1924, the Roman Catholic Mission was built, followed by an Anglican Mission in 1926. The RCMP established a post at Eskimo Point in 1937, providing further stability. But it is only since the establishment of a school in 1959 that many of the people have lived in the community year-round.

Eskimo Point developed hamlet status on December 1, 1977, and is known for its Inuit Cultural Institute, which was established to encourage and preserve the Inuit culture.

In the late 1960s and early 1970s, two airstrips were constructed as a result of local initiative. The first was approximately one and a half kilometres south of the community, while the second was located immediately to the west. Air carriers flying into the community at the time considered both of them to be hazardous and unsafe: neither had been alligned into the prevailing winds, and each had numerous undulations and cobbled surfaces.

Transport Canada selected a new airport site, approximately one kilometre from the community, in the early 1970s. The runway alignment (15-33) favoured the prevailing winds. (Owing to magnetic variation over the years, the runway is now referred to as 14-32). The Department of National Defence (DND) began the construction of a new airport under the Remote Airports Program and finished the civil works under the Arctic Air Facilities Program. The Eskimo Point gravel-surfaced runway was built to 1,219 metres in order to meet DND's air search and rescue requirements, but the runway could be extended to a length of 1,524 metres.

Construction of civil works and access road commenced in 1974-75, and was completed in 1977-78. A passenger cargo shelter was constructed in 1976-77, and a new passenger shelter is currently being built.

A power line was extended to the airport by the Northern Canada Power Commission and the airfield lighting system, including Visual Approach Slope Indicator System (VASIS), was finished in 1978-79. Meteorological instruments, including alidade, anemometer and ceiling projector, were installed during the same year. The non-directional beacon was replaced with solid state equipment and relocated from within the community to the airport in 1978-79.

The airport was first licensed as a public facility in January 1978 for Day-Visual Flight Rules (VFR) use only, and a year later, after the airfield lights were commissioned, the status of the airport licence was enhanced to Day/Night-VFR. An Automatic Remote Controlled Airfield Lighting System (ARCAL) was installed in 1982/83.

Gravel crushing for re-surfacing the aircraft manoeuvring surfaces and stockpiling (a ten-year supply) for future maintenance purposes was completed in 1982/83.

Airport lands, currently under the administration and control of the Department of Indian Affairs and Northern Development (DIAND) will be transferred to Government of the Northwest Territories (GNWT) in the not-too-distant future.

The airport is operated by the GNWT and served by Calm Air and Nunasi Northland using HS-748, Beech, and King aircraft.

In 1987, there were 1,241 aircraft movements and 5,200 passengers.

As there are no roads, the only forms of transportation to the outside world, other than air, are bombardier to Rankin Inlet and barge from

Churchill, which serve the principal industries of trapping, hunting, fishing, handicrafts, mineral exploration, and tourism.

Source:
Transport Canada, Central Region.

Estevan Airport
(Saskatchewan)

The earliest evidence of flying in Estevan can be found in a Report of the Air Board, which mentions aircraft visiting or flying over this city in 1922. In October 1924, E.A. Alton of Winnipeg attempted a mail flight from Estevan to Winnipeg in a Standard J1 biplane: he had to land near Bienfait because of engine trouble. Then in 1928 "Westy" Westergaard, (an ex-World War I pilot who later became known for his bush flying exploits) flew an airplane at an Estevan fair.

The original Estevan Airport was located eight kilometres south of the city and was six and a half kilometres north of the Canada-U.S. border. It was built by the Department of National Defence in l942 for the British Commonwealth Air Training Plan, and became No. 38 Service Flying Training School (SFTS) under the Royal Air Force.

No. 38 SFTS was originally destined for Swift Current, Saskatchewan, but following strong representations made by Estevan's Mayor Harry Nicholson, the location was changed to Estevan. It opened on April 1, 1942, and it was disbanded February 1, 1944. In June 1942, the school had an aircraft strength of thirty two Anson I's, eighty four Anson II's, and fourteen Menasco Moths.

The city of Estevan took over the airport from the Department of Transport in 1946 and entered into a lease for one dollar per year, covering airport land, two hangars, a control tower, drill hall, fire hall, and motor transport section. The airport had three paved runways: 12-30 at 843 metres long; 06-24 and 18-36 at 792 metres long. Estevan Flying Club was organized then and operated the hangar while carrying on student training until 1959. The city was responsible for all maintenance of the airport.

The South Saskatchewan Regiment Reserve Army and the Air Cadet Squadron occupied and used the drill hall. Officers' quarters, sergeants' quarters, and other buildings were turned into housing, largely for returned veterans and their families. St. Joseph Hospital used the hospital building for convalescing patients when there was an overflow at St Joseph's.

At war's end, approximately 150 Cessna T-50s and AT-17s Ansons and Cornell aircraft were stored at the airport. A weather office was opened on the site and operated by the Department of Transport.

In 1947, the Crown Assets Disposal Corporation started disposing of the stored aircraft, many of which were returned to the United States under a lend-lease agreement. An airport grocery store and school opened, and housing continued; the airport was approved as a Customs port of entry.

During the years 1948 to 1949, staff housing was built for hospital employees, and the airport buildings gradually became occupied by such interest groups as the army, air cadets, flying club, and businesses. Approximately 350 people lived on the airport site at that time.

In 1950, the oil boom hit Estevan. Housing was at a premium, and trailers were hooked up to old sewer and water lines, which remained on the airport after the buildings had been torn down earlier. The airport population rose to six hundred as a result of oil and coal company air-traffic, mainly comprising Cessna 180s and Piper Apaches.

Both local and transient flying activity increased during the fifties, and Customs clearance services were strained by the number of sportsmen (hunters and fishermen) using the facility. In 1955, the flying club installed runway lights.

The Estevan Flying Club ceased operations in early 1960, and its assets were sold, but it was re-organized and reactivated in May 1960. Commercial aviation at the site expanded from a single flying school to include spraying, pipeline and power line patrols, charter aircraft rentals, maintenance, and aircraft sales. Traffic continued to increase. The city purchased the airport land and buildings from the Department of Transport in 1972, when a new runway lighting system was installed, and the weather office was relocated in a new, modernized facility.

At the peak of prosperity, there were approximately forty-five buildings and seven hangars on the airport site. Over the years, two structures burned down; two buildings became schools; another two were redesigned as grocery stores; one hangar was converted into a skating rink; and many other facilities were moved or torn down. In 1989, only one hangar and four buildings remained.

The following aviation enterprises operated at the old airport site:

1946 - 60	Estevan Flying Club
1958 - 72	Nicholson Flying Club Ltd.
1972 - 75	Nicholson Flying Service (1972)
1976 - 80	Norm-Air Service
1981 - 83	Geroux Air Service
1984 - 86	Pari-Air
1985 -	Blue Sky Air

In the 1980s, interest in the airport was kindled by the news that the old airport would be sold to the Saskatchewan Power Corporation for the coal underneath it, and a new airport built north of Estevan. During the winter of 1988-89, the old airport served its last pilot and the new facility was opened on May 27, 1989.[1] After the inauguration of the modern site, the old airport was closed down. The buildings are being demolished and it will be used by the Saskatchewan Power Corporation for coal strip mining when the surface is cleared of debris.

The new Estevan Airport is owned by the city and operated under lease by Blue Sky Air Limited. In addition to Blue Sky Air, the only based operator, the airport serves as a location for the Estevan Flying Club, which reorganized in January 1987 as a lobby group participating in the planning stages of the new airport.

There are two paved runways at this airport: runway 08-26, which is 5,000 by 100 feet, [1,524 by 31 metres] and runway 33-15, at 3,000 by 75 feet [914 by 23 metres]. They are lighted for night flying by an Aircraft Radio Control of Aerodrome Lighting System (ARCAL).

Two hangars are located on the site: the larger one houses a twenty-four-hour weather station, a lounge for the flying club, and a lobby.

Source:
Transport Canada, Central Region.

Footnote to Estevan Airport

[1] *The Estevan Airport: A History to 1988*, (brochure), Estevan: The Flying Club.

Eureka Airstrip
(Northwest Territories)

Eureka, on Ellesmere Island, 621 kilometres northeast of Resolute, became a Joint (Canada-U.S.) Arctic Weather Station in 1947.

On April 7, 1947, the first landing was made on the sea ice of Slidra Fiord. Representatives of Canadian and American weather services made a reconnaissance of the area and a suitable site was selected on the north shore. U.S. Army Air Force crews began moving supplies for the weather station from Thule, Greenland, into the Fiord on April 8—the air distance from Thule is 579 kilometres, and aircraft normally completed two flights per day. The ice in Slidra Fiord (where the airplanes landed during the airlift) was found to be 80 inches [203 centimeters] thick which permitted wheel landing. Approximately 50 per cent of the total tonnage was carried by a C-82.

A permanent station staff of six men unloaded the freight (some 110 tons [111,760 kilograms]) and moved it to the site. The team then erected temporary buildings and commenced their weather observing duties. Five buildings were constructed and the permanent station facilities installed during the period April 15 to June 21 without any curtailment of the regular meteorological program. Jamesway huts, used as temporary shelters throughout the first months, are easy-to-assemble prefabricated units 4.8 by 4.8 metres, and may be increased in length by increments of 2.4 metres. An example of the speed with which the huts are made operational: station personnel had landed at Slidra Fiord at 11 a.m. with one of these buildings on board. By 7 p.m., it was up and heated, radio equipment and facilities for weather observations were in operation, and hot meals were available for personnel.

An ice breaker reached the Eureka weather station on August 9, 1947, bringing permanent buildings, more equipment, a year's supply of consumable stores, and two additional station staff. The permanent buildings were built prior to the dark and cold of winter, and more facilities were added in subsequent years.

Two small tractors were airlifted to the station in May 1947, and the six staff made an airstrip during July, to hedge the possibility that rough ice might form in the fiord. This gravel runway, 11-29, is 1585 by 46 metres.

In 1972, the U.S. withdrew from the arctic weather program, which has since been managed by the Canadian Meteorological Service of Environment Canada, and is known as the High Arctic Weather Station.

There are no hangar or servicing facilities at the airstrip, which is operated and maintained by Transport Canada through contract personnel.

DND and Bradley Air Service both maintain separate summer camps at the airstrip, and the station's proximity to a national park, Axel Heiberg Island, Tanquary Fiord, and Lake Hazen makes it the major jumping-off point for tourists and many scientific expeditions. Eureka is also the most northerly permanent civilian site in Canada, and many assault teams going to the North Pole pass through on their way to Ward Hunt Island.

Annual aircraft movements now average 1,500.

Source:
Transport Canada, Central Region.

Flin Flon Airport
Formerly known as Channing Airport
(Manitoba)

The original Channing Airport, located within the limits of the town of Flin Flon, was constructed in 1948 by Arrow Airways. Canadian Pacific Airlines began to serve the airport in 1949.

In 1950, the Department of Transport paid the town a capital grant to improve the airport, and a further grant was considered in 1956. However, the runway, which was 3,300 feet [2,006 metres] long and constructed of crushed rock, was barely adequate for the DC-3 aircraft which were then operated by TransAir on scheduled service, and the surrounding terrain prevented lengthening the runway or improving the approaches. Therefore, rather than spending more money on Channing, a site for a new airport was sought.

In 1959, 8,400 passengers used the Flin Flon (Channing) Airport. TransAir had 1,120 scheduled operations.

The new location was found at Baker's Narrows on the north arm of the Athapapuskow Lake, almost thirty-one kilometres from Flin Flon. In January 1960, the Department of Transport offered to construct a 5,000 by 150 foot [1,524 by 46 metre] runway, provided the town would acquire the land, transfer the title to the department, construct a terminal, and operate the airport. The town accepted the department's terms, and a contract was awarded for the construction of the airport in the winter of 1960-61.

Flin Flon Airport began operating on May 12, 1962, and the town received an airport operating subsidy from Transport.

Canadian Airlines and Calm Air serve Flin Flon with daily flights to and from Winnipeg.

In 1988, the airport handled 3,838 aircraft movements and 17,400 passengers.

Russ Lawrence (1968 - 1971) and Irwin Drinkwater (1971 -   ) have served as airport managers.

Sources:
1. R.L. Clarke, "Airport Notes" (Ottawa: Transport Canada) [unpublished collection].
2. Transport Canada, Central Region.

Fort Frances Municipal Airport
(Ontario)

In 1958, an airport commission conducted an airport development study in Fort Frances. After many years of research, a site was found and a proposal submitted to the town council.

In 1969 the town purchased from Bordair Limited 247 acres [110 hectares], which included a 40 by 60 foot [12 by 8 metre] hangar and a 2,200 foot [609 metre] grass runway. Additional land was purchased, bringing the total acreage to approximately 600 acres [243 hectares]. A 40 by 60 foot [12 by 8 metre] terminal building was constructed, the grass strip replaced by a 4,000 by 100 foot [1,219 by 30 metre] gravel runway with a treated surface, a taxi-way to a 200 by 100 [61 by 30 metre] apron was built, and fuel facilities of 80 and 100 octane gas were installed.

During 1974, the runway was resurfaced with asphalt. A non-directional beacon (NDB) was installed on the airport and later moved to its present site, about seven kilometres northwest of the field. As a port of entry for Canadian Customs, the airport attracted aircraft of all types.

Jet fuelling facilities were installed in 1975 to accommodate the rapid increase of turbine and jet aircraft traffic, and the apron area was expanded to allow additional and safer manoeuvring area, as well as more aircraft parking capacity.

In 1978, a four bay garage was built to house and service airport equipment.

In 1984-85, the federal government granted Fort Frances $2.2 million to construct a much-needed cross runway 2,600 by 75 feet [742 by 23 metres]; a parallel taxiway, which not only allowed access to the cross runway but also opened up a large area for future development; a 500 foot [152 metre] extension to the main runway, bringing its length to 4,500 feet [1,372 metres]; and drainage ditches along the perimeter of the runways.

In 1987, taxi-way Charlie was constructed by the town to open up an area for hangar lot development and aircraft parking lots. Since its construction, one hangar has been built and two other lots leased for future hangar construction. Five aircraft parking lots have also been leased.

Fort Frances plans to construct another taxiway to access additional hangar lots, extend the main runway to accommodate larger aircraft, expand the apron, and either renovate the existing terminal or build a new facility.

Canadian Voyageur Airlines operated the first scheduled flights using a Cessna 402 and a Beech 18. It supplied a connecting link between North Central Airlines into International Falls, Minnesota, and TransAir at Dryden, Ontario. On Air Limited, out of Thunder Bay, Ontario, took over the scheduled run in 1974 and added a connection to Thunder Bay using Islanders. In 1975, the Ontario government purchased De Havilland Twin Otters in order to supply better air services to northwestern Ontario, and operated them under the name of NorOntair, which made northern connections out of Fort Frances to Dryden, Kenora, and Red Lake, and eastern connection to Atikokan and Thunder Bay as well as further connections with Air Canada and Nordair. On March 5, 1989, NorOntair introduced the Dash 8 on a scheduled run from Thunder Bay to Fort Frances and on to Winnipeg, Manitoba.

The airport is currently serviced by two commercial operators who provide charter and medivac (air ambulance) services. Bordaire Ltd. operates two Piper Navajo aircraft and Fort Frances Air operates a Piper Navajo and a Beach King Air 90. Fort Frances is also a very popular fuel stop for military aircraft travelling to and from training sessions. Aircraft from the United States provide the greatest traffic volume, clearing Canada Customs en route to northern sites to fish and hunt. On average, there are 8,200 aircraft movements and 20,000 people through the airport facilities each year, making the Fort Frances Airport one of the busiest in western Ontario.

The airport staff—airport manager, assistant airport manager, two full-time airport attendants, and two part-time attendants—is responsible for all areas of the operation. They fuel aircraft, take and record weather observations, operate Unicom radio, operate and maintain mobile equipment, and maintain the terminal, maintenance garage, and airside. Personnel are also trained as auxiliary fire fighters for crash, fire, and rescue purposes.

Since the airport is owned by the town, the governing body is the town council. Each year, an airport commission is appointed, which is responsible for managing airport operations. The airport manager is accountable to the commission with regard to expenditures and day-to-day operations. Commission and airport management meet once a month to deal with airport issues.

Don Melville held the position of airport manager from 1971 to December 31, 1988. Bill Caul took over the position as of January 1, 1989.

Source:
Bill Caul, Airport Manager, Fort Frances Municipal Airport.

Fort McMurray Airport
(Alberta)

Fort McMurray was founded as a Hudson's Bay Company trading post in 1870. In 1925, the Alberta and Great Waterways Railroad, (now the Northern Alberta Railways) was built to Waterways, southeast of Fort McMurray. At the time, all freight was transferred from trains to barges at Waterways and from there, by the Athabasca, Slave, and Mackenzie Rivers to the north.

Fort McMurray, now a city, is located at the junction of Athabasca and Clearwater Rivers, some 381 kilometres northeast of Edmonton. The major industry in the area is now the giant tar sands development, which accounts for a population increase from 3,387 in 1967 to 34,949 in 1986.

91. Fort McMurray Airport, Alberta, c 1945.

The site of the present airport was originally a toboggan trail that served local traplines until Lute Vewager cleared trees and other obstacles to provide Fort McMurray's first landing strip in 1936. Vewager lived in Fort McMurray and had a light airplane to make frequent trips to Edmonton, where he owned and operated a gravel crushing plant.

In 1942, the U.S. Corps of Engineers cleared the area further and developed a 5,000 by 300 foot [1,524 by 91 metre] packed gravel runway. This aerodrome supported the Canol project[1] by providing an airlink with the railhead at Waterways. Materials were shipped to Fort McMurray, where they were stored or trans-shipped to Norman Wells or other points along the route.

At the end of the war, Canada bought the aerodrome from the United States along with others constructed by the U.S., and the site was taken over by the Department of Transport, which still operates the airport.

Canadian Pacific Airlines served the airport and, from 1946 to 1958, subsidized a taxi service operated by Roy Hawkins to deliver mail and passengers. In 1948, CPAL provided scheduled service to Edmonton at a return fare of $34 and, between 1948 and 1958, used aircraft such as the Lockheed Lodestar, DC-3, DC-4, and DC-6.

In 1950, Fort McMurray Air Services was es-

tablished, becoming Contact Airways in 1955. In 1954, runway 07-25 was lengthened to 6,000 feet [1,829 metres] and paved. The air terminal building and staff houses were moved from the south to the north side of the airport in 1956.

In 1958 Pacific Western Airways took over from CPAL scheduled service to Edmonton in the south and Fort Chipewyan and Uranium City in the north.

Contact Airways built the first hangar in 1964. The use of a new 4,500 foot [1,372 metre] paved taxiway began in 1980, and a permanent control tower in 1981. In 1985, a new firehall was added. A new air terminal building was opened in January 1986. The old one, built in 1962, is now being used for airport operations. Syncrude has based its operations on this site.

In 1988, there were 92,667 passengers and 41,028 aircraft movements.

The following have served as airport managers:

Sabe Lantinga	1948 to 1949
John Hamilton	1949 to 1951
Arnie Ambly	1951 to 1957
Lloyd Goltz	1957 to 1959
Dave Devlin	1959 to 1961
Andy Fortier	1961 to 1969
Wayne Steel	1970 to 1971
Rene Rizzoli	1971 to 1972
Mike Patterson	1972 to 1973
Gordon Rollins	1973 to 1975
Maurice LeFebvre	1976
Ron Miller	1976 to 1978
Ken Howard	1978 to 1980
Steve Baker	1980 to 1982
Dave Knight	1982 to 1984
Shawn Sutherland	1984 to 1986
Joe Hennessey	1987 to 1989
Dave Rayko	1989

Sources:
1. Transport Canada, Western Region.
2. S.J. Baker, Airport Manager, Fort McMurray Airport.

Footnote—Fort McMurray Airport

[1] The Canol project involved the construction of a pipeline from Norman Wells, N.W.T., to Whitehorse, Yukon, to provide gasoline and oil to American defence forces in Alaska. A number of aerodromes were built in Canada by the U.S. to transport men and materials to the construction sites, particularly during the freeze-up of the waterways. The aerodromes built were Fort McMurray, Embarras, Fort Smith, Fort Resolution, Hay River, Fort Providence, Fort Simpson, Wrigley and Norman Wells.

Fort Nelson Airport
(British Columbia)

In 1935, the Civil Aviation Branch of the Department of National Defence began a survey of an airway between Edmonton and Whitehorse by way of Fort St. John and Watson Lake. One of the aerodrome sites selected was Fort Nelson, and work on the airway began in February 1941. With the entry of the United States into World War II, the airway took on a new importance as a

92. Fort Nelson terminal building, B.C.

staging route from Edmonton to Alaska; and a much larger construction program began in the spring of 1942, to meet U.S. Air Force requirements. In 1943, American contractors assumed responsibility for the completion of the original program, including Fort Nelson Airport: the airfield was constructed from 1940 to 1943. Using local timber the USAF produced some of the lumber used for the buildings in a nearby sawmill. The air base was handed over to the RCAF in 1947, when American improvements and buildings were purchased by Canada (see Chapter 10).

The RCAF station population varied from one to three hundred. The airport was used as a staging and search and rescue base. In 1950, construction began on eighty-five married quarters, which were completed by 1952, by which time the airport was a self-contained community complete with a hospital, school, theatre, clubs, skating rink, gymnasium, fire department, and stores.

The first Department of Transport presence on the site was an aeradio station and weather office, established in the early 1940s. Canadian Pacific Airlines began operations in the area in 1942. The RCAF station officially disbanded on July 1, 1958, and all property, buildings, houses, and inventories were transferred to the Department of Transport on October 16, 1958. Over the next several years, most of the military buildings were sold or demolished. The air traffic control tower and operations building were destroyed by fire in 1960 and replaced with a new terminal operations facility later the same year. In the mid-1960s, runway 03-21 was resurfaced and extended. Sixteen married quarters were sold and moved to the town of Fort Nelson.

The license was issued on September 11, 1958, and today the airport has two runways: 07-25, at 1276 metres, and 03-21 at 1951 metres.

The airport is open on a twelve-hour basis,

with various services being provided either on an active or stand-by basis.

There are currently four atmospheric environment employees providing weather services to public and aviation interests.

Fort Nelson is served by Time Air with F28 jet service. The airport is also a base for two helicopter firms: Canadian and Highland; and for three fixed-wing charter operators: Villers Air Services Ltd., Glen-Air Flying Services Ltd., and Bryant Aviation. In addition, the B.C. Forestry Service operates water bombers from the airport.

In 1988, there were 14,595 passengers and 12,972 aircraft movements.

Since the Department of Transport assumed responsibility for the airport, the following personnel have served as airport managers:

Dave McAree	1958 to 1960
M. Krysowaty	1960 to 1962
Ray L'Heureux	1962 to 1964
George Potter	1964 to 1967
Fred Olynek	1968 to 1977
Joe Hennessey	1977 to 1979
David Knight	1979 to 1982
Dave Rayko	1982 to 1988
David Creighton	1988

Today, the airport has a complement of twenty-five Transport Canada personnel; fourteen are Airports Group employees and eight are flight service station employees. The remaining three are with the technical services branch.

Source:
J. Hennessey, former Airport Manager, Fort Nelson Airport.

Fort Resolution Airport
(Northwest Territories)

September 1935, the Department of the Interior began construction of a winter landing strip at Fort Resolution. $2,000 was allocated for the project, which was to assist transportation into the mining areas. By the summer of 1937, a runway 3,500 by 100 feet [1,067 by 30 metres] had been built, but the airstrip was not satisfactory in the following winter, and most landings were made on the ice in the bay nearby. By the winter of 1938-39, two landing strips of 3,500 and 2,000 feet [1,067 and 609 metres] had been developed, and in the summer of 1939, the width of the strips had been increased to 200 feet [61 metres].

The U.S. Air Force assumed control of the aerodrome and made a number of improvements as part of the Canol project[1] in 1942-43. The USAF withdrew and the Department of Transport took over the site on February 15, 1944, and maintained it using War Appropriation Funds. An airport licence was issued in the name of the Department of Transport on November 1, 1948.

Responsibility for the operation and maintenance of the airport was transferred from the Department of Transport to the Government of the Northwest Territories in the fall of 1979.

During the years 1987 to 1989, major renovations were made: the terminal building was retrofitted with cedar siding and the utilities were updated; the runway, taxiway, and apron were upgraded, the lighting system was replaced, and an access road was reconstructed.

Today, Fort Resolution Airport has a 4,150 by 100 foot [1,372 by 30 metres] gravel runway and a non-directional beacon.

Ptarmigan Airways offers scheduled carrier service and Air Providence offers Class III service.

During 1988, the airport had 1,500 passengers and 840 aircraft movements.

Sources:
1. R.L. Clarke, "Airport Notes" (Ottawa: Transport Canada) [unpublished collection].
2. Transport Canda, Western Region.
3. Marvin Zaozirny, Government of the Northwest Territories.

Footnote—Fort Nelson Airport

1 See Footnote under Fort McMurray

Fort St. John Airport
(British Columbia)

In 1938, the Fort St. John Board of Trade sponsored the construction of an airport and approached the Department of Transport for financial assistance. As there was no municipality, the department asked the province to purchase the site and operate the proposed airport that Transport was prepared to construct. The province, however, refused this offer in July 1939.

The department wanted an airport at Fort St. John as part of the new airway planned between Edmonton and Whitehorse, by way of Fort St. John, Fort Nelson, and Watson Lake. When the province refused to participate, the Department of Transport purchased the site and constructed a landing strip 4,000 feet by 400 feet [1,219 metres by 122 metres] that was completed in the spring of 1940.

When the United States entered World War II, the Edmonton to Whitehorse route took on greater significance and was developed into the Northwest Staging Route to Alaska. A big construction program was undertaken in 1942 to connect the existing airfields with the Alaska Highway (which opened to traffic in 1943) and to provide additional emergency fields and navigation aids between Edmonton and North-

way, Alaska. This involved the American forces in a large building program including the Calgary, Edmonton, Grande Prairie, Fort St. John, Fort Nelson, Watson Lake, and Whitehorse sites, and the construction of five landing strips between Fort St. John and the Alaska boundary. In 1943, American contractors assumed responsibility for the completion of the work at a number of airports, including Fort St. John. The U.S. Air Force constructed a completely new facility at a location east of the community which today remains the Fort St. John Airport. The original airport was closed down in the winter of 1943-44. At the end of the war, Canada bought all the facilities that were constructed by the U.S. (see Chapter 10).

The Department of Transport took over Fort St. John Airport on April 10, 1951. However, civilian staff were brought onto the site as early as October 1950. The permanent airport licence was issued in the name of the Department of Transport on December 8, 1951.

Approximately $1.5 million-worth of wartime runway development and reconditioning was completed in November 1958, and extension of the two runways resulted in their current lengths: 11-29, 6,900 feet [2,103 metres]; 02-20, 6,700 feet [2,042 metres]; and an operational width of 200 feet [61 metres].

Alterations and additions to the air terminal building were completed in January 1960 and, shortly thereafter, approach lighting was installed on both runways. The late 1960s saw the construction of the airport maintenance garage and fire hall, and the commissioning of a Visual Omni Range (VOR).

A new terminal was built in 1971-72, and the old facility was modified as an operations building with space provided for CP Air; this building was torn down in 1981. A new operations building was constructed in 1978 and houses air traffic and flight service operations, electronic maintenance, atmospheric environment, and all administrative activities.

In the period 1986-88, all of the major airport infrastructure systems with the exception of the terminal were replaced or upgraded: a new entrance road and parking facility; water, sewer and storm water systems; expanded air terminal apron; new electrical generation and distribution systems; and the overlay of runway 11-29 and its associated taxiways. The fire hall was expanded and the maintenance garage area was rebuilt. All of these changes represent an estimated total capital investment of $6 million.

Canadian Airlines International and its partner Time Air operate daily B-737 and Fokker F-28 services to Vancouver, Edmonton, Calgary, Fort Nelson, Watson Lake and Whitehorse. Major services are also provided by Air BC to the Vancouver and Edmonton markets.

Although the community is marginally remote, the Fort St. John Airport is an important transfer point for oil-field and construction workers, technical support, service personnel and visiting management. It also serves as a vacation departure point for the residents of northeastern British Columbia.

The economic boom and bust nature of the local oil and gas based economy greatly affects the airport's business: the price hike in the 1970's resulted in increased in aircraft movements from 40,542 in 1976 to 76,473 in 1980. Movements declined to 35,198 by 1985, and in 1988 there were only 23,840. The number of passengers was 155,506 in 1976, 259,700 in 1980, and 160,000 in 1985. By 1988, passenger traffic had risen again to 177,576.

The following have served as airport managers:

H.R. Press	1951 to 1956
E.R. Osborne	1956 to 1965
F.W. McCloud	1965 to 1966
H.E. Crandll	1966 to 1972
J. Richardson	1972 to 1974
G. Hollingsworth	1974 to 1977
F. Olynek	1977 to 1983
T.W. Cook	1983

Sources:
1. Transport Canada, Western Region.
2. R.L. Clarke, "Airport Notes" (Ottawa: Transport Canada) [unpublished collection].

Fort Simpson Airport
(Northwest Territories)

Fort Simpson Airport is located on the west bank of the Liard River, approximately fifteen kilometres above the junction of the Mackenzie River. The village of Fort Simpson, sixteen kilometres from the airport, has a population of 980.

The airfield was constructed in 1942-43 by the U.S. Army as part of the Canol project[1]. At the end of the war, Canada bought the aerodrome, together with others that had been constructed by the U.S. in Canada.

The airport is operated by Transport Canada. It has one runway, 13-31, 6,000 by 150 feet [1,829 by 46 metres], with an asphalt surface, and is lighted. The airport also has a closed runway, 17-35, 5,000 by 150 feet [1,524 by 46 metres]. This runway was once one of the longest in the north before the threshold was displaced to shorten it to its present length.

Northwest Territorial Airways and Simpson Air (1981) Ltd. provide scheduled services to Yellowknife. Depending on the flight, aircraft such as Electra, B-737, DC-3, and Twin Otters are used.

In 1988, the airport had 8,321 passengers and 5,256 aircraft movements. Traffic is expected to increase at Fort Simpson with the development of a pipeline.

The following have served as airport managers:

L.R. Sampert	1963 to 1967
R. Knight	1967
Mark Fairbrother	
W. Goodall	1974
R.L. Bye	1974 to 1977
A.G. McDonald	1977 to 1978
R.L. Bye	1978 to 1986
David Omgoituck	1986
D. Polock	1986
B. Roste	1986

Sources:
1. Transport Canada, Western Region.
2. R.L. Bye, former Airport Manager, Fort Simpson Airport.
3. B. Roste, Airport Manager, Fort Simpson Airport.

Footnote—Fort Simpson Airport

[1] See Footnote under Fort McMurray

Fort Smith Airport
(Northwest Territories)

The discovery of oil at Fort Norman, N.W.T., in early 1921, brought the first aircraft into the Canadian Arctic. On May 29, 1921, Elmer

93. Western Canada Airways plane with airmail, Fort Smith, N.W.T., January 24, 1929.

Fullerton, flying the Imperial Oil Company's Junkers airplane Vic, landed at Fort Smith with three passengers on his way to Fort Norman.[1] In November 1928, "Punch" Dickins, flying a Western Canadian Airways airplane with two passengers, landed at Fort Smith on a flight from Edmonton.

The first airmail service was flown to Fort Smith by "Wop" May during the winter of 1929-30. In January 1930, the Post Office asked the Department of the Interior to build a winter airstrip at Fort Smith. The Department of National Defence provided funds and the airstrip was constructed in October 1930 on property of the Roman Catholic Mission near the old hospital, which is on the south side of the present town of Fort Smith. The strip, however, could not be used regularly because it ran at 90° to the prevailing winds. During the summer, float-equipped planes landed on the nearby Slave River, close to the Rapids of the Drowned, inside the town limits.

During the fall of 1934, the airstrip was improved as an unemployment relief project, and another strip was built at right angles to the first. On November 21, Canadian Airways Ltd. was authorized to use the airfield for winter operations only. Both the winter strip and the seaplane base were used regularly by Canadian Airways

94. First airport at Fort Smith, N.W.T.

(successor to Western Canada Airways) and by McKenzie Air Services.

By the winter of 1938-39, a new airfield had been built by the Department of the Interior on the site of the present airport. It had two strips: one running east-west at 3,600 by 300 feet [1,097 by 91 metres], and one aligned north-south at 3,500 by 200 feet [1,067 by 61 metres] . This airfield was the beginning of the 'new airport,' which is located on the south side of Slave River—its boundary extends to the high-water mark of the river.

In the early part of World War II, Canadian Pacific Air Lines (CPAL), the successor of Canadian Airways Ltd., spent $12,000 on airfield improvements.

In 1942, the airfield was taken over by the U.S. Air Force as part of the Canol Project[2], and was expanded considerably. In 1944, Canada purchased the improvements which were done here and at other airports built by the U.S. during the war.

The Department of Transport took over the airport in October 1944. The first air terminal building, made of logs, was operated by CPAL until 1959 and was located on the south side of the airport across the field from the site of the present terminal. The operations building, constructed in 1957, served as a combined passenger and operations facility.

In 1945, when CPAL asked the Department of Transport to reimburse it for the improvements it had made to the airport, Transport agreed (in September 1948) on condition that Transport hold the license and CPAL pay appropriate landing fees and other airport charges. A permanent airport licence was issued on March 1, 1949.

Fort Smith Airport has two runways: 11-29 is 6,000 by 200 feet [1,829 by 61 metres] and was paved in 1957; runway 02-20, of sand and gravel, is not maintained in the winter. It is 4,275 feet [1,303 metres] long. In 1969, the Department of

95. Terminal building at Fort Smith Airport, c. 1942.

Transport constructed a new air terminal building on the north side of the main apron.

Meanwhile, in 1968, a new licensed seaplane base, complete with docks and other facilities, was built ten kilometres from the airport on the shore of Four Mile Lake, which is on the Alberta side of the N.W.T.-Alberta border.

For many years, Pacific Western Airlines provided scheduled service to Hay River, Yellowknife, Edmonton, and Calgary. This service is now provided by Canadian Airlines International. Northwestern Air Lease Ltd. offers flights to Yellowknife, Fort Simpson (via Hay River), and Fort Chipewan, and also provide charter services and flight training with C401, 402, and smaller aircraft. Loon Air provides charter service with fixed wing aircraft on wheel/floats, and rotary wing service is provided by Canadian Helicopters and Canadian Territorial. The government of the Northwest Territories' Renewable Resources and Parks Canada maintain forest firefighting operations at their base on the airport using DC-6, CL215, and B25 aircraft.

In 1988, the airport reported 19,700 passengers and 9,069 aircraft movements.

The following have served as airport managers:

G. Stephenson   to 1945
M. Milt 1945   to 1946

Bill Walls	1946 to 1951
George Matters	1951 to 1952
Jack Smythe	1952 to 1954
Dave McAree	1955 to 1957
Jim Richardson	1957 to 1959
M Smith	1959 to 1962
Archie Bevington	1962 to 1980
Ron Miller	1980 to 1981
Marty Raito	1981 to 1984
Barry Rosity	1984 to 1986
Ray Bye	1986 to 1989

Sources:

1. Transport Canada, Western Region.
2. M.T. Raito, former Airport Manager, Fort Smith Airport.
3. R.L. Clarke, *Airport Notes* (Ottawa: Transport Canada) [unpublished collection].

Footnotes—Fort Smith Airport

[1] F.H. Ellis, Canada's Flying Heritage (Toronto: University of Toronto Press, 1961), p 207.
[2] See Footnote under Fort McMurray.

Fort Vermillion Airport
(Alberta)

Fort Vermillion Airport, four kilometres northeast of the town, has a public licence and is oper-

96. Fort Vermillion Airport, Alberta, 1956.

ated by the Alberta Transportation Department. It has one paved runway, 07-25, at 914 by 30 metres.

Fort Vermillion Airport was established by Canadian Pacific Air Lines (CPAL) in 1950 and licensed in the company's name for use by DC-3 aircraft. The land was owned by the Synod of the Diocese of Athabasca and leased to CPAL for $200 per year.

CPAL terminated service to Fort Vermillion in 1959, when the airport was taken over by Pacific Western Airlines and licensed by them. They suspended service in 1961 because of the deteriorating condition of the airport, and service to Fort Vermillion was cancelled in 1964.

The site became a public airport in 1968.

Fredericton Airport
(New Brunswick)

The Fredericton Airport was built in 1949 by the Department of Transport on land provided by the city, which for many years had tried without success to establish a municipal airport.

The earliest record of the city's efforts is July 1920, when the Fredericton Board of Trade asked the Air Board (the interim federal government organization responsible for aviation in Canada) for aerodrome specifications. In the 1922 official List of Airharbours Available for Use, Fredericton appears as a public seaplane base over 800 yards [74 metres] square that was licensed for Customs. In October 1929, the city again made inquiries from Ottawa. In 1930 and again in 1932, the District Inspector of Eastern Airways examined a number of possible sites, including Embleton, five kilometres northwest of the city and across the Saint John River. When in 1936 and 1937, the District Inspector, at the city's request, yet again examined sites, the development of one at Nashwacksis was recom-

mended. In December 1939, the mayor suggested that Nashwacksis be made a British Commonwealth Air Training Plan aerodrome; but the high cost of development could be not justified by the Department of National Defence.

In 1941, F. Hardwick obtained a private airport licence for a field at Barker's Point near Fredericton, for day operations of light aircraft. The following year, there was a request for airmail and passenger service to Fredericton using the Barker's Point field, but the site was declared unsuitable. In January 1944, the airport licence was cancelled because the site was not being used as an airfield. The licence was reissued in September of that year.

In the winter of 1945-46, James Sturgeon leased Barker's Point Aerodrome from Hardwick, and the licence was transferred to him on February 26, 1946. In the fall of 1947, Maritime Central Airways began scheduled operations with Lockheed 10 aircraft.

On September 20, 1948, a private airport licence was granted to Currie's Flying Service for an airfield at the Nashwacksis site. Gaetano Digiacinto took over Barker's Point Aerodrome from Sturgeon on April 30, 1949, but his licence for the airfield expired on May 1, 1950, and was not renewed. The field was returned to farmland by December 1951, after Barker's Point had served well as an aerodrome for ten years.

In the meantime, the city was continuing its efforts to develop an airport for the community. It had tried to get mail and passenger service for Barker's Point,[1] and the Mayor again approached Ottawa in May 1943. The District Inspector of Eastern Airways was once more instructed to investigate the possibility of finding a site suitable for a main line airport to serve the capital city of New Brunswick. In August, a preliminary report was made on a site nineteen kilometres from Fredericton, near Rusagonis, but no further action was taken. In March 1945, the

97. New air terminal, Fredericton, constructed 1963, enlarged 1988.

city again asked Ottawa for an airport survey and in May, a possible site was found at Lincoln, just fourteen kilometres from Fredericton. A survey was carried out on the Lincoln and Rusagonis sites to determine which one would be the more acceptable. Cost comparisons and zoning protection favoured the Lincoln site, and on April 25, 1947, twenty-seven years after the city's first inquiry in Ottawa, the Minister of Transport announced that the department would build an airport at the Lincoln site, provided the city of Fredericton acquired the land. The city finally expropriated the property in May 1948, and work began in September 1948.

On November 30, 1949, runway 15-33 was far enough advanced to permit Department of Transport officials to land there. Clearing for the second runway, 09-27, began in January 1950.

In March 1950, the Department of Transport and the city agreed that Transport would construct the airport while the City would erect a terminal and other necessary buildings, and be responsible for the operations and maintenance of the airport. The old operations building at Blissville[2] was cut in sections and moved to Fredericton, and an airport licence was issued to the city on April 11, 1950. Beginning April 1, 1951, the Department of Transport paid the airport an operating subsidy of five cents per square

yard of paved surface (185,320 square yards [154,927 square metres]), which was increased to six and a half cents in 1954.

In 1951, the city of Fredericton began operating Fredericton Airport. Staff at that time consisted of an airport manager, an attendant, and two equipment operators.

During 1950-51, Maritime Central Airways (MCA) offered a passenger service into Fredericton, using a Lockheed 10 that carried approximately ten passengers. Later in 1951, these aircraft were replaced by the Douglas DC-3. Along with this passenger service, MCA operated the Forest Patrol Service (with a DeHavilland Beaver) for the province of New Brunswick.

Department of Transport aeradio facilities were moved from the old Blissville Airport to Fredericton in the spring of 1951 and, until 1956, communications staff also provided weather information for pilots. In 1956, full-time meteorological personnel were moved to Fredericton.

As more people began to travel by air, Trans-Canada Air Lines (TCA) extended its service to Fredericton, and in 1952, provided passenger service by DC-3—which was replaced in 1956 by North Star, Viscount, and Super Constellation aircraft. The Vanguard was introduced in 1961.

As traffic increased, so did the size of the airport. In 1958, runway 15-33 was extended to 6,000 feet [1,829 metres], and high-intensity approach and runway lights were installed.

By this time, the financial burden was becoming too great for the city and, early in 1957, the Department of Transport was asked to take over the operation. On November 7, 1959, after extended negotiations, the city of Fredericton turned over the airport and other city-owned assets, including land, buildings, installations and equipment to the Department for the sum of $118,000.

As Fredericton began to be used more fre-

quently as an alternate airport for TCA and for other aircraft, it became necessary to install an Instrument Landing System (ILS)—commissioned in 1959. In 1961, a second taxiway was built, as well as an extension to the aircraft ramp.

In 1963, a $1 million expansion program provided a new terminal building; maintenance garage and firehall; pump-house; water, sewage and fire hydrant system; extended ramp areas; roads; and a car park.

Air traffic activity in the Maritime provinces has changed considerably over the years. Air Nova and Air Atlantic were formed in July and March 1986, respectively, and their influence became evident in early 1988 when, in a newly deregulated environment, they began operating as feeder airlines for Air Canada and Canadian Airlines.[3] The addition of these two partner airlines created a need for more space at the Fredericton Airport. In 1988-89, in an eighteen-month $3.6 million project, the airport was remodelled and enlarged to accommodate the increasing number of passengers, which had reached 208,000 in 1988.

The renovations included expansions to the north and south ends of the building, creating an additional 1,100 square metres of floor space; a new 330 square metre flight services station and atmospheric environmental services weather office, located at the south end above a new larger baggage area and additional space for administration offices and an electronics workshop.

The ground floor passenger waiting area became more spacious, and larger ticket counters and working areas were provided for Canadian Airlines International. Air Canada offices were relocated, and, its ticket counter became the first in Canada to have wheelchair access. As a result of the relocations, space for regional carriers became available for retail development.

Other additions include larger indoor baggage-handling facilities and a conveyor; a new VIP lounge at the centre of the main floor; separate offices for Customs and Immigration; a full kitchen for the restaurant; a new gift shop and bar; and a larger, more convenient security holdroom.

Fredericton Airport is located thirteen kilometres south of the city of Fredericton on Route 112, the main highway that connects Fredericton with Oromocto (five kilometres from the airport) and Saint John. It is served by two scheduled carriers: Air Canada and Canadian Airlines International (and their partner airlines, Air Nova and Air Atlantic). Locally-based firms in the aviation industry include the Fredericton Flying Club, Norfolk Aerial Spraying Ltd., Trans Maritimes Helicopters Limited, Diamond Aviation, Forest Protection and Woodland. There are almost two hundred government and non-government employees on site.

The airport serves a larger land area than any other in the province: from Edmunston and Grand Falls in the north, to Houlton, Maine, in the west, to St. Andrews and St. George in the south, to Cole's Island, Minto, and Chipman in the east. The population of the region is roughly 180,000.

In 1988, there were 207,600 passengers and 33,482 aircraft movements.

The following is the list of airport managers who have served at Fredericton Airport:

Ron Young	1959 to 1960
(City and Transport)	
J.J. Joe Cole	1960 to 1961
Hiram Noel	1961 to 1966
R.J. (Doc) Aubrey	1968 to 1972
L. Clarke	1973
H. Cochrane	1972 to 1975
P. Kelly	1975
J. Courage	1975 to 1976
P.A. Richard	1976 to 1977
E.C. Blake¨	1977

Sources:
1. R.L. Clarke, "Airport Notes" (Ottawa: Department of Transport) [unpublished collection].

Footnotes to Fredericton Airport

[1] Trans-Canada Air Lines had extended its service to Halifax in 1941.

[2] Blissville was one of the one-hundred-mile aerodromes of the Trans Canada Airway, built in 1939.

[3] Transportation Group, University of New Brunswick, Airport Economic Study.

Gagnon Airport
(Québec)

The Department of Lands and Forests of Quebec transferred the site of the Gagnon Airport to the Quebec Cartier Mining Company in 1960 to be used for a public airport. During the same year, the mining company built the airport at its own expense to link the town of Gagnon with other industrial and urban centres. The company operated the airport from 1960 to 1976.

In 1965 the company asked the Department of Transport to take over the operation of the airport, but was refused. On February 1, 1976 after prolonged negotiation, the company transferred the airport to the town of Gagnon for a nominal sum, and the town thus became eligible for an airport operating subsidy.

A new air terminal was built in 1978.

The airport has since been closed, and the land has reverted to the province.

Source:
Transport Canada, Quebec Region.

Gander International Airport
(Newfoundland)

The history of Gander International Airport opens in 1935 when a party of Newfoundland and British Air Ministry officials tentatively selected the site near Gander Lake at Milepost 213 on the Newfoundland Railway. Construction began in June 1936.

The airport was needed for the north-Atlantic Air service, agreed upon by the governments of the United Kingdom, Canada, Newfoundland, and the Irish Free State in December 1935 (see Chapter 9). At that time, there were no suitable long-range landplanes; survey and experimental flights with flying boats (operated by Imperial Airways and Pan American Airways) were planned for 1936; but by 1937, the British expected to be able to use a specially designed long-range landplane (the DH-91 Albatross). The overall plan for the North-Atlantic service involved (a) an experimental summer flying boat service, (b) an experimental winter landplane service, (c) a regular year-round landplane service, or—if (c) was found to be unfeasible—(d) a regular summer flying boat service.

Accordingly, temporary flying boat bases were established at Foynes (Irish Free State),

98. Newfoundland Airport, Gander railway station and post office, 1937.

Botwood, Shediac, Montreal, and terminals at Southampton and Port Washington. Experimental flights were carried out successfully in 1937. Unfortunately, the Albatross did not meet expectations as a long-range airplane and its development for Atlantic service was discontinued in 1938. Nevertheless, construction at Gander continued and was completed on October 31, 1939.

Gander has had several changes of name. At first, it was known as "the airport at Hattie's Camp, near Gander Lake."[1] No one lived in the area, there were no roads, and the site was covered with forest. When construction began in 1936, the place was officially named Newfoundland Airport. The new railway station also took the appellation "Newfoundland Airport" as a designator of location—so the proper address of the area then became "Newfoundland Airport, Newfoundland Airport, Newfoundland"! This name continued to be used until the early 1940s when, after the arrival of the RCAF, it began to be known as Gander. The Newfoundland government retained the name Newfoundland Airport, but the place name became Gander. During the war, the airport became Gander Airport (through common usage) and so remained until 1961, when it became Gander International Airport. The new town, which was constructed west of the airport in 1952, also took the name Gander.

99. Administration building, and staff house, Newfoundland Airport, December 20, 1937.

100. The first airplane to land at Newfoundland Airport—a Fox Moth VO-ADE.

When it was constructed, Gander was the largest airport site in the world, measuring one mile square. Commenting on the site selection, an Air Ministry official, in his report of August 23, 1935, said:

> The aircraft that may ultimately be used on a regular service have not yet been built and their performance cannot be forecast with accuracy. To allow for future requirements, it seems advisable to select landing and alighting areas of large size and with unobstructed approaches.[2]

Another Air Ministry official, H.A. Lewis Dale, Deputy Director of Works, submitted a report to the governor of Newfoundland dated October 26, 1936, following his visit with aviation officials in Canada and the United States:

> I still found differences of opinion as to airport construction, but these differences when probed were less real than they appeared to be superficially. It often transpired that the climatic factor, or the pattern of a particular aerodrome, largely accounted for an apparent contradiction. It is impossible to lay down dogmatic rules for airport design—each case must undoubtedly be decided individually—but I found sufficient agreement to enable me to lay down, as follows, what I believe to be essential to the Newfoundland projects.

Dimensions of Runways

5. In deciding the dimensions of runways, it is necessary to distinguish between runways across an all-way field and runways which themselves provide the pattern of the safe landing ground as at Hattie's Camp. Where there is an all-way field, hard-surfaced runways 200 feet [61 metres] wide are considered adequate as there is no danger should the aircraft overrun the edges. Where the safe-landing area is confined to a strip system (as at Hattie's Camp), 600 feet [183 metres] is the width required. The minimum suggested was 500 feet [152 metres], but 600 feet was more generally approved). For blind landing, a strip of 1,000 feet [305 metres] minimum was suggested, but discussion elicited further opinions that 1,500 feet [457 metres] should be provided. A width of 1,200 feet [366 metres] as shown on plan No. D2 is recommended, as the consensus of opinion was that it would be adequate, especially as it could be widened later if necessary. The length of runways, as shown on the plan, were considered adequate, but not excessive.[3]

Gander had four paved runways, the largest paved area of any airport in the world, and the equivalent of 110 miles [177 kilometres] of twenty-foot [six-metre] highway. The main 'blind landing' runway was 4,800 by 1,200 feet [1,463 by 366 metres], and the other three were 4,500 by 600 feet [1,372 by 183 metres]. The length and width of the main runway were influenced by the fact that there was no alternate airport in Newfoundland and the Albatross had to be able to land at Gander no matter what the weather. The runway was equipped with sodium vapour lights mounted flush down the centre line and as an aid to blind landing, and was served by the Lorenz blind landing system (made by Telefunken of Germany, sold under licence by Marconi Wireless Telegraph Company of England).

This was the forerunner of the post-war ILS (Instrument Landing System). It had a directional beam along the runway and an outer and inner marker beacon, but no glide path.

The original airport had one hangar (whose single door measured 150 by 30 feet [43 by 9 metres]) and an administration building, which provided office space as well as accommodation for single staff members. There were two remote wireless stations (at separate receiving and transmitting sites) and a diesel-electric plant (the airport's only source of electricity). There were twelve houses for married personnel, a general store, a central heating plant, an aviation fuel storage area, a fire station, and a small railway station. No highway connected with the airport, and the railway was the only link with the outside world.

The Newfoundland Airport Club, founded in 1938 and located in the administration building, was the centre of community life for the thirty-four staff members. It had a bar (the first licensed club bar in Newfoundland), showed movies, and ran dances. Today the club has its own building in the town of Gander.

The airport site was chosen because the location had a reputation for good weather and was one of the few large, flat areas in eastern Newfoundland. It had been recommended by Mr. Powell, who had surveyed and worked on the

101. Newfoundland Airport group by staff-house 1939.

Newfoundland railway, Captain Douglas Fraser, a Newfoundland aviator, A. Vatcher, a surveyor, and I. McClure of the British Air Ministry.

Newfoundland—the owner—undertook to construct and operate the airport, and the United Kingdom agreed to pay five-sixths of the capital cost and one-half of the operating cost of the ground organization, plus the full cost of the radio services. Construction of the airport began in June 1936, with T.A. Hall, formerly of the Newfoundland Department of Public Works, chief engineer, and A. Vatcher resident engineer. It was an enormous task, and progress was slow. In 1938, Newfoundland hired a team of engineers from Canada, led by F.C. Jewett and R.A. Bradley,[4] both of whom had worked on the huge Welland Canal project. From November 30, 1938, the staffs of the Air Ministry Radio, Canadian Meteorological, and Newfoundland Control Service (all three from Botwood flying-boat base) were installed at the airport, but construction was not finished until October 31, 1939.

The powerful radio station at Gander was built for the British air ministry by the Marconi Wireless Telegraph Company of England. The chief engineer, J.N. Johnson—he was known as The Admiral, and served in Newfoundland from 1936 to 1939—had also built the temporary radio station at Botwood. The Botwood staff moved to Gander leaving Botwood to be staffed until 1945, during the flying boat season. The Gander station provided point-to-point communication to Ireland, England, the United States, and Canada (St. Hubert and Shediac), ground-to-air communications, and radio direction finding services.

Squadron Leader H.A.L. Pattison, RAF, was a key official in all of these undertakings.[5] He was an RAF signals officer and came to Newfoundland from London in 1936 to supervise the construction and operation of the Botwood radio station for the British Air Ministry. Later, his responsibilities were extended, making him Air

102. Two tanker aircraft of Flight Refuelling Ltd. before original hanger, Gander, 1939.

Ministry liaison officer to Newfoundland and Canada for the Trans-Atlantic Air Service. When the airport was completed in November 1938, he became aerodrome control officer (an English title, equivalent to airport manager in Canada). He also acted as aviation advisor to the Newfoundland government.

On January 11, 1938, the first airplane landed at Gander. It was the Fox Moth VO-ADE, operated by Imperial Airways for the Newfoundland Government, equipped with skis and flown by Captain Douglas Fraser (a Newfoundlander) with Engineer George Lace.

The first airplane to land at Gander from outside Newfoundland was the Monocoupe 90A, registration SE-AGM, which arrived on May 15, 1939, from Bangor, Maine, flown by Charles

103. Black Watch Regiment under canvas, Gander, Nfld., 1940.

Backman, who was delivering it to its owner in Sweden. He took off the next day but failed to arrive and was presumed lost at sea.

On May 19 and 21, 1939, two Handley-Page Harrow airplanes, G-AFRH and G-AFRG, arrived at Gander from Montreal by way of Halifax. These were two-engined bombers converted to aerial tankers and operated by Flight Refuelling Ltd. of England (owned by Sir Alan Cobham). They were stationed at Gander to refuel Imperial Airways flying boats Cabot and Caribou in flight after take-off from Botwood for Foynes. In-flight refuelling was carried out until the end of the 1939 flying boat season and the company's contract terminated on May 31, 1940, because it was decided not to use in-flight refuelling for the 1940 season and thereafter. During their spell in Gander, the Harrows were used to calibrate direction-finding equipment and to test the Lorenz blind landing installation.

During the winter of 1939 they were used in runway snow compaction tests. (Although a strong, smooth surface could be produced, it collapsed at the beginning of the thaw). The aircraft were donated to the RCAF and flown from Newfoundland to Canada in the fall of 1940.

When the development of the Albatross as a transoceanic aircraft was cancelled by Britain in 1938, there was no longer any early prospect of a transatlantic landplane service through Gander. Hence, there appeared to be no immediate use for the airport when it was finished in late 1939. The radio, meteorological, and control staffs at Gander continued to look after the flying boat service, which operated each summer through Botwood until the end of 1945; during the winter, high frequency (H.F.) direction finding (D.F.) service assisted aircraft flying the U.S.-Azores-U.K. route. Heavy wireless traffic (mainly weather information) continued, as did transatlantic weather forecasting. Upper-air observation flights for weather readings at various altitudes were transferred from Botwood (and Norris

104. Nfld. Airport, Gander—Captains & crews, Lockheed Hudson Bombers, en route to England, Nov. 10, 1940. Standing, L. to R. W.B. Lyons, D.L. Gentry, R. Adams, C.M. Tripp, W.C. Rodgers, J.A. Webber, J.D. McIntyre, S.T.B. Cripps, N.G. Mullett, A.M. Loughridge, A. Andrew, N.E. Smith, G.R. Hutchinson, J.W. Gray, D.C.T. Bennett. Kneeling, L. to R. D.B. Jarvis, H.G. Meyers, J.E. Giles, E.F. Clausewitz, K.Garden, W.T. Mellor

Arm) to Gander and continued during 1939 until June 1940. Imperial Airways pilots D.C. Fraser, C.S. Kent and D.B. McGregor flew in a Fairchild 71-C and a Fox Moth owned by the Newfoundland Government. The highest flight was one of 17,000 feet [5180 metres]. The meteorological staff plotted and analyzed flight data.

In the summer of 1940, Gander was designated as the main staging post for the delivery of bombers to Britain. The Atlantic Ferry service, then Canadian Pacific Air Service, set up in October 1940, under Captain "Taffy" Powell, formerly of Imperial Airways. Gander personnel, after three years of experience with flying boat service, provided the support organization and expertise, and carried a heavy burden during the first few months until more personnel could be brought in and trained. The United Kingdom investment in Gander, and the earlier decision to keep the Trans-Atlantic Air Service organization in existence, now began to pay dividends.

The RCAF visited Gander for the first time on February 10, 1940, when two Hudsons flew in from Eastern Air Command at Halifax. On June 4, two Digby aircraft came from Halifax, carrying senior air officers who went to St. John's for discussions with the Newfoundland government.

These meetings led to the stationing of five Digby aircraft from 10 BR Squadron Halifax at Gander for anti-submarine patrol operations. (Four enemy submarines were sunk). The aircraft arrived on June 17, 1940, with Squadron Leader H. Carscallen in charge, so marking Gander's entry into the war. On June 23, the Black Watch Regiment of the Canadian Army assumed the defence of the airport: the strategic position of Gander was now finally recognized.

The following Canadian units served in Gander:

RCAF

10 BR Squadron	flying Digbys and Liberators, April 1, 1941, to August 13, 1945
5 BR Squadron	flying Cansos, November 1, 1942, to May 1, 1943
116 BR Squadron	flying Cansos, November 15, 1943, to June 7, 1944
127 Squadron	flying Hurricanes, August 20, 1942, to July 23, 1943
126 Squadron	flying Hurricanes, July 24, 1943, to June 1, 1944
129 Squadron	flying Hurricanes, June 3, 1944, to September 30, 1944

Army Regiments

Black Watch	June to August 1940
Queen's Own Rifles	August to December 1940
Royal Rifles	December 1940 to April 1941
Victoria Rifles	April to September 1941
Lincoln and Welland	September 1941 to March 1942
P.E.I. Highlanders	March 1942 to March 1943
Picton Highlanders	March to September 1943

From September 1943, anti-aircraft units of the Royal Canadian Artillery became responsible for the protection of Gander.

A large construction program began in autumn of 1940, to provide accommodation and hangars for the RCAF and the army.

On April 1, 1941, Newfoundland handed over control of Gander Airport to Canada for the duration of the war, and from that time it was operated as a military base. RCAF Station Gander was established on May 5, 1941, under Group Captain Lewis, and the Department of Transport established the radio range station.

The U.S. Air Force moved into Gander in May 1941, when the 21st Reconnaissance Squadron arrived with six Douglas B-18 aircraft (the same type of aircraft as the RCAF's Digby). The 41st Reconnaissance Squadron replaced the 21st Squadron in August with eight Boeing B-17 aircraft. The Americans were at Gander as tenants of Canada, which supplied the hangars and other buildings, on what became the 'American side' of the airport. Although the U.S. had not entered the war at the time, their aircraft from Gander did carry out anti-submarine reconnaissance flights off the coast of Newfoundland. The American flag was first raised at the American base on August 8, 1941.

On July 2, 1941, the U.S. Ferry Command flew its initial air service flight from Bolling Field, Washington, D.C. to Prestwick by way of Gander using a converted Liberator bomber. The service was to carry important passengers and mail to England. Six round-trips had been made by mid-October, when it shut down for the winter.

The U.S. ferry service through Gander began on August 15, 1942, when a squadron of tactical B-17s took off for Prestwick. A second squadron of nine B-17s left Gander on August 19. The U.S. ferry service continued throughout the war and, with RAF Ferry Command operations, made Gander, a very active airport.

With Lockheed-10 aircraft Trans-Canada Air Lines began service to Newfoundland on May 1, 1942, and made their first Gander landing on that day. At that time the passenger waiting room and airline offices were located in the old administration building on the north side of the airport.

By mid-1943, Gander "was much the largest RCAF operational base in history, with a population occasionally reaching past 15,000, counting RCAF, USAF, RAF Ferry Command, Canadian Army, Contractors and local civilian personnel employed..."[6]

During Canada's wartime occupation of Gander, the Department of National Defence spent $19,960,170 to expand the facilities for military use, including the extension of three runways to 6,000 feet [1,829 metres]. When control of the airport reverted to Newfoundland on April 1, 1946, the improvements were sold to Newfoundland for $1 million.

Gander was originally planned as a transatlantic air terminal and, in serving as a base for the ferry operations during the war, it fulfilled this role. It began on November 10, 1940, with the first dispatch of a formation of seven Hudson bombers, led by Captain D.C.T. Bennett of the British Overseas Airways Corporation. (He later became Air Vice Marshall Bennett, CBE, DSO of the Pathfinder Force of RAF Bomber Command). Planes arrived safely the next morning at Aldergrove, Northern Ireland. Three more formations left Gander before the end of December. Subsequently, aircraft were dispatched singly.

When the first Hudson arrived in Gander on October 28, 1940, there was no aircrew accommodation. Canadian Pacific Air Service, then

105. Gander Airport—USAF Liberator taxiing, 1941.

manager of the enterprise, therefore hired two sleeping cars and a diner from the Newfoundland Railway and parked them on a nearby siding. These became home for the ferry crews until the staff house, called the Eastbound Inn, was ready on December 19. The ferry organization built two hangars and staff accommodation on the southeast side of the airport in 1941 and soon became self-sufficient. The RAF Ferry Command took over the ferry organization in July 1941, and on October 7, the RAF also took over the radio station from the Air Ministry, (with F.R. Ratcliffe as officer in charge) as well as the transatlantic control unit (which was managed by T.M. McGrath). The Department of Transport continued to supply meteorological services under P.D. McTaggart-Cowan (later known as McFog).

The base remained under the control of Captain I.G. Ross of the British Overseas Airways Corporation until the first RAF Commanding Officer, Group Captain Cottle, assumed command on April 1, 1942. The U.S. Air Force began ferrying B-17s and B-24s through Gander in large numbers in August 1942; and in May 1943, joint RAF-USATC control of the North Atlantic air route was established in the RAF Ferry Command hangar to co-ordinate movements of RAF and USAF aircraft. The Trans-Atlantic Ferry Service[7] was a great success: 6,500 aircraft were delivered safely to the United Kingdom by the RAF, and 10,000 by the USAF. Although there were losses, these were very small—about two per cent.

A final note on ferry operations at Gander concerns the Return Ferry Service, operated for the Ferry Command by BOAC, using converted Liberator bombers. The service flew ferry crews back to Montreal from England so they could pick up new aircraft for eastbound delivery. The Liberators also carried VIPs and urgent freight. On May 4, 1941, Captain D.C.T. Bennett flew the first eastbound flight and Captain James

Youell piloted the first westbound flight.[8] These return ferry flights continued during the war and constituted the first regular year-round transatlantic passenger service—a great advance over the earlier summer flying boat service by way of Botwood. On February 10, 1946, the Return Ferry Service of BOAC completed 2,000 Atlantic crossings. The service was demilitarized on September 30, 1946.

With the end of the war in Europe in 1945, Newfoundland began to consider the return of Gander Airport to a peace-time role. Troops started to move out, although the RCAF and RAF remained until April 1, 1946, and RCAF Lancasters began to fly home from Europe by way of the Azores and Gander on June 6, 1946. The last RAF bomber was delivered to England through Gander on September 6, 1946. BOAC continued to operate the Return Ferry Service through Gander, and on July 1, 1946, inaugurated London-to-New York passenger service with Lockheed Constellations. Meanwhile Trans-Canada Air Lines had continued to operate the Canadian Government Transatlantic Air Service with Lancastrians. Commercial airlines, mainly American, and many of which operated under government contract during the war, indicated their interest in establishing passenger service to Europe by way of Gander.

The first landplane civil passenger service commenced on October 23, 1945, when an American Overseas Airlines DC-4 left Gander for Shannon. Pan American Airways operated its first landplane (DC-4) service through Gander on October 27, 1945. On November 25, 1945, Trans World Airlines operated a Constellation via Gander; and so civil traffic began. The airlines occupied space on both the 'American side' and 'RAF side' of the airport; the civil airport authorities converted some vacant military buildings into living quarters, offices, and restaurants for passengers and civilian personnel.

In 1946, the work of converting military build-

106. Gander, Newfoundland, August 20, 1943.

ings continued, and on April 1, after five years of military control, the RCAF officially returned the airport to Newfoundland.[9] RCAF airport traffic controllers continued to man the tower until June 5, when a Newfoundland staff of ex-Air Force pilots and air crew assumed responsibility. The Department of Transport lent one of its air traffic control experts, Roy Mattern, to the airport to train new personnel.

The RAF officially closed its station on April 1, 1946,[10] but left a number of officers to continue transatlantic control services until May 21, when Newfoundland personnel took over. The Department of Transport later established the Oceanic Air Traffic Control Centre, in accordance with decisions reached at the provisional International Civil Aviation Organization (ICAO) meeting, held in Dublin in March 1946.

On September 14, 1946, a new air terminal was opened in part of the former RAF hangar 22. Nearby, vacant living quarters were converted to overnight passenger accommodation and named "Skyways Hotel." The terminal bar, known as "The Big Dipper," operated twenty-four-hours-a-day and soon acquired a worldwide reputation as a meeting place for Atlantic travellers. By this time, Gander was served by eight international airlines: BOAC, Pan American Airways, American Overseas Airlines, Trans-Canada Air Lines, Trans World Airlines, KLM, Air France, and SILA (Swedish). All transatlantic air traffic—

eastbound and westbound—landed at Gander, which adopted the title, "Crossroads of the World." By the end of 1946, 1,000 passengers a day passed through Gander.

From the beginning, Gander had been a self-contained community, sixty-four kilometres from the nearest town, and in 1946, its nature remained unchanged. During the war, it had grown into a large military camp of about 15,000 people, but now it was reduced to a population of 2,000, half of whom were employed on the airport with the Newfoundland government and the airlines. The new airport administration was responsible for the whole community and supplied living quarters (mainly 544 apartments in converted military barracks), municipal services and utilities, a bakery, a dry cleaning plant, stores, schools, churches, and hotels.

Gander was built by the Newfoundland and British governments to serve the Trans-Atlantic Air Service and was to be financed by both countries. The two governments resumed their joint interests at the end of the war, but those years had changed the original concept somewhat, and now Newfoundland played a more active role. The Civil Aviation Division of the Newfoundland Department of Public Works operated the airport. (Newfoundland was administered by a commission of Government with six commissioners, three appointed by the U.K. and

107. Queen Elizabeth & Prince Philip,
Gander International Airport, June 19, 1959.

three by Newfoundland). Because finances were tight, the government decided that Gander Airport would operate on a cost-recovery basis as far as possible. Any deficit, which was to be budgeted annually, would be shared one-third by Newfoundland and two-thirds by the United Kingdom: Newfoundland's share was not to be less than $250,000 a year. From the start in 1945, maximum revenue was derived from all non-aviation activities. The initial landing fees, which were high—perhaps the highest in the world at the time—were based on fees (for non-scheduled landings) at La Guardia, New York, plus 50 per cent to take into account the higher costs at Gander for snow-clearing, etc. The Gander fee for a DC-4 was $80,[11] and this was increased by 50 per cent on October 1, 1947. The airlines protested these fees and, at one stage, the American carriers threatened to use the U.S. Air Force base at Stephenville on the west coast of Newfoundland instead of Gander. The agreement among the U.S., Britain, and Newfoundland, however, prohibited civil use of Stephenville, except as an alternate airport in an emergency.

The financial position and management philosophy of the airport led to an interesting and unusual relationship between the airport and the airlines. When the airport could not meet all of the airlines' demands (and there were many in the first year of operations), an agreement was

108. Terminal, Gander International Airport. Opened by Queen Elizabeth, June 19, 1959.

reached whereby improvements required by the airlines would be financed jointly by these airlines.[12] The conversion of hangar H22 (on the RAF side) into the airline terminal, opened on September 14, 1946, was financed in this way: the airlines provided the capital funds and agreed to pay operating and maintenance costs. Rents and terminal use fees paid by the airlines were credited against their capital investment. The agreement worked quite well, although there were some differences between the airlines and airport management from time to time. Non-scheduled or non-participating airlines were charged a terminal-use fee of $30 in addition to the regular landing fees.

The airport accounts for the year ending March 31, 1948, show operation expenses[13] at $941,060, revenue at $820,212 (landing fees amounted to $799,924), and an operating loss of $120,848.

In December 1946, Gander installed Ground Controlled Approach (GCA), a mobile radar unit that permitted the controller to 'talk down' an aircraft. Pan American Airways operated the GCA for the airlines that used Gander regularly; operating costs were jointly underwritten by the airlines. Non-participating airlines requesting GCA service were charged $125 per landing. GCA was primarily a military system, and the Gander unit was the first civil GCA system in the world. It continued in operation until 1959, when the Department of Transport commissioned and operated the Precision Approach Radar (PAR). The weather limits for the use of GCA at Gander were 300 feet [91 metres] and half a mile [almost one kilometre]. During the years of GCA operation at Gander, over 30,000 landings were made without incident.

Allied Maintenance of Newfoundland Ltd., which still operates at Gander, was established there in 1948 to provide maintenance, passenger handling, dispatch, and other contract services to

airlines. Its services permitted customer airlines to reduce staff and overhead expenses.

On April 1, 1949, when Newfoundland became part of Canada, the airport staff became civil servants of Canada, and the Department of Transport took over what was then its largest airport, with a staff of 1,176. The operating and maintenance costs for 1948-49 were $2.9 million (not including radio and air traffic control), revenue was $3.2 million—a profit of $238,900, before depreciation. To put these figures into perspective, the total revenue from Department of Transport airports in the previous year was $1.4 million. Airport management at Gander had a great deal of autonomy, far more than usually allowed at a Department of Transport airport—for one thing, it operated on the principle of cost-recovery. Because of its isolation, the airport was self-sufficient in many respects: it hired and fired its staff and issued its own cheques. It took a while to integrate Gander into the Canadian airport system, and, for some time, Gander was 'different' from the standard airport. By the same token, some Gander procedures and practices were adopted for use at other airports. One of these was landing fees. At the time of the Gander take-over, standard landing fees across Canada were much lower; for example, for a DC-4 of 73,000 pounds [33,113 kilograms], Gander charged $120, while the Department of Transport fee was $14.60. Some consideration was given to rescinding the Gander fees. But they were retained—and applied elsewhere in the Transport system of airports where transatlantic landings might occur: for example, at Halifax, Moncton, Sydney, and Goose Bay, and, later, when the range of transatlantic aircraft increased, at Montreal and Toronto.

Gander's cost-recovery policy was discontinued under the Department of Transport, and the airport became part of the Canadian airport system in which operating and maintenance costs came out of annual appropriations, while revenue was credited to the consolidated revenue of Canada. The Airlines' Agreement, whereby the carriers paid the full costs of the air terminal operation, was terminated. The Ground Controlled Approach agreement was, however, allowed to continue until the Department of Transport introduced its Precision Approach Radar in 1959.

Gander soon began to expand and receive new facilities, because of the greater availability of capital funds. Three runways were improved and extended (13-31 to 8,900 feet [2,713 metres], 09-27 to 6,180 feet [1,884 metres], and 04-22 to 10,500 feet [3,200 metres]; one of the original runways was realigned and another, the old no. 2, was abandoned). New runway lighting was installed, and navigational aids introduced, and a new air terminal building was constructed. Queen Elizabeth II opened this on June 19, 1959.

In 1950, authorities decided to create a new town-site west of the airport and move all living quarters and other community activities off the airport. The population at this time was approximately 4,000, and there was a pressing need for housing: many people wanted to own their own homes. There was a demand for shopping facilities; and private enterprise saw that Gander, on Newfoundland standards, was becoming a large population centre. New schools were required, and religious denominations wanted to replace the temporary facilities they had set up in surplus military buildings. In short, as Gander grew as a community, its people wanted a release from Department of Transport control and dependency.

For its part, the Department was anxious to relinquish its responsibility for running a municipality, and realised that an enlarged 'town area' on the airport would encroach on the prime activity of Gander—aviation. So the provincial government, the Department of Transport, and the Central Mortgage and Housing Corporation co-operated in building streets (named after aviators who played a part in the history of aviation in Newfoundland and on the North Atlantic air route), installed services, provided serviced lots, and constructed rental housing. The first fifty Department of Transport houses were ready by 1952. Privately owned houses were erected, and the transfer of population from the airport to the town was underway. In a short time, all non-aviation buildings on the airport were sold and removed from the site. The town took the name of Gander and elected its own council in 1959. The community developed rapidly and soon had two shopping centres, new schools and churches, a vocational school, hotels, and a hospital.

The town of Gander has grown and prospered and, following the construction of the Trans-Canada Highway and a vast network of provincial roads, it has become a service centre for the northeastern part of Newfoundland. This resulted in the diversification of the local economy, and the population (12,000 in 1979) is less dependent on airport employment.

In 1958, there were 9,273 landings at Gander, and 407,000 passengers passed through the airport. In that year, jet aircraft (de Havilland Comet and the Boeing 707) came into service on the North Atlantic routes. The high performance and longer range of these new aircraft soon had their effect. Until this time, nearly every piston-engined aircraft on the Atlantic route had to refuel at Gander, at one of the alternate airports in the Maritime provinces, or at Goose Bay. Now, the Boeing 707 could fly non-stop when conditions were right. In the next few years, as more of the international airlines purchased jet aircraft, Gander's importance began to decline and traffic decreased. However, it still served as a refuelling stop for non-scheduled air carriers, and for many jets when weather or load factors made non-stop crossings impossible.

In 1971, the Department of Transport launched the Trans Ocean Plane Stop (TOPS) program, an international selling mission aimed at getting more business to Gander, particularly from non-scheduled and charter carriers with destinations in the mid-continent of North America and on the Pacific coast. The program has been successful and is still very active. The most frequent users of Gander are American Trans Air, Luftransport, Trans International, Rosenbalm, Federal Express, Heavylift, Scan Air, Flying Tigers, El Al, Nationair Canada, Transwede, Caribbean Air Cargo, Evergreen International., World Airways, Southern Air Transport, Connie Kalitta Services, Air Charter Services, and Gulf Air. In addition, Aeroflot, Cubana, and Interflug regularly refuel at Gander en route to and from Moscow and Cuba. Incidentally, many East Bloc and Cuban citizens have defected to Canada during the stopover.

Eastern Provincial Airlines, Newfoundland's regional airline, had its head office and maintenance base at Gander from 1953 to 1984. EPA was incorporated in March 1949 and had routes in Newfoundland, Labrador, and the Maritime provinces, terminating in Montreal. In 1984, the company moved its head office and maintenance base to Halifax, and in 1985 was sold to Canadian Pacific Airlines.

While Gander may no longer be the aerial crossroads of the world, it is still a vital point on the North Atlantic route; its International Flight Service Station (IFSS), the largest aeradio station operated by Transport Canada, serves aircraft within the 1,152,000 square miles [1,853,914 square metres] of Gander oceanic area. In 1986, Gander IFSS communicated with approximately 115,000 aircraft, in almost half a million contacts.

In 1988, Gander had 124,700 passengers and 43,093 aircraft movements.

The following managers have guided the affairs of Gander Airport over the years:

H.A.L. Pattison

Pattison oversaw the construction of Gander Airport for the U.K. and Newfoundland Governments and, with his other duties in connection with the Trans-Atlantic Air Service, managed it from 1938 to 1941.

RCAF

The RCAF station conducted anti-submarine operations and was a base for Atlantic air ferry activities from 1941 to 1946.

G.D. Middleton

Middleton, a British Air Ministry official, served as airport manager for two years under H.A.L. Pattison, who had become Director of Civil Aviation. Middleton served from 1946 to 1948, when he returned to England.

H.A.L. Pattison

Pattison served again as airport manager during the years of Gander's transition to the Department of Transport airports system, 1949 to 1951. He then became Canadian representative on the Air Navigation Commission at the ICAO.

Eric Winsor

Winsor had been business manager responsible for all commercial activities since 1946. He served as airport manager from 1946 to 1957. He was transferred to Department of Transport headquarters in Ottawa and eventually became Director General of Airport and Construction Services.

Rex Tilley

After RAF service, Tilley had joined Gander staff in 1946 as senior air traffic controller. He served as airport manager from 1957 to 1963. Tilley was later transferred to the regional office of Transport in Moncton and became Regional Manager of Airports.

J.D. James

James became airport manager in 1964 and remained in the position until 1984. He first went to Gander in 1936 during its construction and, in the succeeding years, served in many positions on the airport.

John R. Pittman

Pittman served as manager from 1984 to 1988. Previous to Gander, he had been airport manager at Yarmouth 1981-82, worked in Civil Aviation Branch, Moncton, 1982-83, in Airport Operations, Ottawa, 1983-84. In 1988, he became Director of Airport Operations in Airports Group, Moncton.

Lawrence Lachapelle

Present manager. Previous to Gander, he served as manager, Airport Operations and Services at Calgary International Airport, 1981-88, and acting manager, Terminal and Industrial Services until going to Gander.

Sources:
1. Author's diary and papers
2. Transport Canada, Atlantic Region.

Footnotes to Gander Airport

[1] There was no such place as Hattie's Camp! A man named Hattie cut lumber in the vicinity of Jonaton's Pond and would enter the area just east of Milepost 213 on the Newfoundland railway. The first airport workers referred to Milepost 213 as Hattie's camp. Five and a half kilometers west of 213, section workers on the railway had established a camp near Cobb's Pond, and a couple of families lived there. It became known as Cobb's Camp—a name sometimes erroneously used for the airport. (Information provided by J.D. James, airport mamager, Gander International Airport).

[2] See file 570/35 of the Newfoundland Archives, St. John's.

[3] Ibid.

[4] Jewett later became Chief Engineer for the Department of Transport on the construction of aerodromes for the British Commonwealth Air Training Plan. Bradley became airport engineer with the Newfoundland Civil Aviation Division at Gander after the war, and later, regional construction engineer in the Ontario region of the Department of Transport.

[5] Pattison originally came to Canada in 1933 as a flight lieutenant (RAF) on exchange to the RCAF. He was posted to Camp Borden as a signals specialist to set up the Wireless Service trraining. After seven months, he went to the RCAF Headquarters in Ottawa as assistant staff officer, Air Operations, in charge of organizing the RCAF Signals Service.(Source: W/C F.H. Hitchins, "Air Board/CAF and RCAF, Canadian War Museum paper No. 2" *Mercury Series*, published by the Canadian War Museum, National Museum of Man, National Museums of Canada, August 1972. R 358 400971 H675).

In 1941 the U.K. agreed that Pattison should remain in Newfoundland as officer in charge of the Air Ministry's wireless organization at Gander, and as the liaison officer between Newfoundland. the RCAF and the British Air Ministry, with particular reference to trans-Atlantic flights. In 1944 he was appointed Director of Civil Aviation for Newfoundland. When Newfoundland joined Canada in April 1949, Pattison became airport manager at Gander under the department of Transport. In May 1951 he became Canada's member of the ICAO Air Navigation Commission. Following six years in that appointment, he served as department of Transport's representative at the Canadian High Commission in London. He retired in 1964 and died in England a few years later.

[6] Air Marshall Clare L Annis, "Eastern Air Command Recalled," *CAHS Journal*, Vol. 14, No. 3, (Fall 1976) p. 76. Group Captain Annis was commanding officer, station Gander at the time.

[7] In addition to the landplanes handled at the airport, a

large number of flying boats were ferried overseas through a sub-base at nearby Gander Lake.

[8] This aircraft, Liberator AM260, was the first to land at Gander from England.

[9] Newfoundland paid Canada $1.0 million for improvements, buildings etc.

[10] Newfoundland paid Britiain $200,000.00 for improvements and buildings.

[11] Papers dated October 29, 1948, by the Director of Civil Aviation to the Director of Air Services, Department of Transport, relating to the coming Union of Newfoundland and Canada, Section II, p. 14, and following (unpublished document).

[12] Ibid

[13] This cost includes radio and control tower, but not terminal, staff accommodation, hotel and community services.

Gaspé Airport
(Québec)

In 1951, interested people in the private sector began to develop the current site of the airport. A company, Gaspé Airport Inc., was formed, of which the sole shareholder was the Trans-Gaspésienne Airline Company. The following year, it sold the airport to the municipality of Gaspé for the nominal sum of one dollar.

Transport Canada provided a grant of $42,000 in 1953 to the airport and issued the first public airport licence in 1954.

In 1960, the airport became a link between the Magdalen Islands, Anticosti Island, Ste. Anne-des-Monts, Murdochville, and a number of airports on the north shore routes operated by Air Gaspé Inc., the major user of the airport at that time.

Transport Canada bought the airport for one dollar in 1965, and the following year, began reconstruction—paving the runway, taxiway, apron, and access road—at a cost of $900,000.00. Subsequently, by agreement with the municipality, the operation and maintenance of the airport was transferred to Gaspé, with a subsidy from Transport Canada.

The current air terminal building was constructed in 1973; and in 1974, Transport Canada set up a flight services station.

In 1979, the airport was equipped with an emergency generating system, and in 1981, Localizer for non-precision approach procedure/ Distance Measuring Equipment (LOC/DME) and Visual Approach Slope Indicator System (VASIS) systems were installed on runway 11-29; a Runway Identification Lights (RIL) was deployed on runway 11; and in 1984, Very High Frequency omni-directional Range (VOR) was installed.

The Gaspé Airport was provided with a new waterworks, and sewage systems during 1987-88.

The airport is currently served by Air Alliance and Intair, with regular flights between Montréal, Québec, Mont-Joli, Gaspé, and Iles de la Madeleine. Using DASH 8, ATR42 and METROLINER aircraft, Les Ailes de Gaspé offers a charter service. The airport has 35 staff, and in 1988, 14,600 passengers passed through; there were 5,218 aircraft movements.

Sources:
1. Transport Canada, Quebec Region
2. Louis Boulay, Airport Manager, Gaspé Airport

Gillam Airstrip
(Manitoba)

Gillam, 740 kilometres north of Winnipeg on the CNR Hudson Bay line that runs between The Pas and Churchill, has a gravel airstrip 5,000 by 150 feet, 1524 by 43 metres] one kilometre northwest of the town. Manitoba Hydro constructed the strip in 1966, with a grant from the Department of Transport, so that personnel and equipment might be moved during the construction of the Manitoba Hydro dam sites. It is operated by Hydro, with an airport operating subsidy from Transport.

The air terminal building had been a school house, built in 1957 in the town of Gillam, then moved to its present location in 1969. It was extended in 1979.

Visual Approach Slope Indicator System (VASIS) was installed in 1977 andDistance Measuring Equipment (DME) in 1986.

The following use the airport: Canadian Airlines International; Skyward Aviation; Air Manitoba; Calm Air International Ltd.; Gillam Airways; Custom Helicopters; Northwinds; Nunasi Central Airlines Ltd.; Viking Helicopters Ltd.; Keewatin Air Ltd.; Airwest; Canadian Helicopters.

In 1989, there were 4,470 aircraft movements; 14,000 passengers passed through the airport and approximately 300,000 pounds of freight were hauled by the two scheduled airlines.

Source:
Transport Canada, Central Region.

Gjoa Haven Airport
(Northwest Territories)

Gjoa is one of the airports in the Kitikmeot region, that has been improved in recent years. Reconstruction, completed in September 1983, provided a gravel runway of an excellent grade surface material "that is easy on aircraft tires and propellors..."[1] a great improvement over "the old Gjoa Haven runway, that terrible quagmire of sand that occasionally swallowed small aircraft and made 60-metre landings routine for any type of aircraft."[2]

The runway, 13T-31T is 1,341 by 30 metres.

There is a terminal building and good apron lighting. The Government of the Northwest Territories runs the airport. First Air provided scheduled service from 1987 until November 1989, and Territorial Airways has also operated at this site.

In 1988, there were 1,152 aircraft movements, with 4,100 passengers.

Sources:
1. Government of the Northwest Territories.
2. Transport Canada, Central Region.

Footnotes to Gjoa Airport

[1] John Rogers, Regional Manager, Airport Operations, Arctic Airports Division, Government opf the Northwest Territories.

[2] Transport Canada, Central Region.

Goose Bay Airport
(Labrador)

The Department of Transport built Goose Bay Airport during 1941-42 for the Department of National Defence (RCAF). The construction of the airport was recommended on July 29, 1941 by the Permanent Joint (U.S.-Canada) Board on Defence "in order to facilitate the ferrying of long- and medium-range aircraft across the Atlantic, to enhance the effectiveness of plans for hemisphere defence, to prevent congestion at the Newfoundland Airport (Gander) and to provide greater security for crews and equipment."[1]

The board advised the Canadian government to undertake the construction of an air base in the vicinity of North West River, Labrador, "as quickly as feasible" and that, if Canada was unable to do so, the government of the United States be invited to provide the necessary facilities. Canada agreed to proceed with the project,

and a contract was awarded to the McNamara Construction Co. in September 1941.

Earlier that year, a joint Navy-Air Force and Department of Mines and Resources party began to chart and photograph the coastline of Labrador, and to look for potential airport sites. One of the party, Eric Fry of the Dominion Topographical Survey, found what looked like an ideal site thirty-two kilometres south of North West River; a sandy plateau on which the airport was later built, with a good harbour nearby in Goose Bay, at the southwest end of Lake Melville.

By July 1, Fry advised Ottawa that he had found a promising site, and on July 14, a group of RCAF officers and engineers arrived to appraise it. Ottawa approved their recommendation and, in August, advance parties of engineers and surveyors were flown from Halifax to the site in flying boats. By September 20, preliminary layout work had begun from a camp at the water's edge.

The ice-breaker MacLean was the first ship to arrive at Goose Bay on August 29, carrying heavy equipment and fifty RCAF personnel. On September 30, 1941, three ships, the Sorrel, the Foundation Jupiter, and the O.K. Service, arrived with bulldozers, prefabricated houses, graders, and other construction equipment. It was then a race against time to ship in and unload the material required for winter construction: with freeze-up, the port was closed for six months.

Within three weeks of the arrival of the first ships, a temporary wharf was erected, the roadway from tidewater to the plateau was well under way, and work had started on the airport itself. On November 16, 1941, the resident engineer wired the Department of Transport in Ottawa to report that three gravel runways were cleared to a length of 7,000 feet [2,134 metres] and were suitable for large aircraft. A ski-equipped twin-engine Québec Airways plane was the first airplane to land on the runways at Goose Bay,

arriving on December 3, 1941. The first military aircraft, piloted by P/O Hutchinson, RCAF, landed on December 9, 1941. Aircraft carrying supplies used the snow-compacted runways throughout winter.

The Goose Bay Airport was constructed with the approval of Newfoundland, which granted Canada a 99-year lease to the 120-square-mile site, effective September 1, 1941. The lease covered the operation of the airport as a military base "for the duration of the war and for such time thereafter as the Governments agree to be necessary or advisable in the interests of common defence...The question of its use for civil and commercial operations after the war...will form the subject of discussions between the Governments of Canada, the United Kingdom and Newfoundland, and these discussions will take place not later than twelve months after the war."[2]

The first RCAF detachment commander at Goose Bay was Squadron Leader W.J. McFarlane, who arrived in September 1941 and returned to Gander on November 12. During the winter of 1941-42, only a small detachment of service personnel was required to administer the outpost and maintain the runways. On April 1, 1942, Goose Bay was officially declared RCAF Station Goose Bay and McFarlane returned to become the station commanding officer. The RCAF ensign was hoisted for the first time on March 29, 1942.

Three days after Pearl Harbour, a C-39 of the USAF Ferry Command began to move contractors' personnel and supplies from Moncton to Goose Bay. By mid-February 1942, this service was replaced by Northeast Airlines, operating (under contract to the U.S.) between Presque Ile, Maine, and Goose Bay by way of American bases in Newfoundland. The U.S. was then developing the Northeast Staging Route to Britain—via Greenland and Iceland in which Goose Bay was destined to play a major role.

109. Goose Bay Airport, Labrador, 1943.

Construction continued throughout the winter of 1941-42 so that accommodation buildings and hangars were ready for spring. By April, the officers' quarters were completed and occupied: twenty-four officers lived on the ground floor and forty-eight non-commissioned officers lived upstairs. A 'nose' hangar, capable of housing three aircraft, was also ready.

Goose Bay began ferry operations on April 6, 1942, when a detachment from RAF Ferry Command arrived from Gander: F/Lt. T.M. McGrath and nine airmen. That night, two RAF Cansos and one Liberator left for Prestwick via Greenland (BW8, Sondreströmfjord) and Iceland.[3] On April 17, three Hudsons (flown by Bisson, McVicar, and Evans) left on the first direct flight from Goose Bay to the U.K. The snow-compacted runways were hard enough at night and in the early morning, but because they softened up during the daytime RAF Ferry Command temporarily suspended operations—on April 23, only two weeks after arrival. Three Hudsons then on hand were flown to Gander and from there to the U.K.

Three USAF officers and nine other ranks were stationed at Goose Bay; and during April, several American aircraft flew between Goose Bay and BW8.

When the snow runways began to break up, three gravel strips were built: operations resumed and continued all summer. The runways and taxi strips were paved by the early fall of 1942.

From June 1942, there was a steady buildup of military personnel at Goose Bay, including the American armed forces, and the New Brunswick Rangers arrived to defend the air base. By the end of that month, there were 1,700 service personnel and 700 civilians in this new Labrador settlement.

On June 1, the RCAF turned over Building No. 13 to the U.S. Air Force for use as a mess, and on June 8, Colonel Smith arrived to become the first commanding officer of the American contingent. On July 15, USAF, with Canadian approval, began construction of its own camp on the opposite (south) side of the airport; and on August 1, 1942, USAF base became an independent entity. The first official American flag-raising ceremony in Labrador was conducted on February 1, 1943.

From this time, there was a steady increase in traffic of war planes flown to Britain by the ferry organizations of the RAF and USAF. The planes were dispatched both singly and in squadrons. On June 26, 1942, eighteen USAF B-17 bombers left Goose Bay for the U.K. by way of BW1 and BW8 in Greenland, thus becoming the first American tactical aircraft to reach England by air. The first "BOLERO" air movement was completed twenty-six days later. On July 6, seventy Lockheed Lightning fighters left for England by way of BW1 (Greenland) and Iceland. The RAF continued to delivered long- and short-range twin- and four-engine bombers.

By the end of 1942, buildings had been completed, housing 5,000 service personnel and 3,000 construction workers. In January 1943, twenty-five families that had built huts and camps at Otter Creek were moved to the area now known as Happy Valley.

By June 1943, Station strength was:

RCAF	40 officers
	471 airmen
RAFTC	39 all ranks
Canadian Army	10 all ranks
Civilians	10
YMCA	3
Aircraft	1 Norseman
	8 Hurricanes (129 Squadron)[4]

Essentially, Goose Bay Airport was run by the RCAF, which controlled the operation and communications services used by its own air personnel, while RAF Transport Command and USAF ferry services relied on their own respective units. Meteorological services for the RCAF and RAF were provided by the Department of Transport.

The RCAF conducted anti-submarine operations from Goose Bay; six Canso aircraft from 5 BR Squadron were stationed there in July and August 1943, nine aircraft from 162 BR Squadron in October 1943, and three aircraft from 116 BR Squadron from November 1943 to June 1944. Air defence at Goose Bay was provided by Hurricanes of 129 Squadron from April to October 1943, and by 130 Squadron from October 1943 to March 1944.[5]

Wartime traffic figures are not available for Goose Bay, but we know that in June 1944, 2,598 aircraft passed through the station and for the twelve month period ending September 30, 1945, the airport handled 24,000 aircraft. When the war ended in Europe in 1945, the traffic through Goose Bay, Gander, and Stephenville brought an estimated total of 240,000 personnel back to North America without fatality.[6]

At the end of the war, consideration was given to the future use of Goose Bay Airport as a military base and as a base for commercial aircraft flying the North Atlantic route. Canada's position was relatively clear because it had a 99-year lease to the site, but the USAF were in a different situation: they were tenants of Canada with the approval of Newfoundland, and it was assumed they would withdraw.

The USAF, however, wanted to remain at Goose Bay indefinitely for reasons stated in Permanent Joint Board on Defence papers:

There would be a continuing need for facilities there so long as the United States forces remain in Europe... Air Transport Command will have necessity for retaining existing facilities at Goose Bay for the continued safe operation over the North Atlantic Route. Goose Bay is also an ATC supply point for outlying (U.S.) weather and communications stations in Eastern Canada and Baffin Island and is also an alternate to Stephenville... Goose Bay is considered vital to the defence of the United States and Canada and should be maintained as a military base on such a scale as to provide for the stationing of operational squadrons as required.[7]

After high-level discussions among the United States, Canada, and Newfoundland, it was agreed that the USAF could remain. Canada also decided to keep Canadian forces at Goose Bay as long as U.S. forces were established there—the idea of withdrawing the RCAF, and turning over the airport to the Department of Transport, was temporarily put aside. By the end of 1946, Goose Bay was *the* defence facility in Newfoundland, including Labrador, under the command and control of Canadian forces. On April 1, 1949, Newfoundland became part of Canada.

Following the signing of a twenty-year lease between the United States and Canada in 1953, the U.S. undertook an extensive construction program on the south side of Goose Bay Airport. This included permanent married quarters, dormitories, nine hangars, a chapel, a theatre, base operations, the "Goose Hilton" hotel, and a new hospital.

Between 1952 and 1958, a program of construction was also undertaken by the RCAF on the north side that included married quarters and a school.

On April 10, 1947, the new passenger terminal (located in an RCAF hangar on the north side) was used for the first time by a Trans-Canada Air Lines' North Star on an Atlantic flight.

The post-war use of Goose Bay by commercial aircraft on the transatlantic service was a subject of prolonged discussion between the Canadian, Newfoundland, and United Kingdom governments. Provisions had b een written into the Leased Bases Agreement with the United States and the Canada-Newfoundland-Goose Bay Agreement, stating clearly that the military airports could not be used for civil aviation (other than use related to the war) without the approval of Newfoundland. Newfoundland's position was that "the maximum concentration of traffic at Gander is clearly desirable having regard to our liability in respect of the heavy costs of airport operation."[8] That position was maintained in discussions with Canada and the United States, and the final agreement provided that Stephenville and Goose Bay could be used by civil transatlantic aircraft only in an emergency or as weather alternates for Gander.

In 1957, the Strategic Air Command of the USAF became the host unit at Goose Bay air base with over 3,000 personnel supporting the B-47 mission and the KC-97 alert tankers. The first KC-135 jet tanker landed at Goose Bay in 1960. In 1966, when Harmon Field (Stephenville) closed, USAF Goose Bay assumed many of Harmon's functions, and in 1968 the 95th Strategic Wing moved to Goose Bay from Biggs Air Force Base in Texas.

In 1967, an RAF unit moved into Goose Bay Airport and is still there, providing support for Vulcan delta-wing bombers that come from

110. Goose Bay Airport, early 1970s.

bases in the U.K. to carry out low-level training over Labrador and eastern Québec. Support is also provided to RAF aircraft that stage through Goose Bay on their way to and from points further west.

Towards the end of the 1960s, there was a gradual phasing down in air defence activity and a consolidation of the RCAF base. Operation and maintenance of the airport and the north side were handed over from RCAF (Air Transport Command) to the Department of Transport on August 1, 1967; the USAF kept responsibility for its military base on the south side. Only sixty Canadian Forces personnel remained at Goose Bay to operate radar and air traffic control—this had to remain a military operation under the Canada-U.S. agreement covering the American presence on the airport. On September 1, 1970, thirty Canadian Forces personnel were transferred to Goose Bay to jointly man with the USAF the Manual NORAD Control Centre (MNCC) radar.[9] The Air Defence Command set up a Canadian Forces Station at Goose Bay. On July 1, 1971, the Canadian Forces took full control of the Melville Long Range Radar (LRR) and MNCC. The USAF began reducing its forces at Goose Bay and Canadian Forces families were able to move from the permanent married quarters area of Spruce Park (northeast side) to the

USAF area (southwest corner). Canadian Forces unit operations also moved to the USAF side.

In January 1973, the twenty-year lease to the United States was extended by six months to July 1, 1973, to permit the governments to complete arrangements for the transfer of the U.S. base to Canada. At that time, it was decided that Transport Canada—rather than the Department of National Defence—would assume full responsibility for the airport. On July 1, 1973, the land covered by the lease to the USAF was turned over to Transport together with all the buildings and improvements. A new agreement was signed by the USAF and Transport whereby Transport would operate and provide specified services and facilities to the USAF on a cost-recovery basis for three years until July 1, 1976.

From 1973 to 1976, Transport Canada vacated the north side of the airport, except for some Crown-owned housing and released a large portion of the former RCAF camp to the province of Newfoundland and Labrador for industrial use.

On September 30, 1976, the USAF SAC operation was replaced by a Military Air Lift unit (MAC), whose role was to ship air cargo and service USAF aircraft in transit through Goose Bay. MAC is still there.

On July 1, 1976, the responsibility for the Goose Bay air base was shared by Transport Canada and Public Works. Under the new arrangement, Transport was responsible for the operation of the civil airport and supporting the airside activities of the CAF, USAF, and RAF; Public Works for the administration of all groundside facilities. Transport's staff was reduced from 760 to 115.

Since 1973, the following major projects for upgrading the civil airport have been completed:

1973-74   A new air terminal building was built.
1974-75   New runway approach lighting sys-

111. Goose Bay Airport, early 1970s.

tems; a renovated operations building for telecommunications.

1975   Runway 16-34 was reduced in length to 6,200 feet [1,890 metres] and runway 09-27 reduced in width to 200 feet.

1975-76   A new Instrument Landing System (ILS) was provided.

1976-77   700,000 square yards of non-operational ramp space was taken out of use. Airport staff moved into the renovated administration building.

1977-78   A new Very high frequency Omni-direction Range (VOR) was installed.

1978   The new control tower opened and Transport Canada took over airport traffic control from the Canadian Forces, which had continued to provide that service since the end of the war.

1978   A new VHF/DF; the Visual Approach Slope Indicator System (VASIS) on runway 27 replaced.

1974-79   Former USAF POL system for fuel supply (74,445,000 gallons) was renovated to meet Canadian environmental standards.

Today, Goose Bay Airport has two runways in use: 09-27, at 3,368 metres, and 16-34, at 2,916 metres long.

On April 1, 1988, control and management were transferred from Transport to the Department of National Defence, and the airport is now used as a Low-Level Fighter Training Centre for National Defence and NATO allies.

Under individual bilateral agreements, Canada hosts military training programs for the armed forces of the Federal Republic of Germany, the United Kingdom, the United States, and the Netherlands. The following military operators are based at CF Base Goose Bay:

a) UK Royal Air Force, which carries out low-level flying training from April to November each year. The RAF began training at Goose Bay in 1967 using Vulcan bombers; and in 1984, the Tornado fighter bomber was introduced. A typical RAF exercise involves about ten to twelve aircraft and ground support personnel for a three-week period. The RAF can station twenty-four aircraft at Goose Bay.

b) The Federal Republic of Germany—German Air Force, which has the largest low-level flying training programme at Goose Bay. It began in 1981 with F-4 Phantoms and later introduced Alpha jets and Transall aircrews, then Tornados in 1985. It carries out an average of 3,000 sorties each year, and can station up to twenty-five combat aircraft at Goose Bay.

c) The Netherlands Air Force, which deployed a trial detachment of F-16 crews at Goose Bay for training in 1986. As a result, they decided to conduct flying training operations at Goose Bay on an annual basis, commencing in 1987, and can station up to 25 combat aircraft at the base.

(If NATO selects Goose Bay as the location of a Tactical Fighter Centre for all types of advanced flying training, it would station up to 140 aircraft at the base all year).

All incremental costs for training in Canada are recovered from the participating governments.

Today, about nine hundred civilian personnel

are employed directly or indirectly at the Goose Bay airfield in work which is mainly supportive of allied training, whose economic impact is estimated at more than $50 million.

Although the Department of National Defence manages the airport, Transport administers the terminal and the civil aviation operational area. Its site manager also acts as liaison between civilian operators and the Department of National Defence.

The following operators are currently based at the airport: Newfoundland Northern Air Transport, Labrador Airways, Universal Helicopters, Sealand Helicopters, Labrador Aviation and Allied Aviation.

In 1987, the airport had 70,900 passengers, and, in 1988, there were 8,062 aircraft movements.

D.M. Willmer was the first Department of Transport airport manager, and he took over on August 1, 1967. He was replaced by A.M. Keating in 1969. R.B. Goudie became manager in 1973, when Transport assumed responsibility for both the north and south side complexes. When it also became responsible for providing "mission support" for the 95th Strategic Wing of the USAF (SAC), airport staff was increased from 160 to 760. Goudie was succeeded by J.W. Stannix in July 1975.

Sources:
1. J.D. MacDonell, "35th Anniversary of Canadian Forces Station Goose Bay," unpublished article.
2. Transport Canada, Atlantic Region.
3. National Defence Headquarters, Ottawa.

Footnotes to Goose Bay

[1] *Goose Bay Air Base Act 1945*, Government of Newfoundland (St. John's: King's Printer). The Agreement may also be found in *Documents on Relations between Canada and Newfoundland, volume 1, 1935-1949*, (Ottawa: Department of External Affairs, 1974), Appendix F, pp. 1414-1416.

[2] Ibid.

[3] This was the first proving flight over the proposed short stage route via Greenland and Iceland. The two Cansos were flown by Captains Don McVicar and George Evans, and the Liberator by Captain Louis Bison, all of the RAF ferry command. The Liberator acted as mother ship, and flew back from Prestwick to Montréal over the same route carrying the crews from the two Cansos that had been delivered to the U.K. The Liberator landed at Goose Bay for fuel on April 14.

[4] J.D. MacDonnell, "35th Anniversary of Canadian Forces Station Goose Bay" (unpublished article).

[5] S. Kostenuk and J.A. Griffin, *RCAF Squadron Histories and Aircraft, 1924-1968* (Toronto: Samuel Stevens Hakkert, 1978).

[6] Stanley W. Dzinban, *United States Army in World War II: Military Relations between United States and Canada, 1939-49* (Washington: Office of the Chief of Military History, Department of the Army, 1959), p. 129.

[7] Reference to the Permanent Joint Board on Defence is found in Documents on *Relations between Canada and Newfoundland*, pp. 1024, 1025 and 1029.

[8] Ibid.

[9] This radar had its beginning in the Pine Tree Line built from Newfoundland and along the Labrador coast, 1952-54. The Melville site was started on August 1, 1953, and operated by 641 Aircraft Control and Warning (AC&W) Squadron USAF.

Gore Bay Airport
(Ontario)

The Department of Transport built Gore Bay Airport in 1947 as part of the new Red 23 Airway of the Trans-Canada Airway system-- Toronto, Wiarton, Gore Bay, upper Michigan to Lakehead (now Thunder Bay) and west. Trans-Canada Air Lines (TCA) was then using DC-3 aircraft, and intermediate airports were a safety requirement.

The airport, which opened in the summer of 1947, had two paved runways, 4,100 by 200 feet [1,250 metres by 61 metres], an operations building, and a radio range.

In 1950, runway 10-28 was extended to 6,000 feet [1,829 metres]. It was repaired in 1982 but reduced to 1,524 metres in length for economic reasons.

From 1947 to the mid-1950s, Gore Bay was an active airport, used by TCA and the RCAF as a refuelling stop, for there were no airports at Sudbury or Sault Ste. Marie. Also during this period, the airport was a base for aerial and magnetometer surveys north of Manitoulin Island and Elliot Lake.

In 1975, telecommunications staff left the airport, and communications were directed through the Sault Ste. Marie station.

Since 1988, Manitoulin Air Service has been operating scheduled and charter service at Gore Bay Airport, and the airport is used by many tourist aircraft from the United States. From September 15 to December 31, 1988, the airline transported over 325 passengers to or from the airport, and in that year, there were 2,697 aircraft movements.

There is now one full-time employee at Gore Bay, the airport manager, C. Beange. The first airport manager was S.B. Lee, who went there from Armstrong Airport, who was succeeded by J. Rumley in 1955.

Source:
Transport Canada, Ontario Region.

Grand Forks Airport
(British Columbia)
Grand Forks Airport opened in 1928 at the site now occupied by the hospital, and was relocated in 1946 close to the present arena grounds. The

new airport was built in 1970 by Grand Forks, with assistance from the department of transport, on land provided by the city. Operating costs have been subsidised by Transport Canada since 1972.

The airport has one paved runway (07-25: 1,310 metres long) and a small terminal building. Vernon helicopters and British Columbia's forestry services are based there, as well as eight to ten private or corporately owned aircraft.

In 1988, 2,833 aircraft movements were reported.

Sources:
1. Transport Canada, Pacific Region.
2. The Corporation of the City of Grand Forks.

Grande Prairie Airport
(Alberta)

In February 1927, the town council of Grande Prairie passed a resolution in favour of obtaining a site for an airport. Construction began in the fall of 1928 on a quarter section of land owned by the federal Department of the Interior. The Department of National Defence ceased to have responsibility for the forestry patrol, and the site was returned to the Department of the Interior.

112. Grande Prairie Airport, Alberta, c. 1928.

That department leased the site to the town of Grande Prairie in June 1933 for a period of five years. The site was licensed in the name of the town on May 18, 1937, and was known originally as Johnson's strip. It is now used by the Grande Prairie Gliding Club.

The Department of Transport gave the town a capital grant to finance airport improvements in August 1939. However, on January 23, 1940, the town was asked and subsequently agreed to turn over the airport to Transport so that additional work could be done to improve the facilities in connection with the new air route from Edmonton to Whitehorse. Runway construction began in May 1941. The entry of the United States into the war increased the importance of this air route, which became the Northwest Staging Route. There was considerable new construction, some of which was undertaken by the U.S. to improve its own operations; Grande Prairie was among the sites improved. In fact, the USAF constructed a new airport with two runways in the fall of 1942, and all operations moved there. These American facilities were purchased by Canada at the end of the war (see Chapter 10).

The USAF operated Grande Prairie until 1945 and then turned it over to the RCAF. The Department of Transport took it over on April 10, 1951, and still operates it. The airport licence was issued on December 8, 1951.

The old air terminal was built in 1942, improved in 1944 by the RCAF, expanded by the Department of Transport in 1964 and finally removed in 1980 after having been replaced by the new air terminal that was completed in 1979. Funds for its construction were advanced by the province of Alberta under an agreement stipulating that the Department of Transport would pay the capital back over a number of years. Participation by the province in this project and another at Lethbridge made it possible to provide two

113. United Air Transport from Edmonton, Grande Prairie, c. 1930.

badly needed air terminals several years in advance of the capital program for terminal development across Canada.

The airport is six and a half kilometres from Grande Prairie and 438 kilometres northwest of Edmonton. It has two paved runways: 11-29, at 1,981 metres, and 07-25, at 1,890 metres. Both are 61 metres wide. The airport areas is 465 hectares.

The airport is served by Time Air Inc. and Air BC. Time Air operates Dash 7 and 8 aircraft, along with the F-28 and both originates and terminates flights in Grande Prairie with an average of five daily round-trips. Air B.C. operates Dash 8 and BA-14 aircraft with an average of eight daily round-trip flights. It also originates and terminates flights at Grande Prairie.

The following helicopter companies are based at the airport: Highland Helicopters Ltd., Canadian Helicopters, Canwest Aviation Ltd., Peace Helicopters Ltd., and Precision. Others using the airport include oil company and forest industry aircraft, forestry water bomber bases, Shell Oil, Grandair, Proctor and Gamble, Wapiti Aviation and Grande Prairie Air Service.

In 1980, when the airport enjoyed the effects of the short local economic boom it had 169,000 passengers and 79,750 aircraft movements. In 1988, however, aircraft movements had dropped

114. Terminal building, Grande Prairie Airport, 1956.

to 36,714 with only 103,300 passengers.

CP Air, which had operated at Grande Prairie since 1943, opened a new air cargo facility in 1981. Shortly after the amalgamation of PWA, Time Air and CP Air the company announced its termination of service to Grande Prairie and left on April 29, 1988.

There are currently nine hangars on the airport. The old Tissington hangar burnt down on April 2, 1971, and the Johnson Trusses facility burnt down during 1981.

Over the years, the following have served the Department of Transport as airport managers:

Alex Thurber
Dave Devlin
Doug Willmer
Lloyd Goltz
Don Hector

Sources:
1. Transport Canada, Western Region.
2. R.L. Clarke, "Airport Notes" (Ottawa: Transport Canada) [unpublished collection].
3. D. Hector, Airport Manager, Grand Prairie Airport.

Grise Fiord Airstrip
(Northwest Territories)

The settlement at Grise Fiord (meaning "Pig Fiord" in Norwegian) is located on the southern coast of Ellesmere Island—near ruins of the Thule culture—and is Canada's most northerly Innuit community. In 1957, the RCMP moved their post at Graig Harbour, sixty kilometres west, to Grise Fiord. Relocation of Inuit families from Port Harrison, Quebec, and Pond Inlet appears to have been successful: the Inuit established a co-operative in the late 1960s and a school was built in 1962.

Because the difficult terrain is restrictive, the original aerodrome and the present aerodrome are located in the same area. The present aerodrome does not meet zoning criteria and thus cannot be licensed. Upgrading of the existing runway (609 by 23 metres) commenced in 1976-77 and was completed in 1980-81; an apron was built, a meteorological pad, and access road. (The runway—an unlicensed gravel strip, operated by the N.W.T. government— was constructed to less than the minimum standard length of 914 metres because of difficult terrain). Above-ground airfield lighting was installed, complete with approach lights and hazard beacons. The Northern Canada Power Commission extended the powerline to the aerodrome at the same time.

An interim passenger shelter, a trailer, was installed in the summer of 1985.

Airport lands, which are presently under the administration and control of the Department of Indian Affairs and Northern Development, will be transferred to the government of the N.W.T.

The settlement is served by Kenn Borek Air Ltd. using Twin Otter aircraft twice per week.

In 1987, there were 179 aircraft movements and 167 in 1988. In 1986 and in 1987 there were seven hundred passengers.

Hunting, trapping, fishing, handicrafts, and tourism are the industries of the area.

Source:
Transport Canada, Central Region.

Halifax International Airport
(Nova Scotia)

Halifax International Airport was built by the Department of Transport near Kelly Lake on land provided by the city of Halifax. Operated by the Department of Transport it opened in June 1960 with a temporary licence.

The airport at Kelly Lake was not the first air base in the Halifax area. In 1918, the Canadian government, at the urging of Britain, set up its first military air unit in Canada at Baker's Point near Dartmouth. It was a base for the newly formed Royal Canadian Naval Air Service (RCNAS), which was to operate Curtiss HS-2L flying boats on anti-submarine patrols. Until Canadian personnel could be trained, the air station was operated by the U.S. Navy Flying Corps. World War I came to an end before the RCNAS was ready, and the unit was disbanded (see Chapter 3). In 1920, however, the old base, then known as the Dartmouth Air Station, was used by the Air Operations Branch of the Air Board for the repair and maintenance of its seaplanes and flying boats. The station was included in the published List of Airharbours Available for Use during 1922 as follows: "Halifax, N.S. Government Air Station for Seaplanes—over 800 yards square—licensed for Customs" (see Chapter 7).

As early as July 5, 1919, the city of Halifax town planning board asked the federal government to build an airfield for the Halifax area. The government replied that the civil aviation organization under the Air Board[1] was not yet set up, but that generally the government would expect municipalities across Canada to provide their own airfields.

On January 19, 1927, the Civil Aviation Branch of the Department of National Defence made an offer of technical assistance if Halifax would consider the provision of an airport in the area. This was a time when the government was beginning to consider the feasibility of air-mail service; it announced its plan to assist in the formation of light aeroplane clubs; and, in 1928, the decision was made to construct the Trans-Canada Airway, in which established municipal airports would play an important role. The city of Halifax was, indeed, interested, and many proposed sites were examined and rejected for technical or financial reasons. Finally, in September 1928, a Civil Aviation inspector recommended a site at Bluebell Farm: it was the only one available and would be expensive to develop. The city held a plebiscite in April 1929 and received approval to spend $190,000. On June 16, 1930, construction began on two landing strips: 1,800 by 600 feet [549 by 183 metres], and 2,000 by 600 feet [610 by 183 metres]. An airport licence was issued on January 9, 1931, and the city leased the airport to the Halifax Aero Club[2] for operation and maintenance. Profits, if any, were to be shared equally by the city and the club. The first airplane to land at the airport was a Curtiss Robin of Atlantic Airways, piloted by Cliff Kent, in February 1931.[3]

The Aero Club manager—Don Saunders— also served as airport manager. Saunders had been a captain in the RFC during the First World War and was a well-known pilot in the Maritimes. He later became regional manager of airports for the Department of Transport in the Atlantic region.

During the winter of 1929-30, a contract was let by the Post Office for the conveyance of mail between Halifax and Montréal for connection with ocean steamers. This was later continued on a daily basis with a connection at Moncton until

June 1931, when it was cancelled in the interest of economy.

In 1931, Pan American Airways (see Appendix 26), with a U.S. Post Office contract and a Canadian permit, began to operate a daily service during the summer from Boston and Portland to Saint John and Halifax, with the option of extending the service to Sydney and St. John's. Pan American permits to operate in Canada did not, however, allow it to carry mail or passengers between Canadian points—a rule that did not please residents of Halifax and Saint John.

In a 1931 report, the Superintendent of Airways of the Civil Aviation Branch stated that, at Halifax, "the changes there in the last two years are miraculous; it is now a really good airport and has a good hangar and Club House. Pan American added a small passenger station last year and their daily service during August and September helped to establish confidence in the future of the airport on the part of Citizens."[4] Approximately $225,000 had been spent on the airport.

In 1932, the mayor asked the government to make some improvements to the airport as an unemployment relief project, but nothing was done. In 1937, the new Department of Transport offered the city one-third cost-sharing assistance for airport improvement; and in late 1938, the department finally undertook the extension of the two runways by 200 and 250 feet [61 and 76 metres].

During 1938-39, studies undertaken to see if the airport could be expanded for airline use, led to the conclusion that it could not be adequately developed. It was decided instead that the new Dartmouth airfield being built for the RCAF could be used, while limited improvements to the Halifax airport would make it suitable for light aircraft.

The new Dartmouth Airport was ready in early 1940, and RCAF squadrons operating Digby and

Hudson aircraft moved in. Work on the Halifax airport ceased, and the city leased the site to the government as an army camp. The airport, whose licence was cancelled on October 15, 1941, was closed that year, and a portion of it, located off Chebucto Road and fringing the Westmount housing development, became Saunders Park. A memorial was erected there, marking the site of Halifax city's original airport, commemorating Donald Saunders as "Mr. Flying."

Lack of a suitable airport at Halifax had prevented the extension of Trans-Canada Air Lines' service, but in 1941, TCA began flying to Dartmouth Airport: its trans-continental air service was now completed from coast to coast. Dartmouth continued to serve as the Halifax airport until 1960.

During the war, Halifax retained its interest in having a civil airport. In October 1945, it asked the Department of Transport for technical assistance in locating a site for a new airport. Many locations were examined and rejected during the next few years, and it was not until late 1954 that a site near Kelley Lake, recommended by Trans-Canada Air Lines, was approved. The Department of Transport agreed to construct and operate the new airport, provided the city acquire the land and transfer it to the Department for one dollar. Both parties agreed and construction of the two runways, 8,000 by 200 feet [2,438 by 61 metres], and 6,200 by 200 feet [1,890 by 61 metres], began in November 1955. These were lengthened to 8,800 and 7,700 feet [2,438 and 2,347 metres], respectively, prior to the opening of the airport. Meanwhile, in 1952, the minister of National Defence, on behalf of the Navy (which now operated the Dartmouth Airport) agreed that the Department of Transport could, at its own expense, extend the Dartmouth runways to meet Trans-Canada Air Lines' needs.

The new Halifax International Airport became operational in June 1960 and a licence permitting

115. The first Halifax airport, Nova Scotia, c. 1930.

full Instrument Flight Rules (IFR) operation was issued on July 1, 1960. The air terminal building was officially opened on September 10, 1960.

The airport is located in the county of Halifax, thirty-seven kilometres north of Halifax, the provincial capital. Land near the airport boundary is sparsely settled. The AeroTech Business Park, operated by the Halifax County Industrial Commission, borders Halifax International Airport on the south and east boundaries, and attracts high tech and airport-oriented businesses. Major tenants include Pratt & Whitney Canada and Litton Systems Canada. The closest communities are Enfield, eight kilometres north, and Waverley, eleven kilometres southeast.

In 1960, the airport provided facilities for approximately 180,000 passengers. When it became apparent in the early 1970s that the growth rate at the Halifax International Airport was greater than at the average airport, a long-range development plan for the terminal resulted in a new holding room being opened in July 1976. The original air terminal building contained 182,273 square feet [16,933 square metres] of floor space. The opening of the new facility added approximately 54,000 square feet [5,017 square metres]. In 1988, two temporary passenger walkways were constructed in an effort to improve the service for passengers using

the two major regional carriers. Plans are progressing to establish holdrooms connected to both these walkways.

Since 1985, Halifax International Airport has changed from a terminus operation for central Nova Scotia to a hub/spoke airport operation for the entire Atlantic region.

The number of passengers using the airport has increased from 180,000 in 1960, to 1,700,000 in 1980, and to 2,300,000 in 1988. Aircraft movements totalled 23,671 in 1961, 84,588 in 1980, and 100,042 in 1988.

The domestic catchment area population for approximately 595,000 in 1984, is extended by a tendency for air passengers from southern New Brunswick to use the Halifax International Airport. The catchment area for international travellers is estimated at 1,714,000, drawing passengers from Nova Scotia, New Brunswick, and Prince Edward Island.

The original site expropriated by the city consisted of 2,750 acres [1,113 hectares]. Future expansion will become necessary, and it is hoped that the surrounding lands will remain commercially zoned in order to prevent residential growth in the area. Other changes in the airfield have produced centreline lighting for reduced visibility landings and resurfacing of runways because of increased weight of modern aircraft.

The airport has eleven hangars: Canadian Airlines International Hangar, Halifax Hangars Limited, Atlantic Airways Limited, Air Canada Cargo Centre, Air Canada maintenance hangar, IMP Group Paint hangar, IMP Group small hangar, IMP Group large hangar (used for overhaul and repair of military aircraft), IMP Group Heliport hangar, IMP Group Aerocenter, Air Halifax hangar. An automobile service station operated by Petro Canada Limited, is located at Halifax International.

There are five customhouse brokers, six freight forwarders, five refueling agents, and

three servicing companies established on the airport premises. In the air terminal building, there are five rent-a-car agencies and retail stores, the newest being a Laura Secord candy shop and Beales' Bailiwick, a quality craft shop.

Six scheduled airlines—Air Canada, Canadian Airlines International, Air Nova, Air Atlantic, Air St. Pierre and, most recently, KLM Royal Dutch Airlines—are currently operating at the airport. In addition, there are five agencies offering charter services: Eastern Flying Service Ltd., the IMP Group Ltd., Atlantic Sky Service, Versatile Air Services Ltd., and Cougar Air Inc..

The employee population of the Halifax International Airport stood at 3,000 in February 1988.

The following is a list of the airport managers who have served at Halifax International Airport since its opening in 1960:

E.A.King	1960 to 1961
G.W. Blatchly (acting)	1961 to 1963
D.L. Forbes	1963 to 1964
G.W. Blatchly (acting)	1964
J.J. Cole	1964 to 1968
H.B. Miller (acting)	1968 to 1969
K.J. Robinson	1969 to 1973
G.M. Knox	1973 to 1987
Janet Shrieves	1987

Sources:

1. R.L. Clarke, "Airport notes" (Ottawa: Transport Canada) [unpublished collection].

Footnotes to Halifax Airport

[1] The board itself was only just coming into being; the Air Board Act had been passed on July 16, 1919. The board was the interim department responsible for aviation in Canada.

[2] The club was founded in 1928, initially using two Moth seaplanes that were housed in the old hangar at the Dartmouth Air Station. The aircraft were flown

across to the Halifax side each morning and back in the evenings. The club did not fly in winter. (Source: Ted Watson, Moncton).

[3] According to Watson, Kent was one of six pilots brought to Canada from England by Curtiss Reid of Montréal. He was a pilot with Imperial Airways in Newfoundland in the late 1930s.

[4] Public Archives Canada, MG 30 E243, vol. 7.

Hall Beach Airport
(Northwest Territories)

Hall Beach, located on the northeastern shore of the Melville Peninsula, facing Fox Basin just inside the Arctic Circle, was chosen as a DEW Line site. In 1957-58, the USAF constructed the Hall Beach Airport in accordance with an agreement of May 5, 1955, between the governments of Canada and the United States of America. The USAF continued to operate the airport until 1977, when the Department of Transport assumed responsibility for the operation and maintenance of the strip, including establishment of air/ground communications for advisory services. In 1982, Transport built a terminal building, which comprises two baggage areas, a passenger waiting area, the airport manager's office, and two airline offices rented by First Air and Canadian Airlines International.

There is only one Department of Transport employee on site, the airport manager (currently Ron Vaslett), who occupies one of the two one-bedroom living quarters in the terminal building. The other is occupied by the mechanic. The airport is maintained by contract staff.

There is one gravel runway, 124T-304T, which in 1981-82 was moved twenty-three metres to the east. However, it was soon apparent that the new location was too close to the DEW Line hangar, and so it had to be moved once again. It was later relocated 122 metres to the north and extended to 1,646 by 46 metres.

Hall Beach was the area headquarters for DEW Canada, and the Transportation Centre for the sites from Cam Three eastwards to Dye Main. The depot level maintenance and the communications centre for the DEW Line were all located at Fox Main.

The airport is served by Canadian Airlines International using 737 aircraft with four scheduled services per week, and First Air, using Twin Otter and HS-748 aircraft, with twelve scheduled services per week.

In 1987, there were about 8,000 passengers at Hall Beach.

The principal industries and activities in the area are fishing, hunting, exploration, tourism, and archaeology.

Sources:
1. Transport Canada, Central Region.
2. Pat Wield, Operations Manager, High Arctic Airports, Transport Canada.

Hamilton Airport
(Ontario)

In 1911, one year after the large air meets at Montréal and Toronto, a meet was held in Hamilton, giving citizens their first opportunity to see an airplane in flight. The events were staged from an area known as the O'Heir Survey near the Tuckett Farm on Beach Road. Such well-known aviators as Charles F. Willard, an American barnstormer and exhibition flyer, and J.A.D. McCurdy, the first man to fly an airplane in Canada, took part.[1]

In 1926, J.V. Elliot founded an aviation school on Beach Road near Stewart Park. The hundred acre [forty-one hectare] field was designated as a Customs airharbour in 1928.

In 1927, when the government announced its plan to encourage the formation of light aero-plane clubs, the Hamilton Aero Club was the first to join the scheme. It was founded by Major Robert Dodds MC, a well-known early pilot and aviation personality, who was the club's first president and instructor. He managed International Airways and was later superintendent of Canadian Airways' air-mail operation in eastern Canada. He held many senior appointments in the Civil Aviation Branch of the Departments of National Defence and Transport, and was actively involved in the development of airports for the British Commonwealth Air Training Plan during the World War II. He later became director of Civil Aviation, a position from which he retired in 1958.

In early 1927, when the federal government asked major cities in Canada to consider establishing their own airports Hamilton was one of the first to show interest. Major General Mac-Brien, the managing director of International Airways of Canada, encouraged the city to acquire an airfield site that his company offered to lease for five years and would help to develop.

A new airport site of 227 acres [ninety-two hectares] was acquired two and a half kilometres south of the Elliot field and west of Redhill Creek. It had three sod runways, 2,640, 2,260, and 2,760 feet [805, 689, and 841 metres] long. Although not then finished, it was opened on June 6, 1929. The airport was operated by International Airways, to which the temporary airport licence was issued. The Civil Aviation Branch of National Defence suggested that the licence be in the city's name, and later that year the licence was changed (see Appendix 20).

International Airways was soon taken over by Canadian Airways, and the agreement with the city was dissolved. Construction and maintenance of the airport ceased, but some flying continued. In October 1930, the city agreed to have the airport in good condition for the following spring. This work cost $65,000.

The Hamilton Aero Club moved to the new airport in 1930, and Leavens Brothers' flying operations were also located at the site. In March 1930, the Post Office awarded a contract to Canadian Airways for a daily air-mail service that included Hamilton.

By the summer of 1931, the airport had two hard-surfaced runways and two hangars. One had been built by International Airways and one by the Aero Club. The airport also had field lighting and a beacon to meet the requirements of the Detroit-to-Toronto air-mail service. This service was discontinued in April 1932, as a government economy measure.

The city leased the airport to the Aero Club in October 1931, for the rent of one dollar a year, and the club assumed responsibility for its operation and maintenance.

A civil aviation report dated October 21, 1931, mentioned Hamilton in these terms: "Hamilton Airport is owned by the City, which had spent $300,000 on its development without any assistance from the Government. The airport is managed by the Aero Club for the City. With the exception of Vancouver, no city in Canada has made a larger investment in aviation."[2] In 1931, the Hamilton airport was lighted for night flying, the entire cost of which was borne by the city.[3]

The cancellation of air-mail services in 1932 and the financial strain of the depression caused much opposition to the city's operation of the airport, but by 1935 there was a revival of interest, and the airport committee became very active. It put strong pressure on the government to have Trans-Canada Air Lines or another scheduled airline serve the airport, but without success. The committee was most unhappy about the refusal, because it had been a pioneer aviation centre and its airport investment exceeded that of other cities.

In December 1936, Hamilton Airport became eligible for a capital assistance grant from the new Department of Transport. By early 1938, the proposed improvements had not been made and one runway was declared unsafe. Work began in the summer, and R. Gibson, distributor for Cub Aircraft, proposed to expand his operation at the airport and build an assembly plant. More work was done in 1939. In 1940, the expanded activity of Cub Aircraft and test flying made it necessary to set up air traffic control under rules agreed to by both the Aero Club and Cub Aircraft. Meanwhile, local interest groups in Hamilton began to pressure the city to encourage the industrial development of the valuable airport site.

The Aero Club of Hamilton had a contract with the Department of National Defence to train pilots for the RCAF under the Provisional Pilot Officer Training Scheme. When the British Commonwealth Air Training Plan (BCATP) was set up at the end of 1939, the club suggested there should be an Elementary Flying Training School (EFTS) at the Hamilton Municipal Airport, even though the airport was not then large enough for the air traffic such a school would generate.

In 1940, the Department of National Defence built a new airport for the RCAF at Mount Hope, fifteen kilometres southwest of the city. No. 10 EFTS was established there in October under the BCATP operated by Hamilton Flying Training School Ltd., a subsidiary of Hamilton Aero Club. In 1943, after No. 10 EFTS moved to Pendleton Airport, the RAF established No. 33 Air Navigation School at the airport, also under the BCATP. No. 1 Wireless School moved to Mount Hope from St. Hubert in the last year of the war.

By 1943, the Hamilton Aero Club had completely withdrawn from the municipal airport, and Cub Aircraft became the principal remaining activity.

The future of the municipal airport was discussed again at the end of the war. Although the field was in poor condition, it was near the city, while Mount Hope, which had three hard-surfaced runways, hangars and other facilities, was fourteen and a half kilometres southwest. In spite of the condition of the municipal airport, activities there increased. Cub Aircraft Ltd. were still operating, and Warriors Air Service began in 1945. Narvy Aircraft Ltd. also used the field. In 1946, the latter two companies combined to become Peninsula Air Service Ltd. President, Glen White, became airport manager in 1948. The Hamilton Aero Club, however, did not return to its old quarters, but remained at Mount Hope.

The future of the city airport remained unresolved during the late 1940s. Its condition was poor and its potential for expansion severely reduced by buildings that had encroached on airfield approaches. It was used by light aircraft in daylight only, and by November 1948, only Peninsula Air Service remained. In 1949, Glen White founded Trans Aircraft Ltd. from the old Cub Company, but the Hamilton Municipal Airport had to close in November 1951.

In 1945, the Department of Transport took over Mount Hope Airport on a caretaker basis. Throughout 1946 and most of 1947, the airport was not licensed although it was used, at times, by an RCAF auxiliary squadron and by the Hamilton Aero Club (since August 1946). The club occupied part of hangar no. 3, and obtained an airport licence in December 1947. Club Manager Reg Spence was nominally in charge of civil operations.

In 1952, the city applied for and received the airport licence on the basis that it lease part of the airport, including half of hangar No. 4 (to which the Aero Club would move). The RCAF would be responsible for flying control and airfield maintenance, and the city for civil aviation and airport management. Glen White, who had managed the municipal airport since 1948, became the Manager of Mount Hope for the city

116. Hamilton Airport (Elliot airport), July 1927.

in 1952. He remained president of Peninsula Air Service, which moved to Mount Hope.

In 1950, the RCAF established an Auxiliary Squadron at Mount Hope and, in 1952-53, extended two of the airport's runways to accommodate jet fighter aircraft, and restored night flying. Genaire Ltd. and International Harvester Ltd. leased hangar space from the RCAF, which remained at the airport until 1962, when the city assumed responsibility for its maintenance.

In 1964, Hamilton leased the whole airport from the Department of Transport and appointed a Civic Airport Committee to which the airport managar reported.

Hamilton finally obtained scheduled air service in 1961 when Nordair's Seaway Route was inaugurated linking Montréal, Kingston, Oshawa, Toronto, Hamilton, London, and Windsor. The service ended in 1962. Since 1969, Nordair has operated a scheduled service linking Hamilton with Windsor, Ottawa, Montréal, and Pittsburgh using Boeing 737 aircraft.

On May 1, 1969, the Department of Transport established airport traffic control and an Instrument Landing System (ILS) was commissioned in August of that same year. The airport receives an operating subsidy from Transport Canada. A terminal building was constructed by the city in 1969 with a capital grant from Transport: the building has been enlarged several times.

Hamilton Airport has three paved runways: 06-24, at 1,824 metres long, 12R-30L, at 1,581 metres, and 12L-30R, at 2,438 metres.

The following operators are based at the airport: Glanford Aviation Ltd., the Canadian War Heritage Association, Condor Aviation, Peninsulair, Tempus Air Ltd., Intact Aviation, the Hamilton Flying Club and the EAA.

Canadian Partner and United States Air Express offer scheduled air service.

The Regional Municipality of Hamilton-Wentworth and the Department of Transport have made considerable efforts to promote and upgrade the airport. At the beginning of the 1980s, $48.6 million was spent to build a 2,438-metre runway and to construct a new terminal building and related facilities to attract traffic from Toronto. In 1987, a new air traffic control tower was constructed and commissioned.

That same year, 150 hectares of land, previously a golf course, was acquired to permit the removal of trees and allow for unobstructed use of the new runway.

Following the government's 1985 policy of economic regulatory reform, a number of cargo, charter, and commuter airlines began operating out of Hamilton Airport, including Pan Am Express, Allegheny, Nationair and United Parcel/Purolator, and Canadian Partner. At the time, road access to the airport became an issue which has not yet been resolved, although discussions are ongoing.

On August 18, 1989, it was announced that there would be immediate improvements to the terminal apron, taxiways, power supply, and terminal facilities. Officials also stated that some airlines had agreed to transfer some of their charters to Hamilton. Shortly thereafter, Transport Canada officials met with Air Canada and Canadian Airlines International to determine their needs.

In 1988, Hamilton Airport recorded a total of

117. Elliot Airport, Jack V. Elliot Air Service, Hamilton, Ontario, 1928.

140,000 aircraft movements and over 95,000 enplaned and deplaned passengers.

Peter Ainsworth has been airport manager since 1981: Sid Mitchell had held the position for the previous decade.

Sources:

1. Transport Canada, Ontario Region.
2. Dr. Neil McArthur, *Airport and Community. Five case studies of local airport land use*. Report prepared for Transport Canada.

Footnotes to Hamilton Airport

[1] F.H. Ellis, *Canada's Flying Heritage* (Toronto: University of Toronto Press, 1961), pp. 79-80.

[2] Public Archives Canada, MG 30 E243, vol. 7.

[3] Canada, Department of National Defence, *Report on Civil Aviation* (Ottawa: King's Printer, 1931), p.15.

Hay River Airport
(Northwest Territories)

The town of Hay River is located on the south shore of Great Slave Lake, 1,118 kilometres by road from Edmonton, and has a population of 4,000. It was founded in 1894 by Anglican missionaries. A disastrous flood in the spring of 1963 caused the relocation of the town-site to higher ground, and it is now one of the most modern communities in the Northwest Territories. The airport is three kilometres north of the town.

The United States built the airport in 1942-43 as part of the Canol project which led to considerable development—roads and aerodromes—in the Territories.[1] After the war, Canada bought this and other U.S. built airports from the United States.

Hay River Airport was taken over by the Department of Transport on October 1, 1944, and an airport licence was issued on November 1, 1948. Today, the airport is operated by Transport Canada.

The site has two runways: 04-22, which was 914 metres gravel and 305 metres paved, and 13-31, 1,828 metres long, paved. Initially, the main building was a Quonset hut; but a new terminal building was constructed in 1970.

The airport is served by Canadian Airlines International with connections to Edmonton by way of Buffalo Airways, Carter Air Services, Landa Aviation, and Hay River Air Services. All are based at the airport and provide charter services.

In 1988, the airport had 25,960 passengers and 8,863 aircraft movements. The following have served as airport managers:

Cec Rogers	1944 to 1947
E.R. Osborne	1947 to 1955
J. Unger	1955 to 1956
H. Semple	1956 to 1977
G. Whitlock	1977 to 1978
B. McNeil	1978 to 1980
G. Whitlock	1980 to 1987 (worked at the airport from 1949)
D. Creighton	1987 to 1989

Sources:
1. Transport Canada, Western Region.

2. R.L. Clarke, *Airport notes* (Ottawa: Transport Canada) [unpublished collection].
3. G. Whitlock, former Airport Manager, Hay River Airport.

Footnote—Hay River Airport
[1] See Footnote under Fort McMurray

Igloolik Airstrip
(Northwest Territories)

Among Canadian Arctic sites, Igloolik on Melville Peninsula provides a unique record of unbroken Inuit habitation. Captains Perry and Lyon of the Royal Navy spent the winter of 1822-23 at Igloolik.

In the early 1920s, an Inuit, Umik of Pond Inlet, set up a mission and preached his version of Christianity. A Roman Catholic Mission was established in 1931 by Father Bazin of the Oblate Missionaries. But it was not until 1939, when the Hudson's Bay company set up its first post that the Igloolik did not have to travel to Pond Inlet or Repulse Bay to trade. By 1959, the addition of a school and new government buildings led to the emergence of Igloolik as a settlement of major status in the northwestern Baffin region. The Igloolik Co-operative was incorporated in 1963. The settlement gained hamlet status on July 1, 1976.

The original airstrip 3,600 by 80 feet [1,097 by 24 metres] was developed by the community at the only suitable location within one to three kilometres. The aerodrome facilities included a low intensity airfield lighting kit, a one-room heated passenger shelter, and a Non-Directional Beacon (NDB), which had been funded by the Department of Indian Affairs and Northern Development and installed by Transport Canada.

Transport Canada carried out improvements to the existing aerodrome under the Arctic Air Facilities Policy. The gravel runway was upgraded to dimensions 300 by 100 feet [14 by 30 metres] commenced in 1979, and was later increased to 3,400 by 100 feet [636 by 30 metres], complete with 200-foot [61-metre] overruns. Both ends of the improved runway surface were feathered into the existing overshoot areas, giving a licensed length of 3,800 feet [1,158 metres], with a 450-foot [137-metre] overrun at runway 32 that is usable for take-offs.

The NDB was replaced with solid state equipment in 1977-78. In 1978-79, a powerline to the airport was completed. Communication and meteorological equipment and instruments were installed in 1979. A new passenger cargo shelter was erected in 1979-80; permanent airfield lights were installed in 1983-84—a temporary aboveground lighting kit, funded by the government of the Northwest Territories had been in place prior to this.

Airport lands which are presently under the administration and control of the Department of Indian Affairs and Northern Development will be transferred to the territorial government. The runway is licensed in the name of the government of the Northwest Territories.

The settlement is served by First Air with HS-748 and Twin Otter aircraft, 12 times per week.

There were 299 aircraft movements in 1987 and 681 in 1988. The site had 4,200 passengers in 1986, and 5,100 in 1987.

Hunting, fishing, trapping, and handicrafts are the industries of the area.

Source:
Transport Canada, Central Region.

Iles de la Madelaine Airport
Formerly House Harbour
(Quebec)

Before the Second World War, aircraft visiting the Magdalen Islands landed on a sand beach on the north shore of Grindstone Island. By 1941, Maritime Central Airways was carrying out regular service from Mainland (Maritime provinces) to the beach, and continued to do so until the airport at House Harbour was constructed.

In 1948, the Department of Transport agreed to provide two grants-in-aid of $25,000 each for the construction of airstrips on Amherst and Grindstone Islands, so that a year-round air service could replace the uncertain marine transportation on which communities were dependent. The funds would be made available provided the appropriate municipalities would agree to acquire the necessary land and build and maintain the airstrips.

Under this arrangement, an airstrip for Harve Airport was built on Amherst Island, between 1949 and 1951 from grants totalling $47,600. It was used occasionally by Maritime Central Airways, whose regular base of operations was the beach on Grindstone Island.

From 1949 to 1954, negotiations were conducted intermittently with various municipalities on Grindstone Island. Among the sites considered were Cap-aux-Mules on the south shore, Cap-au-Tran, and Etang-du-Nord. In 1955, the municipality of House Harbour and the Department of Transport (Atlantic Region) agreed that the municipality would purchase the land, the department would construct an airport and House Harbour would operate it.

The airport, consisting of two sand runways, 07-25 and 16-34, each 4,000 by 300 feet [1,219 by 91 metres], was completed in October 1956 at a cost of $195,000. Maritime Central Airways, contracted by the city to operate and maintain the airport, was able to use the strips during summer months, but hard-surfaced runways were needed for year-round service. The Department of Transport constructed two paved runways at a cost of $325,000: 08-26, at 4,500 feet [1,371 metres], and 16-34, at 3,600 feet [1,097 metres]. The

118. Air terminal building Iles de la Madeleine, December 1981.

work was completed in the fall of 1959.

A temporary airport licence was issued in January 1960 and, on the ninth of that month, the airport was officially opened. A permanent licence was issued on June 28, 1965.

In August 1968, the Department of Transport acquired ownership of the airport for a nominal sum of one dollar and, on September 6 of the same year, contracted the operation and maintenance of the airport to Eastern Provincial Airways (which had acquired Maritime Central Airways). The airport was operated under contract by Versatiles Air Service Ltd. during the early eighties. Today, maintenance is provided by Fernand Cyr, who won the contract in 1989.

In 1972, Eastern Provincial Airways asked that runway 07-25 be extended to 5,500 feet [1,676 metres], but the request was refused. The following year, municipal and provincial authorities requested that the runway be extended to 6,000 feet [1,829 metres] and asked for the installation of an Instrument Landing System (ILS), but careful studies revealed that a 6,000 foot [1,829-metre] runway would not be feasible.

Quebecair began an Iles de la Madeleine-Gaspé-Mont Joli-Quebec city — Montréal service on October 27, 1974. The airport is now served by Inter-Canadian, Air Atlantic, Air Alliance, and Icarus.

The airport name was changed from House Harbour to Iles de la Madeleine Airport on December 4, 1975, and on April 1, 1976, in response to municipal and provincial representations, administration of the airport was changed from the Atlantic region to the Quebec region.

In 1988, there were 41,904 passengers and 5,897 aircraft movements.

A new air terminal building was opened in December 1981 and a new runway, 08-26, was built in 1982.

Sources:
1. Transport Canada, Quebec Region.
2. R.L. Clarke, "Airport Notes" (Ottawa:Department of Transport) [unpublished collection].

Inuvik Airport
(Northwest Territories)

For many years, the vast area known as the Mackenzie River Delta was served by the principal settlement—Aklavik, but as activities gradually increased, larger facilities were required. Construction is extremely difficult and costly because of the soil conditions. In 1953, the government investigated the possibility of moving its facilities to a better location. After an extensive reconnaissance of the entire delta area for a new town-site, an engineering team recommended a location on the east channel of the Mackenzie River and named it East Three. The new town was later renamed Inuvik, which is Inuit for 'the place of man.'

One of the first requirements of the new town-site was an airstrip. Construction started in 1956 using a new method of crushed rock-fill placed on top of the permafrost without disturbing it. The runway (6,000 by 150 feet [1,828 by 43 metres]), parking apron, and connecting taxiway were constructed in this manner with a minimum thickness of eight feet [two and a half metres] of crushed rock. Construction was finished in 1958, and the airport licence was issued on November 24, 1958.

By 1959, the airport was providing a twenty-four-hour service and was designated as a Customs port of entry. Since 1959, the apron has been expanded and taxiways and roads have been built to the aviation development area. Many buildings have been constructed, including the terminal, car park facilities, and the control tower. Runways, taxiways, and the apron have been paved. The total expenditure amounted to more than $7.5 million.

The airport is located thirteen kilometres southeast of the townsite, 201 kilometres north of the Arctic Circle and ninety-seven kilometres inland from the Arctic Ocean. By air, Inuvik is 772 kilometres from Fairbanks, Alaska, 1,086 kilometres from Yellowknife, 1,931 kilometres from Edmonton, and 2,092 kilometres from Churchill.

Inuvik, which has grown steadily since its founding, is a major centre in the Northwest Territories, with a strong administrative base and a population of approximately 3,500. Until 1978, the only means of transportation to Inuvik was by air. The completion and opening up of the Dempster Highway, however, has connected the centre to the south by way of Dawson city, Whitehorse, and Fort St. John to Edmonton and Vancouver. Air continues to remain the primary mode of transport for goods and passengers because of the vast distances to the south by road and the lack of ice bridges or ferries during spring and fall.

Canadian Airlines International and Northwest Territorial Airways currently provide fifteen scheduled flights a week using Boeing 737 aircraft between Inuvik and Edmonton with stops at Norman Wells and Yellowknife. Alkan Air provides return service five times a week to Whitehorse, Mayo, Dawson, Old Crow, and Inuvik. Aklak Air has daily service out of Inuvik to delta settlements Aklavik, Fort McPherson, and Tuktoyaktuk, and twice weekly to Sachs Harbour, Paulatuk, and Holman Island. Nahanni Air Service runs return three times weekly between Norman Wells, Fort Good Hope, and Inuvik.

In addition, the following operators are based at Inuvik: Canadian Helicopters, Western Arctic Air Ltd., Sunrise Helicopters Ltd. and Inuvik Air Charter. There is also an RCMP detachment located at the Airport.

The military uses the airport as a Forward Operating Location for its CF-18 fighter jets and support aircraft, and is planning hangars, a mess hall, and a taxiway. During the summer months, the Department of Environment stations an Electra aircraft at the airport for ice reconnaissance. Halfway between the town of Inuvik and the airport at Long Lake, there is a seaplane base for float- or ski-equipped aircraft. Transport Canada controls the land surrounding the lake and leases out waterfront lots.

A large-scale land-fill program was begun by Transport Canada in 1974 to fill the uneven ground in the aviation development area, hence attracting prospective tenants associated with the vast gas and oil exploration activities at the

119. Inuvik air terminal and control tower, N.W.T., 1975.

time. Approximately 188,200 cubic yards of fill blasted from quarries was used over the permafrost—in the way that the runways had been constructed—providing approximately 926,800 square feet [86,100 square metres] of level area with access roads suitable for aviation development. There is a total of thirty-eight Transport employees, housed in Crown-owned accommodation.

Airport activity declined with the cutback in oil exploration. Aircraft movements fell from a peak of 50,800 in 1973, to a low of 21,600 in 1979; in 1988, movements were 20,846. In 1975, there were 46,000 passengers; in 1979, 40,700; in 1988, 76,500.

The following have served as airport managers at Inuvik:

Doc Abrey	1958 to 1963
Ken Wilams	1963 to 1966
Barney MacNeil	1966 to 1978
Dave Funston	1978 to 1980
Barney MacNeil	1980 to 1984
Marty Ratio	1984 to 1985 (acting)
Robert Hess	1985 to 1986 (acting)
Peter Tremblay	1986 to 1988
Jim Logan	1989

Source:

A. Axani, former Acting Airport Manager, Inuvik Airport.

Iqaluit Airport
Formerly Frobisher Bay Airport
(Northwest Territories)

Frobisher Bay, on Baffin Island, was discovered in 1576 by the English navigator, Martin Frobisher, during his search for a passage from the Atlantic Ocean to China. Throughout the eighteenth and nineteenth centuries, the area was frequented by whalers and traders. The present village, named Iqaluit in 1987,[1] is located near the site of a traditional Inuit fishing village. Iqaluit is a regional administrative centre for the Northwest Territories government. It has a large hospital, schools, and a modern hotel, and is now a small town with many of the amenities of the south, despite its harsh Arctic climate.

The United States constructed the Frobisher Bay Airport, now renamed Iqaluit, in 1942-43 with the permission of Canada as part of the so-called Crimson Route. This was to be a short stage ferry route to northern Europe from California by way of The Pas (this facility to be built by Canada), Churchill, Coral Harbour, Chimo and Frobisher,[2] Greenland, and Iceland. By March 17, 1943, a gravel runway, 6,000 by 200 feet [1,829 by 61 metres], had been established. Canada bought the U.S.-built airports for $27 million in 1944. But Frobisher (Iqaluit), remained under control of the U.S. Air Force for some time. Hangars, a radar station, and other buildings were constructed after the war by the USAF; and it was not until 1950 that the RCAF took over the airport.

In 1953-54, the location of the runway was changed from 09-27 to 18-36. It was 6,000 feet [1,829 metres] long. In 1957, paving of the runway was completed and, in 1960, it was lengthened by 3,000 feet [914 metres] to 9,000 feet [2,743 metres] long, with a width of 200 feet [61 metres].

From 1955 until 1958, Frobisher (Iqaluit) was the main supply airport for the construction of the DEW Line.[3] By July 1955, the Foundation Company of Canada, the primary DEW Line contractor, had as many as three hundred aircraft operations a day through Frobisher and requested help in controlling them.

On September 1, 1957, the Department of Transport took over the airport from the RCAF and operated and maintained it for the principal users, Strategic Air Command of the USAF,

120. Iqaluit (Frobisher Bay) Airport, N.W.T.

which conducted in-flight refuelling operations from there. During the peak period, the department employed 225 people. In 1963, the USAF abandoned its Frobisher (Iqaluit) operations and Transport personnel were reduced in number. The USAF gave the federal building, maintenance hangars, radar station and fuel storage to the Department, which, in turn, made the buildings available to the Department of Northern Affairs in 1964. The federal building, which had been a combined operations building and living quarters for the USAF, is now used for airport offices and as a residence for high school students. It is operated by the territorial government.

Iqaluit Airport is sometimes used as an alter-

121. Iqaluit (Frobisher Bay) Airport, 1974.

nate for aircraft flying the polar route between Western Canada and Europe. Canadian Airlines operates a service to Montréal eleven times per week (B-737). Nordair, now Canadian, was the first to put jet aircraft into service in the Arctic in November 1968. Territorial Airways, based at Iqaluit, operates the connection with Yellowknife twice per week and with Ottawa daily, in addition to flights from and to the Arctic airports (Lake Harbour, Cape Dorset, Broughton Island, Pangnirtung, Clyde River, Pond Inlet, Baker Lake, etc.). Air Baffin, also based at Iqaluit, operates a charter flight with twin-engine Cessna-type aircraft. Iqaluit also receives DC-8 and L-1011 aircraft for technical stops from and to Paris and San Francisco.

In 1988, the airport had 55,000 passengers from about 12,000 flight movements.

Airport maintenance is contracted; the manager and the fire chief are Transport Canada employees.

Sources:

1. Transport Canada, Quebec Region.
2. R.L. Clarke, "Airport Notes" (Ottawa: Department of Transport) [unpublished collection].

Footnotes to Iqualuit Airport.

[1] "The name, meaning 'place of fish' in Inuktitut, has long been used by the Inuit for their community at this centre of the eastern Arctic on Baffin Island. In 1971, the municipal Hamlet of Frobisher Bay in the area of the airbase was incorporated. It became a village in 1974, a town in 1980. . . As to the name of the water feature, originally called Frobisher Strait in 1576 by Martin Frobisher, there are no plans to change Frobisher Bay." Alan Rayburn, 'Native Names for Native Places,' *Canadian Geographic* (April/May 1987), p.88.

[2] The location was originally code-named Crystal Two and was an American weather-radio station prior to the construction of the airport.

The Distant Early Warning (radar) Line extended from the Alaska-Yukon border to Baffin Island; it was planned by the United States and Canada, but funded by the U.S.

Isachsen Airstrip
(Northwest Territories)

Isachsen, on Ellef Ringnes Island, 531 kilometres northwest of Resolute Bay, was a Joint (Canada-U.S.) Arctic Weather Station established in 1948.

The first three station personnel were flown in on April 3, 1948, with Jamesway huts and emergency rations and shelters.[1] By April 13, approximately 84 tons of supplies had been delivered to the station site. Most was carried in U.S. Air Force C-54 aircraft, but two loads of bulky grading equipment were brought in by C-82 aircraft, commonly known as 'the flying box car.' By April 21, a total of 161 tons had been airlifted to the station, so completing the operation except for the later delivery of a few miscellaneous items.

The initial station complement was to be six men—three Canadians and three American. An additional American mechanic helped with airstrip construction during the first summer, and because for efficient operation seven men were required permanently, the staff level was kept at this figure. However, for equitability in the Arctic Project, the ratio was changed to four Canadians and three Americans—because Mould Bay was staffed with three Canadians and four U.S. personnel.

The station staff erected all the buildings in the camp throughout the spring and summer of 1948: five Jamesway huts, three tents, and one pre-fabricated wooden building. Two pre-fabricated wooden buildings were added in 1949.

Isachsen continued to grow until September 1978 when the station was closed. Occasional inspections of the site have been made since. The gravel airstrip, 05-23, is 4,800 by 180 feet [1,463 by 46 metres] and has remained usable.

Source:
Transport Canada, Central Region.

Footnote to Isachsen Airstrip
[1] Jamesway huts are described in the chapter under Eureka.

Kamloops Airport
(British Columbia)

A survey for an airport site was made in 1930, and in June 1931 the city of Kamloops leased forty-six acres [nineteen hectares] from B.C. Fruitlands for an airport at the present site. Between 1936 and 1938, a gravel runway, 2,840 by 150 feet [866 by 46 metres], was constructed. In 1938, the city bought the land, plus another thirty acres [twelve hectares]; and this became the airport.

In April 1939, the Department of Transport agreed to grant money to the city for airport development, including runway surfacing, and the city planned to build hangars. The runway was paved in September 1939.

On April 13, 1939, an Aeronca, piloted by Cyril Jackson, made the first official landing at Kamloops Airport; on August 1, 1939, the airport was designated a port of entry under the Customs Act; and the official opening was on August 5, 1939.

Gilbert Flying School moved to Kamloops Airport from Vancouver on April 16, 1942—all civil flying on the coast had been cancelled because of the war—and became the only flying school west of Winnipeg at the time.

Between 1939 and 1945, the airport was developed extensively by the RCAF as an alternate for the United States Air Transport Command, which was ferrying aircraft through Canada and Alaska to the USSR. An additional 861 acres [385 hectares] of land was purchased, the runway was rebuilt, and a taxiway, large parking apron and twelve buildings were added. Construction started in December 1942 and was completed in June 1943. Surplus land was later sold to the Department of Agriculture and the city of Kamloops to reduce the size of the airport to its present 570 acres [231 hectares].

In a ceremony in May 1964, the Governor General of Canada, the Earl of Athlone, named the airport Fulton Field, in remembrance of Wing Commander John Fulton, DSO, DFC, AFC, a native of Kamloops who was the first commanding officer of 419 (city of Kamloops) Squadron.

When Kamloops Airport was passed over to the Department of Transport from the RCAF on August 29, 1945, it had thirteen buildings and one runway a mile [1.6 kilometres] long. In 1947, the airport was leased back to the city of Kamloops.

Central B.C. Airways started operating at Kamloops and, in 1951, the airport became the company's headquarters, with owner Russ Baker in charge. In 1952, it moved its head office to Vancouver and, in 1952, changed its name to Pacific Western Airlines.

On March 13, 1950, Canadian Pacific Airlines inaugurated daily service to Kamloops, using DC-3 aircraft, with connections to Williams Lake, Quesnel, Prince George, and Vancouver.

In 1961, the Department of Transport took over the airport and a period of extensive expansion and building commenced. Runways and taxiways were rebuilt and associated field lighting was installed.

In 1963, the main runway, 08-26, was extended to 5,500 feet [1,676 metres], and Canadian

Pacific began using Convair aircraft. A new air terminal building and maintenance garage were built and officially opened in August 1964.

The aeradio station at Ashcroft was moved to Kamloops in 1966, and provided twenty-four-hour service from April 1.

In August 1967, air traffic control began—operated from a car, until a temporary tower was opened in October. Aircraft movements reached 34,609 that year, and 29,200 passengers passed through the airport.

Pacific Western Airlines took over the service from CP Air in 1968 and provided daily jets to Vancouver and Calgary, with Boeing 737s.

Because of poor visibility during fall and winter, relocation was considered, but an extensive search for a new site, carried out by Transport personnel, was unrewarding.

In 1969, the air terminal building extension was completed, providing more space in the lobby. A coffee shop was added and parking space was expanded. B.C. Airlines—taken over by Pacific Western Airlines in 1970—inaugurated scheduled service to Kelowna, Penticton, Williams Lake, and Prince George.

Construction of a new air traffic control tower, begun in 1970 was completed in May 1971.

In 1972, the airport was threatened by the flooding of the Thompson River, and Transport staff worked around the clock constructing dykes to keep the airport in operation. Much of the site had been flooded in 1948; and during the winters of 1984 and 1985, more than $2 million was spent to riprap the river bank adjacent to the airport.

Runway 08-26 was extended to 6,000 feet [1,829 metres] and during the following year, arrival and departure modules were added to the air terminal building, and the maintenance garage was extended to provide a firehall. By 1974, aircraft movements were up to 60,314 per year and the number of passengers handled had increased to 149,027.

In 1975, a track guidance localizer, a middle marker, an outer marker, and a Non-Directional Beacon (NDB) were put into operation, and in 1976, runway 08-26 was given an asphalt overlay.

Telecommunications equipment was moved from the air terminal building to a nearby trailer in 1977, and a staff lunchroom was built in the air terminal building.

In 1978, the grass runway, 04-22 was rebuilt and paved. It is 914 metres long.

Spurred by a booming economy, major construction projects such as the Mica and Revelstoke dams, and the rapid growth of the city, airport business soared to peaks of 91,943 aircraft movements in 1977, and 235,600 passenger movements in 1981.

In May 1983, construction began on an enlargement of the firehall and maintenance garage, and on Phase 1 of the new air terminal building project. In October, Distance Measuring Equipment (DME) was commissioned. Coupled with the localizer, this lowered landing limits and increased reliability of scheduled services.

In June 1984, Intercity Air started a service between Kelowna, Kamloops and Vancouver using Convairs. The company was subsequently bought out by Time Air, and the service was discontinued in March 1985.

Work on the new terminal building started in 1984 and was completed in 1985. In October 1985, Air BC started service to Kamloops using De Havilland Dash 7 aircraft, and in November, Time Air took over the Prince George-Kamloops-Kelowna route from NT Air, which had flown it under contract to PWA.

In 1986, the old terminal building was completely renovated to become the operations building, providing upgraded quarters for airport administration, electronics maintenance, the flight service station and the Atmospheric Environment Service (AES) weather office. The

Fulton Field plaque was relocated to a viewing mound adjacent to the terminal building and was re-dedicated on May 15, when the operations building was officially opened by Honourable E. Davie Fulton.

Major reconstruction of the southside road (Aviation Way) was undertaken in 1987. Almost a third of the remaining 1943 main apron on the north side was also re-built and two new helipads were installed. In April, Aviair Aviation commenced service from Kamloops to Kelowna, Williams Lake, and Prince George—the route was extended to Dawson Creek in 1989.

In April 1989, Canadian Airlines International (CAIL), successors to PWA, ceased operations in Kamloops, ending twenty-one years of scheduled jet service. CAIL routes were taken over by Time Air, operating De Havilland Dash 7 and Dash 8 aircraft.

The airport's fiftieth anniversary was celebrated in 1989 with special events to commemorate the official opening. Guests included many aviation pioneers: Joe Bertalino, who had barnstormed in Kamloops in 1921 and had subsequently worked as Transport Canada inspector; Sheldon Luck, who flew the first scheduled air-mail flight to Kamloops in 1939; Margaret Rutledge, one of Canada's first female commercial pilots, who co-piloted with Sheldon Luck on flights to Kamloops. Also present were some of those responsible for the development of the airport, including Ian Clark, Mansell Barron (who founded one of the first aircraft maintenance companies on the airport) and former airport managers Bill Rempel and Lloyd Rowland.

Scheduled airline service is now provided by Time Air, Air BC, and Aviair Aviation. Kamloops Air Services, Seymour Air, Highland Helicopters, and Canadian Helicopters offer charter services; and sixteen companies provide aviation-related services while another five provide support services.

Airport business was adversely affected by the recession in the early 1980s, and in 1986 the new Coquihalla Highway to Vancouver further reduced passenger traffic. In 1988, the airport had 137,579 passengers and there were 43,638 aircraft movements.

Various titles have been used for the person in charge of the airport. The following served:

D. Dick	airport attendant 1947
Tom Green	airport attendant 1949
R.K. Hill	airport manager 1953
Ian Clark	airport agent 1951-57
R. Evans	resident manager 1951
W. Rempel	airport manager 1971-76
L.A. Rowland	airport manager 1976-83
Ben Rathbone	airport manager 1983-89

Sources:
1. Lloyd Rowland, former Airport Manager, Kamloops Airport.
2. Transport Canada, Pacific Region.
3. Ben Rathbone, former Airport Manager, Kamloops Airport.
4. Neil Burton, Canadian Airlines International Ltd.,
5. Ian Clark and the Kamloops Museum.

Kapuskasing Airport
(Ontario)

Kapuskasing Airport is located on a site 3.2 kilometres square, approximately three kilometres west of the town. The land had been part of the Dominion Farm and was transferred to the Department of National Defence in 1933. It was selected as the site for a supplementary airfield on the Trans-Canada Airway, and an unemployment relief camp was set up there in the summer of 1933, when construction of the field began. A hangar built in 1935 still stands, and is used as an air terminal and maintenance garage. The relief camp was closed in June 1936, but work continued under control of the Civil Aviation Division of National Defence.

A Department of National Defence aircraft landed at the site on August 20, 1935; and by the winter of 1936-37, the airfield was sufficiently completed to allow the creation of compacted-snow runways—a first for a Department of Transport airport. When, on December 9, 1936, a Canadian Airways Ltd. aircraft piloted by "Punch" Dickins landed, the rolled runway was proven to be satisfactory—although expensive—and the operation was continued until spring.

Construction continued; and on February 27, 1938, Trans-Canada Air Lines made its first landing with an Electra aircraft, continuing the acceptability of snow-rolling for winter runway maintenance. Nevertheless, two runways, 17-35 and 10-28, were paved in 1938, and December 1, Trans-Canada Air Lines(TCA) moved operations to Kapuskasing from the Porquis Junction airfield. A permanent airport licence was issued in February 1939.

When scheduled services began on April 1, 1939, the airport was leased to TCA for operation and maintenance. The Department of National Defence took over the field at the outbreak of war, and it was designated for military use on December 23, 1939.

The runways were reconstructed and new lighting installed in 1944; and in 1946, the RCAF disbanded its operation (124th Ferry Squadron) at the airport.

In 1957, TCA stopped service to Kapuskasing, and Austin Airways took over the scheduled service with DC-3s. Because of low traffic volume, Austin Airways discontinued service in March 1959; the maintenance level of the airport was reduced, and only one runway was kept open.

When Mattagami Skyways began daily service to Timmins in 1962, runway 17-35 was reconstructed in the same year. Mattagami was bought out in 1967 by Georgian Bay Airways, which continued scheduled service to Timmins until 1970, when the service was taken over by White River Air Service.

The Kapuskasing Flying Club was formed in 1976., and now operates four aircraft at the airport.

In 1978, the air terminal was expanded, and, at the same time, the beacon tower, an old landmark, was removed. In the same year, Kimberly Air and Spruce Falls Power & Paper Co. erected two hangars.

Runway 17-39 was resurfaced in 1980, and extended to 4,900 feet [1,493 metres], to accommodate the HS-748 aircraft operated by Austin Airways (now Air Ontario), which provided a cargo service to the Hudson Bay area. The runway was further extended to 9,912 feet [896 metres] in 1982. Runway 10-28 is 2,940 feet long.

Scheduled flights for freight and passengers to Moosonee, Winisk, and Attawapiskat began in 1983, and is now provided by Norontair and Air Ontario. In 1987, 23,200 passengers travelled through Kapuskasing Airport.

In 1984, a new terminal building and associated parking lot were built. Road access was also upgraded for general aviation areas.

As well as Air Ontario and Norontair, the following operators are based at the airport: Spruce Falls, Kimberly Air Services, Frontier Air Services, and the Kapuskasing Flying Club.

The airport is operated by Transport Canada. The following served as airport managers:

George McKnight	1939
Fred Child	to 1960
Bill Benedetti	1960 to 1965
Robert Laberge	1965 to 1990

Sources:
1. Transport Canada, Ontario Region.
2. R.L. Clarke, "Airport Notes" (Ottawa: Transport Canada) [unpublished collection].

Kelowna Airport
Formerly Ellison Field, B.C.

The city of Kelowna has shown a keen interest in aviation from the earliest days of flying. In1913, a Curtiss plane took off from floats on Okanagan Lake, left the floats behind, and landed on wheels at Vernon. In the early 1920s, Captain Trim flew his Curtiss from the polo field east of the present Gyro Park; and Barney Jones-Evans and Lowell Dunsmuir flew from a grass field in east Kelowna. Rutland field opened in 1927; and Radium Hot Springs Air Services operated from Rutland and Vernon in 1929, offering flying instruction and charters. In 1931-32, Yukon Southern Air Services used Rutland aerodrome on its service between Oliver and Vancouver. It continued to be used until 1945, when a new site was required.

In 1946, the citizens of Kelowna authorized the city to buy a parcel of land (then Dickson Ranch) for an airport. A 3,000 by 100 ft [914 by 30 metre] grass strip was completed in 1947, which became known as Ellison Field. (The airport was situated in the district of Ellison, but the property is now part of the city of Kelowna). A small terminal building was constructed in 1947, and the first flight from Ellison Field was made in the late fall of that year. The municipal hangar was built and the airport was licensed in 1948. Cliff Renfrew's hangar was built and Imperial Oil installed a gas pump in 1949.

From 1947, Okanagan Air Services offered flight instruction, charter service, and timber cruising, until 1951, when it formed Okanagan Helicopters Ltd.

122. Kelowna air terminal, B.C., 1947.

In 1957, the Department of Transport gave a grant to the city of Kelowna for airport improvement, and a gravel runway, 3,000 by 150 feet [914 by 46 metres], was constructed. The city then negotiated with the Department for a paved runway, to attract scheduled air service; and in July 1958, Canadian Pacific Airlines came in with a daily DC-3 service to Vancouver. This continued until August 1959. A 5,350 foot [1,631-metre] paved runway was completed in July 1960, which required additional land bought by Kelowna. In return for capital assistance from Transport, title to the whole site was transferred by Kelowna to the Department, which in turn leased the airport back to the city. On July 1, 1960, Canadian Pacific Airlines re-opened its

123. Kelowna Airport, B.C., 1983.

Kelowna-to-Vancouver service—now with Convairs.

Pacific Western Airlines replaced CPAL in 1969 and provided scheduled flights to Calgary and Vancouver using Boeing 737 and Convair 640 aircraft.

A new terminal building was opened on October 26, 1968, and the control tower, commissioned in June 1971, was constructed by the city with a grant from Transport. In 1982 and 1983, a $2.4 million addition and renovation of the terminal building was completed; the terminal apron was enlarged; an itinerant aircraft parking apron was constructed north of the terminal apron; and a heli-pad was built south of the apron.

In 1985, the air terminal building almost doubled in size, to include a new concourse, departure room, baggage handling facilities, a restaurant/bar, gift shops and more space for the airlines, Customs and Immigration and car rentals.

The airport is still operated by the city of Kelowna with an operating subsidy from Transport Canada. Between 1969 and 1973, the city collected an airport user fee, charged to passengers enplaning or deplaning from commercial aircraft.

The airport is served by Canadian Airlines International with B737 aircraft, Air BC with BAC 146 and DH7, and Time Air with Dash 7 aircraft. Also based at the airport are Kelowna Flightcraft Ltd., Southern Interior Flight Centre Ltd., RCMP Air Detachment, Kelowna and District Flying Club, and Okanagan Aero Engine.

In 1988, the airport had 398,034 passengers, and there were 54,153 aircraft movements. (Activity at the airport was at its peak in 1981 with 406,664 passengers and 78,554 aircraft movements).

Plans to extend the runway from 1,624 metres to 2,225 metres, at a cost of $45 million, will accommodate aircraft up to the Boeing 767.

The following served as airport managers:

Ralph Hermansen	to 1968
Eric Davison	1968 to 1972
M.L. Sheehan	1972 to 1980
Roger Sellick	1980 -

Sources:
1. Kelowna Airport site master plan.
2. Transport Canada, Pacific Region.
3. R. Sellick, Airport Manager, Kelowna Airport.

Kenora Airport
(Ontario)

The town of Kenora is located in northwest Ontario at the north end of the Lake of the Woods. In its pioneer days, it was known as Rat Portage—after the water channel used by muskrats as they went from Lake of the Woods to the Winnipeg River. In 1905, the name was changed to Kenora: the "Ke-" was taken from Keewatin (Kenora's sister town), the "-no-" from Norman, Kenora's west suburb, and the "-ra" from Rat Portage.

The Hudson's Bay Company first established a post on the Winnipeg River in the early 1800s, and later moved it to the present townsite, where it was the first building in Rat Portage. Following a dispute between the provinces of Ontario and Manitoba from (1870 to 1884) as to which province had jurisdiction over the area, it was first incorporated as a Manitoba town; but when Ontario took the dispute to the Privy Council in London, England, it won jurisdiction over the area, and Kenora was incorporated as an Ontario town in 1892.

In 1932 and 1933, the Civil Aviation Branch of the Department of National Defence looked for a suitable airport site. Although construction began in October 1933 it was stopped in June 1934, because the site would be too expensive to develop. A new area was chosen, one and a half kilometres from the first, and work began in late 1934 as an unemployment relief project. It was closed down on June 30, 1936 and reopened in August as a civil aviation project. But progress was unsatisfactory and the project closed down again in November 1936. The airport was finally completed in early 1939, with three turf runways: 07-25, at 4,000 by 150 feet [1,219 by 46 metres]; 13-31, at 2,600 by 200 feet [792 by 61 metres]; and 04-22, at 2,700 by 200 feet [823 by 61 metres].

In 1956, runway 07-25 was paved with asphalt. It was extended in length to 6,000 feet [1,829 metres] in June 1978. Runway 04-22 was closed permanently in August 1977. Runways 07-25 and 13-31 are maintained during the summer months, but there is no maintenance on runway 13-31 during the winter months, and it has only low intensity lighting. Visual Approach Slope Indicator System (VASIS) and a medium-intensity lighting system were installed on runway 07-25 as part of the extension project, and illuminated wind cones placed at each end. There are no approach lights on either runway, but the airport is served with an Non-Directional Beacon (NDB) and VHF omni-directional Range (VOR), Tactical Air Navigation Equipment (TACAN) for instrument approaches. Distance Measuring Equipment (DME) is also on site.

Air tourist traffic began to develop in the Kenora area after the war, and a permanent airport licence was issued in the name of the Department of Transport on November 14, 1946, for use by light and medium aircraft. When runway 07-25 was paved in 1956, the airport could handle DC-3 aircraft.

In 1960, an air traffic control unit was established, and a new operations building was constructed in 1967-68. The building was completely renovated as an air terminal in 1973, and a Customs extension was built in 1984.

Strobe lights were installed on runway 07-25 in 1988, taxiways B and C were paved in 1989, and a Customs building the same year.

The airport is served by Norontair using Twin Otter aircraft with fourteen movements per week, Bearskin using Beech 99 aircraft with forty-six movements per week, and Tempus using Convair 580 aircraft with four movements per week.

Charter service is offered by Walstein Air, Air Dale, Austin Airways, Kenora Air Service, and Helitac.

There were 26,200 passengers and 20,857 aircraft movements in 1988.

The following have served as airport managers: Bill Duffield, Andy Quinn, Tom Inverrity, and Jim Richardson.

Pickell's Airport Services currently operates the airport under contract for Transport Canada, and the current airport manager is Earl Pickell.

Sources:
1. Transport Canada, Central Region.
2. R.L. Clarke, "Airport Notes" (Ottawa: Transport Canada) [unpublished collection].

Kingston Airport
(Ontario)

The original Kingston Airport, located on Reid Farm, was north of Concession Street and west of Division Street. On March 1, 1929, the city leased seventy acres [twenty-eight hectares] of land for five years and voted $5,000 to the newly-formed Kingston Flying Club for a hangar and equipment.

The airport had two runways: one running north-south, at 2,300 feet [701 metres], and another running east-west, at 1,280 feet [390 metres]. The airport licence was issued on December 4, 1929. The land lease lapsed in September 1933 and was not renewed, but in 1934, a new lease was issued in the name of the flying club which was still operating at the same site in 1939. The airport licence was cancelled in September 1942 and flying was suspended.

The present airport is a new site at Collins Bay and was constructed in 1940-41 for the British Commonwealth Air Training Plan (BCATP). The location had already been selected in 1938 for a new general aviation facility. The airport was named Norman Rogers Airport for the local member of parliament and minister of National Defence, who was killed in an aircraft crash en route from Ottawa to Toronto in 1940. No. 31 Service Flying Training School (SFTS) RAF was established there in 1941 to train pilots for the Fleet Air Arm: it flew Fairey Battles and later Harvard aircraft. In 1944, the RCAF took over the school and it became No. 14 SFTS.

In January 1946, the airport was transferred to the Department of Transport, leased to the city of Kingston for operation as a municipal airport. It was licensed in the city's name in March 1946. The Kingston Flying Club ran the airport for the municipality; but Transport was not satisfied with the operation and threatened to cancel the licence. Attempts to have Trans-Canada Air Lines serve the city were unsuccessful. From 1953 to 1958 the club earned some revenue from the local naval reserve squadron which housed its aircraft in the club's hangar.

In 1955, local residents who objected to aircraft-noise and to rumoured plans of expansion, asked the Department of Transport to close the airport and move operations to the disused wartime airport near Gananoque, but the city opposed any move.[1] In the same year, the township of Kingston passed a by-law to restrict expansion, as it wanted to subdivide the area east of the airport for housing development; and it

asked Transport to build a new airport north of the city. The Department refused, but in 1959, acquired 112 acres [forty-three hectares] on the east side of the airport to protect the possibility of runway extension.

In 1959, Vicom Corporation (a manufacturer of machine tools and devices) subleased the entire site—except for the flying club area—from the city and, in effect, became the city's agent in managing airport affairs, including the leasing of building space and maintenance. The city subsidized airport revenues to the extent of $3,000 per year for maintenance. The agreement with Vicom lasted until October 1964.

Over the years, many airlines looked at the possibility of establishing scheduled air service through Kingston, and in 1961, Nordair included Kingston on its Montréal-Oshawa-Toronto-Hamilton-London-Windsor route. The service was suspended in August 1962 because of operating losses. In 1963, the Kingston Flying Club tried to provide a non-scheduled class-three service three times weekly to Toronto Island and Montréal; but this ended after five months.

In June 1962, the township presented a brief to the Department of Transport claiming that the airport was a hazard to the orderly growth, and again requested that a new airport be built north of the city. Again, Transport declined to act.

In 1972, after several years of sharing airport management with the township council, the city of Kingston decided to assume full reponsibility, not only for the management of the airport, but also for its development. The city purchased the site from Transport in June 1974 and agreed upon a plan to improve the facility on a cost-sharing basis.

The main runway, 19L-01R, has been extended to 4,600 feet [1,402 metres], new lighting has been installed, an aeradio flight information service set up by Transport Canada, and a new Non-Directional Beacon (NDB) installed. These

124. Aerial view, Kingston Airport, Ontario.

improvements were in place for the 1976 yachting Olympics in Kingston.

An equipment garage was built in 1987, new Flight Service Station (FSS) facilities in 1989, and a new terminal building and the reconstruction of the east-west runway are in the planning stages.

At present, AOG Heliservices, the Kingston Flying Club, and Central Airways are based at Kingston Airport.

Of the wartime hangars, nos. 1 and 2 have been demolished. Number 3 is used by Kingston Tennis World, no. 4 is used by the city, and no. 5, by the flying club and the city. Central Airways took over Toronto Airways' hangar; AOG Heliservices built their hangar and offices in 1981.

Air Ontario and Canadian Partner provide scheduled service (sixteen flights a day, Monday through Friday, with reduced service on weekends).

In 1988, there were 36,900 passengers and 43,716 aircraft movements at this site.

Don Timlin is now airport manager.

Sources:
1. McArthur, Dr. Neil M. *Airport and Community. Five case studies of local airport land use.* Report prepared for Transport Canada.

2. *Wartime base in Kingston now a thriving airport.* Carnet, September 1978.

3. Don Timlin, Airport Manager, Kingston Airport.

Footnote to Kingston Airport

[1] The Gananoque Airport was built under the BCATP as a relief airport for the service training school at Kingston.

Kuujjuaq Airport
Formerly Fort Chimo Airport
(Quebec)

Kuujjuaq Airport, originally known as Fort Chimo Airport, is located in northern Quebec near Ungava Bay and was built by the United States, with Canadian permission, as part of the U.S. Air Force's Crimson Route.[1] This was to be a short stage overland ferry route to northern Europe from California by way of The Pas, Churchill, Coral Harbour, Chimo,[2] Frobisher, Greenland, and Iceland. Construction was started by the USAF in September 1942 and by April 5, 1945, a landing strip 3,000 by 150 feet [914 by 46 metres] had been developed.

The province of Quebec granted a reservation of the airport site, approximately eight miles square, (16.3 hectares) to the Department of Transport effective August 1, 1944. Problems which arose as some Inuit settled within the area reserved for the airport, were eventually solved; and in 1970 a new provincial Order in Council authorized airport use of all lands required.

After the war, Canada purchased the U.S.-built airports in this country for a sum of $27 million. The USAF, however, remained caretaker of the Chimo Airport for a number of years after the war.

In August 1945, the RCAF asked the Department of Transport to maintain the airport for photographic survey operations during 1946 and 1947; and by fall 1947, only twelve American civilians remained in charge of the airport, which was fully transferred to the RCAF in October 1949. In September 1950, Transport took over responsibility from the RCAF on a minimum maintenance basis, using equipment left on the base. Most of this was destroyed by fire in January 1951, following which two employees with home-made drags maintained the strip.

Meanwhile (on February 26, 1948) Mount Laurier Aviation Ltd. was given permission to use the airport to transport mining exploration teams.

During the construction of the DEW Line (1956-58),[3] Chimo Airport became one of the main airports on the Mont Joli-Moncton-Goose Bay-Frobisher route.

On January 31, 1955, a temporary airport licence was issued to Boreal Airways, which operated the airport under lease from the Department of Transport. A new temporary airport licence was issued to Nordair (which took over Boreal) on June 10, 1958. The Foundation Company of Canada, the prime DEW Line contractor at the time, was responsible for maintenance.

Upon completion of the DEW Line, Transport received complaints that the airport was not adequately maintained as an en route facility for aircraft flying to and from Frobisher Bay (Iqaluit). Consequently, on September 30, 1958, the airport lease to Nordair was cancelled, and the Department assumed operation on December 15, 1958, with a temporary licence which was made permanent in September 1966. By then, Fort Chimo Airport was an important base for commercial operations in the Arctic, as well as being an alternate airport for commercial and military aircraft en route to Frobisher Bay.

A rotating beacon was installed in October 1958. At that time, airport users were Nordair, Wheeler Airlines, World Wide Airlines, the RCAF, and Nordair.

90. Fort Chimo (Kuujjuag) Airport, Québec, 1977.

In 1968, major resurfacing began on the main runway, 08-26; and to avoid closing the airport, gravel runway 14-32 was reopened. September 30, 1969, the paving of runway 08-26 was completed.

Nordair provided Class-two service three times a week with DC-4 aircraft, and in March 1969 made its first Boeing 737 jetliner flights; Wheeler Northland and St. Felician Air Services used the airport year-round as a base for charter flights.

In 1972, a new air terminal building was constructed at a cost of $416,112, and an Instrument Landing System (ILS) and Non-Directional Beacon (NDB) were installed. Nordair moved into the new terminal on February 14, 1973.

On August 28, 1980, the name of the airport was changed from Fort Chimo to Kuujjuaq, after the nearby municipality.

The airport road which now connects the village of Kuujjuaq to the existing airport site was Kuujjuaq's first landing strip. Today the airport has two runways, 07-25, at 1,829 metres paved, and 13-31, at 1,646 metres, with a gravel surface.

The airport is currently served by Canadian Airlines International, Air Inuit, and Johnny Mays Air Charter Inc. In 1988, there were 30,200 passengers and 9,185 aircraft movements.

The following have served as airport managers:

Louis Soucy, Joe Valkovik, Yvanoe Phillippe, Paul C. Vautour, R. Allard, J. Cardinal (1979-1981), J. Flowers (1981), Jean-Pierre Bourget (1987), Michel Lafrance (1987-1989), and Robert Duquette (1989).

Sources:
1. Transport Canada, Quebec Region.
2. R.L. Clarke, "Airport Notes" (Ottawa: Transport Canada) [unpublished collection].

Footnotes to Kuujjuag Airport.

[1] See Chapter 10; and under Churchill Airport and Coral Harbour Airport.

[2] The location was originally code-named Crystal One and was an American weather/radio station before the construction of the airport.

[3] This is the Distant Early Warning (radar) line, which extends from the Alaska-Yukon boarder to Baffin Island. It was planned by the United States and Canada, but financed by the U.S. See Chapter 11.

Langley Airport
(British Columbia)

Langley Aerodrome, which opened in 1938, was built by the Department of Transport to serve as an intermediate field for the Trans-Canada Airway. The site was originally called Langley Prairie because it was flat and treeless.

In 1941, after the aerodrome was taken over by the Department of National Defence for the RCAF, improvements were made and it became a relief aerodrome for No. 18 Elementary Flying Training School of the British Commonwealth Air Training Plan at Boundary Bay.

At the end of the war, the Department of Transport took over the aerodrome and leased it to the township of Langley, which continues to operate it.

The airport, located thirty-nine kilometres southeast of Vancouver, is a popular recreational and flying training centre for the lower mainland, and serves single-engine and light twin aircraft. The proximity of Pitt Meadows Airport and the newly-opened Boundary Bay Airport, combined with the economic recession of the early 1980s, led to a drastic 50 per cent reduction in aircraft movements at Langley. In 1980, the site had 203,664 aircraft movements (compared with 279,963 at nearby Pitt Meadows); but in 1988, the number of aircraft movements at Langley was only 121,041.

The airport has two runways: 01-19 is asphalt and 640 metres long; 07-25 is turf and 701 metres long.

The control tower, operated by Transport Canada, was expanded in 1983-84.

Skyway Air Services and the Langley Flight Centre operate flying schools at the airport. Several helicopter companies are based at the site: Helilogistics, Can-Arc Helicopters Ltd., Tundra Helicopters, International Heliflight, and Helo Investments Ltd. Other fixed base operators are Rotech Industries Limited, Double J Aviation, Medco, and Teck Construction.

Sources:
1. Transport Canada, Pacific Region.
2. Michael Zrymiak, township of Langley.

La Ronge Airport
(Saskatchewan)

In 1947, the federal Department of Natural Resources built the first airstrip at La Ronge, Saskatchewan for mail freight and forest fire patrol, using Norseman, Beaver, Stinson, and DC-3 aircraft. It was taken over by the government of Saskatchewan, which started a scheduled air service, Sask Airways. The airport was also used by the smoke jumpers for forest fire fighting from 1958 to the mid-1960s.

Norcanair bought Sask Airways in 1963 and operated DC-3, Beech 18s, Canso, Bristol freighters, Beaver, Single Otter, Twin Otter, Aztec Twin, and C185-C180 aircraft usually on floats during the summer and on skis in winter.

In 1960, La Ronge Aviation erected a hangar on the cross strip (which had been built in 1953); and, starting with a C180, expanded its operation by acquiring a Beaver, Otter, and C185. Today, the company maintains more than fifteen aircraft.

Transport Canada and Saskatchewan built a new airport six and a half kilometres north of La Ronge in 1976. (The old site was razed and built over by urban development). There was a paved 5,000 by 150-foot [1,524 by 46 metre] main runway with high intensity lighting, Visual Approach Slope Indicator System (VASIS), VHF omni-directional Range (VOR), Very High Frequency Direction Funding (VHF/DF), and a twenty-four-hour flight service station. Taxiways A-B-C and the main ramp were paved, a gravel ramp for aircraft parking was built, and a paved ramp was provided for the Saskatchewan Water Bombing Operation. In this same year, Norcanair moved to the new airport with a temporary terminal, and La Ronge Aviation and Athabasca Airways built hangars.

In 1977-78, the government of Saskatchewan erected a large hangar to service their water bomber fleet, which today comprises three Cansos, five Gruman trackers, four CL215s, and five Light Twins as "bird dogs," or spotter planes. Woodland Aero also built its hangar.

Norcanair was bought in 1982 by High Line Airways, which operated a scheduled service to La Ronge and other points north. Then, in 1986, High Line was bought out by Time Air, which now operates a Dash 7 from La Ronge. Vic Protasenko has been base manager for Norcanair, High Line, and Time Air since 1970.

A hangar previously used by Norcanair for storage purposes, became the site of a Shell

Mobil's facility in 1989, for the sale of turbo, aviation gas, and Mobil refuelers.

A new terminal building with a Flight Service Station (FSS) cab was opened in September 1988, and during the following summer the main ramp was extended and paved.

La Ronge is operated by the Saskatchewan government Department of Highways and Transportation and does not receive federal subsidy. Employing more than 140 people, the airport is used by charter companies and tourists.

In 1988, there were 6,400 passengers and 30,343 aircraft movements.

Sid Dziki has been airport manager since 1970.

Source:
Transport Canada, Central Region.

Lethbridge Airport
(Alberta)

Aviation history in Lethbridge began on July 14, 1911, when Eugene Ely landed on a grass area enclosed by the race track at the exhibition grounds. Katherine Stinson, a well-known American pilot who made exhibition flights in Western Canada, used the field on July 27, 1918. (Ely's chief claim to fame was the fact that he was the first man to fly off the deck of a ship, landing on a beach in the state of Virginia).

On the evening of August 7, 1919, Captain Ernest Hoy landed at Lethbridge's second airfield, the Lethbridge Collegiate Institute site. He had made the first aerial crossing of the Rocky Mountains and flown from Vancouver with stops at Vernon, Grand Forks, and Cranbrook, in a 90 h.p. Curtiss JN-4 with a cruising speed of 75 m.p.h. [121 km/h], a ceiling of 7,000 feet [2,134 metres], and a range of four hours. The flight was made through passes rather than over the mountains because of the limited ceiling of the aircraft, with a total elapsed time of 16 hours, 34 minutes—the last stage from Cranbrook to Lethbridge taking 2 hours, 27 minutes.[1]

The site of Lethbridge's third airfield was south of the exhibition grounds which are now part of the Lakeview subdivision—the Collegiate Institute site was found to be too rough. The new location was used for five years by Captain "Jock" Palmer's Lethbridge Aircraft Ltd. until the company was dissolved. The following excerpt from a government report of May 17, 1939 shows Lethbridge's enthusiasm about developing an airport:

Lethbridge was one of the first cities in North America to consider the establishment of a municipal airport. On August 30th, 1920, the City Clerk wrote the Air Board[2] requesting advice in the matter. In September of that year, two sites were inspected, both of which were reported suitable for the purpose and the interest of the city in its airport has continued since that date.[3]

In the published list of airharbours available for use during the year 1922, Lethbridge is shown as having a private-commercial airharbour 600 by 800 feet [584 by 731 metres] in area.

In 1925, Southern Alberta Airlines was organized and Jock Palmer hired as a pilot. Its field was north of the CPR tracks, east of what is now North Mayor Magrath Drive, and south of Fifth Avenue North, and was the first to be properly marked; it had a hangar, beacon, and boundary lights, and it was used until Kenyon Field was developed in 1938. The site was abandoned because of the obstructions presented by grain elevators and a water tower.

The city council's licence application of July 1927 was granted on September 23, 1927. A press notice marking the occasion was recalled in a speech given in 1939:

The Minister of National Defence announces that a licence for a public Customs airharbour has been granted to the City of Lethbridge. The flying field is situated within the city limits and is therefore readily accessible. It is close to the power and telephone lines and the water supply. Its surface is level and the approaches to the field are unobstructed, so that it provides excellent facilities. The few improvements necessary have been carried out by the municipal authorities to the satisfaction of the inspecting officers of the Department, and the Department of National Revenue have concurred in the issue of a Customs Airharbour Licence in order to provide facilities for the entry of aircraft from the United States in southern Alberta.

Lethbridge is the second city in Alberta to take this important step, Edmonton having obtained a licence for a municipal airharbour some time ago.

The establishment of airharbours by municipalities throughout the country will do much to assist the development of aviation by creating facilities for air travel and the prompt response of the city of Lethbridge to the appeal issued by the Department last Spring, to Canadian municipalities to provide such facilities, is exceedingly gratifying.

On January 15, 1930, the Postmaster General signified his approval of Lethbridge as a point of call on the trans-Prairie air mail service thus being inaugurated.[4] This necessitated the installation of lighting for night flying and again the local authorities cooperated with the Civil Aviation Branch in the improvement of their airport to provide the facilities required for the night mail service.

On June 2nd of that year, a by-law was passed by a large majority of the rate-payers of the City of Lethbridge authorizing the expenditure of $80,000 for this work, which was immediately placed in hand. These improvements included the erection of the municipal hangar, the improvement of the surface of the airport and the installation of an airway beacon and boundary lights for the aerodrome. A grant of $4,442.00 was made to the city to assist them in providing an efficient airport lighting system. A radio range station was erected by the Department of National Defence during 1931 to improve the facilities at the airport. The report on these facilities, dated January 12, 1931, states that 'these are now complete and very satisfactory, the lighting beacon being visible from a very great distance.'

The importance of Lethbridge on the trans-Canada airway has always been recognized as it is the point of departure from the Prairie Provinces to make the flight over the Rocky Mountains. Progress in aviation between 1930 and 1937 was extraordinarily rapid, and airports which were large enough for the aircraft of the former period are now too small. To meet the new conditions, the building of a new aerodrome on a larger site,[5] now known as the Kenyon Field, was necessary.

Cooperation in the creation of the new facilities required has been freely and whole-heartedly given by City Council and officers to meet the new conditions. Kenyon Field is one of the finest aerodrome sites on the continent. It is absolutely unobstructed from all quarters and has been well-described as the Pilot's Dream. The improvements carried out during the past two years now provide the most up-to-date and efficient set up for the conduct of high speed, night and day, all-weather, scheduled air service. They include two hard-surfaced runways, one

3,700 by 150 feet [1,128 by 46 metres] and the other 3,400 by 150 feet [1,036 by 46 metres], with connecting taxiways.

The Trans-Canada Air Lines have built their own hangar and office facilities, which provide accommodation not only for the air line operation but also for the Radio and Meteorological services of the Department of Transport. A new radio range station has been built to serve the airport and the Radio and Meteorological staff is on duty twenty-four hours of the day.[6]

Work on the new airport began June 1937. The Department of Transport agreed to make a capital contribution amounting to one-third of the cost.[7] In the summer of 1938, work began on hard surfaced runways to accommodate Trans-Canada Air Lines' operations. On September 9, 1938, a TCA Lockheed 14 made an emergency landing on an uncompleted runway. A permanent licence was issued for the new airport on October 8, 1938, and the licence for the old airport was surrendered by the city. Regular operations began in October 1938, and passengers services started on April 1, 1939.

The new airport, officially opened on June 7, 1939, was named Kenyon Field after Herbert Hollick-Kenyon, a well-known pilot who was the first to fly air mail to Lethbridge in January 1931 by Canadian Airways to Lethbridge from Edmonton and Winnipeg. Hollick-Kenyon flew in the World War I, and then with Canadian Airways in the north, Trans-Canada Air Lines and Canadian Pacific Airlines. In 1935, he became famous as a member of the Ellsworth expedition to Antarctica, and he was airport manager at Toronto (Malton) for a brief period in 1938. The opening ceremonies also honoured Captain Hoy and J.H. Tudhope, who, as superintendent of Airways (in National Defence and Transport), played a leading role in the development of aviation in Canada through the establishment of the

Rimouski-Montréal ship-to-shore air mail in 1927 and, later, the planning of the Trans-Canada Airway, 1928-38.

On December 23, 1939, Lethbridge Airport was designated for military purposes and, in March 1940, the Department of National Defence established a flying training school there under the British Commonwealth Air Training Plan (BCATP). The Department of Transport leased the airport from the city on September 27, 1940, for the duration of the war and operated it as a civil airport despite the fact that it had considerable military traffic.

In 1940 and 1941 respectively, No. 5 Elementary Flying Training School (EFTS) and No. 8 Bombing and Gunnery School were established at Lethbridge under the BCATP. No. 5 EFTS was originally run by Lethbridge Flying Training School Ltd., but in 1941, it was moved to the High River Flying Training School Ltd., a subsidiary of the Calgary Aero Club.

All improvements made to the airport during the war were taken over later by the Department of Transport for civil use.

In May 1948, the city decided against resuming airport operations as Trans-Canada Air Lines had rerouted to the west coast through Calgary. (On the original Trans-Canada Airway, Lethbridge had been the junction for Calgary and Edmonton). The Department of Transport assumed ownership of the airport in 1967.

A new $4 million air terminal building was opened on October 19, 1979, by Premier Lougheed, assisted by federal Transport Minister Don Mazankowski. The building was constructed under an agreement between Transport Canada and the Alberta Department of Transportation: the province put up the capital while Transport, as the airport operator, was to pay back the cost over a number of years and receive title to the terminal. This arrangement allowed speedy implementation. The new terminal

125. Airport buildings, Lethbridge, Alberta, 1944.

replaced the converted RCAF mess hall first occupied in 1947 and renovated in 1968 and 1970.

A new $612,000 firehall was officially opened on August 14, 1986; and an airport maintenance garage, costing $1.2 million, on May 1, 1987.

Today, Lethbridge has two runways: 05-23, 1,981 metres long, and 12-30, 1,493 metres long.

The airport is served by Time Air and Air BC; and the Lethbridge Flying Club, founded in 1945, is based at the airport.

In 1988, there were 47,206 aircraft movements and 109,381 passengers on scheduled air service.

The following have been managers of Lethbridge Airport over the years:

A.W. Westergard	1939
Neil C. Boyles	1959
William Walls	1959 to 1962
John Fifield	1962 to 1976
David Devlin	1975 to 1977
Gerald Baker	1977 to 1979
Myrna Flesch (Bradley)	1979[8]

Sources:

1. Transport Canada.
2. R.L. Clarke, "Airport Notes" (Ottawa: Transport Canada) [unpublished collection].
3. Official Opening Programme of June 7, 1939.

4. Program for the opening of the new air terminal building in 1979.
5. R. Price, Manager, Lethbridge Flying Club.

Footnotes to Lethbridge Airport

[1] F.H. Ellis, *Canada's Flying Heritage* (Toronto: University of Toronto Press, 1961), pp. 178-79.
[2] The board was the government organization responsible for aviation in Canada from 1919 to 1923, when the new Department of National Defence took over. The Department of Transport was established in 1936 and assumed responsibility for civil aviation.
[3] Public Archives Canada, MG 30 E243, vol. 9, memorandum 17 May 1939.
[4] The mail service was discontinued on March 1, 1932, because of the Depression.
[5] This site is nine and a half kilometres south of the city and about 283 hectares in area.
[6] Public Archives Canada, MG 30, E243, vol. 9, from a speech made by the Minister of Transport, 17 May 1939.
[7] In actual fact, the Dominion government was forced to give Lethbridge greater assistance, reasoning that Lethbridge was a small community which had provided and maintained, at its own expense, a good airport for ten years that was quite sufficient for ordinary traffic but not for the high-speed aircraft TCA would be using. In addition, a grain elevator had been built by the Dominion government making the approach to the airport difficult in poor weather. Furthermore, Lethbridge was an important junction point, and the airport there was a key airport.
[8] Flesch was the first woman airport manager in Canada.

London Airport
(Ontario)

In January 1927, the London city engineer asked the Civil Aviation Branch of the Department of National Defence for advice on building an airport. The city had a site in mind, six and a half kilometres south of London at Lambeth. The site was investigated and found to be satisfactory, and a temporary licence was issued on August 10, 1927.

A city by-law, drafted to authorize purchase of the land for $20,000, was defeated on December 5, 1927. On January 28, 1928, however, a group of businessmen put up the money, formed the London Airport Ltd., and acquired the site. A new airport licence was issued to the company on May 3, 1929. By May 10, a hangar had been built. The London Flying Club was formed in 1928 under the government scheme to assist light aeroplane clubs, and based itself at the airport.

In the summer of 1927, there was an aviation event of great local interest: the Carling Brewery Co. of London offered a prize of $25,000 to the first pilot to fly non-stop from London, Ontario, to London, England. This was the same amount won by Lindberg for his New York-to-Paris flight of May 22, 1927. Carling provided the airplane, a Stinson-Detroiter—christened Sir John Carling—and spent about $2,500 to prepare a field at Crumlin near London for the take-off. R.B. Tully and J.V. Medcalf, both of whom had a great deal of experience in the Ontario Provincial Air Service, were chosen to be pilots. They took off at daylight on August 28, 1927, but ran into fog and bad weather near Kingston and returned to London. The flight plan was then changed from a non-stop flight to one travelling by way of Harbour Grace, Newfoundland. They took off again on September 1, were delayed five days in Caribou, Maine, and finally reached Harbour Grace. From there, they took off at 0945 hours on September 7, 1927, and were, unfortunately, lost during the Atlantic flight.[1]

To return to the history of London Airport, airmail service from Montréal to Windsor was due to start in July 1929. In June, the Civil Aviation Branch asked the city to install lighting at the airport under the government's assistance scheme, whereby the government would pay 50 per cent of the cost. The city refused and the Airport Company could not raise the money. Lights were not installed, and the field closed on November 4, 1929. It reopened in January 1931 with a beacon provided by the Airport Company.

On March 30, 1931, the city of London granted the London Flying CLub $5,000 to assist in the maintenance of the airport, and a permanent licence was issued to London Airport Ltd. on May 30, 1931. The air-mail service was discontinued on April 30, 1932, but was later re-established on February 10, 1933, by Trans-American Air Lines Corporation between Detroit and Buffalo via London. By June of that year, Trans-American Air Lines refused to use the airport because it was too small for the three-engined aircraft the airlines used on the route.

Early in 1935, the city asked the Civil Aviation Branch to conduct a survey of the local airport situation and to decide whether the airport could be expanded or a new facility developed at a more suitable location. Over the next four years, many sites were studied, and the city pressed the government to build an airport as an unemployment relief program. In May 1939, Inspector Dodds (later controller of Civil Aviation in the Department of Transport) recommended three possible sites: one five kilometres from St. Thomas,[2] one near Rebecca (six and a half kilometres northeast of London), and one near Crumlin (three kilometres east of the city). The proposal was that if the city would purchase the site, the Department of Transport would develop the airport, exclusive of buildings. In July 1939, the city purchased the Rebecca site, which is the location of today's London Airport, and work began on September 9, 1939.

Meanwhile, on March 29, 1938, London Airport Ltd. decided to close the airport at the Lambeth site effective April 30. The city, how-

ever, again came forward and granted the London Flying Club $500, thereby keeping the airport open. The airport was finally closed on August 7, 1942, and was later used as a naval wireless training station.

On January 24, 1940, London agreed to lease the airport (then under construction) to the federal government for the duration of the war. By March 1940, the Department of National Defence had decided to establish an elementary flying training school (EFTS) and an air observer school (AOS) at London under the British Commonwealth Air Training Plan (BCATP). Three hangars, barrack blocks, and other buildings were erected. Two hard-surfaced runways, 14-32 and 05-23, each 3,100 [945 metres] long, were completed in 1940. The airport opened on July 27, 1940, and was leased to the Department of Transport, which took over and managed it as a civil airport. An airport manager (R.B. Allen) and staff were appointed in December. The airport licence was issued May 6, 1941, for the 'London City Airport.'

The RCAF portion of the airport was known as RCAF Station Crumlin, and the airport was sometimes called Crumlin Airport. No. 3 EFTS opened in June 1940 and operated until July 1942 with fleet Trainers and No. 4 AOS Ansons. It was one of the first eight schools in the BCATP, and was run by the London Elementary Flying Training School Ltd. (a subsidiary company of the London Flying Club). No. 4 AOS was established at the airport in September 1940 under the direction of Leavens Brothers (Training) Ltd. It closed in December 1944.

The Honourable C.D. Howe, Minister of Transport, opened the first terminal building, which housed the civil radio and Trans-Canada Air Lines, in July 1942. The inaugural flight of TCA (a Lockheed 14 aircraft) arrived on the same day.

In 1941, an aircraft overhaul plant was built in the southwest corner of the airport, by Central

Aircraft Ltd., to service Lysanders, Ansons, Fleet Trainers, Fairey Battles, and Mosquitos. The building was sold to Somerville Industries Ltd. in 1947, when Central Aircraft closed down.

In 1943, runways 05-23 and 14-32 were lengthened to 4,145 and 4,000 feet [1,263 and 1,219 metres] respectively, a new runway 08-26 of 3,800 feet [1,158 metres] was built, and National Defence erected two new hangars for No. 4 AOS.

At the end of the war, the city of London refused to accept responsibility for the airport, and the Department of Transport continued to operate it.

In 1947, (when TCA began to fly DC-3Cs) the terminal building was enlarged to provide more space the for airlines, Customs, air traffic control and airport administration. In July 1947, the London Flying Club leased Hangar No. 1, and Leavens Brothers leased Hangar No. 3 for its commercial flying school, which closed down when fire destroyed the hangar, in 1955.

In 1948, hangar no. 4 was destroyed by fire. In September 1949, the city of London 420 (Fighter) Auxiliary Squadron was formed and began operations out of Hangar No. 5 using Harvard aircraft. In 1950, RCAF Station London was established at the airport, and became a North Atlantic Treaty Organization (NATO) Induction and Training Centre. It was re-equipped with Mustangs in 1952; and in 1954, when the NATO Centre was transferred to Centralia, it received T-33 jets. The squadron was disbanded in 1957, and the RCAF station was closed the following year, on September 30.

In 1950, runway 14-32 was equipped with an Instrument Landing System (ILS) and high intensity approach lighting; and in 1955, the year that TCA introduced the Viscount, it was reinforced and lengthened to 6,000 feet [1,829 metres]. Runway 08-26 was reinforced and lengthened to 5,200 feet [1,585 metres] in 1957.

In 1959, Execair Ltd. began operations as a commercial flying school and charter service, and continued until October 1964.

The Meteorological Branch opened a weather office in the terminal building in 1960.

Skyland Aviation purchased hangar no. 2 from the Crown Assets Disposal Corporation in August 1961. The London Flying Club cancelled its lease to hangar no. 1 (which was subsequently declared surplus and demolished) and moved into leased quarters in hangar no. 2 in 1962.

Plans were under way for a new air terminal building south of the bottom of runway 32 in 1963. The city had held discussions with Transport about the future of the airport as early as October 1953, but decided in February 1954 that it would not take it over. In December 1960, the department asked London for title to the land forming part of the airport so that a new air terminal building could be built on it. In 1964, when the city sold the land to the department, construction of the new building began. It was opened on April 10, 1965, and the old building was torn down in 1969.

In 1968, Air Canada began to operate DC9s through London.

Great Lakes Airlines of Sarnia began operations through London using Convair 440 aircraft in April 1973. During the same year, the London Flying Club purchased hangar no. 2.

Runway 08-26 was lengthened to 6,300 feet [1,920 metres] in 1973, 05-23 was shortened to 3,174 feet [967 metres], and 14-32 lengthened to 8,800 feet [2,682 metres] in 1974, permitting use by DC-8, Boeing 707 and 747, and L1011 aircraft.

In 1974, hangar no. 5, the last operational building used by the RCAF, was sold and removed from the site.

On September 11, 1975, the first non-stop London, Ontario, to London, England flight was made by a Boeing 707 of Laker Airways, forty-eight years after Tully and Medcalf's attempt.

On October 31, 1976, Air Canada and Great Lakes Airlines reached an agreement whereby—using Convair 580's—Great Lakes took over all of Air Canada's Toronto to London flights.

As a result of economic regulatory reform in the airline industry, smaller aircraft and more frequent flights were introduced to the London area. Air Canada operated four daily flights to Windsor, Winnipeg, Vancouver, Ottawa, Montréal, and Moncton. It ceased operations in London in 1987. Air Ontario, now a subsidiary of Air Canada, operated daily scheduled service to Sarnia, Cleveland, Toronto, Ottawa, Montréal, North Bay, Sudbury, Sault Ste. Marie, and Thunder Bay. Canadian Airlines International ceased its scheduled flight service in April 1989. City Express ceased operations in October 1988, and Canadian Partner and Air Ontario currently provide scheduled service at London Airport.

Air Ontario, recognizing the economic benefits developing in London, moved its headquarters there. It completed the construction of its offices and hangar complex in 1986. Several charter operators also began operations to serve passengers travelling to Sunspot destinations and Expo 86.

Because of the new carrier services and increased aviation activity, the passenger processing areas of the terminal building became overcrowded. It was suggested that the air cargo area and associated brokers' offices be moved from the terminal to a separate facility. Several developers expressed an interest in constructing an air cargo building, and on February 11, 1988, the minister of Transport announced that the department was prepared to contribute funding to the construction of site services and an access road.

Through a special program carried out from 1983 to 1985, a number of expansion and refurbishing projects were undertaken to meet increasing capacity demand. This included expansion to the restaurant and to the international arrivals area. In 1988, the number of parking spaces at London Airport was doubled.

126. Air terminal, London Airport, Ontario, 1965.

Transport Canada also installed a new radar system at London Airport—expected to be operational by 1990—as part of a major program called the Radar Modernization Program (RAMP), which provides major Canadian airports with state of the art air navigation systems.

In April 1988, Runway 05-23 was decommissioned and converted to a taxiway, a change which permitted the construction that year of a privately owned hangar and fixed base operation facility, and the development of additional commercial lots.

In 1988, more than 300,000 passengers used London Airport. After ten years of service, R.B. Allen retired as airport manager in 1950, to be followed by F.I. Banghart (who had formerly managed St. Hubert, Dorval and Winnipeg). Banghart retired in 1957 and was replaced by Norman R. Craig. When Craig retired in 1971, K.C. Blair took over.

Sources:

1. N.R. Craig, former Airport Manager, London Airport.
2. Transport Canada, Ontario Region.
3. R.L. Clarke, "Airport Notes" (Ottawa: Transport Canada) [unpublished collection].

Footnotes to London Airport.

[1] F.H. Ellis, *Canada's Flying Heritage* (Toronto: University of Toronto Press, 1961), pp. 269-70.

[2] In a letter of March 24, 1939, from the deputy minister of Transport to the London city clerk, the deputy discussed the financial assistance needed to build a new airport for London. He also raised the possibility to London and St. Thomas collaborating to build one airport halfway between the two cities to serve both. Nothing came of the suggestion. (Public Archives Canada, MG 30 E243, vol. 3).

Lynn Lake Airport
(Manitoba)

Lynn Lake Airport is located one and a half kilometres northwest of the town, whose population is 1,600. It serves Lynn Lake and the catchment area of Leaf Rapids, Brochet, Lac Brochet, Tadoule Lake, and Pukatawagan communities.

Canadian Airlines International/Calm Air operates out of the airport, as well as La Ronge Aviation Services Ltd. and Parsons Airways Northern Ltd.

The tourist fishing lodges in the area create considerable traffic from June to September, and the geographical location of the airport is ideal as a jump-off point to the North. The airport is owned by Transport Canada and operated by the Local Government District of Lynn Lake, which receives an annual operating subsidy.

Lynn Lake Airport was developed in 1951 by the Local Government District of Lynn Lake in conjunction with the Department of Transport. At that time, there was no road or rail service. The airport has a paved runway 07-35, which is 1,524 by 46 metres and a gravel runway 08-26, 762 by 30 metres. The latter was reconstructed in 1966. Runway 07-35 was rebuilt in 1982 and an additional paved area was added. The air terminal building was built in 1969 and expanded in 1978. An Aeradio Facility, established in 1966, is staffed on a twenty-four-hour, seven-day-a-week basis. The airport is equipped with VHFomni-directional Range (VOR), Distance Measuring Equipment (DME), Non-directional Beacon (NDB), VHF Direction Finder (VDF), and Visual Approach Slope Indicator System (VASIS).

In 1988 there were about 20,000 passengers and 10,600 aircraft movements.

The following served as airport managers:

Bill Taylor	1961 to 1968
Fred Johnson	1968 to 1973
Ron Dodds	1973 to 1974
Don Taylor	1974 to 1987
George Friesen	1987

Sources:
1. Transport Canada, Central Region.
2. The Local Government District of Lynn Lake—Airport Manager.

Midway Aerodrome
(British Columbia)

Midway is an uncertified aerodrome owned by Transport Canada. It has a 1,250-metre turf runway.

The field was developed in 1936 as an emergency landing field for the air-mail route from Lethbridge to Vancouver and maintained by an aerodrome keeper.

It was used for war purposes from 1940 to 1946, and in 1963 was a water bomber base. It is being used more and more by Visual Flight Rates (VFR) aircraft flying between the Okanagan and the Kootenays.

Maintenance responsibilities are met by a contractor who reports to the airport manager at Penticton.

Sources:
1. Transport Canada, Pacific Region.

2. R.L. Clarke, "Airport Notes" (Ottawa: Transport Canada) [unpublished collection].

Mingan Airport
(Québec)

The United States, with Canada's permission, constructed an airport at Mingan in 1942. It was intended as a base for American aircraft being ferried from Montréal to Goose Bay and from there by the northern route to Europe. At the end of the war, Canada bought Mingan Airport from the United States for $3.6 million.

The Canadian army occupied the site from 1945 to 1950. Northern Wings Ltd. and private aircraft began to use the airport in 1950.

In 1951, the airport became the property of the Department of National Defence which, in 1957, transferred it to the province of Québec. The province planned to open a hotel on the site to accommodate tourists and fishermen; and nearby Patterson Lake was to be used as a seaplane base.

In 1958, the Québec Department of Tourism, Fish, and Game leased the airport and seaplane base to Air Gaspé, which operated a passenger and mail service. In November 1967, Québec leased the airport for three years to the municipality of Longue Pointe de Mingan at a nominal rent. Later the municipality asked that the site be developed as the regional airport. This was opposed by the town of Havre-St.-Pierre because it also had a facility that it wanted Transport to develop as the regional airport.

In 1972, the department gave Mingan a 37-by-10-foot [11 by 3 metre] trailer as a passenger waiting room.

Northern Wings transferred its operations from Havre-St.-Pierre in April 1976 because facilities at Mingan were better, and a new terminal was located in the building used by the St. Laurent Club.

The Mingan Airport became an air traffic centre as a result of the opening of a road between Sept-Iles and Mingan. The airport is now served by Transair on a regular basis.

The airport is operated by the town of Mingan and receives an operating subsidy from the provincial government of Québec.

Source:
Transport Canada, Québec Region.

Moncton Airport
(New Brunswick)

The history of aviation and airports in Moncton began in the winter of 1927-28, and are recorded in "A History of Aviation in the Atlantic Provinces," an unpublished and undated paper written by Don McClure, general manager of the Moncton Flying Club:

The first scheduled air flight out of Moncton took place on January 11, 1928, when a Fairchild 71 took off at noon from the ice of the McNutt Reservoir on the McLaughlin Road with mail and passengers for the Magdalen Islands. The aircraft had arrived in Moncton at 1500 hours on January 7, and between that day and the day of departure

127. Leger's Corner, N. B. 1930. L. to R.
H.S. "Jr" Jones, Art Jarvis, Burton Trerice,
Walter Flemming, Romeo Belanger,
Al Parker, Bill Irvine

hundreds of Monctonians went out to the reservoir to see this 20th century wonder. On the Fairchild's return trip to Moncton on January 12 it was forced to land at Cape Tormentine because of a snow storm and approaching darkness and did not land back in Moncton until the 14th.

Later trips from the McNutt Reservoir to the Magdalens were carried out on January 18 and 24 and on March 3. It was decided then to move the location of the base to a site at Cook's Brook on the Shediac Road. This site was later given the name Aero Lake.

Scheduled airmail service to Prince Edward Island was inaugurated on March 3 with the departure of the Fairchild 71 from the Cook's Brook site. This site proved to be more practical than the reservoir, but it still presented many difficulties. It was strictly a winter "ski" operation. The road to this airport was often blocked with snow, and automobiles could not be used to deliver mail from the post office.

The operator of the mail and passenger service at that time was the Fairchild Airways Ltd. In a letter dated February 15, 1929, the company notified the City Council that, although it wished to serve this part of the country in the future, it could not continue the mail service without better landing conditions.

The need for a proper landing field had also become increasingly apparent to some prominent air-minded Moncton citizens such as Dr. C.R. Baxter, who, in an address to the Moncton Club on February 1, 1929, advocated the formation of a flying club as well as a new airport to serve all the aviation requirements of the city of Moncton.

In April 1929, a private company, Moncton Airport Ltd. (owned by Dick McCully, Charles Baxter, John Humphrey, William Creaghan, Timothy O'Brien, and Dave Houston) bought

land at Leger's Corner, three kilometres east of the city of Moncton. The site was often referred to as "the old race track" and today is known as the Brunswick Downs Race Track in the town of Dieppe. The city of Moncton offered to match dollar for dollar all funds raised by Moncton Airport Ltd. (up to a $1,000 limit) towards the development of a new airport, and work started on April 25, 1929. A small building that had been used at the Cook's Brook location was moved there until a hangar could be built.

The airfield had two runways: one running east-west was 1,500 feet [457 metres] long, while the north-south runway was only 900 feet [272 metres] long. A temporary airport licence was issued June 26, 1929. The airport continued to operate until 1941.

The Moncton Aero Club, founded July 1, 1929, was based at the new airport, as was the International Airways (later Canadian Airways) flying service and school. International provided flying training for the Aero Club, while the latter arranged the social side of the activities. Walter Fowler, later of Trans-Canada Air Lines, was one of the company's instructors. Claude Keating, who later became the first manager of the present airport at Lakeburn, became the Moncton Flying Club's first instructor. The club was reorganized in 1939 and joined the Canadian Flying Clubs Association on April 14, 1939.

The first Maritime Provinces Air Pageant was held at the Moncton Airport on July 1 and 2, 1929, and was an outstanding success. Approximately 45,000 people attended, and pilots and aircraft from across Canada participated. Proceeds from the pageant enabled Moncton Airport Ltd. to pay for the land and the early improvements. On October 29, the company transferred its interest, right, and title in the airport free of charge to the city, and Moncton became a municipal airport. Moncton built a hangar and converted the runways to gravel surfaces in 1930.

International Airways, still only a fledgling

company, continued to operate from the airport and, in 1929, W.H. Irvine was appointed flight superintendent of the airline, and was later replaced by Bob Dodds and Walter Fowler. These three men had successful careers in aviation and became well-known in many air centres across Canada. Irvine became a senior official of the Department of Transport in Moncton and he finished his career as regional controller of Civil Aviation in Vancouver; Dodds later joined the Department of Transport and was prominently associated with the development of the Trans-Canada Airway—he later became controller of Civil Aviation in Ottawa. Fowler became general manager for Air Canada in the Atlantic provinces.

In 1929, International Airways graduated its first class of students, among them Jim Wade, Bert Trerice, Art Snowden, "Junior" Jones, and Claude Keating. In the same year, the airline expanded its mail service to take in Prince Edward Island and Montréal. The company merged with Canadian Airways in 1930, which continued to function at Moncton until 1941. Later, Canadian Airways merged with other small companies across Canada to form Canadian Pacific Airlines. The airline remained in Moncton for some time, using the name Canadian Airways even after the merger.

A new temporary airport licence was issued to the city on November 15, 1929, and the field was to be used on the proposed Moncton-Montréal air-mail route. Canadian Airways leased the field from the city in December of 1930. When, in 1934 the city asked the government to investigate the possibility of further development, the location was unsuitable for expansion. The site of the present airport at Lakeburn, six and a half kilometres east of the city, was chosen in May 1936.

In March 1937, the city discussed with Transport the development of an airport suitable for trans-Canada air service, and a plan was developed for the Lakeburn site: the city would contribute $192,000, and the department $162,000.

There would be one paved runway, 3,200 by 150 feet [975 by 46 metres]. On March 26, 1938, it was agreed that the city would acquire the site and that the Department would undertake all additional expenditures, build the airport, and operate it. The city would share any operating profit until it had been reimbursed for the cost of the land. The land was transferred to the Crown on August 17, 1938, and construction began on the same day. The 3,200 foot [975-metre] east-west runway was completed in August 1939, and the northeast-southwest runway was finished shortly after. The third runway was usable by winter. A temporary airport licence was issued on November 1, 1939, after which Trans-Canada Air Lines (TCA) started day operations.

Aviation in the Moncton area progressed slowly between 1930 and 1938. On July 14 and 25, 1933, General Balbo of Italy, on his way to and from the World's Fair in Chicago, used Shediac Bay, fourteen and a half kilometres north of Moncton for his armada of twenty-four Savio Machetti flying boats. Shediac was also used by Pan American Airways Clipper flying boats on their trans-atlantic service via Botwood, Newfoundland, in 1937 and 1939, and from 1942 to 1945.

In 1940, TCA inaugurated mail and passenger service between the cities of Moncton and Montréal, with Walter Fowler as the first pilot on this route. The service was later extended to take in Halifax, Sydney, Saint John, Fredericton, and Newfoundland. North Eastern Airlines, an American company, operated a service for mail and passengers between Moncton and Boston from 1941 to 1947, providing connections with TCA.

Maritime Central Airways came to Moncton in 1941 and began operating between Charlottetown, Summerside, Moncton, and Saint John. Carl Burke was one of the first pilots on this route; others were Ray Murnaghan, Jim Wade, "Junior" Jones, Bob Mills, and Garnett Godfrey. The airline's operations centre was Moncton, and, later, it extended its service to take in Newfoundland,

Labrador, and Sept-Iles. Eastern Provincial Airways took over Maritime Central in 1963.

In March 1940, the Department of National Defence asked the Department of Transport for permission to establish a service flying training school (SFTS) at Moncton Airport under the British Commonwealth Air Training Plan (BCATP). This was agreed to, subject to traffic control arrangements being made with TCA and Canadian Airways Ltd. The airport remained under the management of the Department of Transport.

The old airport at Leger's Corner remained in use for the flying club and small aircraft until it was closed in April 1941. Although the club ceased operations for the duration of the war, it formed a subsidiary company, Miramichi Flying Training School Ltd. and operated No. 21 Elementary Flying Training School (EFTS) at Chatham, New Brunswick, under the BCATP from 1941 to 1942. After that, No. 21 EFTS moved to Neepawa, Manitoba, and became No. 35 EFTS under the Royal Air Force.

On November 29, 1940, the RCAF set up No. 8 SFTS at Moncton under the BCATP. Two relief airports were also built to ease the traffic at Moncton: No. 1 at Scoudouc and No. 2 at Salisbury. The BCATP schools ceased operations in March 1945. Use of the emergency landing strip at the present air traffic control centre, Riverview, was also discontinued.

In addition to its air force training schools, Moncton airport was a busy repair and overhaul base during the war. Clark Ruse Aircraft Ltd. had a large plant in hangars built by the Department of Munitions on the south side of the airport (the company had another factory at Dartmouth). The two remaining buildings—now used by the Department of Transport—were known as the Clark Ruse hangars for years after the war.

During the war, Moncton Airport was an alternate to Gander for the RAF Ferry Command and the Return Ferry Service of BOAC; and in 1946, it was officially designated as an alternate airport on the Trans-Atlantic Air Service. Moncton's runways were improved to meet the needs of large transatlantic aircraft: in 1948, 11-29 was extended and widened to 6,287 by 200 feet [1,849 by 59 metres].

On August 30, 1946, the city declined the Department of Transport's offer to hand back the airport for operation on a lease basis. A permanent airport licence was issued in the department's name on February 21, 1949.

The first air terminal was located in the TCA hangar. It was later expanded. In 1952, while the Clark Ruse hangar (which also housed the Department of Transport's Regional Air Service headquarters) was being converted into a modern air terminal, the entire structure was destroyed by fire. A new building was started, and the first part of the air terminal was opened in 1953. In 1964, expansion and modifications included the construction of an operations building and a control tower which were occupied in 1965. In 1976, the terminal and operations buildings were combined, resulting in the present air terminal.

Between 1955 and 1958, Moncton became an important air freight centre in support of the DEW (Distant Early Warning) Line[1] radar built along the 68th parallel north of the Arctic Circle from Alaska to Baffin Island. Moncton was used by USAF Military Air Transport Service (MATS) aircraft as a staging point for supplies.

128. Aerial view of Leger's Corner, Moncton, 1929.

Maritime Central Airways was the main contractor for the east sector of the line, and Moncton was its main base.

Over the years, Moncton has undergone many changes. Runway 07-25 was extended to 6,150 feet [1,874 metres] in 1958 and 11-29 to 8,000 feet [2,438 metres] in 1968; (02-20 remains at 3,670 feet [1,119 metres]). Instrument Landing System (ILS) was installed on runway 11-29 in 1941, and on 07-25 in 1961. In 1980, runway 07-25 was changed to 06-24 due to the change in magnetic variation. High intensity lighting was installed in 1960 and 1968.

The Moncton Aero Club, which later became the Moncton Flying Club, was one of the prime movers behind the development of the first airport in 1929. After valuable service to the BCATP under the corporate name of Miramichi Flying Training School Ltd., the club re-formed after the war, became established in the old SFTS no. 5 hangar on the north side of the airport, and has operated very successfully at Moncton Airport ever since. In July 1965, the club hangar leased from the Department of National Defence was destroyed by fire, but the aircraft were saved. The club rebuilt in 1966 on the south side of the airport, and in 1974 built an eight-bay T-hangar to house club and private aircraft.

In October 1966, J.C. Folkins opened the J.C. Folkins Hangar. He was a well-known early pilot in the Atlantic provinces, an airways inspector with Transport, and a supporter of the club.

Today, Moncton Airport serves a catchment area of 300,000 people. In 1988, there were 293,000 passengers and 183,530 aircraft movements.

Over the years, Moncton has been served by the following airlines:

International Airways	1929 to 1930
Canadian Airways	1930 to 1941
TCA (Air Canada after 1964)	1938 to present
North Eastern Airlines	1941 to 1947
Maritime Central Airways (merged with EPA)	1941 to 1963
Eastern Provincial Airways	1963 to 1986
Air Atlantic	1986 to present
Air Nova	1987 to present
Inter-Canadian	1988 to present

The original TCA hangar is now owned by Central Trust II and occupied by Central Trust, Atlantair, and Lanco Aircraft Maintenance; Hangar no. 4, one of the original wartime structures, is Transport's regional flight hangar; the flying club has two modern hangars; and the Department of National Defence still uses five of the wartime SFTS hangars on the northwest side of the airport.

Air Canada, with DC-8s and 767s, now operates one of two national air cargo holding areas at Moncton.

The following have served as airport managers at Moncton since its beginning:

Claude Keating	1940 to 1959
Harold Toole	1959 to 1961
Hardy Crandall	1961 to 1965
A.J. Benny Gaudet	1961 to 1965

(who was a mechanic with the flying club on the 1929 site)

John A. Strugnell	1985

129. Leger's Corner, Airport Moncton, New Brunswick, 1930.

Sources:

1. Transport Canada, Atlantic Region (material collected and edited by A.J. Gaudet).
2. Mills, Roger, ed. *Five Decades of Flying: History of the Moncton Flying Club*. Moncton: Moncton Flying Club, 1979.
3. R.L. Clarke "Airport Notes" (Ottawa: Transport Canada) [unpublished collection].
4. McClure, Don. A History of Aviation in the Atlantic Provinces [unpublished paper].

Footnote— Moncton Airport
[1] See chapter 11.

Mont Joli Airport
(Québec)

The Mont Joli Airport was constructed in 1941-42 for the Department of National Defence to assist the Royal Air Force Ferry Command in its operations across the north Atlantic. It was also used for the British Commonwealth Air Training Plan (BCATP) and RCAF operations. The airport was used by No. 9 Bombing and Gunnery School during winter months and by RCAF Eastern Air Command as a coastal patrol base in summer. It had three paved runways: two 4,000 feet [1,219 metres] long and one 4,300 feet [1,311 metres].

In February 1943, Canadian Pacific Airlines (CPAL—formerly Québec Airways Ltd.), which was based at Rimouski Airport, asked the Department of National Defence for permission to operate from Mont Joli Airport. It had a contract to carry mail and freight to Goose Bay and it found Rimouski too small for the DC-2 aircraft, which the company had obtained from the U.S. Air Force. The Department agreed, because it would be uneconomical to spend money on Rimouski; and the decision was influenced by the fact that a radio range was to be installed at Mont Joli. On March 25, the Department of National Defence agreed that Mont Joli could be used, but on a temporary basis only.

After the end of the war, CPAL was permitted to carry passengers and freight from Mont Joli to the north shore of the St. Lawrence, and to the far north. The Department of Transport undertook winter maintenance of the airport in 1945-46, and following transfer from National Defence on December 15, 1945, a permanent licence was issued in the name of Transport on May 2, 1946.

In 1951, Mont Joli was designated as a supplementary airport on the North Atlantic air route for emergency use only. In the same year, and at the request of the Department of National Defence, Transport extended one runway to 6,000 feet [1,829 metres] as an emergency recovery strip for the Air Defence Command.

By 1952, the airport was being used by Hollinger-Ungava Ltd. for supply to Knob Lake, Québec North Shore, Labrador Railway, and by Québecair (Rimouski Airlines Ltd.). In 1954, a control tower was provided.

During the construction of the DEW Line between 1955 and 1958,[1] Mont Joli was a very busy airport on the supply line to Goose Bay, Fort Chimo, and Frobisher Bay, when twenty-two air carriers operated twenty-four hours a day, seven days a week. These companies moved out in 1958 and, in the same year, Québecair transferred its operations to Rimouski.

There was a great deal of rivalry between Rimouski Airport and Mont Joli, which were only twenty-four kilometres apart. Rimouski had been in existence since 1927, while Mont Joli was built in 1942; but while the Rimouski site had limited possibilities for expansion, Mont Joli was new and had better facilities. A special economic study was done for the Department of Transport in 1958, which recommended that Rimouski be classed as a local airport and that all future development be concentrated at Mont Joli, which would then become the regional main line airport.

In 1959, runway 02-20 was closed. The two remaining runways are 06-24, at 1,829 metres long, and 16-34, 1,219 metres long.

Hollinger Ungava Transport moved its operations to Sept-Iles Airport in 1959, and from 1960 to 1968, Mont Joli was served by Québecair, Hollinger Ungava Transport, and Baie Comeau Air Services.

In 1968 Québecair returned to Mont Joli from Rimouski as Rimouski could not accommodate Québecair's first jet aircraft, the BAC-111. The Mont Joli Airport then started to play its role as regional airport.

A new terminal building was constructed in 1972 and an Instrument Landing System (ILS) was installed in 1974. VHF Omni-directional Range (VOR)/Distance Measuring Equipment (DME) was added in 1978. The flight service station was constructed in 1984.

In 1983, Conifair Aviation began flights from Mont-Joli to Anticosti Island and Schefferville during the hunting season; and in 1988 provided service to Anticosti for the fishing season.

Air Alliance began service in June 1988.

Adjusting to magnetic variations, runway 16-34 was designated 15-33 on July 21, 1989. The threshold of runway 33 was extended 20 metres to a safe length of 1,149 metres.

In 1987, the electronic maintenance centre was built—the first centre of its kind in Québec.

The airport, operated by Transport Canada, processed 78,600 passengers in 1987. There were 14,036 aircraft movements in 1988.

The following served as airport managers:

Albert Guillaut	1945 to 1948
Charles Delisle	1948 to 1953
Rene Billard	1953 to 1957
Albert Thibault	1957 to 1981
Rheaume Allard	1981 to 1982
Jacques Pelletier	1982 to 1989
Francois Matz	1989

Sources:
1. Transport Canada, Québec Region.
2. R.L. Clarke, "Airport Notes" (Ottawa: Transport Canada) [unpublished collection].

Footnote— Mont Joli Airport

1 Distant Early Warning (radar) Line from the Alaska-Yukon boundary to Baffin Island, designed by the United States and Canada, and financed by the U.S. See Chapter 11.

Montréal International Airport (Dorval)
(Québec)

Montréal has been associated with aviation from the earliest days of man's conquest of the air. The first recorded aeronautical event was on July 31, 1879, when Charles Page, Richard Cowan, and Charles Grimley made one of the first balloon ascents in Canada, and covered eighty kilometres in their craft, *Canada*, from Shamrock Lacrosse Field in Westmount to St. Jude near St. Hyacinthe.

Another noteworthy event was the Montréal Aviation Meet, in July 1910 at Lakeside, which was "the most pretentious undertaking of its kind to be held on this side of the Atlantic up to that date."[1] During the meet, on July 2, Count de Lesseps made the first airplane flight over a Canadian city. The first official air mail was flown on June 24, 1919, from Montréal (Bois Franc Polo Grounds) to Toronto (Leaside) by Captain Brian Peck RAF.[2]

St. Hubert, the first civil airport to be built and operated by the Canadian government, opened in 1927. It was Montréal's first official airport, and became the centre of civil aviation in eastern Canada. St. Hubert provided air mail and passenger operations, including Canadian Colonial Airlines' international service to Albany, New York, in 1928 and Trans-Canada Air Lines' transcontinental service in 1938. By 1940, however, it could no

longer accommodate both civil airlines and the expanding air training needs of the RCAF. And when, in the late summer, Canadian Pacific Air Service began the Trans-Atlantic Air Ferry operation for the U.K., the need for a second airport in the Montréal area became urgent.

In 1939, the Department of Transport and the RCAF had begun to give the matter some thought. The department looked at possible sites closer than St. Hubert for a new civil airport to serve Montréal. St. Hubert was considered "too far from the city to make it attractive for short haul, as passengers have to spend too much time getting to and from the airport."[3] Cartierville was a possibility: the owner, Curtiss Reid Airport Co., was anxious to sell the land; but the site was small and hemmed in by obstructions. Finally, the Dorval race course was chosen.

When, on May 20, 1940, the British Commonwealth Air Training Plan (BCATP) aerodrome committee, established the need for an aerodrome for the wireless training school near St. Hubert, the Department of Transport suggested a plan to developing Dorval: "a site under consideration as a civil airport to serve Montréal, with a view to possible development to make the aerodrome suitable for Wireless School Aircraft and an Elementary Flying Training School; the balance of development necessary to meet Transport requirements to be carried out after the war."[4]

The matter was settled and an Order in Council of December 24, 1940, stated that the plan was:

to develop an airport at Dorval for an Air Observer School and Wireless School under the British Commonwealth Air Training Plan, the said airport to be developed also as a Civil Air Terminal for the metropolitan area of Montréal in place of St. Hubert airport which is now used for that purpose and which would then be placed at the disposal of the Department of National Defence for use as a main aerodrome for a Service Training School under the Commonwealth Air

Training Plan, the cost of the work at Dorval to be borne jointly by the Department of Transport and the Department of National Defence in accordance with the interest of each Department, taking into consideration the transfer of the St. Hubert Airport to the Department of National Defence.[5]

Fifteen hundred acres of land were acquired and the first contract for the job was awarded on October 10, 1940. It was hoped that the airport with three paved runways of 4,000 by 200 feet [1,219 by 61 metres], capable of extension to over 5,000 feet [1,524 metres], would be ready by August 1941.

In a statement to the *Montréal Star* on October 25, 1940, the controller of Civil Aviation said that the 1,500 acre [607-hectare] site was larger than any in Canada except Malton, (where the city of Toronto had bought 1,600 acres [648 hectares]). He continued:

In neither case will the initial development require the whole area, but the Dorval site is so near the city that it is essential to secure enough property to provide for future developments and prevent the building of homes, facilities and other obstructions in the immediate neighbourhood of the flightways.[6]

Dorval opened September 1, 1941—a fast job by today's standards. According to staff circular 13/41 of August 5, 1941, the airport was designated by the Deputy Minister as Montréal Airport (Dorval) to distinguish it from St. Hubert Airport. A temporary airport licence was issued to the Department of Transport on September 1, 1941.

Dorval was not used by the BCATP Observer and Wireless schools, as had been envisaged by the Order in Council of December 24, 1940. Instead, the expanded Air Ferry organization, which became the Royal Air Force Ferry Command, moved from St. Hubert into the buildings originally intended for the BCATP.

The operations based at St. Hubert—Trans-

Canada Air Lines, Canadian Colonial Airways, Northeast Airlines Inc. (formerly Boston Main Airways Inc.), Québec Airways, and the RAF Ferry Command—were notified to cease operations at St. Hubert after September 1, 1941, as Dorval would be ready by then. The RAF Ferry Command requested—and were granted—permission to deliver aircraft and park them at Dorval at an earlier date, as their first departures from Dorval were scheduled for 1300 hours (GMT) on September 2.

Operations were transferred to Dorval as planned, and the first airport manager was F.I. Banghart, who had previously filled this position at St. Hubert for nine years. St. Hubert Airport was transferred to the Department of National Defence.

Information Circular 0/39/41 of August 28, 1941, stated:

St. Hubert Airport (Montréal) will be closed to civil air operations and Licence no. 99 cancelled from midnight August 31, 1941.

Montréal Airport (Dorval) will opened for civil air operations on September 1, 1941. Temporary accommodation and limited facilities until further notice.

3 paved runways	N-S	5,270 x 200 feet
	E-W	5,000 x 200 feet
	NE-SW	5,000 x 200 feet

Customs Port of Entry
Men and equipment on field at all hours and on runways occasionally.

The Ferry Command made office space and other facilities available to the civil operation until accommodation was ready, which helped to ease the transfer from St. Hubert.

The conditions under which the Ferry Command occupied Dorval were set out in a letter of May 26, 1941:[7]

26th May, 1941   Dorval Airport
5168-817

Dear Mr. Long:

Thank you for your letter of May 23rd, accepting responsibility on behalf of the Ministry of Aircraft Production for an estimated sum of $1,385,640, covering the original commitment of the BCATP, now transferred to the Ministry, and compensation for extensions to runways, etc., detailed estimates, which are to be submitted by this Department to your office in due course.

I confirm that the above figure is an estimate and that, when the actual cost of construction is known, financial adjustment will be made in accordance with this. Action has been taken to authorize Dibblee Construction Company to proceed immediately with the extensions and revisions in the specifications in regard to strengthening the pavements, etc., and work will be prosecuted with the utmost vigor to completion.

It is also agreed that the use of the airport will be limited to civil air transport operations and trans-Atlantic flying and will not be used for other purposes without the joint consent of this Department and your Ministry; further, that your Ministry shall have the right to erect, at its own expense under conditions acceptable to this Department, any buildings, hangars, etc., necessary for the conduct of your operations, and that any structures erected for this purpose will be part of your Ministry's equity in the airport, such equity to be the subject of negotiation between the Canadian and British governments at the close of hostilities, when a general adjustment of accounts between the two governments is effected.

Yours faithfully,

(C.P. Edwards),

Deputy Minister

H.M. Long, Esq.
Ministry of Aircraft Production, United Kingdom
Royal Bank Building
Montréal, Québec.

This understanding was later set out in formal agreements between the Canadian and United Kingdom governments in Agreement No. 32705 July 30, 1941, and Amendments No. 31149 January 26, 1943, and No. 35939 June 5, 1944.[8]

The Ferry Command was the largest operation on the airport. It built three large hangars, which still stand today, two of which have been converted into the present air cargo terminal. The headquarters administration building (part of which later served as a passenger terminal for the Trans-Atlantic Air Service) housed the Regional Air Administration of Transport Canada until 1988. The Ferry Command operated the crash-fire and ambulance service, and controlled the security of its part of the airport. Transport maintained and managed the airport and controlled civil operations, including the control tower. Trans-Canada Air Lines built its own hangar.

The air terminal building was opened in December 1941. Its curved frontage resembled the original terminal at Washington National Airport.[9] The facility was located between the north end of the hangar line and what is now the transborder finger of the present terminal. All trace of the old terminal has disappeared as it was dismantled soon after the new building opened in 1960.

Originally, there were six hangars on the airport: no. 1 was built by the Department of Transport and leased to Trans-Canada Air Lines (TCA); no. 2 was built by TCA and later sold to Québecair; nos. 3 and 4 were built by the RAF

Ferry Command and had a total of eight bays. At the end of the war, hangars nos. 3 and 4 were taken over by the Department of Transport and leased to airline companies; they were sold in 1964 to Timmins Aviation Terminals Ltd. and converted into the present air cargo terminal. No. 5, built by the RAF Ferry Command, was taken over by the Department of Transport after the war and leased, and was later sold to TCA, which in turn sold it to Nordair in 1962. No. 6 was owned by the RCAF, and was destroyed by fire in 1956.

As Ferry Command operations developed during the war, so did its facilities at Dorval, and throughout its occupancy of the airport, relations and co-operation between the Ferry Command and the Department of Transport were always cordial and effective. By mid-1944, consideration was being given to the eventual winding down of operations, and on June 5, 1944, Agreement No. 35939 (amending Agreement No. 32705) set out the terms for transfer to Canada:

without compensation, of the United Kingdom's equity in the said airport including buildings and hangars on the understanding that the United Kingdom will have the use of the airport and facilities which it now enjoys until the end of the war and for six months thereafter, and that the Canadian government will be responsible for any necessary capital expenditures which Transport Command of the United Kingdom may require to be made on the said airport.[10]

The Ferry Command would continue to pay the operating costs of its hangars and buildings and other facilities, and Canada would continue to pay the costs of operating and maintaining the airport.

As an indication of the level of activities at Dorval at the time, The *Montréal Star* reported on September 8, 1945, that four airlines operating twenty-two schedules and handling five hundred North American passengers a day were using Dorval, "the largest and most important airport in the Dominion." More than 10,000 aircraft had been delivered from Montréal during the war, and there had been 20,000 transatlantic communications flights of more than 3,000 miles [4,828 kilometres] each.

When the war ended in September 1945, the transition to full civil operations began. Since the transfer of operations from St. Hubert in 1941, TCA, Canadian Colonial, Northeast, and Québec Airways had been operating at Dorval. Canadian Pacific Airlines came to Dorval in 1942. BOAC had operated the Return Ferry Service to England for the RAF Ferry Command since May 1941, and TCA had operated the Canadian government Trans-Atlantic Air Service (CGTAS) since July 1943. BOAC's service was demilitarized in September 1946, and TCA took over CGTAS in May 1947. Both companies began to offer their commercial transatlantic scheduled service from the overseas passenger terminal in the former RAF Transport Command administration building; the main terminal was used for domestic traffic.

On February 16, 1946, the Department of Transport took over the buildings, hangars, and facilities, valued about $4.5 million, in a transfer made by Air Vice Marshal G.R. Beamish, (the air officer commanding of Transport Command, No. 45, Group RAF), to C.P. Edwards, deputy minister of Transport. The RAF Group was disbanded at midnight the same day. During the hand-over, Beamish presented a bronze plaque to the deputy minister to commemorate the work of both the civil organizations and the RAF Transport Command formations that had been based there.

The permanent airport licence, no. 231, was issued on December 11, 1946.

Air traffic on the North Atlantic route began to increase quickly with the post-war revival of Europe. A total of 246,359 passengers used Dorval in 1946. Canada entered bilateral agreements with foreign countries, under which mutual air traffic rights were granted to the designated airline of the signatory country, and many new international airlines starting scheduled air service to Dorval: BOAC (1946); KLM (1949); Air France (1950); Lufthansa (1956); SAS (1957); Sabena (1957); and Alitalia (1960) This placed a severe strain on the facilities in the old RAF Transport Command building. In 1952, a total of 589,216 passengers, domestic and international, used Dorval.

The handling of passengers was considerably eased with the opening of the new air terminal building in December 1960, and more foreign air carriers began to serve Montréal:

Swissair	1962
Aeronaves de Mexico	1964
Irish International	1966
Aeroflot	1966
Olympic	1969
Iberia	1969
Czechoslovakia	1970
El Al Israel Airlines	1971
TAP Portuguese Airlines	1971

In addition, Canadian carriers began to serve overseas destinations from Dorval:

TCA Paris-London	1951
TCA Paris-Dusseldorf	1952
CPAL Paris-Lisbon	1957
CPAL Amsterdam and Rome	1965
TCA Brussels and Zurich	1958
TCA Moscow via Copenhagen	1966

The following domestic and transborder (to the U.S.) air carriers began service at Dorval:

TCA[11]	September 1941
Northeast	September 1941
Canadian Colonial	September 1941
Québec Airways	September 1941
Canadian Pacific[12]	May 1942
Eastern[13]	June 1956
Nordair	May 1960
Eastern Provincial	November 1970

Georgian Bay Airways	May 1969
SolairMay	1969
North American Airlines	July 1969
Alleghany Airlines[14]	April 1972
Delta Airlines[15]	August 1972
Pilgrim	July 1974
Atonabee	January 1975
Air Caravane	June 1976
Pem Air	November 1976
American Airlines	January 1977

In November 1975, the new Montréal International Airport opened at Mirabel and all overseas flight operations transferred there from Dorval.

Now to the commercial side of the operation! Some of the first airport concessions for commercial services to the public in Canada were established at Montréal Airport (Dorval):

Ground Transportation
According to the company, the history of Murray Hill Limousine Service in Montréal goes back to 1909. It provided ground transportation services between St. Hubert airport and downtown Montréal from the early 1930s and moved to Dorval when airline operations were transferred there on September 1, 1941. The company held the first ground transportation concession at a Canadian airport. With an absence between 1981 and 1987 Murray Hill has continuously serviced Dorval with buses and limousines.

Restaurants
The Canada Railway News Co.[16] operated the Tea Wing Restaurant in the original air terminal at Dorval—the first airport restaurant in Canada. The company was invited by Transport to operate the airport restaurant when the terminal opened in 1941 because of its long experience with similar services at railway stations. (In 1941, it also operated the RAF Ferry Command cafeteria, and the nearby Dorval Inn—used by air ferry crews. Although both operations continued after the war, they were eventually closed down.)

In 1951, the financial arrangements for the operation were changed and, effective April 1950, the company paid the Department of Transport 5 per cent of gross revenue. The company subsequently had restaurants at other airports, including Toronto (Malton), and was the Canadian pioneer in this industry. The Montréal Airport restaurant received its first liquor licence in 1956.

Flight Kitchens
Canada Railway News Co. operated the first flight kitchen at Montréal Airport in 1941, located next to the RAF Ferry Command cafeteria. Before that time, flight meals were prepared at the Bonaventure Railway Station in downtown Montréal, then from a house in Dorval before moving to the airport.

Car Rentals
The Tilden Drive-Yourself company was given the first car rental concession at Montréal International Airport in 1952. It was an exclusive concession, and at the time, Tilden was the Hertz licencee. In 1953, Tilden left the Hertz organization, but because the airport concession was in Tilden's name, it continued as Tilden Rent-a-Car. Hertz was excluded and did not re-enter the airport until 1957 when a change in Transport's policy permitted a second concessionaire. Avis Rent-a-Car System of Canada began to serve the airport in 1959.[17]

Car Parking
The first car parking concession at Montréal Airport was granted to Stanley Realty Co. (Tilden) in late 1952.

In March 1948, concern was expressed about congestion in the transatlantic terminal. TCA would soon be introducing DC-4M North Star aircraft on the Atlantic route, and BOAC was planning to use Constellations in the summer. Already two aircraft were arriving simultaneously, and Inspection Services was complaining of overcrowding. "Peaking" was about to become a problem, and airlines were asked to revise their schedules. (Peaking of airline activity was then a new airport operations' dilemma, but it is one that still plagues airports today). The Department and the airlines formed a study committee in May 1948 to look at future needs.

On January 27, 1950, the District Inspector of Eastern Airways recommended to headquarters in Ottawa that consideration be given to the problem of jet aircraft noise that could be anticipated at Dorval. His concern was prophetic: the first noise complaint was received from Pointe Claire on May 18, 1951, well before the first jet flight! The problem worsened over the next years and, on September 9, 1959, the city of Dorval asked the Department to prohibit jet operations at the airport during normal sleeping hours. Transport began noise abatement studies, and special flight procedures were introduced at Montréal, Toronto, and Winnipeg. In 1960, airline operations at Montréal were restricted to the hours between midnight and 0700. The noise problem was one of the factors that led to the decision to build a new airport at Mirabel rather than to expand Dorval.

By January 22, 1952, the airport had two main runways which had been extended to 7,000 by 200 feet [2,059 by 59 metres], while the third—the north-south runway—remained at 5,270 by 200 feet [1,550 by 50 metres].

In May 1952, Colonial and Northeast Airlines expressed an interest in having pre-clearance service (provided by U.S. Inspection Services) established at Montréal—it was working well at Toronto with the strong support of American Airlines. But since the Dorval terminal building

130. Original air terminal, Montréal International (Dorval)

was already overcrowded, the Department of Transport could not allow the new facility to be set up. The airlines, nevertheless, acted on their own and, on November 23, U.S. Immigration staff arrived and began to work at the airline counters. On December 22, 1954, the deputy minister of Transport ruled that pre-clearance at Montréal must be stopped until new building facilities could be provided; and in February 1955, the airlines were told to discontinue pre-clearance. But they resisted, and in April, the Department had to agree to let pre-clearance continue on an interim basis.

Construction of the new terminal building finally began in May 1956: Dorval was the busiest airport in Canada with 11,000 scheduled flights and 1,092,000 passengers per year, and bigger facilities were badly needed.

The building took a long time to complete. During construction, there were many major design alterations to meet the changing requirements of the airlines and the newer and larger aircraft then coming into use. The terminal, opened in December 1960, had cost $30 million and was one of the largest and finest air terminals in the world. It was the largest in Canada and had been planned to provide enough space for the airlines and passengers well into the future. Along with better facilities for the air-

lines, it had many good restaurants and bars and excellent shops—provided under Transport's new airport concession development policy aimed at increasing non-aviation revenue.

On September 1, 1955, the department granted Timmins Aviation Ltd. a twenty-year lease of land for a hangar, for general aviation needs and particularly for the use of executive aircraft at Dorval. This was the first commercially owned hangar to be built on a government airport under a land lease for a guaranteed long-term. There was a provision that, while the Crown could cancel "for a public purpose," it would then pay the depreciated value of the building, at a rate that was spelled out in the lease. This was a new government policy to replace the former one in which the Crown might cancel at any time without compensation—which had made private investment in buildings on government airports virtually impossible.[18] The new policy was introduced after long negotiations with Timmins and other interested parties in the aviation industry, and made possible the sale of surplus government-owned hangars and the construction of new ones at Canadian government airports.

In July 1957, Timmins Aviation opened the first air cargo building constructed at a Canadian airport near to the old air terminal. The lease was cancelled on October 31, 1964, and the structure demolished because of traffic congestion and the need to clear the site to improve operations at the new terminal. The owners, who were compensated under the provisions of the lease, bought hangars no. 3 and 4 (the original RAF hangars) and converted them into the present air cargo terminal, which opened in December 1964. The original Timmins Aviation hangar was purchased by Innotech Aviation Ltd. in November 1974 and the cargo terminal by Marathon Terminals Ltd., who took over Timmins Aviation on December 31, 1969.

TCA, now Air Canada, built the first part of its new maintenance base in 1958 in the north east

area of the airport. When the original hangar area, in the southwest area of the airport, became fully occupied, a new general aviation area was developed opposite the Air Canada maintenance base. Execair (Québec) Ltd. built the first hangar there in 1968.

The airport was renamed Montréal International Airport on November 14, 1960.

In 1968, when Dorval passenger traffic had reached 4.5 million, the results of a long-term planning study of the airport were published. It forecast that:

(a) airline passenger traffic would double every eight years;

(b) air cargo would double every three or four years;

(c) general aviation would double every ten years;

(d) approximately 40,000 people would be employed directly in the aviation industry in metropolitan Montréal by 1985; 10,000 were so employed in 1968;

(e) by 1985, 7,500 acres [3,037 hectares] of land would be required for airport activities, plus 2,500 acres [1,012 hectares] for expansion beyond that date (the airport now occupies 3,900 acres [1,325 hectares]);

(f) the airport would be required to operate twenty-four-hours-a-day to allow efficient use of aircraft worth approximately $40 million each;

(g) noise disturbance to adjacent communities had already created social and economic problems, and complaints and petitions were being received in increasing numbers from a widening area; a night curfew on jet operations was already in effect and would be difficult to lift. This imposed an increasing operating penalty on the airport and the airlines.

The study found two possible solutions to these problems:

(a) move people away from the airport, which would not be feasible from a social point of view and would be economically prohibitive;

(b) move the airport from the people; in other words, build a new airport.[19]

If this solution were accepted, it was felt that Dorval could continue to function as a second airport for use by short-haul inter-city traffic using smaller jet aircraft, and by business aircraft, by some classes of general aviation, and for aircraft maintenance and servicing. Traffic would be more evenly distributed throughout the day, and the night-time curfew maintained.

These general conclusions were accepted following more detailed studies, and a new Montréal International Airport, constructed at Mirabel, was opened in November 1975.

The growth of facilities at Dorval had continually failed to meet demands, since its opening in 1960. In 1975, the terminal building with 800,000 square feet [74,320 square metres] of floor space had not only to accommodate domestic, transborder and international airline operations, but all the airline operational and administrative offices—airport management, Customs and Immigration (U.S. as well as Canadian), Health, weather, area and airport traffic control, restaurants, and shops. It had thirty-eight aircraft gates, and car parking facilities for 2,800 cars. In 1989, there were forty-four attached aircraft parking positions. A three-level parking garage for 2,400 cars was built south of the terminal in 1986, bringing the total number of parking spaces in the terminal area to 5,700.

In July 1961, the Department of Transport's underground hydrant refuelling system, the second in Canada, went into operation. (Gander opened the first in 1959, where the two installations were owned by Shell and Imperial Oil). The department sold the system at Dorval to a consortium of airlines.

131. Montréal International Airport (Dorval) Québec, 1944.

Air Canada installed its first passenger loading bridge at the terminal in December 1966.

The transborder finger of the terminal building was extended to handle increased traffic and four new aircraft gates were provided in April 1967.

In May 1970, Air France introduced the first Boeing 747 service to Montréal, and with it came new problems of such large single aircraft loads. This was the beginning of the new era of large aircraft: the jumbo jets.

In the spring of 1973, the new Category II Instrument Landing System (ILS) was put in service. This reduced airport operating limits for specially equipped aircraft and thus improved the regularity of service in bad weather.

In 1975, Dorval had approximately eight million passengers and over ten million visitors; more than 14,000 employees worked at the airport; and 190,051 tons of air cargo were handled.

When Montréal International Airport (Mirabel) began operations in November 1975, the international airlines transferred their overseas operations, including full freighter aircraft, there. Dorval then began a new life, providing domestic air services and transborder services to destinations in the United States.

The intention was to shift most of the commercial flights to Mirabel by 1985 in response to expected increases in air traffic: Dorval was to stay open for certain short-haul flights, general aviation, and aircraft maintenance.

But the original long-range plan was not realized, because the traffic growth predicted for Montréal was never attained. It may be partially attributed to the energy crisis of the 1970s, which had a marked effect on the entire aviation industry. Also, Montréal lost its role as the sole eastern gateway to Europe when bilateral agreements opened up the other Canadian cities to foreign carriers. After years of study and consultations, the government announced in 1982 that Dorval would remain the principal Montréal airport for domestic and transborder flights.

In 1986 government decided to maintain both Dorval and Mirabel, and to integrate them into a single airport system under one airport management structure.

Transport Canada owns and operates the three major airports in Montréal. In general terms, Dorval is the principal airport for domestic and transborder (Canada/United States) flights; Mirabel, the principal airport for international flights and air cargo; and St. Hubert is a satellite airport for pilot training and other general aviation activities.

The following airlines have served Dorval with domestic and transborder services from the dates indicated:

Air Alliance	June 1988
Air Alma	1980
Air Atlantic	November 1988
Air Canada	1941 as TCA;
Air Creebec	December 1988
Air Nova	September 1988
Air Ontario	1983
American Airlines	1971
Business Express	June 1986
Canadian Airlines International	began service in 1959 at Dorval as CP Airlines
Canadian Partner	March 1989
City Express	September 1985

Delta Airlines	August 1972
Eastern Airlines	June 1958
Inter-Canadien (Québecair)	January 1988
Mall Airways	March 1988
Minerve	April 1989
Northwest Airlines	1962
Piedmont Airlines	February 1988
Skycraft	June 1986
US Air	1974
Voyageur Airways	December 1986
Wardair	1975

In 1986, 3.7 million passengers on domestic flights and 1.9 million on transborder flights went through Droval, which also remains a hub for air cargo carried in passenger aircraft. Although its primary function is that of an air carrier airport, Dorval provides a wide range of services for other sectors of aviation: smaller air carriers, air taxis, government and corporate aircraft, private and rental aircraft, and advanced pilot training.

Dorval Airport is an important base for aircraft overhaul and line maintenance; it is the headquarters for Air Canada, as well as the regional office for Canadian Airlines. The airport also houses aircraft manufacturing and assembly operations for Canadair, and a completion centre and maintenance division of Innotech Aviation.

The following companies occupy hangar, cargo, and service buildings on the west (Innotech Aviation) and east (Execair) sides of the airport: Air Canada, Canadian, Marathon, Inter-Canadien, Eastern, Societe immobiliere du Québec, Aircraft Technicians, Flight Safety, Aircom Electronics, Hydro-Québec, Air Dorval, Ross Turner Holdings, Avionnair.

In 1987, there were 175,000 aircraft movements at Dorval, of which 64,195 were general aviation-related.

Although the bulk of air shipments in the Montréal area are handled at Mirabel, cargo operations continue to be a major activity at Dorval Airport. About fifty operators, including airlines, customs brokers, freight forwarders, shipping agents, and Canada Post are located in three cargo buildings in a mixed commercial zone west of the passenger terminal. The largest, cargo building no.1 on Road C, has direct access to an adjacent aircraft parking apron. Airside access for the two smaller cargo buildings on Road B is via a nearby airside security checkpoint.

The assigned cargo role for Dorval airport is to handle shipments on domestic and transborder flights. The cargo is carried either in the lower decks of regular passenger aircraft, or on the lower and upper decks of combi-flights. Pure freighters at Dorval are limited to aircraft not greater than 75,000 pounds gross take-off weight.

In 1986, 29,000 tonnes of air cargo were enplaned and deplaned at Dorval.

The area of the airport site is 1,325 hectares. There are three runways: 10-28, 2,134 metres; 06R-24L, 2,926 metres; and 06L 24R, 3,353 metres.

In 1985, Québec Regional Headquarters of Transport moved from the old RAF Transport Command Building, which it had occupied since the end of World War II, to a new building located west of the air terminal building parking lot. The old RAF building has been demolished and the site used for aircraft parking.

Canadair built an aircraft assembly plant on the airport in 1980 near Air Canada's maintenance base in centre field. The facility, which was expanded in 1988, employs about four hundred people in the manufacture, assembly and flight testing of aircraft components and aircraft.

The following airport managers have operated Dorval airport over the years:

132. Montréal International Airport (Dorval). Terminal building under construction.

F.I. Banghart (1941-1945)

Banghart had been an air-mail pilot with London Air Transport Ltd. in 1927, and he served as airport superintendent and manager at St. Hubert from 1932 to 1941. He later served as airport manager at Winnipeg and London, from which he retired in 1957.

R.A. Joberty (1945-1946)

Joberty became airport manager at Ottawa in 1951.

T.P. Roberts (1946-1947)

Roberts was on temporary duty at Dorval. He was airport manager at Ottawa Airport, 1938 to 1951.

Leigh Capreol (1947-1963)

Capreol had been chief test pilot with de Havilland Aircraft Ltd. in 1929, a pilot for—and partner in—Capreol and Austin, Toronto, in 1934, and a test pilot for the Noorduyn Norseman at Cartierville in 1935.

J.E. Goulet (1963-1968)

Goulet had been airport manager at Québec city from 1947 to 1958. From 1968 to 1970, he was regional manager of airports for the Québec region.

A.R. Habel (A/Manager, 1968-1970)
Habel had been airport manager at Québec from 1966 to 1968 and was an airways inspector in the Department of Transport (Québec Region).

J.E. Goulet (1970-1981)
Goulet was airport manager for this period, except for 1980-81, when he served as director general for the Centraide campaign. During his absence, Jean Marc Labelle served as acting manager.

J.M. Labelle (1982-1988)
Labelle became director general of Montréal airports in the reorganization which placed Dorval and Mirabel in the Montréal airports system under one airport management structure with a general manager at each airport.

Sylvain Lessard (1988-present)
Lessard succeeded Labelle as airport general manager.

Sources:
1. Transport Canada.
2. Master Plan—Mirabel International Airport, Dorval, 1988, Airports Authority Group, Transport Canada.

Footnotes—Montréal International Airport (Dorval)

[1] F.H. Ellis, *Canada's Flying Heritage* (Toronto: University of Toronto Press, 1961), p.68.
[2] Ellis, pp. 55, 68, 71, 136-37; and Madeleine Lasnier, *Aeroport International de Montréal/Montréal International Airport (Dorval)* (Montréal: Department of Transport, Québec Regional, September 1968), p.28.
[3] Canada, Department of Transport, file 5168-817, vol. 1, memo, 6 July 1939.
[4] Canada, Department of Transport, file 5168-817, vol. 2, memo, 20 May 1940.
[5] Canada, Department of Transport, file 5168-817 vol. 4.

[6] Canada, Department of Transport, file 5151-817 vol. 1, 25 October 1940.
[7] Public Archives Canada, J.A. Wilson Papers, MG 30 E243, vol. 9.
[8] Public Archives Canada, RG 24 5240, file 19-55-1, vol. 2.
[9] John Stroud, *Airports of the World* (London: Putnam, 1980), p.57.
[10] Public Archives Canada, RG 24 5240, file 19-55-1, vol. 2, 5 June 1944.
[11] TCA offered two transcontinental services daily.
[12] CPAL began Montréal-Toronto-Winnipeg-Vancouver service in May 1959.
[13] Eastern took over Canadian Colonial that year.
[14] Allegheny merged with Mohawk Airlines.
[15] Delta merged with Northeast.
[16] The company was founded on July 3, 1883. The name Aero Caterers Ltd. came into use on May 23, 1944, and the company is now known as Cara Operations Ltd.
[17] In 1957, Tilden was "represented by Avis in the USA and throughout the world," according to the company's letterhead. Tilden represented Avis in Canada for a time. The Avis franchise for Canada was taken over by the Provincial Transport Company of Montréal, and Avis Rent-a-Car System of Canada was formed in 1958.
[18] Trans-Canada Air Lines built the first hangar at Dorval in 1941 under a fifty-year land lease that could be cancelled by the Crown on sixty days notice.
[19] Madeleine Lasnier, "Aeroport International de Montréal/Montréal International Airport (Dorval)," (Montréal: Department of Transport, Québec Region, September 1968), pp. 10, 12, 22, 26, 28.

Montréal International Airport (Mirabel)
(Québec)

In 1966, the Department of Transport began a study of the projected aviation needs of the Montréal area over the next twenty-five to thirty years and of how these needs could best be met.[1] The study revealed that the Montréal International Airport at Dorval would reach traffic saturation by 1975, and that, even if it was expanded, it would reach its maximum capacity by 1985. Beyond that, additional air terminal buildings and runways would require the acquisition of very expensive land. Even more critical would be the noise problem—the public living near the airport were already protesting and demanding action. And although restrictions were imposed on night flights the annoyance persisted.

After weighing all the factors, the government decided in 1968 that the future aviation needs of the Montréal area could be met only by the construction of a new international airport, one which would be suitable for new generation aircraft and the largely unknown demands of the twenty-first century.

In 1969, a site was chosen for the new airport at St. Scholastique, fifty-eight kilometres from the centre of Montréal and forty-eight kilometres from the Dorval airport. To meet the needs of the foreseeable future, much land was required on a site that was remote from residential and industrial developments. In the largest expropriation ever carried out in Canada, the federal government took 88,000 acres [35,640 hectares] of farm and forest land. In 1973 fourteen small towns and villages, located within the expropriated area, were amalgamated into a single municipality, which the residents, by popular poll, called Mirabel. This was the name of a farm owned by one of the original nineteenth century settlers; and during the World War I, there was a Grand Trunk Railway station called Mirabel in the area.

Although Mirabel was the world's largest airport at that time, its 17,000-acre [6,885 hectare] operational area, however, is slightly smaller than that of the Dallas-Fort Worth complex. Such a large acreage was acquired to ensure that

133. Montréal International Airport (Mirabel).

the areas surrounding the airport would always be free of environmental problems related to aircraft noise, and the runways and approaches were to be built in the centre of the 17,000-acre operational area. All land use and building heights in the peripheral area were to be controlled so that the airport could operate without significant constraints. Phase I of the airport development occupies 5,200 acres [2,106 hectares]. One hundred fifty-seven property owners (including 144 of the area's 820 farmers) had to move to make way for the initial construction; the others were given ten year renewable land leases.

In 1984, the government decided to dispose of 28,755 hectares, which were resold to the farmer owners; and in 1987, 324 additional hectares were declared surplus.

Phase I construction of the Mirabel Airport began in June 1970, and includes two runways and taxiway systems, 11-29 and 06-24, each 12,000 by 200 feet [3,658 by 61 metres], the air terminal building, the control tower, a car parking garage, service buildings, and utilities. An underground refuelling system and air cargo terminal were constructed by the aviation industry. A 361-room hotel, Le Chateau de l'aéroport, was built by Canadian Pacific Hotels Ltd.

Phase I was designed for six to ten million passengers per year. Plans called for six runways and six terminal buildings, capable of handling sixty million passengers[2] by the year 2025. Airport construction, including the air terminal, cost $350 million.

The terminal building is an unusual design, with remote aircraft gates, and minimizes walking distances for passengers. It measures 1,140 by 280 feet [350 by 85 metres] and has up to eighteen arrival and twenty-two departure docks. Aircraft park at three servicing clusters (eighteen aircraft at a time), 1,500 feet [457 metres] from the terminal. Passengers are taken to and from there by twenty passenger transfer vehicles (each carrying up to 120 people). This system avoids aircraft congestion at the terminal, permits a more flexible service, and reduces walking distances. There is an aeroquay for connecting domestic flights, which has six aircraft positions linked to the terminal by four bridges. The free-standing control tower is 215 feet [65 metres] high and was the tallest in Canada at the time. The parking garage accommodates 3,400 cars.

Mirabel Airport was officially opened by Prime Minister Trudeau on October 4, 1975, and operations began on November 29, 1975. Because it has no noise restrictions it may operate twenty-four hours a day—one of the few major airports in the world that has this capability. When the airport opened, all transoceanic scheduled and charter operations were transferred from Dorval, and thirty-three airlines now serve the airport: Aeroflot Soviet Airlines; Czechoslovak Airlines; Royal Air Maroc; Aerolineas Argentinas; El Al Israel Airlines; Sabena Belgian Airlines; Air Canada; First Air; Société Française d'affretement; Air France; Iberia; Air St. Pierre; KLM, Royal Dutch Airlines; Swissair; Air Transat; Lanchile S.A.; TAP Air Portugal; Alia, The Royal Jordanian Airlines; LOT Polish Airlines; Trans-Brasil; Lufthansa German

Airlines; Varig Airlines; Alitalia; Société Minerve (France); Wardair Canada; British Airways; Société Minerve (Canada); Worldways; Canadian International; Nationair; Yugoslav Airlines - JAT; Cubana Airlines; and Olympic Airways.

The air cargo centre groups together five buildings and one common-use loading dock. The dock and loading bridges, were built in 1976 by Air Canada. Buildings A, B, and C provide office and storage space to air carriers, customs brokers, and the Department of Revenue (Customs and Excise). About seventy-five companies are tenants there.

Building D brings together twenty-five brokers and forwarding agents and serves as a cargo and brokerage dispatch centre. Fitted out in 1981, the distribution centre was intended for storage, packaging and distribution of goods.

The following airlines provide air cargo service: Air Charter Systems; Federal Express; Korean Airlines; Air France Cargo; Flying Tigers; Scandinavian Airlines; Cargolux; Japan Airlines; System; Express Air Canada; KLM Cargo; and Swissair Cargo.

In 1987, Transport Canada built an apron and access roads and put in place the infrastructure of the aircraft maintenance area capable of accommodating four hangars.

134. Air cargo terminal, Montréal International Airport (Mirabel).

In 1988, Technair Ltd. erected an administration building and a maintenance hangar with two bays large enough for B-747s. Canadair built one hangar, a three storey building for engineering and administration offices as well as a production plant and technical support for its military division.

A seven-storey administration building houses the offices of seven government departments. Two airport kitchens on the site are operated by Marriot and Cara. A two-storey service centre accommodates building maintenance vehicles and airport grounds services; a special garage takes the large passenger transfer vehicles for servicing. There is a fuelling centre; and air support buildings for Air Canada, Canadian International, and Hudson General, are located near to the control tower. Agriculture Canada has an animal quarantine on site.

The initial transfer of traffic to the new airport was expected to move about 3.7 million passengers a year from Dorval to Mirabel, leaving Dorval with approximately five million passengers. Additional transfers from Dorval were planned so that by 1985 Mirabel would have seventeen million passengers, and Dorval about three million. Unfortunately, these transfers to Mirabel have not materialized and the airport is under-utilized. In 1979, Mirabel handled only 2,750,000 passengers, compared to Dorval's 6,250,000. In 1980, there were 49,059 aircraft movements at Mirabel and 174,458 at Dorval. In 1988, Mirabel handled 2,500,000 passengers, compared to Dorval's 6,500,000. In 1988, there were 70,000 aircraft movements at Mirabel, and 200,000 at Dorval.

There are at least two reasons for the unexpected distribution of traffic: first, the unforeseen down-turn in the economy and the slow-down in traffic growth in 1970; second, and perhaps more important, the change in overseas traffic patterns between Montréal and Toronto, which followed

135. PTV connected to Air Canada 747, Montréal International Airport (Mirabel).

new bilateral air agreements (of the early 1970s) between Canada and several European countries, granting reciprocal traffic rights to national airlines. In return for European gateways for Canadian air carriers, Canada had to give traffic rights to Toronto. The immediate result was that passengers who had previously deplaned at Montréal and transferred to a domestic carrier to fly to Toronto now flew direct to Toronto. The longer range of the new aircraft made it possible for flights from European points to Toronto, Winnipeg, Edmonton, and Vancouver to complete their journeys to these western cities without a stop in Montréal.

The first airport manager of Montréal International Airport (Mirabel) was P.E. Arpin. He was succeeded by Rubin Ginzburg in September 1974.

In 1986, the Department of Transport announced the joint administration of Dorval and Mirabel Airports on a commercial basis. The new integrated management was put in place in April 1988, and Dorval and Mirabel became "The Montréal Airports." Their management reflects a new mission which involves public and private sectors. J.M. Labelle became director general of the Montréal Airports System; Dorval and Mirabel each have a general manager.

Sources:

1. Transport Canada, Québec Region.
2. "Mirabel," *Financial Times of Canada*, (29 September 1975: Special Edition).
3. *Montréal International Airport*, produced by Van Ginkel Associates, September 1968, for the Department of Transport.

Footnotes—Montréal International Airport (Mirabel)

[1] See the section on Montréal International Airport, Dorval.

[2] This was roughly ten times the current passenger traffic at Dorval Airport.

Moosonee Airport
(Ontario)

Moosonee Airport was opened in May 1970 as a result of the provincial program "Highways in the Sky." The construction of the airport was shared by the federal and provincial governments.

Moosonee Airport, operated by the Moosonee Development Area Board, is the gateway to the northern corridor of airstrips situated along Hudson Bay. Commercial aircraft not only service communities along Hudson Bay, but also provide accessibility and supplies to isolated areas to the North.

In 1971, Moosonee Airport received its first subsidy from Transport Canada, which increased to $114,304 by 1977. In 1974, a cross-wind runway was completed at the provincial government's expense, and a new maintenance building was built in 1987.

In 1989, runway 06-24, (1,219 metres), was paved. Runway 14-32 is a 1,067-metre-long gravel surfaced runway that was extended by 305 metres in 1989. A new taxiway was added at the time of the extension.

There has been an enormous increase in air traffic movements at Moosonee for aircraft in the 39,000 to 79,000 pound weight range: 303 movements in in 1976, more than tripled to 998 in 1978. This is due in part to the James Bay Hydro Project, but the main increase comes from the move to more sophisticated and efficient land-based aircraft—for example, HS-748. During 1989, the HS-748 made sixteen flights per week and the ATR-42 made one flight per day, six days a week.

Moosonee, the most northerly railhead in Ontario, will serve increasingly as the hub from which passengers and freight are transferred to aircraft for destinations further north. Plans are being finalized for a rail link and railway terminal warehouse to be built on the airport site in the spring of 1990.

Moosonee airport has scheduled daily flights by Air Québec, Frontier Air and Canadian Partner. Huisson Aviation Ltd. (helicopters), Bushland Charter Service and the Ontario Ministry of Natural Resources are based at the airport.

Moosonee Airport had 6,727 aircraft movements in 1988.

Sources:
1. Transport Canada, Ontario Region.
2. John Kirk, General Manager, Moosonee Development Area Board.

Mould Bay Airstrip
(Northwest Territories)

Mould Bay, Joint (Canada-U.S.) Arctic Weather Station on Prince Patrick Island, is 692 kilometres northwest of Resolute Bay. The initial landing was made on April 11, 1948, with three station personnel and basic supplies. Voice contact was made with Resolute that same evening, with a small portable radio.

A tractor was delivered on April 12, and the airlift continued until April 19, when all the supplies had been delivered except for some bulky grading equipment, which was taken in on April 25. One hundred and seventy tons of supplies were carried into Mould Bay in thirty-two flights without incident. The airlift was carried out from Resolute simultaneously with the establishment of the Isachsen station by the Air Transport Command of the U.S. Air Force. The scale of the operation is evident from the aircraft that were assigned to it: five C-54s, two C-82s, and two C-47s. Approximately one hundred military personnel and about twenty-five civilians were transported to Resolute for this mission.

The staff establishment at Mould Bay was identical in numbers to that at Isachsen the first year: three Canadian and three U.S. personnel, and an additional American mechanic employed on a temporary basis for airstrip construction. The complement was later raised to seven: four Canadian and three American personnel.

The gravel airstrip 09-27, 1,646 by 46 metres is operated and maintained by Transport Canada through contracted staff. There are no hangar or aircraft servicing facilities.

Since 1972, when the United States withdrew, the Arctic weather program has been managed by the Canadian Meteorological Services of Environment Canada. It is known as the High Arctic Weather Station.

In 1980, there were 165 aircraft movements.

Source:
Transport Canada, Central Region.

Muskoka Airport
(Ontario)

Muskoka Airport was built as an emergency landing field on the Trans-Canada Airway. Before the government's decision to locate the field there, the town council of Gravenhurst had made several representations to the authorities in Ottawa. Work on the site actually began in September 1933.

The town asked that the field be named Ferguson Airport after the first aircraft owner in Muskoka; but the Department of the National Defence (then responsible for civil aviation) refused and named it Reary after the nearest post office, six and a half kilometres north of Gravenhurst. The town then asked that the name be changed to Gravenhurst Airport, but again the Department refused. The airport was renamed Muskoka in 1938.

On September 11, 1935, an American aircraft landed—the first on the field.

Both the east-west runway, graded to full length, and the one running north-south were in good condition by November 1935. By May 1936, the work was nearly completed. When the project closed in June 1936, W. Price, the foreman in charge, was appointed caretaker, and work continued on a day-labour basis under the Civil Aviation Division.

During 1940-41, the RCAF used the airport for flying training. In 1943, the field was made available to the Royal Norwegian Air Force (RNAF), which moved its training base from Toronto Island Airport. When the RNAF moved out, the airport licence was issued in the name of the Department of Transport on May 20, 1946.

By 1946, the airport had three turf runways: two 3,100 feet [945 metres] long and one of 3,000 feet [914 metres]. Doherty Air Services Muskoka Ltd. was then based there.

When the RCAF training base (for Sabre jet fighters) was established at North Bay in 1951, an asphalt runway, 6,000 feet [1,829 metres] long, was built by National Defence as an emergency facility in support of the North Bay operations, 161 kilometres from Muskoka. Runway lighting was added between 1952 and 1954.

For a few years in the mid-1950s, Trans-Canada Air Lines offered services into Muskoka, but discontinued because of lack of traffic.

Muskoka is now run by Transport Canada and is the scene of brisk general aviation activity with aircraft sales, service, charter, and maintenance facilities. Townsend Air Services, Air Muskoka, and Orillia Air Services are based at the airport.

There were 34,000 aircraft movements in 1987.

Muskoka Airport is a Customs port of entry and serves much tourist traffic from the United States.

The following served as airport managers:

Major M. Price	1933 to 1951
Bill Benedetti	1951 to 1960
Bill Hough	1960 to 1962
Lloyd Street	1962 to 1980
N.S. (Charlie) Dow	1980 to 1987
Richard Marchand	1987 to present

Sources:

1. Transport Canada.
2. R.L. Clarke, "Airport Notes" (Ottawa: Department of Transport) [unpublished collection].

Nanaimo Airport
(British Columbia)

The Nanaimo Airport was developed by the federal government as an emergency wartime field in 1942, with an asphalt runway 5,000 by 200 feet [1,524 by 61 metres], and taxiway.

The airport is sixteen kilometres south of the city of Nanaimo, near Cassidy on the east coast of Vancouver Island.

The city of Nanaimo has leased the 212 hectare site from the federal government since 1952 for $1.00 per annum, and operates the airport. In 1978, the city received a $455,000 grant from the federal government to repave the runway and taxiway and to construct a new parking apron and complete other improvements. Transport Canada provided all engineering and technical staff.

There is presently no common use air terminal or public parking facility at the Airport. All five scheduled airlines have separate facilities.

Runway 16-34 is maintained at its current length of 1,524 metres and remains classified as a Code 3 (C) Instrument Non-Precision Runway.

The airport is served by Air BC, Time Air, Aquila Air, Sky Link, and Burrard Air. The following provide charter service: Aquila Air, Aviate Air, Burrard Air, and Time Air.

In 1988, there were 117,350 passengers, and 62,929 aircraft movements.

Nanaimo Harbour has scheduled seaplane services by Thunderbird Air and Lyce Air. Air Rainbow provides chartered seaplane service. In 1988, the seaplane statistics were 21,100 aircraft movements and 41,040 passengers.

The following operators are based at the airport: Nanaimo Flying Club, Frank Beban Logging Ltd., S. Madill Ltd., and the Air Cadet League of Canada (Gliding Programme). Nanaimo Aeroservices Ltd. provides aircraft maintenance.

The current airport manager is D.M. Geddes.

Source:

1. City of Nanaimo.
2. D.M. Geddes, Airport Manager, Nanaimo Airport.

Nanisivik Airstrip
(Northwest Territories)

Nanisivik, Canada's first mine north of the Arctic Circle, is situated in Strathcona Sound on the northern tip of Baffin Island. Located seven hundred kilometres north of the Arctic Circle, Nanisivik is connected by an all-weather road to the community of Arctic Bay, a distance of twenty-seven kilometres. The town of Nanisivik, eight kilometres north of the airport and five and a half kilometres south of Strathcona Sound, is considered a development area and is administered by the government of the Northwest Territories.

The airstrip was completed in October 1978 as part of the service for the mine and community at Nanisivik on Baffin Island.

The gravel strip, 106° T - 286° T, is 1,950 by 46 metres, and is operated by Transport Canada. Local traffic averages forty aircraft landings per month; passenger traffic ranges from 450 to 700 per month; annual in-bound freight amounts to 700 tonnes.

The development of the mine and provision of infrastructure were undertaken under an agreement signed at Frobisher Bay in June 1974. Project financing was provided by the government of Canada, Texas Gulf Inc., Metallgesellachaft A.G. of West Germany, and Billiton B.V. of the Netherlands. The mine is operated by Nanisivik Mines Ltd.

The mine produces zinc (with small amounts of lead, as well as silver and cadmium as by-products). Production is expected to continue at least until 1994: the ore is shipped out in ice-breaking carriers during the shipping season.

Air service connects Nanisivik to Iqaluit (Frobisher Bay) twice weekly and takes approximately two hours flying time by jet. Twin Otter aircraft from other Baffin region settlements and Resolute Bay have scheduled flights into Nanisivik.

The annual mean temperature at Nanisivik is -14°Celsius. Permafrost is estimated to extend to a depth of five hundred metres. The rock temperature in the mine is -12° Celsius. Summer thawing rarely extends to a depth greater than one metre. As none of the annual precipitation seeps into the ground, the run-off of rain and melted snow in early July is spectacular and has dissected the landscape with deep gorges.

Nanisivik Mines Ltd. maintains sixty-four family accommodation units ranging from one-bedroom apartments to four-bedroom detached houses. Single status employees are housed in three- and five-bedroom units integrated into the townsite, and one fifty-five room multiple accommodation building. The government has fifteen houses for its employees. Canadian Airlines and Bell Telephone also provide permanent accommodation for their representatives.

A 25-metre diameter dome is located in the town centre. This unique building is utilized for food preparation and dining. All single-status employees are served meals at the Dome and the facility is open to family employees and the public. The building is owned by the Territorial government and is leased by Nanisivik Mines Ltd.

The town population is 350, of whom 100 are children. Inuit make up 25 per cent of the population and have come principally from the Baffin region, but some originally lived as far away as Rankin Inlet and northern Québec. Southern Canadians have been recruited from all parts of Canada, but principally from Newfoundland, northwestern Québec and northern Ontario.

Sources:
1. Nanisivik Mines Ltd., Nanisivik, N.W.T.
2. The Northern Miner.
3. Transport Canada, Western Region.

Natashquan Airport
Québec

Between 1950 and 1954, an airstrip 4,000 by 150 feet [1,219 by 46 metres] was constructed at Natashquan, and aircraft began to use it in Octo-ber 1954. The sand surface, however, was not satisfactory and it had to be covered with gravel two years later.

In October 1971, Transport granted $6,500 to the municipality for runway and ramp improvements, and a trailer was set up as a temporary terminal until the new building, put up by Transport, was opened in 1973.

The runway was still causing problems in May 1972, and Northern Wings threatened to suspend service.

The municipality continued to press Transport for runway improvements. In the fall of 1975, $90,000 was made available by Transport for a contract to re-gravel the runway and put it in shape for use by Northern Wings HS-748 aircraft. It was paved in 1979 and is now 1372 by 30 metres.

Ownership of the airport was transferred to Transport on December 15, 1965. It is operated by Natashquan with an operating subsidy from Transport Canada, first provided in 1970.

The airport is served by Intair, and Varaps Aviation is based at the site. In 1988, there were 11,900 passengers and 4,235 aircraft movements.

Source:
Transport Canada, Québec Region.

Norman Wells Airport
(Northwest Territories)

Norman Wells is situated on the east side of the Mackenzie River, 1,491 kilometres from Edmonton, 685 kilometres from Yellowknife, 458 kilometres from Inuvik, and 144 kilometres south of the Arctic Circle. As a distribution hub, it serves Fort Good Hope, Fort Norman, Fort Franklin, and several smaller communities, fishing lodges, and outfitting camps. It, in turn, is served from Edmonton, Yellowknife, and Inuvik on a regular basis. Transportation is by air year-round, by barges during summer months, and by winter road during four months in winter.

Imperial Oil Ltd. drilled its first successful well at Norman Wells in 1920, and a small refinery was built there in 1921. But the immediate market was limited and transportation south expensive, so it was forced to close. The refinery started up again in 1932 to supply the mines at Great Bear Lake. Production was expanded in 1939 to 840 barrels a day and increased even more during the war.

In 1942, when the Japanese occupied the Aleutian Islands and posed a threat to Alaska and North America, U.S. forces in the Alaskan coastal area needed a secure source of gasoline and oil. The United States, with Canadian approval, built a pipeline from Norman Wells to Whitehorse: this became known as the Canol project. A number of aerodromes in Canada that would connect with the railheads at Waterways and Peace River in Alberta were built to carry men and materials to the construction sites.[1] This was particularly necessary in winter when water routes were frozen. Finished petroleum products from Whitehorse were to be distributed by way of pipeline to Skagway and Fairbanks in Alaska and to Watson Lake in the Yukon. Supplies were brought by barge down the Mackenzie River and by truck up the new Alaska Highway. The project was completed in February 1944, and sixty new wells had been drilled at Norman Wells. There was, however, no longer a need for the pipeline when the allied position in the Pacific improved, and, eventually, it was abandoned and the Whitehorse refinery was moved to Leduc, Alberta.

The Norman Wells Airport, initially developed as an airstrip by the United States Army Force in 1942 in support of the Canol Project, was a 6,750 by 200 foot [2,057 by 61 metre] silt runway. The airfield—one of several—was bought by Canada from the U.S. at the end of the war. The Department of Transport took over the aerodrome on November 1, 1944, and maintained it until October 15, 1946, when it was placed on a caretaker basis. From October 1, 1947, to October 31, 1954, the airfield was maintained by Imperial Oil Ltd. for the RCAF. The Department of Transport then arranged for Imperial Oil to continue maintenance on a fixed fee basis until April 1, 1955, when the RCAF agreed to maintain the field during the balance of that year's spring DEW Line airlift. The Department of Transport took over maintenance in the summer of 1955, and an airport licence was issued in the name of Transport for twenty-four-hour operation on February 22, 1956. During the construction of the DEW Line[2] in 1955-58, Norman Wells was one of the main support airports.

Norman Wells is in the zone of continuous permafrost. Outside the runway area itself, soils commonly contain significant quantities of ice that cause large settlements when thawed. Hence pilings are commonly required for buildings. The soil underlying the runway is denser and drier, and conventional cut-and-fill methods were employed in runway construction.

A new air terminal building was constructed by Transport in 1958. In 1961-62, the runway (6,000 by 150 feet [1,829 by 46 metres]) taxiways and apron were gravelled, and in 1969 were paved with asphalt. Medium intensity runway and approach lighting was installed in 1964. VASIS (Visual Approach Slope Indicator System)was installed in 1971 and VOR (VHF Omni-directional Range) in 1973. A steel "butler type" maintenance garage was erected in 1962.

Norman Wells has developed over the years as a result of increased activities by Esso Resources Canada in oil exploration and drilling. The community attained village status on April 1, 1986.

Canadian Pacific Airlines, which had served the Mackenzie Valley since taking over Canadian Airways in 1940, turned over its operation to Pacific Western Airways in 1960. The first jet aircraft, a Boeing 737, arrived at the airport in 1969. Nahanni Air Services commenced operations in 1973. In 1988, Northwest Territorial Air began L188 Electra schedule service into Norman Wells from points south; Aklak Air announced scheduled service from points north; the government of the Northwest Territories' Forestry department developed a heliport at the east end of the airport; and Chevron Canada Ltd. started operating re-supply aircraft out of Norman Wells.

The airport had 21,466 aircraft movements in 1987, and there were 26,900 passengers.

The following have served as airport managers at Norman Wells:

D. Willmer	1963
E. Davison	1963 to 1965
E. Campbell	1965 to 1966
J. Williams	1966 to 1973
K. Howard	1973 to 1975
R. Rozzoli	1975
D. Hector	1975 to 1977
J. Patterson	1977
R. Bye	1977 to 1978
R. Barradell	1979 to 1984
S. Sutherland	1984 to 1985
R. Dean	1985 to 1986
D. Romanko	1986

Sources:
1. Transport Canada, Western Region.
2. R.L. Clarke, "Airport Notes" (Ottawa: Transport Canada) [unpublished collection].

Footnotes—Norman Wells airport
[1] At Fort McMurray, Embarras, Fort Smith, Fort Resolution, Hay River, Fort Providence, Fort Simpson, Wrigley, and Norman Wells.

[2] The Distant Early Warning Line was planned jointly by Canada and the United States, but financed by the latter. It was built north of the Arctic Circle and extended from the Alaska-Yukon border to Cape Dorset, Baffin Island. About forty-one stations were built; the line was working by January 1, 1958. Most of the sites were inaccessible except by air, and a huge airlift was developed to support construction.

North Battleford Airport
(Saskatchewan)

In 1928, the town of North Battleford asked the Civil Aviation Branch of the Department of National Defence for assistance in finding a suitable airport site, and in July a location was selected in the Buena Vista subdivision, three kilometres from town. Construction was completed and a permanent licence (no. 138) was issued to the town on December 30, 1930. The longest runway was 2,600 feet [792 metres], and the shortest, 1,700 feet [518 metres].

The aviation industry was booming; and the need for commercial air service in this northern community was provided by Cherry Red Airlines and Commercial Airways Ltd. until the early 1930s. The contract for handling airmail in Western Canada was awarded to Western Canada Airways Ltd. of Winnipeg, whose route originated in Winnipeg with several stops in Saskatchewan, including North Battleford. The North Battleford Optimist reported on March 6, 1930: "city officials welcome plane as first batch of air mail comes in." This service lasted only a few years.

M & C Aviation Co. Ltd., Saskatoon, entered into an agreement in September 1931 with the city to base one of its airplanes in North Battleford; and Prairie Airways Ltd. of Moose Jaw also stationed one of its charter aircraft there. "That the charter plane stationed at the airport is a boon to persons throughout this territory requiring medical attention has been demonstrated the past week," reported the North Battleford Optimist on January 5, 1939.

In 1938, a terminal building was constructed, an additional 103 acres [41.7 hectares] of land acquired and runways were improved[1] to the following dimensions: north-south, 2,640 by 500 feet [805 by 152 metres]; northwest-southeast, 2,700 by 300 feet [823 by 91 metres]; and east-west, 2,640 by 300 feet [805 by 91 metres]. City Council called a special meeting to discuss the opening ceremonies, and unanimously decided to name the airport McIntosh Field in recognition of the hard work done by C.R. McIntosh, the member of parliament for North Battleford. War broke out, however, and the opening ceremonies never took place.

In January 1940, the town was asked to lease the airport to the federal government for the duration of the war for use as an RAF training school under the British Commonwealth Air Training Plan (BCATP). North Battleford agreed, and an extensive development of the airport began. On August 29, 1940, the North Battleford Optimist headlined: "Plans Out for Huge Air Project—To include 39 buildings at cost of over a million." The BCATP came into full operation upon completion of the develop-

136. Curtiss biplane, first aircraft at North Battleford, Saskatchewan c. 1912.

ment. No. 35 Service Flying Training School (SFTS) personnel arrived from Britain on July 21, 1941 and were welcomed by an Indian chief in full ceremonial dress. No. 35 SFTS turned out 941 graduates before disbanding on February 25, 1944 when the buildings and facilities were then taken over by the Royal Canadian Air Force. The training school continued for just over a year and disbanded on May 15, 1945. Les Gamwell, the retired airport manager, recalls that he maintained the double runways (inner and outer triangles) for the BCATP with a staff of three in 1944.

When the airport was transferred to the Department of Transport in the fall of 1945, because the town refused to take it back, there were seven hangars, a terminal building, a maintenance garage, and many other buildings. The North Battleford Optimist reported that "certain buildings at the local airport are to be made available to citizens prepared to utilize them as housing" (November 22, 1945). This referred to the housing shortage created by soldiers returning from overseas. It was not until September 1947 that the Department of Transport appointed some airport staff, although Canadian Pacific Airlines had already been operating a daily scheduled service there.

Canadian Pacific, which had purchased Prairie Airways of Moose Jaw in 1942, found it necessary to use smaller aircraft on the service to North Battleford when air traffic declined, and eventually stopped its service on November 1, 1957. Battle River Air Services obtained its licence in March 1947 to operate a non-scheduled commercial air service based at North Battleford. It also provided a flying training school. The company discontinued service in the early 1950s.

By 1955, there were only three hangars remaining, nos. 3, 4 and 7. Hangar no. 7 housed the Western Development Museum from 1948 to

1963 and then served as storage for the museum until 1986, when it was dismantled. Hangar no. 4 housed the Saskatchewan Government Salvage Department and, since early 1970, was owned by Gendall Air Ltd., which ran a charter service. Hangar no. 4 was purchased in 1984 by Odishaw Farms. The hangar housed an Aero Maintenance facility and was also used for storage. Ownership reverted to Transport Canada on January 1, 1989, and was later leased to the city, with Aero Maintenance facilities and aircraft parking continuing. Battleford Airways relocated in August of 1987, leaving hangar no. 3 vacant: it was demolished in the winter of 1988-89. The city now has a fixed base operator looking after hangar no. 4. A new Esso fuel dispensing facility, built in the spring of 1989 supplies aviation gas, and will provide jet fuel in the future.

Modifications were made to the runway system in 1956-57 when a new runway, 12-30, was built. By 1958, lighting had been added to the runways and the second runway, 06-24, had been upgraded.

Mel-Air Services Ltd. obtained a licence to operate a regularly scheduled passenger service in the fall of 1964. Its route started in Swift Current, stopped off at Saskatoon, North Battleford, and Lloydminster, and turned around at Edmonton. The service ended in mid-1969.

The Department of Transport administered the airport until 1970. The city then took over the operation until 1974 when it was returned to Transport Canada, only to revert to the city once more in November 1981.

Early in 1975, the Canadian Transport Commission issued a regular passenger service licence to Miksoo Aviation to operate at North Battleford. Miksoo ended its operation in mid-1978.

Two aviation businesses are now located at the airport. McPhail Air Services, which has been in operation since 1952, providing student flight training, charters, aircraft sales and service, aircraft maintenance, and crop spraying, changed ownership and is now known as Battleford Airways.

Prairie Flying began operating charter service out of North Battleford in October 1989.

In 1970 Transport Canada finished construction of a new terminal building, officially opened on March 2. It contains offices, a waiting room for commercial air carriers, and the airport's telecommunications and atmospheric environment equipment.

Today, the airport has two paved runways: 12-30, at 1,524 metres long, and 06-24, at 891 metres long.

Twelve aircraft are based at the airport. In 1988, there were 5,338 aircraft movements.

A. Vilm was the airport manager from 1981 to 1985. R.J. Thompson has been the airport manager since 1986.

Sources:
1. Transport Canada, Central Region.
2. R.L. Clarke, "Airport Notes" (Ottawa: Transport Canada) [unpublished collection].
3. R.J. Thompson, Airport Manager, North Battleford Airport.

Footnote—North Battleford Airport

[1] These improvements were funded in part by a grant of $10,000 from the Department of Transport in May 1838.

North Bay Airport
Also known as Jack Garland Airport
(Ontario)

North Bay made its first request to the government for an airport as long ago as 1920, but at the time it was government policy that local communities should provide their own aerodromes. Thus it was not until 1937 that the city got an airport.

In 1933, the Department of National Defence (then responsible for civil aviation) chose North Bay as a regional office for the construction of aerodromes and emergency landing fields for the Ontario section of the Trans-Canada Airway.

In 1937, it was decided to build an airport at North Bay as part of the airway. The city was unwilling to undertake the expense and the Department of Transport, despite the government's earlier policy, agreed to build and operate the airport. At that time, the department operated only three civil airports— St. Hubert, Rimouski, and Ottawa (see Chapter 6 for more on this policy). The site selected for the airport was at Carmichael Corner, six and a half kilometres northeast of the city and, by 1938, three runways were under construction.

A terminal building was also constructed in 1938—the first building, designed as a terminal, to be erected by the Department of Transport. (At St. Hubert, there was an administration building, built in 1929; Rimouski had a small administration; and at Ottawa, the Department's only other airport, the terminal was located in the hangar lean-to).

Trans-Canada Air Lines (TCA) made its first

137. First Terminal North Bay Airport, built in 1938.

138. North Bay Airport, Ontario, 1942.

flight into North Bay in August 1938 and began to carry passengers in 1939, using ten-passenger Lockheed 10-A aircraft. At that time, North Bay was the junction for flights from Toronto and Montréal going west.

A hangar, built in 1939 by the Department of Transport for TCA, is currently in use for aircraft storage.

In 1942, the three runways were paved: 08-26 was 4,850 by 200 feet [1,478 by 61 metres], 13-31, 4,600 by 150 feet [1,402 by 46 metres], and 18-36, 4,500 by 150 feet [1,372 by 46 metres].

In the same year, the RAF Ferry Command took over part of the airport as a flight training base. Later, the RCAF Transport Command began training flights from North Bay and established a ferry base there to fly Liberators and Lancasters across the Atlantic. The RAF Ferry Command remained at North Bay until October 1945. Despite these extensive military operations, North Bay remained a civil airport under the management of the Department of Transport, and after the war remained under its administration.

The RCAF returned to North Bay in 1952 when the war began in Korea, and the airport became a regular air force station. The runways and facilities, which had been adequate during the World War II, were not suitable for the new high

139. North Bay Terminal, built in 1963.

performance jet aircraft that used the base. Consequently, runways and taxiways were extended and strengthened, and new tarmac was added. Hangars, a control tower, living quarters, and many other buildings were constructed. Today, the village that houses the military personnel at North Bay Airport is known as Hornell Heights.

In 1963, Transport constructed a new modern air terminal building.

The first control tower at North Bay was built in 1940—a small glass house that was added to the top of the old terminal building. Three controllers were appointed in 1943. The tower was closed at the end of the war and reopened in 1950.

On August 26, 1966, the name of North Bay Airport was officially changed to Jack Garland Airport in memory of the deceased member of parliament for the area, who had taken a special interest in the airport.

Transport Canada, which owns and operates the airport, has its maintenance centre there for Sudbury, Moosonee, Attawapiskat, Peawanuk, Fort Albany, Fort Severn, Fort Hope, Landsdowne House and Webequie.

With 84,541 aircraft movements and more than 104,000 passengers in 1988, the airport is served by the following scheduled airlines: Air Canada, Norontair, Air Ontario, Canadian Partner, Voyageur Airways, and Frontier Air.

The following served as airport managers:

Frank Hughes	1940 to 1942
Lorne W. Hicks	1942 to 1974
James Albeartie	1974

Military Operations

National Defence activities at North Bay include Canada's Air Defence Operational Headquarters. Located together at the thirty-nine hectare military complex are the headquarters for the 22 NORAD Region and the joint Canada-United States Continental Air Defence Organization.

Canada's air defence bases and units are administered through and are operationally responsible to the Defence Headquarters in North Bay. The Radar Control Wing coordinates radar and interceptor units to provide constant surveillance of over two million square miles of Canadian and American airspace.

Located deep below the base on Airport Hill are the Fighter Group, the Canadian NORAD Headquarters, and the Radar Control Wing. Completely self-sufficient, this complex provides day-to-day surveillance of Canada's airspace.

Canada Forces Base (CFB) North Bay supports many lodger units along with the above headquarters. 414 Squadron flies T-33 aircraft on target and electronic counter-measures missions; 414 (Black Knight) Squadron provides training for NORAD crews across North America.

CFB North Bay is the largest single employer in the city. There are approximately 1,400 military employees, including more than fifty U.S. Air Force personnel and 322 civilians working on the base, with an annual payroll about $20 million. In 1989, the federal government announced that CFB North Bay would close within two years, a move which may affect airport operations.

Sources:
1. Transport Canada, Ontario Region.
2. J.G. Albeartie, Airport Manager, North Bay Airport.
3. R.L. Clarke, "Airport Notes" (Ottawa: Transport Canada) [unpublished collection].

Norway House Airport
(Manitoba)

The Norway House Airport is situated on Fort Island west of the Norway House reservation lands on provincial Crown property. Although the airport receives an operating subsidy from Transport Canada, it is owned and operated by the province of Manitoba Department of Highways and Transportation.

In 1966, Deputy Commissioner of Manitoba Northern Affairs was taxed with providing transportation access to northern communities. It was therefore decided to build an airstrip in every northern community with a population of over one hundred people, as the cost of developing road access was prohibitive.

Construction of the airport began in 1968-69. The initial mud runway was eventually replaced by a gravel strip measuring 1,600 by 100 feet [488 by 30 metres], using crushed granite from the drilling and blasting of rock outcrops. The original runway lights were 'homemade'; an old walking plow was used to dig a narrow trench into which was placed plastic water pipe; electrical wiring was then inserted into this pipe, giving 25-foot-candle power that barely met the Ministry of Transport minimum licensing requirements. The vertical light-stands at every 30.5 metres were plastic plumbing stacks.

Prior to the construction of the runway, Lamb Air provided scheduled service on skis/floats between Norway House and Thompson/The Pas. Northlands Airlines offered regularly scheduled service on skis/floats between Norway House and Winnipeg. In 1969, during the construction of the runway, scheduled service was provided by both Lamb Air and Mid-West Airlines, which acquired ownership of Northlands Airlines. By 1970, Mid-West Airlines amalgamated with TransAir, which continued to provide regular scheduled service between Norway House and Winnipeg.

With the completion of a new terminal building, the airport was opened on April 13, 1971, with a ribbon cutting ceremony. (The building was expanded in 1972). A twin otter owned by Mid-West and piloted by Captain Murray Haybrittle was the first plane to use the officially opened airport.

In 1976, Transport Canada provided funds to extend the runway to 1,200 metres. The construction of a road connecting Norway House to Jenpeg and Dunlop facilitated the hauling of gravel to the airport site.

The Norway House Airport currently serves two scheduled air carriers: Northwinds Northern Inc., which, in 1977, filled the void created by Lamb Air's demise; and Perimeter Airlines (Inland) Ltd., which, in 1978, filled the void created by TransAir's discontinuation of service between Norway House and Winnipeg after its amalgamation with Pacific Western Airlines. Two charter air carriers also operate out of Norway House: Mid-Manitoba Air and Muskego Air.

In 1988, theere were 19,021 passengers, 349 tonnes of freight and 5,742 aircraft movements.

The following have served as airport manager at Norway House Airport:

Dick Schott	1968 to 1972
Pier Sienema	1972 to 1976
Frank Paupanekis	1976 to 1983
Glen A. Flett	1983 to present

Source:
Transport Canada, Central Region.

Oshawa Airport
(Ontario)

The Oshawa Airport was built for the RCAF to be used for the British Commonwealth Air Training Plan (BCATP) and became No. 20 Elementary Flying Training School (EFTS).

The site is north and west of the city of Oshawa and occupied 318 acres [129 hectares] of what was then farm land. Although the airport began operations in June 1941, the official opening ceremony did not take place until a year later in June 1942: the Duke of Kent officiated.

No. 20 EFTS was operated by the Ontario County Flying Training School Ltd, which received several efficiency awards, including the 'Cock of the Walk' trophy and the Minister of National Defence for Air Efficiency Pennant. The school closed in late 1944 when the BCATP was phased out.

The city of Oshawa took over the airport after the war and leased the land from the federal government. The Ontario County Flying Club operated the airport for the city until 1961, when the club closed down. The airport, licensed in the name of the city, has been operated for the city by the Oshawa Flying Club since 1962.

The present airport has three paved runways: 12-30, at 1,059 metres long, 04-22, at 819 metres, and 08-26, at 808 metres. There are three hangars, two of which are the original EFTS buildings, and one owned by Atlantis Transportation Services Inc. One EFTS hangar is owned by Skycraft Air Transport Inc. and the other is occupied by Skycraft and the flying club.

The following are based at the airport: Skycraft Air Transport provides scheduled air service, operates a flying school, and runs a charter service; the Oshawa Flying Club offers flying training; and Atlantis Transportation provides aircraft maintenance and storage. The Robert Stuart Aeronautical Collection, an aviation mu-

140. Annual fly-in breakfast, Oshawa County Flying Club, Oshawa Airport, 1955.

seum, is also located on the site, and displays items from 'Camp X,' the spy school which operated near Oshawa during the war.

The airport has a control tower operated by Transport Canada.

Since the war, the primary function has been that of a recreational airport; however, there are a number of passenger, military, and freight-passenger aircraft movements related to local industries accommodated at Oshawa Airport. Skycraft Air Transport operates a scheduled passenger service along the Oshawa-Detroit-Windsor-Ottawa-Montréal route.

In 1989, the airport had 96,091 aircraft movements and 39,600 passengers.

Sources:
1. Robert Stuart.
2. *No. 20 Elementary Flying Training School— RCAF 1941-1944, Oshawa, Ontario* [souvenir booklet published by the Ontario County Flying Training School Ltd.].
3. Transport Canada, Ottawa headquarters.

Ottawa International Airport
(Ontario)

Ottawa Airport was originally known as the Hunt

Club Field. Its history can be traced back to July 19, 1919[1] when a Curtiss JN-4 airplane landed near the Ottawa Hunt and Golf Club, Uplands. This aircraft, the first privately owned machine to land in the capital, was flown from Toronto for its owners, E.J. Draper and W.M. Deisher of Reo Ottawa Sales Co. The next few years saw rapid development of flying activities at Uplands.

But the first airplane flights in the Ottawa region took place earlier. Between September 11 and 14, 1911, Len Hammond flew a biplane from Slattery's Field[2] (between Main Street and Echo Drive) over the crowds attending the nearby Central Canada Exhibition; and on October 8, 1913, W.C. Robinson landed at Slattery's field after departing from Montréal—the first flight between two Canadian cities.

An RAF airplane carrying air mail from Leaside, Toronto, landed in Ottawa on the area behind Rockcliffe Rifle Butts on four occasions in August and September 1918.[3] The Air Board built an aerodrome at Rockcliffe in 1920 for the use of its Civil government Air Operations (CGAO).

On May 14, 1920, the superintendent of flying operations proposed leasing 'the Uplands,' erecting a Bessoneau hangar there, and setting up for an experimental photographic survey of Ottawa.

141. First airmail from Ottawa to Toronto, August 27, 1918.

The total cost of this project was not to exceed $2,500. The proposal was not accepted; instead, Rockcliffe Aerodrome was established because there was already a seaplane base on the nearby Ottawa River, thus making Rockcliffe a combined land-water base.

The Hunt Club Field, owned by Uplands Realty Co., was used intermittently by aircraft, including Department of National Defence planes, but attracted little public attention.

When Charles Lindbergh landed his Spirit of St. Louis at Hunt Club Field, flying in from New York on July 2, 1927, he was greeted by a large crowd and was made a guest of honour during Ottawa's celebration of Canada's Diamond Jubilee of Confederation. The aerodrome was named for him: Lindbergh Field.

There was more public interest in aviation following Lindbergh's visit, and the Department of National Defence (then responsible for all aviation, civil as well as military) was asked to improve Lindbergh Field. The requests were firmly refused: the RCAF had Rockcliffe, and it was the responsibility of the municipality to provide accommodation for civil aircraft. Further, "the site was too far from the city and the soil was too poor to maintain a good turf surface."[4]

Regular flying activity began on January 14, 1928, with the incorporation of the Ottawa Flying Club (under the government's new scheme of assistance to light aeroplane clubs). The club leased the land from Ottawa Uplands Ltd. for $300 a year, and received an airport licence for Uplands on July 26, 1928. Apparently, there was some confusion between the names Lindbergh Field and Uplands Aerodrome, for the Controller of Civil Aviation wrote to the Surveyor General of Canada on April 10, 1929: "After consultation with the operators of the field, it has been decided to request that the name Uplands Aerodrome be adopted."[5]

In 1935, the facilities of the airport (now known as Uplands Field, was operated by the Ottawa Flying Club Ltd.), included a club house and office, one hangar 35 by 40 by 14 feet [10.6 by 12.2 by 4.3 metres], two private hangars for light aircraft, refuelling by Imperial Oil, and a wind-sock.

In November 1935, an official of the Civil Aviation Branch (Department of National Defence) was concerned about the condition of the airport, and recommended that the licence be suspended until the "surface and dimensions of the field have been improved."[6]

In 1937, the Civil Aviation Branch of the new Department of Transport reported that the field was still rough, but it could be easily improved, and two 5,000-foot [1,524-metre] landing strips could be constructed, if necessary. The flying club was asked to spend $3,000 on improvements. The Controller of Civil Aviation wrote in a letter of April 26, 1937: "It is inadvisable to attempt to licence an airport for light aircraft only at the moment Uplands is being used by airplanes of all sizes. This condition is dangerous and the Department no longer feels justified in permitting it to continue. The site must be improved immediately, or abandoned."[7]

The flying club could not finance the improvements and ceased to be the lessee of the property

142. First landing, Ottawa Airport (Hunt Club Field) July 19, 1919.

165

on May 1, 1937, when Laurentian[8] leased the site from Ottawa Uplands Ltd. for a term of ten years at a rent of $720 per year. At Laurentian's request, the airport licence was transferred to them on May 29, 1937. The company agreed to make the improvements required by the Department and to permit the Ottawa Flying Club to continue to operate at the airport. They also agreed to lease additional land required for improvements at $300 a year for five years, renewable.

Soon afterwards, Laurentian approached the Department of Transport for assistance, but Civil Aviation officers pointed out that responsibility for the "provision of airports in municipalities is one which belongs to the municipality concerned, or other interested parties. The only airports provided by the government, apart from St. Hubert Airport, are those established for emergency purposes on the Trans-Canada Airway, in isolated sections."[9] The company also tried unsuccessfully to interest the city of Ottawa—at the time the land could have been bought for $720 an acre. But the city declined and the company approached Transport once more on July 28, 1937. This time, the government agreed to help, and planned to build three hard-surfaced runways, 3,000 by 75 feet [914 by 23 metres], and a hangar, which was to be used by Trans-Canada Air Lines. Work was delayed because Laurentian could get nothing better than a ten-year lease, but it finally bought the land for $25,000. Estimates prepared for airport operations gave projected revenue of $16,520, expenses of $41,640, and capital expenditures of $174,000.

On January 20, 1938, the Controller of Civil Aviation wrote an internal memorandum on the subject of Uplands Airports, from which the following extracts have been taken:

1. Before the necessary improvements can be arranged for a decision must be reached in regard to the tenure of the site and the responsibility for its maintenance.

2. The property is owned by Laurentian Air Services, who purchased it in September from the previous owners, the Uplands Syndicate, Limited, at a cost of $25,000.00.

3. There appear to be three alternatives:

(a) The Department purchase the land outright for the above sum, let contracts for the necessary improvements and maintain the field in future as a Government aerodrome. If this scheme is adopted, the cost of the land and the improvements will be between $175,000.00 and $185,000.00...both the company and the club should be asked to pay a suitable annual charge covering landing fees and the use of the aerodrome.

(b) The Department might enter into an agreement with Laurentian Air Services to retain the ownership of the property and grant the Department a long-term lease (20 years minimum) for its use. The Department could then construct the runways, hangars and other facilities and could operate the airport with the flying club and Laurentian Air Services as tenants. The cost in this case would be as outlined above, except that instead of paying $25,000.00 outright, the Department would pay an equitable annual rental to Laurentian Air Services based on the capital cost of the land, $25,000.00.

(c) An arrangement might be entered into with Laurentian Air Services to retain the ownership of the land and make the improvements themselves, the Department paying an annual fee for use of the aerodrome...the annual rental would be a fair rate on the investment of $185,680.00, plus $15,000.00 as the Department's share in the operating expense.

4. There is one further alternative, to approach the City of Ottawa and proceed on the same lines as had been done in all other cities, namely, that the city should own and

143. Lindbergh's Spirit of St. Louis, Ottawa Airport, 1927.

operate the airport, the Department giving them assistance in its improvements under P.C. 3166. Allowing for the special circumstances of Ottawa, being the capital city with a good deal of government business, a more generous grant than is normally given might be justified.

5. This alternative, however, would inevitably mean delay and it might be possible to obtain the use of this aerodrome before fall at the earliest, in which case there would be no stop at Ottawa on the trans-Canada airway unless the facilities at Rockcliffe could be obtained as a temporary measure. If this were done, the tentative site chosen for the radio range station should be purchased now and the ranges laid out so that they would serve both Rockcliffe and Uplands.

6. An early decision is necessary as to which plan should be followed, in order that preparations may be made to start work by April 15, on the improvement of the airport and the construction of the radio range station.[10]

After negotiation between the Department of Transport and Laurentian, the department agreed to purchased the airport (300.13 acres [126.7 hectares]) from Laurentian for $37,500, and to lease Laurentian the land on which its hangars and buildings stood for one dollar a year for a

144. Hunt Club Field, July 2, 1927.

period of twenty-one years, renewable for twenty-one years. It granted the company the right to operate commercially from the airport, to sell gasoline, and to take off and land its aircraft without paying landing fees. The original lease was dated May 11, 1938 The company's buildings were located in the north corner of the old airport.[11]

Construction began on May 17, 1938. The minister, C.D. Howe, directed that the work be done quickly and that the airport be ready for the opening of Trans-Canada Air Lines (TCA) service. The airport licence was surrendered by Laurentian on May 28, 1938, and cancelled until work on the airport was completed.

Effective May 14, 1938, the Department gave the Ottawa Flying Club a five-year renewable land lease for the site of two hangars built on the Manotick Road, and stipulated that the club must be prepared to move its buildings at its own expense if requested by Transport.[12] The rent was to remain at $300 a year—the same amount that the club had paid Laurentian Air Services. The club also agreed to provide rent-free office space to the airport manager, T. Roberts, in recognition of the government's subsidy and assistance.[13] (The airport manager actually leased the space in Laurentian's hangar).

The airport reopened on August 20, 1938,

under a licence issued to the Department of Transport. There were two runways: east-west, 3,300 by 200 feet [1,006 by 61 metres], and north-south, 3,000 by 200 feet [914 by 61 metres], which had night flying lighting facilities. When Transport took over and developed Uplands, policy still required that such airports should be provided by the communities to be served. (Transport operated only two civil airports, St. Hubert (Montréal) and Rimouski, which were both built for the special reasons described in Chapter 6). The deputy minister of Transport had written to the mayor of Ottawa on March 9, 1937, saying:

The introduction of large high-speed aircraft has created a demand for larger and smoother aerodromes than was considered necessary five years ago and, in other respects, a complete revision of the requirements for airports from which regular operations are conducted.

Provision has been made under Order-in-Council P.C. 3166 whereby consideration will be given to applications from municipalities with aerodromes located on the Trans-Canada Airway for financial assistance in the development of their aerodromes, exclusive of buildings to the extent of one-third of any expenditure made to date by such municipalities, plus one third of any further expenditure which they undertake to make.

It is, therefore, requested that, if your city is interested in taking advantage of the provision for financial assistance, you take immediate steps to investigate your local problems and, where necessary, have surveys put in hand in order that complete information as requested may be available to accompany your application at an early date. Immediate consideration will be given to applications submitted in order that full advantage may

be taken of the forthcoming construction season.[14]

The city refused to become involved. As there was no alternative, the federal government assumed full responsibility. Notes prepared for the official opening of the airport included the following observations:

The Canadian transcontinental airway system would be incomplete without an adequate airport in the capital city. Fortunately, Ottawa lies directly on the route between the Maritime provinces, Québec and the western provinces. It is also very little north of the direct route between Montréal, Toronto and Windsor, so that no divergence of the route is necessary in order to serve the capital.

The rapidly expanding aviation activities of the Department of Transport demand adequate accommodation for the maintenance of the Department's service aircraft. These two needs have been met by the building of a civil airport in Ottawa on this site. It is one of a chain of airports in the principal cities which will serve the traffic requirements of the main centres of population. These airports have been modernized during the past two years by the Department of Transport under generous appropriations granted by Parliament for assistance to municipalities in this work...

Each of these airports will have hard-surfaced runways suitable for all-weather traffic, hangar accommodation to shelter the planes, radio range and communication stations to guide the pilot during his flight and a meteorological station to furnish weather reports. They will all be lighted for night flying, so that flight may continue during the hours of darkness. Accommodation for passenger, mail and express traffic is being provided. The hard-surfaced runways now opened by Mrs. Howe[15] are the first instalment. The lighting and radio services will be installed by the end of September and the hangar, shops and traffic accommodation will be completed before the winter sets in...[16]

The Department of Transport also provided radio (including a radio range) and meteorological services for the airport, housed in leased premises nearby.[17]

On April 1, 1939, TCA began scheduled passenger and mail service at Ottawa and, on the same date, the airport name was changed from Uplands to Ottawa—the fourth name in the airport's twenty-year history.

The airport had grown into a thriving centre of commercial aviation by the time war broke out in September 1939, when Ottawa Airport began to undergo major changes and development. It was used (as RCAF Station Uplands) for pilot training under the British Commonwealth Air Training Plan (BCATP) and was the home of No. 2 Service Flying Training School (SFTS), which gained the reputation of being one of the best units in the whole BCATP. No. 2 SFTS was opened by the Governor-General on August 5, 1940, and was the first of the new BCATP schools. Relief aerodromes for No. 2 SFTS were built at Pendleton and Edwards, Ontario.

Ottawa Airport continued to function during the war as a civil airport under the Department of Transport: civil operations were controlled by Transport and military operations by the RCAF. Although No. 2 SFTS was disbanded on April 14, 1945, RCAF Station Uplands remained until Maintenance Command moved out in 1947.

All land bought and all improvements made to the airport site during the war were at the expense of the Department of National Defence. The first contract, let in May 1940, was to pave four runways, and included the extension of the existing ones. Additional land was acquired east of the airport, along the Bowesville Road, as the building area for the air force camp and for the

Ottawa Car and Aircraft Ltd., which was engaged in the manufacture and assembly of aircraft that were test-flown from the airport.[18] Later in the war, both Ottawa Car and Laurentian Air Services engaged in the overhaul of aircraft engines for the Department of Munitions and Supply.

On August 1, 1940, the Ottawa Flying Club was asked by Transport to stop flying because of the heavy traffic from the training school. Meanwhile, it remained responsible for elementary flying training at St. Eugene Aerodrome—a duty it fulfilled throughout the war; it was allowed to keep its Ottawa airport buildings rent-free for the duration. In September 1945, the club began to fly again from Uplands.

Immediately after the war, civil aviation began to develop, and there were demands for hangar and other space at Ottawa. Canadian Colonial Airlines Inc. asked the Department of National Defence in March 1946 for hangar space, as it had begun to serve Ottawa on the Montréal-Ottawa-Syracuse-Washington route. The RCAF, which had already given Transport half of hangar no. 1 for civil use, suggested that the remainder be used to look after Colonial's requirements. In December 1945, Laurentian Air Services had leased part of its hangar to Customs—it was on the north side of the airport next to the Transport hangar. The latter was used to house TCA aircraft and also served as a passenger terminal. Colonial built a small hut between the two hangars to serve its passengers and accommodate other operations.

In November 1946, the Ottawa Flying Club approached the RCAF for a hangar and other buildings that National Defence had promised "when the buildings were no longer required by the RCAF."[19] National Defence replied that the buildings were still required but would be made available if they became surplus to the RCAF. Some acrimonious correspondence followed

145. Original hangar, Ottawa International Airport, 1945.

(February 12, 1947) in which the club reminded the minister that the company, which the club had established to operate No. 13 Elementary Flight Training School at St. Eugene for the BCATP, had "voluntarily surrendered substantial funds to the Crown and surrendered its charter."[20] In return, it had been assured it would be given certain buildings and equipment at Ottawa Airport to conduct its peacetime operations. An Order in Council had been passed approving the the lease of such buildings at nominal rent to the respective clubs as the Department of Transport considered necessary. The conflict was resolved later in the year.

In March 1947, Uplands once again became a civilian airport and, for three years, the RCAF's only connection was through facilities to permit headquarters officers to maintain pilot proficiency. On May 5, 1947, National Defence transferred four hangars and seven buildings to Transport. The flying club then occupied half of hangar no. 1 and the watch office building. Later, it occupied other buildings and, in 1961, it built its own club house and a small hangar, where it is still located.

In March 1947, the Department of Transport informed TCA of its plans to convert the lean-to of hangar no. 1 (ex-RCAF) into new offices for Canadian Colonial Airlines and Customs and

146. Ottawa International Airport, 1951.

Immigration, and asked if TCA would consider moving its offices there also. (The hangar was near Bowesville Road and it was advantageous to have TCA and Colonial together). TCA declined; and until the new air terminal building was opened in 1960, remained at the old terminal attached to the original hangar on the north side.

The old terminal was enlarged in 1954 by the construction of an annex onto the hangar. This eased congestion in public areas and provided limited space for some commercial activities: snack bar, operated by R.D. Marshall; car rentals (Tilden had the exclusive concession for two years from January 1, 1954, and was the first car rental agency at the airport); and ground transportation (Red Line Taxi Co., which for years had a concession at the Ottawa Railway Station and the Chateau Laurier Hotel, had been granted the airport concession in August 1947).

On December 1, 1950, an RCAF station was again located at the Ottawa Airport, to support expansion of regular and reserve unit activities, and later a fighter unit of Air Defence Command was stationed there. The base was used by Air Transport Command, and in 1954, it became headquarters for Air Material Command. It also housed the Central Experimental and Proving Establishment and the National Aeronautical Establishment of the National Research Council.

New hangars, nos. 10 to 14 inclusive, were built between 1955 and 1957. In 1971, the Aeronautical Evaluation and Test Establishment moved to Cold Lake, Alberta. Canadian Forces Base Ottawa was established on October 2, 1972, as the result of the amalgamation of the former bases at Rockcliffe and Uplands.

In 1950, a large section of the township of Gloucester was expropriated to provide land for the extension of runway 14-32 to 25,000 feet [7,620 metres], a military requirement for the testing of high speed and high performance category aircraft, such as the Arrow. Such a remarkable length was planned for high speed runs to test various aerodynamic forms—the U.S. Air Forces was making similar test at Salt Lake Flats. Although the Arrow did not fly until 1958, the long lead time ensured that the facilities would be in place when needed. But the military requirements were changed; and the runway was extended to only 8,800 feet [2,682 metres] in 1951 and to 9,700 [2,957 metres] in 1961. Currently, the two main runways are 10,000 and 8,000 feet [3,048 and 2,438 metres]. In addition, there are two runways of 3,300 and 3,900 feet [1,006 and 1,189 metres] at the 'old airport' area on the north side of the site. These are restricted to use by small aircraft.

In 1956, the Department of Transport asked the Ottawa Flying Club to consider moving its entire operation to Carp Aerodrome, which the department was planning to develop as a satellite airport for Ottawa, because the mix of airline, air force, and flying club training activities at the Uplands was undesirable: recreational and small general aviation flying could be accommodated better at Carp, and then the runways on the old north airport would be closed. Although the club was prepared to consider a move to Rockcliffe, it refused to go to Carp. In fact, considering that they were "the founders of the Uplands Airport,"[21] the club members felt they were being

treated badly. The chief of Air Staff, RCAF, however, in correspondence with the deputy minister of Transport, stated that he could not permit civil operations to become established at Rockcliffe. The outcome was that the club and other general aviation interests were allowed to continue to use Ottawa. The club and some servicing companies then built their own hangars and T-hangars on land leased from the department.

On May 29, 1959, there was a suggestion that the airport be named Ottawa International Airport to coincide with the opening of the new modern air terminal building: the new designation would eliminate confusion between the names then in common usage (RCAF Station Uplands, Uplands Airport, and Ottawa (Uplands) Airport). The official decision was to call it Ottawa Airport (Uplands).

On August 5, 1959, just weeks before the new $6 million air terminal was due to open, the building suffered $300,000 damage when a USAF jet aircraft being demonstrated at the airport broke the sound barrier as it flew over the building. The force of the blast broke a large part of the vast area of glass on the front of the building; it tore loose metal roof edge flashings and under-roof insulation, bent metal window frames and did other extensive damage. The opening of

147. Ottawa International Airport (Uplands) 1970.

the terminal, by Prime Minister Diefenbaker on June 30, 1960, ushered in a new era in the long history of Ottawa Airport.

The new terminal had a control tower as well as accommodation for the airlines and airport administration. For a number of years, it housed the department's Air Services School for air traffic control, radio operators, and weather observers. An aviation museum was located on the second floor and, in separate buildings at ground level, three full-size historic aircraft were displayed. This display was appropriate, if rather unusual for an airport, and it attracted much public attention over the years. The museum moved away from the airport on August 24, 1964—the day the airport was designated Ottawa International Airport.

In the fall of 1977, an enclosed walkway was constructed to protect passengers from inclement weather and provide better aircraft apron use and management.

A major expansion of the airport was completed in December 1987 at a cost of $52.8 million. The renovated east wing of the air terminal now includes new Customs and Immigration facilities, a new three-track baggage claim, as well as a new first aid post. The west wing was expanded to include additional passenger check-in facilities. The new, larger, passenger hold area is on the second level and a new restaurant-bar was added.

Between the wings is a spacious concourse bathed in natural light with an unobstructed view of the tarmac and runways. A covered walkway links the second floor and the 1,400-space parking lot. Several improvements have been made for the assistance of disabled travellers.

Many changes were made to improve security.

A new free-standing control tower, located in the airfield area west of runway 14-30, went into operation in 1991. The central cab of the old tower will be used by the airports gate assignment unit.

Air Canada, Canadian Airlines International link Ottawa International to most Canadian cities. Air Ontario, Voyageur Airways, First Air, Tempus, Skycraft, Canadian Partner, Inter Canadian, and Air Alliance provide local third level service. Eastern Airlines links Ottawa to the Washington/Baltimore area and Miami. In 1987, US Air was awarded the Ottawa-New York city route, while First Air picked up the Ottawa/Boston route and continued to provide service to Iqaluit and Nuuk, Greenland. In June 1989, KLM Royal Dutch Airlines began service to Amsterdam.

In addition to its airline traffic, the Ottawa International Airport is the home of Transport Canada's Flight Services with its large modern hangar to house and maintain its fleet of aircraft. The Canadian Force's Air Transport Group operation, including the VIP flight and the National Research Aeronautical Establishment, are based there. On the north side of the old field, there are ten enterprises connected with aviation and aircraft servicing. These include the Ottawa Flying Club (established in 1927), Bonavair Ltd., Wagner Air Freight, Inotech Aviation Ltd., and Laurentian Air Services Ltd.

More than four hundred people are employed at the airport by Transport Canada, which owns and operates the facility. Another one thousand are employed by other government agencies and commercial aviation firms—not including personnel at the Canadian Armed Forces Base and the National Research Council Aeronautical Establishment.

In 1988, there were 165,000 aircraft movements (of which 130,000 were itinerant), and 2,748,400 passengers (2,443,283 domestic, 305,117 transborder/international).

The following have served as airport managers at Ottawa International Airport over the years:

T.L.P. Roberts	1938 to 1951
R.A. Joberty	1951 to 1964
D.H. Dupuis	1964 to 1971
J.M. Descary	1971 to 1981
K.G. Current	1981 to 1986
C. Dunwoodie-Legault	1986 to 1987
R. Imbeault	1987 to 1988
B. Bowie	1988 to present

Source:

Transport Canada

Footnotes—Ottawa International Airport

[1] Canada, Department of National Defence, Directorate of History, Uplands file.

[2] The Canadian Aviation Historic Society erected a plaque at 35, Riverdale Avenue recording these events.

[3] Canada, Department of National Defence, Directorate of History, Uplands file.

[4] Canada, Department of National Defence, file 5168-464, vol. 1, memo signed by J.A. Wilson, controller of Civil Aviation, 15 July 1927.

[5] Ibid, 10 April 1929.

[6] Canada, Department of National Defence, Civil Aviation branch, file 5168-464, vol. 1, memo signed by J.H. Tudhope, Superintendent of Airways, 13 November 1935.

[7] Canada, Department of National Defence, file 5168-464, vol. 1, letter signed by J.A. Wilson, Controller of Civil Aviation, and addressed to the Ottawa Flying Club, 26 April 1937.

[8] Laurentian Air Services Ltd. was incorporated and began business at the airport in 1936. It was the second oldest air service company in Canada, Austin Airways being the oldest. Both have since ceased operations.

[9] Canada, Department of National Defence, Civil Aviation Branch, file 5168-464, vol. 1, letter signed by A.D. McLean, Superintendent of Airways, 24 June 1937.

[10] Public Archives Canada, MG 30,E243, vol. 9.

[11] Laurentian's first hangar was building in 1936 and is still in use.

[12] In June 1939, the club was asked to move its club house four hundred feet [122 metres] to the south, as it was an obstruction at the end of the runway.

[13] The J.A. Wilson Papers (Public Archives Canada, MG 30 E243, vol. 9] contain a memo dated May 18, 1938, stating: "Now that this Department has obtained possession of the Uplands Airport property, there is a need to appoint an Airport Manager; a need for some-one during the summer, while work is going on; Mr. T. Roberts, formerly an instructor with Ottawa Flying Club, will apply to be the Airport Manager; temporari-ly to be employed as a labourer until the position can be established and given the duty to supervise flying operations for the summer."

[14] Public Archives Canada, MG 30 E243, vol. 9, De-partment of Transport, file 5100-014, letter signed by V.I. Smart, Deputy Minister, 9 March 1937.

[15] The wife of the Honourable C.D. Howe, Minister of Transport.

[16] Pub lic Archives Canada MG 30 E243, vol. 9, J.A. Wilson Papers.

[17] This was the Tally-ho building, located at the south-east corner of Bowesville Road and the road allow-ance south of the golf club. The Department of Trans-port purchased the land and building in April 1940.

[18] The plant was destroyed by fire in early 1944 and was not rebuilt. The Department of National Defence purchased the land.

[19] Canada, Department of Transport, file 5156-137-3, vol. 1, letter from the Royal Canadian Flying Club As-sociation (RCFCA), 21 November 1946.

[20] Ibid.

[21] Canada, Dept. of Transport, file 5151-464, vol. 2, Ottawa Flying Club president P.E. Arpin, in a letter to the deputy minister of Transport, 11 February 1956.

Pelly Bay
(Northwest Territories)

Pelly Bay has an unlicensed gravel strip operated by the government of the Northwest Territories. The runway, 05T-23T, is 1,448 by 30 metres.

The facility is unique in many ways. It is the only location in the region to have an unlicensed airport whose development remains unscheduled. The people of Pelly Bay were entirely responsi-ble for construction of the present facility, and during the three-year period from 1966 to 1968 built the runway to its present length. They salvaged DEW Line equipment for its construc-tion; and the present runway lighting came from further salvage missions to nearby abandoned DEW Line stations. Over the years, the wiring has been buried to permit easier snow removal.

The unusual taxiway and large wedge-shaped apron were constructed later to ease off-loading from the aircraft hauling fuel for Pelly's resup-ply. In 1980, and again using local initiative, a surplus Quonset unit was relocated from Camp 4 DEW Line, upgraded, and put in place to serve as the Observer/Communicator work area and waiting room. During 1985, more local initia-tive was shown as the hamlet cannibalized the old nursing station and constructed a new airport terminal building.

First Air offers scheduled service to this site. In 1988, there were 1,037 aircraft movements, and 2,100 passengers.

Source:
Government of the Northwest Territories.

Pembroke Airport
(Ontario)

Pembroke Airport was first developed in 1956 by Pembroke Air Services as a base for pilot train-ing and aircraft rental. It had a gravel east-west runway of 2,000 feet [609 metres], a hangar, and some classrooms.

The airport received its first temporary licence in March 1957; and in 1958, a 3,300-foot [1,006-metre] north-south runway was developed, which was extended to 4,000 feet [1,219 metres] in 1967.

In 1966, under the auspices of the Pembroke and Area Economic Council, local businessmen and elected officials wanted a municipal airport in the Pembroke-Deep River area with regular air service between Pembroke and Toronto. The Pembroke Area Airport Commission—representing the city of Pembroke and eleven lo-cal municipalities—studied alternative airport sites, but decided the existing one was the best available, and purchased it in March 1968.

In July 1968, Royalair began operations link-ing Pembroke with Montréal, Ottawa, Peterbo-rough, and Toronto using DC-3, Heron, and Twin Otter aircraft. A small terminal building was erected the same year.

Royalair continued to serve the airport until November 1969 when, for financial reasons, it ceased operations. Then, in May 1970, a group of Pembroke businessmen, opened a new ser-vice—Pem Air which flew between Pembroke and Toronto—the profitable leg of the route.

The airport was closed during the summer of 1977 while runway 17-35 was reconstructed to 4,000 by 100 feet [1,219 by 30 metres] and run-way lighting was installed. During that period, Pem-Air operated out of the Canadian Forces Base Petawawa and resumed regular service at Pembroke Airport in November 1977. In March 1978, the service was extended to include North Bay and Montréal.

The Airport Commission purchased an addi-tional 990 acres [40 hectares] of land in 1977 and a further 200 acres [81 hectares] in 1980.

The airport is operated by the Airport Com-mission, and receives an operating subsidy from

Transport Canada. It has scheduled service to Toronto (Pem Air), charter service, cargo flights, air ambulance, aerial photography, aerial crop spraying, flying schools, military training, firefighting operations, general aviation, and aircraft maintenance.

When the 'temporary' terminal building, erected in 1968, was destroyed by fire in December 1982, further temporary facilities were located in the Pem Air hangar/office complex. But in 1983, this was destroyed by fire; yet again temporary terminal facilities were set up.

The new terminal building was opened in January 1984. A runway extension and taxiway were completed in the same year.

A new hangar/office for Pem Air and a five bay T-hangar for the Pembroke Flying Club were also completed in 1984. The club added a lounge to their hangar in 1989.

Late in 1984, when Transport Canada leased a fleet of airport maintenance equipment to the Airport Commission, the commission hired staff and took over the operation and maintenance that had previously been contracted out.

In 1988, the airport had 12,400 passengers and 1,835 aircraft movements.

Dianne Mau has been the airport manager since 1983.

Source:
Transport Canada, Ontario Region.

Penticton Airport
(British Columbia)

In April 1930, the city of Penticton first showed its interest in having an airport, when it asked the civil aviation authorities for specifications for a site that could be used in conjunction with the proposed air-mail route.

Two proposed locations were examined by the Department of Transport in July 1937. One of these, west of the city and north of Skaha Lake, was part of an Indian reserve, was selected and later developed as the present Penticton Airport. It is seventy-two kilometres north of the Canada-U.S. border.

In March 1938, Transport agreed to a cost-sharing arrangement, provided the city obtained title to the land. Because the land was Indian-owned, the city was unable to acquire it. About this time, a decision was made that Penticton should be a supplementary airport on the Vancouver-Lethbridge airway. Sixty-one hectares of land were expropriated (in the summer of 1940) and preliminary development of the field was completed in 1941. Further work was undertaken at the request of the Department of National Defence during the war to permit its use as an emergency field. The runway was paved and some buildings erected. It was used as an emergency military aerodrome in 1944.

On November 1, 1945, a temporary airport licence was issued in the name of Transport for twenty-four-hour operation, and an aerodrome keeper, Algy Jackson, was appointed. A permanent licence was issued on May 10, 1954.

An additional 120 acres [49 hectares] of land were acquired from the Indian band in February 1946 for airport expansion, and in December of that year, the airport was transferred to the Department of Transport from National Defence. The runway, 5,400 feet [1,646 metres] long, was extended to 6,000 feet [1,829 metres] in 1959. In 1946, the airport was used by Trans-Canada Air Lines and Canadian Pacific Airlines (CPAL). Aeradio service was established in 1948.

A new air terminal building was opened in 1963.

In 1968, CPAL, with DC-6Bs, provided two scheduled flights daily, which Pacific Western Airlines took over in April 1969, using Boeing 737s. The airport was also served by Northern Thunderbird Air Limited.

A mobile control tower was installed in 1969; but, in 1971, the terminal building was expanded to provide a permanent control tower, as well as offices for aeradio and telecommunications staff.

In 1976, a privately-owned aviation centre was constructed on the airport, about one and a half kilometres from the terminal building. It included a twelve-unit motel, a flying training school, and an aircraft overhaul shop. The latter is no longer in operation.

In May 1988, Canadian Airlines International (formerly PWA) withdrew jet service from Penticton. Today, scheduled service is provided by Time Air and Air BC, using turboprop airplanes.

Penticton Airport now serves as a water bomber base for the area. It is also the centre for Rap Attack training, a program that teaches helicopter skills in fighting fires. Penticton is a major port of entry from the United States for fishermen heading north, and the airport hosts aviation buffs during the annual air show.

The following operators are based at the airport: Canadian Helicopters (which operates an international mountain training school), Warner Aviation, Sunrise Aviation, Interior Aviation, and Penticton Aviation (a repair facility).

In 1988, there were 84,600 passengers and 48,725 aircraft movements.

The following have been airport managers:

Algy Jackson	1945 to 1968
W. Mitchell	1968 to 1970
W. Remple	1970 to 1979
R.J. MacKay (acting)	1979 to 1980
G.C. Baker	1980 to 1983
Lauren Pennycook (acting)	1984 to 1986
Janet Brown (acting)	1986 to 1987
Jim Warman	1987

Sources:
1. Transport Canada, Pacific Region.
2. R.L. Clarke, "Airport Notes" (Ottawa: Transport Canada) [unpublished collection].
3. Jim Warman, Airport Manager, Penticton Airport.

Pitt Meadows Airport
(British Columbia)

In May 1961, the Department of Transport announced its decision to build a new airport at Pitt Meadows that would serve as a satellite of Vancouver International Airport. It would also have a seaplane base on the adjacent Fraser River. The site was 700 acres [283 hectares] in area and, initially, the airport was to have two graded landing strips, 2,500 by 500 feet [762 by 152 metres], one gravel and the other grass.

The airport opened on July 20, 1963. Pitt Meadows is thirty-two kilometres northeast of Vancouver International Airport and serves the area north of Fraser River from Mission city up to and including Vancouver. It is a general aviation satellite airport, catering to flying training, commercial charter operations, and aircraft maintenance businesses, and has ramp and dock facilities, built in 1965.

The Aero Club of B.C.[1] moved its entire operation from Vancouver International to Pitt Meadows on June 1, 1963. The club, which had begun its life near the Minoru Park Race Track on Lulu Island in 1915, had moved to a farmer's field at Pitt Meadows in 1916. So, for the club, the move in 1963 was really a return to home.

Pitt Meadows quickly became a busy airport and, by the end of December 1965, traffic was averaging 6,000 movements a month. But by February 1967, runway 07-25 showed signs of breaking up. Both runways were paved in 1969.

A new parallel asphalt runway, 08R-26L, was opened in June 1970, and today, the airport has

148. 1969 Control Tower, Pitt Meadows, B.C.

three runways: 08L-26R, 762 by 23 metres, 08R-26L, 1,311 by 33 metres (extended in 1986), 762 by 33 metres and 18-36, 762 by 23 metres.

A portable control tower began operations in September 1967, and the permanent tower was opened in August 1969.

By 1974, Pitt Meadows had 242,679 aircraft movements—the largest number at any Transport Canada airport; and in 1979, with a total of 287,034 it ranked second. Traffic dropped off in the early 1980s, due to the recession and the opening of Boundary Bay Airport in 1983; and by 1988 there were only 121,891 aircraft movements.

In 1975, a new seaplane ramp was built providing access to the airport for float aircraft; there were 5,703 float aircraft movements in 1978, and 3,800 in 1988.

The following operators are based at the airport: the Aero Club of B.C. (flying club), Airborne Enterprises Ltd. (flying school and aircraft parking), Altair Aviation Services (flying school, charters, pilot supplies), Zool's Professional Aircraft Maintenance, Avionics Canada Ltd. (avionics sales and service), Command Aviation Services Ltd. (fuel concession and hangar space), ALC Airlift (helicopter and fixed wing operations), Messerschmidt Aviation (aircraft painting), Prism Helicopters Ltd. (heli-

copter operations), Hyack Air Ltd. (hangar space, aircraft maintenance), Meadows Aero Lease Ltd. (flying school and T-Hangar rentals), Pitt Air (Aircraft maintenance and T-Hangar rentals), Rowan Industries Ltd. (T-Hangar rentals), Cam Aero (Aircraft maintenance), Skyhaven Aviation Ltd. (T-Hangar), Southside Management (private T-Hangar), P.K. Upholstering, and P.K. Pilot Supplies.

The following have served as airport managers:

G. McNeil	1961 to 1970
D. McNeil	1970 to 1979
D.J. McArthur	1980
H. Underhill	1981 to 1987
R.M. Fynn	1987

Source:
1. Transport Canada, Pacific Region.

Footnote—Pitt Meadows Airport

[1] The Aero Club of B.C. was the first flying club in Canada, founded on December 15, 1915 (Rudy Morin, *The Aero Club of B.C.*, unpublished article).

Port Hardy Airport
(British Columbia)

From 1942 to 1945, Port Hardy Airport was an RCAF operational base and coastal patrol facility. It was also a supplementary airport on the Alaska Air Route.

In 1946, the Department of Transport took it over for civil operations, and the airport was licenced on February 14, 1946. It was an approved alternate and refuelling point on Amber Airway No. 1 from Seattle, Washington, to Anchorage, Alaska. On January 12, 1950, it was approved as an alternate on the North Pacific route.

Port Hardy Airport is situated at the northern end of Vancouver Island. It is served by three scheduled airlines, but schedules are often changed because of the seasonal industries supporting Port Hardy. Sport fishing attracts most of the airline users over the summer months and there is sporadic commercial fishing. Logging camps in the area are seasonal operations and are affected by heavy snow in winter and forest fire in summer.

The control tower was constructed in 1956, and the new air terminal building was opened in 1963. The tower was de-commissioned in 1975, and in 1988, was redesigned and renovated to accommodate a flight aervice and weather office. Customs service is provided at the airport from May to September.

The runways, taxiways, and aprons were reworked between 1965 and 1969. Runway 11-29 was grooved in 1970—the first airport to be done in Canada.[1]

Today, the airport has three runways: 11-29, 1,524 metres long; 07-25, 1,219 metres; and 16-34, 1,219 metres but not maintained.

In 1988, there were 39,800 passengers, and 22,251 aircraft movements.

The airport is served by Time Air, Air BC and Pacific Coastal Air. Vancouver Island Helicopters Ltd. is based at the airport.

The following served as airport managers:

K.J. Robinson	1945 to 1946
C.E. Huntley	1946 to 1954
E. Wilson	1954 to 1977
R. Jones	1977 to 1980
H. Toom	1980 to 1982
D. Burns	1982 to 1986
R. Newton	1986 to 1988
B. Harwick	1988

Sources:
1. Transport Canada, Pacific Region.
2. R.L. Clarke, "Airport Notes" (Ottawa: Transport Canada) [unpublished collection].

Footnote—Port Hardy Airport

[1] Grooves were cut across the runway to improve lateral drainage especially after heavy rainfalls. This improved braking of the aircraft.

Powell River Airport
(British Columbia)

The town of Powell River is located on the British Columbia mainland, about 128 kilometres northwest of Vancouver. It was originally established and operated by MacMillan Bloedel Ltd., and is now administered by the District of Powell River, who own and operate the airport under an operating subsidy from Transport Canada. The airport is located on eighty-one hectares of provincial Crown land.

The area was first surveyed for an airport site in 1945, and in 1948, the Powell River Aero Club began the construction of an airstrip. The airport was taken over by the Village of Westview in 1951, and a licence was issued in June 1952 for a 2,800-foot [853-metre] gravel strip.

In 1953, Queen Charlotte Airlines began scheduled service with DC-3 aircraft, and the airport was later served by Pacific Western Airlines and Powell Air.

The air terminal building was opened in 1955, and the runway, 09-27, was paved to 3,760 feet [1,146 metres] in 1964.

From time to time, there were discussions and studies concerning the future of the Powell River Airport. The site was not a good one: it could not be enlarged and, until September 1981, could not be used for night flying. In 1960, the municipality acquired 447 acres [181 hectares] of land at Black Point for a new airport. The matter was reviewed in 1968, and again in 1973, when the community decided to continue operations at the existing site. However, the land at Black Point has been kept available.

In 1980, the British Columbia government provided funds for the improvement of the airport, including the removal of trees and obstructions on the approach to runway 09, and the installation of runway and taxiway lighting and two hazard beacons. On September 21, 1981, the airport licence was amended to allow night operations. A weather station was opened in April 1982.

In 1982, the Powell River Airport was served by four commercial airlines which provided regular scheduled service: Air BC (the major carrier), Pacific Coastal, Skylink, and Aquila Air. Charter service was provided by two locally based companies, Sun Coast Air and Riverside Helicopters. Other users included the following: MacMillan Bloedel Ltd.; Nav Air (Loomis Courier); Industrial Equipment Ltd.; the B.C. government; the RCMP; and Airsea Rescue.

The runway was resurfaced in 1987, and in 1988, a solar beacon was installed on the north hazard beacon site.

In the first six months of 1989, the airport had 18,357 passengers.

Sources:
1. Transport Canada, Pacific Region.
2. Update: Corporation of the District of Powell River.

Prince Albert Airport
(Saskatchewan)

As early as the spring of 1927, talks were initiated locally to determine a suitable location for an airport at Prince Albert. Captain Mercer of the Royal Canadian Air Force suggested a site south of the city near the extension of 6th Avenue West.

Coincidentally, the city accommodated float plane traffic by the placement of buoys on the river.

During 1929, the 150 acre [61-hectare] Norman Russel Farm was purchased for the airport, and is now part of the 255-hectare total airport property. The only funds available to improve the airport in 1929 were from the $290 real estate commission that was refunded on the land sale. The $290 was put to good use, as it covered the cost of cutting all the weeds, plowing, disking, harrowing, and sowing the runways with brome grass.

The Department of National Defence improved Prince Albert Airport in 1940, preparing for a flying training school under the British Commonwealth Air Training Plan. It had two training units based there during the war: No. 6 Elementary Flying Training School, operated by the North Saskatchewan Flying Training School Ltd. (a subsidiary of the Saskatoon Flying Club) and No. 6 Air Observer School, operated by the Prince Albert Air Observer School Ltd.

In 1946, the city of Prince Albert took over the airport and has operated it ever since, with an airport operating subsidy from Transport.

Saskatchewan Government Airways, formed in 1947 and based in Prince Albert, provided passenger service, forest patrol, fire suppression, and air ambulance service. In 1962, the name of the company was changed to Sask Air and, in 1965, it was purchased by Norcanair. Subsequently, Norcanair was purchased by Time Air in January 1988 and consequently became part of the Canadian Airlines International Group.

In 1949, when the Prince Albert Airport expanded to its present size of about 630 acres [255 hectares], the main runway, 08-26, which is 5,000 by 200 feet [1,524 by 61 metres], was paved. The turf runway, 16-34, is 2,500 by 100 feet [762 by 30 metres].

A flight service station established by Transport-Canada in 1950 was initially in hangar no. 21, and moved to the Norcanair hangar in 1968. Eventually, it took its present location between the air terminal building and the Athabasca Airways hangar. The terminal building, constructed at a cost of $1 million, was officially opened on June 24, 1985.

As part of Canada's national aviation network, Prince Albert Airport is jointly owned and operated by Transport Canada and the city of Prince Albert. It is licensed for day and night operations and is the principal IFR (Instrument Flight Rules) and VFR (Visual Flight Rules) operation in Northwest Saskatchewan.

Transport Canada Flight Service Specialists offer a twenty-four-hour flight safety service and a full take-off and landing advisory.

Customs and Immigration services are available at the airport on prior notice for commercial airlines and general aviation traffic.

The Prince Albert Airport is the home base for the government of Saskatchewan forest fire water bombing operations. P.A. Aviation offers pilot training and charter flights, and Athabasca Airways helicopters operate private and charter flights and a summertime fire patrol. In addition, the RCMP has a base at the Prince Albert Airport from which it serves all Saskatchewan and particularly Northern Saskatchewan.

The needs of Prince Albert and Saskatchewan are further met by Time Air, located in the air terminal building, and Prairie Flying Service, operating out of Regina. Both airlines offer flights five days a week in and out of Prince Albert.

Prince Albert Airport averages 31,000 aircraft movements per year and, with the increased mineral and mining activity primarily north of Prince Albert, aircraft movement could average 35,000 in the next two to three years.

Doug Charrette is the present airport manager.

His predecessors were A. Quinn and William Lougheed.

Sources:
1. Manuscripts of the History of the Prince Albert Chamber of Commerce, 1988.
2. Transport Canada Brochure, Prince Albert Airport, 1985.
3. W.H. Lougheed, former Airport Manager, Prince Albert Airport.
4. D. Charette, Airport Manager, Prince Albert Airport.
5. Main, J.K.R. *Voyageurs of the Air*. Ottawa: Queen's Printer, 1967.

Prince George Airport
(British Columbia)

As early as February 23, 1920, the Air Board[1] asked the city of Prince George if it were interested in establishing an aerodrome. The city declined, however, because of the cost.

The first recorded flight made into Prince George was on August 2, 1920, when three De Havilland 4-B biplanes of the U.S. Army Air Service landed on Central Avenue, Prince George, to refuel; a fourth plane arrived on the next day. The four aircraft formed the first Alaska Air Expedition that had left Mitchell Field, New York, on July 15, bound for Nome, Alaska. They had already landed in Canada at Saskatoon, Edmonton, and Jasper. One aircraft sustained some damage in the landing at Prince George. The four aircraft left for Alaska on August 13 by way of Hazelton, B.C.,[2] Wrangell, Alaska, and Whitehorse, Yukon, and reached Nome on August 23. They began the return flight on August 26 and landed at Prince George—one in late September and the rest in early October. All four eventually arrived at Mitchell Field on October 20, 1920.[3]

By July 1922, the city had established an aerodrome 2,400 by 300 feet [731 by 91 metres] across First Avenue. Then in 1928, faced with the growing number of aircraft passing through the region, the city bought a 165-acre [65-hectare] tract of land one and a half kilometres south of the town. The land, near the intersection of highways 97 and 16, is now used as a golf course.

The city had an aerodrome with two runways, 2,200 by 300 feet [670 by 91 metres] in April 1932. It was not until December 1, 1938, however, that the field met the standards required for a licence; one was issued on that date in the city's name. In late 1939, the Department made a capital grant to the city of Prince George for improvement of the airport as part of the Vancouver-Fort St. John air route to Alaska.

In 1937, United Air Transport Company, owned by Grant McConachie, secured a contract from the Post Office to fly mail to isolated points in British Columbia, and selected Prince George as a base.

A new airport site on a high bench of the Fraser River, parallel to the Quesnel Highway and eleven kilometres east of the city, was surveyed and purchased in 1940. Construction began almost immediately for the Department of National Defence. The main runway, 14-32, was built in 1941, and the airport was completed in July 1942 as an RCAF station forming part of the Vancouver-Whitehorse staging route. The U.S. Air Force constructed a number of buildings on the airport, which were later purchased and taken over by the Department of Transport.

In 1940 and 1941, Pan American Airways operated the Seattle-to-Fairbanks route by way of Prince George, Juneau and Whitehorse.

Pan American built a radio station and an administrative building at Prince George in late 1940.

149. Terminal building, Prince George Airport, c. 1951.

The old city airport was closed on March 31, 1944, and the new one was used by Pan American Airways[4] and by CPAL, the RCAF, and the USAF. On August 9, 1945, final construction of the airport was completed. The site consisted of 2,034 acres [823 hectares] of land and had three 5,000-foot [1,524-metre] runways forming the traditional triangle. The speed of completion rather than durability appears to have been a major consideration, and consequently serviceability became a problem after the war.

On August 1, 1946, with the war over, the airport was transferred from the control of the RCAF to the Department of Transport. The airport licence was issued on that date, and surplus wartime buildings were sold and removed.

By 1951, the poor quality of the runways became evident. CPAL, which had begun twice weekly service with DC-4 aircraft, had to revert to DC-3s, as the runways were being severely damaged by the weight of the aircraft; and all aircraft larger than DC-3s were prohibited.

Central B.C. Airways began to serve Prince George in 1951, and were taken over by Pacific Western Airlines in 1953. CPAL began DC-6B service in September 1957.

Runway 15-33 was resurfaced and strengthened in 1952, and runway 06-24 was similarly upgraded in 1956. A USAF B-29 made an emer-

gency landing on 19-01 on November 23, 1953, and sank forty-six centimetres into the tarmac. The runway was not rebuilt until 1959. Runway 15-33 was extended to 6,400 feet [1,951 metres] in 1964, and to 7,400 feet [2,255 metres] in 1975.

The Prince George Flying Club was established on the airport site in 1959. It put on the first air show in the area on May 17 of that year.

By 1961, air traffic had increased to the point that the old control tower had to be restored and airport control reintroduced for sixteen hours a day.

Three pulp mills which opened within two to five miles of the airport between 1965 and 1966, caused visibility problems at the airport: zero-to-half-mile visibilities occurred 50 to 75 per cent more often than before.

In November 1968, CPAL introduced Boeing 737 jet service at Prince George.

A new air terminal building was opened on September 15, 1973, and a new control tower was built the same year.

The airport has three runways: 15-33, 7,400 feet [2,256 metres] (extended to that length in 1975); 06-24, 5,625 feet [1,715 metres]; and 19-01, 3,300 feet [1,006 metres], day VFR (Visual Flight Rules) only.

Scheduled air service is provided by Canadian Airlines International, Air BC, Central Mountain Air, and Aviair Aviation.

The following operators are based at the airport: Northern Mountain Helicopters, Highland Helicopters, Northern Thunderbird Air, Carrier Lumber, and the B.C. Forest Service (air tanker base).

In 1988, there were 258,000 passengers and 48,255 aircraft movements.

The following served as airport managers:

J. Knowland	1946 to 1953
K. Thompson	1953 to 1954

S. Sanderson	1954 to 1976
J.P. Williams	1976 to 1979
G.C. Baker	1979 to 1980
W.D. Harley	1980 to 1987
Christine Legault	1987

Sources:

1. Transport Canada, Pacific Region.
2. R.L. Clarke, "Airport Notes" (Ottawa: Transport Canada) [unpublished collection].

Footnotes—Prince George Airport

[1] The Air Board was the government organization responsible for aviation at that time. The Department of National Defence became responsible in 1923, and the new Department of Transport, in 1936.

[2] Hazelton is included in the list of airharbours available for use during 1922 as private-commercial, for seaplanes and airplanes.

[3] F.H. Ellis, *Canada's Flying Heritage* (Toronto: University of Toronto Press, 1961), pp. 187-92.

[4] Pan American operated under U.S. Navy contract from September 1942 to July 1944.

Prince Rupert Airport
(British Columbia)

Prince Rupert Airport is located on Digby Island, west of the city of Prince Rupert and the Rupert Harbour. It is approximately 708 kilometres from Vancouver, British Columbia, and serves a population base of about 30,000 people. The airport was built on Digby Island after a five-year search for a suitable location by the Department of Transport. Prior to the construction of the airport, air travellers going to Prince Rupert arrived after a roundabout route: first, they flew Canadian Pacific Airlines on a DC-4 to the Sandspit Airport, where they boarded amphibian aircraft, usually Cansos, for the flight to the water aerodrome located at Seal Cove in Prince Rupert.

A 6,000 by 200-foot [1,829 by 61 metre] runway, as well as an access road and dock, were built between 1957 and 1959. The main access road runs from the airport to the ferry dock. Construction was difficult, as 10 to 12 feet [3 to 3.7 metres] of muskeg had to be removed and filled with rock before the runway could be built.

In 1960-61, navigational aids, power facilities from the mainland, and meteorological services were completed.

An airport licence was issued in Transport's name for 'day operation only' in 1961, and Canadian Pacific Airlines started regularly scheduled service.

In 1962, the air terminal building, instrument landing system, and staff dwellings were built. The staff accommodations were later removed.

In 1971, the combination firehall/maintenance building was constructed next to the air terminal building.

Access to the airport is unique because air travellers going in and out of Prince Rupert have the opportunity to travel by three modes of transportation: land, sea, and air. Both of the major airlines that operate out of the airport provide bus transportation from their downtown offices to the airport. After boarding buses, passengers travel to the ferry dock on the city side, where buses and passengers board a ferry operated by the city of Prince Rupert, for the twenty-minute trip to Digby Island. At Digby, the buses proceed to the airport, where the passengers take the air trip to Vancouver.

The ferry dock on Digby Island was turned over to the National Harbours Board (now Ports Canada) in 1974. In 1987, a new ferry docking facility was built to replace the original dock.

Two major airlines now operate regularly scheduled jet service out of the Prince Rupert Airport: Canadian Airlines International with a fleet of Boeing 737s, and Air BC with British Aerospace 146 aircraft.

Transprovincial airlines operates non-scheduled flights into the airport, as does North Coast Air. Helicopter service is provided by Vancouver Island helicopters.

In 1988, there were 131,400 passengers and 9,450 aircraft movements.

The following persons have served as airport managers at the Prince Rubert Airport:

O.C. Fisher	1960 to 1970
D. Kirby	1970 to 1977
H. Merth	1977 to 1981
D. Laurent	1982 to 1983
R. Munroe	1983 to 1985
J. Terpstra	1986 to 1989

Source:

Transport Canada, Pacific Region.

Princeton Aerodrome
(British Columbia)

Princeton Aerodrome is an uncertified airfield located on the outskirts of the municipality of Princeton in British Columbia.

The airstrip was developed by the Department of National Defence as part of the overall aviation plan for World War II. The Department of Transport took over the site after the war ended and has since maintained it through contract arrangements. The manager of Penticton Airport is responsible for its operations.

Princeton Aerodrome has an asphalt runway, 1,200 by 23 metres. A NDB (non-directional beacon) is located at the site, which is a point on the main VFR (Visual Flight Rules) route linking the Kootenays and northern British Columbia with Vancouver. A flight service station is based on the airport grounds.

A few older buildings remaining from the war are occupied by the Air Cadets, who use the aerodrome as a centre for glider flight training during summer months. The British Columbia Forestry Service directs firefighting operations from this location.

Source:
Jim Warman, Airport Manager, Penticton Airport.

Québec Airport
(Québec)

In May 1928, the controller of Civil Aviation visited Québec city to meet with the mayor, at the latter's request, to discuss the establishment of an aerodrome to serve the city. The mayor hoped that the federal government would provide the facility. The controller explained the government's policy and wrote:

The Department [of National Defence] considered the provision of aerodromes throughout the country as a matter for the local authorities and, save where they required a base for their own use, would not enter into this field. If they provided a flying field in one city they would be called on to do so everywhere. It was immaterial to the Department whether further action was taken by the municipality itself, or by a commercial operating company, provided

150. Fairchild 71, CF-AAT, Canadian transcontinental Airways Ltd., Ancienne Lorette, PQ, 1930.

that the field met the requirements of the Air Regulations. The Department would assist in the choice of the field and do all in its power to help the establishment of good facilities.

3. I pointed out that the Dominion Government, in letting air mail contracts, was really carrying a large portion of the burden of extending airways and could not be expected to do more. Travel by air was now increasing and if any communities wished to encourage it in their district, they must provide adequate accommodation.

4. In reply to a question by His Worship as to our action in having provided fields at Montréal and Rimouski, it was pointed out that the Montréal field had been purchased solely to help the development of long-distance travel by airship and if it had not been for the airship scheme, the St. Hubert property would not have been purchased. As regards Rimouski, the locality there would expect little benefit from the field, as little or no local mail service would be provided. The industrial and commercial communities of Québec, Montréal, Ottawa, Toronto, Winnipeg and the West would benefit from the speeding up of the mail service in a way that Rimouski would not, and the terminal field there was, on this account, considered as in the direct interest of the Dominion as a whole and, therefore, had been provided by the Dominion authorities. It was pointed out to the Mayor that in Toronto and Ottawa the Contractors [i.e. airmail carriers] had made arrangements for their own fields, quite independent of any assistance or grant from the Dominion government, and that western communities were establishing fields either municipally or commercially owned...[1]

The original Québec Airport was established by Canadian Transcontinental Airways at St. Louis in the municipality of Ste. Foy, west of Québec

151. Québec (Ancienne Lorette) Airport, February 10, 1944.

city, with two strips, 3,000 feet [914 metres] long. A report of May 12, 1938, written by the controller of Civil Aviation gives the history of the St. Louis Airport:

1927-36—Canadian Transcontinental Airways was formed by citizens of Québec to operate in eastern Canada in 1927. They obtained a contract for the operation of the winter air mail service from Montréal to Rimouski along the north shore of the St. Lawrence. In 1928, they purchased the airport site at St. Louis as a base for their uses and the field was granted a permanent private airport licence on March 7, 1929. They constructed three hangars and other facilities on the airport. In 1930, this company was absorbed by an amalgamation of several companies into Canadian Airways, who then became the owners of the airport property and have maintained it since then. Owing to the removal of the base of the lower St. Lawrence winter air mail service from Québec to Rimouski two years ago, Canadian Airways have little use for the Québec Airport and, in conversation, have stated they only made one landing during the past year. Local pilots in Québec have used it intermittently, however.

November 4th, 1936—The city Clerk of Québec wired the Honourable Mr. Power, strongly endorsing the request made by the Chamber of Commerce that Québec Airport be made a 'national airport.' This evidently means that the Dominion government should build and maintain it. The Department of National Defence have stated that the Royal Canadian Air Force have no plans for the future which would involve the establishment of an airport at Québec.

March 7th, 1938—Mr. Romeo Vachon, District Superintendent, Canadian Airways, and Manager of Québec Airways, advised the Department that his company was taking steps to close the airport from May 1, 1938.

April 21st, 1938 - Mr. Vachon and Mr. Dickins, of Canadian Airways, discussed the maintenance of the airport and advised that an annual rental of $6,000 would be required, plus a charge of $2,000 for maintenance of the airport.

May 6th, 1938—Mr. R. Vachon reported that he had had a further discussion with Mayor Borne relative to the maintenance of the airport and said that the Mayor stated the city would take no action in the matter. He further reported that the airport and boundary markers had been removed and the airport, as such, abandoned and that it might be ploughed up at any date.

2. The present site provides fair facilities in an east and west direction. Owing to the slope of the land, the north and south aspect is not good, however, and it is doubtful whether it would be advisable to propose building a field for first class air line operations on that site. Surveys have been made at different times during the past ten years with a view to determining whether a better site could be found and it may be stated that there is no site so convenient which would

152. Air terminal buildings, Québec Airport.

give better facilities. To attain a really good site it may be necessary to move farther from the city, probably a distance of 10 or 12 miles out.[2]

When surveys were conducted in May 1938 for the location of a new airport to serve Québec, a site at Ancienne Lorette was recommended because of its easy access to the city, sixteen kilometres to the northeast. The outbreak of war finally gave Québec the airport city authorities had, until then, requested in vain. In October 1939, the Department of Transport, on behalf of the Department of National Defence, tried to get options on the Ancienne Lorette site for use as a training field for the RCAF under the British Commonwealth Air Training Plan. The matter was left in abeyance as the price asked for the property was too high. In 1940, however, construction of the field for use as an Air Observer School eventually began and the field opened in the spring of 1941. The new airport became the home of No. 8 Air Observer School (AOS) and No. 22 Elementary Flying Training School (EFTS). The flying school was run by the City of Québec Elementary Flying Training School Ltd.—which was not affiliated with a flying club. It flew Ansons and Fleet Finches. No. 8 AOS was operated by Québec Airways, a

subsidiary of Canadian Pacific Airlines. By 1942, the airport had become the major flight training school in eastern Canada. Both schools closed down on March 31, 1945.

The airport at Ancienne Lorette was 239 feet [seventy-three metres] above sea level and sixteen kilometres west of Québec city. It had three paved runways: 12-30, 3,000 feet [914 metres]; 06-24, 3,300 feet [1,006 metres]; and 02-20, 2,800 feet [853 metres], all 150 feet [46 metres] wide and between 1941 and 1943 the airport operated only during daylight hours. During 1941, the first hangars and buildings were erected for No. 8 AOS.

It was not until 1943 that the airport facilities were substantially improved with the installation of runway, taxiway, and approach lights. The Québec city radio beacon came into operation in September 1943, the year that Canadian Pacific Airlines (CPAL) began operating flights on a more or less regular schedule between Montréal, Québec city, Mont Joli, and Sept-Iles.

No major changes took place at the airport until the end of the war in Europe, when the BCATP flying school was disbanded. All the airport facilities might well have been closed down were it not for CPAL, which used the airport during the post-war years.

At the end of the BCATP operations on March 31, 1945, the Department of Transport took over the operation of Québec Airport, while the land and other facilities remained under the ownership of the Department of National Defence. The airport was formally transferred to Transport in the fall of 1946 because the Québec authorities had no interest in taking it over. A permanent airport licence was issued on December 11, 1946.

In the following years, there was gradual growth in civil aviation at the Québec Airport so that by 1948 -1949, it was necessary to extend runway 12-30 at both ends to its present length of 5,700 feet [1,737 metres].

In 1954, to improve air service, TCA and a new airline, Québecair, proposed to set up operations at Québec city. In 1954, runway 06-24 was extended at the northeast end to a length of 6,000 feet [1,829 metres]. It is now 2,743 metres long.

TCA and Québecair began operating at the airport in 1955 with two or three flights a day using DC-3 and Lockheed aircraft. In the same year, construction began on the first air terminal[3] and on the ramps and loading areas.

The terminal was officially opened on December 17, 1957. It included a section for Customs and for TCA, Québecair, and Timmins Aviation. It had a control tower, meteorological and telecommunications services, and Department of Transport administration offices. The airport was designated as an alternate for aircraft on the North Atlantic air route.

In 1959, an ILS (Instrument Landing System) was installed along with high intensity approach lights, and an Airport and Airways Surveillance Radar (AASR) system for air traffic control was completed.

The buildings erected during the war were gradually transformed in the post-war year: some were torn down and others sold. In 1948, one of the buildings became the St. Augustin Hospital for the chronically ill and was still in operation until 1962. Hangar no. 4 burned down in 1946, and hangar no. 3 was sold in 1964. This left hangars nos. 1 and 2, which were bought that same year by the Aero Club de Québec[4] and the Tapis Rouge Aero Service, respectively. Hangar no. 1 has since been replaced, and hangar no. 2, which was used as a terminal building after the war and later owned by Québec Aviation, is now occupied by Inter Québec Airlines.

In 1947, the province of Québec began air service operations for forest protection and for the surveillance of hunting and fishing, and in the fall of 1964, opened a hangar. Also in 1964, a weather radar system was introduced in Québec City, and, in 1965, a VOR (VHF Omni-directional Range) navigation system was set up. This was followed in 1967 by the installation of a Tactical Air Navigation Equipment (TACAN) system.

Jet aircraft arrived at Québec Airport in 1964 and, in 1965, runway 02-20 was withdrawn from service, thus bringing an end to the era of the triangular-shaped airport constructed in 1939 and 1940.

As the volume of air traffic at Québec Airport increased rapidly, plans were made for lengthening runway 06-24 and the construction of a new airport terminal, which was opened in 1973. The old terminal was transformed into an administrative building. Runway 06-24 was lengthened to 7,500 feet [2,286 metres] in 1974.

Québecair began to offer direct charter flights to destination points in Europe in 1976 and 1977; Nordair and the James Bay Society established flights to points in the north of Québec (for example, Fort Chimo).

In 1979, the principal runway was lengthened from 7,500 to 9,000 feet [2,286 to 2,743 metres]. A new access road was built, and the apron ramp was reinforced in 1981. Between 1982 and 1984, improvements included the enlargement of carparks and the aircraft traffic area, and the installation of a loading bridge, thereby adding additional aircraft stands. In 1985, the planning of common use facilities in the air terminal building (counter, office, baggage room) was completed and that of a new general aviation area was started. A major project to rebuild the movement area was concluded during the summer of 1988.

The following air carriers serve Québec Airport: Air Alliance, Air Canada, Air Inuit, Air Nova, Air Transat, Air Ontario, Canadian International, Gulf Air, Inter-Canadian, Inter-Québec, Minerve Canada, and Nationair, with a total of approximately eighty flights daily. Operators use a variety of aircraft including Dash-8, ATR-42, HS-748, Convair 580, F-28, F-100, DC-08, DC-09, B-727, B-737, and the L-1011.

The headquarters of Inter-Québec, Air Alliance, and Conifair are located at Québec Airport; the air service of the government of Québec also operates F-27 aircraft there, as well as the air ambulance Challenger and its maintenance base for the aircraft tankers, CL-215 and Canso.

General aviation (Transportair, Aero-Propulsion, Myrand Aviation, Aviation Leclerc, private proprietors, etc.) use a large variety of small aircraft such as the PA-18, PA-3, Cessna 150, and Cessna Citation; and two companies, Viking Helicopters and Heli-Max, operate helicopters. A multitude of services are offered: freight transport, recreation flights, training flights, pilot schools, air photography, transport by helicopter, and aeronautical maintenance.

As the clearance airport for the military at Bagotville—the Valcartier military base, situated in the vicinity—Québec Airport is the scene of impressive exercises and numerous military movements, as troops are transported both inside and outside the country. The activities generally involve helicopters and C-130 and B-707 aircraft.

The following aviation organizations are also located at the airport: Québec Association of Air Carriers, the Association of gens de l'air du Québec, and les Ailes Québec.

Currently, the Québec Airport, which occupies 632 hectares, serves the provincial capital and is one of the busiest sites in Québec: 650,000 passengers pass through the airport (estimates for the year 2001 foresee more than 1,203,000) and 120,000 landings and takeoffs are carried out each year. Transport Canada employs approximately 140 persons there and 1,400 directly related jobs are generated. Airport activity totalled $37.5 million and the total economic impact of the airport amounts to $67 million.[5]

The following served as airport managers:

W. Wrathall	1945 to 1946
J.E. Goulet	1947 to 1958
J.T.E. Sheridan	1959 to 1965
A.R. Habel	1966 to 1968
L.R. Brochu	1969 to 1976
N. Caron	1976 to 1983
S. Tining	1984 to 1987

Sources:
1. N. Caron, former Airport Manager, Québec Airport.
2. Transport Canada, Québec Region.

Footnotes—Québec Airport

[1] Public Archives Canada, MG 30, E243, vol. 9, memorandum, 15 May 1928.

[2] Public Archives Canada, MG 30 E243, vol. 9.

[3] The same design was used for terminal buildings at Saskatoon (1955) and Windsor (1958).

[4] The Aero Club de Québec ceased operations in 1973

[5] Canada, Department of Transport, Economic Impact Study: Québec Airport, 1989.

Quesnel Airport
(British Columbia)

In December 1940, the village of Quesnel expressed interest in having an airport, and had located a site, five kilometres from downtown and within city limits, capable of accommodating a 6,000 foot [1,829-metre] runway. The Department of Transport agreed that another airport between Prince George and Williams Lake would greatly improve the air route. It was not until 1942, however, that the Department of National Defence developed an airport at Quesnel for use in Western Hemisphere Operations (WHO) during the war.

The airport was taken over by the Department of Transport in 1946, and an airport licence was issued on April 1, 1946.

The runway, which was paved in 1958, no.13-31 is currently 1,670 metres long.

A new air terminal building was constructed in 1967, a new departures lounge added in 1979, and a new arrivals area in 1981. A new combined services building was put up in 1984-85.

Scheduled service to Quesnel is provided by Air BC and Time Air using Dash 7 and 8 aircraft.

The following are based at the airport: Northern Mountain Helicopters, Sharp Wings (charter and flying school), and West Fraser Mills (hangar).

There were 30,100 passengers in 1988 and 14,310 aircraft movements.

The following served as airport managers:

W. Turner	1946 to 1959
P. Nowesad	1959 to 1978
J. Gunn	1978 to 1981
R.J. MacKay	1981

Sources:
1. Transport Canada, Pacific Region.
2. R.L. Clarke, "Airport Notes" (Ottawa: Transport Canada) [unpublished collection].

Rankin Inlet Airstrip
(Northwest Territories)

Rankin Inlet is located on the west coast of Hudson Bay, 515 kilometres north of Churchill.

The gravel airstrip, 13-31, originally 3,800 by 150 feet [1,158 by 46 metres], was built in the late 1950s to serve the North Rankin Nickel Mine. Ownership was transferred to the Department of Transport in 1960, (with the Department of Indian and Northern Affairs continuing to be the operator), and in 1975, it was taken over by

the hamlet of Rankin Inlet, with Transport providing funding for maintenance.

In 1976, extensive development began at the airstrip: the strip itself was lengthened to 5,000 feet [1,524 metres]; a terminal building and maintenance garage were constructed, and navigation aids improved.

Construction is currently under way to upgrade the runway surfaces to accommodate a DND Forward Operating Location for CF-18 aircraft.

The airstrip is now operated by the government of the Northwest Territories.

Rankin Inlet is served by Calm Air, NWT Air, First Air, Nunasi Northland and Keewatin Air Ltd.

In 1988, there were 7,976 aircraft movements and 23,300 passengers.

Sources:
1. Transport Canada, Central Region.
2. Municipality of Rankin Inlet.

Red Lake Airport
(Ontario)

Red Lake is a mining community 153 kilometres northeast of Kenora and 169 kilometres northwest of Sioux Lookout.

The Red Lake Airport is located a half kilometre from the community of Cochenour in the township of Golden, about five kilometres from Red Lake. The population of Golden and environs is about 8,400; the economy depends upon two gold mines in nearby Balmertown.

Before the airport was built, the community was served by seaplanes and ski-planes operated by the pioneer airlines: Wings Ltd., Starratt Airways, and Canadian Airways, which carried passengers, mail, and freight to and from Winnipeg, Kenora, Sioux Lookout, and Hudson. It was claimed that "Red Lake became the busiest airport in the world for the summer months of 1936 and handled 50 per cent more air freight than any other airport in the world in 1937."[1] All this activity was by seaplane—and ski-plane during the winter—in support of mining in the area.

In 1945, the Department of Transport began preliminary surveys for an airport site, through rugged terrain of rock and muskeg. Although proceedings began in 1947, it was not until February 2, 1956, that a firm agreement was made between Transport and the province of Ontario whereby the chosen site was set aside for development as a permanent airport,[2] which was to be maintained by the Department of Transport. In 1946, a single gravel runway, 07-25, was constructed, 4,000 by 150 feet [1,219 by 46 metres], and was ready on May 29, 1947, for CPAL daily Lockheed Lodestar service from Winnipeg. Construction was completed in August 1949; but the runway was not paved until 1969. It was totally reconstructed in 1987. and the runway bearings were changed to 08-26 in 1979.

The airport was maintained for Transport by CPA until the airlines' route was transferred to Central Northern Airways, which then maintained the field. A temporary airport licence was issued in Transport's name on May 17, 1951, although the department had not received title to the land from the province and had no staff at the airport. For this reason, the licence was allowed to lapse on July 1, 1952. A new licence was issued to Transport on October 17, 1956, and arrangements were then made with Central Northern Airways to operate and maintain the airport for day use only.

In 1959, the Department of Transport took over the airport and appointed staff. Lighting was installed that year, and the licence was amended on November 19, 1959, to permit twenty-four-hour operation.

In 1981, the township of Golden took over operations and maintenance of the airport from Transport Canada.

Department of Transport buildings include a terminal building, maintenance garage, weather station, and a field electrical building. The airport is equipped with an NDB (Non-directional Beacon) and a VOR (VHF Omni-directional Range).

Norontair flies out of Red Lake twice daily flying to Dryden, and Perimeter, once daily to Winnipeg. Sabourin Airways serve the northern communities, and Bearskin flies to Thunder Bay and Winnipeg twice daily.

Aircraft movements have increased from 6,620 in 1973 to 17,000 in 1988. In 1983 there were 15,300 passengers; 24,700 by 1987.

The airport has a manager, Brian Anderson, and a staff of five. Fifty people and upwards are employed at Red Lake Airport, depending on the season.

Sources:

1. Transport Canada, Central Region.
2. R.L. Clarke, "Airport Notes" (Ottawa: Transport Canada) [unpublished collection].

Footnotes—Red Lake Airport

1 Donald F. Parrott, *The Second Gold Rush to Red Lake*, (published by the author, 1976), p.53.
2 The provinciad difficulty obtaining zoning easements from one of the mining companies involved.

Regina Airport
(Saskatchewan)

Regina had an airfield as early as 1919, located at the corner of Mill Avenue and Cameron Street, and licensed under the newly introduced Air Regulations on April 22, 1920, when Airharbour Licence No. 1 was granted in the name of the Aerial Service Co. Ltd.[1] In 1922, when the Air Board published its first List of Airharbours Available for Use, there were thirty-seven in all. Regina was classified as 'Private Commercial-Aeroplanes-area 800 yards square.'[2]

Lieutenant Roland J. Groome and Edward Clarke formed the Aerial Service Co. Ltd. in Regina in 1919. On May 26, 1919, Groome was the pilot on the flight between Regina and Moose Jaw that carried specially printed copies of the Regina Leader between the cities. A week before, on May 19, 1919, Groome and Bob McCombie flew a Curtiss JN-4 from Saskatoon to Regina on what was the first successful cross-country flight in Saskatchewan. Groome became the first licensed commercial pilot under the new Air Board Regulations and received licence no. 1 on July 1, 1920. McCombie received air engineer's certificate no. 1 at the same time. One of the company's Curtiss JN-4 airplanes bore the first registration letters to be used in Canada, G-CAAA, issued on April 20, 1920. After a distinguished career in aviation, Groome lost his life in an aircraft accident on September 20, 1935, while he was an instructor for the Regina Flying Club.[3]

A second airfield, known as Lakeview Aerodrome, was opened by Jack Wright and R.J. Groome in 1927.

153. Regina Airfield, July 1919.

The city of Regina was very air-minded in the early 1920s and made plans to set aside forty acres [sixteen hectares] of land for future airport development. The Regina Flying Club was formed in 1927, and in order to qualify for benefits under the government's new plan to assist light aeroplane clubs and associations (see Appendix 9), bought 160 acres [sixty-five hectares] of land that year for the development of an airport. This was Regina's third airport site. The city bought land from the club later in 1928, and a start was made on the development of the present Regina Airport, three kilometres west of the city. The official opening, however, was not held until September 15, 1930.

In the ensuing years, additional property was purchased, a hangar was built, two runways were paved in 1932, and airport lighting was added. These improvements gave Regina a modern municipal airport.

The first air-mail test flights through Regina started on December 10, 1928, on the Winnipeg-Regina-Calgary-Saskatoon-Edmonton route, operated by Western Canada Airways, which later became part of Canadian Airways Ltd. The prairie section of the new Trans-Canada Airway which began in 1929, was first to be built because of the relatively easy terrain. A teletype circuit between Winnipeg and Moose Jaw, had a drop in Regina in 1930; and a chain of radio beacons, with one at Regina, was set up in the same year. In 1931, major improvements were made to the airport, and a radio range was installed in 1938. And in 1932 asphalt runways were built at Regina, making it the only airport so equipped between Montréal and Vancouver.

The first night air-mail service through Regina was inaugurated in 1930 by Canadian Airways Ltd. In 1938, TCA began its first transcontinental air-mail and passenger service between Montréal and Vancouver, with Regina as a regular stop; and Prairie Airways Ltd. operated a daily service with two-engined Beechcraft from Regina to Moose Jaw, Saskatoon, Prince Albert, and North Battleford.

During 1938, runway 07-25 was constructed and 12-30 rebuilt. In 1939, as the city was unable to finance it, the Department of Transport built an administration building with a control tower, which was officially opened in February 1940.

When the war broke out, Regina Airport was taken over by the federal government for the duration of hostilities. It was operated by the Department of Transport as a civil airport, but was dominated by a flying training school for the British Commonwealth Air Training Plan (BCATP), run by the RCAF. The Department of National Defence built three hangars and made further improvements to the airport for its new role. In November 1940, No. 15 Elementary Flying Training School began operations. It was managed by the Regina Elementary Flying Training School Ltd., a subsidiary company of the Regina Flying Club. No. 3 Air Observer School was also established at the airport.

In 1945, BCATP operations came to an end and the RCAF hangars and other buildings were taken over by the Department of Transport, which continued to operate the airport until 1955.

In November 1952, a new runway, 08-26, was completed. Soon after, TCA introduced North Star aircraft service at Regina. An ILS (Instrument Landing System) was installed in 1955. A new air terminal building was opened on October 12, 1960 and, in 1967, runway 12-30 was extended by 1,000 feet [305 metres]. The present airport has two runways: 12-30 at 7,900 feet [2,408 metres] and 08-26 at 6,200 feet [1,890 metres], with widths of 200 and 150 feet [61 and 46 metres], respectively. Runway 08-26 was resurfaced in 1988.

The city of Regina resumed operation of the airport in 1955; but even with a subsidy from the

154. Administration building, Regina Airport, c. 1941-42.

Department of Transport had financial problems. After prolonged negotiations, Transport bought the airport from the city for $2.3 million and assumed responsibility for its operation on January 1, 1972. The enlarged terminal building was opened in September 1986. About five hundred employees work at the airport today.

There are nine hangars at the site: one pre-war, two wartime, and six privately owned. The pre-war hangar, built in 1930, is used by the Saskatchewan Executive Air Service as its main operations base. The two remaining wartime hangars are used by the Regina Flying Club and Prairie Flying Services.

The following air carriers operate scheduled services:

Air Canada	DC-9, Boeing 727
Canadian Airlines	Boeing 737
Time Air	F-28, Dash 7,
Convair	580, F-27
Prairie Flying	Cessna 402

Time Air operates in Saskatchewan, flying F-27s, Convairs, Dash 7s, F-28s to points in northern Saskatchewan, as well as offering daily non-stop service to Minneapolis and St. Paul, Minnesota.

Air Canada and Canadian Airlines provide direct daily (or more frequent service) to Toronto, Winnipeg, Vancouver, Calgary, Edmonton, and

Saskatoon. Time Air provides daily service to Minneapolis, St. Paul, Winnipeg, Calgary, Saskatoon, and various points in the northern Saskatchewan region. Prairie Flying, flies daily to Prince Albert, Saskatchewan.

The airport serves a variety of charter activity, especially during the winter vacation period, to destinations in Arizona, Mexico, Nevada, Florida, and Hawaii.

There are six aviation service outlets at Regina Airport that provide charter flights, flying instruction, or aircraft maintenance services.

The following airlines have discontinued service: Norcanair (1987); Pacific Western Airlines (1987); Canadian Pacific (1987); and Frontier (1986).

In 1987, the airport had 601,700 passengers; in 1988, there were 82,745 aircraft movements.

The following served as airport managers:

Captain R.A. Dalhaye	1939 (Transport)
Bob Joberty	to 1950 (Transport)
Norm Street	1950 (Transport)
Dennis Rennick	to 1967 (Regina)
Don Campbell	1968 to 1971 (Regina)
Don Campbell	1972 to 1975 (Transport)
Ray Jennings	1976 to 1987 (Transport)
Wayne Harley	1987 (Transport)

Sources:
1. Transport Canada, Central Region.
2. Transport Canada, Public Affairs, Regina.
3. R.H. (Ray) Crone of Regina.
4. Saskatchewan Archives Department.

Footnotes—Regina Airport
[1] "Canadian Airharbours", *Aviation and Aircraft Journal* (24 October 1921), p.482.

[2] See Chapter 7. For the definition of "airharbour," see Appendix 18. The Air Board was the government body responsible for the control of civil aviation in Canada at the time.

[3] F.H. Ellis, *Canada's Flying Heritage* (Toronto: University of Toronto Press, 1961), pp. 158-59.

Repulse Bay Airport
(Northwest Territories)

Repulse Bay (Rae Isthmus, Melville Peninsula) was first visited in the early 1740s by Captains Middleton and Moore. By 1850, it was one of the great centres of the Arctic whaling industry. Shortly after the demise of the Hudson Bay whaling industry in 1916, the Hudson's Bay Company established at Request Bay the first trading post used by the nomadic people of the Pelly Bay, Igloolik, and Repulse Bay areas. Revillon Furs followed in 1923, and a Roman Catholic mission was founded in 1932. The present permanent settlement began in the early 1960s, when the first rental homes were introduced; and today's principal activities are hunting, fishing, trapping handicrafts and tourism.

The airstrip is unlicensed and operated by the government of the Northwest Territories (GNWT), and the original was first developed over a course of years by community groups. Its current dimensions are 1,158 by 30 metres. The Department of Indian Affairs and Northern Development funded the NDB (Non-directional Beacon) equipment, while Transport Canada technicians completed the installation in the late 1960s or early 1970s.

When a site more suitable than the original location was not found, and following a field survey in 1975, Transport Canada upgraded the existing aerodrome in 1976-77 under the Arctic Air Facilities Policy.

In the spring of 1977, Transport agreed to construct a gravel runway, 3,400 by 100 feet [1,036 by 30 metres], which was completed in 1981-82.

With the extension of the powerline to the airport in 1979-80, permanent airfield lighting installation was completed in 1983-84. The meteorological instruments and communications equipment were temporarily installed in the community in 1976-77 and relocated at the airport in 1982-83. The NDB was upgraded to solid state equipment in 1977-78, and a passenger shelter was completed in 1982-83.

Airport lands which are currently under the administration and control of the Department of Indian Affairs and Northern Development will be transferred to the government of the Northwest Territories in the near future.

Repulse Bay is served by Calm Air, using HS-748, Beech King Air, and Twin Otter Aircraft; and by Nunasi, using HS-748 and Beech King aircraft.

In 1987, there were 395 aircraft movements, and 2,100 passengers.

The main industries of the area are hunting, fishing, trapping, handicrafts, and tourism.

Source:
Transport Canada, Central Region.

Resolute Bay Airport
(Northwest Territories)

Cornwallis Island, on which Resolute Bay is situated, is about 3,100 miles square in area. The island was discovered and named by Captain W.E. Parry in 1819 while he was searching for the Northwest Passage. Many ships visited Cornwallis Island during the search for the Sir John Franklin Expedition of 1845, and Resolute Bay was named after the HMS Resolute, commanded by Captain Henry Kellett, who led an expedition in 1850-51.

There are four protected Inuit villages near Resolute, two of which are located in the beach

155. Terminal building, Resolute Bay Airport, N.W.T., 1974.

area south of the fuel tank farm. The sites contain the largest concentration of old Inuit archaeological remains on Cornwallis Island.

In January 1947, the United States and Canada agreed to the development of a network of Arctic weather stations. The plan envisaged the establishment of two main stations that could be reached by sea, one in Greenland and one in the Canadian Arctic, which would serve as advance bases from which a number of smaller bases could be established by air.

Resolute, at 74°43'N and 94°57'W, became the main base in the chain because of its central location and its potential as an airport-seaport complex. The weather station was a joint operation of Canada and the United States (JAWS) from 1947 until 1972, when the U.S. withdrew from the Arctic Weather program.

In 1949, an ionosphere station and buildings for the Dominion Observatory were set up, and telemetry equipment was added at a later date. The ionosphere equipment is used for tracking satellites, including the Alouette. Both it and the telemetry equipment were turned over to the Department of Communications in 1969-70.

The airport was constructed by Tower Company Ltd. in 1950, for the RCAF who established its base in 1949 and maintained the runway and

facilities. The weather station was moved from the beach area to the airport in 1953.

On August 7, 1958, the airport had an unusual visitor when the U.S. Navy Airship ZPG2 arrived from Churchill and moored by an RCAF crew to a temporary mast erected 300 yards [274 metres] west of the runway. The airship was en route from Weymouth, Massachusetts, to Ice Island T3 (79° N 121° W) to visit a group of scientists on an International Geophysical Year project.

The ship left Resolute early August 9, but it was unable to land at T3 because of bad visibility. After circling the base for an hour, mail was dropped and the airship returned to Resolute, seventeen hours after departure, with thirty-six hours of fuel remaining. It proceeded directly to Churchill, where it arrived on the evening of August 10, forty-four hours after the original departure from Resolute. The airship was back at its home base in Weymouth on August 12.

The RCAF continued to operate and maintain the airport until April 1, 1964, when the Department of Transport assumed responsibility and awarded a maintenance contract to a private firm. This arrangement still continues.

With the takeover from the RCAF, the Telecommunications Branch of the Department of Transport inherited the marine-aeradio station, which maintains a point-to-point service with other sites in the High Arctic, and provides air-to-ground communications with aircraft operating locally and with aircraft flying the polar route to and from Europe. During the summer shipping season, ship-to-shore communications are maintained.

The first commercial aviation operation in the High Arctic was established in Resolute in 1963, when W.W. (Weldy) Phipps founded Atlas Aviation. Phipps had first flown into Resolute in 1953 with a Canso of Spartan Air Services. He was joined by his wife, Fran, who later (1972)

became the first woman to reach the North Pole. Flying a Super Cub, Beaver, and Single Otter, Phipps pioneered the use of balloon tires on aircraft in the Arctic.

In 1966, Atlas Aviation bought a de Havilland Twin Otter, registered as CF-WWP, which became the first commercially registered Twin Otter in Canada. This aircraft, which also had balloon tires, crashed south of Eureka in 1973 and was salvaged for parts.

Atlas Aviation was sold in December 1971 to Kenting Aviation of Calgary and operated under the name of Kenting Atlas Aviation. To expand and provide on-site servicing, Kenting built a large hangar in Resolute Bay in 1972. After a brief tenure with Kenting Atlas, Phipps retired from aviation to his property in Prince Edward Island, and Kenting Atlas sold its Resolute fixed-wing operation to Kenn Borek Air in 1976.

With the world anxious for new sources of energy, many Canadian and international companies looked to Canada's Arctic. An influx of approximately forty exploration companies, along with federal government scientific groups, descended on Resolute during the late 1960s and early 1970s and, with Resolute as a hub, they conducted field operations throughout the Arctic.

The increased activity in the High Arctic

156. Resolute Bay Airport, N.W.T., 1981.

in 1972, when Bradley Air Services established its base. One of the partners in Bradley was Dick DeBlicquy, who had flown in the Arctic since the early 1950s with the RCAF and with Spartan Air Services on the DEW Line.

The unexpected activity brought the Department of Transport into the hotel business—the Airhotel, as it was known. Accommodation and meals had to be provided for 189 residents and to transients. (The dining facilities once served over seven hundred meals in one day). There is hot water heating from a central heating plant, as well as hot and cold running water, showers, and flush toilets. Many distinguished persons have been accommodated, including Her Majesty Queen Elizabeth II, Princess Margaret of the Netherlands, governors-general, and prime ministers.

In order to meet the increased demands of aviation and exploration of 1970, the fuel storage facilities had to be increased: thirteen million litres capacity was added, and expanded again in 1971-72 to the present total of sixty-eight million litres. These facilities are now leased to Imperial Oil Ltd.

The tenancy of the exploration companies in Resolute Bay placed such a heavy demand on the electricity supply that in 1972, a $1 million diesel generating station was installed by the Department. In 1975, the electrical generating and distribution facilities were turned over to the crown corporation, the Northern Canada Power Commission.

Resolute Airport has two gravel runways: 17-35 is 1,981 by 61 metres, with a concrete button 46 metres long at the end of 35. This runway has an ILS (Instrument Landing System), high intensity runway and approach lights, and strobe lights. The second runway, 10-28, was constructed in 1968 and expanded in 1972 to 1,219 by 46 metres; 10-28 has medium intensity runway and approach lights and strobe lighting. Other navigational aids are the VOR (VHF Omni-directional Range) and DME (distance Measuring Equipment). The runways are maintained with the same type of equipment used at southern Canadian airports.

In 1983, Transport converted the Airhotel to a staffhouse complex and began renovations to make more comfortable quarters for the permanent staff close to their places of work. Within the complex are a sauna, games room, TV lounge, and library; and all staff quarters are connected to a satellite TV antenna that distributes ten Cancom channels.

The working relationship between the contractor's staff and Transport Canada's Regional Office is close and unique, due to Region's active participation through the years. Resolute is the only airport in Transport's Central Region operated and maintained entirely by contractors. Through the contractors, Transport supplies manpower and support services to the weather sites at Mould Bay and Eureka, and to Nanisivik and Hall Beach as part of the Complex Maintenance Centre responsibilities. No one is able to predict that activities will return to the levels of the 1970s, but indications are encouraging that there will be an upturn. Recently, the airport has become a busy place, with the commissioning of an Atmospheric Environment Service (AES) hangar, a heating/water treatment plant, and a water pumphouse on Strip Lake; rehabilitation and resurfacing of runway 17-35 and apron 1; recabling of this runway and replacement of its approach light system; and capital projects identified for a new field electrical centre, firehall, air terminal building, flight service station, and staff house.

Resolute Bay Airport is served from the south by Canadian Airlines International Limited from Montréal and Edmonton with the B737C. In March 1969, Nordair was the first company to operate a commercial passenger-carrying jet across the Arctic Circle. From 1974 to 1978, TransAir provided service from Winnipeg with the Boeing 737.

The airport has Crash Fire Fighting Reserve Services (CFR) staffed by fully trained volunteers. CFR equipment includes an all-terrain foam vehicle with 5,000 litres of water and 700 litres of foam, as well as a water tanker with 7,000-litre capacity. Volunteers are trained on site by the fire chief.

The airport had 10,800 passengers and 5,510 aircraft movements during 1988.

The first maintenance contract was administered on behalf of the Department of Transport by D.G. MacLachlan, regional superintendent of Northern Airports, Central Region, from April 1, 1964, until his retirement in January 1972. One of the buildings in the Resolute accommodations complex, the MacLachlan Inn, bore his name. During the early years, on-site airport management was provided for six-month periods by Stan Westhover, Bill McKay, Art Kennedy, Tom Kilpatrick, Ed Osborne, and Bill McLeod.

Upon the retirement of MacLachlan, E.R. Osborne assumed the position of regional superintendent of Northern Airports. This title was changed in 1974 to manager, High Arctic Airports. Osborne's contribution to Resolute was recognized by the Resolute Airport Arctic Circle Club when it named its new library/TV lounge Osborne Hall. Osborne retired in December 1975 and was succeeded in May 1976 by J. Valkovic. In August 1983, John Goodman, a former contract employee, was named airport manager. He was succeeded in July 1989 by John Colthart.

Sources:
1. P. Wield, Operations Manager, High Arctic Airports.
2. Transport Canada, Central Region.
3. Greenway, K.R., W/C, RCAF, "To the Top of the World by Airship" *CAHS Journal*, 18 (Fall 1980), No. 3, pp. 83-86 and 92.

Rimouski Airport
(Québec)

Rimouski Airport is important historically because it was established in 1927 by the Department of National Defence at the same time as St. Hubert Airport. It was thus the second civil airport built by the government, even though the policy at that time was that all civil airports should be owned and operated by municipalities.[1]

Rimouski was required to provide support for the Post Office's experimental air-mail service, in which mail was moved to and from transatlantic ocean liners. The service was designed to speed up mail delivery between Canada and England, and was the first step towards a transatlantic air service. The mail, transferred between ship and shore by the St. Lawrence River pilot boat from Father Point, was to have been flown from Rimouski to Montréal by seaplane, but because the water was too rough, landplanes were used. In due course, the air-mail route between Rimouski and Montréal was lighted to improve the regularity of the service. In January 1933, the St. Hubert-Rimouski airway was sarcastically described as St. Hubert-Montmagny-Rivière du Loup-Rimouski by way of the railway—referring to the pilots' reliance

157. First airmail service, Rimouski, Québec, May 5, 1928.

upon the rail line as a visual navigation aid.[2] Emergency fields were recommended every forty-eight kilometres with lighting at each.

The first mail sent from Rimouski to St. Hubert by landplane was carried in November 1927, and the service continued until 1938.

The airport, two and a half kilometres from Rimouski, was a grass field near the public wharf, and the land was leased from several farmers. The original airport was T-shaped, 1,800 by 2,200 feet [549 by 670 metres], and the landing strips were 550 and 800 feet [168 and 244 metres] wide. Regular operations for the 1928 shipping season began in April.

In 1929, the airport—known as Rimouski Wharf—had a permanent day licence and was owned by the Dominion government. A mail contractor operated the site, whose only facility was a hangar. Henri Richard was employed as the first aerodrome caretaker in 1928 and served in that capacity until 1957.

In September 1930, the controller of Civil Aviation was advised to purchase the land, "especially in view of the fact that further development work is required to bring this airport up to the standard of a government-owned airport."[3]

Airport licence no. 138 was issued to the Department of National Defence on October 17, 1930, for Rimouski Airport (day use only) for "Lots 91, 96, 102, 105, 110 and 120 in the Parish of Rimouski."[4]

From the outset, the department had trouble with the owners of the land, who held out for higher rents than the government considered reasonable. The property was eventually expropriated on May 26, 1931, at a cost of $30,045.

A plan of the airport, dated November 26, 1936, shows a hangar, a number of small buildings, and a gasoline pump, all located in the northwest corner.

In January 1938, Québec Airways complained that its passengers were being harassed by the

158. 1928 Hangar, Rimouski Airport c. 1942.

solicitations of taxi drivers and asked that a taxi zone be established and that cabs be prohibited from crossing the landing area.

On November 24, 1939, the controller of Civil Aviation advised the chief of Air Services that "the present site (Rimouski Airport) is, and has been for 12 years, of great use. It cannot be enlarged economically, however."[5]

By 1943, operations were constrained by the size of the airport. When on February 11, the District Inspector of Eastern Airways reported that CPAL would be operating two DC-2 aircraft under Post Office contract three times weekly into Goose Bay with mail, passengers, and cargo, and the airport was too small for DC-2s, development of Rimouski was considered to be uneconomical. The field could only be extended east and west—and would probably be abandoned after the war. Meanwhile, the RCAF had built a new airport at nearby Mont Joli for the British Commonwealth Air Training Plan (BCATP); and after some persuasion by the Department of Transport, the Department of National Defence reluctantly permitted CPAL to use Mont Joli—on a temporary basis.

About the same time, CPAL asked Transport for improvements to the hangar and for a 2,000 by 500 foot [609-by-152-metre] extension of the airport to the west because "demand for air services to important communities on the north shore of the St. Lawrence and to Goose Bay has increased tremendously due to war circumstances and operations out of Rimouski airport have expanded accordingly."[7] The airport was then unsuitable for Boeing 247D or DC-2 aircraft; but the RCAF was reluctant to allow CPAL to operate from the new airport at Mont Joli. The result of this request was that Transport gave CPAL permission to move a fence at Rimouski and rent the additional land from the owner.

As of July 11, 1944, the airport was known as Rimouski. It was located east of town on the south shore of St. Lawrence River, 274 metres from the riverbank. The west end of the airport was directly south of the government wharf. Runways were southwest by northeast, 2,350 feet [716 metres] and north-south 1,800 feet [549 metres] (south side rough and irregular), and there was no lighting.

In December 1945, the town asked the Department of Transport to expand the airport, but the department was unwilling to do so because of site limitations and the proximity of Mont Joli airport.

Transport entered into an agreement with CPAL on January 8, 1946, under which the latter would maintain the Rimouski Airport "as a licensed public airport; rates to be charged in accordance with the Information Circular 0/7/34 or Staff Circular 8/41 or others prescribed by the Lessor; all schedules of charges to be approved by the Minister."[8]

Effective October 1, 1946, the town of Rimouski leased the airport from the Department of Transport for five years (lease number 40188), which was renewed from year to year thereafter until 1974, when a new twenty-year lease was granted.

An airport licence was issued in the name of the town of Rimouski on March 17, 1947, listing runway 10-28 at 2,200 by 100 feet [671 by 31 metres].

In June 1947, with the consent of Transport, the town subleased the airport, including the administration building, workshop, and hangar, to Rimouski Airlines for one year and year-to-year thereafter, subject to Department of Transport lease number 40188 of 1946.

The town and Rimouski Airlines—the principal users of the airport—had plans to extend the airport at their own expense. But when, in April 1950, the town asked the department to give it the land forming the airport, and later offered to buy it, the Department was of a mind to close the airport altogether. It decided not to accept the advice of the Air Transport Board, which felt that Rimouski Airport was important to the operation of Rimouski Airlines, despite the proximity of Mont Joli Airport.

Although the Department of Transport had yet to make a decision about the ownership of the airport grounds and their possible transfer, the town expropriated land on the east side to expand the airport, arguing that if the airport had to be moved in the future, the town would more easily carry out the transaction. But Rimouski was reluctant to spend money on airport improvements unless it owned the land; and, for its part, Transport was not interested in improving the airport. The town wanted Transport to transfer title to the airport (which included a 1928 hangar and a 1926 administration building, both built by the government) for one dollar. In 1951, the Department refused to sell because of the bad precedent this might establish, opting instead to continue to lease the airport to the town. The Department also considered that the town's proposed new airport site outside the town was unsuitable.

On December 31, 1951, the town reported airport revenues of $27,337, expenses of $41,664, and a deficit of $14,327. Rimouski Airlines paid the town $450 a month on a lease basis and also paid the costs of maintaining the airport.

The town proposed a landing strip and runway layout in June 1952 that was approved by Transport, and provision was made for its construction in 1953-54. Estimates of $350,000 were made for a "new or improved single strip at Rimouski, provided the town acquires the land and agrees to continue to operate the airport."[9]

On July 27, 1953, a contract was let for a runway of 3,400 feet [1,036 metres] at a cost of $350,000, and the town agreed to expropriate the extra land. When its action was challenged, Rimouski suggested that Transport expropriate the land and be reimbursed by the town; but this was found to be legally impossible. Transport was asked once more to expropriate in its own right—a move opposed by Premier Duplessis (January 20, 1954) as he claimed that this was the right of Québec.[10] In December 1954, Rimouski officials presented a brief to the minister of Transport, outlining the importance of the airport to Rimouski and asking for a second runway, a terminal building, and hangars to meet the needs of Québecair[11] and the community.

The construction of a new paved runway, 07-25, 3,475 feet [1,059 metres] long, was completed in late summer 1955.

In 1955, the city acquired a war-surplus hangar at Gander and had it removed and rebuilt at Rimouski Airport. Work was completed on May 1, 1956.

On January 17, 1957, both the city and the Department of Transport expropriated more land to extend the runway.

In 1957, Transport made an economic study of Rimouski to decide on the best course of future action for the airport. Its report noted that:

Québecair had 2,054 DC-3 arrivals in 1955, and 2,891 in 1956. More passengers originated/terminated at Mont Joli than at Rimouski; Rimouski traffic was mainly with the North Shore, Québec city, Anticosti, Gaspé. Mont Joli had heavy cargo traffic connected with the construction of the DEW Line in the North. Land ownership at the airport was divided between Transport (majority), city and Québecair, with the two latter owning the buildings. Québecair owned the land for the proposed second runway.

Investment: Transport $380,000
             city $ 30,000

The report recommended that:
- it would be wasteful to maintain both Rimouski and Mont Joli, which are only 24 kilometres apart; Mont Joli was the better airport;
- that one airport should be designated for the Rimouski-Mont Joli Area;
- that Rimouski be a local airport and Mont Joli be the regional mainline airport.

On July 13, 1958, the passenger terminal, hangar, and five DC-3 aircraft, all owned by Québecair, were destroyed by fire. Québecair reconstructed the terminal and built a new hangar west of the old site during the winter of 1958-59.

In November 1958, Transport agreed that Québecair could build a winter extension to the runway towards the east, if Québecair covered the costs of and purchase and construction. The extension of 1,125 feet [343 metres] would give a total usable length of 4,600 feet [1,402 metres], which was needed for the operaton of the F-27 aircraft.

Québecair moved its F-27 maintenance facilities from Rimouski to Dorval in February 1961. DC-3 maintenance operations remained in Rimouski until January 1969, when the headquarters of Québecair was moved to Dorval because BAC-111 aircraft could not be operated from Rimouski.

Rimouski is still licensed in the name of the city, and Transport Canada continues to own sixty-one hectares of the site. The old lease was cancelled and superseded by a new one, number 10020, on March 13, 1974, for a term of twenty years, renewable a further term of twenty years.

Over the years, the following air carriers have operated at Rimouski Airport:

Canadian Airways Ltd.	1927 to 1938
Canadian Transcontinental Airways Ltd.	1927 to 1928
Québec Airways Ltd.	1938 to 1942
Canadian Pacific Airlines Ltd.	1942 to 1946
Rimouski Airlines Ltd.	1946 to 1953
Québecair Inc.	1953 to 1969

Until September 1989, the airport housed the Aero Club de Rimouski, when club operations were discontinued. The flight training school, l'ecole de Pilotage de Chicoutimi, is now run by Air Satellite de Baie Comeau, the airline which provides scheduled service at the airport. Helimax , a helicopter company based at the airport.

Source:
Transport Canada, Québec Region.

Footnotes—Rimouski Airport

[1] See Chapter 6 for the rationale.
[2] Public Archives of Canada, Department of National Defence, file 5151-Q208, vol. 2.
[3] Public Archives Canada, Department of National Defence, file 5151-Q208, vol. 1.
[4] Ibid.
[5] Public Archives Canada, Department of Transport, file 5168-537, vol. 1.
[7] Public Archives Canada, Department of Transport, file 5168-537, vol. 1, CPAL letter to the deputy minister of Transport, 26 February 1943.
[8] Public Archives Canada, Department of Transport, file 5151-Q208, vol. 5.
[9] Public Archives Canada, Department of Transport, file 5168-537, vol. 2, internal memorandum, 4 October 1952.
[10] Public Archives Canada, Department of Transport, file 5168-537, vol. 3.
[11] Québecair was the result of the merger of Rimouski Airlines Ltd. and the syndicat d'Aviation du Golfe Inc., bought out by Romeo Crevier of Rimouski, January 1, 1953.

Rouyn Airport
(Québec)

In March 1933, General Airways of Rouyn obtained a licence to establish a seaplane base for daytime use on Tremoy Lake (formerly Osisko Lake). In winter, the company operated from an ice landing strip. Dominion Skyways obtained a seaplane base licence in March 1938.

In 1948, CPAL began service into Rouyn using Lake Tremoy as a seaplane base. At that time there was no runway, and the airline used Canso amphibian aircraft.

In March 1948, the city of Rouyn asked the Department of Transport for assistance in locating a site for the construction of an airport. The present site was chosen in December 1948, and work began in August 1949 with an initial grant of $25,000 from the Department. The city agreed to operate and maintain the airport. A paved runway, 08-26 of 4,200 feet [1,280 metres], was completed in 1950. With further financial assistance from Transport, the runway was extended to 4,500 feet [1,372 metres] in 1953, to 5,600 feet [1,707 metres] in 1958, and to 6,500 feet [1,981 metres] in 1978.

A temporary airport licence was issued to CPAL in August 1950, to permit the operation of their Lodestar and DC-3 aircraft on their service to Rouyn. In April 1953, CPAL built a small terminal building—by then, it had two flights per day.

The Department of Transport began to pay the city an airport operating subsidy in April 1956 to help defray the costs of running the airport.

In November 1958, the Gardner Company, which operated an aviation school, erected a hangar; Noranda Mining, Timmins Aviation Ltd., and Lamothe Construction operated aircraft at the airport and the RCAF made occasional flights.

From 1958 to 1960, Québecair had a DC-3 service from Québec to Rouyn by way of Parent and Senneterre, and Austin Airways DC-3s flew from Kapuskasing and Timmins to Rouyn. These services were discontinued because of a lack of traffic. During the 1960s, Rouyn Airport was a base for aerial survey and photography offered by Austin Airways, Selco Exploration, Kenting Aviation, and Aero Photo du Québec.

Trans-Canada Air Lines began to serve Rouyn in November 1955 using DC-3 aircraft, when it took over the CPAL service and in 1958, it introduced Viscount Turboprop planes.

The city tried unsuccessfully to transfer the airport to Transport in 1965, because of financial difficulties, but on March 22, 1968, Transport took possession of the airport for one dollar and then leased it back for one dollar per year—to be operated by the city with a Transport subsidy.

A new terminal building was completed in July 1969, with Transport paying $74,000 of the cost. The airport was closed from June to November that year to permit resurfacing of the runway.

The city made another unsuccessful attempt to transfer administration of the airport to Transport in May 1970, and in July 1972 appointed Francis Lavigne as manager.

Air Canada introduced DC-9 aircraft to the Rouyn service in 1974; Québecair began its service on August 12, 1974, with F-27 aircraft, and connections to Québec five days per week. Prop-air, which also served the airport made its headquarters at Rouyn in 1981, when it acquired the assets of Air Brazeau, and set up a five-day per week courier service to Montréal. It was later to get the contract (in 1987) for cargo storage and handling for Hydro Québec's James Bay project;

and it began a regular flight service between Rouyn-Noranda and Gatineau.

Meanwhle, in 1974, the city built a 1,204-square-metre hangar for lease to Air Brazeau. And it was in the same year Flight Information Service was established: it took charge of night services at Val d'Or and Matagami airports in 1982; and in 1988 occupied a new four-storey building at the airport.

Between 1976 and 1980 many improvements were made—the runway was repaved; the terminal building expanded; the maintenance garage extended. And in 1982, an ILS (Instrument Landing System) system was put into operation.

In 1989, Air Alliance established regular Dash-8 flights between Rouyn-Noranda, Montréal and Québec, twice per day, six days per week and Inter-Canadian introduced its new F-100 and ATR42 for regular flights serving Rouyn-Noranda, Montréal, and Québec.

The number of passengers embarking and disembarking at Rouyn-Noranda exceeded 88,000 in 1987.

Sources:
1. Transport Canada, Québec Region.
2. J.L. Gauthier, Air Canada, Rouyn-Noranda Region.

St. Andrews Airport
(Manitoba)

St. Andrews Airport was developed for use as a satellite of Winnipeg International Airport to solve traffic problems arising from the large number of ab initio pilots being trained at the busy international airport. When it opened, there was an immediate reduction in congestion and in aerial incidents between the small, slow-flying aircraft and the heavier, faster, scheduled transports.

The airport is nineteen kilometres north of the city of Winnipeg on Highway 230. The airport's elevation is 231 metres above sea level, at latitude 50° 04'N and longitude 97° 04'W. It is owned and operated by Transport Canada.

The airport is located almost in the centre of the old Red River settlement: river lots established by the Métis and early Scottish settlers between 1854 and 1870. The lots were from 30 to 300 feet [9 to 91 metres] wide and extended five kilometres from the river. The airport, comprising 1,170 acres [474 hectares], extended from Lot 9 to Lot 52 in the rural municipality of St. Andrews.

The history of St. Andrews begins before Manitoba became a province. Several old hand-hewn stone houses are located along the river bank from Winnipeg to Selkirk, and the town contains the only intact stone-walled fort in western Canada—Lower Fort Garry. Eight kilometres from the airport is the village of Lockport. Here, locks were built on the rapids to make the Red River navigable from Lake Winnipeg to well within the U.S. border. Much of the early freight moved on the Red River, including a great deal of the sand, gravel and stone to construct the city of Winnipeg.

In 1962, construction on St. Andrews Airport began with two runways, 18-36 and 12-30,

159. St. Andrews Airport, 1974.

2,500 by 500 feet [762 by 152 metres]—graded and seeded to grass—and connecting taxiways. The airport opened in 1964. Because the sod runways had to be closed during every spring break-up and also after a heavy rain, construction began in 1968, to provide two hard-surfaced all-weather runway. An industrial area on the airport was also initiated, and the west side of the airport was reserved for building lots, 100 by 250 feet [30 by 76 metres]. In 1970, a third runway was constructed, 04-22, for student instruction and for crosswind operations.

To accommodate increasing traffic, a runway parallel to 18-36 at 3000 by 75 feet [914 by 23 metres] was built in 1978, with a connecting taxiway and three holding bays at the 18, 36 and 04 ends of the runways. In 1983, the infield taxiways were built; and in 1988 runways and taxiways were resurfaced.

The traffic also called for control towers: a temporary tower was built in May 1967; and work which began the following year provided a permanent tower in 1969. Visual contact with the new 18-36 runway required a new control tower, which was built in 1981. A Very High Frequency Direction Finder (VHF/DF) was installed in 1989.

The first tenants of St. Andrews Airport were the Winnipeg Flying Club and Fly for Fun, Inc., to be followed by Point West School of Aviation and St. Andrews Airways. Today, there are twenty operators based at St. Andrews Airport. Services now available include flying schools (fixed wing), a helicopter school, charter aircraft, aerial spraying, aircraft engine repair and maintenance, aircraft engine overhaul, commercial hangar space, aircraft maintenance and repair, aircraft rentals, restaurants, a helicopter simulator (the only private simulator in Canada), an ultra light aircraft manufacturing company, aircraft fuel cells repairs, and a travel agency.

With the establishment of helicopter operations, a helicopter pad was constructed in 1978.

St. Andrews is proud to boast that this is a first in western Canada. Helicopter night flying training is now possible.

Air traffic movements increased steadily from 9,176 in 1965 to 153,669 in 1973, reaching a high of 231,714 in 1977, and then declining to 92,490 in 1986. By 1988, movements had risen to 115,044.

The following served as airport managers:

Bob Beattie	1964 to 1971
Earl Pickell	1971 to 1977
F. Buck	1978 to 1979
Joe Hennessey	1979 to 1980
Gary Fries	1981 to 1985
Ralph Haines	1986 to present

Sources:
1. Transport Canada, Central Region.
2. Ralph Haines and Cathy Goodman, St. Andrews Airport.

St. Anthony Airport
(Newfoundland)

The St. Anthony Airport is located at the top of the Great Northern Peninsula of Newfoundland, approximately fifty-six kilometres from the town of St. Anthony. It is the only airport on the peninsula with regular air service.

St. Anthony has a population of approximately 3,000 (1976) with a catchment area of 18,000. The town is the site of the Grenfell Regional Health Services Hospital, which has 140 beds, and operates its own 'flying ambulance' to provide comprehensive medical and passenger transportation services for Labrador, northern Newfoundland, and remote areas of Québec.

St. Anthony's connections with aviation go back to the early 1920s and 1930s. In 1922, Major F.S. Cotton landed his ski-plane on the

harbour ice on his experimental air-mail service to northern Newfoundland. In 1931 and after, Douglas Fraser and Arthur Sullivan used St. Anthony (on skis and floats) in their early commercial air services.

The first airport, located twenty-six kilometres from town, was constructed during the period from 1963 to 1966 with financial assistance from the Department of Transport. It was to be maintained as a public facility by the town of St. Anthony.

The town was unable to keep the airport up to adequate standards and Transport assumed operation and maintenance responsibilities on November 1, 1971. The Department entered into a contract with Eastern Provincial Airways to operate the airport, but the company withdrew from the agreement after one year. A similar contract was granted to the Canadian Marconi Company, effective November 1972, but it, too, withdrew from the contract on December 31, 1973. Transport moved in its own personnel, on January 1, 1974.

The terminal building, a temporary structure, was constructed in 1975 and expanded in 1977 to accommodate an aeradio facility. Queenair, Twin Otter, Navaho Twin, and Turbo Beaver aircraft, were used—for the most part—by Labrador Airways (Class III service) and the Grenfell Mission, which had a hangar at the airport.

The runway provided only 91 per cent wind coverage under all-weather conditions, which had to allow for a fifteen knot crosswind. This fell below Transport Canada's required 98 per cent; and usability of the airport ranged around a low 81%. Re-orientation, or new construction would have been too difficult and costly to be feasible; and consequently a new airport at a site known as Hare Bay, was urged by local people.

Work at Hare Bay began in 1984; completed at a cost of $12.5 million, it was ready for occupancy on June 15, 1987. The site is located on

540 hectares of land underlaid by a table head formation of limestone. St. Anthony Airport has one 1,219 metre asphalt runway and provides VFR (Visual Flight Rules) service with sixteen-hour CFR (Crash Fire Rescue) coverage.

It has a two-storey terminal building, housing administration offices and also a flight service station; a combined services building, with maintenance workshops and CFR facilities; and a pumphouse.

The two principal passenger-carrying operators are Labrador Airways and Air Nova-Lab Airways, serving the Labrador Coast area with Twin Otter aircraft. Air Nova provides Dash-8 service with scheduled runs from Deer Lake, Blanc Sablon, and Goose Bay.

There were 9,700 passengers in 1987, and 6,000 itinerant aircraft movements.

Dan Ollerhead has been airport manager since January 1974.

Source:
Transport Canada, Atlantic Region.

St. Catharines Airport
(Ontario)

There has been an airport in the St. Catharines area since 1928 when the St. Catharines Flying Club operated in the first field just south of the Queen Elizabeth Highway in the vicinity of the Garden City Raceway. The fiftieth anniversary of the flying club was celebrated in 1978.

In 1935, the Department of National Defence (then responsible for civil aviation) judged the old field unsafe, and the club was forced to relocate. That same year, with the assistance of St. Catharines' Mayor Mac Lockhart, the club leased a portion of the Welstead property (161 acres [24.7 hectares]), the present airport site, with an option to purchase. In consideration of the financial assistance from St. Catharines, the club agreed to transfer all its rights to the city and to operate the facility as a public airport until the city wished to take it over, at which time the club would retain ownership of its buildings.

In late 1939, when it became evident after the declaration of war that the British Commonwealth Air Training Plan (BCATP) would be operated throughout Canada with the help of the flying clubs, the St. Catharines Flying Club applied to become an elementary flying training school (EFTS). Approval was given with the understanding that St. Catharines would turn over the airport to the Crown for one dollar. The city exercised its option, purchased the property from Welstead for $8,000, and turned it over to the Crown.

No. 9 EFTS opened on October 10, 1940.[1] The airport was then a sod field which, under heavy rain and snow that autumn and winter, became inoperable. In the spring and summer of 1941, the Department of National Defence put in hard-surfaced runways, at a cost of approximately $225,000. Further drainage had to be installed, and the investment of the Crown reached half a million dollars.

After the war, when the flying club resumed operations the city leased the airport from the Department of Transport for one dollar a year, and the flying club was given free hangarage under a special Order in Council by which flying clubs were recognized for their work with the BCATP.

The airport was funded by the city of St. Catharines, which spent $65,000 on it between 1935 and 1940. There were two tenants on the field: Genaire, which managed the airport for the city from 1951 to 1957, and the flying club, which managed it for the Airport Commission from 1958 until a full-time manager was hired in 1966.

In 1955, the Junior Chamber of Commerce, after doing a nine-month study on the facilities, functions, and value of the airport to the community, recommended to the city that the airport be improved. Their report emphasized the need for an improved water system and runway lighting.

The city presented these findings to the deputy minister of Transport. Pressure was put on the department by H.P. Cavers, MP for Lincoln, by John Smith, mayor of St. Catharines, and by Murton Seymour. The government then agreed to put in medium intensity night lighting, which was operational by 1959. A year later, an NDB (Non-directional Beacon) was installed so that the airport could be used for IFR operations as well as VFR (Visual Flight Rules) operations.

Until this time, St. Catharines had had a three-man Airport Management Board. Then, a brief presented to the Board by the Junior Chamber of Commerce recommended closer managerial supervision of the airport property; and the Chamber would cooperate in establishing a committee to look into this matter. The Airport Management Board appointed Harry Edmonstone and Donald Forgie to its membership and elected the latter as chairman in 1957.

At the request of the Junior Chamber of Commerce Airport Committee Frank Clayton, Von Kaufman, Jack Leach, and Dick Robertson looked into airport management functions, and opportunities to increase revenues. They recommended that a commission be formed, and that the surrounding municipalities be asked to support the airport.

The Niagara District Airport Commission was formed in 1958. It consisted of council and business members and was supported by St. Catharines, Niagara Falls, Niagara-on-the-Lake, Niagara township, Louth, Merriton, Stamford, Port Dalhousie, Grantham, and Thorold town and township. With the incorporation of regional government and with amalgamation, there are now four supporting municipalities: St. Catharines, Niagara Falls, Niagara-on-the-Lake, and Thorold.

The flying club managed the airport until April 1966 when a full-time manager was hired. At that time, a large expansion was taking place: a 5,000 foot [1,524-metre] runway, a terminal, new runway lighting, a new water system and a sewage lagoon were constructed. The total cost of the expansion was around $600,000, of which $130,000 was paid for by the commission and $490,000 by the Department of Transport. Supporting municipalities paid an extra 15 cents per capita towards the expansion loan, which was paid off in 1974.

Further expansion took place in 1970, when the control tower was erected (fully funded by the federal government) and in 1971, a weather office in the terminal. (Rental for the weather office paid off the loan for construction). In 1974, Hayes-Dana erected a hangar to house its aircraft (now a Lear jet). In 1975, the commission put up the first phase of the equipment garage, which was completed in 1976, and which has a total of eight bays to house all maintenance equipment. In 1976, the flying club sold the old recreation hall to Niagara Nautic to be used for boat construction.

St. Catharines Airport is primarily a general aviation facility with training, recreational, charter, and privately owned aircraft.

Several airlines have attempted operations in the past twenty years. The first was Southern Provincial, which operated from St. Catharines to Toronto Island, Welland, and Brantford in 1957. Its main problem was that the airports did not have lighting facilities, and this curtailed operations during the winter months. In 1967, in conjunction with Expo, Nordair ran charter flights for people wishing to visit the Falls—the service was used more by people from the Niagara area visiting Expo. The airline, however, had only planned for a short term, and did not continue flights after Expo was over. From August 1968 to November 1969, Royalair flew to Toronto International, Ottawa, Peterborough, and Montréal from St. Catharines. Although its service began to build up, the airline had problems with equipment and personnel changes, and eventually went bankrupt. Air Niagara operated from the St. Catharines Airport to Toronto International from July 1970 to January 1971, but did not earn the revenue it had expected. It also experienced equipment problems. In 1975, Bradley Air Services applied for a licence to operate from the airport to Toronto Island, Fort Erie, and Toronto International. The company received approval from the Canadian Transport Commission in 1976.

The following operations are based at St. Catharines Airport: the St. Catharines Flying Club, Niagara Nautic, Genaire Limited, Hayes-Dana, Niagara Helicopters, and Air Niagara.

Customs has an office in the terminal and is on-call from the Queenston-Lewiston Bridge twenty-four hours a day, seven days a week, as the airport is a commercial port of entry.

The airport has three paved runways: 10-28, 610 metres; 01-19, 911 metres; and 06-24, 1,524 metres. There were 46,000 aircraft movements in 1987.

The following have served as managers:

R. Strodbrau	1933 to 1934
F. Gillies	1934 to 1937
R. Wingfield	1937 to 1939
Pat Pattison[2]	1939 to 1945
George Dunbar	1946 to 1949
Moe Louch	1949 to 1950
Bob Calendar	1951 to 1963
Earl Gilks	1963 to 1965
Blanch Quinn	1965 to 1966
Ted Taylor	1966 to 1986
Greg Bailey	1986 to present

Sources:
1. Transport Canada, Ontario Region (with notes from P. Pattison, former Airport Manager).

Footnotes—St Catherines Airport
1 The school was operated by St. Catharines Flying Training School Ltd., a subsidiary of the St. Catharine's Flying Club.
2 Pattison had been manager of the first airport from 1931 to 1935. He was manager of the flying school from 1933 to 1941. "Announcement," *CAHS Newsletter*, No. 28. (December, 1980) p.4.

St. Hubert Airport
(Québec)

St. Hubert was the first civil aerodrome to be built by the Canadian government and was a departure from policy which, for years, had stated that municipalities were responsible for providing aerodromes serving their communities.

The were two reasons for the establishment of St. Hubert. The first—and more important— reason was to serve the airship service from England. Prime Minister MacKenzie King, at the Imperial Conference in London in 1926, promised Canada's involvement in Empire Air Communications by airship, through the provision of an airship base in Eastern Canada. The second reason was to provide a base for the airmail service between Montréal and Rimouski, which connected with ocean liners sailing between

160. Curtiss JN-4, St. Hubert, Québec, 1928.

161. Fairchild FC-2W2, first Canada-U.S. mail serrvice, St. Hubert, Québec, 1928.

Canada and England. The mail was put on board or picked up by the river pilot boats in the St. Lawrence, off Father Point, Québec. Landplanes were used on the Rimouski-Montréal service because of rough water in the St. Lawrence; but as there was no licensed aerodrome in Montréal, part of St. Hubert property was to be used for this purpose.

Because it did not want to create any dangerous precedent, the Department of National Defence approached the city of Montréal before taking any action. In a letter of January 13, 1927 (see Appendix 8), the city of Montréal was asked to consider whether it could provide its own aerodrome. The department wrote to the city again on April 21, 1927 to tell the mayor of the need for an airship base, and asking about the possibility of combining an "airship site with a municipal aerodrome, as the characteristics required for both services do not differ materially." Montréal declined, and the Department of National Defence proceeded on its own, bought the land, and paid the full cost of construction (see Appendix 7). Subsequently, when the mayor of Québec city tried to use St. Hubert as a precedent for an airport in his city, the Department wrote: "the Montréal field had been purchased solely to help the development of long-distance travel by airship and, if it had not been for the airship

scheme, the St. Hubert property would not have been purchased."[1] But in 1931, the department seemed to be a little uncomfortable about its departure from policy. In a memorandum dated September 18, 1931, J.A. Wilson, controller of Civil Aviation, wrote to the deputy minister:

St. Hubert has been developed as a national airport, like Croydon, near London, Le Bourget, near Paris, and Tempelhof in Berlin. Whether, in view of the benefit the City of Montréal has derived from its establishment, relieving the City authorities of the necessity of furnishing their own airport, an endeavour should be made to obtain from them a yearly grant towards its maintenance, should be considered. The City undoubtedly gains by the location of such a fine establishment at its doors. It should be clearly understood, however, that St. Hubert has a national interest as well as a local one as the airport of Montréal. It was built by the Dominion Government following a decision on National policy, into which purely local consideration did not enter.[2]

Two Air Ministry officials from London visited Canada in May and June 1927. (One of the officials was Major G.H. Scott, who had commanded the British Airship R-34 on its return flight from England to New York in 1919). With

162. New Club House (1929) Montréal Light Aeroplane Club, St. Hubert, Québec.

163. St. Hubert, Québec, c. 1929-30.

Canadian officials, they inspected possible areas for an airship base, from Sydney, Nova Scotia, to as far inland as Toronto, and selected a site near St. Hubert as the most suitable. Their recommendation was accepted, and the project was approved by Order in Council No. 1233, dated June 24, 1927. The Department of Public Works bought a triangular-shaped site of 729 acres [295 hectares] at $200 an acre, near to the CNR station, seven miles east of Montréal on the Chambly Highway. Public Works also undertook the engineering work. The target date for completion of the airstrip, mooring tower, hydrogen production plant and ancillary buildings was the fall of 1928, when the first airship flight was expected. The tower and airship facility were to be located in one corner of the triangle.

Part of the site, not near the mooring tower, was planned as a public airharbour. A temporary aerodrome was ready for use at the end of November 1927, and the first airplane—preceding completion of the site—landed on November 1. On November 11 a Fairchild monoplane operated by the Department of Defence Air Service for the Post Office landed with the first landplane air-mail from Rimouski. A temporary wooden hangar was available for use that winter.

Good progress was made during 1928 and the mooring tower, 210 feet [64 metres] high, was

194

erected. The tower head was built in England (under Air Ministry supervision), together with two others: one for South Africa, one for Egypt. The first flight by Airship R-100 was now expected in May 1929.

The Report on Civil Aviation for 1928 contains the following statement:

St. Hubert is also being developed to form a great public air terminal aerodrome which may be used on equitable terms by all desiring to do so. In November 1927, the demand for aerodrome facilities became urgent and a temporary aerodrome was cleared and graded, adjacent to the airship tower, for use while the permanent aerodrome was under construction...

It also reports that a permanent hangar, 80 by 120 feet [24 by 36 metres] was completed, a flood light, obstruction lighting, and a flashing beacon were installed, and a radio station and weather service were provided. The report goes on: "the airport, when complete, will rank as one of the most efficiently equipped airports in the world." While senior officials of the Deparment of Defence may have worried about the policy implications of St. Hubert, the technical staff were enthusiastic about their first civil airport and used it for the development and testing of airport equipment and procedures.[3]

164. Canadian Airways Ltd., sign and personnel, St. Hubert, Québec, 1929-1930.

165. St. Hubert, Québec, c. 1930.

Many firsts in the development of civil airports in Canada were recorded at St. Hubert: the first landing fees and airport user fees were introduced in 1927 (for details, refer to Appendix 19); and the passenger toll of ten cents a passenger carried for hire is particularly interesting—many people assume that such a fee was an innovation of the 1970s.

Two runways—the first hard-surfaced runway in Canada—1,800 and 2,000 feet [549 and 609 metres] long and 150 feet [46 metres] wide were built at St. Hubert in 1929. In the same year, the administration building was completed to house aerodrome staff and the offices for wireless, meteorology, the post office and Customs. It also had a passenger waiting room: it was the first air terminal building.

As well as being the terminal for Rimouski-Montréal airmail, St. Hubert was the airport for Canadian Colonial Airways international airmail service between Montréal and Albany, New York, which began October 1, 1928. Passengers were also carried on that route when the mail load permitted. The airport, therefore, was the terminal for the first international passenger freight and mail route between the United States and Canada. From October 1 to December 31, 1928, 985 Canadian and foreign aircraft arrived and departed, and there were 1,387 passengers.

Domestic airmail service was extended to Ottawa and Toronto in 1928.

St. Hubert was licensed as a public Customs airport on March 30, 1929 (it had opened on May 1, 1928):

It soon became the centre of civil aviation in eastern Canada[4] and has continued to be the sole airmail and customs aerodrome for Montréal. The Department was thus encouraged to continue the development of the aerodrome at the same time as the airship base...St. Hubert is the only all-weather field in the Montréal district and the only one lighted for night...Montréal holds a key position in North America. It was because of this that St. Hubert has been developed on the scale that it has...[5]

Other historic firsts for St. Hubert included:
(a) a radio range: "an experimental radio range or beacon" was erected in 1928 by the Royal Canadian Corps of Signals. A new low frequency five-tower range was installed in 1936;[6]
(b) airport traffic control: control service and a control tower began in February 1939 with C.C. Bogart in charge;[7]
(c) snow removal: in 1938, snow blowers were purchased and first used at St. Hubert, Ottawa, Malton, North Bay and Moncton. Snow-rolling and compaction were no longer suitable for the

166. Aerial view of St. Hubert Airport with airship R-100 at mooring mast, August 1930.

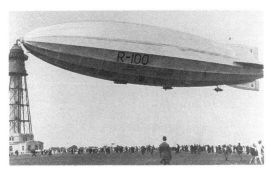

167. Airship R-100 at mooring mast, St. Hubert Airport, Québec, August 1930.

higher speed aircraft at eastern airports, even though they remained satisfactory in western and central Canada, where snow conditions were quite different.[8]

The year 1930 was memorable in the history of St. Hubert Airport.[9] It was the year in which the long-awaited airship service, for which the airport had been built, made its first flight.

The airship base was under the command of Lt. Cdr. A.B. Pressey, Royal Canadian Navy, who had been lent to the Civil Aviation Branch of the Department of National Defence for airship duties. He, with four naval ratings, had been sent to the Royal Airship Works at Cardington, England, to gain experience in airship operations. The mooring tower crew was completed by ten local men who helped in laying out the cables, making connections and working the mooring winches. The Royal Canadian Corps of Signals untook the responsibility for the Canadian end of the system of radio communication between the airship and the bases at Cardington and St. Hubert; and special meteorological office and observatory were established at St. Hubert.

Because of the great public interest in the arrival of the first airship, planning for the event required close cooperation between the city of Montréal, the Province of Québec and the respective police forces. All roads were put in

first class condition and completion of the approaches to the new harbour bridge was hastened so as to give alternative crossing of the St. Lawrence. The CNR, whose main line adjoins the airport, built special sidings to accommodate passenger traffic to and from the airport and ran supplementary trains for the thousands of visitors. The Airport Manager made special arrangements to service the large number of visiting airplanes and for the control of many pleasure flights during the stay of the R-100.

The big day was August 1, 1930. Airship R-100 arrived over St. Hubert after midnight July 31 and circled until dawn, dropping its mooring cable at 0430 hours on August 1. "Mooring was successfully completed without untoward incident in the record time of 23 minutes. Considering that this was the first mooring made to the tower at St. Hubert and that, of the mooring crew of 14, ten had never seen an airship before, this was a noteworthy achievement."[10] The total time for westbound flight was 78 hours, 52 minutes.

On August 9 and 10, the R-100 made a courtesy non-stop flight over Ottawa, Toronto, Niagara Falls, and back to Montréal, where it moored at sunset. It left for Cardington at 0930 hours on August 13, with a crew of 42, and 13 passengers, including Group Capt. E.W. Stedman, Chief Aeronautical Engineer, Department of National

168. Stuart Graham reviewing weather reports at St. Hubert, c. 1930-31.

169. Lockheed 12-A at St. Hubert, Québec, May 1937.

Defence. The return flight was uneventful and R-100 moored at Cardington at 1100 hours, August 16, after an elapsed time of 57.5 hours.

The round trip of R-100 was a great success. The practicability of a summer service by airship between Montréal and Britain had been tested and the results were fully up to expectation. The operation at St. Hubert had gone well and the Report on Civil Aviation in 1930 offered the opinion "that the installation mooring tower and equipment was the most up-to-date in the world."

The arrangements for handling the public also worked well. During the ten-day visit of R-100, over one million people went to St. Hubert to see the airship; 8,000 visitors had been shown the airship's interior while it was moored at the mast; and over 3,000 landings were made on the airport by visiting aircraft.

Unfortunately, the sister ship R-101 was less successful. It crashed in France on October 5, 1930, on a flight to India. 46 passengers and crew (many of whom had visited Canada in the R100) were killed, including the British Minister of Air. There were only seven survivors.

The tragedy brought an end to the project Empire Airship Service. Although the airship facilities at St. Hubert were maintained for a number of years in the hope that the use of the airship would be revived. this did not come

196

about; and Britain now looked to the airplane to provide empire air communications. The mooring tower, which had been completed on March 31, 1930 at a total cost of $376,082.35—all paid by Canada—was dismantled in 1938.[11]

It may be of interest to note the amount of revenue collected at St. Hubert from its opening on May 1, 1928, to 1931.[12]

1928	$ 3,368
1929	$ 9,999
1930	$23,750
1931	$13,060

In 1930, operation and maintenance costs (including the airship tower) were $65,000.

Airport statistics for the first four years of operation are as follows:[13]

	1928	1929	1930	1931
Canadian Aircraft Landings	122	287	572	325
Foreign Aircraft Landings	69	698	1183	745
Passengers (In and Out)	166	1387	1716	1026

Over the next years, St. Hubert continued to expand and develop: new runways and hangars were built; in 1938, Trans-Canada Air Lines (TCA) began service from the airport using Lockheed Electras, carrying ten passengers, and

170. St. Hubert Airport, Québec. New control tower (middle), built in 1985.

continued to operate from St. Hubert until 1941, when it moved to the new Montréal airport at Dorval.

In January 1939, airport charges were revised to provide for "a service charge for the use of the airport at the following rate:
$100 per month for the first schedule.
$ 50 per month for the next on each succeeding schedule.

Second or succeeding sections of an established schedule will be charged a landing fee at the established rate as a service charge for using the airport."

Canadian Associated Aircraft Ltd. built a plant at St. Hubert in 1939 for the assembly of Handley Page Hampden bombers for the RCAF, and the first Hampden was flight-tested in August 1940. In 1941, the plant was taken over by Canadian Vickers Ltd. for the assembly of Canso (PBY 5-A) aircraft, the first of which was flight-tested in December 1942. The company moved production to Cartierville in 1943, and the plant was taken over by Fairchild Aircraft and used as a flight test facility.[14]

In June 1940 the Departments of Transport and of National Defence jointly considered the establishment of an air observer school at St. Hubert (under the British Commonwealth Air Training Plan [BCATP]), and a service flying training school (SFTS). The discussions were broadened to include the possibilities of an airport at Dorval; and a Order in Council of December 24, 1940 authorized

the said airport to be developed also as a Civil Air Terminal for the metropolitan area of Montréal in place of St. Hubert...which would then be placed at the disposal of the Department of National Defence for use as a main aerodrome for a Service Flying Training School...the cost of the work at Dorval to be borne jointly by the Departments of Transport and National Defence, in accor-

171. St. Hubert Airport, Québec. New control tower built in 1985.

dance with the interest of each Department, taking into consideration the transfer of the St. Hubert airport to the Department of National Defence.[15]

In September 1940, the Canadian Pacific Air Service began to operate the Trans-Atlantic Ferry Service for the British government at St. Hubert.[16] Aircraft were gathered there from factories in the United States, serviced, and then ferried across the Atlantic by way of Gander. The organization took over an RCAF hangar and contributed a great deal of air traffic to the already busy airport—which also accommodated terry crew training. The RAF Ferry Command, as the organization was then called, moved its operations to Dorval on September 1, 1941, where it took over the buildings originally intended for the air observer and wireless schools.

When Dorval opened on September 1, 1941, St Hubert's civil licence (no.99) was cancelled at midnight, August 31. It was taken over by the Department of National Defence, RCAF, and its long history as a civil airport came to an end until it was opened again in 1968.

When St. Hubert was closed to civil traffic, Trans-Canada Air Lines, Canadian Colonial Airlines (at St. Hubert since 1928), Northeast Airlines and Québec Airways moved to Dorval.

The RAF Ferry Command moved at the same time.

The first Airport Manager at St. Hubert was Mr. F.I. Banghart, who had been an airmail pilot with London Air Transport Ltd. in 1927. In 1932, he was the 'working superintendent' and watchman of the airport when, due to the economic crisis of the time, staff and expenses were cut to the minimum. He was Airport Manager in 1935, transferred temporarily to Malton in August 1940, to take over that airport from the city of Toronto for the Department of Transport, and later became Airport Manager at Dorval (1942-45), Winnipeg (1947-50) and London (1950-57).

After the war St. Hubert became one of the RCAF's main fighter stations, and was the Canadian headquarters of NORAD (North American Air Defence Command). But in the late 1950s and during the 1960s, there were fewer activities at St. Hubert; and in the latter part of 1968, RCAF Squadron 414 moved from St. Hubert to Ottawa Airport. (Transport paid $443,000 towards the cost of the relocation).

Meanwhile in 1965, United Aircraft (Pratt & Whitney) moved its flight operations from St. Jean Airport to St. Hubert, where the company constructed its number 4 factory on land formerly owned by Transport Canada. It has direct access to the airport and has three buildings: a plant, a hangar, and an administration building. United Aircraft is the most important user of the airport, and has scheduled runs between its plants in Toronto and West Virginia to St. Hubert. Also, there are flights by a Boeing 720B (converted from a 707) which is used as a test plane during certification tests of turbo prop engines.

On October 1, 1968, the Department of Transport took control of St. Hubert, when it again became a civil airport, and a satellite for Montréal. All general aviation (flying schools, aircraft servicing companies, etc.) moved to St. Hubert from Cartierville Airport (which was then closed to traffic other than that of Canadair Ltd), and occupied hangar 12. A year later, Transport moved into its new administration and maintenance building, and hangar 12 was sold to private industry.

In 1970, runway 06R-24L was built, and today, the airport has four runways: 06L-24R at 2,390 metres, 06R-24L at 1,219 metres, 18-36 at 1,143 metres, and 10-28 at 945 metres.

Between 1977 and 1982, St. Hubert had the greatest number of aircraft movements in Canada, averaging 280,000 takeoffs and landings annually, of which 182,000 were local flights. It is a Customs port of entry, with an annual average of about 1,000 aircraft and 3,500 passengers, eighty per cent of whom are tourists.

St. Hubert, you will recall, had its first control tower—Canada's first—in 1939. This was replaced by the RCAF in 1954; and in June 1985, a new $2.4 million tower was opened. A plaque at the airport marks the fiftieth anniversary, celebrated in 1989.

In 1973, with the established of the CGEPS the Edouard-Montpetit Aerotechnical School was established at St. Hubert.

On September 10 and 11, 1988, St. Hubert was host to Expo Air, one of the most reputable air pageants in Canada, which attracted no less than 60,000 people. The pageant, which was formerly held at Mirabel International Airport, being quite successful, was held again in 1989 at St. Hubert.

Another first in the history of St. Hubert was on November 16, 1989, when Intair began offering regular flights: daily connections are provided to Toronto, Ottawa, and Québec with ATR-42 aircraft— the first regular passenger service at St. Hubert since airline operations were moved to Dorval in September 1941. Intair has built its own terminal on land leased from the airport.

The new Canadian Space Agency is to be located at St. Hubert Airport, on 86 hectares of airport land reserved by Public Work Canada.

Sources:
1. Transport Canada, Québec Region.
2. Michel Lafrance, Airport Manager.

Footnotes—St Hubert Airport

[1] Memorandum from the controller of Civil Aviation to the deputy minister of National Defence regarding the aerodrome in Québec City, 15 May 1928. Public Archives Canada, MG 30 E243 vol. 9.

[2] Public Archives Canada, MG 30 E243, vol. 7.

[3] In fact, St. Hubert's role was expanded in a submission to the Governor-in-Council on October 4, 1927, "before construction of the mooring mast is begun and in order that the site may be used as an airbase for the investigation of the airways in eastern Canada, certain preliminary work...is proposed to be done this fall, clearning, levelling, etc., and construction of a hangar." Public Archives Canada, RG24 vol. 35, 36. file 921-28-109.

[4] The Montréal Light Aeroplane Club was based there; in 1927, the club was given permission to build its own hangar on land leased from the department.

[5] Public Archives Canada MG 30 E243, vol. 7, extract from a memorandum from J.A. Wilson, controller of Civil Aviation, to the deputy minister, arguing in favour of continued operation at St. Hubert at its current level, despite the financial depression of the day, 18 September 1931.

[6] J.R.K Main, *Voyageurs of the Air* (Ottawa: Queen's Printer, 1967), pp. 323, 325.

[7] William Ellwood, "Air Traffic Control—Then and Now," *CAHS Journal*, vol. 15, no. 3, (Fall 1977), pp. 72-76.

[8] Canada, Department of Transport, Annual Report, (Ottawa: King's Printer, 1939-40), p. 23.

[9] Canada, Department of National Defence, Report on Civil Aviation, (Ottawa: King's Printer, 1930), p. 67 and following.

[10] Canada, Department of National Defence, Report on Civil Aviation (Ottawa: King's Printer, 1930), p. 69.

[11] Public Archives Canada, MG 30 E243, vol. 9.

[12] Canada, Department of National Defence, Report on Civil Aviation (Ottawa: King's Printer, 1931), p.73.

[13] Canada, Department of National Defence, Reports on Civil Aviation (Ottawa: King's Printer, 1928 to 1931).

[14] K.M. Molson and H.A. Taylor, *Canadian Aircraft Since 1909* (Willowdale: Canadian Aviation Historical Society, 1983), p. 24.

[15] Canada, Department of Transport, file 5151-817, vol. 1.

[16] In May 1941, the ferry operation was taken over by the Atlantic Ferry Organization (ATFERO) for the Ministry of Aircraft Production, and finally by the Royal Air Force Ferry Command in July 1941.

Saint John Airport
(New Brunswick)

The present airport is the second one to serve Saint John. The first airport was at Millidgeville on a site near the present firefighter academy. The representative of the Department of National Defence (responsible for civil aviation until 1936) chose this location in April 1928 following an exhaustive survey of the district, made at the request of the city. Atlantic Airways Ltd. operated the airport, which had two runways, one 1,800 feet [549 metres] long and the other 2,200 feet [610 metres]. The site consisted of 102 acres [forty-one hectares].[1]

In 1931, Pan American Airways (PAA), see Appendix 26, which held a U.S. Post Office contract, began to operate a daily summer service from Boston and Portland to Saint John and Halifax with the option of extending the service to Sydney and St. John's, Newfoundland.

However, PAA's permit to operate in Canada did not allow them to carry mail or passengers between Canadian points, a regulation that did not please residents of Halifax and Saint John.

In November 1931, the superintendent of airways of the Department of National Defence reported that he found the Saint John Airport much improved, and the runways had been lengthened. He also discovered, however, that there was not much activity since PAA had discontinued daily service. The Saint John Flying Club (established 1929) and two small companies based their aircraft at the airport.

In the early 1930s, Millidgeville acquired something of a reputation as an international airport when it was used by aviators attempting to fly the Atlantic. Several flights landed there en route from New York to Harbour Grace, Newfoundland, which was their departure point for Europe.

In 1931, Ruth Nichols, the well-known American aviatrix, hoped to be the first woman to fly the Atlantic solo. She arrived at Millidgeville en route to Harbour Grace on June 22 in her gold and white Lockheed Vega, but crashed during her attempt to land the fast monoplane on the short runway. She was injured and was flown back to New York by Clarence Chamberlain, who had flown the Atlantic in the Columbia in June 1927.

On the same day, Hoiriis and Hillig left Millidgeville for Harbour Grace in their Bellanca Liberty. They crossed successfully and landed in Germany on June 25.

Amelia Earhart, with Bernt Balchen, arrived at Millidgeville from New York on May 19 in her crimson Lockheed Vega. She had already flown the Atlantic as co-pilot with Wilmer Stultz in a tri-motor Fokker seaplane, Friendship, from Trepassey Bay, Newfoundland, on June 18, 1928. She was the first woman to fly the Atlantic, and she now wanted to be the first woman to make the trip solo. She succeeded when she flew alone from Harbour Grace to Londonderry, Ireland, on May 21, 1932.

On August 19, James Mollison, in his Puss Moth, Hearts Content, landed in a field at Pennfield Ridge, eighty kilometres from Millidgeville, completing the first solo flight across the Atlantic from east to west.

George Hutchinson and his 'flying family' landed at Millidgeville in his Sikorsky Amphibian, *City of Richmond*, on August 23. He carried his wife, two children and a crew of four and hoped to fly to Scotland by way of Labrador, Greenland, and Iceland. The plane was wrecked in Greenland, but no one was injured.

After these rather newsworthy events, the airport settled down to a more normal existence.

The controller of Civil Aviation, Department of Transport, in a report of March 28, 1938, wrote that:

Millidgeville was chosen as being the best available within a reasonable distance of the City. Development has, therefore, been somewhat costly and the the airport limited in size. Up to 1932 the City spent a total of $183,175 on the site and the adjacent seaplane base at Millidgeville. Recognizing that the City had backed the project whole heartedly when times were good and that certain further improvements were required, to make the site safe, and in view of the acute unemployment situation in the City, the Department of National Defence established a project on the airport for the relief of single, homeless men and further expenditures were made. The project was closed down in the fall of 1935...the City would be entitled, on the basis of their original expenditure, to a grant of approximately $61,000.00. If they desire to proceed with further improvements, it is recommended that these...involve the removal of certain outcrop of rock, the diversion of Millidge Avenue, the extension of the east-west runway across the existing road into clear country beyond...Though the site will never be one which will permit of its use by very large aircraft in all conditions of visibility, the airport has already proved itself a safe airport for smaller types of aircraft and with the work recommended can be greatly improved to permit its safe use by medium class aircraft under fair conditions of visibility.[2]

One runway at Millidgeville was paved in 1938.

During World War II, an RCAF airport was constructed at Pennfield Ridge, eighty kilometres southwest of Saint John, and operated under the British Commonwealth Air Training Plan (BCATP) as the base for No. 2 Air Navigation School and No. 34 Operational Training Unit. At the end of the war, the airport was taken over and run by the Department of Transport for a number of years. For a time, Saint John was served from both sites, with Maritime Central Airways operating from Millidgeville and Trans-Canada Air Lines from Pennfield.

During the war, there was a dramatic increase in the size and the number of aircraft and an ever-increasing volume of air traffic and cargo. By the early 1940s, the city fathers realized that the airport at Millidgeville was quickly becoming inadequate for Saint John, and sought assistance from the Department of Transport to build another larger airport. Accordingly, on May 15, 1943, a search was commissioned, and by December of the same year, an engineering survey was made of the present site. The Department of Transport gave its approval in 1944 and advised the municipality to purchase the site at a recommended price of $200,000. It lies, sixteen kilometres east of Saint John, and comprises 1,776 acres [719 hectares]. The transaction was

172. Saint John Airport (Millidgeville), c. 1930.

completed on February 26, 1946, and title was vested in the city.

The Department agreed to construct the airport, which was to be operated and maintained by the city. The agreement was signed by the department and by the city on March 20, 1950, but the actual construction began in March 1949. A year later, runway 05-23, 1,676 by 200 metres, was completed, and 14-32, 1,554 metres in length, soon after. On September 2, 1949, the first aircraft landed on the rough gravel surface during construction of runway 05-23. It was a Cessna plane, piloted by James Wade and carrying Senator Riley and a party of VIPs. In February 1950, the first night landing was accomplished by an RCAF Dakota. The terminal building was started in 1951.

The Millidgeville airport licence was cancelled in 1951, and the site was used for a housing development.

Beginning on January 1, 1952, the Department of Transport paid the city an operating subsidy.

The first scheduled airline flight to the new Saint John Airport was a Maritime Central Airways' DC-3, flown by Captain Jones of Apohaqui, New Brunswick, which landed there on August 11, 1951. In order to make the transfer of service from the Millidgeville site to the new airfield easier, MCA used an automobile as a

mobile ticket office until the air terminal building was ready. Six weeks after the first scheduled flight, the radio range was completed and commissioned for service.

Although it was operating throughout the latter half of 1951, the airport was not officially opened until January 8, 1952, the same day as the opening of the air terminal building. At that time, J.K. Kennedy was chairman of the Airport Commission and William Arrowsmith was the first airport manager. The facility came to be known as Turnbull Airfield, after W.R. Turnbull of Rothesay, New Brunswick, a pioneer aeronautical researcher and inventor.[3]

Turnbull Airfield hosted its first air show on Dominion Day, July 1, 1953, with participants from across Canada and from many foreign countries. It was an outstanding success. Air travel through Saint John continued to grow at a rapid pace and, by 1954, plans were underway for an extension to the air terminal building to accommodate Customs service. The need for a control tower was pressing. Plans for its construction were approved in 1955 and the building was completed in July 1956. Before it was finished, the Airport Commission advised the Department of Transport, in November 1955, that it would be charged an annual assessment of nine dollars per square foot of tower space. After considerable negotiation, the Department purchased the land and building in March 1957 for the sum of $102,000. The following year, in October 1958, the ILS (Instrument L:anding System) was commissioned.

At the same time as the public side of the airport was developing, private enterprise was also becoming interested in the new site. In 1953, the Irving Organization constructed a 120 square foot [11-square-metre] hangar, 30 feet [9 metres] high; sliding doors took up 70 per cent of the east wall. Two years later, the Saint John Flying Club erected a combined hangar and social building near the southwest corner of the Irving Transportation Ltd. hangar. This building was destroyed by fire on July 6, 1975.

On May 14, 1957, the municipality proposed that an estimated $432,000 be spent on an extension for the air terminal building. Because of uncertainties about relative financial responsibilities of Transport and of the city, discussions went on for years. Eventually the city asked the department to purchase the airport and assume responsibility for its operation. But that was not to happen until 1968; and in the meantime, plans for the terminal extension were approved. In the spring of 1960 tenders were called for demolition of approximately 40 per cent of the terminal and for the construction of a major extension to the remaining 60 per cent. The work was completed in June 1961.

A new taxiway was constructed from the southeast end of the aircraft parking ramp to the button of runway 32 to expedite ground movements of aircraft. The project was completed in July 1962: the new area was 2,750 by 75 feet [838 by 23 metres], black-topped throughout, running parallel to runway 14-32.

With the arrival of jet passenger service to Saint John, a longer runway was required, and work began in July 1963, to extend runway 05-23 by 2,000 feet [609 metres]. The work was completed in September 1964 by adding to the 05 end of the runway. Both runways were resurfaced in 1968.

In 1967, Carrigan Insurance Company built a combined hangar and flying club room from which they operated a scheduled air service to various parts of New Brunswick under the name of Air Brunswick. This was later bought out by Air Canada. A fourth hangar was added to the site in 1972, when Aircraftsmen Ltd. built a concrete and metal structure for the sale and maintenance of aircraft, and for the operation of a charter service by Atlantic Central Airlines.

After ten years of intermittent negotiations, the city and the Department reached an agreement, effective April 1, 1968, under which the city and county of Saint John sold its lands, premises, and equipment at the airport to Transport for the sum of $835,000. By mutual agreement, the entire airport staff was retained, with J.E. Mahoney as airport manager.

In June 1973, 3,400 square feet [316 square metres] were added to the groundside of the terminal building, and a further addition of 1,700 square feet [158 sq metres] was made to the southeast corner in 1977, to accommodate baggage pick-up and passenger exit.

Private enterprise increased its activities, too. In the fall of 1975, Fundy Aviation Ltd. erected a metal hangar on a concrete slab. Unfortunately, the door had not arrived when a hurricane hit the airport on February 2, 1976. The wind lifted the building straight up and blew it over the hydro line into a field about 150 feet [46 metres] away, where it collapsed into useless rubble. Miraculously, none of the five aircraft in the hangar at the time was damaged. Undaunted by this setback, the hangar was rebuilt on the same pad in 1976 and now serves as a flying school and aircraft maintenance hangar. Approval was also granted to another private company to build a maintenance hangar on the site of the old Saint John Flying Club, which had been destroyed by fire in July 1975.

A $1,560,500 combined services building was constructed to house the vehicle maintenance garage, general trade shops, and fire hall in 1980.

During the beginning of 1980, traffic volumes continued to increase, but then took a downswing, which lasted until 1984. Passenger traffic went from a high of 205,032 in 1980 to a low of 163,815 in 1983— attributable to the high oil prices of the early 1980s and the start of major rehabilitation of airport runways in 1983.

In the summer of 1983, a new service road was constructed to connect the new combined

service building and airport maintenance facilities to the air terminal complex. Runway 14-32 was recapped with asphalt in 1983, and runway 05-23 was similarly resurfaced in 1984. A new High Intensity Approach System was installed on the 05 approach to runway 05-23. To complement the improvements already done, the next step was to refurbish the existing air terminal building. This project started in the fall of 1984 and carried through to a 1985 completion, at a cost of $1.2 million, in time for the Canada Summer Games, which were hosted by Saint John.

With deregulation, traffic at Saint John has grown to 36,800 aircraft movements, carrying 251,000 passengers for 1988. The airport is served by Air Canada, Canadian Airlines, Air Nova, Air Atlantic, and Inter-Canadian.

The airport plays an important role in the economy of Saint John and currently has approximately 228 full- and part-time employees. Overall, the airport places about $22.8 million directly into the local economy.

The following airport managers have served since 1951:

William M. Arrowsmith	1951 to 1953	(city)
Donald Crookshank	1953 to 1955	(city)
J.E. Maloney	1955 to 1968	(city)
J.E. Maloney	1968 to 1978	(Transport)
M.D. Campbell	1978 to 1982	(Transport)
H.G. Rossiter	1982 to present	(Transport)

Sources:

1. Transport Canada material (provided by A.J. St. Croix, J.E. Mahoney, G. Jones, S. MacGregor, and W.A. Black).
2. Helmer Biermann "Millidgeville—The Dream of a Great Airport" *Atlantic Advocate* (September 1980), pp. 18-23.

Footnotes—Saint John Airport

[1] United States, *Airports in Canada and Newfounland*, (Washington: U.S. Printing Office, 1930).

[2] Public Archives Canada, MG 30 E243, vol. 9.

[3] Turnbull built a wind tunnel in 1902 to test aerofoils and wind flow. It was the first one in North America. He was the first Canadian to tackle the purely theoretical aspects of aeronautics. Turnbull became interested in the design and construction of the air propellers and wrote his first paper in 1902. In 1918, he began experiments with controllable pitch propellers and invented the first successful one, which was flown for the first time at Camp Borden, Ontario in 1927 (see F.H. Ellis, *Canada's Flying Heritage* (Toronto: University of Toronto Press, 1961), pp. 3, 13-15.).

St. John's Airport
(Newfoundland)

St. John's Airport, near Torbay, was built as a military aerodrome in 1941. At that time, Newfoundland was not part of Canada, but was administered by the Commission of Government under the chairmanship of the governor of Newfoundland, who was appointed by the British government. With the outbreak of war in 1939, Canada immediately became concerned with the defence of Newfoundland. Speaking in the Canadian parliament on September 8, 1939, Prime Minister King declared that "the integrity of Newfoundland and Labrador is essential to the security of Canada," and that, in contributing to the defence of Newfoundland, Canada would not only be defending Canada, but also assisting Britain.

The question of establishing an airport near St. John's was first raised in Ottawa on February 29, 1940 by Sir Edward Emerson, commissioner for Justice and Defence for Newfoundland, when he met with officials of the Department of External Affairs to discuss the protection of Bell Island against raids by German submarines. At that time, 30 per cent of the iron produced in Canada was smelted at Sydney from ore obtained from the Wabana Mines on Bell Island in Conception Bay near St. John's. The defence of Bell Island presented a special problem of direct interest to both the government of Canada and the government of Newfoundland. Canada was interested because of the ore, and Newfoundland because the industry provided employment for Newfoundlanders and revenue for the government. In his discussion on the defence of Bell Island, Sir Edward raised the question of the advisability of establishing a Royal Canadian Air Force station for reconnaissance aircraft at St. John's.

A report of the Joint Board of Defence (comprising Canada and the United States) dated October 4, 1940, set out the responsibilities of Canada and the United States for the defence of North America. In this report, one of the activities to be undertaken by Canada was to provide, if possible, a fighter aerodrome near St. John's.

During the last part of 1940, convoys on the Atlantic carrying vital supplies and materials were endangered because of German U-boat operations, and the very lifeline of Britain was in danger of being cut off. Air protection for the convoys became of prime importance and, in order to give this type of protection, it was essential to have an aerodrome near St. John's from which to operate.

On March 13, 1941, the secretary of state for External Affairs informed the governor of Newfoundland of Canada's intention to develop an aerodrome at Torbay to accommodate RCAF operations.

The government of Newfoundland agreed to this on April 17, 1941, with the understanding that all the expenses of development would be borne exclusively by the government of Canada and that if the aerodrome were to be used as a civil airport this would require the consent of the Newfoundland government. With this understanding and subject to the settlement of details with appropriate departments of the government of Newfoundland, it was agreed that the Canadian government could purchase privately owned lands and that Crown lands were to be placed at the disposal free of charge, either as an outright grant or on a lease, for a period commensurable with the capital investment.[1]

After studying the weather, topography, and access to the site, an area near the picturesque fishing village of Torbay was selected—just a few kilometres from Lester's Field, where Alcock and Brown took off on the first non-stop flight across the Atlantic on June 14, 1919. The Aerodrome Committee[2] asked the Department of Transport to submit an estimate for two 4,000 by 150 foot [1,219 by 46 metre] runways, taxiways, aprons, hangars, and related facilities. The submitted figure of $1,436,000 was submitted and was approved, and McNamara Construction Company, the successful bidder, began construction on April 28, 1941.

The first landing at Torbay took place on October 18, 1941, while the runways were still under construction. Three U.S. Air Force B-17 bombers landed after circling the airport a number of times as a signal for the trucks and construction equipment to vacate the runway. The landings caused concern and annoyance to the Department of Transport, which was supervising the runway construction, because of the danger to both construction workers and the crews of the airplanes involved— especially when made without notice or permission, as was the case with these three airplanes.

Another and more dramatic landing was made on October 31, 1941, during a weather emergency. The BOAC Liberator AM-262, flown by Captain S.T.B. Cripps on the Return Ferry Service between Prestwick, Scotland and RAF Ferry Command Headquarters in Montréal, was en route from Prestwick to Gander with a crew of five and fifteen passengers. Two of the passengers were the Honourable Colonel Ralston, Canadian Ministry of National Defence, and Major General Crearer, the chief of the General Staff. By the time the aircraft had passed the point of no return, an early snow storm, which Gander had been experiencing during the day, became worse, making landing at Gander impossible. The bad weather had extended all along the eastern seaboard, thus preventing a landing east of Montréal. Owing to the critical range of the aircraft, the situation became an emergency. The senior controller of the RAF control office in Gander, T.M. McGrath, called RCAF Group Headquarters in St. John's, explained the situation, and asked if the Torbay Airport was fit for use. On being informed that although runway 08-26 was not completed it had reached the stage where it could be used for landing, Gander diverted Cripps to St. John's, where he made the first 'official' landing at the new airport at 1630 hours. As the airport had no instrument landing aids at that stage, the St. John's radio station, VONF, which was usually off the air at this time of day, was requested to remain on air and was used by Cripps as a homing beacon. The aircraft suffered some damage to its nose wheel during the landing at Torbay and was delayed there until November 2, when it flew to Gander. It finally reached Montréal on November 3.

On November 26, 1941, twenty RCAF airmen arrived at Torbay. On the same afternoon, four Hudson aircraft landed. The aircraft crews and the twenty ground crew (airmen), under Squadron Leader M.P. Martyn, were housed at the airport for the first night in tar-paper-covered shacks heated by pot-bellied stoves. This was the beginning of the RCAF Station Torbay. It was January 1942 before accommodation was ready for the rest of the station personnel. The station was to have two roles: (a) the defence of

shipping in St. John's Harbour; and (b) anti-submarine operations and convoy patrols. U.S. Air Force aircraft were later accommodated at Torbay Airport.

Eastern Air Command, Halifax, which controlled RCAF operations in Newfoundland, established No. 1 Group Headquarters in St. John's on July 10, 1941, to control anti-submarine air operations in the northeast Atlantic area and the air defence of Newfoundland and Labrador. It was disbanded on June 30, 1945.

During the war, the following squadrons served at RCAF Station Torbay with aircraft as noted:

125 Squadron	-June 9, 1942, to June 24, 1943, using three Hurricane fighters
5 CAC	-Detachment of three Lysanders April 23, 1942, for coastal artillery co-operation
128 Squadron	-June 24, 1943, to March 15, 1944, using Hurricane fighters
145 BR Squadron	-formed at Torbay, as a Bomber Reconnaissance Squadron; May 30, 1942, to October 26, 1943, using Hudsons and Venturas
11 BR Squadron	-October 26, 1943, to June 17, 1944, using Hudsons and Liberators
5 BR Squadron	-May 10, 1943, to August 1, 1944, using Cansos
160 BR Squadron	-August 3, 1944, to June 15, 1945, using Cansos
10 BR Squadron	-June 11, 1945, disbanded at Torbay, August 15, 1945

One enemy submarine was sunk on October 30, 1942, by a Hudson of 145 Squadron, operating out of Torbay.

By virtue of the U.S.-U.K. Bases Agreement of 1940,[3] the United States was given a ninety-nine-year lease to three areas in Newfoundland. These were to be developed into major military bases for the protection of the United States and

the ocean approaches to the northeast part of the continent. Bases were constructed during 1940-41 at Harmon Field (Stephenville), Argentia, and Fort Pepperell (St. John's). After Pearl Harbour and the entry of the United States into the war in December 1941, the U.S. wanted to develop a major U.S. Air Force unit at Torbay Airport, but Canada did not agree and the plan was dropped.[4] In 1941, Canada did offer the United States use of Torbay as may be required for servicing purposes.

"In April 1944, the RCAF agreed to permit use of hangar space [at Torbay] to accommodate the personal plane of the U.S. Commanding General of nearby Fort Pepperell and in order to provide for routine inspections and minor repairs to other U.S. Air Force aircraft..."[5] From this modest beginning, the American presence at Torbay grew, but only in the role of communications and transportation in support of the U.S. Headquarters, Newfoundland Base Command at Fort Pepperell. Later, in September 1946 and in February 1948, leases were granted to the USAF for Hangars No. 3 and 4 and other buildings. The leases provided for thirty days notice of cancellation.

When the Department of Transport took over the airport from the RCAF on April 1, 1946, it became a civil operation. Although the USAF were good tenants, the large number of military personnel at the airport had caused some problems to the civilian management. On a couple of occasions, when the USAF carried out security exercises, civilian personnel were denied access to the airport; and this finally led to the airport being taken over by the RCAF on April 1, 1953, when it once again became RCAF Station Torbay. The USAF then became the guests, or tenants, of the RCAF. Transport retained control of the air terminal area in the southwest corner of the airport. The airport remained under RCAF control until April 1, 1964, when the Department of Transport once more assumed management, and the RCAF transferred its search and rescue service to summerside, Prince Edward land.

The original airport construction consisted of runways 08-26 and 17-35 and taxiway B, which were completed by December 1941. Runway 08-26 was lengthened to 5,000 feet [1,524 metres] in 1942, while 17-35 was widened to 200 feet [61 metres] in 1942 and lengthened to 7,000 feet [2,134 metres] in 1958.

Runway 02-20 was constructed in 1942 to a length of 4,000 feet [1,219 metres] and a width of 200 feet [46 metres]. Runway 11-29 was constructed to a length of 4,900 feet [1,493 metres] and a width of 200 feet [61 metres] in 1943. It was extended by 1,800 feet [549 metres] to the east and 300 feet [91 metres] to the west in 1954, and its entire length was rebuilt. It was further extended in 1968 by adding 300 feet [91 metres] to the east and 1,200 feet [366 metres] to the west. It was recapped with asphalt in 1967, and the centreline and touchdown lights were installed in 1970. The first Category II ILS(Instrument Landing System) in Newfoundland and the fourth in Canada was commissioned on runway 29 on March 25, 1977.

Runway 11-29 has an interesting history. It was constructed by the government of Canada to meet American requirements. Construction began before obtaining formal permission from the government of Newfoundland, and part of the runway was on property that the government of Newfoundland had granted the United States, to meet its requirements. The Canadian government was very concerned by this, as it felt that facilities constructed by or for the United States government in Newfoundland outside the U.S. bases should be on property owned by Canada. As a result of negotiations, the U.S. gave up its right to the land; and on June 18, 1943, United States legation in Ottawa advised the Canadian government that, because of changing technical

and strategic conditions, there was no longer any need for American construction at Torbay. By this time, the construction of 11-29 was well under way; however, the Canadian authorities were not too concerned about the matter, as they felt that the runway would be the most used one on the airport.

Ramp No. 1, located on the east side of the airport and now known as the general aviation ramp, was constructed in 1942. Taxiway F and Ramp No. 11 (known as the terminal building ramp) were constructed in 1942 to serve the civil operation.

On March 15, 1943, the Air Officer Commanding Eastern Air Command wrote to the Secretary of Air, Department of National Defence, complaining of the difficult situation that resulted from TCA's operations at Torbay. He stated that it was not unusual for three aircraft to arrive daily with no accommodation for the handling of the flights except one inadequate corner of hangar no. 2. There were no toilet facilities, and passengers had to walk through an operational hangar to the RCAF facilities on the far side. He noted, too, that there was no evidence of construction in the civil area previously agreed to for the use of TCA where the following facilities had already been provided: a taxi-strip, a concrete parking area, a cleared area

173. Airport terminal, St. John's, Newfoundland.

for an administration building, and an entrance road from the main highway between St. John's and Portugal Cove.

The air officer commanding felt the situation created a security problem, and that congestion of the taxi-strip interfered with the RCAF operations. He requested that high priority be given to the completion of the TCA development as greatly increased use of the airport was anticipated due to intensification of submarine warfare off the Newfoundland coast.

A frame terminal building was completed late in 1943 and served until it was replaced by the present building on October 6, 1958. A new taxiway was constructed in 1973 which provided an alternate access to the terminal building ramp.

The original building was converted into offices and housed the telecommunications operations, which subsequently moved to the present tower operations building when it opened on March 9, 1976. The old terminal was demolished in July 1978.

The first control tower at the airport was located on top of hangar no. 1 and was operated by the RCAF. It was destroyed by fire on March 17, 1946. The Department of Transport built the second control tower in late 1951, but it was not occupied until December 1952. Temporary airport traffic control was provided from a box-like structure on the old administration building from June 18, 1952, to meet the demands of the U.S. Air Force.

The question of title to land at Torbay was the subject of much correspondence. The government of Canada was anxious to acquire property rights to the airport. The Secretary of State for External Affairs wrote to the Canadian High Commissioner in Newfoundland on October 21, 1941, stating that if the government of Newfoundland insisted on a leasehold agreement for Crown lands, this would lead to an unsatisfactory situation where portions of the aerodrome property bought directly from the owners would be owned outright by Canada, while other parts would be under lease. The matter was resolved at a conference held at St. John's on October 27, 1941, when it was agreed that the government of Canada was to receive a grant in fee simple to Crown lands from the Newfoundland government. This was confirmed by Article 4 of the agreement between Canada, Newfoundland, and the United Kingdom, respecting defence installations in Newfoundland, in St. John's on April 8, 1946, and in London on May 3, 1946. It stated that title in fee simple to lands of Torbay Airport and its subsidiary installations should be vested in the government of Canada, in accordance with the understanding between the governments of Canada and Newfoundland, at the time of construction of the airport. Article 4 also stated that Torbay Airport may be operated as a commercial airport by the government of Canada for air services between Newfoundland and Canada, in accordance with such laws and regulations in force from time-to-time in Newfoundland as may be applicable to civil aviation.[6] The agreement also stated that the airport was to be available to Newfoundland civil and military aircraft on terms not less favourable that those applicable to Canadian civil and military aircraft and for emergency landing by any civil or military aircraft. All fees imposed on civil aircraft were to go to the government of Canada. Any revenue from landing fees or other charges in excess of the cost of operating the airport for civil purposes was to be paid to the government of Newfoundland.

With the construction of the airport at Torbay, the government of Newfoundland was anxious to see air services established between Newfoundland and Canada. When first approached, TCA refused to undertake the service as it was not considered economically viable. With the consent of the Dominion's office in London, the

Newfoundland government authorized Harvey and Company to negotiate with Northeast Airlines of the United States to provide the service. Leonard Earle of Harveys went to Ottawa on October 2, 1941, to seek permission from the Canadian government for the use of Torbay Airport for such a service. In spite of TCA's reluctance to provide air service, the Canadian High Commissioner in Newfoundland wrote to the Secretary of State for External Affairs on October 15, 1941, setting out the reasons why Canada should establish a commercial air service between Newfoundland and Canada. While in Ottawa and Montréal, Earle called on H.J. Symington, president of TCA, and J.A. Wilson, director of Civil Aviation. He tried to pursuade TCA to extend its service from Moncton to St. John's. He carried with him letters of support from Sir Wilfred Woods, senior member of the Commission government, and from Air Vice-Marshall McEwan, the air officer commanding the RCAF in Newfoundland.

Symington did not think it was possible to operate into Newfoundland, because no more aircraft could be acquired during the war. Wilson agreed with Symington, and he also questioned whether there would be sufficient traffic to justify a service even as far as Halifax after the war. Earle then asked what TCA's reaction would be to permitting an American airline to use the airport. Wilson arranged a meeting with C.P. Edwards, deputy minister of Transport, who gave Earle a sympathetic hearing. The RCAF was interested in TCA using Torbay, as it was short of transport and would welcome the service. There was a quick change of heart in Ottawa, because by the time Earle returned to St. John's, the secretary of state for External Affairs had written to the High Commissioner in Newfoundland, asking that steps be taken to approach the Newfoundland government to obtain permission for the operation of a regular air-mail, pas-

senger, and express service from the terminal in the Maritimes to Gander Lake Airport and from there to Torbay by Trans-Canada Air Lines. The letter contained assurances that the proposed service would, in all respects, be equal to that given on the Canadian transcontinental route.

The first airplane operated by TCA on the scheduled service arrived at Torbay at 1615 hours local time on May 1, 1942, with the following passengers on board: Canadian Army Nurse Baker, Nurse E.E. Buffet, Sergeant F.B. Cahill, RCAF, J.L. Courtney, and J.P. Courtney. The crew consisted of Captains Trerice and Fowler and the stewardess, Dorothy Reid. The plane was a Lockheed Lodestar and, after an hour's stay, the aircraft took off with the following outbound passengers: Mrs. F.J. Quinn, M.T. Rodgers, W.M. Knapp, Tas Whipper, A.L. Malloy, and L.K. Chaplin.

On March 17, 1946, a fire which swept the east side of the airport caused $1.5 million in damages, as it destroyed a large hangar, four USAF airplanes, the control tower, and several vehicles. Six thousand gallons [27,276 litres] of gasoline were also lost.

Fred Milley was appointed the first airport manager on April 1, 1946, and continued to administer the airport until February 6, 1949, when he resigned to take another position. After Confederation on April 1, 1949, Tom McGrath became airport manager. He was transferred from Gander, where he had been operations manager; he had been associated with that airport from its initial years. Following McGrath's transfer to the Department of Transport in Moncton, L.V. MacDonald was appointed airport manager on October 21, 1949, and he continued in this position until his transfer to Moncton on May 25, 1953. On April 1, 1953, the airport once again came under military control when the RCAF took charge. The RCAF assumed responsibility for the operation and maintenance of the runways and the other facilities and buildings on the military side (east) of the field, except for those leased to the USAF. The Department of Transport continued to operate the civil air terminal, meteorological service, and other facilities associated with the radio range and ILS (Instrument Landing System).

M.F. Lawlor was appointed airport manager on April 1, 1964. He accepted the transfer of facilities on behalf of the Department of Transport from the Department of National Defence and set up an all-civil operation. The airport was then known as St. John's Airport. Following Lawlor's retirement, Harold B. Hefferton was appointed airport manager on December 10, 1985. He was previously the operations manager at St. John's Airport and had previously held other management positions at both St. John's and Gander International Airports.

Since April 1, 1964, the airport has experienced tremendous growth and has undergone many changes. In 1970, it was designated as an international airport for use only by general aviation aircraft of not more than 30,000 pounds gross weight. The restriction, which had an adverse affect on the volume of traffic and on the potential for development, was rescinded in 1974 following numerous complaints from the business community and other concerned bodies. In 1986, Air Canada was given permission to operate its London, England, international passenger flights to and from St. John's with the inaugural flight occurring on August 29, 1986. These flights previously operated through Gander International Airport.

All buildings on the east side of the airport, known as RCAF Station Torbay (with the exception of the hangars and of buildings 13, 14, 15, 16 and 37) were sold through the Crown Assets Disposal Corporation (CADC) to the government of Newfoundland and Labrador in January 1965. Hangar no. 4 was sold through the CADC on September 5, 1968, to Air Transit Limited, and became the first privately owned hangar at the airport. The building is now used to provide aircraft storage and ground servicing for general aviation aircraft. In 1983, Aero Flight Holdings completed construction of a new hangar to provide aircraft storage and ground servicing for general aviation aircraft. It houses the head office of the C.H.C. Helicopter Corporation, which is the largest commercial helicopter company in Canada and the second largest in the world. In 1989, Air Atlantic, partner of Canadian Airlines International, completed construction of a head office and a hangar facility at St. John's Airport. Transport Canada finished a new combined services building in 1986, which comprises the airport fire hall, the maintenance garage, and a number of trade workshops and offices. (These were previously housed in old wartime hangar no. 2). Transport Canada has constructed a new general services building in the general aviation area of the airport. The building provides helicopter hangar space, flight information services, a weather briefing office, and aviation regulation and inspection services for international general aviation.

The Newfoundland Flying Club and the Avalon Flying Club had been in existence at the airport for a number of years. Building 37 was sold to the Avalon Flying Club in June 1964 and was used as its headquarters. The first privately owned flying school was established there by Squires Flying Service Ltd. in 1970 and operated out of hangar no. 4 until the company constructed its own hangar in 1972. Squires ceased operations in June 1975 when the flying school was taken over by Terra Nova Development Ltd., under the name of Aztec Aviation Flying School.

Currently, St. John's Airport, 140 metres above sea level, consists of approximately 634 hectares. It is located in the northeast corner of

174. Former RCAF buildings, St. John's, Newfoundland, 1981.

the Avalon Peninsula, approximately nine and a half kilometres northwest of the city of St. John's. The small point of land on which the airport is located is surrounded by water on three sides: it is bounded on the east by the Atlantic Ocean five kilometres from the field and on the west by Conception Bay, approximately eight kilometres away.

Because of the hilly terrain and the nearness of open water, weather conditions vary considerably and are greatly affected by small changes in wind direction and speed. Another important influence is the Labrador current, which flows southward along the east coast of Newfoundland, curves westward south of the Avalon Peninsula, and meets the warm Gulf Stream southeast of Newfoundland in the area of the Grand Banks. The airport must, therefore be equipped with the best landing aids; and as a result of improvements made since 1977, the use of the airport during the past few years has been greatly increased.

The airport not only serves the capital city, St. John's, which is the centre of commerce, government, education and specialized health care services in Newfoundland, but a catchment area of the Burin and Avalon peninsulas, as well as Clarenville and half of Bonavista Bay.

Eastern Provincial Airways with its base on St. John's, first started operating from the airport in January 1949, with summer service to Gander and Buchans, three times weekly, flying Cessna Cranes. Aircraft were maintained from January 1949 until October 1953 at Hangar No. 2 at St. John's Airport. In November 1953, the company moved its head office and maintenance facilities to hangar no. 21 at Gander International Airport, and in 1955, Lockheed 10s were used to provide service from Gander to Deer Lake, Frenchman's Cove and St. John's. In 1961, scheduled service with a C-46 aircraft, began service, from the Island of Newfoundland to the Labrador towns of Goose Bay, Twin Falls (now Churchill Falls), and Carol Lake (now Wabush and Labrador city). In 1963, the C-46 aircraft were retired, Handley Page Dart Heralds were purchased, and Maritime was bought by Eastern Provincial Airways which moved its head office to Halifax, Nova Scotia, in 1984 and was subsequently sold to Canadian Pacific Airlines in 1985.

The airport is served by two major airlines: Air Canada and Canadian Airlines International. Air Canada uses DC-9, Boeing 727, Boeing 767, DC-8 and, on occasion, Boeing 747 and L-1011 aircraft, with flights routed through Halifax, Montréal, and Toronto. Canadian Airlines International operates Boeing 737 aircraft and has routes to all major Canadian sites. Air Nova and Air Atlantic provide a connector/commuter service for the larger air carriers, and Atlantic Airways also operates a scheduled service at the airport. They use various types of aircraft, including Dash 8, BA 146, King Air, and Merlin.

In 1987, there were 63,086 aircraft operations, while the two scheduled airlines had 627,316 passengers.

Sources:

1. Frank Lawlor, former Airport Manager, St. John's International Airport (using material from the St. John's Daily News and Evening Telegram).
2. Leonard Earl.
3. Transport Canada.
4. H.B. Hefferton, Airport Manager, St. John's International Airport.

Footnotes—St. John's Airport

[1] These two principles applied to all lands required for the Canadian forces in Newfoundland.

[2] This was a joint committee of the Departments of National Defence and Transport that oversaw the choice of aerodrome sites and the completion of construction programs for the RCAF and the British Commonwealth Air Training Plan facilities.

[3] The Newfoundland and Bermuda bases were given "freely and without consideration" as distinct from the U.S.-U.K. agreement for American bases in British territory in the Caribbean, for which the United States 'paid' with fifty over-age American destroyers. These agreements were implemented more than a year before the U.S. entered the war.

[4] Three American B-17 aircraft made the first landing at Torbay in October 1941.

[5] Extract from a report of the Canadian High Commission, St. John's, to External Affairs , Ottawa, 24 November 1948.

[6] After the war, Canada retained ownership of Torbay Airport. The RCAF operated it until April 1, 1946, when responsibility was transferred to the Department of Transport.

St. Thomas Airport
(Ontario)

St. Thomas Airport , constructed in 1940 as part of the British Commonwealth Air Training Plan, was Relief Station No. 1 for No. 14 Service Flying Training School at Aylmer, Ontario, and lies east of the city, off highway 3 near Yarmouth Centre.

After withdrawal of the RCAF, St. Thomas leased the airport from the Department of Transport in 1945 for a rent of one dollar a year and assumed the responsibility for its operation and maintenance. In 1949, St. Thomas entered into an agreement with Elgin Airways Ltd. to operate the airport for a fee of $200 per month. The airline managed the airport until 1959.

After that time, Northcana Ltd. operated the site for the city until December 1961, when it was succeeded, in February 1962, by N.A. Distributors (Canada) Ltd., which managed the airport until September 1962. Then Hicks and Lawrence Ltd. assumed control as a result of winning public tender called by the city. The company was given a lease for five years at an annual rental fee of $1,000 and the payment of taxes on the property.

In 1965-66, the city considered purchasing the airport from the Department of Transport, but the plan fell through, and the purchase was not effected until 1971. Since that time the city has run the airport.

The city installed new runway lighting and extended runway 09-27 to 3,000 feet [914 metres] in 1973. These improvements were made to encourage local industries owning executive aircraft to use the airport. A new administration building was erected in 1971.

There are twenty hangars on the site, six of which were built during 1989.

The airport has three paved runways: 09-27, 1,539 metres; 15-33, 805 metres; and 03-21, 805 metres.

St. Thomas Aviation (flying school), Central Ag-Air Ltd. (aircraft repairs and agricultural spraying), Hicks and Lawrence Ltd. (major overhauls and agricultural spraying), Can-du Air (helicopters), and Supermarine (spraying outfit) are based at the airport.

There were 47,792 aircraft movements in 1988.

Sources:
1. Transport Canada, Ontario Region.
2. Roger Simpson, Airport Attendent, St. Thomas Airport.

Salmo Aerodrome
(British Columbia)

Salmo Aerodrome, developed in the 1930s as an intermediate aerodrome on the Trans-Canada Airway, is owned by Transport Canada and was leased to the village of Salmo in 1955.

It is a single turf strip 975 by 91 metres located in the middle of the village golf course, and the club house doubles as a terminal building. The strip is only usable during the summer.

The Nelson Daily of June 28, 1960, had a news item reporting that the Salmo golf course would open on July 1 and "will have a ground rule unique in the books of golfdom. It will state that 'all golfers will clear the course on the approach of an aircraft'. This is because the broad flat terrain does double duty as a light airfield, as well as an attractive golfers paradise. It will make it convenient, too, for aircraft owners in neighbouring communities to drop in for a game at any time."

The Salmo District Golf Club is negotiating with both the federal and provincial governments to purchase the golf course, with the understanding that it remain an emergency landing field. It is not used extensively by aircraft and there are no more than once-a-week landings by small planes. There is no revenue derived by the golf course in conjunction with aircraft and no fees are collected.

Sources:
1. Transport Canada, Pacific Region.
2. K.W. Henderson, Secretary of Salmo Golf Club.

Sandspit Airport
(British Columbia)

Sandspit Airport was developed on the northeast tip of Moresby Island of the Queen Charlotte Islands by the Department of National Defence as an emergency landing strip for Pacific War Operations in 1943. It was first intended to call the airport Lawson after Bill Lawson, Superintendent of Airways for the Department of Transport, but there was strenuous opposition from local residents.

The airport was transferred to the Department of Transport on August 1, 1946, and an airport licence was issued in the name of the department on June 16, 1947.

The air terminal building was constructed in 1951.

The paved runway, 12-30, improved in 1960 and repaved in 1978, 1,560 metres long; a turf runway 08-26, is 914 metres long.

The following air carriers serve the airport:

Canadian Airlines International	- scheduled
Trans-Provincial Airlines	- scheduled/charter
Skylink	- scheduled
Canada West	- scheduled/charter
Frontier Helicopters	- charter
Sandspit Helijet	- charter
Vancouver Island Helicopters	- charter

In 1988, there were 40,400 passengers and 13,025 aircraft movements.

The following served as airport managers:

A. Fowlic	1946 to 1953
A. Davies	1953 to 1956
W. Mitchell	1956 to 1957
I. McCaskill	1957 to 1959
J. Gidman	1959 to 1961
R. Cormier	1961 to 1965
W. McKinnon	1965 to 1967
J. Hawkins	1967 to 1987
B. Hawick	1987 to 1988
S. Hoeg	1989

Sources:
1. Transport Canada, Pacific Region.
2. R.L. Clarke, "Airport Notes" (Ottawa: Transport Canada) [unpublished collection].

Sarnia Airport
(Ontario)

The site of the Sarnia Airport was originally owned by the operator of a flying school there. Development of the airport, which opened in 1957 with a north-south grass runway of 2,000 feet [609 metres], was financed by the city and local industries. It was licensed for day operation of light aircraft; and its first operator was Sarnia Airlines Ltd.

With financial assistance from the Department of Transport, the city built a new hard-surfaced runway, 05-23, 2,989 feet [911 metres] long. In August 1958, the airport was licensed for day and night flying.

In December 1960, the city conveyed title of the airport land to the Department of Transport and the site was then leased to Sarnia as a municipal airport. The city subleased to Great Lakes Airlines for operation.

In 1965, Sarnia, with financial assistance from Transport, built and paved a new runway, 14-32, 3,000 feet [914 metres] long. It built a hangar and a terminal building in 1967 and, in 1968, runway 14-32 was extended by 1,000 feet [305 metres].

In 1969, Sarnia acquired main line status through the Great Lakes Airlines' regular commercial air service.

Transport completed further improvements to the airport in 1971-72, including the extension of runway 14-32 to 5,100 feet [1,554 metres], and the city became eligible for an operating subsidy in 1972.

The airport is served by Air Ontario (formerly Great Lakes Airlines), Canadian Partner, and Huron Aviation. Huron Aviation also provides charters, flight training, and aircraft maintenance and is a fixed-base operator on the airport. Dow Chemical Company operates a hangar at the airport.

Despite efforts by Transport Canada to encourage Sarnia to continue to operate the airport, the city council passed a resolution on July 15, 1985, asking Transport to assume responsibility. The following year Transport Canada issued a contract to Scottsdale Aviation to operate the airport on behalf of the Department. The contract, which expired on May 30, 1989, was awarded again to Scottsdale for another two-year term, ending June 30, 1991. All airport services are contracted out.

In 1987, there were 13,700 aircraft movements and 50,300 passengers.

Source:
Transport Canada, Ontario Region.

Saskatoon Airport
(Saskatchewan)

Saskatoon's first contact with aviation goes back a long way. In 1911, a Curtiss airplane owned by Bob St. Henry arrived by train, and made its first flight at Saskatoon on May 17, from a prairie grass strip west of the city limits. Glenn Martin, an American later known as a designer and builder of bomber aircraft, came to Saskatoon in 1912 and flew a Pusher biplane, which he had designed and built, at the annual Exhibition. In

175. Keng Wah Aviation hangar, Saskatoon, 1920.

1913, when Saskatoon set aside a quarter section of land west of the exhibition grounds at the southwest edge of the city as an aerodrome, W. Featherstone set up an aviation school there with a Farman biplane. Then came World War I, and local aviation ceased.

In April 1919, Lieutenant Stan McClelland, ex-RAF, established a commercial flying operation at a field on 22nd Street West and Dundonald Avenue, one and a half kilometres northwest of the St. Paul's Hospital, and built a hangar there for his Curtiss JN-4 biplane. The field was used by four DH-4B airplanes of the U.S. Army Air Service on July 25, 1920, on their way from New York to Nome, Alaska; and on October 10, three of the aircraft landed at the McClelland field on their return journey.

At the same time as McClelland was setting up his field, another was established four and a half kilometres north, near Hudson Bay Slough. It was operated by Keng Wah Aviation between 1919 and 1922 and was used to train young Chinese from the United States, Canada, and from China for Dr. Sun Yat-Sen's Revolutionary Army.[1]

Saskatoon is shown in the List of Airharbours for 1922 as having two public-commercial airharbours (see Chapter 7): one was 400 by 600 yards [366 by 549 metres], and the other, 300 by

400 yards [274 by 366 metres]. The latter was granted Airharbour Licence No. 2 on April 22, 1920, to McClelland Aircraft Ltd; the other was granted Airharbour Licence No. 49 on September 6, 1921, in the name of R.J. Groome of Regina.[2]

In February 1920, the city asked the Air Board[3] to establish an aerodrome in Saskatoon for the province of Saskatchewan. But because government policy required a community aerodrome to be the responsibility of the local municipality, the city took no further action.

In January 1927, the Department of National Defence, Civil Aviation Branch, asked Saskatoon to consider establishing an airport. By this time, the Department was giving some thought to air-mail services and was launching its scheme to assist in the establishment of light aeroplane clubs across Canada. The city was interested and the Department sent an officer to help select a suitable site. In May 1928, a site was chosen and recommended for development and use by the Saskatoon Aero Club. The city acquired the land (sixty-five hectares) in July, and the site was licensed for day use on June 1, 1929. There were two runways: north-south, 1,760 feet [537 metres] long and, east-west, 2,640 feet [805 metres]. With a grant from the department, the city installed airport lighting in June 1930. The

176. Saskatoon, Saskatchewan, 1930.

old airport site is now a small part of the present complex on the northwest edge of the city. It was then situated in the rural municipality of Cory and became part of the city on January 1, 1971.

Saskatoon Airport was first developed in 1928 as the home of the Saskatoon Aero Club (later the Saskatoon Flying Club), which operated from the airport and received financial grants from the city.[4] Flight training began in May 1928, when the club received a DeHavilland Moth from the federal government; and by the end of 1929, it was the second largest aeroplane club in the country. Dick Mayson acted as airport manager during this time.

Western Canada Airways started the first air-mail service into the area in 1930, linking all the major cities of Western Canada. Service was discontinued on March 31, 1932, a casualty of the depression. In January 1937, the city asked for a grant to improve the airport, but the Department of Transport would give no assurances of help because the airport was not on the Trans-Canada Airway, and expansion depended on Post Office approval of air-mail service between Regina and Saskatoon. Finally, a $20,000 grant, under the one-third cost-sharing scheme, was approved in April 1938. The city constructed three runways during the summer of 1938 and further work was done in 1939.

177. Fokker F.XIV CF-AIL (Western Canada Airways Ltd.). First prairie airmail service, Saskatoon, March 3, 1930.

In 1938, Prairie Airways Ltd. added Saskatoon to its Moose Jaw-Regina, Saskatoon-Prince Albert-North Battleford route, providing daily passenger service and mail service.

About the same time, the Saskatoon Flying Club entered into an agreement with the Department of National Defence to give primary flying training to provisional pilot officers of the RCAF. This contract continued until the beginning of the war, when the club became a part of the British Commonwealth Air Training Plan (BCATP) as No. 6 Elementary Flying Training School (EFTS) at Prince Albert operating as The Northern Saskatchewan Flying Training School Ltd.

In January 1940, the city agreed to lease the airport to the federal government for the duration of the war. The RCAF took over and it became the home of No. 4 Service Flying Training School (SFTS) until November 1945. Early in 1940, work started on five large hangars, barracks, classrooms, workshops, a hospital, and a control tower. No. 4 SFTS was a very busy school, and two relief stations—no. 1 at Vanscoy and no. 2 at Osler—were set up to reduce traffic at Saskatoon. BCATP operations Saskatoon came to an end on March 31, 1945.

The Department of Transport took over maintenance of the airport from the RCAF in November 1945, because the City reneged on an earlier agreement. By 1948, instrument landing systems were installed on Runways 08 and 32. The next year, a control tower was put into operation.

In October 1950, the RCAF established a training station on the airport, and on January 1, 1952, No. 1 Advanced Flying Training School (AFTS) began to train RCAF, RAF, and Atlantic Treaty air crews. By the end of 1952, permanent married quarters had been completed and station personnel moved in. RCAF Station Saskatoon, in addition to No. 1 AFTS, supported other RCAF units in the Saskatoon area, including No. 23

Wing Headquarters, No. 406 Auxiliary Squadron, No. 3043 Technical Training Unit (Auxiliary), and No. 4002 Medical Unit (Auxiliary). In 1964, the auxiliary units were disbanded and the RCAF closed its entire station during the summer when four hangars were handed over to the Department of Transport.

Trans-Canada Air Lines started scheduled passenger service to Saskatoon in July 1947 using DC-3s. It introduced the North Star in 1950, the Viscount in 1955 and the DC-9 in 1967.

Department of Transport improvements included the construction of a new air terminal building in 1955. (The same plans were later used for terminals at Québec and Windsor). The airport became a Customs port of entry in September 1954. The primary runway 08-24 was lengthened in 1954 and again in 1960. Today, it is 2,530 metres long and 61 metres wide. Runway 14-32 was rebuilt and lengthened in 1963 and is now 1,890 metres long. Transport continued to run the airport, since the city once again refused an invitation, made in October 1955, to take over.

Consolidation of the air carriers has left Saskatoon with two major companies in 1989: Air Canada and Canadian Airlines International Ltd. Time Air Inc. operates out of Saskatoon as a Canadian Airlines partner. Saskatoon is curently

178. Old air terminal, Saskatoon, Saskatchewan, built in 1955.

served with B-737, DC-9, B-727, F-28, Convair 580 and 640, and Dash 7 aircraft.

In the late 1970s, Saskatchewan Air Ambulance began offering its service from the airport. There are two flying schools on the airport: Mitchinson Flying Service Ltd. and Saskatoon Flying Service Ltd.

Of six hangars on the airport one was built during the war. Hangar no. 2 is occupied by Highline Drilling; no. 3 by Cameco; no. 6 by Time Air; no. 7 by Central Aircraft Maintenance; no. 8 by Mitchinson Flying Services; and no. 9 by Athabasca Airways.

A new air terminal building of modern design, built by Transport Canada, was officially opened on November 29, 1975. The old terminal, which was renovated in 1977, now serves as the operations building and accommodates Customs and Immigration Services.

In 1989, when Saskatoon Airport celebrated its seventieth anniversary, the minister of Transport dedicated the Wall of Fame—a pictorial composition on the history of the Saskatoon Airport and its aviation pioneers.

The early 1980s saw a general recession and a reduction of air traffic. However, an improved economy combined with aviation deregulation has more recently turned this around. In 1988 there were 625,000 passengers and 113,148 aircraft movements.

The following served as Airport Managers:

Phil Nicholas	1946 to 1964
Michael Krystowaty	1964 to 1979
Ernest Michaulk	1980 to 1985
William Restall	1985 to present

Sources:

1. R.L. Clarke, *Airport Notes* (Ottawa: Transport Canada) [unpublished collection].
2. Transport Canada, Central Region. Winnipeg.
3. R.H. Crone, *Aviation Pioneers in Saskatchewan,*
Saskatchewan History Journal vol. 28, no. 1 (Winter 1975) [published by the Saskatchewan Archives Board].

Footnotes—Saskatoon Airport

[1] "Airports '79, 50 Years in Flight", Saskatoon Star Phoenix, (May 31, 1979), supplement.

[2] "Canadian Airharbours," *Aviation and Aircraft Journal*, (October 21, 1921), pp, 482 and 531.

[3] The Air Board was the government body that, at the time, had responsibility for aviation in Canada. The Department of National Defence replaced the board on January 1, 1923, and had responsibility for aviation until the formation of the Department of Transport on November 1, 1936.

[4] The flying club ceased operations in 1950.

Sault Ste. Marie Airport
(Ontario)

Sault Ste. Marie's recorded origins are traced to the founding of a Jesuit mission in 1668 at Saut de Sainte Marie. Its earliest significance to the white man lay in its strategic location as a funnel through which all waterborne traffic between Lake Superior and the other Great Lakes must pass. Today, the system of locks and canals which bypass the rapids of the St. Mary's river is claimed to be the busiest in the world.

Twin cities have grown up on both sides of the international border that approximates the centre line of the St. Mary's River; however, Sault Ste. Marie, Ontario, has far outstripped its Michigan namesake in terms of population. The industrial development of the Canadian "Soo" is linked directly to the founding of Algoma Steel Corporation in 1900, which has employed upwards of 10,000 individuals of the approximately 80,000 population.

Requests made to the federal government for an airport at Sault Ste. Marie date back to April 1929, but, for twenty-five years, no steps were taken to establish one. Then, in November 1954, the Department of Transport announced that an airport would be built at a site in Park township, twenty-six kilometres southwest of the city.

In 1956, 1,560 acres of land were acquired, and, the following year, a contract was awarded to construct two asphalt runways, 04-22 and 11-29, each 6,000 by 200 feet [1,829 by 61 metres]. Coincident with the completion of this work in 1960 was the erection of a combined maintenance garage and air services building, and a temporary terminal building. The following year, the construction of a car park and other groundside improvements was authorized.

On August 1, 1961, all major facilities, except the ILS (Instrument Landing System) commenced operation, and the airport was declared suitable for TCA Vanguard operations. Until that time, TCA had provided service to Sault Ste. Marie, Ontario, by using Kinross Airport near Sault Ste. Marie, Michigan, about twenty-six kilometres away and across the U.S.-Canada border.

The TCA route, across United States territory, had been established in 1947, following a decision made by the Department of Transport and TCA to realign the airway to allow shorter and quicker service from Toronto to Winnipeg: it was called the Great Lakes Airway. The original airway follows a route north of the Great Lakes through Kapuskasing and Armstrong; the new airway permitted TCA to serve Sault Ste. Marie, Ontario, and Thunder Bay, (at that time known as the Lakehead (Fort William-Fort Arthur)) on the Toronto-Winnipeg route. TCA was then flying DC-3 aircraft; and Department of Transport requirements specified intermediate aerodromes at approximately one hundred mile intervals. Accordingly, additional aerodromes were provided by Transport between Toronto and Sault Ste. Marie at Gore Bay on Manitoulin Island and at

Wiarton, near Owen Sound; and the field at Graham was enlarged. Transport arranged with the American authorities to provide aerodromes in Michigan at Canada's expense. Three were required: Kinross, a small airport already in existence, but requiring improvements; and two new fields at Grand Marais and Houghton. The Houghton County had been negotiating with the Civil Aeronautics Administration (CAA) in Washington for a small airport. The parties concerned decided to use Canada's contribution and, with a CAA grant, thus built a larger airport). A radio range station was required at each of the three sites and these were paid for by Canada. Initially, TCA was required to operate and maintain Kinross, later receiving reimbursement for these costs from Transport. Kinross eventually became a U.S. Air Force base, and TCA was a tenant. It was called Kincheloe Air Force Base in 1961. The Houghton Memorial Airport was dedicated to the memory of those who served their country on September 11, 1948, and the plaque recognized the contribution made by the Canadian government to the development of the airport.

TCA began service via Kinross on July 1, 1947. Through a special Canada-U.S. agreement, TCA passengers bound for Sault Ste. Marie, Ontario, were not allowed to stop anywhere

179. Ontario Provincial Air Service, Forestry Branch base, Sault Ste. Marie, Ontario, 1928.

180. First TCA service, Sault Ste. Marie, Ontario, August 1961.

while they were in the U.S., and were to be carried between the two Sault Ste. Marie cities by bonded motor vehicles. However, Americans could use the airline when going to or from Canadian destinations. TCA used Kinross from June 18, 1947, to July 31, 1961.

Within two years of opening, the temporary terminal at Sault Ste. Marie, Ontario, was considered inadequate. The Department of Transport yielded to public pressure and awarded a contract for the construction of the present terminal, which began service in July 1964. It was expanded in 1985, and again in 1988.

By 1970, traffic justified air traffic control service, which began in June from a mobile tower. In September, the staff moved into their permanent tower on top of the terminal building.

Since that time, site development has continued, the principal undertakings being the erection of a new services building, a fire hall, and, most recently, a structure to house administrative and maintenance functions. Airport tenants have themselves contributed three large hangars and some smaller structures.

"The Soo" is served today by Air Ontario and Canadian Partner, which provide direct service to Toronto, and by Norontair, which offers service to Toronto and Thunder Bay, and through-service to Winnipeg with stops at Dryden and

Kenora. Norontair operates Twin Otters on a scheduled service from several northern communities to connect with the major carriers at Sault Ste. Marie.

The Ontario Ministry of Natural Resources water bombers operate out of the airport, as do a number of charter firms: Ranger Lake Helicopters, Clarm-Aire Ltd., Air Dale Ltd., and Algoma Airways (which also operates a flying school).

In 1987, there were 56,000 aircraft movements and 272,500 passengers.

The following have served as airport managers:

J. Murphy	1961 to 1966
H. Mingle	1966 to 1980
J. Bell	1980

Sources:
1. Transport Canada, Ontario Region.
2. J. Bell, Airport Manager, Sault Ste. Marie Airport.
3. Material regarding three Michigan airports: Public Archives Canada, RG 70-6, Vol. 165-1526-10; RG-21, file 57,41G, 1948.
4. Alice Gibson Sutherland. *Canada's Aviation Pioneers*. Toronto: McGraw-Hill Ryerson Ltd., 1978.
5. James A. Pung. "The Houghton County Airport, 1944-1970," 1969 [unpublished transcript].

Schefferville Airport
(Québec, on the border of Labrador)

A 4,200 by 150 foot [1,280 by 46 metre] runway was constructed in September 1947 at Hana Lake, six and a half kilometres northwest of Schefferville to meet the needs of prospecting and mining in the region. It later became a public airport under the operation of Hollinger North Shore Exploration Company.

In October 1948, the runway was enlarged to 4,300 by 200 feet [1,310 by 61 metres], and a small terminal that included an aeradio station was constructed.

A licence for the operation of a seaplane base nearby, at Knob Lake, was issued in October 1950.

A new runway, 4,600 by 250 feet [1,402 by 76 metres], was constructed at Schefferville on the present site in November 1954, and a new seaplane base was established at Squaw Lake. Operations at Hana Lake and the Knob Lake seaplane base ceased in July 1954.

The airport came under the jurisdiction of the town of Schefferville in September 1955, and the licence stipulated that it must be operated as a public airport.

From 1953 to 1957, the Mid-Canada (radar) Line was under construction along the 59th parallel from Hopedale, Labrador, to Dawson Creek, British Columbia. Because the proposed sites were isolated, the helicopter was vital. Suppliers were flown into Knob Lake (Schefferville) Airport by conventional craft, and were then helicoptered by RCAF's 108 Communications Flight—which at the peak of its operations had twenty-five helicopters. The Mid-Canada Line came into operation in 1965; the Canadian Armed Forces unit left in September, and the airport became the responsibility of the Department of Transport.

In March 1959, Canadian Marconi Company contracted to operate and maintain the airport, and continued to do so until August 1977; then Québecair took over until August 1982, when Transport Bravo Inc. assumed responsibility.

A new terminal opened in 1967. It was formerly a Marconi Company hangar on the southwest side of the runway, 18-36—which was extended to 5,000 feet [1,524 metres] and paved in 1968.

The Société d'Energie de la Baie James (SEBJ) began operations at Schefferville in October 1974; and it and Airgava leased land from Transport in 1975.

The closure of the iron mine in 1983 led to a large migration of the town's inhabitants. The region still attracts mining activity, but hunting and fishing are the most important economic activities, and attract a large number of tourists between the months of June and September.

In 1987, the airport dealt with 10,400 passengers and 13,881 aircraft movements. Typically, 79 per cent of the annual movements take place during the summer season.

Québecair served the airport until November 1981, when Air Schefferville (Laurentian Air Service), and based at the airport, became the subcontractor for Québecair.

Sources:
Transport Canada, Québec Region.

Sept-Iles Airport
(Québec)

In December 1929, Trans-Continental Airways began to develop two landing strips of 2,400 feet [731 metres] long, at Sept-Iles with the intention of improving winter air-mail service. Further development of the airfield as an unemployment relief project was recommended to the government in 1932, but nothing was done until Québec Airways completed construction of two 2,900

181. Sept-Iles Airport, 1929. Trans-Continental hangar, Rue Brochu.

182. RCAF installations, constructed in 1943, Sept Iles.

foot [834 metre] strips, and obtained a temporary airport licence on April 8, 1939.

The present airport was constructed for the RCAF in 1942 as a base for operations against German submarines that were attacking shipping in the Gulf of St. Lawrence, and for aircraft being ferried to England by way of the northern route through Goose Bay. The first landing strip was made of steel mats and was used while the three permanent runways were being constructed of stabilized concrete. This new process consisted of laying forty-six centimetres of coarse rock, twenty-five centimetres of gravel, and fifteen centimetres of fine gravel and sand. Cement was worked into the gravel by sheepsfoot rollers, watered and graded. The surface, once set, made a rugged and uneven runway. There were no expansion joints and the surface soon deteriorated and cracked. The runways, 6,000 by 200 feet [1,829 by 61 metres], were paved in 1951. By October 15, 1944, the airport was placed on a caretaker basis, as the U.S. Air Force had established a similar facility at Mingan, approximately 161 kilometres to the east.

On December 26, 1945, the airport was transferred to the Department of Transport, a licence issued on February 18, 1946, and has been operated by the Department ever since. In 1946, the old Canadian Trans-Continental Airways field

183. Old and new terminal, Sept-Iles.

was abandoned and Canadian Pacific Airlines (CPAL) transferred its operations to the Department's airport. On December 1, 1947, it was decided that Sept-Iles Airport would be retained, and the USAF airport at Mingan (which was purchased by Canada at the end of the war), would be abandoned. Mingan was transferred to the province in 1951 and is now operated by the town of Mingan.

When Transport took over the airport in 1945, the buildings were in poor condition and required a great deal of repair. Until the heating plant was converted to oil in 1947, it was fired by two wood-fed boilers, for which the airport staff had to cut their own firewood.

Former airport manager George Langlois described the development of the airport in 1948 in the following manner:

In June 1948, the Iron Ore Company of Canada started on their Knob Lake project by building a railroad from Sept-Iles to Knob Lake (distance 355 miles [571 kilometres]) and the first phase of the project consisted of building landing strips every 10 miles [16 kilometres] on the right-of-way. This project brought Sept-Iles Airport into prominence as the hub of aviation of Eastern Québec as all supplies, materials and equipment had to be airlifted to the various air-strips. Aircraft were chartered from all of Canada and, at one time, 35 aeroplanes were operating 24-hours-a-day and 365-days-a-year. This created untold problems as freight, materials, food, equipment, etc., had to be stored pending airlifting to various sites. A hangar, two garages, various material storage sheds, and movable dwellings for eighty pilots and engineers were erected as these facilities were non-existent in the Village of Sept-Iles.

Over the years, Sept-Iles has become an important transportation centre. It has the railway to the northern mines, the shipping port for ore carriers, and the transfer and supply point for passengers and freight to Schefferville (Knob Lake), Wabush, Labrador city, Fermont, and Basse Côte Nord.

Sept-Iles Airport is also the maintenance centre for Aviation Québec Labrador, Inter Québec, QNS&L, and the Québec Cartier Mining Co.

In 1954, the administration building left by the RCAF was replaced by an air terminal building with a control tower. This was followed by the installation of ILS (Instrument Landing System), VOR (VHF Omni-directional Range), and VH D/F (Very High Frequency Direction Finding).

In 1978, Transport Canada opened a new air terminal to the south of the former one. Constructed at a cost of $5.5 million and covering 6,000 square metres with car parks and access roads, the terminal can handle one million passengers annually.

The airport, which has three paved runways: 05-23, 1,798 metres; 09-27, 2,003 metres; and 13-31, 1,840 metres, is served by Inter Canadian, Air Alliance, Air Labrador Québec, Iron Ore Co. Aviation, Alexandair, Heli-littoral, Viking Helicopters, Québec Cartier Mining Company.

Sept-Iles Airport provides direct employment for about 250 persons and its presence creates approximately 125 indirect jobs. It generates approximately $11.5 million annually in spin-offs, which represents gross salaries and operating expenses.

In 1987, there were 122,900 passengers and 34,468 aircraft movements.

The following have served as airport managers for Transport Canada:

George Langlois	1946 to 1971
Joe Valkovic	1971 to 1973
Raynald Imbeault	1973 to 1975
Robert Francis	1976 to 1978
Pierre Coutu	1979 to 1981
Suzanne Levis	1982 to 1985
Ronald Menard	1985 to 1989
Alain Bastarache	1989

Sources:

1. Transport Canada, Québec Region.
2. J.L.G. Langlois, former Airport Manager, Sept-Iles Airport.
3. R.L. Clarke, "Airport Notes" (Ottawa: Transport Canada) [unpublished collection].

Sioux Lookout Airport
(Ontario)

Sioux Lookout Airport, one and a half kilometres north of the town, was one of the one hundred-mile intermediate aerodromes on the Trans-Canada Airway.

Construction of a turf runway began in 1935 as an unemployment relief project, and it was ready for use late in the following year. In 1938, a paved runway was constructed. Essential buildings were erected from 1936 to 1937, and a permanent licence was issued in the name of the Department of Transport on November 18, 1946.

The airport is now operated by the town of Sioux Lookout and has two runways: 16-34 is paved and 1,280 by 30 metres; 03-21 is gravel and 689 by 23 metres.

In 1984, an air terminal building (which also houses a new flight service station) was constructed, as well as a parking lot with a capacity for fifty parked cars.

Anticipated plans for the spring of 1990 involved changing the existing gravel runway 03-21 into a taxiway and renovating the taxiway into an apron area, so as to alleviate aircraft movement problems.

Three air charter companies are based at the airport: Weagmoe Air, Bearskin Lake Airways, and Frontier Air.

In 1987, there were 43,900 passengers and, in 1988, there were 28,318 aircraft movements.

Sources:
1. Transport Canada, Central Region.
2. R.L. Clarke, "Airport Notes" (Ottawa: Transport Canada) [unpublished collection].
3. Calvin Hart, Public Works Superintendent, Municipality of Sioux Lookout.

Smithers Airport
(British Columbia)

The Smithers District Chamber of Commerce started to develop the first Smithers airfield in 1929, on land which the Chamber had bought three kilometres from the village. Ownership of the land was later transferred to Smithers. Money for the project was provided by the Chamber of Commerce, the village, and donations from public-spirited citizens. In March 1933, the Chamber of Commerce asked the federal government (Departments of Labour and National Defence) for a financial contribution as a labour relief measure to complete the work already begun on the airfield's grass runway: it wanted to extend the runway, widen the cleared area, and level and prepare two more runways. The first airplane to use the airfield was flown by Jimmy

Mattern, the famous American aviator who was flying from Alaska, and landed at the Smithers Aerodrome on July 26, 1933.

The village of Smithers applied for an airport licence in March 1936.

In December 1940, the existing grass airfield was declared inadequate. The Department of Transport carried out a detailed survey for the Department of National Defence, to find a site that could be used as an emergency facility on the Prince Rupert to Alaska route. Land was expropriated in November 1941, and construction began approximately three kilometres northwest of Smithers.

On May 6, 1943, the airfield, with a 4,400 foot [1,341-metre] asphalt runway, was officially opened as RCAF Station Smithers. The station was disbanded on March 31, 1944, and on the following day, No. 17 Staging Unit was formed. This was disbanded on August 11, 1945. From 1943 to 1945, construction of airport support facilities continued; but there was little air activity and Smithers was used mostly for the storage of aircraft and as a staging point, for Hurricanes, Harvards, and Venturas.

After the war, the airport was transferred to the Department of Transport and a licence was issued in the name of Transport on April 1, 1946.

Aircraft activity continued to be limited between 1945 and 1951; but aeradio facilities were provided, and winter maintenance of the runway was achieved by rolling and packing the snow. Although Lake Kathlyn (adjacent to the airport) was used by float aircraft, it could not be formally developed as a seaplane base, as it did not meet the minimum Department of Transport requirements.

Passenger service was introduced in 1953 by Canadian Pacific Airlines (CPA) DC-3s, with flights to Terrace and Prince George three times a week.

In 1955, the runway was overlaid and extended to 5,000 feet [1,524 metres]. CPA introduced

Convair aircraft to Terrace, and Smithers was designated as an alternate.

With the opening of the new airport at Prince Rupert in 1961, Smithers was no longer required as the alternate to Terrace. CPA flights were reduced to weekend service only, and airport winter maintenance was reduced to the rolling and packing of runways.

In 1970, a new terminal was opened; and Pacific Western Airlines introduced Boeing 737 jet service in June 1973.

Today, the airport, which is operated by Transport Canada, and has one paved runway, 14-32, 5,000 by 150 feet [1,524 by 46 metres]. It is serviced by the following scheduled airlines: Canadian Airlines International, offering two jet flights daily to and from Vancouver with a stop at Terrace; Skylink Airlines, with two flights daily to and from Vancouver with a stop at Terrace; Central Mountain Air, with service to Prince George, Terrace, Dease Lake, Brown Creek, Studee Valley, and Stewart.

The following operations are based at the airport: Northern Mountain Helicopters; Highland Helicopters; Smithers Flying Training; B.C. Ministry of Forests (tanker base); McKnight Aviation Services; and Van Alpen Exploration.

The following have served as airport managers:

P. Theibolt	1946 to 1949
A. Davies	1949 to 1958
P. Lychak	1958 to 1964
F. Hill	1964 to 1974
L. Rowand	1974 to 1975
A. Fewster	1975 to 1982
J. Perry	1982 to 1989

The airport had 47,800 passengers in 1988 and there were 20,245 aircraft movements during that year.

Sources:
1. Transport Canada, Pacific Region.
2. R.L. Clarke, "Airport Notes" (Ottawa: Transport Canada) [unpublished collection].

Spence Bay Airport
(Northwest Territories)

The airport, located on the Boothia Peninsula, Northwest Territories, is licensed and operated by the government of the Northwest Territories.

The present facility is a vast improvement over what existed to serve the community a few years ago. The old runway, still evident at one end, is on the present south VASIS (Visual Approach Slope Indicator System) pad. It was short and narrow with poor quality binding material that created many soft areas.

The present gravel runway, initially developed to Arctic C standard (3,000 feet [914 metres]) in 1977 has been extended to 3,600 feet [1,097 metres]. But both facility users and the community believe that further expansion would make the runway comparable with other airports of the region, and attract larger aircraft on scheduled services.

Spence Bay, like most small communities of the Kitikmeot, takes pride in its airport: this is evident in its neat and organized appearance.

With the addition of a fuel dispenser unit and an ARCAL (Aircraft Radio Control of Aerodrome Lighting) unit installed in 1985, the airport offers a full range of services to the air carriers of the region. First Air has a scheduled service at Spence Bay.

In 1988, there were 871 aircraft movements and 3,700 passengers.

Sources:
1. The government of the Northwest Territories.
2. Transport Canada, Central Region.

Springbank Airport
(Alberta)

Springbank Airport, thirteen kilometres west of Calgary, was constructed on the former McLaurin farm and began operations in February 1969. The initial site was 1,040 acres [421 hectares]. Transport Canada owns and operates the airport.

The site was constructed to serve as a satellite of Calgary International Airport for low-speed aircraft and flying training. Springbank has two paved runways: 07-25, 3,400 feet [1,036 metres], and 16-34, 3,000 feet [914 metres] long. Both were resurfaced in 1973; and overlays to all runways and taxiways were effected in 1988.

In February 1970, night flying operations were authorized, and a new control tower opened in December of the same year. The flight service station was moved from Calgary International Airport to Springbank Airport in 1988.

The facility serves recreational, private, commercial, corporate, and flying training operations. The following enterprises are based there:

Flying Training:	Calgary Flying Club
	North American Air Training College
	Calgary Flight Training Centre
	Mount Royal College
Charter:	Calgary Flight Services
	North American Air
Lease/Overhaul/Storage:	R.J. Peacock Holdings
	Cavalier Aviation
	Mustang Maintenance
	Rocky Mountain Aircraft
Aircraft Storage:	Arnold T. Hangars
	Arrowhead Aero-motive
Avionics:	Okanagan Avionics

184. Control tower, Springbank Airport, Alberta, 1978.

Traffic increased from 7,651 movements in 1969 to a peak of 241,058 in 1979, almost reaching the saturation point; however, the recession in the early 1980s resulted in a drastic downturn with a low of 114,133 movements in 1988 and an overall ranking of 20th. The first quarter of 1989 has shown a substantial increase in traffic over the same period in 1988.

The following served as airport managers:

Jake Wiens	1969 to 1973
Don Hector	1973 to 1976
Joe Hennessey	1976 to 1977
John Kish	1977

Source:
Transport Canada, Western Region.

Stephenville Airport
(Newfoundland)

Stephenville Airport was constructed in 1941 by the United States under the terms of the Leased Bases Agreement of March 27, 1941, negotiated between the United States and the United Kingdom.[1] It is located on the west coast of Newfoundland, 451 air kilometres west of St. John's, eighty kilometres from Corner Brook (the principal city on the west coast), and 322 kilometres west of Gander. Today, the airport serves an area population of 50,000.

The ninety-nine year lease from Newfoundland to the U.S. was for land at Stephenville, Argentia, and St. John's, and gave retroactive authority for land already taken over and on which construction had already begun. The land was "free from all rent and charges, other than compensation to be mutually agreed on to be paid by the United States, in order to compensate the owners of private property for loss by expropriation or damage arising out of the establishment of the said bases and facilities."[2] "In August 1943, the British government offered to assume even these costs as a reverse lend lease charge, and the offer was accepted."[3] Upon the determination of the lease, the lands were to revert to the Crown in right of the government of Newfoundland.

The initial lease for Stephenville covered 867 acres [351 hectares] of land, and construction there actually began on March 10, 1941.

The United States was not at war at the time (early 1941) that the bases at Stephenville, Argentia, and St. John's were set up. When the first American troops arrived in St. John's in January 1941, their role was to defend U.S. military and naval installations in Newfoundland and to co-operate with Canadian and British forces in defending Newfoundland and Canadian coastal zones. They were also there to support the American naval forces and, in prescribed boundaries, to destroy any German or Italian naval, air, or ground forces encountered.[4]

When established in April 1941, the base was called Stephenville Air Base, but in June of that year, it was redesignated Harmon Field in honour of Captain Ernest Emery Harmon, an ace of the U.S. Army Air Corps who was killed in an air crash in 1933. On February 13, 1948, the base was renamed Ernest Harmon Air Force Base.

From April 1, 1941, until September 1, 1943, the base was under the control of the Newfoundland Base Command, U.S. Army and was assigned to Eastern Base Command. On September 1, 1943, Harmon was placed under control of the Commanding General, North Atlantic Wing, Air Transport Command (later Military Air Transport Service). On October 1, 1950, Harmon became part of the newly formed Northeast Air Command, which was dissolved on April 1, 1957, and Harmon was transferred to the Eighth Air Force of Strategic Air Command.

The following units operated Harmon during the history of the base:

1388th Army Air Force Base Unit	—May 1941 to January 1948
1226th Air Base Group	—February 1948 to October 1950
6602nd Air Base Wing	—October 1950 to August 1952
6602nd Air Base Group	—August 1952 to June 1954
6605th Air Base Wing	—June 1954 to April 1957
4081st Strategic Wing	—April 1957 to 1966

Building construction in 1941 was of the temporary frame type. From 1947 through 1949, eight two-storey, 125-man permanent frame dormitories; 247 family housing units; a six hundred-seat theatre; a headquarters building; forty-eight-man bachelor officer quarters (BOQs); two five-hundred-man dining halls; and four sixty-eight-man civilian dormitories were built. The third major construction program was carried out between 1951 and 1957 when $95 million was spent to reconstruct the runway, taxiway, apron and ramp systems and to build eleven hangars, including the alert hangar and the double cantilever heavy bomber hangar. Many other features needed to make Harmon a modern facility were

constructed, such as a one-hundred-bed hospital; seven BOQs; four dining halls; two six-storey, seven-hundred-airmen dormitories; a fuel system; central heating plant; a modern grade-school; and two hundred family housing units.

After VE Day in May 1945, two major movements of aircraft to the United States took place over the North Atlantic ferry route. The AAF White Project, for the return of tactical aircraft for redeployment to other theatres, involved the movement of 3,004 aircraft by July 15—which, incidentally, returned over 50,000 personnel with the loss of only one aircraft and no lives. The Green Project called for the air transportation to the United States of personnel eligible for discharge. Under this project, in a ninety-day period ending in mid-September, 160,000 passengers were transported without fatality, and, by mid-September, passengers transported under the WhiteProject had exceeded 80,000. Throughout these movements, the major burden was borne by the main bases at Stephenville, Gander, and Goose.[5]

In 1957, Transport, with the approval of the American authorities, built a small air terminal at Stephenville for the use of Canadian air carriers. It was located on the boundary of the air base so that the public using it would not have to enter American property, while on the airside it had access to the runways. Under an agreement with Transport, the terminal was operated and maintained by TCA.

On December 7, 1965, the American government notified Canada, under the provisions of the 1941 Leased Bases Agreement, of its intention to abandon Harmon Field on December 31, 1966, and it began to reduce the scale of operations in May 1966.

Because the Department of National Defence had no need for Harmon Field, the Department of Transport took it over as a civil airport on June 30, 1966. A licence was issued in August, and Transport has continued to manage the site—Stephenville Airport—since then.

By Cabinet decision of March 3, 1966, the government of Canada gave a quit claim in favour of Newfoundland of all reversionary interests in the U.S. Base at Harmon Field, provided that the province of Newfoundland would transfer lands and appurtenances to the federal government as might be required for the performance or provision of services that were normally a federal responsibility.[6]

At takeover, the airport personnel consisted of forty people and included the airport manager, an office supervisor, the fire chief, a supervisor of airfield and building maintenance. Sufficient tradespeople, equipment operators, mechanics, electricians and security personnel were employed to maintain the airfield and about twenty Department of Transport buildings.

The Telecommunications Branch of Transport moved its operations from St. Andrew's in 1966, and in May 1969, occupied a new centre in building 161. In August 1974, the Canadian Coast Guard moved from Corner Brook to Stephenville to make a combined marine-aeradio station of twenty personnel. This arrangement was changed in 1979, when the Canadian Coast Guard took marine radio operations to a building outside the airport boundary.

In 1966, the air traffic control branch of Transport began its operation of the former American control tower, but closed down after two years, because there was too little traffic.

Stephenville has been one of the designated weather alternates for Gander since the beginning of regular passenger service across the Atlantic in the autumn of 1945. Because of the limited range of the aircraft then in use on the Atlantic route, the airport was used extensively in its alternate role. American carriers tried to get permission to use Stephenville instead of Gander on a regular basis, as they felt landing fees at Gander were too high. However, the Bases Agreement precluded the use of Stephenville for civil aviation purposes except in emergencies.

In 1949, TCA (to become Air Canada) began providing regular flights to Halifax and Montréal under an agreement with the USAF. Air Canada continued flights from Stephenville to Montréal and Toronto using DC-9 and Boeing 737 aircraft until June 1969, when the airline ceased operations at the airport.

Eastern Provincial Airways (EPA) had commenced flying through Stephenville in 1967 with daily flights to points in Newfoundland and capital cities in eastern Canada, using B-737s on all its flights. EPA ceased operations at Stephenville in January 1986, when the service was taken over by Air Atlantic, using Dash 8-type aircraft.

Stephenville's main runway, 10-28, is 3,048 by 61 metres. A secondary crosswind runway 02-20, 1,341 by 46 metres, is used for daytime VFR (Visual Flight Rules) only.

The following have served as airport managers since Transport took over the operation of the airport:

Hiram Noel	1966 to 1974
Lester C. Clarke	1975 to 1978
Frederick C. Smith	1978 to 1980
Alphonsus Hawco	1980 to 1984
David W. Bussey	1984

In 1988, there were 65,500 passengers and 11,056 aircraft movements.

Sources:
1. Transport Canada, Atlantic Region.
2. Transport Canada, Stephenville Airport.

Footnotes—Stephenville Airport

[1] The agreement provided for ninety-nine year land leases to the U.S. in Newfoundland, Bermuda, the Bahamas, Jamaica, Antigua, St. Lucia, Trinidad, and British Guiana for the establishment of U.S. military bases. In the case of Newfoundland and Bermuda, the base rights "were given 'freely and without consideration.' The other base rights in the Caribbean area were granted in exchange for fifty over-age American destroyers." Stanley W. Dzinban, United States Army in World War II: *Military Reactions between United States and Canada*, 1939-1945 (Washington: Office of the Chief of Military History, Department of the Army, 1959), pp. 164 and 165.

[2] Government of Newfoundland, The American Bases Act, no. 12, 1941.

[3] Dzinban, p. 165.

[4] See Dzinban, p. 157 and following.

[5] Dzinban, p. 192.

[6] Canada, Department of Transport, file 5151-1108, vol. 2 and 3.

Sudbury Airport
(Ontario)

In 1952, the Department of National Defence built a single strip, 6,600 feet [2,012 metres] long at Sudbury for use as an emergency landing field for CF-100 aircraft operating out of North Bay.

The community was well aware of the value of commercial air service to the Sudbury area, and an airport committee was established to explore the possibilities. On February 25, 1953, the Sudbury Airport Committee was empowered to proceed with arrangements to build a second runway and a terminal at the airfield and also to try to get TCA to serve the city with a regular service.

An arrangement was made whereby (a) TCA would provide service if and when a second runway was built; and (b) the Department of Transport would build a second runway if Sudbury built the terminal.

The terminal, built by the city with contributions from the International Nickel Company of

Canada, Falconbridge, and the Department of Transport, was completed on February 28, 1955.

TCA began regular service on February 1, 1954, and on April 1 of the same year, the federal government leased the airport to the city for one dollar a year.

In 1968, an ILS (Instrument Landing System) went into service on runway 04-22. In the same year, Manitou Airways built a hangar for its flying school and aircraft maintenance.

From 1954 to 1972, the airport was operated by an airport commission that included representatives of the city of Sudbury and the towns of Copper Cliff and Falconbridge. The introduction of regional government in 1972, saw the commission phased out, and the airport became a section of the city's transportation department.

In 1972, a control tower was manned by the Department of Transport. In 1973, a new air terminal building was opened as part of a six-year improvement program. Runway 04-22 (2,012 metres) was resurfaced in 1977, and 11-29 (1,524 metres), was similarly upgraded during the following year.

Norontair began service to Sudbury in 1971 with connections to Sault Ste. Marie, North Bay, Timmins, and Elliot Lake. First Air operates to North Bay and Ottawa. Air Canada provides service to Toronto and Thunder Bay, and Voyageur flies to Toronto Island. Air Ontario and Canadian Partner also offer scheduled service.

The following operations are based at the airport: Voyageur (maintenance base), Imperial Esso (operated under contract by Voyageur), Cambrian Aviation (which runs Shell refuelling), the Ministry of Government Services (an air ambulance), the Sudbury Flying Club, and the Ministry of Natural Resources (fire attack base).

The city operates the airport under an agreement with Transport Canada and receives a subsidy to cover the operating deficit.

In 1988 Sudbury had 86,706 aircraft movements and 236,400 passengers.

The following served as airport managers under the city:

Clarence Clark   1954 to 1976
O.G. Myers   1976

Sources:
1. Transport Canada, Ontario Region.
2. O.G. Myers, Airport Manager, Sudbury Airport.

Swift Current Airport
(Saskatchewan)

Swift Current Airport, located eight kilometres east of the city, was developed in 1937 as one of the hundred-mile airports on the Trans-Canada Airway, and supplied weather and navigation services.

In 1940, when the airport was developed by the Department of National Defence as an RCAF training station for the British Commonwealth Air Training Plan, three paved runways and associated taxiways were constructed for the RAF No. 39 Service Flying Training School and No. 4 Air Navigation School.

The airport was taken over by the Department of Transport in 1946, which operates it today. TCA began scheduled service through Swift Current in 1947.

The site has three paved runways: 12-30, 1,295 metres; 03-21, 869 metres; and 07-25, which is not maintained. Runway 03-21 and the east taxiway were rebuilt in 1988.

The airport has a small wartime terminal building and two hangars, one of which was used as a museum for old farm equipment until 1969; it is now vacant. The other hangar houses Swift Current Flying Service.

The airport was the base of Mel-Air, which operated non-scheduled services from 1960 to 1970. Southern Frontier provided scheduled service to Regina, March to July 1980, and to Calgary, March 1980 to January 1981. Swift Current Flying Service also provides charter service.

In 1988, there were 11,366 aircraft movements.

The following served as airport managers:

Department of Transport   1947 to 1970
Al Smith (Smith Air)   1970 to 1976
Ed Bellay (Smith Air)   1976 to 1980
Randy Barlow   1980 to 1982
Ed Bellay   1982 to 1984
Dave Halliday   1984 to 1988
Cal Townsend   1988 to present

Sources:
1. Transport Canada, Central Region.
2. R.L. Clarke, "Airport Notes" (Ottawa: Transport Canada) [unpublished collection].
3. Cal Townsend, Airport Manager, Swift Current Airport.

Sydney Airport
(Nova Scotia)

The first Sydney Airport, developed in June 1929 through the efforts of the Cape Breton Flying Club, was located at MacMillan Farm, halfway between Sydney and Glace Bay. Two landing Strips 1,800 feet [549 metres] long, were constructed, and, on August 3, 1929, the site was given a temporary airport licence. In 1927, the federal government offered to finance a municipal airport if the city acquired the land, but the proposal was not accepted.

In August 1938, the Department of National Defence began the construction of a new airport at Sydney for the RCAF at a site thirteen kilome-

185. Sydney Airport, Nova Scotia, 1931.

tres east of Sydney on Route 4. This was to have three-runways, each 4,000 by 200 feet [1,219 by 61 metres]. The flying club airport was closed down when the new RCAF site was completed in 1940.

Further developments occurred between 1940 and 1943, including the extension of the runways to 5,000 feet [1,524 metres] to meet operational needs. The airport was used throughout the war by bomber reconnaissance aircraft of the RCAF, which were engaged in anti-submarine operations off the Atlantic Coast and in the Gulf of St. Lawrence. Sydney had a fighter squadron for local defence.

The RAF Ferry Command and the Return Ferry Service used Sydney as a staging point and as an alternate on their transatlantic operations.

RCAF Station Sydney was closed down on December 31, 1945, and the Department of Transport took over operation of the airport on March 5, 1946, in support of Trans-Canada Air Lines' service to Sydney. All the buildings not required by Transport were declared surplus and sold; the airport was designated as an alternate for the North Atlantic air route, and a licence was issued on March 10, 1947.

In October 1950, runway 07-25 was relocated and also extended to 7,070 feet [2,155 metres]. During the following years, most of the hard-surfaced areas deteriorated, partly through lack of maintenance. In 1958, Transport's regional office in Moncton recommended the development of a new airport because of the high cost of renewing and developing the existing area. But Ottawa did not agree, and runway 01-19 was extended to 6,000 feet [1,829 metres] in 1958. In March 1962, runway 14-32 was closed because of its poor condition. A large-scale rebuilding program followed, which included the construction of a new terminal building in 1967.

The western half of the runway 14-32 was reactivated for summer operation in 1976. The ILS (Instrument Landing System) on runway 07 was replaced in 1977, and VASIS (Visual Approach Slope Indicator System) was installed on runway 25. A new ILS was installed on runway 19 in 1978 to replace one destroyed in a storm in October 1974. Runway 01-19 was recapped in 1977, and 07-25 was similarly upgraded in 1980. The main ramp and taxiway K were extended in 1982.

Today the airport has three runways: 01-19, 1,829 metres; 07-25, 2,155 metres; and 14-32, 914 metres.

From 1966 to 1978, hangars were constructed by Eastern Flying Services Ltd., Okanagan Helicopters Ltd., Transport Canada, and Versatile Air Services.

186. First Sydney Airport, Nova Scotia, c. 1930.

Sydney is served by Air Canada, Canadian Airlines International, Air Nova, Air Atlantic, and Air St. Pierre. Cape Breton Flying School, Eastern Flying Services Ltd., Versatile Air Services, and Bras d'Or Construction are also based at the airport.

Sydney Airport serves Cape Breton Island, with a population of 166,116 (1986), and in 1988 had 183,000 passengers and 17,462 aircraft movements.

The following have served as airport managers since 1946:

C.J. MacDonald	1946 to 1947
E.A. King	1947 to 1959
H.O. Toole	1959 to 1960
J.J. Cole	1961 to 1964
D.M. Willmer	1965 to 1966
J.R. MacIntyre	1966 to 1983
F.J. Whelan	1983

Sources:
1. Transport Canada, Atlantic Region.
2. R.L. Clarke, "Airport Notes" (Ottawa: Transport Canada) [unpublished collection].

Terrace Airport
(British Columbia)

Terrace Airport was constructed in 1943 for the Department of National Defence as part of the Home War Establishment on the route from Vancouver to Prince Rupert via the Fraser Valley, approximately thirteen kilometres from the city of Terrace.

The airport was transferred to the Department of Transport in 1946, and a temporary licence for day operations was issued on April 15, 1946. An aerodrome keeper was appointed that year. A permanent licence was issued on July 8, 1947.

In 1949, winter maintenance of the airport was discontinued because other area airports—Smithers and Sandspit—were available.

Canadian Pacific Airlines began scheduled service to Terrace in 1951 because of the Alcan development at Kitimat, and airport maintenance was resumed. The site was licensed for night operation in December 1956 and became a Customs port of entry in November 1958.

From 1957 to 1959 the airport was upgraded to main line status. A new air terminal building was constructed in 1968 and the main runway was rebuilt in 1974. Today, the airport has three paved runways: 15-33, 1,829 metres long; 09-27, 1,620 metres; and 03-21, 1,638 metres (all are 61 metres wide). The air terminal building was improved in 1978, and, in 1988, a second floor was constructed on top of the old flight service station (FSS), to give the new FSS a better view of the runway, and to house Atmospheric Environmental Services (AES).

The airport has a catchment area of approximately 40,000 people and serves two main cities, Kitimat and Terrace. It is served by five air carriers: Canadian Airlines International, Air BC, and Skylink, all providing service to Vancouver via either Prince Rupert or Smithers; Trans Provincial Airlines, with scheduled and freight service to areas north of Terrace; and Central Mountain Air, with scheduled air service to Prince George via Smithers.

General aviation is represented by several private aircraft owners and operators.

Coastal Mountain Flying School provides *ab initio* flying training. It began operations in Smithers using Terrace as a satellite school, but in 1989 Mark Adam, the owner, moved the school to Terrace.

In 1988, there were 89,700 passengers and 13,973 aircraft movements.

The following served as airport managers:

H. Leusley	1949 to 1954
W. Mitchell	1954 to 1968
S. Harris	1968 to 1976
W. Mitchell	1976 to 1978
G. Lund	1978 to 1981
T.W. Cook	1981 to 1983
Darryl Laurent	1983

Sources:
1. Transport Canada, Pacific Region.
2. R.L. Clarke, "Airport Notes" (Ottawa: Transport Canada) [unpublished collection].

The Pas Airport
(Manitoba)

The Pas has the distinction of being the destination of the first known charter flight in Manitoba—perhaps in all of Canada. In October 1920, Hector Dougal, who was running a freelance air service, Canadian Aircraft, out of Winnipeg, was approached by F.J. Stanley, a fur trader from The Pas with a proposition to fly him into his home town. With this flight, he became renowned in the eyes of his townsmen as the first to fly into that northern outpost. The direct distance is about 483 kilometres—but to fly direct was out of the question in those days. Dougal had an Avro 504, rigged as a three-seater; an air engineer, Frank Ellis, an early aviation pioneer and later author of Canada's Flying Heritage, was the third member of the party. The route chosen lay north of Portage la Prairie over Gladstone, Dauphin, Swan River, and Hudson Bay Junction. After many difficulties and several unscheduled stops, they made it into The Pas four days after leaving Winnipeg (a trip that takes a couple of hours today). After carefully reviewing the situation, the intrepid airmen decided they had had enough and shipped the aircraft back to Winnipeg by rail.

As early as 1921, the Manitoba government Air Services initiated limited summer forestry patrols with HS-2L flying boats operating from Norway House Grace Lake. The Pas again came into the aviation picture in 1928, when it was a point of call on Punch Dickins' famous 4,000-mile [6,437 kilometre] swing through the Northwest Territories. (He started in Winnipeg and returned via The Pas, taking about forty hours over a period of twelve days). The Pas was also frequently used by Northern Aerial Mineral Explorations and Dominion Explorations in 1928 and 1929; and many other bush pilots regularly called at The Pas during these pioneer days.

The Pas Airport was constructed in 1942 as part of the Crimson Route[1] for the U.S. Air Force, which wanted a staging route from the American west coast to Europe, with shorter stage lengths than the northeast route via Goose Bay and Greenland. Canada showed little enthusiasm for the project at the time, but it was completed, nevertheless, with some Canadian aid. The route was conceived as running from the rich industrial areas of northern California, across north Hudson Bay, south Baffin Island, Greenland, and Iceland to the United Kingdom. Canada constructed the airport at The Pas; the U.S. (with Canadian approval) built airports at Churchill, Coral Harbour, Fort Chimo, and Frobisher. Although the route was never used for ferrying purposes, the Canadian airports played a very important role during the construction of the DEW Line in 1955, and in the development of the Arctic.

In 1942, Canada began construction at the Clearwater Lake site, thirty-two kilometres northeast of The Pas and 483 kilometres northwest of Winnipeg. The additional facilities and services required to bring the base up to USAF standards as a military field were paid for by the American government, and included navigation and communications equipment, operations buildings, barracks and associated facilities. In May 1943, the military decided that The Pas Airport was no longer needed. As a result, the runway requirements were scaled down, and only those projects that had reached 50 per cent completion were finished.

The Pas Airport was operated by the USAF until the end of the war, with Canadian radio operators; and it was used to a limited extent by military aircraft of both countries. But Canada had not supported the Crimson Route: it doubted that the route would ever be used. However, since the government did not want to leave any loophole for American legislators to claim property or other special rights in Canada, it purchased the American installations. Canada spent more than $27 million to ensure its sovereignty.

In October 1944, the Department of National Defence advised the Department of Transport that the USAF would be vacating The Pas. Transport took possession in September 1945, but because of budget constraints at Transport, National Defence paid the maintenance costs until the spring of 1947. A temporary licence was issued in the name of Transport on October 25, 1946, and RCAF buildings and land were formally transferred on January 27, 1947. The permanent licence was issued on July 8, 1947.

Soon after World War II, the RCAF began to use The Pas as a base during aerial photographic

187. The Pas Airport, Manitoba.

surveys. Charter operators were also attracted to the airport. In 1947, Canadian Pacific Airlines began a scheduled air service on the Winnipeg-Dauphin-The Pas-Flin Flon route, and Transair, (then known as Central Northern Airways), began a charter service. Canadian Airlines International and Territorial Helicopter are based there.

The airport provides electrical and building upkeep for Flin Flon, Lynn Lake, Thompson, Ennadai, Gillam, Norway House, Island Lake and Swan River.

The Pas has two runways: 12-30, built in 1942-43, rebuilt in 1965, and reconditioned in 1986; 08-26, built in 1942-43 and partly rebuilt in 1964 and 1965. In 1966, taxiway C was restored, security fencing installed, and the runways rewired.

The concrete ramp area, which was rebuilt in 1965, is large enough to accommodate several large aircraft.

The following have served as managers:

Jack Smythe	1947 to 1953
Alex Clarke	1953 to 1957
Wilf Morley	1957 to 1960
Gordon Docking	1960 to 1964
Andy Quin	1964 to 1967
George Elliott	1967 to 1969
Bill Scales	1969 to 1975
E.C. (Bud) Codd	1975 to 1984
D. Fahlgren	1984 to present

Sources:

1. Transport Canada, Central Region.
2. R.L. Clarke, Airport Notes (Ottawa: Transport Canada) [unpublished collection].

Footnote—The Pas Airport

[1] See Chapter 10.

Thompson Airport
(Manitoba)

Thompson Airport, located nine and a half kilometres north of the city, was originally built by the International Nickel Co. in 1961 to support the company's mining operations, and had one runway of 3,000 feet [914 metres].

The airport was transferred to the Department of Transport in 1963 and is now operated by the Local Government District of Mystery Lake under lease from Transport, and with an operating subsidy.

Runway 05-23, 5,400 by 150 feet [1,646 by 46 metres], was paved by Transport in 1964 to accommodate turbine aircraft, and was extended to 5,800 feet [1,768 metres] in 1972. The second runway, 14-32, constructed in 1971, is gravel, and 2,500 by 100 feet [762 by 30 metres]. An ILS (Instrument Landing System) was commissioned during 1970, followed by a VOR (VHF Omni-directional Range) in 1971, a DME (Distance Measuring Equipment) in 1973, and a VHF-DF (Very High Frequency Direction Finding) in 1975. A temporary control tower was installed in 1971, with a permanent control tower building commissioned in October 1974.

The air terminal building was completed in 1967, financed by a capital grant from Transport, and was doubled in size in 1971. During 1987 and 1988, additional hangar lots were added to the north side of the airport, and delta taxiway was constructed to accommodate new tenants. As of 1989, tenants on the north apron are Manitoba Government Air, RCMP Air Division, Custom Helicopters, Calm Air International, Northwinds Airlines, and Air Manitoba.

The airport is served by Canadian Airlines International with flights to Winnipeg, Flin Flon, and The Pas. It is also a base for Calm Air International, Northwinds Airlines, Northern Inc., Skyward Aviation, Nunasi Central Airlines,

Custom Helicopters, Manitoba Government Air, and the RCMP. Water bombers are based at the airport during the firefighting season.

In 1969, there were 12,380 aircraft movements, which increased to 41,319 in 1988; the airport had 81,700 passengers in 1979, and 105,200 in 1988.

Douglas R. Gillon became the Thompson airport manager in 1982, succeeding C.W. Weir. Don C. Taylor is the current manager.

Sources:

1. Transport Canada, Central Region.
2. Local Government District of Mystery Lake.

Thunder Bay Airport
Previously known as Fort William Municipal Airport and, later, Lakehead Airport
(Ontario)

In January 1927, the Department of National Defence (then responsible for civil aviation) wrote to a number of cities across Canada, including Fort William,[1] suggesting that they provide airports to serve their respective communities. Fort William showed some interest, and, with the neighbouring city of Port Arthur, asked the department to locate a suitable site for the airport.

On March 19, 1929, an airport licence was issued to the Fort William Aero Club. This covered a site called Bishop Field, thirteen kilometres west of the city near the municipal golf course, and had an airstrip 2,000 feet [609 metres] long. The condition of the airport soon deteriorated and, in June 1931, the city of Fort William gave the club $1,200 to improve it. The licence lapsed on October 29, 1935, as the club did not renew its lease to the property. But on April 1, 1937, both the lease and the licence were renewed and, by August, the field had been extended to include two runways, 3,000 and 2,000 by 100 feet [914 and 609 by 30 metres]. Obstructions on the approaches, however, reduced the effective lengths to 1,900 and 1,600 feet [579 and 488 metres].

In October 1937, Fort William asked the new Department of Transport for help in constructing a new airport. A site was selected a half-kilometre south of Arthur Street in the township of Neebling; and in May 1938, the department agreed to give the city a grant to help construct the airport. These initiatives arose because Canadian Car and Foundry Co. Ltd. (Fort William), a Division of Hawker Siddley, was awarded a large contract in September 1937 to built a two-seater aircraft for Turkey: the Neebling site was close to the plant. Two hundred and forty acres [ninety-seven hectares] of land were purchased by the city, and work began on August 15, 1938. By March 1939, one runway was in operation. In November 1939, the department agreed to increase its grant. An airport licence was issued to the city on December 4, 1939.

Meanwhile, the club airport, Bishop Field, was sold to Canadian Car on May 11, 1937, and a licence was issued to the company for a private airport on May 19, 1938. The club was given free use of the field, and its instructor, O.J. Weiben, acted as airport manager. The licence was cancelled on May 1, 1940.

At the outbreak of the World War II, the aviation committee of the city recommended that the federal government assume control of the airport for use as a flying training field. The Department of Transport took over the airport by lease, effective July 2, 1940, and, while it remained a civil airport, the RCAF established No. 2 Elementary Flying Training School (EFTS) there under the British Commonwealth Air Training Plan (BCATP). The school was operated by Thunder Bay Flying Training School Ltd., a subsidiary of the Lakehead Flying Club. At the time, the airport had three grass landing strips.

After additional land was acquired in 1942, concrete runways 12-30 (4,120 feet [1,256 metres]) and 07-25 (4,700 feet [1,433 metres]) were constructed in the same year.

The EFTS closed in June 1944, and the RCAF turned over the buildings to the Canadian Car and Foundry Co. Ltd. for the remainder of the war. The Department of Transport took over the site in February 1946.

In March 1946, Transport offered to return the airport to the city, which declined to accept it. The airport licence, which was still in the city's name, was cancelled and reissued in favour of the Department of Transport on October 18, 1946.

The name of the airport was changed from Fort William Municipal to Lakehead Airport on May 28, 1947; and following the amalgamation of the cities of Fort William and Port Arthur in 1970, it was named Thunder Bay Airport. Trans-Canada Air Lines began serving Lakehead Airport on July 1, 1947. A new terminal building was opened in March 1953.

In 1952, the Department bought the airport land from the city of Fort William and also acquired the additional acreage necessary for extending runways 12-30 to 5,300 feet [1,615 metres] and 07-25 to 6,200 feet [1,890 metres]. In 1968, approximately ninety-eight acres [forty hectares] of land (122 metres from and parallel to Arthur Street) was bought, bringing the overall area of the airport to approximately 790 acres [320 hectares].

Improvements were made to the landing facilities: in 1948, a low intensity approach lighting system was installed on all the runways and, in 1950, an ILS (Instrument Landing System) was commissioned. In 1956, high intensity runway lighting was completed on runway 07-25, and high intensity approach lighting was installed on runway 07.

On August 2, 1958, the airport had an unusual visitor when the U.S. Navy Airship ZPG2 landed for fuel on a flight from Akron, Ohio, to Churchill, Resolute, and Ice Island T/ at 79°N and 121° W. The airship was on its way to a scientific party working at T3 on an International Geophysical Year project, and left Thunder Bay on the same day after a short stop.

The terminal building was extended in 1964 (there was a further extension in 1978), and in the same year, a new operations building housed the control tower which had been located on the roof of hangar no. 1, since traffic control began in June 1954. The present tower was opened in 1987.

Hangars no. 1 and 2, built during the war, were destroyed by fire on November 29, 1957.[2] Hangars 2 and 2A, occupied by Superior Airways (later Austin Airways), and hangar no. 3, occupied by Great Lakes Paper Company, now Norontair, were also of war vintage. Hangar No. 2 was destroyed by fire in 1969. The other hangars, occupied by Thunder Bay Flying Club, Kearney Aircraft, Viking Helicopters, I.N. Paterson, and Confederation College, were constructed in the post-war period. In 1977, the flying club constructed an additional hangar and aircraft handling facilities on the south side of taxiway C. This hangar is now occupied by Trans-Canada Pipelines.

The airport has a maintenance complex which serves Atikokan, Sioux Lookout, Armstrong, Big Trout Lake, Lansdown House, and Pickle Lake.

In 1982, runway 07/25 was rehabilitated, and $7.4 million allocated for infield development expansion, increased the commercial aviation and general aviation areas. In 1985, two new aprons were constructed: Apron 2 for itinerant aircraft parking, and Apron 1A, as stand parking for the third level carriers. To complement Apron 1A, the north end of the terminal was renovated to create the present Departure Area #2. Approach 12 was replaced in 1986 and an Apron 1 overlay was completed in 1987.

As a result of the deregulation of the airline industry in 1987, major air carriers have amalgamated and commuter airlines created. Thunder Bay Airport has since become a hub and spoke airport, linking northwest Ontario to Winnipeg in the west and Toronto in the east. As a result the present terminal services have been strained to meet the demand.

In 1980, Thunder Bay Airport had scheduled services from Air Canada, Nordair, Norontair, Bearskin Lake Airways and Austin Airways. Charter service was offered by the Thunder Bay Flying Club, Lakehead Flying School, and by Austin—which on November 15, 1980, took over the trans-border service of Republic Airlines (formerly North Central).

Thunder Bay Airport is currently served by Air Canada, Canadian Airlines International Ltd., Air Ontario, Canadian Partner, Bearskin Airlines, Norontair and Frontier Airlines, on scheduled service. Thunder Bay Flying Club, Mid-Can Air, and Awood Air provide charter service. On April 1, 1989, Air Ontario (formerly Austin) ceased trans-border service—it is now offered by Bearskin Airlines.

Over the past ten years, there has been additional hangar development by Awood Air, Canadian Pacific Forest Products, the Apron 5 Hangar Group, and the Ministry of Government Services.

In 1989, the airport directly employed 887 people and contributed an additional 924 jobs of spin-off employment. It has an annual economic impact of $172 million, of which $82 million is directly related to airport activities.

In 1967, the airport had 89,602 itinerant aircraft movements and 65,154 local ones. Passenger traffic was 140,000 in 1967; Aircraft movements in 1988 were 109,267, while total enplaning and deplaning passengers reached 591,900.

In 1982, W.A. Scales retired as airport manager. He was succeeded by Hans Toom. Paul Conrad became manager on April 3, 1989.

In 1989, Thunder Bay Airport celebrated its fiftieth anniversary in conjunction with Air Traffic Services' fiftieth anniversary and the Thunder Bay Flying Club's sixtieth anniversary.

Sources:

1. Transport Canada, Central Region.
2. R.L. Clarke, "Airport Notes" (Ottawa: Transport Canada) [unpublished collection].

Footnotes—Thunder Bay Airport

[1] In 1970, the cities of Fort William and Port Arthur amalgamated to form the city of Thunder Bay.

[2] The control tower was also destroyed. Control operations reopened the next day in hangar no. 3.

Timmins Airport
(Ontario)

The Timmins Airport, opened on September 11, 1953, is located eleven kilometres north of the city in Jessop township. The 2,283 acre [924 hectare] site was purchased from the Department of Lands and Forests.

In 1949, the Porcupine Chamber of Commerce[1] formed an airport committee to study the community's needs for an airport and the possibilities of providing one. The Department of Transport agreed to provide financial aid, and construction of a 4,000 by 200 foot [1,494 by 1,829 metre] runway began June 1953.

The air terminal was opened in June 1955, when operations were transferred to Timmins from Porquis Junction, and the latter's airport licence was cancelled.

The airport was operated by the city until 1961 when it was taken over by the Department of Transport.

In 1964, as a result of a large find of copper ore, traffic increased to the point where added terminal facilities were required. As an interim measure, the temporary terminal building at Sault Ste. Marie Airport was moved to Timmins and added to the original terminal.

The airport has grown over the years and now has two runways, one 4,903 feet [1,494 metres] long and the other, 6,000 feet [1,829 metres]. In November 1973, a new terminal building and an adjoining administration/operations building were opened, as well as a new aircraft apron, car parking, and entrance road. The old terminal—from Sault St. Marie— was sold and removed from the airport and is now a cottage.

An ILS (Instrument Landing System) was installed on runway 03 in 1982.

Commercial development strategies implemented during in the mid-1980s have served to make Timmins Airport more self-sufficient. These include land-leasing to Lloyd Richards for construction of a hangar, selling terminal and airport land space for outdoor and indoor signage, and converting the car parking lot into a concession operation—which increased revenues from the previous year by 74 per cent.

Service is provided by Air Canada, Norontair, Air Ontario, Frontier Air, Canadian Partner, and Air Creebec—which serves the north along both sides of James Bay and Hudson's Bay, and transports both passengers and cargo. Currently, there are ten flights daily from Timmins to Toronto.

Timmins Flying Club offers flying instruction and has a small aircraft repair shop.

The airport had 191,600 passengers in 1988, and there were 39,519 aircraft movements.

The following have served as airport managers under the Department of Transport:

Frank Jessop	to 1961
Desmond Dupuis	1961 to 1964
Arthur Phelps	1964 to 1968
Herbert Cochrane	1968 to 1970
David Dick	1970 to 1979
John Bell	1979 to 1980
Richard Koroscil	1980 to 1983
Steve Baker	1983 to 1988

Source:
Transport Canada, Ontario Region.

Footnote—Timmins Airport
[1] The city of Timmins now encompasses Porcupine and South Porcupine, which in 1949, were separate communities. The businessmen of Porcupine initiated the action for an airport. The Porcupine Chamber of Commerce is now the Timmins Chamber of Commerce.

Tofino Airport
(British Columbia)

The Department of National Defence constructed Tofino Airport on the west coast of Vancouver Island in 1940 for the RCAF. At one time, it was the third-largest air force base in Canada, and during the war flew Harvard, Kitty Hawk, Hurricane, Hudson, and Canso (amphibian) aircraft.

When the air force base closed in 1945, the airport was taken over by the Department of Transport, which still operates it. The Parks Board does summer maintenance under contract. The airport is not maintained in winter and is licensed for day use only. It has three concrete runways: 07-25, 10-28 and 15-33, each 1,524 metres long.

The sixteen-hour-a-day flight service station, which provides weather and other flight information for the unpredictable climate of the west coast of Vancouver Island, will be replaced in 1990 with a contract aviation weather reporting station (CAWRS).

A nine-hole golf course was constructed and opened for play in 1985.

The airport proved to be a vital element in the Exxon Valdez oil spill response during the winter of 1988, and is a valued part of tourism promotion for both Tofino and Ucluelet.

Source:
Transport Canada, Pacific Region.

Toronto Buttonville Airport
(Ontario)

Private enterprise has played a relatively minor role in the development of airports in Canada, but a notable exception is that of the Toronto Airways development of Buttonville Airport. From a meagre grass strip in the 1940s, Buttonville has grown to be one of the most highly sophisticated privately owned airports in North America. Over $20 million has been invested in runways, taxiways, buildings and equipment required for reliable 24-hour all weather aviation services. The airport receives no grants or subsidies from any level of government.

The airport is located in the town of Markham and within the hamlet of Buttonville. The town of Richmond Hill is immediately west of the airport.

Aircraft have flown from the present airport site since 1940. However, it was not until 1944 that Maracle and Shaw, partners in a venture called Mohawk Airways, founded Buttonville Airport when they arranged to rent a portion of the present site (approximately 130 acres [53 hectares]) from Douglas Hood.

In November 1944, the field was approved and licensed for light aircraft, day flying only. It had a single grass strip.

In 1945, F.F. Gillies of Gillies Flying Service assumed ownership of Buttonville Airport and the airport licence was extended to permit the operation of ski planes in winter. A hangar was erected near the northern boundary, and two—and later, three—landing strips were prepared.

In 1951, Joe Gerace became a partner in Gillies Flying Service which was subsequently renamed Donway Flying Service whose prime function was the training of student pilots, although a number of other services were added. In 1953, Jim Leggat located his aircraft engine overhaul business on the field, and a flying club—largely made up of graduates of the flying school—also occupied quarters on the site.

In 1957, Gillies retired and Gerace became the licensee. He continued to operate Donway Flying Service until 1963, when he entered into a partnership with Michael Sifton and Charles Dunn to form a new company known as Toronto Airways, which purchased the company, the airport and the land. This marked a major turning point in developing the airport into a first-class, all-weather aviation facility.

The first stage was to convert one of the three grass strips, runway 03-21 into a 3,000 by 100 foot [914-by-30-metre] paved runway, fully lighted for night flying and complemented by a parallel taxiway and high-speed turn-offs to expedite air traffic; two new modern fireproof hangars, 50 by 80 feet [15 by 24 metres], were constructed to house engine rebuilding and service shops to meet maintenance needs; a new refuelling island was built to accommodate five planes at one time from its underground tanks and high-speed pumps; a new 3,500 square foot [325-square-metre] administration building was constructed to house a large central lounge and restaurant facilities; and a 200-car paved parking area was provided for airport customers and the public.

On September 14, 1963, the rejuvenated Buttonville Airport was officially opened by an air show attended by between 25,000 and 35,000 spectators. Services offered on the airport at that time included complete flight training including instrument ratings, radio and navigation and link trainer instruction. In addition, fixed base operators such as Leggat Aircraft Limited, Trans Aircraft Company and Eastern Communications Limited provided private and business aircraft operators with complete ground services repair and overhaul, sales and service, etc.

During this period, Buttonville Airport was also designated a customs port of entry for flights to and from the United States.

Between 1982 and 1986, Torontair operated a commuter service, with Beech 99s and serving Elliot Lake, Kingston, Rochester, Ottawa, and Montréal. The service was suspended following heavy losses.

The new facilities attracted more business and air traffic, necessitating additional services. By 1967, it was apparent that consideration must be given to the introduction of air traffic control. After surveys and extensive negotiations with the Department of Transport, it was agreed that Toronto Airways would build a control tower, and on January 31, 1967, the Department of Transport introduced air traffic control at Buttonville Airport, and a 'Buttonville Tower' control zone, three miles in radius, was established. Buttonville is the only privately owned and operated airport where air traffic control is provided by Transport Canada, which pays rent for tower space.

During 1968-69, increased air traffic and business necessitated further developments: the Department installed a non-directional beacon on runway 21 and approved an instrument approach procedure to this runway; new threshold strobe lights were placed on runway 03-21 by Toronto Airways as part of the instrument approach system. Contracts for $300,000 worth of capital improvements during 1969 included the construction of an additional paved runway 15-33, 2,550 by 75 feet [777 by 23 metres], complete with a parallel taxiway and high-speed turnoffs. On the northeast corner of the airport, a new completely self-contained heliport, with its own landing path, aprons and storage hangars, was built to house a helicopter flying training and charter operation, along with radio station traffic control helicopters. The T-hangars were moved from the north side of the field to the east, adjacent to the heliport. A heated concrete block hangar, 240 by 120 feet [73-by-36 metres], was constructed on the space vacated by the T-hangars to increase the accommodation of fixed base operators and aircraft storage. During this period, Seneca College chose Toronto Airways and Buttonville Airport to introduce its three-year aviation technology course.

In 1968, air traffic movements increased to 170,565, ranking Buttonville Airport ninth in Canada; and in 1969, at 212,031, it ranked fourth.

In 1970, a new terminal facility was planned and built to house all flight operations, with new lounge facilities, offices for fixed base operation sales, ground school and instrument training facilities.

Hydro wires often present problems to airports; and Buttonville was no exception. On the approach to runway 21, an arrangement made with Ontario Hydro to mark and light hydro poles was sufficient, because this location is in a valley. But, on the approach to runway 15, 35-foot [10-metre] Hydro lines necessitated a displaced threshold, and presented a continual hazard. When negotiations with Ontario Hydro to move these hydro lines underground were unsuccessful, Toronto Airways, at a cost of $40,000, underwrote the project.

With the rapid development of Buttonville Airport during 1968-69, Armdale Company, the parent company of Toronto Airways needed more lands for airport expansion. Negotiations resulted in an additional eighty-seven acres [thirty-five hectares] of farm land, located immediately south of the existing 130 acre [fifty-three hectare] airport.

From 1970 through 1977, airport development continued at a rapid pace. Paved parking areas were increased to accommodate more than 200 paved aircraft tiedowns; a new high-speed taxiway was constructed to expedite traffic flow off runway 15; VASIS (Visual Approach Slope Indicator Systems) were installed at the end of runways 03 and 21 to improve safety and to assist day, night and instrument approaches on the runways; an internal north-south paved road was built on the eastern perimeter of the airport to provide access for the development of the easterly section of the airport; five new hangars totalling 166,000 square feet [1,542 square metres] were constructed, with adjacent taxiways, aprons and parking areas, to accommodate two new fixed base operators and inside unheated aircraft storage for more than 160 aircraft. A new equipment garage was located in one of the hangars for field maintenance equipment, which included two new snow ploughs and a new snow blower. A 36-by-12-metre addition was made to the helicopter hangar to accommodate increased sales and operations; the paved parking area northeast of the terminal was expanded to take an additional 120 cars; refuelling facilities were improved, to provide all grades of gasoline and some turbo fuels. Two aircraft hangars west of the terminal were converted to three classrooms, an aviation specialty shop, and new offices to house administration staff, Transport Canada, and inspection and medical services.

In 1976, a 1,200 foot [366-metre] extension to runway 15-33, (increasing its length to 1,143 metres), was complemented by a parallel taxiway with high-speed turn-offs to expedite traffic flow. Medium intensity lighting and a VASIS were subsequently installed. The runway was subsequently extended to 1,219 metres.

In 1973, Armadale Company, decided to move from the Toronto Dominion Centre to the airport.

The two-storey building, designed and constructed during the winter of 1973 was occupied in July 1974. Located on the southest corner of the airport, it provides an additional 12,000 square feet [1,115 square metres] of office space.

During 1977, hangar area was increased by150 feet [46-metre], and Toronto Helicopters, was expanded to accommodate a Province of Ontario Air Ambulance Helicopter Operation. During the 1980s, the airport became a major Medivac centre: Toronto Helicopters, under contract with the Ontario Ministry of Health, and ministry Medivac personnel based on-site, provide 24-hour emergency air ambulance service to communities in a 150-mile radius of Toronto.

The current airport licence issued to Toronto Airways Limited, licenses Toronto-Buttonville Airport as a public airport for day and night operations. While the licence does not mention it, a privately owned non-precision instrument approach is provided on runway 15.

Buttonville, designated by Transport Canada as a satellite to Pearson International (Toronto), has been one of the ten busiest airports in Canada, in terms of aircraft movements, for over twenty years—with an annual average of 190,000.

Air commuter operations were introduced to Buttonville in 1979, when Toronto Airways formed a new division known as 'Torontair' with eight-passenger Piper Chieftain Aircraft, flying twice daily to Elliot Lake. Torontair subsequently extended the service to Kingston, Ottawa, Montréal, and Rochester. But in 1986, Torontair moved its commuter flights from Buttonville to Pearson International, to avoid the repositioning costs involved in providing its customers with direct connections to major scheduled air carriers, domestic and international flights.

On September 5, 1989, Canadian Partners introduced a new scheduled air commuter service from Buttonville, flying Dash-8 aircraft on four return flights daily to Ottawa and Montréal. Two additional companies propose to initiate services from the airport.

In 1983, a new Localizer/DME (Distance Measuring Equipment) was installed for an approach on runway 15, flight tested and commissioned on March 5, 1983. This established the only IFR (Instrument Flight Rules) used exclusively for general aviation in the Toronto core area.

In 1985, Transport Canada relocated the Toronto Area Flight Services Station to Buttonville, where it occupies leased space in the air terminal annex.

The present facilities at Buttonville Airport may be regarded as a model of careful planning and development. The airport has two paved runways, 15-33, 1,220 by 30 metres, and 03-21, 785 by 24 metres. Toronto Airways not only operates the airport, but has a flying school and charter service. Among the 17 companies located at the airport are Toronto Helicopters, Seneca College's Aviation Technology Course and a number of aircraft service industries, which offer a full spectrum of services and employ more than 380 full-time and part-time personnel.

Although Toronto Buttonville Airport has room to grow and develop and has a flexibility to adjust its operations to meet the requirements of the Toronto area, its long-term future is in some doubt. The owners of the airport have negotiated with Transport Canada over many years for financial assistance—especially since 1982 when Buttonville ewas designated a 'satellite airport' to Lester B. Pearson International Airport. However, Transport refused, because Buttonville airport was privately owned—unlike Toronto Island Airport and other satellites associated with major cities across Canada. Meanwhile, Buttonville runs at a loss: although it may set its own fee schedule for aircraft services—landing, parking, storage and so on—these have to be competitive with other airports that receive an operating subsidy. The airport owners offered to sell out to Transport Canada, but again were refused.

Because of operating deficits, the high costs of maintenance and expansion and the escalating value of the airport's 60 hectares of land, the owners are being forced to consider closing the airport and selling the land for redevelopment.

Sources:

1. This text draws upon the paper entitled *A Brief History of Toronto Buttonville Airport*, prepared by Ian H. McCuaig of Toronto Airways Ltd. in 1977, supplemented by notes received from him in April and December 1989. It is published with the approval of the company.
2. Master Plan Report by Transport Canada.

Toronto-Lester B. Pearson International Airport
Formerly Toronto International Airport, and
Malton Airport
(Ontario)

In the 1929 List of Public Airports, Aerodromes, and Seaplane Ports (see Appendix 20), Toronto had two airports, one aerodrome, and one seaplane port: De Lesseps Airport, owned by Toronto Airport Ltd.; Leaside Airport, owned by the Toronto Flying Club; De Havilland Aerodrome, owned by De Havilland Aircraft Co. of Canada Ltd.; and Toronto Harbour, owned by the Harbour Commission (seaplanes). ·

Leaside, built by the Royal Flying Corps in 1917 as a first world war flying training school, was the most active airport in the Toronto area until it closed in 1931. "The city of Toronto paid $3,000 per year to the Toronto Flying Club , to cover their operation of the Municipal Airport." [1] The club opened its own airport (now part of Downsview Airport) in June 1931, and operated there until it moved to Malton in 1942. The air-

188. The Chapman farmhouse, the first air terminal at Malton Airport.

port was the principal Customs point of entry for visiting aircraft until Malton opened in 1939.[2]

The provision of a new municipal airport for the city of Toronto was under active consideration early in 1931, when the mayor called a meeting of aviation—interest representatives to discuss the matter. On April 21, 1931,[3] the controller of Civil Aviation met with the manager of the Toronto Harbour Commission, the mayor and the Board of Control of the city of Toronto. The Harbour Commission wanted to build a combined seaplane port and airport on Toronto Island, but there was strong opposition from cottagers living on the island and from others who wished to see the area developed only for recreational and park purposes. (The controversy continues to this day.) The Department of National Defence (then responsible for civil aviation), while maintaining that the new airport must be provided by the municipal authorities, steered clear of involvement in site selection, but offered technical advice. It expressed the view that the time was not ripe for the development of a combined airport-seaplane port because of the magnitude of the plan. Instead, it favoured the quickest and cheapest solution, i.e. the maintenance of the seaplane port by the Harbour Commission and the immediate development of an airport elsewhere. In 1932, the seaplane base was

located on the harbour front, but the Harbour Commission planned to move it to the western entrance of the harbour and to construct a ramp, a hangar, and other buildings on Toronto Island. Although the site was considered satisfactory, it had a serious disadvantage: because there was no bridge across the harbour entrance, the base would be accessible only by boat.

J.A. Wilson describes the recommendation made to the city:

It was strongly recommended to the city that they should secure an adequate airport elsewhere and spend, in the first place, only sufficient to give the essentials for a safe landing at all seasons together with the minimum hangar and office accommodations necessary for the present traffic. Any plan for the development of such a site should provide for the future expansion as conditions warrant. If, at a later date, the growth of aviation showed that the Harbour site would be advisable, there need be no financial loss. An alternate field in the north end of the city would be required and, even if it was not, the increment of the site value would more than compensate for any improvements made if the airport had to be abandoned later, which is not considered likely.[4]

After the discussions in 1931, things moved very slowly, and the Harbour Commission reviewed its plans for an airport on the island. The Department of National Defence expressed its concern for the condition of the flying club airport and felt American and Canadian pilots should be warned to keep away from Toronto during those winter months when the ground was not frozen. Owing to the importance of Toronto as an airmail centre, however, they continued to allow the mail to be flown out that winter in spite of the poor facilities.

The question of the new airport dragged on. In September 1933, the special airport committee (city and Board of Trade) was ready to recommend to the outgoing city council the purchase of three hundred acres [121 hectares] of land in the north of the city. The mayor proposed that the flying club site be developed, arguing that, while it was not as good as other possible ones, it was suitable. There was, however, a problem: one of the conditions under which unemployment relief could be granted to municipalities in the development of airports was that the site be owned by the municipality and not be disposed of without the consent of the federal government. The Toronto Flying Club airport did not satisfy this condition because the site was owned by Canadian Airways Ltd. and leased to the club.

The club site was still under consideration in July 1934, and the committee was prepared to recommend to the city "that the present grant of $2,500 per annum to the Club be increased to an amount of $15,000 per annum for five years, to enable the Club to: (a) pay the rentals; (b) spend $10,000 to $12,000 per annum on improvements."[5]

The following is a two-year chronology of important events:[6]

February 1, 1935: Ottawa promised it would build a million-dollar airport, the "finest in all Canada," in Toronto. Two sites were under consideration: Barker Field and the Toronto Flying Club property.

May 14, 1935: Eleven of twenty city councillors and the Board of Trade favoured building an airport (airharbour) on Toronto Island, linked to the mainland by tunnel. Opponents believed the money would be better spent on housing and building a courthouse; furthermore, the frequency of fog and the proximity of buildings were seen as drawbacks.

May-June, 1935: Parliament debated the island airport and tunnel proposal. The Liberals (and island residents) opposed it; the Toronto Harbour Board and Mayor McBride were in favour.

September 20, 1935: The tunnel contract was let to the Dominion Construction Corporation for $976,264.

October 30, 1935: Prime Minister Mackenzie King stopped the work. Toronto Council, with only four members opposed, sued for continuation.

December 13, 1935: The island tunnel was definitely out and the search started again for an airport site.

October 14, 1936: Intercontinental Airways declared it would build its own Toronto airport, but Acting Mayor Robbins rejected the private enterprise offer and applied instead to the federal government for financial assistance.

October 20, 1936: A committee was formed to study Toronto's airport need.

November 1, 1936: The Department of Transport, headed by Minister Howe, was formed by merging the Department of Railways and Canals, Department of Marine, and the Civil Aviation Branch of the Department of National Defence. The new Department of Transport had full responsibility for civil aviation.

December 14, 1936: Toronto and Ottawa agreed to seek a site for an airport, with Ottawa contributing $150,000 towards its construction costs.

December 26, 1936: E.L. Cousins, general manager of the Toronto Harbour Commission, recommended a site north of the city, where he said, there was room for 5,000-foot [1,524-metre] runways.

A site was finally chosen in 1937 and, on August 31, nine farm properties totalling 1,050 acres [425 hectares][7] were purchased for the city of Toronto. The chosen site became the Toronto Municipal Airport at Malton. On December 10, 1937, the Department of Transport entered into an agreement with the city of Toronto providing for the payment of grants of $450,000 by Transport over a period of four years to cover the construction of Malton and Toronto Island

Airports. Malton Airport was completed in September 1938 and had two hard-surfaced runways (3,000 by 150 feet [914 by 46 metres]), a grass landing strip, full lighting, weather reporting, and a radio range. The first air terminal was in the Chapman farm house near the Sixth Line (now Airport Road). In 1939 the city constructed a wooden terminal building, identical to the one built at the same time at the Toronto Island Airport. It was 116 by 38 feet [35 by 12 metres] and accommodated passengers and baggage on the first floor and radio services and the airport manager's office on the second floor. It also had a control tower but initially had no air traffic controllers.

The first official landing at the new airport was on August 29, 1938, by an American Airlines DC-3. Trans-Canada Air Lines' first landing was made by a Lockheed Electra on August 31, 1938. TCA began services to Toronto on October 18, 1938.

The airport on Toronto Island, completed in 1939, had two paved runways and a terminal building, and with the seaplane base was a combined land-sea airport. Because of high buildings in the area, the Department of Transport had insisted that there be an alternate airport for use in bad weather—this was one of the reasons for constructing the airport at Malton.

189. 1st landing by American Airlines at Malton, Toronto, August 29, 1938.

The Island Airport was to be used by smaller aircraft.

The two airports cost the city of Toronto $1.8 million, of which $500,000 was federal government grants. Malton was considered "a good site, well removed from city smoke and fog."[8] It became TCA's principal operating base for the trans-continental service, and in 1939, TCA built a modern hangar (near the old Chapman farmhouse). "With Malton and Toronto Island, Toronto is now perhaps better equipped than any other city in North America."[9]

By agreement, the city of Toronto gave responsibility for the control, management, and operation of Malton to the Toronto Harbour Commission, which received its licence on January 24, 1939. That month, the Commission leased the airport to the Department of Transport for one year, ending December 31, 1939. The licence remained in the Commission's name until November 30, 1961, when Transport assumed full ownership. TCA operated the airport for the department, under contract, until the spring of 1940, when an airport manager was appointed and airport traffic control was established. In April 1940, F.I. Banghart, airport manager at St. Hubert, was sent to Malton on temporary duty "to organize the Department's management at that airport, which was formerly run by TCA and

190. First TCA daily Montréal to Vancouver Malton, October 17, 1938.

191. Malton Airport, Ontario, April 23, 1939.

Toronto Harbour Commission. He will be absent from St. Hubert probably a month.[10]

In March 1939, the mayor of Toronto wanted to rename the airport Bishop's Field in honour of Canada's first war ace, but council did not agree. As a matter of interest, an airport land plan of February 26, 1940, showed the name Toronto Municipal Malton Airport, Bishop's Field.

The National Steel Car Company built an aircraft factory in the northeast corner of the airport in 1938: this was the beginning of the aircraft manufacturing industry at Malton.

In 1939, Canadian Associated Aircraft Ltd. built a plant nearby to the north, which was later leased to National Steel Car. The first military aircraft built at Malton by National Steel Car was a Lysander II, which was test-flown on August 17, 1939. The Company began construction of Hampden bombers in November 1939 and Ansons the next year. In 1942, the plant was taken over by the government and reorganized as Victory Aircraft Ltd. for the construction of Lancaster bombers. The first Lancaster was christened on August 7, 1943, and the first Lincoln bomber, the largest built in Canada, flew in October 1945. The Victory Aircraft plant closed in November 1945, when A.V. Roe Ltd. took it over and, in 1946, started the design of the Avro Jetliner and also the CF-100 for the

RCAF. The former was the world's second passenger jet (the DH Comet was the first) and the first in North America. It made its maiden flight at Malton in 1949 but never went into production and Avro dropped its development in late 1951 so the company could concentrate on producing the CF-100 fighter. (The first CF-100 flew at Malton on January 19, 1950). Avro designed and built the famous Arrow fighter, which first flew at Malton in March 1958. The plant was later taken over by de Havilland of Canada in 1962 and subsequently by McDonnell Douglas of Canada, in 1969 to make DC-9 wings and components. It is still operating.

The war had a great influence on the development of Malton. First came the establishment of the aircraft manufacturing industry on a very large scale. Then, in December 1939, the airport was chosen as the site for No. 1 Elementary Flying Training School (EFTS) and No. 1 Air Observers School (AOS) under the British Commonwealth Air Training Plan.[11]

The airport was taken over by the government from the city of Toronto under a lease dated January 14, 1940, at a rental of one dollar a year for the duration of the war and six months thereafter, and was operated by the Department as a civil airport. Hangars and other buildings were erected by the Department of National Defence on the east side of the airport to form two camps, No. 1 EFTS and No. 1 AOS. These hangars served civil aviation for years after the war until they were removed in 1961 to make way for airport development.

On June 24, 1941, American Airlines inaugurated service between Toronto and Buffalo using DC-3 aircraft. TCA began Toronto-New York service on May 10, 1941 with Lockheed Lodestars.

In April 1946, when the city of Toronto decided it did not wish to have the Malton Airport returned to its control while it was losing money, the Department agreed to continue to run the airport, and leased it for a period of ten years.

A new terminal was built in 1949, a one-storey brick structure that became known as the apron building. It was erected in front of the old terminal adjoining the aircraft apron and had a design capacity of 400,000 passengers a year. The two buildings, enlarged in 1954 and 1959, served as the air terminal until the opening of the aeroquay in 1964.

In October 1946, when the RCAF handed over its Malton buildings to Transport, hangars became available for lease to aviation interests. Among the earliest allocations were the following:

H1 located south of the terminal buildings; leased by TCA and became its first all-freight building in May 1954;

H2 south of H1; leased by Sanderson aircraft and was destroyed by fire in February 1958;

H3 located in the southeast corner of the airport, west of the 28 end of the old runway 10-28; occupied by Transport and used for itinerant aircraft storage;

H4 near H3; leased to Eatons and to other owners of executive aircraft;

H5 near H4; leased to A.V. Roe Ltd. and destroyed by fire in March 1955;

H6 near H5 and the end of the hangar line; leased by Toronto Flying Club; the club moved to Malton in 1942 and transferred its operations to King City Airport, north of Toronto, in 1962; the club ceased operations in 1972.

TCA's original hangar, built in 1939 and known as H12, was located southeast of the apron building. In 1952, TCA built another hangar near no. 12, which, at that time, was the largest in Canada (817 feet [249 metres] long). In 1970, the company (now Air Canada) built its 747 hangar in the same general

area. Hangars 3, 4, and 6 were removed in 1961 to permit redevelopment for the new terminal complex, which was opened in 1964. Two hangars purchased by Millard Properties Ltd. were rebuilt in the new general aviation area on the north side of the airport in 1963. The area was developed in 1958 to provide hangar sites for companies engaged in aircraft storage and servicing; it also served as a place for them to build their own facilities under long-term land leases with the Department of Transport. Hangar no. 12 was purchased by Transport from TCA in 1954 and leased to Genair Ltd. (after public tender) for operation as itinerant aircraft storage and servicing. It was removed in 1970 as part of the redevelopment plan.

The first concession at Malton was a small coffee shop in the terminal building, opened in 1941 by Canada Railway News Co. (founded July 3, 1883), the predecessors of Aero Caterers Ltd., which is now Cara Operations Ltd. Cara continued to operate the restaurants in the airport until 1984. Canada Railway News also operated the first flight kitchen at Malton in the old farm house that had served as the airport's first terminal building from 1937 to 1939. Before the flight kitchen in the airport began operations in 1941, flight meals were supplied from the company's

192. 'Modern' terminal at Malton airport c. 1939-40.

railway terminal restaurant in downtown Toronto at Sunnyside.

The first car rental concession opened at Malton in 1950 with Gordon Secord of Hertz Rent-a-Car Co. of Ontario the licencee. Tilden Rent-A-Car came to the airport in 1954.

Air Terminal Transport provided bus and limousine service at the airport since 1951, taking over the Carter Livery Service that had provided service to the airport in the 1940s. Air Terminal Transport operated as Airline Limousine Service from 1951 to 1961. The company changed ownership in 1961, but continued to serve at the airport until May 1965, when Charterways took over. In 1972, Charterways dropped Air Terminal Transport, but retained Airline Limousine Service until March 1974. After that, a number of ground transportation operators were licensed.

Paid car parking began at the airport in 1951, the first such operation at a Department of Transport airport. By 1957, it had grown to 1,050 spaces.

A turnstile was installed on the public observation deck of the apron terminal building in 1950—another first at a Canadian airport.

From the end of the war, traffic at Malton grew steadily as these total passenger figures show:

1946	180,307
1952	558,820
1962	1,480,000

In 1962, passenger traffic at Malton surpassed Montréal International Airport for the first time.

To keep up with the growth of traffic at the airport, the Department of Transport steadily improved the facilities: in May 1948, the ILS (Instrument Landing System) system was commissioned; in August 1957, runway 14-32 was extended by 5,500 feet [1,539 metres] to 11,050 feet [3,368 metres]; 10-28 was extended to

7,200 feet [2,194 metres] (later reduced to 4,000 feet [1,219 metres]); and, in 1962, a new parallel runway, 05R-23L of 9,500 feet [2,895 metres], was completed.

The name of the airport was changed to Toronto International Airport (Malton) on November 28, 1960. (It had been named Malton International Airport in October, but was altered at the request of the mayor of Toronto).

In October 1953, the city of Toronto proposed to sell Malton to the Department of Transport and develop the Island Airport to handle all types of aircraft at a profit to the city. Negotiations continued over the next few years and agreement was reached in February 1957 between the Minister of Transport, the corporation of the city of Toronto and the Toronto Harbour Commissioners, under which Transport agreed to build a new runway and a 36,000 square-foot [3,344-square-metre] hangar at the Island Airport at an estimated cost of $1.5 million. The hangar was to be leased to the city for twenty-five years at an annual rent that would amortise its cost. For its part, the city agreed to transfer Malton Airport to the Department of Transport for one dollar. The transfer was made on April 12, 1957.

In 1960, Malton began to play a full international role in addition to its service to the United States, when on March 1, British Overseas Airways Corporation became the first European airline to gain traffic rights.

Transport took over the airport's emergency-crash services from A.V. Roe Ltd. in 1959.

In 1958, a major redevelopment of the airport began that was to include construction of a new air terminal and administration building complex in the southeast corner of the airport. Although the original plan called for four aeroquays to be built progressively as air traffic increased, only one aeroquay was completed— largely because of the high cost. The aeroquay was opened by Prime Minister Lester B. Pearson on February 28, 1964. It cost $27.5 million and was designed to handle 1,400 passengers an hour and 2 million passengers a year. The unique design featured minimum walking distances from aircraft to terminal, and became'a show place in airport design.' The building was circular, allowing aircraft to park around the circumference, while cars parked in a vertical structure in the centre, entering by a tunnel under the aircraft parking area. By 1966, aircraft movements had doubled to 20,000 and passenger traffic had increased to the point where the aeroquay was already inadequate.

As well as passenger traffic, air cargo demands increased, and the need arose for a central air cargo handling facility. Before this time, each airline had handled its own cargo in whatever space could be made available. In 1963, after negotiations with the Department of Transport and the airlines, a Toronto enterprise, WIG-MAR Investments, built an air cargo centre north of the aeroquay, adjoining the aircraft apron which served that building. The site had been designated for a future aeroquay in the terminal complex plan, but was not required for that purpose for another twenty years. The land was therefore redesignated for air cargo use under a term-certain land lease of twenty years, but when airport plans changed later the time restriction was removed. The Air Cargo Centre was opened in 1964 with the commissioning of Air Canada's cargo terminal. It has been expanded several times since then and, in 1980, provided 35,000 square-metres of floor area. (One expansion was used as the'charter terminal' in 1971).

In 1980, the following airlines had space in the Air Cargo Centre: Air Canada, CP Air, British Airways, Alitalia, Swissair, Air France, American Airlines, Eastern Airlines, and KLM. In 1975, 164,000 tonnes of air cargo were processed at the airport. In 1988, the figure was 273,000 tonnes—more than 40 per cent of all Canada's air cargo.

In January 1963, Malton Fuelling Facilities Corporation, a consortium of airlines, installed a hydrant refuelling system to serve the aeroquay. Consolidated Aviation Services became established at the airport in 1976. Ten airlines were using the airport by 1967. The dates on which they started are shown in the right-hand column:

Air Canada	Domestic	18/10/38
	transborder	(as TCA)
	international	
American Airlines	transborder	24/06/41
Canadian Pacific	domestic	4/10/52
	& overseas	
BOAC	overseas	1/03/60
Eastern Airlines	transborder	2/10/66
Mohawk[12]	transborder	1/11/66
United Airlines	transborder	1/08/67
North Central[13]	transborder	1/08/67

General traffic was growing by 15-to-20 per cent a year. Air Canada alone had more than one hundred flights per day.

Early in 1968, Transport announced that it would build an interim terminal to relieve passenger traffic congestion while plans were being made for the future of the airport. The local residents, complaining of the noise, had organized

193. Terminal buildings, Toronto Municipal Airport (Malton) late 1950s.

into a strong pressure group to oppose the expansion of Malton. Before plans for Terminal II were far advanced, the need for something more than an interim building became evident, as Malton could not be enlarged to meet long-term demands. In December 1968, the minister of Transport announced that the federal government would not proceed with the full expansion of Toronto International Airport at Malton: instead, a new airport would be built far from any residential areas. The site chosen was Pickering, and planning was directed towards development of the new airport. But it also ran into public opposition and, despite the 1975 findings of the Airport Enquiry Commission endorsing the building of a new airport, plans for Pickering were dropped in the same year.

Terminal II (unlike Terminal I) was designed to a linear plan so as to accommodate wide-body aircraft. Construction began in 1969, but as it progressed, the concept changed, the project became a much larger one, and delays arose. Consequently, the Department of Transport had to find temporary means of meeting the pressing need for passenger facilities. By 1970, 6.4 million passengers were passing through the airport; in January 1971, the airport had its first Boeing 747 when Alitalia diverted to Toronto from New York; by April 1971, Air Canada had introduced the 747 on its Toronto-Vancouver service. Therefore, in 1971, as an emergency measure, the Department of Transport entered into an agreement with the owners of the air cargo terminal (which was near the aeroquay) to advance its plans for air cargo expansion and to lease the empty shell to the Department for use as a temporary terminal for summer charter flights. Thus, the charter terminal came into being in June 1971, with all necessary facilities, including Customs and Immigration, and it could handle three DC-8 aircraft at a time.[14]

The first stage of Terminal II opened in June 1972, and at first, handled only charter flights.

194. Toronto International Airport, 1970s.

The charter terminal was given up at this time and reverted to its intended use as an air cargo warehouse. In October 1972, Air Canada moved some flights to Terminal II and, with the whole concept of Terminal II now changed, moved its entire operation there in April 1973.

Resulting from new bilateral air agreements between Canada and other countries, the following overseas airlines began to serve Toronto on direct flights: BWIA (British West Indies Airlines) (May 21, 1969), Air Jamaica (March 1, 1972), Alitalia (November 2, 1972), Lufthansa (April 29, 1973), KLM (April 1, 1974), Swissair (April 1, 1975) and Air France (May 21, 1976).

Additional domestic carriers began to serve Toronto: Air Ontario (September 9, 1969), Pem Air (May 7, 1970) and Nordair (February 4, 1979). In 1989, there were sixty-eight major air carriers operating out of the airport: thirty-four scheduled airlines, twenty charter carriers, and fourteen pure freight carriers, providing air service to over three hundred destinations in sixty countries. More than twenty general aviation companies are based at the airport: they involve commercial and private aircraft, fuelling operations, and avionics equipment manufacture, sales, operation, and maintenance.

Since the opening of the aeroquay and Terminal II, extensive alterations have been made to

improve and increase passenger handling capability. An extension to Terminal II was completed in November 1977; and a connecting parking structure increased the airport public car parking capacity from 5,300 spaces to more than 10,000.

In spite of these improvements, the airport was still very congested. Passenger volume increased by 56 per cent from 1971 to 1974, from 6.7 million to 10.5 million; and in 1979 Toronto International Airport handled 14 million passengers. Transport Canada noted that "halting of construction of the Pickering project and the re-affirmed positions of the Federal and Provincial governments in not proceeding with further expansion of Toronto International Airport (Malton) leave the overloading problem at Malton unresolved."[15]

In 1981, a $28 million improvement programme began in Terminal One and, in the same year, Transport announced an airport master plan for improved services for the travelling public over the next ten years, and described long-term options. Proposals included construction of a third passenger terminal, expansion of the air cargo operation, expansion and development of air carrier maintenance facilities, further improvements to ground transportation facilities, air traffic services, air navigational and airside facilities. The master plan was approved the following year and the work began.

The new air traffic control centre, which cost $15 million, was commissioned in April 1981. In September of the same year, Air Canada and CP Air finished major expansion programmes to cargo buildings A and C. Both Air Canada and CP Air also completed major new maintenance hangars with B-747 handling capability. Wardair completed a new 747 capacity hangar on a site developed by Transport Canada at the western side of the airport.

On January 1, 1984, the airport was officially renamed Lester B. Pearson International Airport

(LBPIA), after the late prime minister and winner of the 1957 Nobel Peace Prize. (This was the airport's fourth name change: Toronto Municipal Airport, 1937; Malton International Airport, October 1960; Toronto International Airport (Malton), November 1960).

Runway 06R-24L, the most heavily used runway at LBPIA, was grooved in 1984, to increase surface drainage so that braking is improved during wet conditions.

Transport Canada introduced passenger transfer vehicles (PTVs) at Pearson International in 1985 to ease the shortage of aircraft parking gates, by parking passenger aircraft at gates distant from the two terminal buildings. As required, these vehicles are brought to a special dock at the terminal and 124 passengers boarded. The vehicle then moves to the parked aircraft, raises the passenger compartment to aircraft-door level so that passengers may board the aircraft. At first, there were two PTVs, owned by Air Canada and Transport. During the past few years, Transport acquired three more PTVs (from Edmonton International Airport, when that airport discontinued the use of PTVs), and contracted all four to Air Canada.

During the summer of 1986, Air Canada initiated a helicopter shuttle service between Cherry Beach, downtown Toronto and Terminal Two, but the service was discontinued because Etobicoke residents complained about the noise.

Construction began in 1990 on a $40 million extension project in Terminal Two. When completed, the international section of the terminal building will be able to accommodate 1,800 passengers per hour.

On June 10, 1989, Lester B. Pearson International Airport marked its fiftieth anniversary.

Terminal Three, whose construction began on May 2, 1988, began operation in early 1991. Northwest of Terminal One and the air cargo terminal area, the complex cost $520 million. It is unique for a Transport Canada airport in that it was designed, built, financed, and operated by the private sector on federally owned land leased to the company. In announcing the project in April 1988, the Minister of Transport said "...for the first time in Canada, private sector funds will be used to finance a major air terminal."[16]

This arrangement had its beginnings in 1986, when Transport called for an "expression of interest" from the private sector to provide the terminal. Proposals were received from four consortia, and of these, the submission of Airport Development Corporation was chosen. An agreement was signed in November 1987, and the ground leased in April 1988, permitting construction to begin.

The Airport Development Corporation, under terms of the forty-year lease, was to construct and operate a twenty-four-gate, world class passenger terminal serving domestic, transborder, and international airlines. In addition to the terminal, the project includes a 3,000-car parking garage, a first-class hotel, offices, trade and convention facilities, and office development along Airport Road. The lease agreement defines the conditions under which the new terminal and related developments are constructed and operated, and provides the federal government with a share of revenues from all land development. Transport Canada will retain its long-standing responsibilities for airside service facilities, aviation safety and security, and will monitor all aspects of the development. Transport will also ensure that an integrated three-terminal system will function in the best interests of all passengers at Pearson Airport.

Terminal Three is designed to handle the following traffic up to 1996: domestic flights, 1,000 passengers per hour; transborder flights, 600 passengers per hour; international flights, 1,000 passengers per hour.

The following airlines are expected to move to the new terminal: Canadian Airlines International, Canadian Partner, American Airlines, Eastern Airlines, British Airways, KLM Royal Dutch Airlines, and Lufthansa German Airlines.

Terminal One, which opened in 1964, has a total area of 56,180 square metres. Its original capacity was 3.2 million passengers annually. Its current (1989) capacity is six million passengers annually. It has twenty-three boarding gates.

Air carriers now serving Terminal One:

Air China	Inter-Canadian
Aerolineas Argentinas	KLM Royal Dutch Airlines
Alitalia	Mall Airways
American Airlines	Northwest Airlines
Business Express	Olympic Airways
BWIA International	Pemair
Canadian Airlines	International United Airlines
Canadian Partner	Varig Brazilian
Comair	Wardair
Eastern Airlines	

Regular charter carriers are Nationair and Worldways
Seasonal carriers are, Luftransport, Martiair, Sterling Airways, Novair International.

Terminal Two opened in 1972 and has a total area of 84,978 square-metres, with thirty-one boarding gates. Its original capacity was six million passengers annually; its current capacity (1989) is nine million passengers annually.

Air carriers now serving Terminal Two:

Air Canada	Korean Airlines
Air France	Lot Polish Airlines
Air Jamaica	Lufthansa German Airlines
Air Ontario	Pakistan Airlines
Air Toronto	Sabena Belgian Airlines
British Airways	Swissair

Cubana
El Al
Finnair
JAT Yugoslav Airlines

TAP Air Portugal
Thai Airways
US Air
Voyageur

Regular Charter Carriers:

Air Niagara Express   Guyana Airways
Air Transat   Odyssey
Canada 3000 (Air 2000) Vacationair
Crownair   Minerve Canada
First Air (Bradley Air Services)

Seasonal Carriers are Iberia Airlines and Sky-world (Points of Call)

Pearson International has three main runways and 25 taxiways. Runway 15-33 measures 3,368 by 61 metres; runway 06L-24R, 3,200 by 61 metres; and runway 06R-24L, 2,896 by 61 metres. A fourth runway, 10-28, has limited general aviation use and functions primarily as a taxiway.

The airport is the busiest airport in Canada, and in 1988, it handled 348,406 aircraft movements and 20,632,701 passengers. To reduce flight delays, the minister of Transport has imposed a limit of seventy flights per hour; and to cope with the noise problem restrictions have been imposed on aircraft operations between 11 p.m. and 7 a.m.

On August 18, 1989, the minister of Transport announced a strategy for aviation in southern Ontario. This plan includes a proposal for two new runways at Pearson International Airport, major renovations to both Terminals One and Two, re-routing of some charter flight traffic to Hamilton's Mount Hope Airport and increased enrolment in Transport Canada's air traffic controller training program.

Back in the 1930s, when the decision was made to build Toronto's airport in Malton, many people wondered who would use an airport so far out of the city. Now, decades later, the city completely surrounds the airport, which is bordered by three municipalities: Toronto (Etobicoke), Mississauga, and Brampton. There has been widespread residential and commercial development during the past decades and the encircling communities have prospered because of their proximity to the airport. Almost 34,000 jobs with firms and government agencies are directly tied to the airport. There are over 15,000 on-site employees working with airlines, aviation support, passenger services and the federal government agencies. In 1987-88, LBPIA generated $129.8 million in revenue and incurred $80.2 million in operational expenses for a gross profit of $49.6 million (before depreciation and capital charges).

The following have served as airport managers of Toronto International Airport since its inception in 1938:

Air Commodore Herbert Hollick-Kenyon	November 1938
Trans-Canada Air Lines (by contract for the Department of Transport)	1939 to 1940
F.I. Banghart (on temporary from St. Hubert Airport)	1940
G.W.C. Dingwall	1940 to 1957
R.E. Harris	1957 to 1972
H.E.A. Devitt	1972 to 1976
D.C. McAree	1976 to 1984
E. Warrick	1984 to 1987
C.S. Heed	1987

Sources:

1. Transport Canada, Ontario Region.
2. S.F.J. Frink, *Toronto Lester B. Pearson International Airport: Facts & Figures*, Transport Canada, 1989.

Footnotes—Pearson International Airport

[1] Long, C.D., *Toronto Airports - Before Malton*, CAHS Journal (Winter 1965), p. 93.

[2] Ibid, p. 96.

[3] Public Archives Canada, J.A. Wilson Papers, MG 30 E243, report of meeting.

[4] Ibid.

[5] Public Archives Canada, J.A. Wilson papers, MG 30 E243, 4 July 1934.

[6] Toronto International Airport: A Chronology, prepared for Transport Canada by Yorkminster Publishing Ltd., (Willowdale: March 1978).

[7] Today, the airport occupies 1,792 hectares.

[8] Public Archives Canada, MG 30 E243, vol. 9, a Department of Transport report, 5 August 1939.

[9] Ibid.

[10] Public Archives Canada, MG 30, E243, vol. 3, a memorandum by J.A. Wilson.

[11] No. 1 AOS opened on May 27, 1940, and closed in March 1945. No. 1 EFTS opened on June 24, 1940. It was disbanded in July 1942 to make room for the expansion of No. 1 AOS. No. 1 ETFS was operated by Malton Flying Training School Ltd., a company formed by the Toronto Flying Club to meet the requirements of the BCATP.

[12] Mohawk was bought by Allegheny in 1972 and, in 1979, became U.S. Air.

[13] North Central became Republic Air in 1980.

[14] Before the opening of the charter terminal, the airport provided a free bus service to charter operators who would agree to process their passengers off-airport at near-by hotels and bus the passengers directly to the aircraft.

[15] Toronto Area Airports Project, CATA, Transport Canada, July 1976.

[16] Transport Canada press release, no. 103/88, 55 April 1988.

Toronto Island Airport
(Ontario)

What was once Toronto's main airport was called Port George VI—the official name for Toronto Island Airport. But the name faded from memory as quickly as the original plans to locate a major airport at Hanlan's Point (site of the Curtiss Flying School flying boat base on Toronto Island, 1915). Aviation needs grew too quickly for the site.

In the 1930s, as the aircraft industry began to grow rapidly and the airplane became accepted as a regular form of transportation, Toronto's airport facilities, consisting of several small privately owned airfields around the city, were unable to cope.

Discussions began in the late 1920s and early 1930s between city officials and members of the Department of Transport to decide on a suitable location for a major city airport. A special committee was set up to assess possible sites.

Out of the final possibilities, it was decided in 1937 that the main airport should be located on an expanded site at Hanlan's Point, with a back-up emergency landing field to be constructed on the flat land in the Malton area.

The Toronto Harbour Commissioners were given the responsibility of developing and operating the two airports. At that time, about fifty families lived at Hanlan's Point on Toronto Island, with yearly leases. In the winter, they walked across the ice to the mainland. In June 1937, they were served notice to vacate the properties by December of that year, and city council authorized several surveys of the island area to find a suitable site for the relocation of the homes. Eventually, Sunfish Island was chosen as an ideal spot to set up a residential area, and funds were set aside for the construction of public facilities, including roadways and watermains with a bridge to Ward's Island and the ferry docks. The homes were moved in the spring of 1938 to their new location on Sunfish Island, which was renamed Algonquin Island. A few residents who preferred to move to the southern end of Hanlan's Point paid for removal costs and, in return, obtained three years' free rent from the city.

Meanwhile, workmen had been grading and clearing the land at Hanlan's Point in preparation for construction of the airfield. The contract was let for the dredging of 1.8 million cubic-yards of fill to create the additional land necessary for the runways; huge bulldozers were moved in to grade the area; as a by-product of the dredging, the Long Pond regatta course was created.

Once the land was prepared, 150 acres [61 hectares] were sodded and two 3,000 foot [914-metre] runways were paved, as were taxi-strips and a parking apron.

The Harbour Commissioners constructed a seaplane ramp as well as a retaining wall and ferry slips in the north and south piers of the Western Channel. The cable ferry, constructed in the commissioners' yard on the Keating Channel, was completed in December 1938. Tests were carried out during the winter and, in the spring, the ferry was put into service across the Western Channel to provide access to the airport.

The airport administration building was completed in the spring of 1939—it was identical to the one built at Malton in the same year and is still in use as a terminal. It has been listed as an historic building by the city.

The first plane landed at the Island Airport on February 4, 1939; and during the year, a total of 7,252 aircraft movements were recorded. It was that year, and in commemoration of the visit of King George VI, that the city council designated the Island Airport Port George VI. The name was duly recorded, but has since been forgotten.

Construction at Malton Airport continued simultaneously with that at the island, and Malton was officially opened inn August 1938.

While Transport took over Malton airport, the city retained control of the Island Airport; and the Toronto Harbour Commissioners operated the field on its behalf. However, the declaration of war in September 1939 brought major changes to the two airports. Malton expanded rapidly. Urgently needed aircraft industries were located close to the airport. Training schools moved in under the British Commonwealth Air Training Plan; and passenger services were extended.

The Island Airport became a training base for the members of the Royal Norwegian Air Force who had fled their occupied country. At 'Little Norway' (as it was known), hangars, dormitories, recreational facilities, drill hall, hospital, and messes were built.

In 1943 the Norwegian camp was transferred to larger quarters in Gravenhurst (Muskoka Airport) and the Royal Canadian Air Force took over, naming it Lakeside Camp.

After the war, the Island Airport became a tremendously popular civilian airport. Aircraft movements jumped from 3,719 arrivals and departures in 1945 to 13,031 in 1946. Aircraft companies, including Central Airways, which is still located at the island, moved in to offer training for pilots as the interest in aviation grew, and every day the newspapers had a new slant on the activities.

Private business aircraft, which were gaining popularity, used the airport because of its proximity to the downtown area. And by 1953 it was necessary to install airport traffic control. The island tower, operated by the Department of Transport, was opened in December 1953 by Mayor Lamport.

Meanwhile, Malton became the base for all the major airlines' continental and international flights. In February 1957 the government agreed to take over Malton and, in exchange, would carry out improvements at the Island Airport for the city.

196. Toronto Island Airport, 1940.

Consequently, the Island Airport was enlarged, a new 4,000-foot [1,219-metre] runway was constructed in 1961, and taxiways were built. In 1963, a 36,000 square foot [3,344-square-metre] hangar was erected, and new lighting was installed to permit night flying.

The Toronto Harbour Commissioners took full responsibility for the operation of the Island Airport on July 1, 1962, and hoped that, under its administration, the Island Airport would be eligibe for federal funding. Although it was the busiest airport in Canada in 1961 with a total of 212,735 landings and take-offs, it continued to lose money.

The biggest problem was that of surface access. The cable ferry (which had run since 1938) could not operate in bad weather. Originally, the ferry was a temporary measure until a tunnel could be built under the Western Gap. Although the federal government appropriated $1 million to build the tunnel as an unemployment relief project—and work actually began on October 11, 1935—when the Conservative government was defeated by the Liberals later that month the project was cancelled. Improved access to the Island by bridge or tunnel has been considered many times since, but nothing has been done; and, today, the city of Toronto remains firmly opposed to the idea.

The ferry continued in operation for twenty-five years, and in 1963, was temporarily replaced by tug service. Talks were held on the problems of access but, by this time, the cost of building a tunnel was prohibitive. In 1964, the 'Maple City' ferry was put into service across the 400-foot [122 metre] gap.

The Island Airport remains popular for pilot training and for visiting businessmen, but its problems persist. Access across the Western Gap via the Maple City ferry is limited, and the proximity of downtown highrise buildings prevents the installation of automatic landing systems.

Despite the airport's popularity and the large number of aircraft movements, its operating deficit increased. The commission made many requests to the Department of Transport for financial assistance, but the airport was not eligible for an operating subsidy. The Department, however, found a way to help, and, for the years 1975 to 1981, paid the Harbour Commission a special annual grant to match the airport's operating deficit. Then, under an agreement of 1983, the Harbour Commission continued to operate the airport, with financial assistance from the Department of Transport. Any surplus from airport operations was to be divided equally between the Transport and the Commission.

In March 1974, the Joint Committee for Toronto Island Airport was convened with representation from the federal, provincial, metro and city governments and from local community organizations. The airport's Intergovernmental Staff Forum (ISF) was established in 1975 to provide technical assistance to the airport site. The ISF, in turn, was directed by the Policy Steering Group, consisting of the federal and provincial ministers of Transport, the federal minister of State for Urban Affairs, the chairman of Metro Toronto, the mayor of Toronto, and the chairman of the Board of the Toronto Harbour Commissioners.

After looking at a range of possible uses for the airport, the ISF evaluated three in detail: it could be used for general aviation only; general aviation and Short Take-Off and Landing (STOL); or recreational use, with or without housing. The report favoured general aviation/STOL while the city wanted general aviation only. The differing opinions sparked further debate, which solved nothing.

During 1980 and 1981, the Canadian Transport Commission (CTC) held hearings on an application by one of five carriers that had tendered STOL Services between Toronto Island, Ottawa, and Montréal. The city of Toronto intervened on the grounds that changing the airport into the city's second commercial airport would run counter to municipal efforts to promote recreation and housing on the waterfront. It also suggested the cost of a STOL service would exceed any benefits it could provide.

The issue of the airport's future remained a matter of local interest until February 1981, when Toronto's city council recommended that an agreement be reached with the federal government and the Harbour Commission to develop the airport for general and limited STOL service, provided the city's waterfront objectives would be protected. In June of that year, a Memorandum of Understanding (MOU) was signed by the

197. Toronto Island Airport, 1989.

federal government, the city, and the commission. A year later, the CTC granted a licence to City Center Airways to operate the STOL service.

On June 30, 1983, a fifty-year Tripartite Agreement superseding the MOU was signed providing for continued use of city land at the island for a public airport for general aviation and limited commercial STOL service. Under the agreement, jet-powered flights are permitted only for medical evacuations, emergencies, and during the Canadian National Exhibition Air Show. Noise abatement procedures were part of the agreement, which was amended in 1985 to permit operation of the De Havilland Dash 8 aircraft. City Express (formerly Air Atonabee) began operations at Toronto Island in 1984, when Air Atonobee was acquired, renamed and moved from Peterborough.

In 1984, the Department of Transport began a $21 million program to improve facilities for general aviation and limited STOL service at the Airport. Projects included a new air traffic control tower, two Microwave Landing Systems (MLS) and expansion of the terminal apron; the tower and one MLS are in use, and installation of the second is nearly complete.

At present, Toronto Island Airport's 1,219-metre runway can handle aircraft carrying up to

198. Air Terminal Building, Toronto Island Airport, 1989.

fifty passengers over distances in the 482 to 644-kilometre range.

In mid-January and early February 1989, the Royal Commission on the Future of the Toronto Waterfront had its initial meetings with the public. Commissioner David Crombie heard from airlines, pilot associations, the city, federal and provincial Departments of Transport and the general public—to name a few—when issues of importance with regard to the airport and its related transportation services were raised. The report is now before the apporpriate authorities.

The airport has three runways: 08-26, 1,219 metres long; 15-33 and 06-25, each 914 metres long.

The following are based at the airport:
City Express:
    Passenger service between Toronto, Ottawa, and Newark, New Jersey.
Central Airways Corp.:
    Sightseeing, charter, air taxi, and flying instruction (Central Airways is one of Canada's oldest civil aviation schools; it began at Barker Field, sixteen kilometres away, and moved to the island shortly after the end of the war).
Air I:
    Flying Instruction, charters.
Harbour Flying Services:
    Charters.
Skyking Airlines International:
    Toronto to Boston, Massachussetts.
Aircraft Maintenance:
    Eagle Aircraft Repairs
    C.J. Hacksaw Metal Shop
    Central Airways Corp.
Aerial Advertising:
    Specialty Air Services Ltd.
Aircraft Sales:
    Ontario Star Aircraft Co. Ltd.
Radio Shop:
    Island Avionics
    Toronto Avionics

Aerial Photography:
    Central Airways Corp.

In 1987, there were 197,600 aircraft movements and 400,000 passengers. The Island Airport, which ranks yearly among Canada's busiest, had its record of 240,339 aircraft movements in 1967.

The following served as airport managers:

W.E. Johnson	1939 to 1947
I. McCuaig	1947 to 1972
Jerry Thornton	1972 to 1987
Alex Home	1987

Sources:
1. *History of Toronto Island Airport*, Public Affairs, Toronto Harbour Commission.
2. *The Future of Toronto Island Airport: The Issues*; Royal Commission on the Future of the Toronto Waterfront, May 1989.
3. Transport Canada, Ontario Region.
4. *Toronto Island Airport, 1939-1989*, Toronto Harbour Commission.

Trenton Municipal Airport
(Nova Scotia)

A group of young Pictou County men in the late 1920s got together with the intent of building an airport. The location decided upon was the present site at the top of the hill in Trenton—it was reasonably flat with an elevation of 317 yards [97 metres], making it an ideal site. The airport was started when government funding was not available for such projects.

The group of enthusiasts organized dances and other activities to raise funds to hire help at a reported wage of 15 cents per hour. The site was covered by scrub growth and thick alders; and since there were no power tools in that era, clearing was by pick, shovel and axe.

There were four years of construction before Jimmy Wade, an early Canadian aviation pioneer flying a tiny De Havilland Gypsy Moth, made the first landing at Trenton on June 29, 1932.

At its opening in September 1932, the airport was officially named the Mollison Airport, after James Mollison, a leading twenty-seven-year-old British flyer—a name that has long since been forgotten by most. Mollison flew his Puss Moth across the Atlantic in August 1932, the first western solo crossing of the ocean, from Portmarnock, Ireland, to a forced landing at Pennfield Ridge, New Brunswick. Having given permission to use his name, Mollison decided during one of his flights to pay a visit. He dropped out of the sky, bounced his wheels on the runway and then flew away, going about his business.

In 1981, the six municipal units in Pictou County recognized the importance of the airport to economic development and formed a Joint Municipal Airport Committee for the purpose of upgrading the site. As a result of this cooperative approach, the province of Nova Scotia agreed to share in the cost of providing much-needed equipment: a new tractor with snow blowing and bush cutting attachments was purchased in 1982; a new runway lighting system, obstruction lighting, and a rotating beacon were installed the following year; and in 1984, weather observation equipment and a non-directional beacon were added. Repairs were also made to the runway and taxi apron.

Following the Joint Municipal Airport Committee's request of the Department of Transport to provide funding, construction commenced on a runway extension in 1986 and was completed the following year; and the terminal was begun in the latter part of 1987 and completed in mid-1988. The opening ceremonies for these improvements were held on August 27, 1988.

Within the terminal building visitors may enjoy a pictorial history of the airports, development.

From the humble beginning of a short grass runway, there is now a 1,219-metre paved strip with air-to-ground communication on the unicom frequency of 122.8 mhz. and a new 3,000-square-foot modern airport terminal building.

Future plans for the airport include the establishment of an airside industrial park, hangars, and security fencing.

The airport is owned by the town of Trenton and operated by Butler Air Services Ltd.

Source:
This section draws upon *Trenton Municipal Airport*, supplied by the town of Trenton, Nova Scotia.

Trois-Rivières Airport
(Québec)

The Trois-Rivières Airport was constructed between 1959 and 1961 by the municipality of Trois-Rivières with a grant from the Department of Transport. In 1960, ownership of the land was transferred from the municipality to the federal government.

The airport was officially opened on October 22, 1961, as a day and night VFR (Visual Flight Rules) public airport. It had a 6,000 by 150 foot [1,829-by-46-metre] runway and a 200 by 300 foot [61-by-91-metre] apron. The St. Maurice Aero Club, a flying school and charter operation, moved its base to the new airport from Cap de la Madeleine.

In January 1962, the municipality undertook the operation of the airport, and an airport committee was formed under Alderman A.O. Dumas.[1] A parcel of land was leased to Roger Leblanc (Helicoptère Aviation Ltd.), who became the first airport manager. In June 1962, the nearby airport at Cap de la Madeleine closed down and its Customs service was transferred to Trois-Rivières.

In 1963, Leblanc erected a hangar at the airport, and the municipality constructed a terminal building. On September 2 of the same year, Trans-Canada Air Lines inaugurated daily service to Montréal and Québec with Viscounts. In the same month, the Department of Transport began to pay the municipality an airport subsidy. M. Tardif, the Air Canada representative, became airport manager.

Air Canada discontinued service to Trois-Rivières in 1967, and, at the same time, the federal subsidy came to an end. However, a maintenance garage was constructed in 1970 with financial assistance from Transport; and in 1978, the Department made a grant towards runway repairs and another in 1982 for the construction of a parallel taxiway.

Cartier Aviation began a flight training school and charter services in 1975.

At present, the following operators are based at the Trois-Rivières airport: Saint-Maurice Aero Club (flying club), Nadeau Air Service Inc. (flight training and charter service), Max

199. Opening of Trois-Rivières Airport, Québec October 22, 1961.

Aviation, Aero-Technique (aircraft maintenance services), Pro-Magnum, and Laminair Developpement Services Ltée. (aerial photography).

Source:
Transport Canada, Québec Region.

Footnote—Trois-Rivières Airport
[1] Dumas later became the regional administrator of Transport Canada's Air Administration in Québec.

Tuktoyaktuk Airport
(Northwest Territories)

Tuktoyaktuk is a community of approximately 975 people (over 90 per cent of whom are Inuit) on the Arctic coast of mainland Canada. The local economy is supported by oil exploration of three major companies.

The Tuktoyaktuk airport is located at 69°26'N and 133°01'W on 144 hectares of land south of the community and west of its industrial area. It was initially constructed in 1957 by the United States Air Force when the DEW Line[1] radar base was established. In 1973, ownership of the property by the Department of Indian Affairs and Northern Development was confirmed, and Transport Canada assumed operating responsibility. During the late 1970s, with intensified oil exploration, there were dramatic and sustained increases in aviation activity; Dome Petroleum, the major user, constructed a runway extension.

The airport is classified as Local-Commercial, Class IV under the Transport Canada system. It serves the needs of the residents by supporting regular Class III Services, connecting mainly to Inuvik, with Twin Otters and DC-3s. Its other major role is the support of petroleum exploration, with B-737s. Other functions include support of the vestiges of the DEW Line opera-

tion, a base for local activity resupply—using helicopters predominantly—and an emergency alternative for Inuvik.

In 1978-79, the gravel airstrip was lengthened to 5,000 feet [1,524 metres] and widened to 130 feet [40 metres], and a taxiway and ramp were added. Navigational aids, such as VOR/DME (VHF Omni-directional Range/distance Measuring Equipment) and an MLS (Microwave Landing System) have been installed.

The runway has an estimated excess capacity to meet demand through 205l; and land has been reserved at the end of the runway for a possible extension of 1,000 feet [305 metres].

Provision has been made for a partial taxiway paralleling the most easterly half of the runway on its north side. This will serve the commercial development area, which could be developed south and east of the present AMOCO Petroleum facilities.

A maintenance garage/firehall was constructed near the air terminal building in 1984-85 at a cost of about $950,000.

Aklak Air and Western Arctic Air are based at the airport.

In 1988, the airport had 13,972 passengers and there were 11,371 aircraft movements.

The following served as airport managers:

R. Barradell	1974 to 1977
E. Tooke	1977 to 1980
Orest Peech	1980 to 1981
Peter Frank	1981 to 1982
K. Laine	1982 to 1983
B. Roste	1983 to 1984
R. Ellis	1984 to 1986
M. Michaud	1986 to

Source:
Transport Canada, Western Region.

Footnote—Tuktoyaktuk Airport
[1] The DEW Line was the Distant Early Warning (radar) Line planned jointly by the United States and

Canada but financed by the U.S. It was built north of the Arctic Circle and extended from the Alaska-Yukon border to Cape Dorset, Baffin Island. Forty-one stations were built, and the line was working by January 1, 1958. Many sites were inaccessible except by air, and a huge airlift was developed to support the construction.

Uranium city Airport
(Saskatchewan)

In the 1930s there was a gold strike in the Beaverlodge area of northwestern Saskatchewan, and the Goldfields camp sprang up around what was known as the Box Mine. The mine closed in 1942, and Goldfields became a ghost town; but with the discovery of uranium, a mill was put into operation in the area—Canada's second uranium mine.

Uranium City Airport (it was changed from Goldfields in 1956) was licensed for operation in February 1952. By then, it had developed to a graded landing strip, 4,200 by 200 feet [1,280 by 61 metres], and was located between the north end of Beaverlodge Lake and Ace Lake. It was licensed for night flying on December 18, 1952. Eldorado Mining and Refining Ltd. (changed to Eldorado Nuclear Ltd. on June 5, 1968), then the owner and operator of the airport, received from Transport (on loan) a rotating beacon in March 1953. By October 1958, the runway was paved, its length increased to 5,000 feet [1,524 metres] and the airport became a subsidized municipal airport. In the same year, medium intensity lighting was installed.

In 1959-60, the airport was transferred from the Saskatchewan Department of Natural Resources to the federal Department of Transport, which leased the airport to Eldorado Nuclear Ltd. A combination radio beacon and transmitter building, along with an operations building, were completed on June 30, 1962; renovation to the operations building was finished in March 1967. Eldorado Nuclear Ltd. closed their mining operations in August 1983.

The airport is owned by the Department of Transport but is operated by the province of Saskatchewan (Department of Highways and Transportation).

It is served by Time Air with Dash-7 aircraft. Athabasca Airways and Uranium city Air Ltd. provide charter service.

In 1988, there were 279 aircraft movements and 2,900 passengers.

The present airport manager is Ken Johnson.

Source:
Transport Canada, Central Region.

Val-D'Or Airport
(Québec)

In 1949, the Department of Transport made a grant of $25,000 to the city of Val-D'Or for the construction of an airport, and in 1950, a 4,000 foot [1,219-metre] paved runway was built.

Canadian Pacific Air Lines began service from Montréal to Val-D'Or with DC-3 aircraft in May 1950. That same year, the Department of Transport made a further grant of $62,000 for additional airport development. By agreement between the Departments of National Defence and Transport in 1951, the runway was to be extended to 6,000 feet [1,828 metres] during 1952.

The Department of National Defence took over the airport in 1954. A large air force camp was built in the next year and a military base was established. From 1955 to 1962, the station was used as an advance base by CF-100 jet fighters operating out of Uplands and North Bay.

The runway, 18-36, was extended to 8,000 feet [2,438 metres] in 1956 and to 8,200 feet [2,499 metres] in 1961.

In 1962, the decision was made to operate CF-101 aircraft out of Val-D'Or, and a major new construction program began. The civil area of operations was relocated on the east side of the airport at Department of Transport expense. On November 19, 1962, the first CF-101 arrived. The runway was extended again for military purposes—this time to 10,000 feet [3,048 metres]—and the airport became an advance defence post. The control tower was operated by the RCAF.

At the end of 1962, the Department of Transport made a contract with Trans-Canada Air Lines for the management of the air terminal and the civil apron. A new terminal building was constructed in 1967-68, and the apron was enlarged in 1972.

The Department of National Defence closed the airport for two months in 1972 so that two inches [five centimetres] of pavement overlay could be added to the runway.

An ILS (Instrument Landing System) was installed in 1972 and, the same year, Nordair and Quebecair moved into the new terminal. Air Canada added two flights a day, Nordair began a new direct Montréal-Val-D'Or service, and Québecair began service from Québec city to Val-D'Or.

In January 1975, the Department of National Defence announced that the armed forces would move out of the Val-D'Or base on April 1, 1976; their number was gradually reduced over the following twelve months. The Department of Transport took over responsibility for the airport on April 1, 1976, and made plans for the airport's redevelopment.

Austin Airways began service at Val-D'Or Airport in 1980, and two new scheduled airlines opened up in 1982: Air Creebec and First Air. In the same year, Nordair began scheduled cargo operations between Val-D'Or, Kuujjuaq, and Frobisher Bay.

June 5, 1987, marked the inauguration of the new airport complex on the west side of the runway, constructed at a cost of more than $10 million. It consists of two taxiways, an apron ramp, a new air terminal (with an area three times greater than the previous one), cargo space and a new road.

Air Canada, Canadian International, Inter-Canadian, First Air, Air Creebec, Air Alliance, Voyageur Airways, and Propair currently offer regular jet or turboprop service. La société de conservation du Nord-Ouest bases three CL-215 water bomber aircraft at the airport during the summer season.

Val-D'Or airport serves as the centre for dispatching mail and is the supply point for northern Québec localities.

The following served as airport managers:

G. St. Pierre	1975 to 1977
Guy Bertrand	1977 to 1979
R. Allard	1979 to 1981
R. Menard	1981 to 1985
D. Bleau	1985

Source:
Transport Canada, Québec Region.

Vancouver International Airport
(British Columbia)

Vancouver International Airport on Sea Island is close to Lulu Island, the place where aviation began in Vancouver. On March 25, 1910, Charles Hamilton, an American, made the first airplane flight in western Canada at the Minoru Park Race Track on Lulu Island, flying a Curtiss pusher biplane. In April 1911, also at Minoru Park Race Track, William Templeton and his cousin, William McMullen, test-hopped their home-built plane. Templeton served in the Royal Naval Air Service (1915-17) and later became the first manager of the Vancouver Municipal Airport. In 1912, Minoru Park was again used as a flying field when William M. Stark flew his Curtiss biplane on exhibition flights. He also carried passengers.

The Aero Club of B.C. was formed with William Stark as its instructor on December 15, 1915. It was the first flying club in Canada. For a time, the club flew from a site near the Minoru Race Track before moving to Pitt Meadows in 1916. On August 7, 1919, Captain Ernest Hoy took off from Minoru Park in his Curtiss JN-4 on the first flight through the Rockies.[1]

In 1920, the Air Board, government agency responsible for aviation in Canada, established a seaplane base at Jericho Beach,[2] Vancouver for the use of the Board's government Civil Air Operations Branch, which was responsible for all flying for the government, e.g. patrols, forest protection, customs, surveys, photography, and transportation. The Branch flew HS-2L and F-3 flying boats and Avros on floats. The station was later administered by the CAF (in 1922) and by the RCAF (in 1923).

On October 17, 1920, a DH-9 landplane of the newly-formed Canadian Air Force alighted in Vancouver (at Brighthouse Park race track, near

200. Vancouver Airport, B.C., July 24, 1931.

Richmond[3]) at the end of the first cross-Canada flight. The trip began in Halifax on October 7 and was made in stages by seaplane to Winnipeg and from there to Vancouver by landplane. The concluding leg of the flight was made by Captain G.A. Thompson, who became a well-known pilot in western Canada. He later served for a number of years as the district controller of Air Services for the Department of Transport in Vancouver.

In 1928, Charles Lindbergh refused to visit Vancouver "because there is no fit field to land on."[4] In the same year, the city of Vancouver leased a field near Landsdowne Park on Lulu Island to assist the Aero Club of B.C. This became the city's first airport, with two runways: east-west, 2,691 feet [820 metres], and north-south, 1,260 feet [384 metres]; a hangar, 64 by 40 feet [19.5 by 40 metres]; and a waiting room.[5] It was used by B.C. Airways for its Vancouver-to-Victoria service with the Ford tri-motor airplane.

Meanwhile, negotiations and planning proceeded to establish a more satisfactory airport. A site on nearby Sea Island was recommended, and was approved by the city of Vancouver, which purchased 475 acres [192 hectares] for $300,000. The new airport was also to have facilities for seaplanes.

At the laying of the foundation stone of the administration building on September 13, 1930, William Templeton, the first airport manager, said, "We had an airport, but no night lighting, no weather bureau, no radio aids and, of course, no business."[6] The 1930s was the barnstorming decade of aviation, the day of the thrill ride. Unofficial air traffic statistics for 1931 show 2,652 passengers were carried on sightseeing flights over the city, while only 536 passengers arrived at the airport on 309 flights from other points.[7]

Vancouver Municipal Airport was formally opened on July 22, 1931, by the Premier of

British Columbia, the Honourable Simon Fraser Tolmie. It had a single runway, 2,400 by 100 feet [732 by 31 metres], an administration building and two hangars.[8] The Aero Club of B.C., which joined the federal government's light aeroplane club scheme in 1929, was the first flying organization to move to the new airport. Other early operators at the airport were Dominion Airways, Sprott-Shaw School of Aviation, Brisbane School of Aviation, and Aircraft Devices of B.C. (a flying school and repair shop).[9] There was a seaplane harbour on the south side of the airport which is still in operation.

The following extract from a letter of July 8, 1931, to Squadron Leader A.T. Cowley (National Defence's Air Services representative in Regina) from J.A. Wilson, controller of Civil Aviation, provides an interesting comment on the operation of the Vancouver Airport:

The municipal authorities do not realize the importance of making the charges for the use of their airport as reasonable as possible so that the aircraft operators will use the municipal airport rather than establish facilities of their own. We have written Templeton impressing this view on him. If the city authorities are reasonable, a company would be ill-advised not to use the facilities provided by the municipality at

201. Vancouver International Airport, 1931.

great expense and they will certainly forfeit much good will if they do not do so.[10]

In 1932, Alaska Washington Airways opened a Vancouver-Victoria-Seattle service for which the airport established its first weather service. This consisted of an exchange of information with Boeing Field in Seattle, three times daily, by phone. During the same year, Canadian Airways operated from Vancouver to Victoria.

On July 1, 1934, after some urging by Templeton (the airport manager) United Airlines, a major American transcontinental airline, began passenger, mail, and cargo service from Seattle to Vancouver using a ten-passenger Boeing 247 airplane. The following year, Canadian Airways began a passenger and air-mail service from Vancouver to Seattle flying a De Havilland Rapide, and later, a Lockheed 10-A.

On March 9, 1935, the city of Vancouver passed a resolution recommending that the Department of National Defence take over the municipal airport and use it as a national airport. The Controller of Civil Aviation was not in favour, and he wrote to the Deputy Minister on April 14, 1935. The reply is of interest as a statement of government policy at the time:

1. I concur in the opinions of the Senior Air Officer, set forth in his memorandum of April 1st. The taking over of the Vancouver airport as an RCAF base is, therefore, not recommended.

2. The problem, therefore, is whether there is any justification for taking it over as a civil airport, to be maintained by the Department for the use of the civil aircraft using Vancouver as a base.

3. The policy of this Department from the beginning has been that each locality must provide and maintain its own airport. The building of the Canadian airway system has always been considered as a cooperative effort, under which the localities served should provide terminals, while the Department would provide the added facilities necessary for safe air navigation on any airway, that is, the intermediate fields in districts where there were no municipalities; the lighting, where required for night flying, and communications, such as radio, teletype services and meteorological services.

4. If the Department should now take over the Vancouver airport, similar demands would be made by many other cities. Regina has already been pressing for the same solution of its financial difficulties. During the past few years, at least two and a half million dollars have been spent by the cities of Canada on airport development. There is no reason why Vancouver should receive preferential treatment over other cities, such as Calgary, Edmonton, Regina, Moose Jaw, Saskatoon, Hamilton, Saint John, Halifax, Moncton and Sydney. The maintenance of all these city airports would throw an intolerable burden on the Department and, as civil aviation develops, there would be continual pressure for the expenditure of more money to keep pace with the growing requirements of the airways. It can readily by seen that this solution presents the gravest drawbacks.

5. The only reason why requests that the Department should relieve the cities of their airports are not being received is because of the unavoidable delay in establishing the trans-Canada airway and its main connections. The city airports were all built with the encouragement and advice of the Department to provide the main bases on the airway, and the municipal authorities are disappointed that, having supplied the airports, greater use is not being made of them. The constructive solution is to press forward with the establishment of the trans-Canada airway and give the cities the service they expected when the airports were built. If this were done, little would be heard in future of the airport being an unnecessary burden. Revenues would quickly rise and, though for some years, they might not meet the whole of the interest and sinking fund charges, there is no doubt that the airports would pay an operating profit at least and the communities would be content to make up the deficit on account of the increase in efficiency of their communications.

6. As had been pointed out elsewhere, the cost of finishing and operating the trans-Canada airway would not be excessive and probably would not exceed that of operating the city airports, which would be of little use without it. The constructive solution is, therefore, on these lines, instead of on the negative proposal that the Department relieve the city of its burden.[11]

Other cities were also having financial problems and airport development suffered in

202. Lockheed 12-A CF-CCT, Vancouver, July 29, 1937. End of transcontinental flight.

consequence. The federal government was able to assist Vancouver when, in December 1936, the new Department of Transport introduced a program whereby it would contribute one-third of the cost of developing terminal airports, the balance to be paid by the municipalities and provinces.

Earlier in 1936, the Civil Aviation Branch of the Department of National Defence provided an aviation and meteorological office at Vancouver Airport; and the Royal Canadian Corps of Signals was in charge of communications.

Between 1936 and 1938, developments at Vancouver included two hard-surfaced runways, 3,000 feet [914 metres] long, taxiways, and field lighting, in addition to a grass landing strip. A low frequency, low course radio range was installed in 1937.

On September 1, 1937, the new Trans Canada Airlines (TCA) began its first scheduled passenger and mail service when it flew between Vancouver and Seattle, having taken over this service from Canadian Airways. On March 6, 1938, TCA began regular air-mail service between Vancouver and Winnipeg, and on December 1, 1938, between Vancouver and Montréal. Transcontinental passenger, mail, and express service was inaugurated between Montréal, Toronto, Winnipeg, Lethbridge, and Vancouver on April 1, 1939.

203. C.D. Howe, Minister of Transport, and crew, July 29, 1937, Vancouver.

In 1937, Grant McConachie's Yukon Southern Air Transport, which later merged with Canadian Pacific Airlines, connected Vancouver by air with Prince George, Fort St. John, Fort Nelson, and Whitehorse.

World War II brought many changes to Vancouver Airport, when it was chosen as a site for an Elementary Flying Training School (EFTS) under the British Commonwealth Air Training Plan. No. 8 EFTS, which opened in 1940, was operated by Vancouver Air Training Co. Ltd., a subsidiary company of the Aero Club of B.C; and brought thousands of pilots to the airport for training. From time to time during the war, operational units of the RCAF were based at the airport, including bomber reconnaissance, fighter, army cooperation, transport, and communications aircraft. Commercial flying increased and the Boeing Airplane Company built a large plant on the south side of the airport in 1939.[12] Canadian Pacific Airlines bought and occupied the plant after the war, and sold it later to Pacific Western Airlines.

In August 1940, the Department of National Defence took over the Vancouver Municipal Airport for the duration of the war and six months thereafter. The airport continued to function as a civil airport under the management of the Department of Transport, using the pre-war city staff. During the war, extensive improvements were carried out by the federal government, including lengthening and strengthening existing runways, and constructing additional hangars and other buildings.

The airport was returned to the city on October 31, 1947, and, at that time, the Department of Transport began to pay an operating subsidy.

By the end of the war, Vancouver had become a busy airport, with the following operators:
Aero Club of B.C.

Canadian Pacific Airlines
    —under Grant McConachie, operated to the Prairies and the Arctic
Queen Charlotte Airlines
    —later to become Pacific Western Airlines; under Russell Baker (formerly of Central B.C. Airways) serving Western Canada
B.C. Airlines
    —serving the B.C. coast
Vancouver "UFly"
    —later to become West Coast Air Services
Okanagan Air Service
    —under Carl Agar, developed from a crop dusting operation of one helicopter into the world's largest helicopter company
Trans-Canada Air Lines
    —since 1937; became Air Canada in 1965

Other airlines serving the airport were United Airlines, which had offered service to Seattle since 1934, and British Commonwealth Pacific Airways, which became Qantas Airways in 1946. It was the first scheduled overseas air carrier with service to Australia to use the airport.

In 1948, the airport, at times called Vancouver Municipal Airport or Sea Island Airport, was renamed Vancouver International Airport.

The airport's international status was further enhanced in July 1949, when Canadian Pacific Airlines began its North Star service to Hawaii,

204. Vancouver International Airport, c. 1958.

Canton Island, Fiji, and Australia; and in September to Tokyo and Hong Kong.

The original airport administration building destroyed by fire in 1949, was replaced by a temporary structure, the north terminal, in March 1950, and extended in 1952.

An ILS (Instrument Landing System) and high intensity approach lighting were installed in 1948. A new runway, 08-26, 8,600 feet [2,621 metres] long, was constructed in 1953 to replace the old main runway, 07-25, and was later extended to the present 11,000 feet [3,353 metres]. In 1961, a cross-wind runway, 12-30, 7,300 feet [2,225 metres] long, was completed.

A good source of revenue, unique to Vancouver Airport, was a tax of twenty-five cents per passenger inbound through Customs, which contributed to the operating profits summarized below. At the end of each year, the airport's net surplus was paid over to the city.

Operating Profit	1951-52	1952-53
Before depreciation	$37,274	$95,243
After depreciation	$ 1,362	$55,979

In 1955, TCA launched a five-times-a-week all-cargo service; Canadian Pacific Airlines inaugurated polar service to Amsterdam; and Pacific Western Airlines (PWA) was operating thirty-two aircraft up the coast and into the interior of British Columbia. PWA joined Queen Charlotte Airlines and B.C. Airlines in offering this in-province service.

By 1956, passenger traffic stood at 654,000, and the terminal facilities had to be expanded again. On July 1, 1957, the west terminal was opened; the north terminal was extended again in 1963.

It had become clear that a major new terminal development would be required to take care of the projected traffic growth at Vancouver. The

city began to plan accordingly and approached the Department of Transport for capital assistance. Under the airport financial assistance policy at the time, Transport could offer capital grants only for the public (non-revenue) space in the building—and this would not be enough for such a major project as at Vancouver's. After prolonged negotiations between the city and the department—and following a municipal plebiscite—the federal government agreed to purchase the city's investment in the Vancouver airport and assume full responsibility for its operation and development. Transport paid $2.5 million for land, buildings and equipment, took over the airport on June 1, 1962, and began to plan a new air terminal complex in the central area, north of the intersection of runways 12-30 and 08-26. Since the conception of the airport in 1929, the city had contributed a total of $1,239,365, while the federal government's input had been $12,820,979.[13]

In 1961, TCA opened a new maintenance complex on the north side of runway 08-26. It was expanded with the construction of a second hangar for wide body aircraft in 1973. CPA operations and maintenance centre opened in 1970 is located on the north side of the main entrance road to the terminal, Grant McConachie Way— named after CPA's founder.

The new terminal complex, which cost $32 million, became operational on September 10, 1968. It was opened on October 25, and had a design capacity of 3.5 million passengers per year.

The old terminals on the south side were converted to other uses: the west terminal became an air cargo terminal in 1968 and was operated by Western Freight Forwarding until 1973; the old north terminal became a general aviation terminal in 1970 and was operated by Central Western Airfreight until February 27, 1976, when it was destroyed by fire.

The northern half of the air cargo terminal was converted to a commuter and general aviation passenger terminal in 1978, and is operated by Transport Canada. It is now known as the South Terminal.

In 1973, Central Western Air Freight, now International Aviation Terminals, opened a modern air cargo facility in the central area near the new air terminal. In 1988, the company completed its latest expansion and now has 9,290 square metres of combined office and warehouse space. Air Canada, which has its own air cargo terminal, added 2,787 square metres of warehouse and office space in 1987, and a further 1,672 square metres in 1988.

In 1988, Transport Canada purchased a Main Deck Cargo Loader (MDL)—a highly specialized machine which can load up to 18,144 kilograms of freight from the top deck of a 747 Combi and other cargo aircraft. The airlines pay the airport $350 per hour for its use. This is a unique arrangement, and the MDL is the only one owned by a Transport Canada airport.

Expansion of the airport has been a continuous process since it was taken over by Transport Canada. Passengers totalled 854,000 in 1962, 2,248,000 in 1969, and 6,476,500 in 1979, when Vancouver ranked third for passenger traffic out of all Canadian airports. In 1988, it was second

205. Vancouver International Airport, c. 1976.

only to Toronto-Lester B. Pearson International Airport, and had more than nine million passengers. In 1988, the airport had 287,000 aircraft movements, compared to 129,730 in 1968.

Road access to the airport on Sea Island had been a long-standing problem. There was only one bridge—the Moray Channel—to connect Sea Island to Vancouver via Lulu Island over the Oak Street bridge. To alleviate the congestion, Transport built two bridges: the Dinsmore Bridge in 1969, which gave access via Richmond; and in 1975, the Arthur Laing bridge, originally called the Hudson Street Bridge, to give direct access to the city of Vancouver.

In February 1971, the Department of Transport opened its new area air traffic control and aeradio centre on the south side of the airport, to replace the premises, built in 1936 near the old north terminal. In 1973, Transport began an expansion program for the air terminal complex that enlarged the cafeteria, the public waiting areas, and passenger hold rooms; it provided a new international arrivals area, as well as additional baggage facilities and parking lots. In 1977, the parking garage under the terminal building was converted to provide more space for inspection services, Canadian and American. And in 1980, floor area was added to the terminal, and car parking was increased to a capacity of 2,400 cars. (There are also 1,000 spaces in the economy public parking area). Another expansion and modernization is underway at an estimated cost of $58 million.

The terminal has twenty-seven aircraft gates serving twenty hold rooms. Twenty-six of the gates have bridges owned by air carriers. The Airport is served by twenty-six scheduled airlines, linking Vancouver to over forty countries around the world:

Main terminal	South terminal	Charters
Air B.C.	Aquila Air	American Trans Air
Air Canada	Burrard Air	Canada 3000
Air China	Canadian Helicopters (formerly Okanagan)	Canadian Armed Forces
Air New Zealand		Finnair
American Airlines	Harbour Air	Great American Airways (SilverWing)
British Airlines	Pacific Coastal	Holidair
Canadian Airlines International Ltd.	Pacific Rim Vancouver Helicopters	Lot-Polish Air Lines
Cathy Pacific Airways	Wilderness Air	Nationair (National Defence)
Continental Airlines	Helijet Airways**	
Delta Airlines		
Horizon Air		Nomads
Japan Air Lines		Odyssey
KLM Royal Dutch Airlines		Points of Call
Korean Air		Worldways
Lufthansa German Airlines		
Qantas Air Lines		
Skylink Airlines*		
Singapore International Airlines		
Time Air		
United Airlines		
Wardair Canada		

  *Scheduled flights from both terminals
  **Operates from a heliport east of the main terminal

The following operators are based at the airport: Canadian Airlines International, Air Canada, and Air BC.

Hangars on the airport are owned/occupied as follows:

Canadian Airlines International
    —the airlines' main maintenance complex.
Air Canada
    —a major maintenance complex.
Innotech Aviation
    —aviation service centre
MacMillan Bloedel Flight Operations
    —company's own aircraft. This is one of the original hangars, built in 1930. It is leased by Transport Canada. Over the years, the hangar was occupied by Trans-Canada Air Lines, Malaboo Searo Club and BNP Airways (B.C. Electric, Northern Construction and the Powell River Company).
Air BC
    —Company operations. This is the second of the original hangars built in 1930, and owned by Transport Canada. It has been occupied by Canadian Airways, Canadian Pacific Airlines, Aero Surveys, Bristol Aero Engines, Pioneer Chain Saws and Air West Airlines. The hangar apron leads southward to the seaplane slipway.
Sea Island Group
    —occupies one of the old CP Air (Canadian Airlines International) hangars on the south side of the airport.
British Columbia Institute of Technology (BCIT)
    —occupies the old CP Air Britannia hangar. The third of CP Air's hangars on the south side, known as the Boeing plant, was dismantled in 1980.

Over the years, the city of Vancouver and later the Department of Transport acquired more and more land on Sea Island for immediate and long-term use in the expansion of the airport. Today, the airport occupies almost all of the 1,620-hectare[14] island, except the village of Burkeville. Most of the land acquired in recent years was obtained by expropriation against strong public opposition.

As part of the expansion announced in 1973, the Department of Transport planned to construct a new runway, parallel to the main 08-26, 3,353 metres long, and north of the terminal complex. Without it, Vancouver would remain, effectively, a one-runway airport. In 1973, when an airport planning committee, chaired by Ivor Jones, was set up to hear public opinion, strong opposition developed from all communities likely to be affected by aircraft noise. At this time, an environmental impact study was required by law, and public hearings had to be held before construction could begin. Local opposition grew and the project was delayed. The matter is currently being reviewed once more in light of the airport's increased traffic and the forecast demands of the future.

To increase the capacity for airside movements, simultaneous IFR (Instrument Flight Rules) approaches were permitted on both runways (08-26 and 12-30) beginning in February 1989. In September 1989, stub runway 26 Alpha was opened for light aircraft departures by making use of Taxiway Alpha. The conversion from taxiway to runway, which required threshold marking and procedure revision, takes some pressure off the main runway and provides an option for aircraft entering the field from the South Terminal.

The seaplane base, now managed and maintained by two operators, Seahurst and Harbour Air, is a vital part of transportation to remote logging and fishing camps.

For a number of years, an interfaith ministry was provided at the airport by Tom Eldon, an ex-CP Air captain, who gave counselling for airline and airport employees and offered guidance to the travelling public. The service ceased for a time, but has been reactivated and is now offered by Layne Daggett as a non-denominational service with the assistance of neighbouring parishes. The chapel is on the third level of the terminal, in space donated by Transport Canada.

Overall, 13,500 people are directly employed at the airport, which is a major generator of economic activity in British Columbia, accounting for $2.7 billion revenue. The airport collected $52,704,000 in revenue for 1987-88, had total expenses of $43,386,000, and produced an operating surplus of $9,378,000.

Vancouver International Airport is one of four major airports currently operated by Transport Canada, that the federal government is considering transferring to local authorities. In July 1989, the federal minister of Transport signed a Memorandum of Understanding in Vancouver to begin negotiations for such a transfer: the airport would remain a federal asset with air traffic control and security under Transport Canada, but administration and economic planning would be handled by a local Board of Directors.

The following have served as airport managers at Vancouver International Airport:

WilliamTempleton	1931 to 1950 (under the city of Vancouver and, during the war, the Department of Transport)
William L. Inglis	1950 to 1976 (under the city of Vancouver until June 1962, when the Department of Transport took over the airport)
Lorne Howel	1984 to 1985 (on an interim basis)
Lorne Howell,	1985 to 1987
FrankO'Neill	1987 to present

Sources:
1. "Vancouver International Airport", Transport Canada, Master Plan Project.
2. *History of Vancouver International Airport,* Transport Canada, Public Affairs, British Columbia Region.
3. Transport Canada, Pacific Region.

Footnotes—Vancouver Airport

[1] F.H. Ellis, *Canada's Flying Heritage* (Toronto: University of Toronto Press, 1961), pp. 32-33, 64-65, 84, 113-115, 178-179.

[2] William Templeton, mentioned above, participated in the selection of the site. Years later, he was involved in picking the site of the present airport on Sea Island.

[3] Ellis, p. 184.

[4] John Scott Mitchell, *Vancouver International Airport: Historical Information and Chronological Listing,* (Vancouver Airport Planning Project, c. 1975).

[5] United States, *Airports in Canada and Newfoundland,* (U.S. Printing Office, 1930).

[6] *Flying High: The 50th anniversary of Vancouver International Airport 1931-1981,* Canada, Transport Canada, TP3118E, unnumbered page.

[7] Ibid.

[8] The administration building, constructed in 1930-31, was the second one in Canada. The first was at St. Hubert in 1929. The hangars, built in 1930, are still in use. One is leased by MacMillan Bloedel Flight Operations and the other by Air BC.

[9] *The Magnificent Distances: Early Aviation in British Columbia, 1910-40,* Provincial Archives of British Columbia, pp. 42, 43.

[10] Public Archives Canada, MG 30 E243, vol. 1.

[11] Public Archives Canada, MG 30 E243, vol. 8.

[12] The Department of Munitions and Supply built a new plant in 1940 and passed it over to Boeing for operation. They assembled Catalinas (PBYs) commencing in 1942, and by 1943 had 7,733 employees. Another plant built in Vancouver by the government was turned over to Canadian Pacific Airlines (CPAL) and operated as a repair and maintenance depot for Stranraers, Hudsons, Grumans, and other aircraft of the RCAF Coastal Command. (See Leslie Roberts, Canada's War in the Air (Montréal: Alvah M. Beatty, 1943,))

[13] *Flying High.*

[14] The original airport site was 475 acres [192 hectares] in 1931.

Victoria International Airport
(British Columbia)

In 1930, there was a private airport owned by British Columbia Airways Ltd., "located on the southeastern extremity of Vancouver Island."[1] Before the establishment of Victoria Airport, air service between Vancouver and Victoria was by seaplane.

In October 1937, the Department of Transport felt there was a need for a large military airport on southern Vancouver Island and favoured Sidney as the site; and, in 1938, the Departments of National Defence and Transport formed a joint committee to plan such an airport.

Construction began in the summer of 1939; runway paving started in September; the airport was ready for use in 1940. The runways were rebuilt and extended in 1941 and completed in 1942. Extensive building construction was undertaken to accommodate the Royal Canadian Air Force, the Royal Air Force, and the Royal Canadian Navy.

The airport, then known as Patricia Bay, was base for bomber reconnaissance and fighter units, and was the home of two operational training units (OTU), No. 3 OTU (RCAF) and No. 32 OTU (RAF), No. 18 Elementary Flying Training School (operated by Boundary Bay Flying Training School Ltd., a subsidiary company of the Aero Club of B.C.) under the British Commonwealth Air Training Plan (BCATP) was also stationed there. The RCAF and RCN occupied the section of the airport known as the West Camp, and the RAF, the East Camp; The RAF left the airport in 1944.

In December 1942, the Department of National Defence gave permission for Trans-Canada Air Lines (TCA) to use the airport for a scheduled service to Vancouver. The service began in 1943 with two daily flights using fourteen-passenger Lockheed aircraft. By September 1946, TCA had three daily flights, and Seattle was later added to the route. This resulted in eight daily flights at Victoria.

The department set aside an area on the east side of the airport for civil use development in October 1947. The airport was transferred to Transport Canada on May 18, 1948, and a temporary airport licence was issued on January 18, 1950, retroactive to 1948. The permanent licence was issued in the name of the Department of Transport on September 8, 1950. RCAF units remained on the airport until 1952.

By 1955, activity had increased to 77,000 aircraft movements, and the seaplane harbour was reactivated. In addition to TCA, the principal users of the airport were Pacific Western Airlines, Fairey Aviation Ltd. of Canada (aircraft repair and overhaul), the Victoria Flying Club, Vancouver Island Helicopters, and Pacific Aviation Services.

On May 22, 1959, the name of the airport was changed from Victoria (Patricia Bay) to Victoria International Airport.

In 1961, runway 08-26 was extended to 6,000 feet [1,829 metres], and an ILS (Instrument Landing System) was installed on the 26 approach. In 1971, the runway was extended again, this time to 7,000 feet [2,134 metres], to accommodate DC-8 operations.

In 1964, a new air terminal building was opened to replace the old facility, which was a converted wartime hangar. A new control tower was also erected. The terminal building was enlarged in 1974 to accommodate increased passenger traffic.

Today, Victoria International Airport has three runways: 09-27, 2,134 metres; 02-20, 1,533 metres; and 13-31, 1,524 metres. In 1988, it had 717,000 passengers, and 29,197 itinerant aircraft movements.

The airport is served by Air Canada, Air BC, Time Air, Burrand Air, Horizonair, Airspeed Aviation, and Air Southwest.

The following airport managers served Victoria:

K.J. Robinson	1948 to 1954
J. Knowland	1954 to 1977
J.E. Mills	1977 to 1983
G.C. Baker	1983 to 1988
L.L. Brown	1989

Sources:
1. Transport Canada, Pacific Region.
2. R.L. Clarke, "Airport Notes" (Ottawa: Transport Canada) [unpublished collection].

Footnote—Victoria Airport
[1] *Airports in Canada and Newfoundland*, United States, (US Printing Office, 1930).

Villeneuve Airport
(Alberta)

Villeneuve Airport, located near the hamlet of Villeneuve, thirty-one kilometres northwest of the city of Edmonton, was opened in October 1976.

It has two paved runways, 08-26 and 16-34, each 1,067 by 30 metres. Of the 573 hectare site 162 hectares are at present used for the airport, and the remainder is leased for agricultural use.

Villeneuve was built as part of an overall aviation master plan for the Edmonton area after discussions with local officials, the city of Edmonton, and the province. The role of Villeneuve Airport complements that of the municipal airport at Edmonton, owned and operated by the city of Edmonton, and the international airport, owned and operated by Transport Canada. All the interested parties agreed on a primary 'special use' concept for the three airports: Villeneuve was to be used for flying training and recreational flying to relieve the municipal airport.

The airport site was chosen from twelve possibilities by a selection committee (formed in 1973), following public meetings and an environmental study.

The airport has an initial design capacity of 250,000 aircraft movements a year. In 1988, there were 70,940 movements.

Improvements to the facilities and airport access include: a new air traffic control tower in 1982; a field electrical centre in 1983; and, in 1988, the paving of all major and secondary roads leading to Villeneuve Airport along with airport access roadway system and parking lots.

The following operators are based at the airport: Global Aircraft Industries Ltd. (formerly Liberty Aviation); R & R Aviation Ltd. (formerly Aero Aviation Centre); Lutheran Association of Missionaries and Pilots - LAMP; Northern Aero Services (formerly Edmonton Flying Club); and a new operator (formerly Herald Aviation).

The following served as airport managers:

John Kish	1976 to 1977
Ross Monroe	1978 to 1980
Ray Proulx	1980
Cliff Sorge	1980 to 1984
Judi Eriksen	1984 to 1987
Ray Proulx	1987 to present

Source:
Transport Canada, Western Region.

Wabush Airport
(Newfoundland-Labrador)

The Wabush Airport serves the northern communities of Wabush with a population of 2,637, Labrador city with a population of 8,664, and Fermont, Québec (Mount Wright), with a population of 3,200. The towns are dependent upon air transportation, although there is a railway line which carries iron ore to Sept-Iles, and a road which connects to Baie Comeau, Québec.

The first airstrip in the Labrador City-Wabush area was of gravel, constructed in 1957 at Ross Bay Junction (sixty-four kilometres northeast of Wabush), 3,900 feet [1,189 metres] long. It accommodated DC-3 and Viscount aircraft, which carried construction workers and materials while the railroad was being built.

As construction advanced in Labrador West, Ross Bay was abandoned for a site closer to the mine; and in 1959, a 4,000 foot [1,219 metre] airstrip was built at Duley Lake, thirteen kilometres southwest of Wabush. then, in 1960, another location was established on the outskirts of Labrador city in the area known today as Tamarack Drive.

The existing airport was built in 1961 as a joint venture by Wabush Mines Limited, Iron Ore Co. of Canada (IOCC), and Québec Cartier Mining. In 1963, an air terminal building was constructed by Crosby Enterprises Ltd. The airport was operated by Northern Airport Limited, which was co-owned by Wabush Mines and IOCC until April 1, 1973, when Transport Canada took complete control of all airport facilities. Before the takeover, Transport Canada, through its grants and aid program, improved the airport by lengthening and paving the existing runway, 01-19, to 6,000 feet [1,829 metres] in 1963, installing airport lighting and, in 1971, an ILS (Instrument Landing System). Transport Canada made further improvements in 1971, including major renovations to the passenger terminal.

In 1978, Transport Canada began an $11 million program to construct a new terminal complex consisting of an air terminal building and operations facility, a car park, access roads, a firehall, maintenance garage, a new taxiway, and apron. The terminal building, opened on August 19, 1981, is located at the north end of the

206. Wabush Airport, Labrador, August 1981.

runway and has access to the Wabush-to-Labrador city highway.

When Transport Canada first took over the airport, it gave a five-year maintenance contract the Marconi Co. Ltd. from April 1, 1973. But the contract was terminated on December 11, 1974, when Transport took over the entire operation.

The following operators serve or are based at Wabush Airport: Canadian (formerly Eastern Provincial Airways, which served from 1960; EPA took over from Maritime Central Airways); Inter-Canadian (formerly Quebecair, which served from 1960; originally it was Maritime Central Airways); Air Schefferville (since 1981); Air Alliance (January 1989); Air Atlantic (June 1989); Iron Ore Company of Canada; Wabush Mines; and Québec Cartier Mining.

The airport, which serves a catchment area with a population of 14,500, had 74,200 passengers and 9,250 aircraft movements in 1988. In 1987, approximately 1,100 tonnes of cargo and mail were processed.

The following have served as airport managers:

Patrick Kelley	1971 to 1973
Robert E. Howard	1973 to 1976
Francis Whelan	1976 to 1983
Paul Vautour	1984 to 1988
Eugene McDonald	1988

Sources:
1. Francis Whelan, former Airport Manager, Wabush Airport.
2. Transport Canada, Atlantic Region.

Watson Lake Airport
(Yukon Territory)

In the 1930s, Watson Lake was a stopping place for United Air Transport, which later became Yukon Southern Air Transport Ltd., and was subsequently taken over by Canadian Pacific Airlines. It was one of a chain of airfields across the Canadian northwest between Edmonton and Whitehorse, which was to follow the route used by the pilots of Yukon Southern.

In 1939, the federal government authorized the planning of airfields at Grande Prairie, Fort St. John, Fort Nelson, Watson Lake, and Whitehorse; and, by January 1940, site surveys had been completed. Construction of the fields began in 1941 as early as weather permitted. At Watson Lake, an area fifteen kilometres northwest of the town was chosen. A site of forty acres [sixteen hectares] was hewn out of the heavily treed countryside, and much filling was needed in a deep depression and a creek that bisected the length of the 5,500-foot [1,676 metre] airstrip. The proximity of the lake itself made further lengthening of the airstrip impossible; and the water body was an obstacle to the main runway approaches.

The logistics for the construction were a formidable undertaking. Men and equipment went to Fort Nelson from Fort St. John over a 483 kilometre winter road. Steamers carried supplies to Wragnell for the base at Watson Lake. Then, smaller boats took them from Wragnell up the Stikine River to Telegraph Creek, Dease Lake and Lower Post—the same route used during the Klondike gold rush. A tote road was then pushed through to Watson Lake from Lower Post.

By late 1941, the Northwest Staging Route fields were usable by daylight in good weather. Minimal landing fields, emergency lighting, radio aids, meteorological equipment and limited housing were in place. At this time during World War II, American warplanes such as the P-39 Aircobra, the P-40 Warhawk fighters and the Douglas C-47 transports were being ferried from Great Falls, Montana, to Alaska. From there, Russian pilots took over and flew the aircraft into Russia by way of Siberia. Because of the relative inexperience of the American ferry pilots and the rugged environmental conditions, the American authorities were forced to press for improved airport facilities and navigation aids, to match up to their own standards of operation.

Watson Lake benefitted from the upgrading program because it was a refuelling spot for American crews. An operations building and control tower were built, and the ramp area and the main and cross-wind runways were paved. Permanent airfield lighting for the main runway was installed, and a large military hangar was erected. The old B.C.-Yukon Air Service Ltd. hangar is still in use. The airfield complex was almost completely an American-operated facility. It grew to accommodate a large complement of personnel with the associated barracks, staff housing, mess halls, apartments, and storage facilities.

On June 23, 1944, Canada and the United States signed an agreement covering the disposal of airfields and buildings constructed by the U.S. in Canada: Canada would buy them, but the U.S. had rights to their use until the end of the war. At that time, the operation of the airport became the responsibility of the RCAF. The Canadian Army took over the maintenance of the Alaska Highway—which connected with the Northwest Staging Route bases, so that the bases would have an overland supply route—as well as the road which connected the airport to the town of Watson Lake.

With the departure of the Americans from the airport in 1946, Canadian Pacific Airlines became its prime user with Lodestar and DC-3 aircraft on the Watson Lake run that was part of its northwest route. Seven single dwellings, built by the RCAF and by Transport during the late 1940's, gave a more permanency to the airport's operation. The airport was a self-contained facility, utilizing many of the wartime installations—a curling rink, a theatre, a hobby workshop, messes, barracks, and a large sportsfield—which attracted airport personnel and townspeople alike.

The Department of Transport took over the airport from the RCAF on April 1, 1957; and, in 1961, barracks and storage buildings were demolished or removed—many to the town. The Lakeshore radio beacon was commissioned in 1962; then, in 1964, the former RCAF playing field was subdivided for homes. The site began to take on more of the complexion of a civic airport.

Jet service to the Watson Lake area began in October 1968 with CP Air's Boeing 737s, and improvements to the airport continued. In 1969, a new maintenance garage/firehall/sand storage complex was built—a concrete block building which replaced the aging log garage located in the main ramp area of the airport. In 1973, the operations areas and the public waiting room in CP Air's building were enlarged, and a freight storage area for CP Air was also added to the air terminal building.

A VOR/DME (VHF Omni-directional Range/Distance Measuring Equipment) air navigation facility was commissioned in 1975 on a site five kilometres directly south of the airport. An ILS (Instrument Landing System) for runway 26 was commissioned in 1981.

Time Air operates a Fokker F-28, to points south of Watson Lake, six days a week. Trans North Turbo Air flies north to Whitehorse every Tuesday and Thursday. At present, there is one charter operation based at the Watson Lake Airport: Watson Lake Flying Services. The airport is a major stopping and refuelling point for light aircraft travelling between southern Canada, and the U.S., and Alaska.

An overnight camping area has been developed for use by itinerant pilots who prefer to stay at the scenic airport. Picnic tables, fire pits, and firewood are supplied in the tenting area.

There are twenty Transport Canada employees at the airport, twelve with the Airports Group, seven at flight services, and one in the technical services branch. Many of these employees live in Crown-owned housing on-site. They have developed the Transport Canada Recreation Association (TCRA) and offer such facilities in the lodge as darts, a pool table, children's area, canteen and cooking area for public or private functions, a TV room and recreation area. Several activities are held each year for TCRA members and the populace of the town of Watson Lake, including an outdoor Curling Bonspiel in late winter, a family fishing derby in the summer, and a mixed slow-pitch tournament in the fall.

A decline in mineral exploration reduced the amount of airport activity in 1988, when there were 9,081 aircraft movements and 10,087 passengers from commercial scheduled flights.

The following have served as airport managers at the Watson Lake site:

E.S. Hall	1957 to 1961
Leo Martell	1961 to 1967
Vern Fitzpatrick	1967 to 1975
Don Gordon	1975 to 1977
Ken Howard	1977 to 1978
Al MacDonald	1978 to 1979
Ross Munro	1979 to 1983
Marcel Michaud	1983 to 1984
Rick Proulx	1984 to 1985
John Terpstra	1985 to 1986
Eleanor Blasetti	1986 to 1988
Jim D. Spring	1989 to

Source:

Steel, C. Wayne. "History of Watson Lake Airport". Transport Canada, Western Region. [unpublished report].

Whale Cove Airstrip
(Northwest Territories)

In the early 1700s, the Hudson's Bay Company extended its interests northward to the Whale Cove area: although the area had already been explored by Captain Thomas Button in 1613, it went in search of minerals.

Whale Cove, on the west shore of Hudson Bay, was not established as a permanent settlement until the summer of 1959. Prior to this date, there had been a settlement at Pistol Point, inland from Whale Cove, when the Department of Northern Affairs relocated a number of the inland Caribou Inuit (who had survived the famine years of 1957 and 1958) to Whale Cove, where they might adapt to the availability of coastal resources.

In 1966, following a field survey to select a site for an emergency airstrip, Transport Canada selected a location ten kilometres from the community. Work on the aerodrome was undertaken by the Department of National Defence in 1971; a gravel runway, 4,000 by 150 feet [1,219 by 45 metres], was built and a small parking apron. The civil works were completed in September 1973. The community gained hamlet status on July 1, 1975.

Although the original aerodrome was built by the Department of National Defence under the Remote Airports Program, later improvements were initiated by Transport Canada, under the Arctic Air Facilities Policy of 1979-80.

A passenger shelter was built in 1987 and the meteorological instruments, located within the community from 1967 to 1977, were relocated to the airport.

Improvements to the runway (covering an area of 1,036 by 30 metres), and to the access road were completed in 1980-81. Medium intensity airfield lights with VASIS (Visual Approach Slope Indicator system) and FEC (Field Electrical Center) were partially installed in 1981-82 and completed during the following year. A twenty-five kilowatt generator was installed in the field electrical centre in 1982-83 to supply power for the airfield lights, and a power line run from the community was completed in 1985.

Whale Cove is served by Calm Air, with ten scheduled flights per week, using HS-748 and Beach King Air aircraft. Keewatin Air Ltd. provides charter service.

There were 1,131 aircraft movements in 1987 and 984 in 1988, with 1,600 passengers in 1987, and 1,500 in 1988. The airstrip is unlicensed and is operated by the government of the Northwest Territories.

The industries of the area include hunting, fishing, and trapping. For transportation other than air, the community has barge service from Churchill; there is no road access.

Source:
Transport Canada, Central Region.

Whitehorse Airport
(Yukon)

In 1927, Yukon Airways and Exploration was formed as the first commercial airline in the Yukon Territory. It was based at "Cyr's wood lot on the hill above Whitehorse," which is the location of the present Whitehorse Airport.[1] It was here that four U.S. Army Air Service DH-4B biplanes landed in August 1920 en route to Nome, Alaska, from New York, and again on their return flight. The field was used regularly by aircraft flying in the area and en route to Alaska. In 1934, these included the Martin Bombers of the U.S. Army.

In 1929, the cleared area was a strip 1,800 feet [549 metres] long. By August 1933, a north-south gravel runway, 3,700 by 300 feet [1,128 by 91 metres], had been developed, along with a cross-runway of 1,500 feet [457 metres]. The field was under the control of the territorial government. Local residents paid for most of the work.

Air transport between Carcross, Whitehorse, and Fairbanks, Alaska, became increasingly important, and by July 1934, the landing strip had been widened to 500 feet [152 metres] and the cross strip extended to 1,600 feet [488 metres], but the field was too soft for heavily loaded aircraft. For a time, the field was operated by the White Pass and Yukon Railway, but the site remained Crown land.

A temporary licence, for day use only, was granted to the government of the Yukon on January 8, 1935.

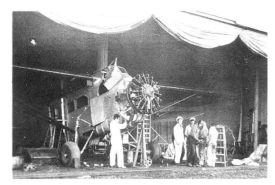

207. *Steamboat Hangar*, Whitehorse Airport, Yukon Territory, c. 1942.

208. CP Airlines hangar, Whitehorse, Yukon Territory, c. 1943.

On July 7, 1937, Grant McConachie, president of United Air Transport Ltd. flew the first airmail between Edmonton and Whitehorse.[2] In those days, Whitehorse was the hub of aerial activity and was used by aircraft from United Air Transport, Northern Airways, British Yukon Navigation Company, Canadian Airways, the RCAF,[3] and Pacific Alaska Airways.

Improvements were made to the field in 1937 when additional land was cleared at the northeast end. The runway was extended to 4,500 by 100 feet [1,372 by 30 metres] and realigned into the prevailing wind. A second runway, 2,000 feet [610 metres] long, was developed at 90° to the first. These improvements were made as a result of the new airway between Edmonton and Whitehorse, via Fort St. John, Fort Nelson, and Watson Lake.

Pacific Alaska Airways (owned by Pan American Airways) began operations at Whitehorse on April 1, 1935, with Lockheed Electras, flying a scheduled service to Fairbanks from Juneau by way of Whitehorse. In the same year, the company built an emergency field at Burwash Landing, Yukon, and provided men and equipment to assist the territorial government in improving and maintaining the Whitehorse Airport. The airline also built an administration building and radio station at Whitehorse in 1935. The original

Pacific Alaska terminal and workshop were at the top of the old road that comes up the clay cliffs about 1,000 feet [305 metres] south of the old RCAF hangar on the east side.

Pacific Alaska continued to operate the Juneau-Whitehorse-Fairbanks service until the winter of 1940 when, in co-operation with Pan American Airways, scheduled service was extended from Seattle to Fairbanks via Prince George, Juneau and Whitehorse, using Lockheed Lodestars and, later, DC-3s. In September 1942, all Pan American operations on the route to Alaska were taken over by the U.S. Navy, and were managed under contract by Pan American until July 1944, when civil operations were resumed. Pan American remained at Whitehorse during the war. From 1940 to 1961, when the air terminal was moved to Hangar A on the west side, the old Department of Transport operations building on the east side was used as an operations centre and ticket office. At the termination of the Navy contract in 1945, the workshop was moved from its original location to Hangar B on the west side. Pan American closed the operations at Whitehorse in December 1963. Over the years, they operated a variety of aircraft: Lockheed 10 and 14, DC-3, DC-4, B-337 Stratocruiser, and DC-6.[4]

The Whitehorse Airport was taken over by the federal government for the duration of the war.

209. Terminal and hangar, Whitehorse, Yukon Territory, c. 1976.

In June 1941, the Department of National Defence approved a major expansion of the airport for use by the RCAF: the main runway was paved and, in 1942, was extended to 6,600 feet [2,012 metres]. Improvements were also made to the second runway.

In December 1941, when the United States entered the war, the Edmonton—Whitehorse route assumed new importance. In 1942, Whitehorse had a key place in the development of the Northwest Staging Route to Alaska. The U.S. Air Force developed the west side of the airport and the RCAF, the east side. Today, the east side is largely unused, as operations are carried on from the west side in the wartime hangars. All American improvements were purchased by Canada for $8 million at the end of the war.[5]

The Department of Transport assumed responsibility for civilian services on the east side, formerly used by the RCAF, in 1948, and the RCAF moved to the former USAF area on the west side. Finally, Transport Canada took over the whole airport in September 1958, and on September 11, a temporary airport licence was issued. Transport Canada established its offices in hangar A and used the old (RCAF) garage and workshops on the west side of the airport.

The air terminal remained on the east side until about 1961 when a new terminal was

210. Control Tower and Operations Building, Whitehorse, Yukon Territory, 1976.

constructed in hangar A. In 1982, construction began on a new air terminal building, just south of hangar A. This new building was officially opened on December 7, 1985, and hangar A was demolished shortly after.

Telecommunications, weather services and air traffic control were located in the old tower at hangar H until the new operations building—near hangar A on the west side—was completed in the spring of 1971. The old operations building was torn down in 1972.

RCAF hangar H was the only building remaining on the east side; it was destroyed by fire on October 1, 1984.

The following airlines serve Whitehorse:

Canadian Airlines
—connections to Fort St. John, Edmonton and Vancouver
Air BC
—connections to Vancouver and Prince George.
Alkan Air
—connections to Faro, Dawson, Mayo, Old Crow, Inuvik, Ross River.
Air North
—connections to Dawson city, Old Crow, Watson Lake, Fairbanks, Juneau.
Delta Air
—connections to Yellowknife.

The following charter operators are based at the airport: Air North Charter and Training, Alkan Air, Trans North Turbo Air, Whitehorse Flying School, Delta Air Charter Ltd., Aerokon Aviation, Tagish Air Services, Big Salmon Air, and Capital Helicopters.

In 1988, there were 133,585 passengers and 53,228 aircraft movements.

The following have served as airport managers since Transport took over:

— Robinson	1958 to 1960
D. McKery	1960 to 1962
A. Thurber	1962
W. Morley	1962 to 1964
J. Richardson	1964 to 1973
J. Williams	1973 to 1974
D. Bedier	1974 to 1976
B. Restall	1976 to 1981
D. Devlin	1981

Sources:
1. Transport Canada, Western Region.
2. E.D. Campbell, former Acting Airport Manager, Whitehorse Airport.
3. R.L. Clarke, "Airport Notes" (Ottawa: Transport Canada) [unpublished collection].
4. Pan American World Airways, New York.

Footnotes—Whitehorse Airport
[1] *The Yukon News*, Seprember 8, 1975
[2] F.H. Ellis, *Canada's Flying Heritage* (Toronto: University of Toronto Press, 1961)p. 322.
[3] Bruce Gowans, "The Restoration of BGR", *CAHS Journal*, vol. 19, no. 1, (1981), p. 24.
[4] According to E.D. Campbell, former Acting Airport Manager, Whitehorse Airport.
[5] See Chapter 10.

Wiarton Airport
(Ontario)

The Department of Transport constructed Wiarton Airport in 1947 as a supplementary facility on the new airway system that would replace the route north from Toronto to North Bay and Kapuskasing and westward to Armstrong and Kenora. The new airway was a direct route westward over the Great Lakes region via Wiarton, Gore Bay, and over northern Michigan to the Lakehead.

The airport opened on August 1, 1948, with two 4,100 foot [1,249-metre runways] and a radio range station. It was located on 800 acres [324 hectares] of land just east of the town of Wiarton on what was known as Jones Range in Keppel township.

In 1954, runway 05-23 was extended to 6,000 feet [1,829 metres] to accommodate jet aircraft—primarily the T-33 jet trainer. A VHF Omni range was installed in 1956, and Tacan, in 1965.

Wiarton Flying Club and Owen Sound Air Services were based at the airport until 1984. The latter is the Cessna dealer, and operates a pilot training centre.

The Wiarton Airport is a designated Customs port of entry, staffed by Customs personnel from Owen Sound. Twenty-four-hour service is available, but there is an additional charge after normal working hours.

In 1970, a new operations building was constructed to accommodate the airport manager, Customs, and a public waiting room. It also provided space for telecommunications personnel who operate a combined Coast Guard and flight services station.

In 1974, runway 11-29 was closed owing to its deteriorated surface. It was reopened as a gravel strip for light aircraft in 1981. Runway 05-23 was refurbished in 1981, but reduced to 1,981 metres [6,500 feet].

Currently, there are no scheduled airline operations at Wiarton Airport. Charter service is provided by Brucelandair International.

The airport caters to the local permanent population, local business, and to tourist traffic in the summer. In 1988, there were 8,713 aircraft movements, the majority of which occured during the spring, summer, and fall.

The following served as airport managers at Wiarton:

J.H. Sanderson	1947 to 1949
Don MacLachlan	1949 to 1952
Chas. Bowens	1952 to 1953
Geo. McKnight	1953 to 1968
Clayton Brady	1968 to 1989
Allen Bluhm	1989

Sources:
1. Transport Canada, Ontario Region.
2. R.L. Clarke, "Airport Notes" (Ottawa: Transport Canada) [unpublished collection].

Williams Lake Airport
(British Columbia

On June 11, 1934, an airport licence was issued to the village of Williams Lake for a site with a landing strip 2,700 feet [823 metres] long and 400 feet [122 metres] wide. The field was cut by two arterial highways and the licence lapsed on September 28, 1937. In the fall of 1940, the village made improvements to the field, assisted by a one-third cost-sharing grant from the federal government; and during the war, further improvements were made at the expense of the Department of National Defence. These were transferred to the Department of Transport in September 1945. A temporary airport licence was issued to the village on December 20, 1946, to allow Parmatta Airways to base a charter service at the field. By June 1950, the field had a single strip, 5,200 by 200 feet [1,586 by 61 metres]; but the terrain prevented further expansion, and in 1953, the village asked that a new site be developed as a main line airport to replace the supplementary airport at Dog Creek.[1]

In September 1956, Transport Canada began construction of the new facility. In September 1959, the single paved runway, 11-29, 7,000 by 200 feet [2,134 by 61 metres], was completed, and the airport was in operation, licensed for day use only, on October 24, 1960—hence Canadian Pacific Airlines (CPAL) could use the airport when rain made the village field too soft for use. The new airport was put in full twenty-four-hour operation on December 14, 1960, and on December 19, CPAL began regular service with DC-3 aircraft to Vancouver, Quesnel, and Prince George. The airport was officially opened on July 5, 1961, and the village airport was closed down.

B.C. Airlines took over the route from CP Air in 1969 and Pacific Western Airlines (PWA), in turn, succeeded them in 1970 using Convair 640 aircraft. PWA introduced Boeing 737 aircraft on the route in 1974.

In 1976, the runway and apron were resurfaced. Subsequently the terminal building has been expanded and the carpark enlarged.

Air BC and Time Air offer scheduled service to and from Williams Lake Airport.

The airport has a number of base operations, including B.C. Forest Service Water Bombers, Vital Aviation, Northern Mountain Helicopters, Sharp Wings, Canadian Helicopters, Av Air, and Shell.

Air traffic at the airport has varied, as follows:

1965	5,573 movements
1973	37,753 movements
1976	22,056 movements
1977	26,234 movements
1980	29,154 movements
1988	20,638 movements

The airport is owned and operated by the Department of Transport.

The following served as airport managers:

J. Westover	1960 to 1964
W. Hough	1964 to 1969
A. Axani	1969 to 1976
L. Roland	1976 to 1977
W. Garbutt	1977 to 1987
M. Colmant	1987 to 1989
B. Bramah (Acting)	1989

Sources:
1. Transport Canada, Pacific Region.
2. R.L. Clarke, "Airport Notes" (Ottawa: Transport Canada) [unpublished collection].
3. B. Bramah, Acting Airport Manager, Williams Lake

Footnote—William Lake
[1]Dog Creek Airport was not closed, but continued to operate on a limited basis. Its facilities were moved to Williams Lake Airport in 1960.

Windsor Airport
(Ontario)

The history of Windsor Airport goes back to 1920, when a group of First World War pilots formed the Border Cities Aero Club. Some of the same men organized the aviation committee of the Chamber of Commerce in 1924 "to be prepared when it became practical to develop flying."[1]

Inspired by Lindbergh's successful flight to Paris in May 1927, local enthusiasts promoted a non-stop flight from Windsor, Ontario, to Windsor, England. Phil Wood, an American, had tried without success to be a member of the crew of the Sir John Carling, which was to fly from London, Ontario, to London, England,[2] so he bought a Stinson-Detroiter monoplane to take part in the Windsor-to-Windsor flight. Wood engaged C.A. "Duke" Schiller, who was then a pilot with the Ontario Provincial Air Service, to fly it, and Wood planned to accompany him as co-pilot. The airplane was named the Royal Windsor. The two men took off from the site of the present airport on September 1, 1927, the same day the Sir John Carling left London, Ontario, for England via Harbour Grace. Both planes ran into bad weather and Schiller and Wood landed at St. Johns, Québec. They arrived

211. Windsor (Walker) Airport, Ontario, c. 1930.

at Harbour Grace on September 7, a few hours after Tully and Medcalf had taken off for England. The Royal Windsor was delayed in Harbour Grace by a gas leak, and by the time it was repaired, Tully and Medcalf were long overdue in England; two other aircraft had been lost in the Atlantic the previous week; so friends prevailed upon Schiller and Wood to abandon their flight. They returned to Windsor from Harbour Grace[3]—but not before they conducted a long flight over the Atlantic in search of Tully and Medcalf, without result.

The idea of developing an airport for Windsor persisted, and in 1928, a branch of the Aerial League of Canada was formed. Three organizations, the aviation committee of the Chamber of Commerce, the Border Cities Aero Club, and the Aerial League, worked together to this end.

Soon afterwards, in the summer of 1928, the Border Cities Aero Club established a turf field at Walkerville. The airport east of Walker Road, was licensed on September 11, 1928, and declared a Customs port of entry on July 20, 1929. The property consisted of 280 acres [113 hectares] and was named Walker Airport by the Aero Club as a tribute to the Walkers, who not only leased the property to the club for five years, rent free, but in addition, gave $10,000 to assist in building a hangar. For several years, the

club received grants from the border municipalities to help them maintain the airport.

The airport was formally opened on September 8, 1928, with a large air show. One item on the programme was the International Air Race from Windsor to Los Angeles for $10,000 in prizes. The rules required that the pilots be Canadian; eight obligatory stops were specified. There were five entrants, but only two finished the race. Drury and Oliphant (London Flying Club) were first, and Whyte and Campbell (Hamilton Aero Club), second.[4]

The airport was used by Canadian Airways during 1930 and 1931 on the daily airmail service. As schedules called for night flying during the winter months, the Department of National Defence (Civil Aviation Branch) undertook to light the airfield at a cost of $9,000. The airmail route was cancelled in 1932, but the lighting remained in operation because the route was flown at night by American Air Lines and Central Air Lines, which had permission to cross Western Ontario on their flights to Detroit.

During the depression, the subsidies from the border municipalities ceased, and the Aero Club found it difficult to maintain the airport. In 1934, the club advised the Civil Aviation Branch that it would have to vacate—not only because of financial difficulties, but because Walker Farms

212. Original hangar, Windsor (Walker), 1940s.

255

213. Windsor Airport, Ontario, 1946.

Ltd. wanted the land back. A large portion of the acreage was, therefore, given up, and the remaining portion was temporarily licensed as an airport on June 12, 1936, in the name of John Canfield.

Throughout 1937, the Department of Transport and the Chamber of Commerce continued discussions on airport development. In February 1938, it was estimated that a 3,000 foot [914-metre] lighted runway could be developed at the Walker Field for $311,000, and in May, the department agreed to build an airport for Windsor on a site to be provided by the city. Following the rejection of a location on the Huron Church Line, it was decided to develop the Walker site. In the meantime, on September 30, 1938, the Walker Airport licence had been cancelled because Mr. Canfield did not renew his lease.

In September, the city asked if the department would agree to operate the airport for five years or until it was self-liquidating—the city, at that time, had no funds to underwrite any losses. The department agreed to run the airport until December 31, 1941, if the city would then take over. The Walker Field was re-licensed in the name of the Border Cities Aero Club on January 24, 1939.

In February, the Department submitted two proposals for the development of the Walker Airport and asked for an early decision, as otherwise, TCA service could not be extended to Windsor. The city acquired the Walker site for $54,000 in August, and Transport began to operate the airport. In June 1940, the city transferred the airport land to Transport for ten years, with an option to re-purchase in 1950. The Department paid the city $176,000 for the preliminary development of the airport.

Following a decision of the Department of National Defence to establish a flying training school at the Windsor Airport, under the British Commonwealth Air Training Plan (BCATP), No. 7 Elementary Flying Training School (EFTS) began operations in July 1940. It was managed by Windsor Elementary Flying Training School Ltd., a subsidiary of the Border Cities Flying Club.

Three runways, 3,750, 3,400, and 3,000 by 200 feet [1,143, 1,036 and 914 by 61 metres], were completed in July, as were the administration building and control tower. The Department of Transport operated the site as a civil airport; TCA began operations on August 1; and the airport was opened officially by the Honourable C.D. Howe, Minister of Transport, in October 1940.

When No. 7 EFTS ceased operations in 1945, the RCAF buildings were transferred to the Department of Transport.

In June 1948, two runways were extended to 5,250 and 5,200 feet [1,600 and 1,585 metres] to permit the operation of TCA's North Star aircraft. In 1954, runway 07-25 was extended to 6,900 feet [2,103 metres] to accommodate the airline's new Viscounts.

On February 16, 1950, the city of Windsor advised Transport Canada that it did not intend to exercise its option to take over the airport on October 15, 1950.

A new air terminal building (with Customs facilities) was completed in 1958, with the same design as the terminals at Québec city and Saskatoon. Many of the war surplus buildings were removed, and improvements were made to the airport. TCA introduced Vanguard aircraft in 1960. In 1962, Canadian Pacific Airlines began DC-8 flights to Mexico city—initially on a restricted basis because of runway length. These flights continued on a regular basis until November 1970. Runway 07-25 was extended to 7,900 feet [2,408 metres] in 1969, the year that Air Canada introduced DC-9 jet service.

One of the oldest aviation companies in Canada, Leavens Brothers, was based at Windsor Airport for many years, and in 1954 purchased the old equipment hangar. The Chamber of Commerce's "Wings over Windsor" had this to say about it:

One of the oldest aviation companies in Canada. They flew Curtiss Jennies from the end of W.W.I. and were most down-to-earth people. The Leavens Bros. were in this area for a long, long time. At first, they operated the 20-mile run from Leamington to Pelee Island. Later, when federal authorities rescinded the Leamington airport licence, they moved their operations to Windsor. But, for 25 years, the Company provided the only

214. New terminal building, Windsor Airport, 1958.

real link for Pelee Islanders to the mainland. Leavens' air service was part of the activity at Windsor Airport until 1963.[5]

In 1976-77, the air terminal building—which had 265,800 passengers and 78,000 aircraft movements—was expanded.

Because of concerns about the environmental effects of the airport on the Windsor community, a Citizen's Advisory Committee was formed in 1974 to help plan additional aviation facilities that would accommodate a predicted growth in air traffic beyond 1990. Meanwhile, work was begun in 1976 as an interim measure to relieve congestion in the air terminal building's public areas at peak passenger traffic periods.

From 1983 to 1985, the airport went through extensive improvements as a result of the federal government's Special Recovery Capital Projects Program. These included the construction of a firehall addition; resurfacing of runways 07-25 and 02-20, taxiways, aprons, and carpark areas; upgrading of water and electrical distribution; and replacement of high-intensity approach and runway lighting systems.

Today, Windsor is served by Air Canada using DC-9, and by smaller commuter-type carriers such as South West Air, Skycraft Aviation, Air Ontario, Ontario Express, Sims Air, and Windsor Helicopter. The airport is also the home of the Windsor Flying Club, the founders of the Windsor Airport.

In 1988, Windsor Airport recorded 73,735 aircraft movements and 283,100 passengers.

The following have served as airport managers since 1954:

Don MacLaughlan	1954 to 1957
James Armstrong	1957 to 1963
M. Krisowaty	1963 to 1964
G.W. Blatchley	1964 to 1965
Bill Glover	1965 to 1971
Art Phelps	1971 to 1974
John Gowan	1974 to 1977
George Leid	1977 to 1979
John Bell	1979 to 1980
David Dick	1980 to 1983
Richard Koroscil	1983

Sources:

1. Windsor Airport staff, Transport Canada.
2. R.L. Clarke, "Airport Notes" (Ottawa: Transport Canada) [unpublished collection].
3. "Wings over Windsor: Golden Anniversary Celebration",*Windsor Chamber of Commerce Briefs,* Vol. VII, No. 7, July-August 1978.
4. Public Archives Canada, MG 30 E243 vol. 9, Controller of Civil Aviation memo, 12 April 1939.

Footnotes—Windsor Airport

[1] "Wings over Windsor: Golden Anniversary Celebration", *Windsor Chamber of Commerce*, Vol. VII, No. 7, (July/August 1978).
[2] In the summer of 1927, the Carling Brewery of London, Ontario, offered a prize of $25,000 to the first pilot to fly non-stop from London, Ontario, to London, England. Carling provided the airplane, a Stinson-Detroiter, christened *Sir John Carling*. T.B. Tully, and J.V. Medcalf, from the Ontario Provincial Air Service, were chosen to fly the aircraft. They left on August 22, 1927, ran into fog and bad weather near Kingston, and returned to London. On September 1, they left again and this time planned to refuel at Harbour Grace, Newfoundland. They were lost over the Atlantic.
[3] F.H. Ellis, *Canada's Flying Heritage* (Toronto: University of Toronto Press, 1961), p. 271.
[4] Ellis, pp. 285-86.
[5] *Wings over Windsor.*

Winnipeg International Airport
(Manitoba)

Before the days of Winnipeg Airport, there was an active airfield at St. Charles, ten kilometres west of the city, which had been established in 1919 by the British Canadian Aircraft Company (later Canadian Aircraft Ltd.)[1] In October 1920, two DH-9 aircraft on the CAF's trans-Canada flight —sent to Winnipeg by train—took off for Vancouver. The first stage of the flight from Halifax to Winnipeg had been made by seaplane.

In November 1927, Western Canada Airways (later Canada Airways Ltd.) erected an aircraft repair workshop at the foot of Brandon Avenue on the bank of the Red River, where airplanes were flown in on floats or skis. As the only seaplane base in Winnipeg, it was used by visiting aircraft; and although a field behind the workshop was used on occasion by wheel-equipped aircraft, it was not good enough to become an aerodrome.[2] Western Canada Airways moved its flying school from the Brandon Avenue base to the airfield at St. Charles in 1928, and to Stevenson Aerodrome (Winnipeg) in 1929.

Stevenson Aerodrome opened on the site of the present Winnipeg International Airport on May 27, 1928. It was built by the Winnipeg Aeroplane Club on 160 acres [sixty-eight hectares] of prairie grassland that was leased from the rural municipality of St. James, then a Winnipeg suburb. The lease, dated July 5, 1928, provided for compensation to the club for its improve-

215. Unveiling plaque, Stephenson Aerodrome (Winnipeg International Airport) May 1928.

ment to the field if the lease were terminated by the municipality.

In 1927, the Winnipeg Aviation League was formed, and sponsored the Winnipeg Aero Club, under the federal government's light aeroplane clubs' scheme of 1927. The club was reorganized as the Winnipeg Flying Club, which began flying on May 28, 1928, and received its charter on October 29, 1929. It entered into a new twenty-one-year lease with the rural municipality of St. James on November 16, 1929, under which it was to develop and operate an airport for the City of Winnipeg and the rural municipality of St. James. A permanent airport licence was issued in the name of the Winnipeg Flying Club in 1929.

The field was opened on May 27, 1928. It was named Stevenson Aerodrome in tribute to Captain Fred J. Stevenson, a well-known World War I pilot and Canadian bush pilot, who lost his life in the crash of Western Canada Airways' Fokker Universal at The Pas, Manitoba, on January 5, 1928. In 1959, at the request of the Department of Transport and with the approval of the councils of Winnipeg and St. James, the name Stevenson Field was changed to Winnipeg International Airport. This was in accordance with the policy of naming airports for the nearest town and meeting International Civil Aviation require-

216. De Haviland Moth, Winnipeg Flying Club, decorated for 1929 air show.

217. Northwest Airways, Winnipeg International Airport, Manioba, 1931.

ments for international airports. A mahogany sculpture in memory of Captain Stevenson, is located in the present air terminal building, and continues the association of the airport with pioneer aviation in the Winnipeg area

In the early years, the only facilities at the aerodrome were a small hangar and a hut. The Winnipeg Flying Club built a club house when private pilots and commercial companies moved in and began to use the field. Then, in 1934, No. 112 Army Cooperation Squadron RCAF (of what was termed the Non-Permanent Air Force) was formed with a hangar at Stevenson Field and five Gypsy Moths. At the outbreak of World War II, the squadron went overseas to fight in the Battle of Britain. They later became 402 (Fighter) Squadron, which was disbanded in 1945 and re-formed in 1946 as an auxiliary unit.

In 1929, the airport was designated as the eastern terminus of the western airmail route; and the following year, when it became a Customs port of entry, federal and municipal funds enabled it to install field lighting.

The first major air carrier to use the field was Western Canada Airways—subsequently renamed Canadian Airways Ltd. in 1930.[3] It constructed a hangar and a maintenance facility there, and made Winnipeg its headquarters.

Northwest Airlines (now Northwest Orient) was the first international air carrier to use the airport. On February 2, 1931, it began an air-mail, passenger, and freight service from Pembina, North Dakota, to Winnipeg, with a Hamilton Metalplane and, later, a larger Ford Trimotor.

Between 1930 and 1932, Canadian Airways flew the prairie air-mail service from Winnipeg to Calgary, serving Regina, Moose Jaw, Medicine Hat, Saskatoon, North Battleford, and Edmonton. The airline also flew from Winnipeg to Pembina. Some of its aircraft were Fokker F-14, Consolidated Fleetster 20, Laird LCB-200 Speedwing biplane, B-40B4, and Stearman 4-EM.

In those days, the runways were sod and clay; the passenger terminal was a lean-to on the side of a hangar, and the snow was compacted, not cleared. On request, a Customs officer came to the airport to inspect international flights.

On September 28, 1937, the Winnipeg Flying Club hangar was destroyed by fire and replaced by a new one that burned down on March 21, 1938. Even before these fires, the club was having financial problems and, on May 25, 1937, it returned the airport to St. James on receipt of $2,500 for its improvements. The club, however, continued to manage the airport.

218. Hangar and "passenger station," Stevenson Field, Winnipeg, Manitoba, 1932.

219. Fokker F14 mailplane refuelling, Stevenson Field, Winnipeg, Manitoba.

Trans-Canada Airlines (TCA) began operations in 1937. It had chosen Winnipeg as its operating headquarters and training centre. This, together with the Trans-Canada Airway system, was responsiblefor airport development. By 1938, Winnipeg had four civil hangars, one RCAF hangar, three hard-surfaced runways (two 3,000 by 150 feet [914 by 46 metres] and one 3,200 by 150 feet [975 by 46 metres]), and the airport had grown in size to eight hundred acres [324 hectares]. Boundary lights had been installed, and a radio range station and weather forecasting facilities were in operation. Airport traffic control was established in 1940.

In May 1937, the city of Winnipeg and the rural municipality of St. James agreed to form an airport commission to acquire lands and undertake the planning and development of the airport, which was then leased to the Winnipeg Flying Club and licensed in its name. The commission (approved by an act of the provincial legislature on February 25, 1938, which authorized it to construct and operate the airport) obtained grants from the federal government, and contributed funds itself, for various works to make the airport suitable for TCA's oeprations.[4] The Department of Transport constructed the third runway, east-west at 3,200 by 150 feet [975 by 46 me-

tres] in November 1938; and in the following year the two original runways were rebuilt.

On April 1, 1939, TCA began trans-Canada scheduled service for passengers, mail, and express between Montréal, Toronto, Winnipeg, Lethbridge, and Vancouver.

At the outbreak of World War II the federal government took over the Stevenson Field from the commission for the duration, and the Department of Transport assumed management and control under Agreement No. 32218 of October 25, 1940. Legal and financial control were assumed on January 1, 1941.

Although the airport continued as a civil facility throughout the war, it was a site for flying training under the British Commonwealth Air Training Plan (BCATP). In 1940, the Winnipeg Flying Club opened Central Manitoba Flying Training School Ltd. which, in December 1940, moved to Portage la Prairie as No. 14 Elementary Flying Training School. This moved to Assiniboia in July 1942, and closed in July 1944.

When the BCATP was established, Winnipeg at once became the focal point for training in the priaries: in 1940, No. 2 Training Command was established with headquarters in downtown Winnipeg; at Stevenson Field, No. 14 EFTS was set up with its Tiger Moths as forerunners of the Observer Training Units—for which Winnipeg was destined to become so widely known; No. 3 Wireless School operated Fleet Forts from the east side of the field, while No. 5 Air Observer School (AOS) flew its Ansons from the present civilian terminal area, and later from the south side. Both the EFTS and the AOS were operated by civilian companies. In November 1944, No. 2 Training Command was redesignated No. 2 Air Command, embracing the Western (Canada) part of the BCATP. The Command was disbanded in 1947.

During the war many buildings and hangars were built:

| BCATP | No. 14 EFTS—moved to Portage la Prairie in December 1940 No. 5 AOS (Air Observer School); No. 3 Wireless School. |
| RCAF | Flying Training; City of Winnipeg Squadron was mobilized at Stevenson Field and went overseas No. 170 Ferry Squadron No. 8 Repair depot. |

Aircraft Factories:

MacDonald Brothers—Ansons (bomber and trainer) overhaul work; Mid-West Aircraft—Hawker Hurricane components; engine overhaul.

In addition, TCA's operations expanded, and Northwest Airlines continued to operate.

In November 1946, Department of National Defence offered most of the buildings at the repair depot immediately east of the airport boundary to the Department of Transport.

At the end of the war, the Airport Commission refused to take the airport back from the Department of Transport—despite the agreement of October 25, 1940—so the Department continued to operate it. On April 15, 1947, a temporary licence was issued to the department to replace the permanent licence issued to the Winnipeg Flying Club in 1929. A permanent licence was

220. Winnipeg International Airport, Manitoba. Old Terminal modernized in 1952.

issued on January 24, 1957. Following lengthy negotiations between the commission and the Department bought the land holdings of St. James and Winnipeg in 1961-62. Rents and concession fees were collected by the commission up to December 31, 1961, even though the airport had been operated by the Department of Transport. The agreement (No. 32218 of October 25, 1940), under which the Department took over the airport on behalf of the Department of National Defence for the duration of the war, was cancelled on June 8, 1964: the Department of Transport was the owner and operator of the airport.

In the spring of 1947, the Department of Transport expropriated land for a new runway, 18-36, 6,200 by 200 feet [1,890 by 61 metres]. It was completed in August 1948 and, at that time, a second runway, 13-31, was under construction. Two ILS (Instrument Landing System) were installed on the new runways in 1948.

In March 1947, RCAF Station Winnipeg was formed, consisting of No. 111 Composite Flight, (with its mixed bag of communications and rescue aircraft), and 402 (Auxiliary) Squadron No. 11 Group of Northwest Air Command—which was located in Winnipeg briefly until it moved to Edmonton in 1951 as Tactical Air Command. No. 14 Training Group took its place to administer the western training stations that were coming back to life as a result of the Korean War. No. 14 Group was absorbed in the fall of 1959 when Training Command Headquarters moved from Trenton to Winnipeg.

The buildings and plant of Station Winnipeg in 1947 were those inherited from wartime units and were grouped on the south side of Stevenson Field. At the outbreak of the Korean War, basic training units were moved from both coasts and concentrated in the prairie provinces. Winnipeg was chosen as the centre for observer training. Navigator training, which, in the post-war years,

had taken place at Summerside P.E.I., resumed at Winnipeg in 1951 to cope with the flood of trainees from a dozen NATO countries.

The renowned military actitivy called for a great expansion of all facilities. The year of 1952 saw the construction of three hangars, instructional buildings, and all the necessary ancillary buildings that form part of a modern air station. By the time instruction at Summerside had been phased out and all navigators were being trained in Winnipeg, No. 2 Air Observer School was the largest aircrew training depot in the RCAF.

In February 1951, the Winnipeg Flying Club opened a new club house and hangar, 18 by 24 metres. The latter was taken over by the Department of Transport in 1976 and was demolished in 1980.

A modernized terminal, opened on December 15, 1952, was an extension to the TCA hangar, which had previously housed the passenger terminal. The new facility, with three aircraft parking positions accommodated airline offices, ticket counters, a baggage conveyor system, and a waiting room. It remained in use, despite its many changes, until the the new air terminal complex opened in 1964.

In 1954, Winnipeg was the fourth-largest civil airport in Canada in terms of traffic with 134,964 aircraft movements. In addition, the airport was handling more military traffic than any other civil airport in Canada. Winnipeg housed the RCAF's No. 2 Air Navigation School; it was also home for Canada's largest NATO air training school; and it was also a supply point for the DEW Line (Distant Early Warning radar system) airlift to the north in 1955-58.

A new runway, 07-25, was built in 1955, and in 1957, runway 13-31 was extended to 8,700 feet [2,652 metres]. In 1960, runway 18-36 was extended to 11,000 feet [3,353 metres], to permit TCA's DC-8 flights to London.

Training Command of the integrated armed forces was formed at RCAF Station Winnipeg on

January 1, 1966. RCAF Station Winnipeg was redesignated Canadian Forces Base (CFB) Winnipeg on April 1, 1966. Training Command was replaced by the Canadian Forces Training System on September 2, 1975, and Air Command became operationally effective on the same date (for planning purposes, it had been formed on June 30, 1975), with headquarters at CFB Winnipeg. In 1960, the Department of Transport announced plans to build a satellite airport at St. Andrews and to move to it all small aircraft operations, including the Winnipeg Flying Club. This plan met with strong opposition, and the controversy continued until 1970, when the Club acceded. It built a hangar at St. Andrews in 1977.

The new air terminal complex was officially opened on the east side of Winnipeg International Airport on January 17, 1964: it had taken almost four years to build at a cost of $18 million. The terminal had forty acres [sixteen hectares] of concrete aircraft apron and, with the new passenger facility, these improvements were a sharp contrast to the previous cramped facilities adjoining the TCA hangar. The airport now began to enjoy modern first-class passenger accommodation equal to that at Ottawa, Montréal, Toronto, and Edmonton. Since 1959, Winnipeg—like Toronto and Montréal—has had pre-clearance services provided by the U.S. Inspection Services for the United States.

Improvements made over the years now gave Winnipeg International Airport the following:

Runway 18-36	11,000 by 200 feet [3,353 by 61 metres].
Runway 13-31	8,700 by 200 feet [2,652 by 61 metres].
Runway 07-25	7,000 by 200 feet [2,134 by 61 metres].

There were twelve civil aviation hangars and seven RCAF hangars.

TCA's facilities had also grown over the years. In 1968, the company, now renamed Air Canada,

221. Terminal opened January 17, 1964
Winnipeg International Airport, Manitoba.

opened its new air cargo terminal immediately south of the passenger terminal. In 1975, it built a new engineering and maintenance complex on the west side of the airport. The cargo terminal was expanded in 1982, and the maintenance complex was expanded in 1983 with the addition of a second hangar. International Aviation Terminal Ltd. built two large cargo depots adjacent to Air Canada in 1983.

In 1966, the airport terminal had 630,000 passengers, doubling to 1.3 million in 1971. There were now thirty-four major buildings on the site. Civil aviation was concentrated on the east side of the airport, and the Canadian Armed Forces occupied the west side. Four airlines—Air Canada, CP Air, Northwest Orient, and Trans-Air—operated scheduled air services. The Winnipeg Flying Club continued operations but on a reduced scale, having already moved some of its activities to St. Andrews.

Currently, the following airlines serve Winnipeg International Airport:
Air Canada (April 1937 as TCA)
Northwest Orient (1931 as Northwest Airways)
Perimeter Aviation Ltd. (September 1979)
Bearskin Lake Air Service (February 1981)
Trans-Canada Pipe Lines (company operation)
Northwest Territorial Air Services (March 1981)
Air Manitoba

Midwest Helicopters
Manwest Aviation
Province of Manitoba—Air Division
RCMP—Air Division
Air West
Canada 3000
Time Air
Air Ontario
Norontair
Ministic Air Ltd.
Federal Express
Ontario Express

Four aerospace companies at the airport are engaged in manufacture and overhaul: Aero Recip Canada Ltd., Douglas Aero Engine, Bristol Aerospace, and Standard Aero Ltd. Several airplane sales agencies and numerous private aircraft are also based there. Since 1920 the airport site, which has now grown to 1,741 hectares, has been a portal for northern aviation, and it is still a DEW Line supply base.

Winnipeg International Airport also continues to serve as a large military (air) base.

The Department of National Defence, on the southwest and west side, houses Air Command Headquarters; Canadian Forces School of Aerospace Studies; Canadian Forces Air Navigation School; Canadian Forces School of Meteorology; The Central Flying School; 14th Training Group Headquarters; Air Reserve Squadron Headquarters; 402 Air Reserve Squadron (City of Winnipeg); 429 Transport Squadron; 412 Trnasport Squadron Detachment and Canadian Forces Base Winnipeg.

The following companies and operators own hangars on the airport:

Air Canada
—a second hangar built and put in service in 1983.
Western Canada Aviation Museum
—owns several original TCA buildings and hangars.

Canadian Airlines International
—leases a hangar from Transport Canada.
Perimeter Aviation
—leases two hangars from Transport Canada and owns one hangar.
Transport Canada
—six, several of which are slated for demolition.
Royal Canadian Mounted Police
Trans Canada Pipe Lines.
Hudson Bay Company (on city property).
Bristol Aerospace (on city property).
Standard Aero Limited (on city property).
Air Manitoba
—leases a hangar from Transport Canada.
Air West & Midwest Helicopter
—lease part of a hangar from Transport Canada.
Pace Aviation owns one hangar.

The Winnipeg Flying Club, founder of the Winnipeg Airport and its manager up to 1940, moved the last of its operations to the satellite airport at St. Andrews in 1977. It officially closed down its operations at the international airport on November 27, 1976, and the Department of Transport bought its club house and other buildings for $200,000.

In 1977, Winnipeg International Airport had two million passengers—ranking fifth in passenger volume. The airport master plan provides for the expansion of the present site by another 121 hectares, the construction of a new runway parallel to 13-31, the relocation of the thresholds of two runways to provide noise relief, and major extensions to the air terminal complex. Between 1984 and 1989, substantial improvements to the airport were carried out at a cost of $100 million, including $32 million for the air terminal, $34 million for the area control centre, $8 million for apron 1, and $4 million for runway 18-36.

In 1988, there were153,344 aircraft movements and 2,459,800 passengers.

The following served as airport managers:

Conrad Johannesson	1928 to 1935
Clifford Kaake	1936 to 1941
Frank Hughes	1941 to 1945
Floyd Banghart	1945 to 1953
Keith Robinson	1953 to 1958
J.E. Smyth	1958 to 1975
Norman Street	1967 to 1968 (acting)
J.E. Smyth	1968 to 1976
Fred Eyolfson	1976 to 1978
George W. Elliott	1978 to 1989

Sources:

1. R.L. Clarke, *Airport Notes* (Ottawa: Transport Canada) [unpublished collection].
2. *Winnipeg International Airport 1928-1978: a half century of aviation history*, Transport Canada.
3. Thomas Legg. *Beyond the Fifth Decade, a history of aviation training by the Winnipeg Flying Club*, 1977.
4. Western Canada Aviation Museum.
5. Canadian Forces Base Winnipeg.
6. George Elliott, former Airport Manager, Winnipeg International Airport; now Executive Director, Western Canada Aviation Museum, Winnipeg.

Footnotes—Winnipeg International Airport

[1] K.M. Molson, *Pioneering in Canadian Air Transport* (Winnipeg: James Richardson & Sons Ltd., 1974), pp. 37-38; and F.H. Ellis, *Canada's Flying Heritage* (Toronto: University of Toronto Press, 1961), pp. 159, 182, 234.

[2] *The Bulletin*, (15 May 1930), pp. 1-5. [published by Western Canada Airways Ltd.].

[3] During 1940-41, Canadian Pacific Railway acquired controlling interest in several feeder airlines in western and northwestern Canada, including Canadian Airways; these were integrated as Canadian Pacific Airlines (Ellis, p. 325).

[4] The commission wound up its affairs in 1965.

Woodcock Aerodrome
(British Columbia)

Woodcock is an unlicensed aerodrome owned by the Department of National Defense and maintained by Transport Canada as an emergency landing strip.

Located on VFR (Visual Flight Rules) mountain valley route, it was developed in 1942 by the Department of National Defence as an emergency fighter runway for the RCAF. The airport is now used for general aviation, and by flying schools as a touchdown point on cross-country trips.

Sources:

1. Transport Canada, Pacific Region.
2. R.L. Clarke, "Airport Notes" (Ottawa: Transport Canada) [unpublished collection].
3. Daryl Laurent, Airport Manager, Terrace Airport.

Wrigley Airport
(Northwest Territories)

In the fall of 1938, the local staff of the Department of Mines and Resources attempted to develop a winter landing strip at Wrigley, but were unable to make it safe.

Then, in 1942-43, the U.S. Air Force developed a runway at Wrigley as part of the Canol project.[1] The USAF withdrew on November 1, 1944, and the Department of Transport took over operation and maintenance. At the end of the war, Canada purchased the airport from the U.S.

The Department of Transport withdrew its staff from Wrigley in October 1946, and the site was placed under a caretaker. The Department of National Defence took over in December 1947, but maintenance of the field ceased on October 14, 1953. The airport was licensed to CPAL on January 30, 1954—for daytime use—and the Department of National Defence abandoned the airport on December 1, 1954, when CPAL assumed full responsibility. The airport licence was amended to permit twenty-four-hour operations on December 29, 1954.

The Department of Transport accepted transfer from the Department of National Defence on June 1, 1955, assumed operation and maintenance from CPAL on June 30, and received a licence. Wrigley became a main line airport with DC-3 service; but when DC-4 and DC-6 aircraft were introduced by CPAL, the airport was no longer used for scheduled service and reverted to the status of local airport.

The operation and maintenance of Wrigley Airport was transferred from Transport Canada to the government of the Northwest Territories on October 1, 1978. There are currently two staff on site, an airport maintainer and an observer/communicator.

The airport has a 3,500 by 100 foot [1,067 by 31 metre] runway with a crushed gravel base. The lights are equipped with ARCAL (Aircraft Radio Control of Aerodrome Lighting) for twenty-four-hour lighting.

In 1989, there were 1,510 aircraft movements at the airport.

Sources:
1. R.L. Clarke, *Airport Notes* (Ottawa: Transport Canada) [unpublished collection].
2. Transport Canada, Western Region.

Footnote—Wrigley Airport

[1] The Canol Project involved the construction of a pipeline from Norman Wells, Northwest Territories, to Whitehorse, Yukon, to provide gasoline and oil to American defence forces in Alaska. A number of aerodromes were built in Canada by the United States to transport men and materials to the construction sites, particularly during the freeze-up of the waterways. The aerodromes built were Fort McMurray, Embarras,

Fort Smith, Fort Resolution, Hay River, Fort Providence, Fort Simpson, Wrigley, and Norman Wells.

Wynyard Airport
(Saskatchewan)

The airport is six and a half kilometres north of Wynyard and is jointly owned by the town and the rural municipality of Big Quill.

Following many difficult air ambulance landings, four Wynyard residents met in December 1957 to explore the possibility of developing an airstrip. Under the chairmanship of Barry Needham, Walter Magnusson, George Bolt, and Kelly Park, began the task of seeking out appropriate land.

The Department of Transport found and later approved a portion of land four miles north of Wynyard, and supplied regulations concerning the building of the airstrip.

Now, funds were needed! When attempts to secure a loan failed, subscribers were sought. Substantial donations were given by individuals within Wynyard and a contribution of $1,000 by the Wynyard Lion's Club was of considerable help. Money was also raised by the town of Wynyard and the rural municipality of Big Quill. Through all the fund-raising, the airport committee saw its membership gradually increase: a project that had started as a struggle by four interested citizens had become a community effort.

The Memorial Airport, as it had been named, consists of one runway, 838 by 60 metres, with a grass surface, whose official opening was part of the town's jubilee celebration. The "Smokers"—a flying display team from Manitoba—held 3,000 spectators spellbound on July 30, 1961, when the Wynyard Memorial Airport came into existence.

Wynyard lies about mid-way on the heavily travelled VFR (Visual Flight Rules) route between Edmonton and Winnipeg. The runway has radio-controlled lights that can be turned on or off in the air by selecting 123.2 MHZ.

The aerodrome is home to four light aircraft, one helicopter, and two ultra-light aircraft. The airport committee has approached the federal government many times for financial assistance to have the runway paved, but without success to date.

Duane Grummett is the present manager.

Sources:
1. Transport Canada, Central Region.
2. Airport Committee, Wynyard Airport.

Yahk Aerodrome
(British Columbia)

The Yahk Aerodrome was developed in 1931 as an intermediate field on the Lethbridge-Vancouver airmail route and used exclusively as an emergency strip—unlicensed, turf, 875 by 75 metres, owned by Transport Canada. It was located in a narrow valley on a well-used VFR (Visual Flight Rules) mountain route to Cranbrook from the U.S. and the Creston area.

Demand for the aerodrome became negligible owing to its proximity to the Creston and Cranbrook airports, and it fell into a state of disrepair. It was officially closed on November 4, 1988, and Transport Canada declared the Yahk Aerodrome surplus later that month.

The regional district of central Kootenay has expressed an interest in using the land (nearly 550 hectares) as a potential landfill site.

Source:
Transport Canada, Pacific Region.

Yarmouth Airport
(Nova Scotia)

In 1936, the Department of National Defence selected a site for an airport outside the east boundary of the town of Yarmouth. Construction began in 1937 and continued until completion in 1939, shortly after the beginning of World War II.

The Air Base had three 5,000 feet [1,524-metre] runways: 02-20, 06-24, and 15-33. There were twelve hangars, with associated service and personnel accommodation, split between two 'camps.' East Camp was operated by the Royal Air Force under the British Commonwealth Air Training Plan for Fleet Air Arm Training. It was also the home of No. 1 Naval Air Gunners School. West Camp was operated by the RCAF for anti-submarine patrol operations. Approximately 175 aircraft, including Swordfish, Walrus, Hurricanes, Hudsons, and Cansos operated out of Yarmouth. One of these Yarmouth aircraft, a Hudson BW-625 of 113 BR Squadron, RCAF, flown by Squadron Leader Small, sank a German submarine U-754 southeast of Sable Island on July 31, 1942. This was the first kill for Eastern Air Command.[1]

At the end of the war in 1945, the Department of National Defence asked the town of Yarmouth to take over the operation and maintenance of the airport, but the town declined. The Department of Transport took over the airport in 1946 and continues to operate it today.

Maritime Central Airways began serving Yarmouth in 1946, and was replaced by Trans-Canada Air Lines in 1947.

The first flying school was started in 1946 with one Piper Cub (DCY) and, at a later date, another Cub (DGO) and a Stinson Voyager (FOZ). Financial difficulties forced the club to close, but a few years later, the Gateway Flying Club was formed. That, too, eventually shut down its operations because of lack of interest. The Yarmouth Flying Club, established in 1973, was forced to close because it had no aviation licence. Then, in September 1979, Scotia West Aviation Ltd. began an aviation service at Yarmouth airport; and although it still operates, Tri-Country Flying Association, a new flying club, was formed in 1982. The club held a highly successful flying show in September 1982 that stimulated new interest in private flying.

After the war, all buildings were dismantled and removed from the site, with the exception of two hangars and some service buildings. A small air terminal with Customs and Immigration facilities was constructed in a lean-to on the south side of hangar no. 5.

Runway 02-20 was extended by 600 feet [183 metres] in 1958 using concrete construction, and was closed in 1965. Runway 06-24 was completely rebuilt in 1965, and the terminal ramp was enlarged. An ILS (Instrument Landing System) was installed on the runway in 1967. Today, two runways are in operation: 06-24 and 15-33, 1,829 and 1,525 metres long, respectively.

Yarmouth was served by Air Canada (1987) with flights to and from Halifax and Boston, as well as a scheduled class-3 service offered by IMP Aviation. Unscheduled services are provided by Bar Harbour Airways, East Coast Airways, and Union Camp Airways. The airport is now served by Air Nova and Air Atlantic, which operate Dash-8 type aircraft. Air Nova provides daily flights (Halifax-Yarmouth-Boston) while Air Atlantic provides a flight every Saturday (Halifax-St. John's-Yarmouth).

The airport serves a population of 65,000 in the catchment area, and in 1988, had 34,900 passengers and 8,854 aircraft movements.

The following served as airport managers:

N. Power	1945 to 1955
C. Allum	1955 to 1960
R.E. Dease	1960 to 1978
D.W. Bussey	1978 to 1980
J.R. Pittman	1981 to 1982
R.I.G. Romkey	1982 to 1988
Acting Appointments	1989 to present

Sources:
1. Transport Canada, Atlantic Region.

Footnote—Yarmouth Airport
[1] S. Kostenuk and J.A. Griffin, *RCAF Squadron Histories and Aircraft 1924-1968*, Toronto: Sanuel Stevens Hakkert, 1978, p 46.

Yellowknife Airport
(Northwest Territories)

The airport at Yellowknife—the capital of the Northwest Territories—was built in the summer of 1944 at the expense of Canadian Pacific Airlines (CPAL) under the direction of Walter Gilbert, the district manager. Construction took six men five days and cost $450. The single strip ran parallel to Long Lake. At that time, there was no road from the Yellowknife town-site to the airport—a distance of five kilometres—and passengers using the airport had to take a float plane shuttle between the town and the strip. They were called "elevator trips" locally, because they were mostly up and down. In the winter of 1945, equipment was brought in from Fort Simpson and a five and a half kilometre road was built from the Town to the airstrip.

The Department of Transport took over the operation of the airport from CPAL in 1946.

In 1946 and 1947, two new gravel runways were built, about half a kilometre south of the original airstrip. CPAL's DC-3, CF-CUE was, on August 11, 1947, the first aircraft to use the northwest-southeast strip after the officially opening.

222. Terminal (1963), tower (1972)
Yellowknife Airport, N.W.T.

Northern Flights Ltd., (owner of the first DC-3 to be placed in public service in the Yellowknife area), began operations in June 1946. It flew to Edmonton, Peace River, and Fort St. John. Max Ward, later the founder of Wardair, was a pilot with the company.

On August 1, 1946, CPAL began service to Edmonton via Fort Smith and Fort McMurray, and in October 1953, began to fly DC-4s.

The Department of Transport began major improvements to the airport in 1954, when two runways were paved. Tender specifications required twenty-four-hour operation of the contractor and completion by September 1, 1954. Consequently, in April 1954, the team of Curry and Lamoureux brought in 120 tons [121,920 kilograms] of heavy construction equipment by tractor train, across the ice of Great Slave Lake from Hay River in three and a half days.

An unusual event at the airport was 'Bull Dog Three' (February 23 to March 8, 1955) when Canadian Army and RCAF striking force manouevres included an airborne assault against the airport and its installations.

In 1956, Pacific Western Airlines Ltd. took over the operations and facilities of Associated Airways Ltd. at the airport.

On May 10, 1957, Yellowknife became an alternate airport, when CPAL announced its

223. Seaplane base, Old Town area, Yellowknife, N.W.T.

non-stop DC-6B Empress flights from Vancouver to Amsterdam. The thirteen-hour, 6,115 kilometre, route over Yellowknife is 2,376 kilometres shorter than by way of Edmonton and Montréal.

A modern terminal building was constructed in 1963, and a new control tower was added to it in 1972. By this time, air traffic at Yellowknife had increased considerably, and the terminal was enlarged in 1973. Construction of a new public parking lot was completed in 1988, followed by a terminal expansion in 1988-89, and a complete renovation of the existing terminal in 1989-90.

Today, the airport has two paved runways: 09-27, 1,524 metres long, and 15-33, 2,286 metres long.

First Air began a scheduled service from Iqaluit and Ottawa in 1957, giving Yellowknife three scheduled services with aircraft carrying more than sixty passengers: CAIL (Boeing 737); NWTA (Lockheed Electra); and First Air (Boeing 727). In 1989, Yellowknife had eight scheduled air carriers to points in the Yukon, Alberta, Manitoba, Ontario and all major centres in the Northwest Territories:

CAIL | Buffalo Airways Ltd.
NWTA | Simpson Air Ltd.
First Air | NWWT Air LeaseLtd.
Ptarmigan Airways Ltd. | Delta Air Ltd.

The following operations are based at the Yellowknife Airport:
NWT Airways Ltd.
Canadian Helicopters Ltd.
Trucking Ltd.
R & S Executive Services Ltd.
Echo Bay Mines Ltd.
Robinson Trucking Ltd. (light aircraft parking)
Ptarmigan Airways Ltd.
Renewable Resources (Water Bomber Base)
Spur Aviation
Department of Indian Affairs and Northern Development (Warehouse)
Latham Island Airways Ltd.
Custom Moving
CAIL Freight Depot
Esso
Department of National Defence
Royal Canadian Mounted Police
Petro-Canada
Great Slave Helicopters Ltd.
Business Connection (NWTel)

In 1988 there were 186,553 passengers and 62,262 aircraft movements.

The following have served as airport managers:

K. Williams	1966 to 1973
G. Richardson	1974 to 1979
M. Lefebrvre	1980 to 1981
S. Baker	1982 to 1983
R. Barradell	1984

Sources:
1. Transport Canada, Western Region.
2. Ryan Fowler. *Historical Background of the Yellowknife Airport.* [author's collection].

Yorkton Airport
(Saskatchewan)

The history of Yorkton dates back to 1882, when the first settlers arrived in the area under the auspices of the York Farmers' Colonization Company, which began a settlement known as York City. The name was later changed to Yorkton and, still later, the settlement was relocated to its present site.

Yorkton Airport, five kilometres north of the city was built in 1940 for the British Commonwealth Air Training Plan and was the home of No. 11 Service Flying Training School (SFTS0 of the RCAF.[1] The Airport was taken over by the Department of Transport on June 27, 1947.

Originally, the airport had four hard-surfaced runways, but only two remain. Runway 03-21 was rebuilt in 1959 to 4,800 feet [1,463 metres], and 12-30 is gravel, 3,000 feet [914 metres] long. A new taxi-strip was constructed in 1965.

In 1940, the airport had six double hangars, an operations building with a control tower, a hospital, and numerous other buildings, only a few of which remain. The operations building serves as a terminal, aeradio station,and airport manager's office. Two hangars are still in use, one by Yorkton Flying Service and the other by Leon Manufacturing, to store bulk fertilizer.

Gordon E. Taylor was Airport Manager in 1981. The airport is now maintained by contract with Pacific Building MaintenanceLtd., and the Airport Maniger is A. (Red) Launttamus.

There were 8,841 aircraft movements in 1988.

Source
Transport Canada, Central Region.

Footnote—Yorkton Airport

[1]No. 11 SFTS had two relief airports, No. 1 at Sturdee, Saskatchewan, and No. 2 at Rhein, Saskatchewan.

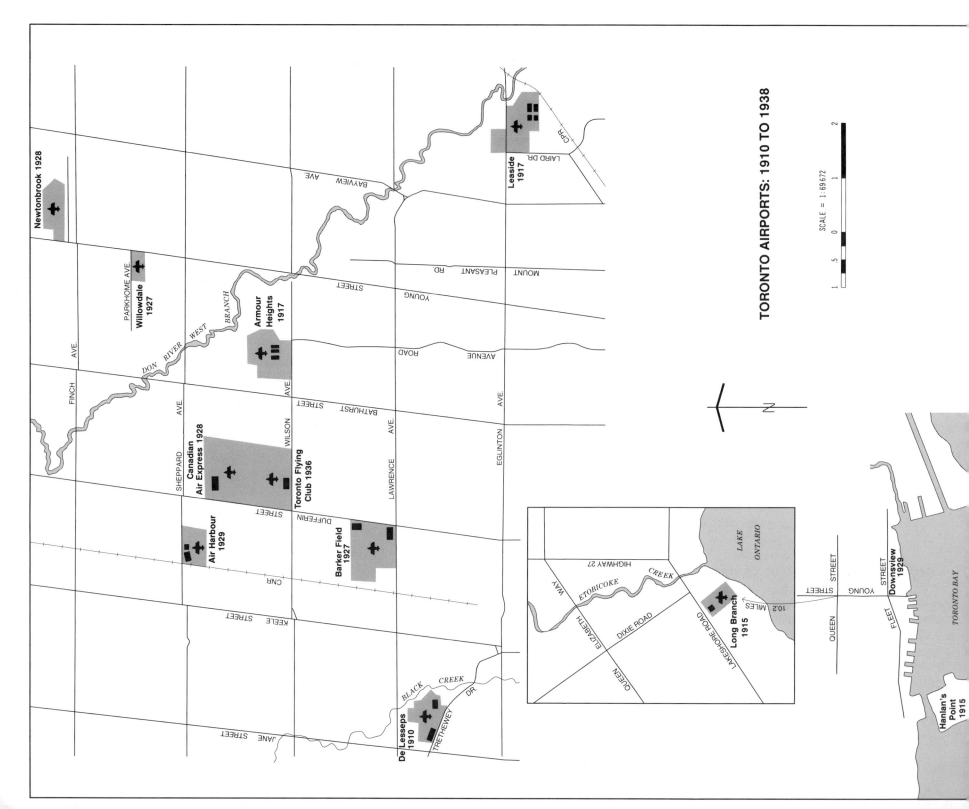

TORONTO AIRPORTS: 1910 TO 1938

Newtonbrook 1928

Willowdale 1927
PARKHOME AVE.

Armour Heights 1917

Leaside 1917
LAIRD DR.
CPR

BAYVIEW AVE.

MOUNT PLEASANT RD.

YOUNG STREET

Canadian Air Express 1928

Toronto Flying Club 1936

Barker Field 1927

Air Harbour 1929

De Lesseps 1910

DON RIVER WEST BRANCH

FINCH AVE.

SHEPPARD AVE.

WILSON AVE.

DUFFERIN STREET

BATHURST STREET

ROAD

AVENUE ROAD

LAWRENCE AVE.

EGLINTON AVE.

KEELE STREET

CNR

JANE STREET

TRETHEWEY DR.

BLACK CREEK

N

Long Branch 1915

HIGHWAY 27

LAKE ONTARIO

ETOBICOKE CREEK

DIXIE ROAD

ELIZABETH WAY

QUEEN

LAKESHORE ROAD

10.2 MILES

YOUNG STREET

QUEEN STREET

FLEET STREET

Downsview 1929

Hanlan's Point 1915

TORONTO BAY

SCALE = 1:69672

SCALE

1 .5 0 1 2

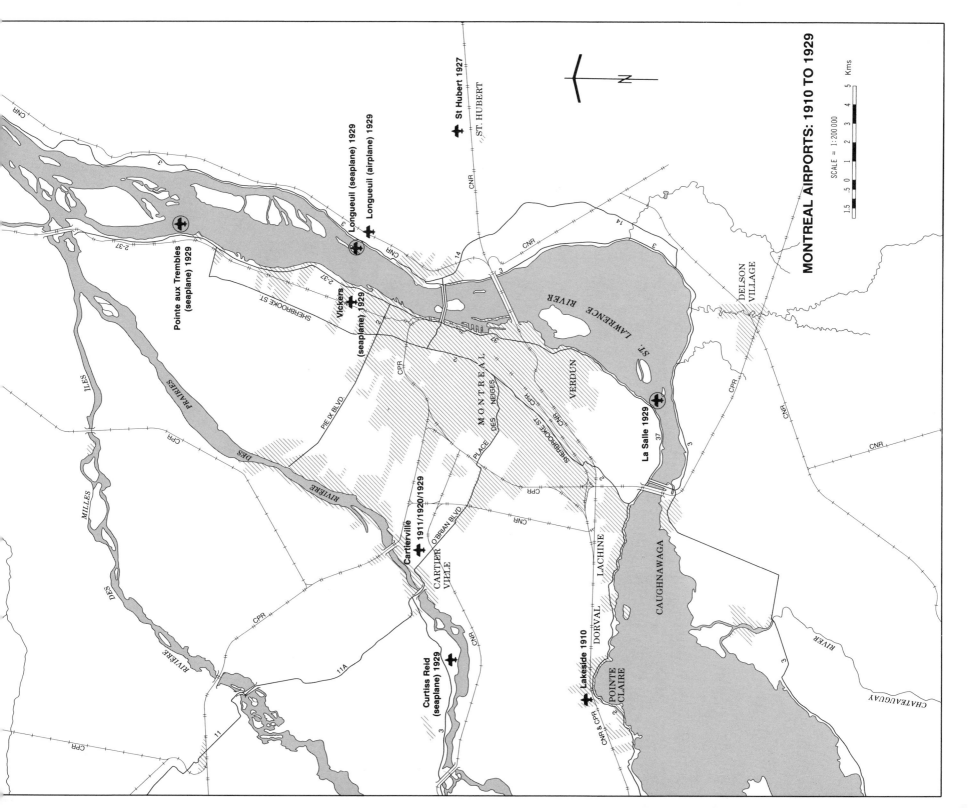

MONTREAL AIRPORTS: 1910 TO 1929

SCALE = 1:200 000

1.5 .5 0 1 2 3 4 5 Kms

TRANS CANADA AIRWAYS MAP
MARCH 31, 1937

APPENDIX 1

Description of Bessoneau Hangar

(Extract from a paper by A.V.M. Stedman RCAF, Public Archives Canada, MG 30 E243, Vol. 17)

Among the gift material received from England after the first war were some Bessoneau hangars. These were canvas-covered hangars with good wooden frames; they had been extensively used in France and an experienced gang could erect one in a few hours. We soon found that they could not stand up safely under the heavy snow loads they were liable to experience in this country, but, because we had no money for constructing permanent hangars, we had to use them. It was decided that we could use two hangars to make one, by halving the distance between frames, and then covering the framing with wooden siding and ready roofing. I believe that Major Dave Barry, of the Royal Canadian Engineers, who looked after our construction work, was responsible for the idea of doubling up the frames. The resulting hangars stood up well, but the canvas curtains, instead of doors, the earth floor and the lack of heat were serious disadvantages. They were the only shelter available at the time at High River and Rockcliffe and were certainly better than none.

APPENDIX 2

John Armistead Wilson, CBE

Throughout this history, frequent mention is made of J.A. Wilson, and extensive quotations and extracts are taken from his papers and articles.

During his long career in the Public Service of Canada, he played a leading role in civil aviation and strongly influenced its development in this country. He has been frequently referred to as "the father of civil aviation in Canada."

It is appropriate, therefore, that a brief biographical note be included in this book.

1879	born in Scotland on November 2
1905-10	worked in Canada as a professional engineer
1910	entered the Department of Naval Service of Canada as Director of Stores and purchasing agent
1918	became Assistant Deputy Minister of Naval Service with special duties in connection with the organization of the Royal Canadian Naval Air Service
1919	was a member of the first Air Board
1920	became Secretary of the second Air Board
1923	became Secretary of the Canadian Air Force in the new Department of National Defence and was in charge of civil aviation.
1927	became Controller of Civil Aviation in a re-organization of the Department of National Defence on July 1
1936	appointed Controller of Civil Aviation in the new Department of Transport
1941	became Director of Air Services in the Department of Transport
1945	awarded the Trans-Canada trophy (McKee trophy) for 1944 in recognition of his long service to civil aviation
1945	retired from the Public Service of Canada (Director of Air Services) in July, anfter more than twenty-seven years in aviation
1954	died on October 10, 1954, in his seventy-fifth year

APPENDIX 3

Air Administration in Canada in 1919

(Public Archives Canada, RG 24 DOC 3564 1011-1-15)

Approved by the Honourable A.L. Sifton, Chairman of the Air Board, for publication in the Special Aviation Issue of a number of leading newspapers in Canada.

The situation with regard to aviation is a curious one. It was only in 1909 that Bleriot made the first flight across the English Channel, and in the five years that intervened before the commencement of the war, flying hardly developed beyond the experimental stage. During the war, it underwent enormous development and expansion, all, however, from a special point of view, namely, war efficiency. Machines were built solely for war purposes; personnel was trained solely for war duty. Granted increased military strength, money was practically no object, and little, if any, consideration was given to prime or operating costs. The air situation is rather more extraordinary than would be the position of motor transport if, for fifteen years of peace, the automobile had been developed solely for, say, the purpose of the game of polo, and personnel in tens of thousands had become engaged in developing it and its connected industries with the sole object of winning matches. If then motor polo was suddenly prohibited, to adapt automobiles to the thousand and one useful purposes for which it is now employed would involve a completely new orientation by the individuals engaged in their design and manufacture and a seeking out of new uses by them and all others interested.

With regard to air, the difficulty is even greater since for purposes of war the belligerent governments have been the sole possible purchasers of aircraft and almost the sole employers of air personnel. There is, consequently, an incli-

269

nation on the part of many people to look to the government to continue to bear the whole burden and a disinclination to individual effort. The problem is, consequently, two-fold. It is essential not only that the thinking of all flying and manufacturing personnel and of the public should be directed to the use of aircraft for purposes of peace, but also that they should realize that an attempt by the government to do everything must necessarily involve stagnation. A government department must be prepared to convince Parliament of the soundness of its proposals before money can be obtained, and Parliament--as well on account of the number of its members as for other reasons--is a much more difficult body to convince than a board of directors. In so experimental a field as civil flying an attempt on the part of the government to restrict all other activities except its own would inevitably mean the arrest of progress. The rapidity of advance in any science is generally in proportion to the number of minds independently engaged upon the solution of its problems.

Commercial flying is important as well from the military as from the civil point of view. No country can, in peace, afford indefinitely to maintain a large air force exclusively devoted to military duties. Either the expense of the maintenance of such a force would be enormous or its strength would be so small that its effect in war would be unimportant. War strength in the air must necessarily depend upon commercial air strength. Upon the commercial air personnel, and upon aircraft used for commercial purposes every country must principally depend for its flying officers and airmen and for its military aircraft. The encouragement and development of commercial aviation is, consequently, the most obvious and important duty of an administration which hopes to have available, in the event of foreign attack, an air force to assist in resisting it.

In this respect Canada is probably in a better position than any of the belligerent countries. It alone of all the belligerents came out of the war without a developed military air organization and the adoption at the last session of Parliament of the Air Board Act places Canada in a most favourable position in regard to the development of air strength both civil and military. That Act constitutes a Board of seven members, headed by one of the Ministers of the Crown, and having upon it one person appointed by the Minister of Militia and Defence to represent the land forces, and one appointed by the Minister of Naval Forces to represent the naval forces. The present remaining four members have been selected from among the personnel of some of the departments of government interested, but they may be replaced, as the organization develops, by individuals with wide air experience. To this Board is entrusted every governmental activity in relation to air, including not only the widest powers (under the Governor General in Council) of regulating commercial air traffic of all kinds, but also of providing for the constitution, discipline, pay and all matters connected with the organization of a military air force.

Acting upon the general principles above indicated the first care of the Board will be the participation of regulations governing air traffic generally. In so doing, it will have the benefit of the Convention relating to the Air Navigation which was drawn in Paris during the Peace Conference, and also of the English Air Navigation Regulations, published at the end of April last, and prepared with a knowledge of what the International Commission in Paris was likely to report.

The Convention has not yet been ratified, but its value as a guide, even if not ratified, is very great indeed, since it goes into somewhat minute detail. It provides against any contracting state permitting the flight within its territories of an aircraft which is not registered, and confers upon each state the right to fly with its registered aircraft over the territory of all other contracting states. It lays down elaborate rules with regard to lights and signals, customs regulations, maps and meteorological reports, provides for the issue of certificates by each contracting state to some or all of the pilots, engineers and navigators engaging in an aerial traffic and lays down a minimum standard for such certificates.

Carrying out the principles of the Convention, the English Regulations require every pilot of an aircraft to obtain a government certificate before he goes into the air (except for training purposes) and distinguishes between certificates to pilots of private aircraft and pilots of freight and passenger aircraft. It is only for aircraft of the latter categories that certificates are required for navigators and engineers. The Regulations further require certificates in the case of those ground engineers who must, on every day before the flight of a passenger or freight aircraft, go over it and certify to its fitness on that day for flying.

Canadian regulations along these lines are now under consideration by the Air Board, and their issue should not be long delayed, although the number of difficulties to be met is numerous. It is important to impose no handicap on the development of air navigation which, consistently with the observance of existing laws and the safety of the public, it is not absolutely essential to impose. The problem presented, therefore, is to find means of providing those very necessary safeguards, while at the same time avoiding anything in the nature of unreasonable obstacles or burdensome restrictions. In this regard the action taken in other countries is not altogether helpful. In each of them air navigation is still more or less dominated by the military organization created during the war. These organizations do not, perhaps, yet fully realize that their respective countries are now at peace and that future war strength depends primarily upon the efficiency of the civil air administration and the development of commercial air navigation. Their influence,

consequently, tends in the direction of air activities which are capable of being performed by military organizations rather than towards developing the commercial possibilities of the air. At least military ideas are apt to colour the Governmental attitude towards air navigation. In Canada, on the other hand, we have no existing military organization. Attention can be primarily devoted to commercial flying and to giving it every encouragement which circumstances and prospects justify. The Air Board is not, however, likely to suggest that Parliament should provide the money, equipment and facilities necessary to do the pioneer commercial work. It is unlikely, for example, to present machines to companies which propose to operate them for commercial purposes, or by the promotion of exhibitions or races to direct attention to aviation in its most dangerous and least useful form. It is also improbable that the Air Board will find it advisable to acquire many more aerodromes than are required for actual government duty, and this number is likely to be exceedingly small. It would be practically impossible to provide aerodromes on the same basis as wharfs and harbour facilities. There are comparatively few places, even among those situated on the water, which require wharf or dock accommodation, or are capable of development as harbours. On the other hand, every city and town, inland and coastal, and, indeed every village throughout the country is a possible terminal or way-port for aerial traffic. An attempt on the part of the government to assume the responsibility for the general provision of aerodromes would, in view of the comparatively small amount of money which must necessarily be available, result (by the discouragement of local initiative) in the retardation of the development of air navigation, which, to a degree still little understood, depends upon ground organization rather than upon mere flying capacity. The only possible avenue for governmental intervention in regard to the acquisition of aerodromes is in the direction of the provision of emergency landing grounds on recognized air routes upon which facilities have been provided by the municipalities but these are separated by such distances that intervening landing grounds are necessary to the safety of aircraft on the route. Terminal landing grounds for every urban area must necessarily be provided by the inhabitants of that area. Every city and town must have one within a very short time. Every village should. An urban municipality without an aerodrome will not be on the air map.

Apart from the provision of intermediate emergency landing grounds, the activities of the air administration will be three-fold.

In the first place, commercial air traffic must be wisely regulated. It must be carried on by certified officers who can be depended upon to make it (as it can doubtless be made) as safe as traffic by railway. The essentials of good aerodromes under our conditions must be determined and municipalities advised as to the selection and upkeep of grounds; the establishment of air routes must be considered and the selected routes mapped and defined; meteorological inquiries must be pursued in co-operation with the Meteorological Service and the results distributed and compared; methods of marking airharbours and of signalling must be studied and improved. In short, everything possible must be done to increase the safety of air navigation to make its development as easy and as rapid as the economics of that navigation permits.

Secondly, distinctively Government duties such, for example, as surveying and forest protection must be undertaken, if, as is expected, their performance by air is likely to yield more satisfactory and, from a national point of view and in the widest sense, more economical results. Experiments must be undertaken to ascertain whether Canada's great northland is capable of development by air. It can certainly be so explored with rapidity and thoroughness possible in no other way. The preservation of the forests on the public domain can probably be ensured by air patrols, and other avenues of activity will doubtless be opened up as the field is intensively studied.

Finally, such a system must be worked out as will provide the country with an air force available for duty if a threat to the country is made. The creation of such a force involves some difficult problems. It takes very much longer to train an air fighter than it does to train a fighter on land. The degree of skill required is of the highest, and the equipment made use of is not only enormously expensive, but, unlike ordnance, it very quickly becomes obsolete. In proportion to its population Canada has an air personnel probably larger than any other country, and it will be one of the first duties of the Air Board to consider how that personnel can be organized and how wastage from it can be replaced. It seems clear that it is financially impossible that that organization should take the form of a large professional air force: means must be found to create an effective organization, most of the members of which are primarily civilians and are yet trained and ready for war.

If the Air Board intelligently regulates commercial aviation, carefully investigates the possibility of performing government services more efficiently by air than by present methods, efficiently carries out such government services as are undertaken, and so lays the foundation for a Canadian Air Force that the organization built up with undue expense in peace may be depended upon in war, it will have difficulties enough to overcome and problems enough to solve without attempting to monopolize the air. That, like the sea, must remain free to those who desire to use it on "their lawful occasions."

Canadian Airharbours

First licences issued by the Air Board under the new Air Regulations of January 1920

LICENCE	PLACE	DATE	LICENCEE	CATEGORY
1	Regina, Saskatchewan	22-4-20	Aerial Service Co.	Commercial; SW of City; 50°25'N 104°30'W
2	Saskatoon, Saskatchewan	22-4-20	McClelland Aircraft Ltd.	Commercial; 2 miles SW of City; 52°08'N 106°43'W
5	Edmonton, Alberta	07-5-20	May-Gorman	Commercial; $3^{1}/_{2}$ miles NW of City; 53°35'N; 113°33'W
7	Hanna, Alberta	10-5-20	Holdbrook & McLeod	Commercial; $^{3}/_{4}$ mile SW of Town 51°38'N 111°56'W
8	Montréal, Québec (Cartierville)	03-7-20	Canadian Division of the Aerial League of the British Empire (operated by R&W Air Service)	Customs Airharbour 7 miles N of Montréal City; near St. Laurent 45°30'N; 73°50'W
10	Armour Heights, Ontario	17-5-20	Bishop-Barker Aeroplanes Ltd.	Customs Airharbour; near Toronto; 43°43'N; 79°24'W
11	Winnipeg, Manitoba (River Park)	18-5-20	Winnipeg Airco Ltd.	Commercial; at Riverpark, West Winnipeg; 49°51'N 97°08'W
12	Winnipeg, Manitoba	18-5-20	Canadian Aircraft Company Ltd.	Commercial; 5 miles West of City; 49°53'N 97°18'N
16	Lac à la Tortue, Québec	02-6-20	Laurentide Co. Ltd.	Commercial, Sea Plane 3 miles SE of Grande Mère; 46°36'N 72°40'W
17	Virden, Manitoba	29-5-20	Town of Virden	Customs Airharbour; $1^{1}/_{2}$ S of Town; 49°50'; 100°30'W
18	Sault Ste. Marie Ontario	07-6-20	Spanish River Pulp & Paper Mills Ltd.	Commercial Seaplane; on St. Mary's River; 46°31'N; 84°21'W
23	Brandon, Manitoba	26-6-20	Brandon Aerial Services	Commercial; $^{1}/_{2}$ mile west of City; 49°50'N 99°58'W
24	Leaside, Ontario	25-7-21 (sic) [may be 1921]	The Ericson Aircraft Ltd.	Customs Airharbour; NE of Toronto; 43°42'N 79°21'W
25	Comox, British Columbia	12-7-20	Vancouver Island Aerial Transport, Co.	Commercial Seaplane; $^{1}/_{2}$ mile SW of Town; 49°39'N; 124°54'W
27	Camp Borden, Ontario	19-7-20	The Air Board, Ottawa	Airharbour; (Military and Civil Government) 4 miles SW of Argus; 44°17'N; 79°56'W
28	Roverval, Québec	07-7-20	The Air Board, Ottawa	Commercial; Seaplane Station N of Ottawa; 48°32'N; 72°13'W
29	Chicoutimi, Québec	23-7-20	Price Bros & Company Ltd.	Commercial; Seaplane; on Saguenay River, West of Town; 48°30'N 71°05'W
30	Rockcliffe, Ontario	28-7-20	The Air Board, Ottawa	Aeroplane & Seaplane Station; Ottawa River,

LICENCE	PLACE	DATE	LICENCEE	CATEGORY
				opposite Kettle Island; 45°28'N; 75°39'W
31	English Bay, Vancouver, British Columbia	04-8-20	The Air Board, Ottawa	Seaplane Station at Jerico Bay, near Vancouver; 49°16'N; 123°17'W
32	Deseronto, Ontario	13-8-20	G.H. Harrold	Customs Airharbour; 3½ miles west of Deseronto; 44°10'N; 77°08'W
33	Yorkton, Saskatchewan	10-8-20	Donald Brown	Commercial; 51°16'N; 102°33'W
35	Lethbrodge, Alberta	28-8-20	Lethbridge Aircraft Co. Ltd.	Commercial; at Lethbridge Exhibition Grounds, 2 miles east of City
37	Fredericton, New Brunswick	16-11-20	City of Fredericton	Customs Airharbour; Seaplane; on St. John River; 45°58'N; 66°39'W
39	Darmouth, Nova Scotia	02-3-21	The Air Board Ottawa	Seaplane Station; 4 miles SE of Darmouth; 44°38'N; 63°31'W
40	Hampstead, Québec	18-2-21	Plante Aerial Service	Commercial; ½ mile N of Town near Montréal; 45°33'N; 73°42'W
41	High River, Alberta	07-05-21	The Air Board, Ottawa	Commercial`2½ miles NE of Town; 50°36'N; 113°51'W
42	Moose Jaw, Saskatchewan	25-5-21	City of Moose Jaw, operated by Western Aeroplane Co. Ltd.	Customs Airharbour; near City; 50°24'N; 113°51'W

LICENCE	PLACE	DATE	LICENCEE	CATEGORY
43	Bowness Park, Alberta	02-6-21	McCall-Hanrahan Aero Service	Commercial; 6 miles of W of Calgary; 51°06'N; 114°13'W
44	Burrard Inlet, British Columbia	01-6-21	The Aircraft Manufacturers Ltd.	Commercial Seaplane; Vancouver Harbour; 49°16'N; 123°06'W
45	Lake Minnewanka Alberta	27-6-21	A.W. Faulkner	Commercial Seaplane; 7 miles NNW of Banff, 3 miles W of Bankhead; 51°15'N; 115°25'W
47	Victoria Beach Manitoba	20-8-21	The Air Board, Ottawa	Commercial Seaplane; Victoria Harbour; 50°42'N; 96°33'W
48	Niagara Falls, Ontario	08-9-21 cancelled 28-10-21	Niagara Air Service	Commercial; Niagara River, 2 miles S of Niagara Falls
49	Saskatoon, Saskatchewan	06-9-21	R.J. Groome	Commercial; 3 miles NW of Saskatoon; 52°10'N; 106°43'W

This table was prepared from the article, "Canadian Airharbours", in *Aviation and Aircraft Journal*, October 17 and 24, 1921, pages 448-450, and pages 481-482, held in the Library Museum of Science and Technology, Ottawa.

APPENDIX 5
The Canadian Air Force

The establishment of the Canadian Air Force (CAF) in 1920 was an important event in the history of Canadian Aviation and in the evolution of government policy. It represented the beginning of military aviation in this country and was the third and final phase of the work which the Air BOard set out to achieve. The CAF became the first regular Air Force in 1922 and the Royal Canadian Air Force in 1923.

The following, taken from an official memorandum dated November 2, 1923,[1] provides some background:

During the summer of 1918, two Air Services were formed for active war work—the Royal Canadian Naval Air Service, for anti-submarine patrol work in connection with the naval convoys on the Atlantic Coast, and two squadrons of aircraft for work in England and France in connection with the Canadian Corps. The latter was part of the Canadian Expeditionary Force and its administration was under the Department of Overseas Military Forces. At the time of the Armistice in November 1918, the organization of neither was complete and both were subsequently demobilized...The following extracts from a memorandum dated April 2, 1919, explaining the provisions of the Act (The Air Board Act), show the situation existing at that time in regard to air defence:

In considering section 5, the question of formation of a separate Air Force arises. It is not considered that the time is opportune for formation of such a body. The whole question of the defence of the country in its Military, Naval and Aerial aspects will be under consideration during the next few years. The scheme of Air Defence may best be developed in conjunction with the new Military and Naval Schemes after mature considera-

tion. For this reason, no attempt has been made to develop under the Air Board for the present any scheme for a separate Air Force....

———

In the beginning of 1920 it was felt that some action must be taken in regard to the formation of a Canadian Air Force. Many thousands of Canadians had served in the Air Service during the War and were anxious to continue their training...P.C. 395 was passed, accordingly, on February 18, 1920, authorizing the establishment of the Canadian Air Force on a non-permanent basis.

———

Camp Borden was established as a training depot and officers and men were employed for its administration and as instructors to train the ex-officers and men who volunteered to join the new Force. These, in joining, agreed to serve for one month in every twenty-four. The administrative and instructional staff were employed for longer periods, usually six months.

———

When the Department of National Defence was formed in 1922, the Air Board organization was discarded. "Aviation" was considered as being synonymous with an "Air Force" and the whole of the Services, civil as well as military, were included under the Director of the Canadian Air Force, who was made responsible to the Chief of Staff for the execution of his duties by Order In Council 3145, dated June 29, 1922.

The story of the creation of the non-permanent Canadian Air Force, the formation of the Department of National Defence, the disbandment of the Air Board, the establishment of a permanent air force, and its development into the Royal Canadian Air Force, is a fascinating and complex one. The story has been written in interesting detail by W/C F.H. Hitchins.[2] Rather than attempt

to make a précis of this paper, extensive excerpts have been taken from it and reproduced here.

When it was decided to establish a Canadian Air Force in 1920, the Air Board made a submission to the Governor in Council setting out the following:

In view of the consideration above set forth, and for the purpose of laying a foundation for the organization of a Canadian Air Force on the general lines indicated, the Air Board recommended three steps:

(a) that former officers and airmen of the Royal Air Force be invited to offer their services as members of the Canadian Air Force upon the conditions that in peace time they would not normally be called upon for active duty for more than five weeks in any two years (including time spent in travelling to and from training centres), that they would receive pay only for the time so spent on active duty, and that for airmen the term of enlistment would be four years;

(b) that the Canadian Air Force be administered through provincial Air Force Associations, of which the Lieutenant Governors would be asked to serve as honorary presidents; the duties of each association, which would receive a small grant for a secretary and office accommodation, would be to maintain the paper war formations of the CAF in its province, keep a roster of officers and airmen and select them, in turn, for their biennial tour of training; and

(c) that negotiations be opened with the Air Ministry to arrange that officers of the CAF who were on the Reserve of the RAF be released from any obligations in the latter capacity which might interfere with their duties in the CAF...(p. 10)

———

On February 18, 1920 the government approved the recommendations of the Air Board for the formation of a non-permanent, non-professional Canadian Air Force...

On the same day that this Order-in-Council was passed (23 April, 1920), Major-General Sir Willoughby Gwatkin was appointed Inspector-General of the Canadian Air Force with the rank of Air Vice-Marshal. In the next few weeks, the six positions authorized for the small CAF headquarters staff were filled. Lieut.-Col. A.K. Tylee, OBE was appointed as Commanding Officer, with the provisional rank of Air Commodore...

By letters patent dated 8 June 1920, six members of the Air Board were incorporated as the 'Canadian Air Force Association', the purpose of which was 'to promote the efficiency and advance the interests of the Canadian Air Force and to assume such share of the administration of such force...as may be authorized by the Governor in Council'. Within the Association, seven principal branches were organized, the three maritime provinces being grouped together in one branch. All the commissioned officers ordinarily resident in the several provinces comprised the membership of the branches with the respective lieutenant-governors serving as honourary presidents...(p. 12)

— — —

In May, arrangements had been made with the Department of Militia and Defence for the Air Board to take over the airfield and buildings which had been constructed at Camp Borden for the use of the RFC/RAF during the war. The transfer was officially made on 5 July 1920, and an Advance Party was soon at work preparing the station and aircraft[3] for the inauguration of training...

While the Advance Party was at Camp Borden one officer reported for training. He was W/C J. Stanley Scott, the Controller of Civil Aviation in the Air Board, who was placed on duty, taken on strength for the normal training period (without pay) and posted to Camp Borden on 16 August. He completed his training period eleven days later and was then granted leave from the CAF, returning to his Civil Service position in the Air Board. Like W/C Scott, most of the civil servants employed by the Air Board also were appointed to or enlisted in the CAF and donned uniform for the normal training period when called up for duty with the CAF. These men, filling the dual role of civil servants under the Air Board and officers or men in the CAF, represented the only permanent thread through the period from late 1919, when the Air Board began to develop, until April 1924, when the permanent RCAF came into being. (p. 16)

— — —

Administration of the CAF was to be assumed in considerable measure by the Canadian Air Force Association to which a charter had been granted in June 1920. Under the regulations of August 1920 the provincial branch executive committees of the Association were charged with keeping rosters of officers and airmen ordinarily resident in their provinces, selecting them for training or for courts martial, courts of inquiry and other duties, and with taking such action as might be directed for the recruitment, administration and mobilization of the CAF in the provinces (Section 21).

Normally officers and airmen would be posted for duty at a centre during not more than four weeks in every two years, with at least twelve months between each period of training (Section 49). With their consent, however, personnel could be posted for duty at training centres for periods of up to six months, and could be specially employed on staff duty at air force headquarters or training centres, or on other special duty, for periods of not more than one year; under special circumstances these periods could be extended by the Air Board...(p. 18)

— — —

With the training centre now organized at Camp Borden, the CAF began to function as a non-permanent, non-professional force. Ex-officers of the RAF were granted appointments in the CAF, placed on duty for the normal training period and posted to No. 1 Wing; (at Camp Borden) at the end of the one-month course the officers were, in most cases, posted to headquarters and granted leave without pay until called up for the next tour of duty...(p.20)

— — —

The next step in the development of the air force occurred in 1922:

A bill to create one Department of National Defence was introduced in the House of Commons by Mr. Graham early in the 1922 session and received Royal assent on 28 June. The act incorporated the former Department of Militia and Defence, Department of Naval Service and the Air Board in one Department of National Defence which was charged 'with all matters relating to defence, including the Militia, the Military, Naval and Air Services of Canada'. The section of the Air Board Act of 1919 which provided for the appointment of an Air Board was repealed, and the powers, duties and functions formerly vested in that Board were transferred to the new Minister of National Defence. To allow time for the reorganization of the three departments which would be necessary before their amalgamation could be completed, it was provided that the act would come into force on a date to be set by proclamation. The effective date was subsequently fixed as 1 January 1923. (p. 91)

— — —

....In reorganizing the air services, prior to the establishment of the new department, the first step was to consolidate the Flying Operations Branch with the CAF. Hitherto all civil government flying operations had been carried out by this branch of the Air Board, and all air stations except Camp Borden had been under its control. The personnel of the branch were appointed by the Civil Service Commission and employed as civil servants; yet virtually all members of its staff were also commissioned or enlisted in the CAF and had been granted leave from their civil duties when necessary to do training or other service with the CAF. This strange duality could be somewhat confusing. Pilots serving with the Operations Branch as civil servants were normally referred to by their Army style service rank (e.g. Captain); many of them were also employed at one period or another on the administrative and instructional staff of the CAF and then assumed Air Force ranks (e.g. Flight Lieutenant). Furthermore, at Camp Borden, which was the CAF's only station, both branches of the Air Board maintained establishments, the shops and stores being under civil management while the training and general administration were under Air Force discipline. This division continued until July 1922, when the equipment branch at Camp Borden was taken over by the CAF, and its civil service personnel were put in uniform. Only the camp maintenance staff remained civilian. The change to Air Force discipline 'simplified the administration and enabled reductions to be made in the numbers employed.' (p. 92)

— — —

Although the new organization of CAF headquarters became effective on 1 July 1922, the several air stations of the Operation Branch were not affected immediately. As the operation season was then well under way and all stations were busy on flying activities for various departments, it was decided to defer their reorganization from civil to service administration until the end of the flying season in the fall. The changes necessary to bring them into the new scheme were then made gradually and as far as possible without disturbing their work. During the operational season, any new appointments required at the stations were made from CAF personnel and, in the autumn, when the season's work was completed, the civil staff of the stations was incorporated in the CAF by commission or enlistment. Civil employees who did not wish to join the CAF were granted one or two months' leave with pay to find new employment. The final formal change was made on 25 November 1922 when the air stations at Vancouver, High River, Victoria Beach, Ottawa, Roverval and Dartmouth were officially redesignated CAF Units, and the air station superintendents became commanding officers. (p. 94)

— — —

For three years, from June 1919 to June 1922, the Air Board had functioned as a separate branch of the government that was essentially civilian in character except for one of its components, the Canadian Air Force, which had a large body of reserve officers and airmen but only a small semi-permanent service staff. After June 1922 the civilian components of the Air Board were gradually consolidated in the Canadian Air Force which, on 1 January 1923, became a part of the new Department of National Defence

and was placed under the control of the Chief of the General Staff. Through the next four and a half years service flying, civil government air operations, technical services, and the control of civil aviation were all Air Force functions administered by Assistant Directors. Organized and operated now on service lines, this new Air Force began to re-equip with new aircraft and train new pilots. Symbolic of the change in status of the CAF from its original position as one component in the Air Board to its new status as the sole government air service was a change in its title. Some time earlier the suggestion had been made that it should seek the distinction 'Royal'; and in the spring of 1922 the idea was revived...

On 5 January 1923, when the reorganization was completed and the new department had officially come into being, formal application was made to the Secretary of State for External Affairs. The Canadian Air Force had now been reorganized as a permanent branch of the Canadian defence forces and hoped that the Governor-General would petition His Majesty to confer the title Royal upon it (granted in March 1923). 'Such a distinction would be most highly prized by all ranks and would add greatly to the prevailing esprit-de-corps.' Thousands of Canadians had served as pilots, observers and airmen during the war, and 'by their efficiency, gallantry and devotion to duty, added lustre to the name of Canada'. The reconstituted CAF had been reorganized almost entirely from the survivors of that body of officers and men. (p. 98)

During 1923, the major role of the RCAF was the conduct of flying operations for other departments of the government. Between 1 April 1923 and 31 March 1924 the service logged 2090.25 hours of flying.

More than two-thirds of this total was on civil operations--forest patrol, photography and survey, transportation, preventative patrols, and the like--the forest protection work alone accounting for 36% of all the RCAF's flying. Only 681.30 hours were classified as service flights. (p. 101)

————

Civil government air operations in 1923 were carried out entirely by service personnel not, as in previous years, by civilian employees of the Air Board. Another highlight of the year's work was the appearance of the first new aircraft to replace the obsolescent war-time types that had been used since 1920. (p. 105)

Footnote—Appendix 5

1 Public Archives Canada, MG 30 E243, vol. 6, J.A. Wilson, secretary, RCAF, to the deputy minister of National Defence.
2 Canadian War Museum, Paper No. 2, "Air Board, Canadian Air Force and Royal Canadian Air Force."
3 Seventy-three "gift" aircraft were assembled and tested.

APPENDIX 6

Letter from
The Secretary of the Air Board
to
The Deputy Minister and Comptroller of Naval Services
(Public Archives Canada, MG 30 E243, Vol. 1.)
G.J. Desbarats, Esq., C.M.G.,
Deputy Minister & Comptroller
Department Naval Service
Ottawa

November 2nd, 1922

Dear Mr. Desbarats,

There are certain matters in connection with the Air Service I should like to put before you when you are taking over the Deputy Headship of the Department of National Defence.

For convenience I will divide what I have to say into three parts-

First, past policy and progress; second, the present situation; and third, the future.

(1) After the Armistice the late Government decided definitely that the time had not yet come for Canada to embark on a policy of maintaining a permanent military or naval air force. Both war time organizations were demobilized and legislation was subsequently passed creating a Board for the control of Aeronautics.

The text of the Air Board Act should clearly the intention that the control should be chiefly civil in character. Following out the policy laid down the Air Board's organization was in the main a civil one.

There are three phases to this work:
(a) Control of Commercial Aviation;
(b) The conduct of flying for other Government Departments (Civil Government Operations);
(c) The organization of the C.A.F.

These three phases are distinct and separate in their purpose, their requirements, and their aims. The interests of one or other is often diametrically opposed to those of the others. Two of them deal with purely civil matters, the third with military affairs (including Naval).

The Air Board organization was formed to suit the policy laid down and the circumstances with which it had to deal. There was [sic] accordingly two civil branches and one military. Each functioned separately and each was represented on the Board which dealt with all matters of policy arising.

(a) The control of Commercial Aviation was exercised through a staff of civil servants, with the necessary aeronautical knowledge and experience to carry out this work. This system has given absolute satisfaction. It has work without friction and has had very considerable success in gaining and keeping the confidence of commercial firms. This has been no easy task and has called for the exercise of judgment and tact at all times.

(b) It was soon discovered that many Government Services, especially those operating in the remoter parts of the country, could be helped and their efficiency increased by the use of aircraft. Permission was, therefore, obtained to establish Civil Stations at different parts of the country, engage civil personnel through the Civil Service Commission for their operation, and carry out such work. Three such stations were started in 1920 and operated during the latter part of that season, and others in 1921 and 1922. The success of the work at each station is proved by the increasing demands for flying from all services. I need not go into details as to the work done. Its value has been recognized everywhere. The usefulness and possibilities of Civil Government Operations have been proved beyond question.

(c) The question of the creation of the CAF was a matter of much greater difficulty. The lines of development were not so obvious, the need was not so urgent, nor would any action taken bring such immediate visible returns. After most careful consideration of many alternatives, it was decided that, as the Government was not then prepared to grant sums sufficient to maintain a permanent Air Force of adequate size to be of any practical use in time of War, it would be best to proceed, in the first instance, with a moderate programme of Air Force training by giving Refresher Courses to those officers and men who served in the Flying Service during the War. As far as possible the whole organization was made non-permanent in character. The reasons underlying this decision are given in Order-in-Council

No. 395, date 18th February 1920. This Order-in-Council is the sole existing authority for the formation of any Canadian Air Force. Its intention and aims are clearly set forth authorizing the recruitment of a non-permanent training unit only. Recruiting for the Air Force was commenced during the summer of 1920 and the preparation of Camp Borden for training put in hand. Training started on October 1 of that year and was continued along the lines laid down until recently when lack of funds necessitated its discontinuance.

Many initial difficulties were encountered. Training has not always been as efficient as might be desired. This was foreseen, however, and specific mention of it is made in the Order-in-Council. Modifications, to meet these faults, were made, with the result that it is safe to say that in June of this year, when the control passed to the Military authorities, there could not be found in Canada any more efficient Government establishment than that maintained by the CAF at Camp Borden. Discipline was good, the personnel was of exceptional quality, the Camp well-kept, the workshops efficiently managed and the stores depot in admirable condition. More fully trained instructors in all subjects except flying were found to be an urgent necessity.

The experience gained in all three branches showed that the organization was sound and was providing a satisfactory basis for the control and development of Aviation in Canada with the funds available for the purpose.

(2) There was no necessity or reason for discarding without enquiry this plan of organization in the formation of the Department of National Defence. It would have in no way interfered with the consolidation of the "non-effective" services which is in process.

All three phases of aviation are now being placed in one directorate, and that directorate made responsible to the Chief of the General Staff. The intention is that the whole of the work of all three branches shall be carried out by the permanent Air Force personnel without regard to whether it is Civil or Military in character. The staff of all three branches is being transferred from the Civil Service to the Air Force, with the understanding that it will be a permanent force. This action has not been confined to flying officers or mechanics on duty, but has extended to messengers, draftsmen, the clerical and stenographic staff and other persons employed in purely office work.

The past policy was that only those persons who would be actually called upon to go into the field in time of war or emergency should be members of the Air Force and that positions that could be filled equally well by Civil Servants should remain civil. The militarization of the staff has been extended even to those officers in charge of the control of Commercial Aviation so that we now have this phase of the work entirely carried out by military personnel who report through the Director of the Canadian Air Force to the Chief of the General Staff. There is no excuse for this state of affairs. It is surely fundamental that the Government relations with commercial firms should be controlled by the Civil Head of the Department and not military officers.

In addition, there has been no expressed intention of the present Government to alter the aviation policy initiated by the late Government. On the contrary, the whole trend of discussion during the last session of Parliament and the public utterances of the members of the Government has been towards the decrease of military establishments. The permanent Naval Services has been replaced by a Naval-Militia and the Permanent force has been considerably reduced. No authority exists, as far as is known, for the creation of a permanent Air Force. The powers given under the Air Board Act, Section 5, are indefinite and vague. Though they served to cover the establishment of a training camp on a non-permanent basis, they might not be held as sufficient to warrant the establishment of a permanent Air Force with numerous bases throughout the country. Order-In-Council 395 clearly states that the C.A.F. shall be of non-permanent character.

This change has been made in direct opposition to the advice of all responsible officers who have had experience in the Government Air Service. Those making it had a very inadequate appreciation of the situation at the time the decision was made. Their views and ideas as to policy and development have materially changed since that time, but the scheme of organization apparently has not varied with this fuller knowledge. Operations and ideas as to policy, which were described as "lunacy" and "dreams" by the late Deputy Minister six months ago, have continued to be carried out with the full support of the military authorities. The policy laid down in June by the Chief of the General Staff:

(1) The creation of an Air Force trained in its duties for war; and

(2) The conduct of Civil Operations so far as the remaining funds allow; has evidently been discarded through the pressure of circumstances, as practically all Air Force training has ceased while the civil operations have been continued and extended.

The plan of organization, approved on 30th June last, calls for the establishment of four Air Force Stations, at Dartmouth, Camp Borden, Winnipeg and Vancouver. These sites were chosen solely with military considerations in view. Two of them are unsuitable for any work immediately in sight. Camp Borden will provide a training establishment for the Canadian Air Force ample for many times the present requirements. To distribute the training to more than one centre while the force remains on its present scale is to decrease its efficiency and increase its cost. At Halifax, there are practically no civil operations to be undertaken and so long as the funds are not available for the creation of Naval Air Squadrons, the maintenance of a station there is a waste of money. North of Winnipeg, a great field for civil operations exists. These, however, can only be carried out by water machines. It was proposed to withdraw the excellent station at High River where land machines only are used and establish it at Winnipeg and work the operations in both districts from a base there. There is no work for land machines at Winnipeg. The proposal is detrimental to the existing operations in Western Alberta and Northern Manitoba. It is further proposed that the Station at Vancouver should be moved to Esquimalt so that it would be near the Military and Naval bases. This move will ruin the operations now so usefully done from Vancouver.

These proposals show how dangerous it is to allow Civil Government Operations and the C.A.F. to be combined. Such a policy can only result in confusion, the handicapping of both servbices and inefficiency in each. Civil Operations, to be successful, must be considered on their merits alone and the same with Air Force training. The desirability of the separation of training and operations is recognized in the Militia Service by placing each in a separate directorate. In peace time all Military Operations are in the nature of training. Air Operations of the kind being done now in Canada are in no way training, but the actual carrying out of real business on a practical scale.

(3) The Department of National Defence should aim at the strengthening of Aviation in all its phases. Air strength in Canada cannot depend on the Government's effort alone, but must rest principally on the development of Commercial Aviation. To this end every effort should be made to assist such firms in their work.

An Aircraft Industry is an essential part of the Defence programme in Canada. Government orders alone cannot sustain this. It also must look principally to the Commercial firms.

Government Civil Operations are necessary but should be confined to the assistance of Federal Departments in their work. This is an entirely legitimate field and a most valuable one which will provide ample scope.

This being the case, there are three obvious courses to follow:

(a) The encouragement of Commercial Aviation so that the country may be strong in the Air and possess a sound Aircraft industry;

(b) The conduct of Civil Government Operations for the experience it will give in the development of Aviation generally, the opening up of new fields for aviation, the improvement of machines and equipment, and the increase in efficiency it can bring to the work of other Government Services;

(c) Adequate training facilities so that all aviation personnel, civil and military, may have the benefit of thorough preliminary training in aeronautics and, in addition, training in Air Force duties in times of emergency.

To achieve these three aims, some unprejudiced thinking is required and a clear realization of the duties and responsibilities which the Department assumes when the Air Board ceases to exist. This apparently has not been given so far. Recognition must be given to the fact that there are three distinct phases of the work and that two of them are civil in their nature and should be controlled by the Civil Head of the Department.

The control of commercial aviation is so obviously a civil matter that nothing need be said here as to the advisability of recognizing this in the organization and placing it where it properly

belongs directly under the Deputy Head.

In order that Civil Government Operations shall be conducted with the sole aim of assisting the work of other Government services, they should be separated from the training of the C.A.F. The personnel engaged in this Branch should belong to the Civil Service. They should all take their CAF training regularly and the greatest freedom of exchange should exist between the two branches. As their aims and objects are entirely dissimilar and the objects which they serve often are opposed, they must not be mixed, however. Civil operations provide the best kind of training for military work and all C.A.F. personnel should be given opportunities to serve on Civil Operations. Still, to mix training with operations is fatal. It is in no way necessary. Interchange of personnel will give what is required in both services. The adequate training of the CAF requires a great deal of attention and much work to place it on a sound basis. This is purely military work and as such properly falls within the sphere of the military authorities. A great field of work exists here for those officers of the Headquarters who are interested in aviation.

I trust that these remarks will make the situation clear to you and indicate the dangers and difficulties of proceeding along the present lines. Those who have most knowledge of the subject are utterly opposed to the present plan. Unfortunately their advice has not been sought nor has it been taken when offered. Their opinions have been over-ridden by others who events have proved to have held a wholly inadequate knowledge of the subject. Fortunately it is not too late to put matters on a better basis. I sincerely trust that action may be taken before long to go into the matter thoroughly, with a view to arriving at a sounder scheme of organization than that now proposed.

If there is any further information you desire

on any of the points raised, I shall be very glad to supply it at any time.

Yours very truly,

(J.A. Wilson)
Secretary of the Air Board

APPENDIX 7

Press Release (1927)
Regarding St. Hubert Airport.

(Public Archives Canada, MG 30 E243, Vol. 6)

The Minister of National Defence announces that negotiations for the purchase of a parcel of land near Montréal, containing approximately one square mile, for the site for the mooring mast, have been practically completed. The site selected is that recommended by Major G.H. Scott and Mr. A.R. Gibbs, the officers of the Air Ministry who visited Canada in the early summer to assist in the choice of a suitable location, after personal inspection of many locations in different parts of Eastern Canada.

It lies on the south shore of the St. Lawrence River, some six miles from the centre of the City of Montral, approximately four miles from the Longueuil ferry-wharf and adjacent to St. Hubert Station on the main line of the CNR. The main road from Longueuil to Chambly touches the west corner of the property. It is part of an open, level plain, well drained, of good surface and in every way suitable for its purpose.

Detailed surveys of the site are being made and the foundations for the mooring tower will be proceeded with as soon as possible. The steel work for the structure will be fabricated during the winter months in order to be ready for erection in the spring. The telescopic arm of the mast head, to which airships are moored, is being made in England along with two others for similar mooring towers in South Africa and in England. Plans and specifications for the subsidiary buildings, mooring winches, gas plant, water and fuel supplies are now receiving consideration, with a view to their construction next summer.

The site will, in addition, make a very fine aerodrome. Some time must elapse before the airstrip scheme reaches the stage when airships carrying passengers and mail can be run on a scheduled time table. In the meantime, the field will not be idle as it is proposed to prepare runways for the use of aeroplanes. Its situation in the centre of a level plain stretching many miles in every direction gives unobstructed approach on all sides and a clear take off into any point of the compass a mile long is possible.

It is proposed to use the site during the fall and winter as a base for the flying in connection with the investigation of the possibilities of air mail services in Canada. Plans are being drawn up for the erection of a hangar and other facilities for the operation of the aircraft at the site. Experienced officers who have visited the site state that every desirable characteristic for a good air terminal is present. Good access by road and rail, power lines and water supply, perfect approaches, good drainage, a level surface, abundant space and absence of obstructions on all sides, all make possible the development of an air base equal to any on the continent.

APPENDIX 8

Letter from the Deputy Minister of National Defence (Air Service)
to
the Mayor of Montréal
(Public Archives Canada, RG 24 3533, 121-1.3)

Ottawa, January 13, 1927
His Worship the Mayor of Montréal,
Montréal, Québec

Your Worship:

The successful establishment of air lines for the carriage of mail, express and passengers in many countries will undoubtedly lead, in the near future, to a demand for similar facilities for fast communication by air in Canada. The policy of the Dominion Government in the development of civil aviation since the Armistice has been towards providing air services in those fields, such as forestry, surveying and transportation in the remoter parts of the country, where other facilities are lacking. There was an urgent demand for aircraft in these fields and it was felt that the initial development of regular air transport lines could be better left to those countries where the population is greater, the traffic heavier and the climatic conditions less severe.

This policy has been successful as flying is now an essential part of such work in many parts of Canada. We are now in a position, also, to take advantage of the experience gained in the operation of air lines in Europe, America and elsewhere. This shows that, where the municipalities have assisted in the establishment of air routes, by providing flying fields, development has been greatly simplified.

Several municipalities have already taken action to assist the development of aerial transport in this way. The City of Edmonton has recently licensed an airharbour within its borders and has set aside a suitable tract of land for this purpose. Haileybury, in northern Ontario, has its licensed airharbour from where, during the past three years, aircraft have been operated into the Rouyn gold fields. Fredericton, N.B., and Virden, Man., also hold licenses for airharbours.

The Department, having in view future development, desires to draw the attention of the Canadian municipalities to the desirability of planning in advance and so being ready to take advantage of air transportation. The Department is prepared at any time to cooperate with the municipalities by lending any assistance it can and giving advice on any points arising. Should you wish an officer of the Air Service to visit your city, inspect any location and advise you on its suitability, please notify this Department.

I am, Sir,
Your obedient servant,
(signed)

G.J. Desbarats,
Deputy Minister

APPENDIX 9

Standard Conditions For Light Aeroplane Clubs and Associations

(Department of National Defence, Report on Civil Aviation 1927)

1. Conditions of Grant

Any approved association or club applying for assistance in the formation of a light aeroplane flying organization must make the following arrangements for its efficient maintenance:

(a) Provide a flying field or seaplane station which fills the requirements of the Air Regulations 1920.

(b) Provide for the housing, repair and maintenance of all aircraft and equipment supplied by the Department of National Defence to the satisfaction of the department.

(c) Arrange for the services of an instructor with such qualifications and on such terms as are approved by the Department and for a licensed air engineer for the maintenance in an airworthy condition of the aircraft and equipment.

(d) Have a roll of at least thirty members who are prepared to qualify as pilots and, in addition, not less than ten further members who have qualified already and are desirous of continuing to fly.

2. Issue of Equipment

(a) <u>Initial Equipment</u>: -to any approved club or association meeting these requirements, the department will issue two aeroplanes with engines complete, type to be specified by National Defence Headquarters, this equipment to be used only for the proper purposes of the club or association.

(b) <u>Additional Equipment</u>: -should the aircraft and equipment issued under the preceding clause of this condition be insufficient to meet the demand for flying instruction in any approved club or association, the Department of National Defence may, at the request of such club or association, make a further issue annually, for a period of five years to any such club or association providing, at the same time and at its own cost and expense aircraft and equipment of a value equal to that which it has requested the department to issue as aforesaid; the type of aircraft and equipment issuable by the department and to be provided by the club or association under this clause to be that specified by the department.

(c) <u>Ownership of Equipment</u>: -all aircraft and equipment issued by the Department of National Defence to any approved club or association shall remain the property of His Majesty the King.

3. Certificate Grant

The Department of National Defence will grant to each approved club or association the sum of $100 in respect of each member thereof who qualifies in such club or association *ab initio* for a Private Pilot's Certificate in accordance with the requirements of the Department of National Defence, the grant made to any club or association for such training not to exceed $3,000 during one financial year.

4. Flying

The enjoyment by any club or association, or by any member thereof, of any of the privileges granted by these conditions, shall in no respect relieve said club or association, or any of its members from any of the provisions of the Air Regulations, 1920, and amendments thereto. No aircraft or equipment issued by the Department of National Defence shall be used in or in connection with any flight made for hire or reward, nor shall any person who is not a member of such club or association be carried in such aircraft or in any aircraft provided by such club or association under the provisions of these conditions.

In the event of any contravention of this condition, or of any provision of the Air Regulations, 1920, or amendments thereto, by any club or association or by any member thereof, the Department may withdraw all aircraft and equipment issued by it to said club or association and suspend all flying operations of said club or association.

5. Periodical Inspection

Periodical inspection of aircraft and equipment will be made by qualified aircraft inspectors of the Department of National Defence, without cost to the club or association.

6. Government Responsibility

Neither His Majesty the King nor any of His officers, servants, agents or employees, nor any Department of the Government of Canada shall be under any responsibility or liability for or in respect of any injury, loss or damage to persons or property incurred or suffered by any approved club or association or any of its members, servants or employees or any third party in respect of or arising out of or in any way connected with or attributable to the operations of the said club or association or the supply, inspection and maintenance of aircraft or equipment and defects in aircraft or equipment issued by the said club or association with the approval of the department or any negligence on the part of the officers, servants, or agents of the department or otherwise.

7. Flying Accidents

A board of inquiry may be convened by the Department of National Defence to investigate any flying accident.

8. Management

Each club or association must be duly incorporated and must assume entire responsibility for all matters of its interior organization and management.

9. Disposal of Equipment

No aircraft or equipment furnished under any grant made may be used or disposed of except as the Department of National Defence may authorize.

10. Termination of Flying

On any club or association ceasing to function, all aircraft and equipment issued by the Department of National Defence must be returned, subject only to its consumption by fair wear and tear during the operation of the club or association.

11. Period of Agreement

Each agreement with any approved club or association will terminate on the expiration of five years from the 1st of April, 1928, but on the failure of any club or association to carry out any of its obligations or for any other cause (which shall not be limited by special reference to the foregoing) sufficient in the opinion of the Department, the Department may terminate the agreement at any time and withdraw any aircraft and equipment issued by it to such club or association.

12. Security Bonds

Each approved club or association must give a bond or other form of security satisfactory to the Department guaranteeing that the club or association will make good at its own expense any damage or injury to the aircraft or equipment issued by the Department whether occurring through its own neglect, or fault or non-compliance with these conditions, or the Air Regulations, 1920, and amendments thereto.

APPENDIX 10

Memorandum for File
Regarding Airmail Service

(Public Archives Canada, MG 30 E243, Vol. 6)
866-8-1 February 23, 1927

Air mail Services

1. Mr. Coolican, Assistant Deputy Postmaster General, called on the Director, R.C.A.F., at 5:00 p.m. today, to discuss proposals for these services. After general discussion, it was decided that the first and most important item was the construction of a civil airharbour at Montréal. It was agreed that the municipal authorities should be approached with a view to ascertaining whether they were prepared to assist by providing a suitable landing field, if so, the Department would undertake expenditures, as outlined in the present estimates, for preparation of the field, construction of buildings, etc. Mr. Coolican and the Director, R.C.A.F., arranged to proceed to Montréal in March for this purpose.
2. It was decided that the Post Office Department should draw up a notice calling for tenders for the carrying of air mails from Father Point to Montréal during the summer season, and from Saint John and Halifax during the winter season on the basis of a price per trip, an average of two trips a week during the year to be allowed for. The advertisement should contain particulars of the ground facilities which would be available.
3. Mr. Coolican definitely stated the wish of his Department to operate any air mail services by contract from the outset, rather than have them operated by a Government service. This was the policy of the Post Office Department in dealing with all services involving the carriage of mails.
4. Preparation of aerodromes, buildings and all other services would be undertaken by this Department, in accordance with the provisions made in the Estimates 1927-28.
5. In the first instance and for a limited time, it was not proposed to institute a surcharge on the overseas mail, or which the delivery would be hastened by conveying it from the seaboard to Montréal by air, but that when the service was successfully started and the public accustomed to its use, such a charge might be instituted later.
6. It was agreed that if the C.P.R. could, directly or by contract with a commercial aviation company, undertake the contract, it would be advantageous. Mr. Collican would therefore keep them posted as to the plan of operation.
7. The entry of an American company into Montréal was considered. Mr. Coolican stated that his Department would be prepared to let a contract to any responsible company who were prepared to run such a service, on the basis of $5.00 per pound. A surcharge would be imposed on mails to be forwarded by air, sufficient to meet this expense. The service would therefore be self-sustaining.

He stated that he had already advised General O'Ryan, Managing Director of the Colonial Air Lines, of these terms, and that the company was prepared to enter Montréal on this basis. He would send the Department copies of the correspondence relating to this.

J.A. Wilson,
Secretary,
Royal Canadian Air Force

July 28, 1927

Investigation of Airways
C.A.W.

The attached memo, signed by the Minister and the Postmaster General shows the action approved. Steps should be taken as follows:

1. Recommend type of aircraft to be purchased with funds made available by the Post Office Department.
2. Proceed with investigation of Rimouski-Montréal route to determine the feasibility of its operation,
   (a) as a seaplane route,
   (b) as a land plane route.
3. Select temporary bases at Rimouski and Québec. At Montréal, Vickers may be used but the location of suitable permanent base should be studied.
4. Report any work required in connection with these bases and assistance which will be necessary in making investigational flights.
5. When planes are purchased, preparations for winter flights should be considered.

J.A. Wilson,
Controller of Civil Aviation.

July 26, 1927

Air Mails

The successful operation of air mail services in the United States, Europe, Australia and other countries has led to the consideration of plans for similar development in Canada, by officers of the Department of National Defence and Post Office.

They recommend that, as certain provision has been made by Parliament for the preparation of airways and the carriage of mails by air, immediate steps be taken, as far as funds permit, for the thorough investigation of the conditions under which such services will operate in Canada and of the location of the best routes and their equipment for safe and regular operation.

They further recommend that, as an initial step, a thorough study be made of conditions and experimental flying be undertaken between Montréal and Rimouski before the close of navigation and, if investigation and experience warrant, during the winter months, as conditions permit, betweem Montréal, St. John and Halifax, to obtain information on the ground of the cost of such service, the work required to establish safe operating conditions on these routes and the best type of aircraft for their efficient operation. During this investigation, mails can be carried when conditions allow up to 600 pounds weight, but, until the preparation and equipment of the routes is completed, no regular service on schedule should be undertaken.

The undersigned therefore approve the immediate purchase of two single-engined commercial aircraft, suitable for such work, from funds voted in the appropriations of the Post Office Department for air mail services, and their operation experimentally by the Air Service, Department of National Defence, between Montréal and Rimouski till the close of navigation and, after that, if the interim experience and investigation warrant and sufficient funds are available to make experimental flights, between Montréal and St. John and Halifax, to investigate the operating problems on these two routes, such mails to be carried in the course of the investigations as may be considered feasible, the Post Office Department to make all necessary arrangements for handling the mails. Full reports of the results of these investigations to be submitted to the undersigned.

Minister of National Defence

Postmaster General

APPENDIX 11
Memorandum on Air Transport Policy

From the Controller of Civil Aviation
To the Deputy Minister of National Defence
(Public Archives Canada, MG 30 E243, Vol. 7)

March 17, 1933

Air Transport Policy
D.M.

1. Canada today presents unequalled opportunities for the useful and economic development of air transport. No country has obtained more immediate returns from the application of aeronautics to its problems and nowhere are the advantages to be gained from further developments more outstanding.
2. The temporary halt in progress caused by the depression makes it doubly necessary that our objects should be clearly defined so that in the interim period a wise policy of safeguarding our interests may be maintained till progress can be resumed. It should be clearly understood that the stoppage is not general and that it has so far effected [sic] only one small phase of aviation, i.e. airway development and inter-city air services in Canada. Progress has been continued with an astonishing growth of traffic all over the world. In Canada, commercial air services, other than inter-city lines, show a continual increase in mail, passenger and freight traffic.
3. A difficult situation is arising because of our

stoppage of progress in inter-city airways. This has two phases:

(a) Penetration by United States air lines; and

(b) The disorganization of Canadian operations.

4. The United States airway system consists of three main trans-continental routes, two coastal routes (from Miami to Boston and San Diego to Seattle) and numerous inter-city connections. This network has 48,379 miles of authorized airways, of which 19,500 are lighted for night-flying. The daily mileage flow over it in 1932 was approximately 144,000, of which 110,000 miles were flown under contract with the United States Post Office. The Aeronautics Branch, Department of Commerce, are responsible for the construction and maintenance of the airways, including intermediate aerodromes, lighting for night flying, teletype, two-way radio communication service and radio direction beacon installations; the Department of Agriculture supplies the meteorological service and the Post Office supports the operating companies by contracts for the carriage of mail by air. The system result of consistent support from the Government on a clearly defined objective over a period of six years.

5. There are three major operating systems: United Air Lines, American Airways and Transcontinental and Western Air Express. Each operates a transcontinental system and each has been built up gradually by the amalgamation of numerous smaller companies.

6. Through a similar process of amalgamation, the Pan American Airways' system has been built up to operate all airways in the Caribbean Sea, South America and Alaska.

7. This consistent support has enabled these companies, after heavy losses in the early years of their operation, to become self-sustaining. All now show an operating surplus. The average payment to the air mail operators has, at the same time, been reduced from $1.07 per mile in 1929 to 57 cents per mile in 1932. This has been possible through the development of passenger and express traffic to supplement the mail revenue. The operating efficiency is high, public confidence in the airway system has grown and a steady increase in passenger traffic has followed.

8. The air line operators in the United States, ambitious to extend their operations and increase their traffic, have studied the Canadian situation continuously. In 1928, an effort, on their part, to obtain control of the eastern Canadian airways was only defeated by the timely action of the Canadian group now interested in Canadian Airways Limited, who, with the moral support of the Government, stepped into the breach, took over the financially weak Canadian companies and formed them into a strong group.

9. Another result of their pressure from the United States was the initiation by the Government, through this Department, of the programme of airway construction, which has resulted in the survey of the trans-Canada airway and the support of the Post Office, who let contracts for the operation of the airway. Up to that time, no effort had been made to support any inter-city air services in Canada and the resources and energy of the air service had been directed towards the conservation of forests in the remoter parts of the Dominion, air surveys and transportation to districts inaccessible by ordinary means of transportation.

10. The operation of the trans-Prairie airway and that from Moncton, via Montréal and Toronto, to Windsor and Detroit, by a Canadian company effectively blocked this penetration for the time being. The United States operators were content to cooperate and exchange traffic at airports convenient to the border with Canadian operators. Now that the Canadian services are no longer operated , the pressure from the United States is being resumed.

11. The activities of Pan American Airways on our Atlantic coast are well known. They now hold a ten-year contract for a service from Boston to Halifax and St. John's, Nfld., with the generous subsidy of $2.00 a mile. Part of this service was operated during the summer of 1931 and their agents have been active in the Maritime Provinces and Ottawa during recent months. The same company operates the airway system in Alaska and is interested in obtaining rights to connect this system, through Canadian territory, with the main American airways. They have also purchased from Trans-American Air Lines the airway concessions in Greenland and Iceland for the survey and operation of the Arctic air route.

12. American Airways, through their subsidiary, Canadian Colonial Airways, have operated since 1938 a highly efficient mail and passenger service from New York to Montréal. Their intention is to extend their service to Ottawa and Québec as soon as conditions justify. They are now tendering on the Montréal-Rimouski air mail service. Should they be successful in obtaining this contract, (and by reason of their backing elsewhere, if they wish it, they can probably tender a price which will be far below any profitable bid from a Canadian firm) they will control the combined air mail-steamer service with all its potentialities.

13. Through another subsidiary, Canadian Air Express, American Airways operated a service from Buffalo to Toronto in 1931. They own the only aerodrome in Toronto fit for

use at all seasons of the year. Further expenditures on it are now under contemplation and it may be anticipated that American Airways will not neglect development in the Toronto district, where they can tap a population of three quarters of a million. They recently purchased Trans-American Air Lines, which for some years, had flown, nonstop, across Ontario between Detroit and Buffalo. In order to obtain the higher foreign air mail subsidy from the United States Post Office, they now call at London and, therefore, already have a strong foothold in Western Ontario.

14. North West Airways, (in which American Airways have substantial holdings), operating from Chicago to Pembina via Minneapolis and Fargo, wish to extend their lines into Winnipeg. So far this has been prevented by the maintenance, by the Post Office, of a remnant of the trans-Prairie air mail service, 57 miles long, joining Pembina with Winnipeg. The formation of a Canadian North West Airways, with headquarters in Winnipeg, is now under consideration so as to tender for the Winnipeg-Pembina air mail service at the first opportunity and thus secure entry into Winnipeg.

15. United Air Lines, a subsidiary of the strongest United States aviation group have at different times, discussed the extension of their activities into Canada. Hitherto they have been content to recognize the prior claims of Canadian operators (good customers for Pratt and Whitney engines, made by another subsidiary of the same holding company). These considerations apparently no longer rule and they now wish an entrance into Vancouver and through central British Columbia to the Yukon and Alaska.

16. It will thus be seen that three of the four major American aviation corporations are prepared to extend their lines into Canada at the first opportunity. From a purely operating point of view and neglecting all other factors, Canada could probably obtain immediate and efficient service by allowing this penetration and encouraging these great organizations to develop our airways. It is for the Government to consider whether the immediate benefit of this course outweighs the fact that control of Canadian aviation would inevitably pass to New York.

17. To understand the effect of the depression on Canadian aviation, it is necessary to review briefly its past. When civil flying began after the war, Canada was in the fortunate position of having in her outlying districts a field where aircraft could play an immediately useful part and compete on even terms with existing means of transport. Other countries, lacking this outlet, concentrated their energies on inter-city services for passengers, mails and express. Such services are competitive with old established transport services by rail, road or water. To compete successfully the air lines must offer a saving of time with equal safety, comfort and cost.

18. Generally speaking, the air lines of the world have not reached the stage when traffic revenue meets operating cost. Many of them are now fast approaching it but to a large extent they are still maintained by subsidies from their Governments. Without generous and continuous Government support, air transport systems on the scale of Imperial Airways; the major American systems; the three French lines, Aeropostale, L'Air Union and the Compagnie Aerienne Francaise; Deutsche Lufthansa, the German group; "SABENA" the Belgian; and "KLM", the Royal Dutch Companies, could not have been built up.

19. In Canada, conditions are widely different. The greater part of our commercial flying has been done in the "bush" by relatively small companies. The subsidy element, so important elsewhere, has been absent. When the Government work has been done it has been let by tender on a straight payment by results basis with few exceptions. In such "bush" operations, an elaborate organization is not essential. Results are primarily dependent on the personality of the operating staff, their resource and skill in meeting onerous conditions without adequate facilities in the way of bases, communications, weather reports, and the many factors which go to build up successful air line operations elsewhere.

20. As has been noted in paragraphs 8 and 9 above, it was not until 1928 that any action was taken by the Canadian Government to interfere with the natural development of Canadian flying beyond enacting the Air Regulations. We had been content to develop our own type of operation, irrespective of progress elsewhere, and to wait till, in the course of time, progress in aeronautical science had evolved more efficient aircraft, capable of competing with other forms of transport on equal terms, and till public opinion was educated up to the value of air transport and would patronize inter-city services on a large enough scale to make them pay.

21. The pioneer operators in Canada were mostly pilots who had gone fresh from school or college to the war and had had little business training or experience. They loved flying, were certain of its success, were willing to work for it and to risk their friends money by investing in the new means of transport. They failed to realize, however, that public opinion was still largely skeptical and that successful airway operations could only be built up by years of steady development, involving expenditures on a large

scale. Commercial aviation ventures have been formed by the score, have lasted for a year or two and then passed out of the picture through lack of support and proper financial management.

22. Stronger groups were gradually evolved through the amalgamation of smaller companies and far-seeing business men, watching progress in other countries and realizing the opportunities for development in Canada, began to take a hand in the financing and control of the new development. Western Canada Airways, formed by Mr. James A. Richardson in 1926, was rapidly expanding with the opening up of new mining districts in Western Canada. In the East, Captain H.S. Quigley had been a leader from the earliest days and was the largest and most successful operator in the Province of Québec. After his death, his companies, the original Canadian Airways and Patricia Airways, were combined with the Laurentide Air Service, the Elliott Air Service of Hamilton, and others, into Interprovincial Airways by Major General J.H. MacBrien. Over-expansion, lack of experience and inadequate equipment soon brought the company into financial difficulties. Its sale to United States interests, who offered to take over the business on generous terms, was only prevented by the intervention of Mr. Richardson and others, who persuaded the original investors to retain their interests and so hold control in Canada. A new corporation, the Aviation Corporation of Canada, was formed for this end, and eventually, the Eastern and Western companies were joined in 1930 in the present Canadian Airways Limited. Canadian Transcontinental Airways Limited, a Québec organization, Commercial Airways Limited, a Québec organization, Commercial Airways Limited, of Edmonton, and Spence-

McDonough Airways Limited were later absorbed. By reason of these amalgamations the capital structure of Canadian Airways Limited today represents much of the capital invested, at different times and from various sources, in commercial flying in Canada.

23. The management of the Canadian Pacific Railway had been studying aviation continually since the Armistice (it was their action in applying for an extension of the Canadian Pacific Railway Charter to include the operation of aircraft that made the Government take action in 1919 to pass the Air Board Act and Air Regulations). It is known that some of its officers had backed some of the unsuccessful pioneer companies. Their experience resulted in a cautious attitude on the company's part towards the new form of transportation during the succeeding decade. The growing success of aviation left little doubt in their minds, however, that it would shortly be a factor to be reckoned with in transportation.

24. The formation of a strong national company in Canada and its support by the Government, through the Post Office and this Department, led the Canadian Pacific Railway to favour participation in Canadian Airways. The Canadian National Railway, disorganized in the post-Armistice period, were making rapid progress and the management was fully alive to the importance of aviation. By 1930, both companies wished to take a hand in the game. It was most desirable that they should not do so as competitors but should support a common programme for development. After some difficult negotiations, this was achieved and authority was given by Order-In-Council in November, 1930, for the investment of a quarter of a million dollars by the Canadian National Railway in Canadian Airways, while the Canadian Pacific Railway invested a similar sum.

25. In this way, by gradual evolution, a strong national Canadian company was built up, with the support and encouragement of the Government, to operate the main trunk airways of the Dominion from coast to coast. They held important air mail contracts for the carriage of mail, were operating a daily service from Moncton to Montréal, Toronto and Detroit and from Pembina, on the international boundary, south of Winnipeg, to Winnipeg, Regina, Lethbridge, Calgary and Edmonton. Connections had been arranged through the United States air mail service between Detroit and Pembina for the carriage of Canadian air mail, pending the construction of a Canadian airway through northern Ontario, surveys for which were in hand, while an extension from Lethbridge to Vancouver to complete the trans-Canada system was contemplated by the Post Office as soon as the Department could equip the airway through the mountains. The company also operated the Rimouski-Montréal air mail service and had taken over the Québec-Seven Island--Anticosti winter air mail service and the Mackenzie Basin service, by the absorption of the bankrupt companies Canadian Transcontinental Airways and Commercial Airways of Edmonton, respectively. The magnitude of these scheduled operations called for an extensive organization for their proper financial and business management, very different from anything hitherto required in Canada.

26. The result of the crisis and the consequent cancellation of all the inter-city air services is being severely felt by Canadian Airways. In the fiscal year 1930-1931 they had a revenue from the Post Office for the carriage of mail of $1,228,260. During the present fiscal year, the total air mail payments to them will not exceed $120,000. The remaining air mail

contracts are those in the North country, which were originally let on a highly competitive basis at a very low price. Several of the more important of these contracts are now being put up for public tender by the Post Office Department and it is feared that this policy will result in further reductions in price, owing to the competition of smaller companies which cut rates continually, only to go bankrupt in a few years.

27. It is known that Canadian Airways lost heavily on their operations during 1931 and 1932. Fortunately, their cast position at the beginning of the crisis was strong and they have been able to stand such losses. They cannot continue to do so indefinitely, however, and unless they are assured of the continuation of their air mail contracts at a remunerative price, they would be foolish to continue to lose the remainder of their capital. Should they be forced to wind up the company now, the result will be deplorable. The strong group who supported Canadian aviation through the pioneer stage and through whose efforts the northern districts have been made accessible, the C.P.R. and C.N.R., whose cooperation in the development of aviation is essential to sound development, will lose their investment. Canadian aviation, as a whole, will not recover for many years from such a set back and the door will be left wide open to penetration by the strong American companies. There is no other organization in the country to take their place. Years of patient effort will be lost at a time when important developments are only waiting better times.

28. This Department's aim in supporting the formation of a strong national Canadian company has been, all through, to develop an organization which could successfully operate, not only the trans-Canada airway but

could cooperate, on equal terms, with other strong national groups, such as Imperial Airways and Pan American Airways, in the trans-Atlantic and trans-Pacific airways.

29. It is recognized that during the present financial stress additional financial support cannot be spared for aviation, nor is this essential. Judicious expenditure of the appropriations now before Parliament for air mails should be sufficient to save the situation, as other similar companies the world over have been. This, together with their growing freight and passenger traffic and economies in management, should enable them to earn their operating expenses till the crisis is passed.

30. The following definite recommendations are made to meet the situation:

(1) Any air mail contracts now held by Canadian Airways should be continued at equitable rates to be fixed by negotiation. Where the rates have been forced down to an unprofitable figure by competition they should be raised.

(2) The summer air mail service connecting with steamers at Rimouski should be supplemented by a similar weekly service to Halifax in winter.

(3) A triangular air mail and passenger service between St. John, N.B., Moncton and Halifax should be established to run 5 days a week. (If funds do not permit for operation throughout the year, a six month summer and fall service is suggested).

(4) The possibilities of a Vancouver-Seattle service by Canadian Airways should be examined so as to give Vancouver a direct connection with the United States air mail system.

(5) The possibilities of a service to give Toronto connection through Canadian Airways with the United States airway system should be examined.

(6) The Government should recognize their investment of $250,000 in Canadian Airways by the appointment of a Director to the Board to fill the vacancy left by the death of Sir H. Thornton, Vice-President of the Company.

(7) The two railway companies should give more active support to Canadian Airways where possible and arrange for through bookings for passengers and express at points where trains connect with airways.

(8) As soon as financial conditions permit a resumption of the trans-Prairie air service and its extension to Vancouver, this should be done.

(9) The Belle Isle combined air and steamer service operated last summer should be resumed at the earliest possible date under contract with Canadian Airways.

(10) The construction work on the trans-Canada airway as a relief measure should be continued and extended.

31. Submitted.

J.A. Wilson,
Controller of Civil Aviation.

Appendix showing operating returns, Canadian Airways, is below:

Canadian Airways Limited
Comparative Condensed
Operating Statistics

	1930	1931	1932
Mileage flown			
Mail	1,382,195	1,336,107	227,372.5
Other	585,929	496,687	1,006,835.0
Total	1,968,124	1,832,794	1,234,207.5
Hours Flown			
Mail	13,491	13,618.08	2,936.56
Othe	7,534	5,525.13	13,775.54
Total	21,025	19,143.21	16,712.10

Mail, Freight & Express (lbs.)

Mail	333,923	459,459	299,066.11
Freight&Express	501,439	764,449	1,870,136.04
Total	835,352	1,223,908	2,169,202.15

Passengers (Revenue Passengers Only)

On Mail Lines	3,545	2,371	807
On Other Lines	5,255	5,676	8,156
Total	8,800	8,047	8,963

Note:

Total mail carried by all commercial
aircraft operators in 1932   413,687

Total freight carried by all commercial
aircraft operators in 1932   3,000,000 pounds
(approx.)

APPENDIX 12

*Memorandum on Assistrance to Municipalities
for Airport Improvements*

From the Controller of Civil Aviation
To the Deputy Minister of Transport
(Public Archives Canada, MG 30 E243, Vol. 8)
921-1-29
Ottawa, Ont.,
November 2nd, 1936

Assistance to Municipalities in the Provision and
Improvement of Airports
Deputy Minister,
Department of Transport.

It is recommended that authority be granted to
assist municipalities in the provision of new airports or the improvement of existing airports on
the following terms:-

1. To qualify for assistance in the construction
   or improvement of a municipal airport the facilities proposed shall be certified by the
   Controller of Civil Aviation as being necessary in connection with the operation of a
   scheduled air transport service approved for
   licence by the Minster of Transport.

2. The grant made by the Dominion Government shall not exceed one third of the value
   of the investment made by the municipality
   in the airport, including land, buildings,
   lighting system and other necessary works.

3. The municipality shall provide a site for an
   airport which shall meet the specifications
   and conditions prescribed and laid down by
   the Controller of Civil Aviation of the Department of Transport under the provisions
   of the Aeronautics Act, Chapter 3, Revised
   Statutes of Canada, 1927, and the Regulations made thereunder.

4. The said site shall be reserved exclusively as
   a public airport, and shall be maintained as
   such by the municipality in accordance with
   the requirements of the Department of Transport, the municipality agreeing that the said
   site shall not be disposed of or used other
   than as a public airport without the consent
   of the Minister of Transport.

5. The municipality shall prepare, in conjunction with the staff of the Civil Aviation
   branch, plans, specifications and estimates to
   be subject to the approval of the Deputy
   Minister of Transport and no work shall be
   undertaken under this agreement without
   such approval being obtained in advance.

6. The municipality shall arrange for the execution of the approved works to the satisfaction
   of the duly authorized representative of the
   Department of Transport, shall provide for
   its supervision by qualified engineers during
   its execution and for the payment of fair
   wages to all classes of labour employed
   during construction.

7. Only such works as are necessary for the
   safe and efficient operation of aircraft shall
   be undertaken under this agreement, including adequate landing and taking off
   areas for aircraft, hangar, workshop and office accommodation, facilities for the convenient handling of mail, passenger and express traffic by air, lighting for night flying,
   and other essentials.

8. The municipality shall take such steps by
   zoning by-laws or other means to protect the
   approaches by air to the airport so as to prevent the subsequent construction of high
   buildings, power lines or other obstructions
   which might be a hindrance to the safe navigation of aircraft landing on or taking of
   from the airport.

The information furnished on the attached
statement showing the investments already made
on the various airports is accurate but may not
be, in all cases, absolutely up to date, as further
improvements may have been made on some airports since it was compiled. The estimates of the
costs of the necessary improvements, on the
other hand, are not based on accurate surveys of
the position at each airport and are, therefore,
subject to revision in the light of further knowledge based on detailed surveys of the requirements.

J.A. Wilson,
Controller of Civil Aviation.

*The Cost of Development chart goes after this.

COST OF DEVELOPMENT OF MUNICIPAL AIRPORTS
TRANS-CANADA AIRWAY

Location	Ownership	Investment Site	Improvement	Required		Estimated Cost
Victoria		Nil				
Vancouver	Municipal	$262,000.	$289,000.	Lighting System		$16,000.
Grand Forks	Municipal	$2,500.	500.	Additional acreage, 20 ac. @ $50.	$1,000.	
				Seeding & surfacing 65 ac. @ $40.	2,600.	
				Circle Maarker, 100' circle	100.	
				Boundary markers, 20 sets & $21	440.	
					4,140.	4,140.
Trail	Municipal	Not available	5,000.	Seeding & surfacing 35 ac. @ $40	1,400.	
				Boundary markers, 10 sets @$21	210.	
					1,610.	1,610
Cranbrook	Municipal	Not available		Additional acreage, 4 ac. on S. @ $50.	200.	
				Work on old road for expansion	300.	
				Seeding & surfacing 23 ac. @ $25	575.	
				Boundary markers,set of 6 @ $21.	126.	
					1,201.	1,201.
Fernie	Municipal	Not available	29,000.	Seeding & surfacing 22 ac. @ $40.	800.	
				Boundary markers, 7 @ $21	147.	
				Lighting (no provision)		
					1,027	1,027
Lethbridge	Municipal	4,500.	25,212.	New hangar	30,000.	
				Additional acreage 80 ac. @ $40.	3,200.	
				Seeding & surfacing 80 ac. @ $40.	3,200.	
				Boundary markers, 12 @ $21.	252.	
					36,652.	36,652
Calgary	Municipal	12,000	48,486.15	Seeding & surfacing 82 ac. @ $40.	3,280.	
				Boundary markers, 28 @ $21.	588.	
Edmonton	Municipal	55,000.	65,000	Seeding & surfacing runways: 8 ac @$40.	320.	
				New hangar (based on cost of Emsdale)	50,000.	
				Boundary markers, 22 @ $21.	462.	
					50,782.	50,782.
		336,050	462,198.12			115,280.

289

Location	Ownership	Investment Site	Investment Improvement	Required		Estimated Cost
Brought forward		$336,050.	$462,198.12			115,280
Medicine Hat	Municipal	5,000.	18,000.	Seeding & surfacing 7 ac. @ $40.	280.	
				Boundary markers, 16 @ $21	336.	
					616.	616.
Moose Jaw	Municipal	46,074.	30,178.72	Seeding & surfacing 2 diagnols: 8 ac. @ $25.	200.	
				Boundary markers, 16 @ $21.	336.	
					536.	536.
Regina	Municipal	16,000.	110,000.	Additional acreage on W., 20 ac. @ $50.	1,000.	
				Resurfacing 70 ac. @ $40.	2,800.	
				16 sets of boundary markers @ $21.	336.	
					4,136.	4,136.
North Battleford	Municipal	4,000.	14,700.	Not applicable		
Saskatoon	Municipal	9,370.	25,267.62	Clearing brush, 60 ac. @ $20.	1,200.	
				Seeding & surfacing 16 ac. @ $40.	640.	
				Boundary markers, 16 @ $21.	336.	
					2,176.	2,176
Brandon	Municipal			Seeding & surfacing 16 ac. @ $40.	640.	
				Boundary markers, 16 @ $21.	336.	
					976.	976.
Winnipeg (Stevenson)	Leased Municipal	Leased	87,400.	Engineer's estimates are being prepared for a complete revision of this project.		
Toronto	Private	138,933.	51,236.	Not applicable		
Hamilton	Municipal	215,000.	95,000.	Not applicable		
Kingston	Municipal	7,000.	14,600.	Requires enlargement		
				Increased acreage	7,000.	
				Grading and surfacing	10,000.	
					17,000.	17,000
Brantford	Municipal	6,000.	7,000.	Not applicable		
North Bay				Purchase of site, 120 ac. @ $25.	3,000.	
				Grading & surfacing 5,800 ft. runway 300 ft. wide	42,250.	
				Boundary markers, 18 @ $21.	378.	
					45,628.	45,628.
		$783,427.	$915,580.49			140,720.

Location	Ownership	Investment Site	Investment Improvement	Required		Estimated Cost
Brought forward		$783,427.	$915,580.49			$140,720.
Ottawa	Private					
Montréal	Dominion Gov't					
Moncton	Municipal	6,000.	20,000.	Rough estimate of cost of setting up new site (Lakeburn) 200 ac. @ $100.	20,000.	
				Grading & surfacing 2 diagonal rundways100 yds. wids. 50¢ per lineal ft. per strip of 20 ft. wide	55,000	
				Lighting (average figure)	12,000.	
				Hangar (on Emsdale cost)	30,000.	
				Administration building (on Lethbridge cost)	19,000.	
					136,000.	$136,000.
Saint John	Municipal	25,000.	135,000.	Now adequate.		
Halifax	Municipal	7,500.	145,000.	Site limited. Runways are 1,800 & 2,000 ft., require lengthening	20,000.	20,000.
TOTAL		**$821,927**	**$1,215,580.49**			**$342,348.**

APPENDIX 13

Extracts from Memorandum of
May 12 and 14, 1945

From the Controller of Civil Aviation
To the Acting Deputy Minister
(Public Archives Canada, RG 12, Vol. 2381)

"The stimulation which flying has received during the war years is well known and advantage should be taken of the existing intense public interest to develop the potentially enormous civil aviation industry. By being in a position to deal expeditiously with enquiries and guide development, the Airports Section of the Civil Aviation Division would be able to convert activities smoothly and efficiently from war to civil re-establishment. This would be in the national interest.

"The airport is the medium by which the civil aviation industry can best be developed and expanded to its obvious potential. The greater the number of airports, the greater the demand will be for aircraft and the greater will be the employment in the industry in the manufacture of aircraft and accessories, and in their servicing and maintenance. Since by Privy Council decision, the administration of Civil Aeronautics comes under the Federal Government, it follows that the Federal Government should take the lead in co-ordinating the interests and activities with the provinces, municipalities and others in the establishment of airports.

"It will be accepted as fundamental that, irrespective of the agency which operates a main line airport, the standard of operation and maintenance will require to be such that it will at no time cause any unreasonable decline in the efficiency of scheduled airline operations. The municipalities, particularly those owning airports, have, during the war years, become aware of the cost of maintaining such a standard and, without doubt, have been considering the implications of such standards to the continued ownership, operation and maintenance by the municipality.

"It, therefore, follows that main line airports will fall into one of the following categories:
(a) Federally owned and operated;
(b) Municipally owned and operated;
(c) Municipally owned and leased to the Government for operation and maintenance, as at present;
(d) Municipally owned, with a grant in aid from the Dominion Government.

"While it may be readily admitted that standardization can be more readily achieved through complete ownership operation and maintenance by the Dominion Government, it is submitted that the overall cost will be less if these functions are carried out by the municipality. But, what is considered more important, the municipality would be encouraged and compelled to take an interest in the airport facility, and the functions would be distributed.

"Obviously, a number of municipalities could not afford to maintain their airports to the standards required without assistance, and it would be necessary to determine the basis upon which such assistance would be made available, that is to say, on a flat-rate or percentage basis.

———

"In the event that the municipality refuses to continue the operation of the airports as a municipal function and it became a charge on the Government, the municipality should, in turn, write off its investment and transfer its interest to the Dominion Government without charge. From informal discussions which have taken place, those municipalities that feel that the expense of operation is beyond their ability would be quite willing to act in this manner.

———

"Apart from operation and maintenance, the Government should be prepared to accept a large share of the cost of extensions and improvements as these, in their entirety, will, for the most part, be beyond the ability of the respective municipalities.

———

"Exclusive of the airports where main line connection will be made, only a few of the airports adjacent to communities, which may become points of call on feeder line services, are municipally owned. The remaining existing airports in this category are the result of the Air Training Plan. There remain a number of communities that will undoubtedly seek feeder line service, but at which no airports have yet been constructed.

"The Civil Aviation Division has reviewed the complete list of R.C.A.F. aerodromes in use under the training plan and had eliminated a large number entirely as having no post war value. As these are declared surplus and revert to this Department, their entire disposition is recommended and they are turned back to Crown Assets Allocation Committee.

"The potential use to which the remainder could be put has been considered and the complete list has been forwarded to the Air Transport Board for their study and comment. Pending a review by the Board, no action is being taken to dispose of these aerodromes, should they become surplus. . . .

Consideration will have to be given to the policy whereby surplus aerodromes may become available to communities to which feeder line services may operate or to communities desiring to have the aerodrome available for general purposes.

———

"Aerodromes, in connection with feeder line services, may possibly require the application of the same policy, with minor modifications, as that which is adopted for main line airports. Here again, however, it is suggested that every effort should be made to encourage the communities to have an active interest in the airport, perhaps with the assistance of the province and ultimately in some cases by the Federal Government."[1]

Footnote—Appendix 13

[1] In elaboration of these extracts, the Controller of Civil Aviation wrote the Secretary of the Air Transport Board on July 24, 1945. See Appendix 15.

APPENDIX 14

Order in Council PC3166 regarding Financial Assistance to Municipalities for Airports
(Public Archives Canada, MG 30 E243, Vol.8)

Certified to be a true copy of a Minute of a Meeting of the Committee of the Privy Council, approved by His Excellency the Governor General on the 14th December 1936.

The Committee of the Privy Council have had before them a report, dated December 11th, 1936, from the Minister of Transport, representing:

That the efficient operation of the trans-Canada airway is contingent on the provision of proper airports in the principal cities;

That during 1928-1929 a number of cities on the route provided airports at their own expense;

That progress in aviation has brought larger and faster aircraft into use, and facilities which were satisfactory at that time no longer meet the needs of modern air services;

That the financial position of the cities today makes it difficult for them to undertake the necessary improvement of existing airports or the provision of new airports suitable to modern requirements.

The Minister, therefore, on the advice of the Chief of Air Services, concurred in by the Deputy Minister of Transport, recommends that a measure of financial assistance be granted to municipalities on the trans-Canada airway to the extent of not more than one-third of the amount already expended by municipalities on approved airports; also not more than one-third of the amount which any municipality on the trans-Canada airway may agree to expend on improvements to existing or new airports on the airway, provided that, in determining the proportion to be paid by the Government to these municipalities, expenditures on hangars or buildings shall not be taken into consideration, and

That, subject to the above mentioned conditions, the Department of Transport be authorized to enter into agreements to assist municipalities on the trans-Canada airway to improve existing airports or provide new airports, such assistance not to exceed one-third of the value of the investment already made (exclusive of buildings) or now proposed to be made, by the municipality, in the airport, any agreement involving an expenditure of over $5,000 to be approved by the Governor in Council.

The Committee concur in the foregoing recommendation and submit the same for approval.

(Signed) E.J. Lemaire
Clerk of the Privy Council

The Comptroller
the Treasury.

APPENDIX 15
Letter regarding Municipal Airports

From the Controller of Civil Aviation to the Secretary of the Air Transport Board
(From Department of Transport File 5161-1, Vol. 1)

Ottawa, Ontario, July 24, 1945.
Walter T. Patterson,
Secretary,
Air Transport Board,
No. 3 Temporary Building,
Ottawa, Ontario.
Dear Mr. Patterson,
As agreed at the meeting on July 11th in Mr. Henry's Office, there is provided herewith further information showing operation and maintenance costs of, and revenue from, main line airports in Canada, as an elaboration to the memorandum on this subject, dated May 12th, 1945, to the Acting Deputy Minister. A brief history of the circumstances under which aid has from time to time been extended to the municipalities is also given.

Statements relating to airports do not include costs for the operation of radio ranges, meteorology, or airport and airway control, as these are items which are applicable to the airways' system as a whole.

The following list shows the principal municipal airports on the trans-continental airways' system with maintenance and revenue figures for the 1943-44 period. The figures for maintenance cover only direct costs for the operation of the airport, such as snow rolling, grass cutting, clearing of ditches, building repair and maintenance, etc. The revenues are derived chiefly from landing charges for scheduled airline operations at the rate of One Hundred Dollars ($100.00) per month for the first schedule, and Fifty Dollars ($50.00) per month for the second and each such succeeding schedule. A very small revenue is obtained from non-scheduled and itinerant aircraft in accordance with the scale of charges set up in Information Circular 0/7/34. Office space in departmental buildings is charged at the rate of One Dollar ($1.00) per square foot per annum, and hangar floor area on a lease basis at the rate of Forty Cents (40¢) per square foot per annum.

These charges include light, heat and janitor services.

	Maintenance	Revenue
Vancouver, B.C.	$ 55,414	$ 9,735.
Lethbridge, AB	17,191	5,871.
Grande Prairie, AB	No RCAF record	
Edmonton, AB	51,276.	10,364.
Calgary, AB	47,444.	3,488.
Medicine Hat, AB	No RCAF record	
Regina, SK	30,349.	6,759.
Saskatoon, SK	No RCAF record	
North Battleford, SK	No RCAF record	
Winnipeg, MB	24,743.	5,944.
Fort William, ON	14,625.	No RCAF rec.
Malton, ON	67,058.	13,423.
London, ON	25,949.	3,264.
Charlottetown, PEI	4,842.	204.
[sic]	$338,901.	$59,250

The following is a list of the principal airports owned and operated by the Federal Government. Their establishment became the responsibility of the Federal Government through lack of action on the part of the municipalities and the necessity for completing the gaps in the airways' system. The figures for "Expenses" and "Revenue" are for the period 1945-46. The extraordinary expenses at Montréal, North Bay and Ottawa are attributable for wartime service demands.

	Expenses	Revenue
Moncton, NB	$ 49,326.	$ 10,861.
Montréal (Dorval), PQ	157,367.	15,496.
North Bay, ON	51,963.	5,083.
Ottawa, ON	66,594.	8,283.
Windsor, ON	22,780.	6,150.

As a matter of record, the following municipal airports were leased for war purposes:-

Kamloops, B.C.	Operated by the RCAF
Saint John, N.B.	Operated by the RCAF
Amherst, N.S.	Operated by Canada Car & Foundry
New Glasgow, N.S.	Operated by the Dept. of Transport
Goderich, Ont.	Operated by the RCAF
St. Catharines, Ont.	Operated by the RCAF
Cap de la Madeleine, P.Q.	Operated by the RCAF
Prince Albert, Sask.	Operated by the RCAF

The capital cost of bringing main line airports up to the standard required for D.C. 4 aircraft has been included in estimates forwarded to the Department of Reconstruction. For the two-year period 1946-47 and 1947-48, this was approximately Sixty Eight Million Dollars ($68,000,000).

From the tabulation on "Maintenance" and "Revenue" for the principal municipal airports for the year 1943-44, it will be seen that the revenue amounts to less than one-fifth of the direct cost of operation. As mentioned above, the principal source of revenue is obtained from scheduled airline operations. At the time the charges for such operations were established, an attempt was made to arrive at a figure in line with similar charges in the United States while, at the same time, taking care to ensure that they did not impose an undue hardship on Canadian airline operators. Any appreciable revenue from itinerant or small aircraft on the basis of the scale of charges in Information Circular 0/7/34 should not be anticipated, since the tendency will be for light aircrafts to operate from the be serviced at smaller and less expensive airfields. Canadian Pacific Air Lines has, from time to time, complained that these charges are unduly high. We have had no comment from Trans-Canada Air Lines or other operators and no attempt has recently been made to ascertain whether these charges are justifiable on an economic basis.

At such time as larger equipment is placed in operation, such as T.C.A.'s D.C. 4 aircraft, it may be that consideration should be given to a corresponding increase in landing fees. For example, the charge for an aircraft with an all-up weight of 70,000 lbs. might be three times as high as for an aircraft weighing 20,000 lbs. If, as appears probable, the number of schedules operating from the principal airports is doubled within the next five years, and the schedule of charges is increased on a basis as mentioned above, the revenue from this source alone might be expected to increase five or six times.

The question of landing charges has international significance and it can be anticipated as a subject for discussion by the Provisional International Civil Aviation Organization. Decisions reached by PICAO will be binding only so far as international airports are concerned, but it may be expected that these decisions will have an effect on domestic decisions leading to the standardization of charges, as will decisions reached with reference to domestic charges for airports in the United States.

The figures given for maintenance cover the requirements for wartime, as well as civilian operations, and are probably considerably higher than would be encountered for purely civil purposed for aerodromes of the same size. However, the principal airports will be greatly increased in size for civil purposes, which will mean increased costs of maintenance. It may be expected that such maintenance will be comparable to, or greater than wartime maintenance for smaller airports, but the amount cannot be accurately determined as maintenance costs do not increase pro rata with the size of the airport.

It is generally conceded that the capital cost of airport establishments cannot be financed from revenue. However, in a number of instances in the United States and Europe, other sources of revenue have been sought with a view to financing airport maintenance. In these instances, supplementary revenue is obtained from automobile parking, public observation enclosures, conducted tours, operation of restaurants, and the judicious allocation of concessions.

The Airport Manager in Amsterdam advised that in 1936 some Six Hundred Thousand (600,000) odd people paid charges varying from Ten Cents (10¢) to Twenty Five Cents (25¢) for the privilege of observing aircraft operations and for conducted tours through the hangar. The Manager of the Washington National Airport advised about two years ago that, by means of charges for car parking, turnstiles for persons visiting the observation area and for restaurant concessions, etc. operated on a flat rate plus a percentage, he hoped to meet operational costs of the airport, amounting to approximately Five Hundred Thousand Dollars ($500,000) per annum. It is felt, therefore, that consideration should be given to encouraging the public to use the airport as a social centre. As the majority of airports land is acquired for zoning purposes or in the process of negotiation which is surplus to operational requirements. By landscaping and the judicial use of concessions, some of this surplus land might be made revenue producing.

The following figures give the items of operating expenses in percentages, and are taken from a survey of municipal airports made by the American Municipal Association, and appear in the Fifth Annual Edition of Airport Regulations 1945-46:-

Operating Expenses

Total Salaries	53%
Field Area	7%
Light, Heat and Power	8%
Field Lighting	6%
Hangars	5%
Runways	5%
Field Rent	4%
Insurance	3%
Taxes	1%

Automatic Traffic Control	1%
Miscellaneous	7%
	100%

The following table on revenue is taken from the same source as above. It is not clear whether the aggregate revenues given in this study balance the expenses. If not, it must be assumed that either a subsidy or a deficit is not shown on the revenue sides:-

Revenue

Hangar and storage	25%
Gas and Oil	23%
Other Rental	19%
Landing Fees	19%
Concessions	8%

(On air terminals the concession revenue is much higher)

Commission and Other Income	4%
	100%

To sum up: there seems to be reasonable hope that, at mainline airports, revenue may be made to pay operating and maintenance expenses within a reasonable period. Such being the case, Federal grants to tide over the municipalities in the interim period, as suggested in the memorandum of May 12th, would appear to be justified.

Brief History of Federal Assistance for Municipal Airports

Order-in-Council P.C. 322 of February 22nd, 1929, authorized the Department of National Defence to make a contribution in the form of a grant of Ten Thousand Dollars ($10,000.00) for any one airport. The Department also undertook to provide, free of charge, one airport beacon at each lighted airport site; such beacon to remain the property of the Department, but to be installed and operated at the expense of the municipality concerned. These steps were taken in order to facilitate the inauguration of the air mail service which was started the following year.

Most of the municipalities on the prairies and a few in the East took advantage of this offer. With the exception of a few of the rotating beacons, most of the lighting equipment concerned has become obsolete.

The Unemployment Relief Projects Administration undertaken during the depression years, 1931-35, did not affect any of the airports now used as main line stops on the trans-continental airways system.

When in 1936 it was decided to establish a trans-continental airline, it was apparent that a number of the municipalities where stops were intended would have to improve their airports to accommodate the new type of flying equipment coming into use. P.C. 3166 of the 14th of December, 1936, was, therefore, passed authorizing the Civil Aviation Division of the Department of Transport to grant financial assistance to municipalities on the trans-Canada airways system to the extent of not more than one-third of the amount already expended by such municipalities on approved airports; also not more than one-third of the amount which any municipality on the airways system might agree to expend on improvements, exclusive of hangars or buildings. All of the principal municipal airport on the trans-continental system, the names of which are given in the first list above, were granted assistance under this scheme. The assistance was later extended to the airports at Prince Albert, North Battleford, Peace River, Cap de la Madeleine, New Glasgow and a number of other points where it appeared to be in the national interest to do so.

As the development of the airways system proceeded, it became apparent that airports were required to serve municipalities that could not reasonably be expected to bear more than a small share of the cost of constructing them. It was, therefore, decided that, at such points the Government would bear the cost of constructing and maintaining the airport if the municipality would provide land. This procedure was followed at Moncton and North Bay. Windsor later on came into this category when the Dominion Government purchased the airport for a period of ten years for the sum of One Dollar.

In order to complete the airways system, it was necessary to provide airports at the Cities of Montréal and Ottawa, neither of which had evinced much interest in airport development. The Department already had a site at St. Hubert which it proceeded to improve to the necessary standard. At Ottawa it was found necessary to purchase the land and build the airport without any assistance whatever from the municipality.

At the outbreak of war, the Department of Transport was instrumental in leasing all the main municipal airports on the trans-continental system for use by the R.C.A.F. for the nominal sum of One Dollar per year.

Yours truly,
(A.D. McLean),
Controller of Civil Aviation

Municipal Airports, Not Main Line, Leased for War Purposes:

Kamloops	Leased by RCAF
St. John	Leased by RCAF
Amherst	
New Glasgow	
Goderich	
St. Catharines	Leased by RCAF
Cap de la Madeleine	
North Battleford	
Prince Albert	

APPENDIX 16

List of Municipal Airports Receiving Operating Subsidy of five Cents a square Yard of Paved Area

(As of December 1, 1956)

Airport	Effective Date
Edmonton*	November 1, 1946
Medicine Hat	April 1, 1947
Prince Albert	April 1, 1947
Vancouver*	November 1, 1947
Brandon	June 1, 1948
Calgary*	July 1, 1949
Fredericton	April 1, 1951
St. John, N.B.	June 1, 1952
Sudbury*	February 1, 1954
Trenton, N.S.	April 1, 1955
Regina	July 1, 1955
Timmins	June 6, 1956

*At these airports, Department of National Defence paid an additional subsidy in lieu of landing fees.

APPENDIX 17

Report of the Interdepartmental Committee on Airways and Airports Policy
(Department of Transport File 5161-1, Vol. 7)

DOC (AAP 508)
OTTAWA, Ontario
18th October, 1950.

The authority of the Department of Transport to construct and operate airports, airways and aids to navigation arises from Part 1 of the Aeronautics Act which places upon the Minister of Transport full responsibility and authority in this connection. The main principles followed by the Department in establishing airports and airways were described to Parliament by the Minister of Transport in 1948. They may be surmised as follows:

(a) The progressive development of mainline airports, to permit the utilization of the most modern types of aircraft at the minimum capital outlay consistent with safety and economy of operation.

(b) The development of a minimum number of international airports consistent with Canada's position in the international civil aviation field and our obligations under international air agreements.

(c) The encouragement of and assistance to municipalities for the development of airports throughout Canada, where it seems desirable that such airports should be developed, maintained and operated by municipalities, to standards set out by the dominion government.

(d) The assistance in the establishment of airstrips at air bases feeding remote areas, for the purpose of stimulating the development of Canada's natural resources.

(e) The assumption of the costs of maintenance and operation of those airports which are under the control of the Department of Transportation, and to assist municipalities in the maintenance and operation of essential airports where the cost is a strain on municipal resources.

(f) The provision and maintenance of aerial aids to navigation, such as radio ranges, instrument landing systems, where necessary, meteorological services and air traffic control, as necessary, to ensure the regularity and safety of air navigation.

The following report presents in greater detail the policy which the Interdepartmental Committee on Airports and Airways believes should be pursued. It is based on the foregoing principles laid down by the Minister and represents in general the policy pursued by the Department of Transport as it has evolved to meet existing circumstances.

The Airways System

The report deals separately with airports and aids to navigation, but is based upon the concept of our main airways and air routes system.

An airway is a defined track over which the following facilities are provided:

(a) Track guidance and fixes by means of radio aids to navigation,

(b) airports adequate for the types of aircraft normally using the airway,

(c) communications, and

(d) traffic control, where necessary.

An air route is a given track over which instrument flight may be approved by the Department of Transport but which, by reasons of light traffic density and the operational limitations of the route, does not justify or require aids to navigation and communications facilities to the same standard as any airway.

The report makes provision also for those airports, usually of a lesser nature, which are not located on an airway or air route but are required to serve the special needs of a community or area.

At present the existing pattern of airways and air routes covers reasonably well the requirements of the Canadian economy for air services and while changing conditions will, in time, lead to the development of some new airways and routes it would appear that the main need of the immediate future will be for development, maintenance and improvement of the existing pattern rather than the establishment of new airways.

Federal responsibility in the matter of provision of airports and other facilities should be defined in the following fashion:

Airport Construction and Improvement

In this section "improvement" means any engineering project involving the reconstruction, strengthening, lengthening or widening of existing runways, taxi strips or aprons, and the construction of new runways, taxi strips or aprons and engineering work incidental thereto.

(a) The federal government should assume responsibility for the construction or airports or improvement of existing airports to satisfy the requirements of the present main airways systems. These systems comprise (1) the terminal and principal airports, which are complete with lighting and all necessary buildings, as well as instrument approach system, where considered necessary, and (2) intermediate or 100 mile airports, complete with lighting and necessary aids to navigation, such as radio ranges or beacons.

Note: In connection with (1) above, the federal responsibility is not to be construed as including the responsibility for the construction of buildings on airports.

(b) Where the national interest requires an airport which does not constitute part of the main airways system and the municipality or other corporate body cannot be induced to participate, or is non-existent, the federal government should assume full responsibility for the construction of an airport or for the improvement of an existing airport. This clause would cover the construction of airports as required on essential air routes, or other vital locations, and would include such lighting, buildings and aids to navigation as may be required by reasons of traffic density and/or operational necessity.

(c) Where a municipal airport forms part of the airways system and there is advantage in improving the municipal airport rather than constructing a new federal airport, a grant-in-aid to the municipality should be made, or the construction might be carried out by or for the federal government.

(d) The federal government should also make grants-in-aid for the construction of smaller airports which are not part of the airways system in the following systems:

(i) where there is a substantial need for an airport to promote the development of natural resources including tourist traffic or where traffic potential in the area is high; and

(ii) where an air service for mail and other communications is necessary to serve an extremely isolated community.

Such grants-in-aid should be made wherever possible to the municipality in the area but may, upon occasion, require to be made to commercial companies, (e.g. mining and lumbering industry) where no municipality exists. Grants-in-aid for airports related to development of natural resources should be made after consultation with the Department of Resources and Development and/or Mines and Technical Surveys and should only be made to a private company in cases where a grant would have been made had a municipality existed. The grants-in-aid should be limited to a maximum of $25,000 for small municipal airports except in unusual conditions and should be on the condition that the recipient will first, at no cost to the federal government, provide the property involved. Experience has shown that the previous objective of equal sharing of costs between the federal government and the municipality is not achievable, in most cases small municipalities are not in a position to share costs equally with the federal government. Grants-in-aid for those lesser airports not comprising part of the airways system should continue to be voted separately in the estimates.

(e) The department should continue to construct airports in the Northwest and Yukon Territories upon the recommendation of or after consultation with the Department of Resources and Development. Consideration should be given to the responsibility for the provision of funds (whether Resources and Development or Transport) for construction of airports in this category in accordance with the principles stated above; i.e., where the airport would normally be provided under the above policy funds should be provided by the Department of Transport, and where the airport is to meet a special need of the Territories Administration funds should be provided by the Department of Resources and Development.

Airport Maintenance

Ordinary airport maintenance should be the responsibility of the operator of the airport in every case whether the airport is owned wholly or in part by the operator of the airport.

Airport Operation

The federal government should continue to operate the airports comprising the main airways system, and those airports deemed to be necessary in the national interest wherever federal operation is necessary for maintenance of the airports concerned. It has been the policy to encourage municipalities to take over airports, and certain airports on the airways system are presently operated by municipalities. In such circumstances where the cost is a strain on municipal resources the federal government provides a subsidy designed to protect the municipality against undue operational losses.

Municipal operation has been encouraged in order to create municipal interest in and support of aviation generally. Moreover it may result in savings to the federal government through reductions in staff employed. On the other hand, those airports which are showing profits or at least meeting operational costs will normally be the ones taken over by municipalities and the federal government will be left with the deficit-producing airports. Further consideration should be given to these factors to determine whether the federal government should continue to pursue the objective of encouraging municipal operation and thereby municipal interest at airports on the airways system or whether the expense involved in federal operation of airports would justify the federal government retaining in future all airports on the airways as a means of reducing its losses.

In the case of airports other than those comprising the main airways system or those deemed necessary in the national interest, the federal government should not assume responsibility for operation.

Aids to Navigation, Air Traffic Control

The federal government should continue to assume responsibility for the construction, operation and maintenance of radio aids to navigation and for air traffic control, where necessary, on the main airways and air routes systems, provided in the case of air routes such facilities are an operational necessity. Determination of the standards of facilities to be provided must depend on technological development but the department should provide the overall minimum which is considered necessary for operational use. Where a commercial air service believes that an additional facility is necessary and is willing to provide it, it should be allowed to do so subject to the consent of the federal authorities. If, however, more than one company is using a privately-owned radio aid to navigation and there is a general public requirement for that aid, then the Department of Transport may take over, or financially assist, the operation of that facility whether or not that facility is on a main airway or essential air route.

The necessity for overall federal responsibility in this connection arises from the following factors:

(1) It is essential that each system operate as an integrated unit with standard equipment and uniform procedure under one authority.
(2) It is essential that the personnel operating such system be trained to a uniform standard and be responsible to a certain authority.
(3) The cost involved cannot rightly be assessed against any particular airport or municipality.
(4) These systems interlink with other international systems.

Strategic Requirements

In determining the policy which it proposes to adopt in construction or improvement of airports, in the development and improvement of the airways system, and in the provision of aids to navigation and traffic control, the civil authorities should continue to work in close co-operation with the military authorities in order to provide co-ordination of military and civil requirements wherever feasible. Civil authorities in reaching decisions on civil aviation should consult with and take into consideration the interests of the Department of National Defence to ensure that strategic interests are not being overlooked. Similarly, the Department of National Defence should continue to consult with the civil authorities and take into consideration possible civil use in reaching decisions regarding military airports and facilities.

Numerous examples of this co-operation during and since the last war can be found, and the work of the Committee itself which was set up with this in mind is contributing materially.

International Obligations

The federal government as a signatory of the International Convention on Civil Aviation and various bilateral air agreements has assumed certain obligations in the matter of provision of facilities suitable for international aviation and for adoption of common international standards and practices. In reaching its decisions on airport construction and aids to navigation and traffic control, it should continue to make these decisions in conformity with the international obligations assumed by Canada.

APPENDIX 18
Definition of Aerodrome, Airharbour, and Airport

A history of Canadian airports should include a definition of the terms used over the years to refer to the areas reserved for the arrival and departure of airplanes.

The best authority for these terms in Canada is the Air Regulations as amended from time to time. The first Regulations, Air Regulations 1920 (made under the authority of the Air Board Act, and approved by the Governor in Council December 31, 1919) include these definitions:

PART I

2. (i) "Airharbour" means and includes:-
(i) any building or other work, whether floating or fixed, used or purposely adapted for the construction, repair, handling, protection, refuelling or storage of aircraft designed to alight on water when such building or other work is adjacent to water upon which aircraft is constructed, repaired, handled, protected, re-

fuelled or stored in, at, or by such building or work alight or from which they take off, together with the adjacent area of water.
(ii) any area of supporting surface other than water used or purposely adapted for the alighting or taking off of aircraft, together with any buildings or other works connected therewith.
excepting, however, any such building, work or area used as aforesaid:
(i) only owing to stress of weather or other emergency, or
(ii) only for the domestic or household purposes of the owner of the building, work or area, and not used or intended to be used for commercial purposes or for the alighting or taking off of commercial aircraft. New.[1]
(j) "Seaplane station" means an airharbour for flying machines, the supporting surface at which is water. New.
(k) "Aerodrome" means an airharbour for flying machines, the supporting surface of which is not water. New.
(l) Airship harbour means an airharbour for airships or balloons. New.
(m) "Customs airharbour" means an "airharbour appointed by the Air Board with the concurrences of the Ministers of Customs and Immigration as an airharbour at which aircraft from abroad may alight, and from which aircraft bound abroad may take off. See ICAN[2] Art. 15; Annex II, 1."
18. No place, building, or work shall be used as an airharbour unless it has been licensed as herein provided.

The term "airharbour" seems to have been a Canadian innovation according to the explanation contained in the Submission of the Air Board, December 22, 1919, from which this extract is taken:

"Part III Airharbours. Much of this part is new, the International Convention having failed to distinguish between alighting places for airships, seaplanes and aeroplanes respectively. The only word used in the Convention for all of these is the word aerodrome and directions are given with regard to aerodromes which are not capable of being complied with at alighting grounds for either airships or seaplanes."[3]

As a matter of interest, ICAN, while referring to "aerodromes" frequently, did not define the term at all.

The term "airport" was first used in Reports on Civil Aviation in 1927, although licences were still being issued to "airharbours." The amended Air Regulations 1938 include these new definitions (it will be noted that the term "airharbour" has been deleted):

PART I - Section 2

(i) "Aerodrome" means and includes an area of land or water or other supporting surface normally used for the arrival and departure of aircraft
(j) "Airport" means an aerodrome designated by the Minister as such and constituting a centre for aerial traffic and containing installations necessary for such traffic
(k) "Customs Airport" means an airport appointed by the Minister with the concurrence of the Minister of National Revenue and the Minister of Mines and Resources as an airport at which aircraft from abroad may alight and from which aircraft bound abroad may take off.

The table entitled "Summary of Airports, Airfields and Anchorages - March 1946"[4] includes amended definitions as follows:

"Airport" is defined as any aerodrome at which facilities available to the public are provided for shelter, servicing or repair of aircraft, and for receiving or discharging passengers or cargo.

"Airfield" is defined as any aerodrome other than an airport.

In Air Regulations 1951 these definitions appear:

1.2.3 aerodrome means a defined area on land or water (including any buildings, installation and equipment) intended to be used either wholly or in part for the arrival, departure, movement and servicing of aircraft;

1.2.6 airport means an aerodrome designated by the Minister as such and constituting a centre for aerial traffic and containing installations necessary for such traffic;"

In Air Regulations 1960 the definitions were as follows:

aerodrome means any area of land, water (including the frozen surface thereof) or other supporting surface used or designed, prepared, equipped or set apart for use either in whole or in part for the arrival or departure, movement or servicing of aircraft and includes any buildings, installations and equipment in connection therewith; (*aérodrome*) airport means an aerodrome for which, under Part III, an airport licence has been issued by the Minister; (*Aéroport*)

In the Aeronautics Act 1985, aerodrome and airport are defined as follows:

"Aerodrome" means any area of land, water (including the frozen surface thereof) or other supporting surface used, designed, prepared, equipped or set apart for use either in whole or in part for the arrival, departure, movement or servicing of aircraft and includes any buildings, installations and equipment *situated thereon or associated therewith.*

"Airport" means an aerodrome *in respect of which a Canadian aviation document is in force.*

The differences between the definitions of 1960 and 1985 are underlined. They are refinements in legal drafting rather than substantive changes. In fact, except for the more legalistic wording, they do not differ from the definitions of 1938. If anything, the 1938 wording is clearer.

It is interesting to look to the International Civil Aviation Organization (ICAO) to see how they define "airports" and "aerodromes." In the 1983 edition of Annex 14 to the convention on International Civil Aviation, entitled "Aerodromes", this definition appears:

Aerodrome: A defined area on land or water (including any buildings, installations, and equipment) intended to be used either wholly or in part for the arrival, departure and surface movement of aircraft.

ICAO has no definition for airport, and despite many years of debate, the matter has not been resolved. It was considered by the council of the ICAO in March 1976. The Canadian representative on the council, in a letter to the author February 1, 1979, says: "In reality, it seems to be a linguistic problem arising from the use of four languages at ICAO and that 'aerodrome' and 'airport' are regarded as being synonymous and there is not likely to be any change in the near future." A proposal to replace the term "aerodrome" by the term "airport", while favoured by many nations, was not accepted because for many the two terms had different connotations in their national regulations. The term "airport", although not defined, is used extensively in ICAO technical documents.

In so far as Canada is concerned, "aerodrome" is the generic word and "airport" is a specific type of aerodrome. This seems to reflect ICAO's failure to define an airport and ignores the fact that "airport" has world wide acceptance as the name of a place used for the arrival and departure of aircraft. The word "aerodrome" is rarely used and widely regarded as part of early aviation history.

T. M. McGrath
1981 & 1989

Footnotes—Appendix 18

[1]"New" means Canadian wording not found in the International Convention.

[2]International Convention on Air Navigation (ICAN), 1919.

[3]Public Archives Canada, MG30, E243, Vol. 10.

[4]Department of Transport Report, 1945-46.

APPENDIX 19
Authorized Landing Fees, Storage Charges, and Terms of use for St. Hubert Airport (1927)

Published in the Department of National Defence Report on Civil Aviation,1927 (Ottawa: King's Printer, 1927), p. 74.

Use by Public

A number of commercial aircraft operating companies use St. Hubert for passenger, freight and mail services. A school of flying is conducted. The Montréal Light Aeroplane Club have rented space for their operations. It is the terminal for the International Air Service between New York and Montréal. Landing fees, storing charges and terms on which land may be leased to commercial operators, to erect their hangars, is set forth in the following schedule:

	*Light up to 3,000 lbs. weight	*Medium 3,000 to 6,000 lbs. weight	*Heavy over 6,000 lbs. weight
Landing fee, including storage on ground for one day, or part thereof	$ 1.00	$ 2.00	$ 3.00
Storage fees per aircraft per day or fraction thereof including landing privileges:-			
(a) Ground space	1.00	2.00	3.00
(b) Hangar space	2.00	3.00	4.00
Dead Storage, ground space only, limited to 14 days	.50	1.00	2.00
Monthly hangar storage fees per aircraft, including landing privileges	30.00	45.00	60.00
Heated hangar space per aircraft per diem, including landing privileges	3.00	4.00	5.00
Monthly heated hangar storage fees per aircraft, including landing privileges	40.00	60.00	75.00
Passenger toll for each passenger carried for hire except passenger in transit		.10	
Light aeroplanes in use by clubs and club members			
Monthly charges per aircraft in operation		15.00	
Mechanician service per hour		1.50	From 8 hours to 17 hours daily.
Mechanician helper per hour		1.00	

Rental of ground for building purposes. All plans of proposed buildings must be submitted for approval to Department of National Defence. $50 per acre annum.

All aircraft must be registered at the office of the aerodrome superintendent.

All commercialand other aircraft in transit not attached to the aerodrome or operating therefrom must be registered immediately upon arrival and be checked out upon departure.

Landing fees must be paid at the time of registration.

Tolls for passengers must be paid at the close of each day by the operators of passenger-carrying aircraft.

All fees for planes in transit must be paid in cash.

No landing fee or service charges shall be collected for aircraft in the service of the Department of National Defence.

No landing fee or service charges shall be collected fromvisitng aircraft of the United States Army, Navy, Marine and Department of Commerce.

*Weights given are total authorized weight according to Certificate of Airworthiness.

APPENDIX 20
1929 List of Licensed Public Airports, Intermediate and Private Aerodromes, Public Seaplane Ports, Seaplane Anchorages in Canada

Location	Name	Class	Altitude	Latitude	Longitude	Identification	Runway areas	Owner
Amherstburg, ON	Pioneer Airways Airport	Airport, Public	500 ft.	42 07 50	83 04 30	100 ft Circle, Band, 4 ft.	1,800 x 2,600 ft.	Pioneer Airways, Ltd. 425 Ouelette Avenue, Windsor, ON
Belleville, ON	Leavens Brothers Aerodrome	Aerodrome,	286 ft.	44 10 0 N	77 19 0 W	50 ft. Circle, Band, 4 ft. Greek Cross, arms, 20 ft.	Runways	Leavens Bros. Air Service Service, Belleville, On.
Brandon, MB.	Brandon Airport	Airport, Public	1,308 ft.	49 52 0 N	99 56 0 W	100 ft Circle, Band, 4 ft.	Total area circular, diameter 2,000 ft. under development	Brandon Aero. Association Ltd., 909 Rosser Ave., Brandon, MB.
Brantford, ON	Brantford Municipal	Airport, Public	775 ft.	43 10 0 N	80 17 0 W	100 ft. Circle, Band 4 ft.	1,500 x 1,100 ft. Landing 2,200 Strip being developed, November 1929.	City Engineer, City of Brantford, ON
Calgary, AB	Municipal	Airport, Public	3,438 ft	51 4 0 N	114 0 2 W	100 ft. Circle, Bandt, 4ft.	Runways	Corporation of the City of Calgary, Calgary, AB.
Cap de la Madeleine, PQ	Municipal	Airport, Public	120 ft.	46 22 0 N	72 32 0 W	100 ft. Circle, Band, 4 ft.	Runways— N.S. 1,300 FT E.W. 2,600 FT.	Fairchild Aviation Co., Grand Mère, PQ
Cartierville, PQ (See Montéal)								
Como, ON		Seaplane anchorage, Private	1,497 ft.	47 54 0 N	83 34 0 W	Equilateral triangle with sides 15 ft; Band, 2 ft. 6 in. with cross.	Como Lake area 6 x 2 miles	Ontario Provincial Air Service, Parliament Bldgs Toronto, ON.
Chatham, ON	N.A. Thompson's Field.	Aerodrome, Private	550 ft.	42 20 24 N	82 9 0 W	50 ft. Circle; Greek Cross, arms, 20 ft.	Total area 1.390 ft. only.	Norman A. Thompson, 136 William St. N., Chatham, ON
Digby, NS	Connor's Field	Auxiliary Aerodrome	350 ft.	44 35 0 N	65 45 0 W	50 ft. Circle; Band, ft., with Bar, length 20 ft.	E.W only	Rufus R. Connor, Chy-an-Dour Farm, Digby, NS
Edmonton, AB	Blatchford Airport	Airport, Public	2,185 ft.	53 35 0 N	113 30 0 W	100 ft. Circle, Band, 4 ft.	Runways	City of Edmonton, Edmonton, AB
Emma Lake, SK		Seaplane anchorage, Public	1,600 ft.	53 35 0 N	105 54 0 W	Equilateral triangle sides, 15 ft.; Band, 2 ft. 6 ins.	2 miles, 6 miles	Western Canada Airways, Ltd., 804 Trust & Loan Bldg., Winnipeg, MB
English Bay, BC	Western Canada Airways Seaplane, Port	Seaplane Port, Private	Sea level	49 17 0 N	123 07 30	Equilatral triangle, sides, 25 ft.; Band. 4 ft. with cross.	Adjacent water, unlimited	

Location	Name	Class	Altitude	Latitude	Longitude	Identification	Runway areas	Owner
Fernie, BC	Fernie Municipal Airport	Airport, Public	3,313 ft.	49 30 0 N	115 05 0 W	100 ft. Circle; Band, 4 ft. with arms 30 ft. indicating runways.	Runway, N.-S 2,500 ft., remaining under development	City Clerk, City of Fernie, Fernie, BC
Fort Francis, ON		Seaplane anchorage, Private	1,122 ft.	48 37 0 N	93 24 0 W	Equilateral triangle, sides, 15 ft.; Band, 2 ft. 6 in., with cross.	Rainy Lake area	Ontario Provincial Air Service, Toronto, ON
Fort William, ON	Bishops Field Airport	Airport, Public	715 ft.	48 23 0 N	89 21 0 W	100 ft. Circle; Band, 4 ft.	Total area	Fort William Aero Club, Fort William, ON.
Fredericton, NB	Municipal	Seaplane anchorage, Public Customs	18 ft.	45 80 6 N	6 39 0 W	Equilateral triangle, sides, 15 ft., Band 2 ft. 6 in with bar	St. John River	City of Fredericton, Fredericton, NB
Grand Forks, BC	Municipal	Airport, Public	1,750 ft.	49 2 0 N	118 30 0 W	100 ft. Circle, Band, ft.	3 runways, 2,400 ft.	Corporation of the City of Grand Forks, Grand Forks BC
Grand Mère (see Lac à la Tortue)								
Haileybury, ON	Municipal	Seaplane anchorage, Public	588 ft.	47 30 0 N	79 40 0 W	Equilateral triangle, sides, 15 ft.; Band, 2 ft. 6 in., with bar	Lake Temiskaming	Board of Trade, Haileybury, ON.
Hamilton, ON	Municipal	Airport, Public	255 ft.	43 14 0 N	79 47 25	100 ft Circle; Band, 4 ft.	Runways, 1,800 ft. and 2,000 ft.	City of Hamilton, Hamilton, ON
Kingston, ON	Curtiss Reid Seaplane port	Seaplane Port, Public	280 ft.	44 14 6	76 28 0 W	Equilateral triangle sides, 25 ft.; Band, 4 ft.	1 mile 3/4 mile	Curtiss Reid Aircraft Co., P.O. Box 2407, Montréal, PQ
Kingston, ON	Kingston Airport	Airport, Public	350 ft.	44 14 0 N	76 30 0 W	100 ft., Circle; Band, 4 ft.	Runway, N.E-S.W., 1,700 ft remainder under development	Secretary, Kingston Flying Club, Kingston, ON
Kitchener, ON	Kitchener and Waterloo Municipal Airport	Airport, Public	1,086 ft.	43 29 0 N	80 31 0 W	100 ft. circle; Band, 4 ft.	NW-SE 2,400 ft. NE-SW 2,200 ft; Landing area under development.	Kitchener and Waterloo Municipal Airport Committee, City Hall, Kitchener, ON.
Lac à la Tortue, PQ		Seaplane anchorage, Private	439 ft.	46 36 0 N	72 40 0 W	Equilateral triangle, sides, 15 ft.; Band, 2 ft. 6 in., with cross.	Lac à la Tortue	Fairchild Aviation Co. Grand Mère, PQ
Lake Waskesiu, Prince Albert, AB	Prince Albert National Parks Branch Airport	Seaplane Port, Public	1,740 ft.	54 0 0	106 3 0 W	Equilateral triangle, sides, 25 ft.; Band, 4 ft.	Lake Waskesiu Total area, 80 miles N of Prince Albert	Prince Albert National Parks Branch, Prince Albert, AB
Leaside, Ontario (see Toronto)								
Lethbridge, AB	Municipal	*Airport, Public, Customs	2,980 ft.	49 43 0 N	112 50 0 W	100 ft Circle; Band; 4 ft.	Runways	Corporation of City of Lethbridge, Lethbridge, AB

Location	Name	Class	Altitude	Latitude	Longitude	Identification	Runway areas	Owner
London, ON	London Airport	Public Airport	874 ft.	42 55 0 N	81 17 0 W	100 ft. Circle; Band, 4 ft	Total area	London Chamber of Commerce, London, ON
Longueuil, PQ	Fairchild Aircraft Ltd. Seaplane Port	Seaplane Port, Public	25 ft.	45 33 39 N	73 29 44 W	Equilateral triangle, sides, 25 ft.; Band 4 ft.	Area, 1 mile square	Fairchild Aircraft, Ltd., 505 Confederation Bldg., Montréal, PQ
Longueuil, PQ	Fairchild Aircraft Ltd., Airport	Airport, Private	50 ft.	45 33 29 N	73 29 25 W	Circle, diameter outside 100 ft.; Band, 4 ft. Greek cross, arms, 40 ft	Runways, 4, 200 x 1,850 ft.	Fairchild Aircraft Ltd., 505 Confederation Bldg., Montréal, PQ
Matapedia Lake, PQ		Seaplane anchorage, Private	500 ft.	48 27 0 N	67 33 0 W	Equilateral triangle, sides, 15 ft., Band 2 ft. 6 in, with cross	Lake area 3 ft. 10 ft.	Compagnie Aérienne Franco Canadienne, 266 St. James St, Montréal, PQ
Medicine Hat, AB	Municipal	Airport, Public	2,200 ft.	50 2 0 N	110 40 0 W	100 ft. Circle; Band, 4 ft.	Total area, sod 2,400 x 2,400 ft.	Corporation of the City of Medicine Hat, Medicine Hat, AB
Minaki, ON		Seaplane anchorage, Private	1,066 ft	49 59 0 N	4 40 0 W	Equilateral triangle, sides, 15 ft.; Band, 2 ft. 6 in., with cross	Lake region of Winnipeg River, area 6 x 1 1/2 miles	Ontario Provincial Air Service, Parliament Bldg. Toronto, ON
Moncton, NB	Moncton, Airport Ltd. Airport	Airport, Public	25 ft.	46 5 0 N	64 45 0 W	100 ft. Circle; Band, 4 ft.	Runways— 2,000 ft. E-W 1,700 ft. SE- NW 1,600 ft. NE-SW.	Moncton Airport, Ltd., Moncton, NB
Montréal, PQ	Vickers' Airport	Seaplane port, Private	25 ft.	45 34 0 N	73 32 0 W	Equilateral triangle, sides, 25 ft., Band 4 ft. with cross.	St. Lawrence River.	Canadian Vickers Ltd., P.O. Box 550, Montréal, PQ
Montréal, PQ (Pointe aux trembles)		Seaplane anchorage, Private	25 ft.	45 39 0 N	73 29 0 W	Equilateral triangle, sides, 15 ft.; Band, 2 ft. 6 in., with cross	St. Lawrence River area 1/2 x 3 miles	Compagnie Aérienne Franco Canadienne, 266 St. James St., Montréal, PQ
Montréal, PQ	Curtiss Reid Seaplane port	Seaplane Port, Public	61 ft.	45 31 0 N	73 45 30	Equilatral triangle 25 ft.; Band, 4 ft.	Sheltered water, 2 x 1/2 miles	Curtiss Reid Aircraft Company, P.O.Box 2407, Montréal, PQ
Montréal, PQ	La Salle Airport	Airport, Public	50 ft.	45 25 0	73 36 0 W	100 ft. Circle;	Total area, 1,800 ft.	Dominion Aircraft Co., Ltd., 305 Castle Bldg. Stanley at St.Catherine Sts., Montréal, PQ
Montréal, PQ(St. Hubert)	St. Hubert Airport	*Airport, Public Customs	87 ft.	45 31 0 N	73 25 0 W	100 ft. Circle; Band, 4 ft.	Runways	Department of National Defence, Controller of Civil Aviation Branch, Ottawa, ON

Location	Name	Class	Altitude	Latitude	Longitude	Identification	Runway areas	Owner
Montréal, PQ (Curtierville)	Reid Airport	Airport, Public	100 ft.	45 32 0 N	73 42 0 W	100 ft. Circle; Band, 4 ft.	Total area	Curtiss Reid Aircraft Co. P.O. Box 2407, Montréal, PQ
Moose Jaw, SK	Municipal	*Airport, Public Customs	1,800 ft.	50 02 0 N	105 35 0 W	100 ft. Circle; Band, 4 ft.	Total area, 2,400 ft. square	Corporation of the City of Moose Jaw, SK
Oba Lake, ON		Seaplane anchorage, Private	1,200 ft.	48 40 0 N	84 13 0 W	Equilateral triangle sides, 15 ft.; Band 2 ft. 6 in. with cross	Oba Lake area 12 - 2 miles	Ontario Provincial Air Service, Toronto, ON
Orient Bay, ON		Seaplane anchorage, Private	852 ft.	49 27 0 N	88 9 0 W	Equitateral triangle sides 15 ft.; Band, 2 ft. 6 in. with cross	Lake Nipigon area	Ontario Provincial Air Service, Toronto, ON
Ottawa, ON	Uplands Airport	Airport, Public	272 ft.	45 20 0 N	75 41 0 W	100 ft. Circle; Band, 4 ft.	Total area	Ottawa Flying Club, P.O. Box 747, Ottawa, ON
Port Arthur, ON		Seaplane anchorage, Public	602 ft.	48 26 0 N	89 14 0 W	Equilateral triangle, sides, 15 ft.; Band, 2 ft. 6 in., with bar.	Port Arthur Harbour	Port Arthur, ON of Port Arthur, Port Arthur, ON
Québec, PQ	Canadian Trans-continental Airways Airport	Airport, Public	300 ft.	46 46 0 N	71 17 0 W	100 ft. Circle; Band, 4 ft.	Total area	Canadian Transcontinental Airways, 111 Côte de la Montagne, Québec, PQ
Québec, PQ (Sillery)	Compagnie Aerienne Franco Canadienne	Seaplane Port, Private	Tide-water	45 46 0 N	71 16 0 W	Equilatral triangle sides, 25 ft., with cross	St. Lawrence River area	Compagnie Aerienne Franco Canadienne, Edifice "Le Soleil", rue de la Couronne, Québec, PQ
Regina, SK	Municipal	*Airport, Public Customs	1,896 ft.	50 28 0 N	104 40 0 W	100 ft. Circle; Band, 4 ft.	Total area	Corporation of the City of Regina, Regina, SK
Regina, SK	University Air Industries Airport	Aerodrome, Private	1,936	50 25 0	104 38 0	Circle, diameter outside 50 ft; Band, 4 ft.; Greek cross, Arms, 20 ft. Band, 4 ft.	Runways— E & W 2,640 ft. N & S 2,600 ft.	Universal Air Industries, Suite 4, Black Block, Regina, SK
Rimouski, PQ	Rimouski Airport	Public Airport	78 ft.	48 28 0 N	68 30 0 W	100 ft. Circle; Band, 4 ft.	Total area	Department of National Defence, C.C.A. Branch, Ottawa, ON
Remi Lake, ON		Seaplane anchorage, Private	794 ft.	49 27 0 N	82 9 0 W	Equilateral triangle, sides, 15 ft., Band, 2 ft. 6 in., with cross	Area of Remi Lake, 3 x 4 miles	Ontario Provincial Air Service, Toronto, ON
Roberval, PQ		Seaplane anchorage, Private	350 ft.	48 32 0 N	72 13 0 W	Equilateral triangle, sides, 15 ft.; Band, 2 ft. 6 in., with cross	Lake St. John area, 20 x 30 miles Montréal, PQ	Canadian Airways, Ltd. 180 St. James St.,

Location	Name	Class	Altitude	Latitude	Longitude	Identification	Runway areas	Owner
Saskatoon, SK	Municipal	Airport, Public	1,600 ft.	52 11 0 N	167 41 0 W	100 ft. Circle, Band, 4 ft.	Runways— E-W, 1,760 ft. N-S 2,640 ft.	Corporation of the City of Saskatoon, Saskatoon, SK
Saint Félicien, PQ	Curtiss Reid Seaplane port	Seaplane Port, Public	302 ft.	48 40 0 N	72 27 0 W	Equilateral triangle, sides, 25 ft.; Band 4 ft.		Curtiss Reid Aircraft Co., P.O. Box 2407, Montréal, PQ
St. Catharines, ON	St. Catharines Airport	Airport, Public	400 ft.	43 9 0 N	79 11 0 W	100 ft. Circle; Band, 4 ft.	Serviceable landing area defined by markers.	Haney Repair Service, 50 Niagara St. St. Catharines, ON
Saint John, NB	Milledgeville Airport	Seaplane Port, Public	50 ft.	4 17 0 N	66 50 W	Equilateral triangle; sides, 35 ft.; Band	1/2 mile and unlimited adjacent water.	Atlantic Airways Limited, P.O. Box 953, Saint John, NB
Sault St. Marie, ON		Seaplane anchorage, Private	938 ft.	46 31 0 N	84 20 0 W	Equilateral triangle, sides, 15 ft.; Band, 2 ft. 6 in, with cross	St. Mary River, 4 x 1 mile	Ontario Provincial Air Service, Toronto, ON
Sioux Lookout, ON		Seaplane anchorage, Private	1,171 ft.	50 5 0 N	91 75 0 W	Equilateral triangle, sides, 15 ft.; Band 2 ft. 6 in., with cross	Pelican Lake area, 4 x 1 1/2 miles	Ontario Provincial Air Service, Toronto, ON
Sioux Lookout, ON		Seaplane Port, Private	1,171 ft.	50 6 0 N	91 75 0 W	Equilateral triangle, sides, 25 ft.; Band, 4 ft., with cross		Western Canada Airways, Winnipeg, MB
Sioux Lookout, ON	Northern Aerial Minerals Exploration, Ltd.	Seaplane Port, Public	1,171 ft.	50 5 0 N	91 55 0 W	Equilateral triangle, sides, 25 ft., Band, Band, 4 ft.	Abram Lake, area 6 x 2 miles	North Aerial Minerals Exploration, Ltd., 100 Adelaide St. W. Toronto, ON
Stratford, ON	Stratford Municipal Airport	Airport, Public	1,191 ft.	43 21 0 N	81 1 0 W	100 ft. Circle; Band, 4 ft.	Total area, some surface improvements, drainage, etc., under development.	Industrial Committee, City of Stratford, Stratford, ON
Sudbury, ON		Seaplane anchorage, Private	820 ft.	46 28 0 N	80 59 0 W	Equilateral triangle, sides, 15 ft.; Band 2 ft. 6 in., with cross	Ramsay Lake area, 3 1/2 x 2 miles	Ontario Provincial Air Service, Toronto, ON
Swanson Bay, BC	Western Canada Airways Seaplane Port	Seaplane Port, Public	Sea-level	53 3 0	128 28 0 W	Equilateral triangle, sides, 25 ft.; Band, 4 ft.	Deep inland water. No beach, ample water.	Western Canada Airways Ltd., Winnipeg, MB
Sydney, NS	Cape Breton Flying Club Ltd.	Airport, Public	30 ft.	46 10 30	60 3 0 W	100 ft. Circle; Band, 4 ft.	Runways— N.-E 1,900 ft. N.-W 1,800 ft.	Cape Breton Flying Club, Sydney, NS

Location	Name	Class	Altitude	Latitude	Longitude	Identification	Runway areas	Owner
Témiscouata, PQ		Seaplane, anchorage, Private	482 ft.	47 27 0 N	68 37 0 W	Equilateral triangle, sides, 15 ft.; Band, 2 ft. 6 in., with cross.	Area of Temiscouata, Lake, 3 x 25 miles	Compagnie Aerienne Franco Canadienne, 266 St. James St., Montréal, PQ
Timagami, ON		Seaplane anchorage, Private	989 ft.	47 5 0 N	79 48 0 W	Equilateral triangle, sides, 15 ft., Band, 2 ft. 6 in., with cross.	Area of Lake Timagami,	Ontario Provincial Air Service, Toronto, ON
Three Rivers, PQ		Seaplane anchorage, Public	Tide-water	46 19 0 N	72 33 0 W	Equilateral triangle, sides, 15 ft.; Band, 2 ft. 6 in, with bar	Area St. Lawrence River, 2 x 25 miles	Canadian Airways, Keefer Building, Montreal, PQ
Toronto, ON	De Lessepps Airport	Airport, Public	400 ft.	43 42 0 N	79 30 0 W	100 ft. Circle; Band, 4 ft.	Total area	Toronto Airport, Ltd., Weston, ON
Toronto, ON	Leaside Airport	Airport, Public	426 ft.	43 42 0 N	79 21 0 W	100 ft. Circle; Band, 4 ft.	Runways— E-W, 2,640 ft. N-S 1,800 ft.	Toronto Flying Club, 21 Richmond St. W., Toronto, ON
Toronto, ON	Toronto Harbour	Seaplane Port, Public	245 ft.	43 38 45	79 22 0	Equilateral triangle, sides, 25 ft.; Band 4 ft.	10,000 x 5,500 ft., Inner Harbour Slipway foot of Scott St.	Harbour Commission, Fleet Street, Toronto, ON
Toronto, ON	DeHaviland Aerodrome	Aerodrome, Private	650 ft.	43 45 0 N	79 29 0 W	50 ft. Circle; Band, 4 ft. with cross	Total area, 2,275 ft. E-W 1,330 ft. N-S	DeHaviland Aircraft of Canada, Ltd. 372 Bay St., Toronto, ON
Trail, BC	Trail Municipal Airport	Airport, Public	1,360 ft.	49 4 0 N	117 37 0 W	100 ft. Circle; Band, 4 ft.	Landing strip, 2,000 x 300 ft., now useable, suitable for light aircraft, remainder under development.	City Engineer Corporation, City of Trail, Trail, BC
Vancouver, BC	Municipal	Airport, Public		49 18 0 N	123 7 0 W	100 ft. Circle; Band, 4 ft.	Runways— E-W 2,671 ft. N-S 1,260 ft.	Corporation of the City of Vancouver, Vancouver, BC
Vegreville, AB	Watt's Airport	Airport, Public	2,200 ft.	53 31 0 N	112 3 0 W	100 ft. Circle; Band, 4 ft.	Total area, 800 yds.; good sod.	M.C. Watts, Vegreville, AB
Walkerville, ON	Walker Airport	*Public, Customs, Airport	580 ft.	42 15 0 N	83 0 0 W	100 ft. Circle; Band, 4 ft.	Total area	Aviation League of the Border Cities, Windsor, ON
Winnipeg, MB	Stevenson Airport	Airport, Public	775 ft.	49 48 0 N	97 14 0 W	100 ft. Circle; Band, 4 ft.	Runways— N-S 3,400 ft. E-W 3,200 ft.	Winnipeg Flying Club, P.O.Box 2265,
Winnipeg, MB	Western Canada Airways Airport.	Airport, Public	765 ft.	49 53 0 N	97 7 0 W	100 ft. Circle; Band, 4 ft	Total area	Western Canada Airways, Ltd., Winnipeg, MB

Location	Name	Class	Altitude	Latitude	Longitude	Identification	Runway areas	Owner
Winnipeg, MB		Aerodrome, Private	764 ft.	49 49 0 N	97 9 0 W	50 ft. Circle; Band, 4 ft. with cross	Total area 2,200 ft. N-S 1,600 ft. E-W	J.R. Morgan, Morgan Nicholson, Ltd., Union Trust Bldg., Winnipeg, MB
Winnipeg, MB		Seaplane Port, Public	760 ft.	49 49 0 N	97 9 0 W	Equilateral triangle, sides, 25 ft., Band, Band	Red River	J.R. Morgan, Morgan Nicholson Ltd., Union Trust Bldg., Winnipeg, MB
Woodstock, ON	William's Airport	Aerodrome, Private	1,125 ft.	43 4 30	80 46 0 W	50 ft. Circle, Greek cross, arms 20 ft.	Total area 400 x 500 yds.	T.F. Williams, R.R. No. 1 Woodstock, ON
Victoria, BC		Airport, Private	150 ft.	48 24 0 N	123 19 0 W	100 ft. Circle Band, 4 ft.	Total area 2,400 x 1,350 ft.	British Columbia Airways Ltd., 900 Fort St., Victoria, BC
Virden, MB	Virden Airport	Airport, Public	1,451 ft.	49 50 0 N	100 57 0 W	100 ft. Circle; Band, 4 ft.	Total area	Virden Board of Trade, Virden, MB.

*Licensed for Custons

NOTE:

(a)   A number of airports licensed above are under a state of development. Recommendations have been made to operators to identify the safe effective landing area or serviceable runways by means of cones, chrome yellow and black.

(b)   In the spring and fall, owing to frost elimination and heavy rains, pilots not acquainted with the conditions are recommended to communicate with the operators of airports before proceeding.

This Table has been reproduced from Department of National Defence Reports on Civil Aviation, 1929. pp 88-92.

APPENDIX 21
Aircraft and Crews that used Harbour Grace Airfield, Newfoundland,
for Transatlantic Flights - 1927 to 1936

Aircraft	Crew	Details
Stinson SMT, Detroiter "The Pride of Detroit"	William Brock, Pilot; Edward Schlee	Arrived August 26, 1927, from Old Orchard, Maine, Departed August 27. Arrived London (Croydon) 23 hours, 19 minutes later.
Stinson SMT, Detroiter "Sir John Carling"	T.B. Tulley J.V. Medcalf	Arrived September 6, 1927, from Old Orchard, Maine. Departed September 7; Lost at sea. The pilots were Canadian and the flight was sponsored by Carling Brewing Company of London, Ontario.
De Havilland DH 60 Moth	Lt. Cmdr. H.C. MacDonald	Aircraft arrived at St. John's by ship; assembled there and flown to Harbour Grace. Departed October 17, 1928 for London. He was lost at sea having been last seen 700 miles east of Newfoundland.
Barling NB-3 "Golden Hind"	Urban F. Diteman	Arrived in St. John's (Lester Field—from which Alcock and Brown took off on their successful Atlantic flight June 14, 1919) from Fredericton, New Brunswick on October 9, 1929. The aircraft was christened "Golden Hind" in St. John's and flown to Harbour Grace on October 19. He departed for London on October 22 and was lost at sea.
Fokker F. VII/3M "Southern Cross"	Charles Kingsford Smith, Captain Everett Van Dyke, Co-pilot J.P. Saul, Navigator J.W. Stannage, R/O	Arrived 8:25 a.m. June 25, 1930 from Port Marnock (near Dublin) Ireland, bound for New York non-stop; landed at Harbour Grace to refuel after a flight of 30 hours 28 minutes. They left for New York on June 26.
Bellanca WB-2 "Columbia" "The Maple Leaf"	J. Errol Boyd, Pilot Harry P. Connor, Navigator	Arrived from Charlottetown, P.E.I. September 23, 1930. After a long delay due to weather over the Atlantic, they departed Harbour Grace on October 9. Twenty-four hours later they landed at Tresco in the Scilly Islands, off Cornwall. Boyd was the first Canadian to fly the Atlantic. "Columbia" was the first aircraft to cross the Atlantic twice. Its first crossing was on June 4, 1927, when Clarence Chamberlain, Pilot, and Charles Levine, passenger, flew non-stop from New York to Berlin in 42 hours. Boyd added the name "The Maple Leaf" to the aircraft, which still carried the name "Columbia" on the rudder.
Bellanca CH 300 Pacemaker "Liberty"	Halger Hoiris, Pilot Otto Hillig	Arrived from Saint John, N.B., June 22, 1931. They departed on June 24 and 32 hours later landed at Cressel, Germany. They reached their final destination, Copenhagen, on June 26.
Lockheed Vega "Winnie Mae"	Wiley Post, Pilot Harold Gatty, Navigator	Arrived from New York June 23, 1931. They departed four hours later and landed near Chester, England, on June 24, 17 hours, 17 minutes later. They completed their around the world flight in New York on July 1st in the elapsed time of 8 days 15 hours 51 minutes.
Lockheed Sirius "Justice for Hungary"	Alexander Magyar George Endresz	Arrived from New York July 13, 1931 and departed on July 15. They landed the next day at Bieski, Hungary, 12 miles short of their destination, Budapest, because of a shortage of fuel. They flight time was 26 hours 12 minutes.

Aircraft	Crew	Details
Lockheed Altair "Miss Liberty"	Louis T. Reichers	Arrived from Newark, N.J., May 13, 1932. He departed the same day for Dublin, Ireland, ran out of fuel and landed in the sea near the Irish Coast. He was picked up by the "SS President Roosevelt".
Lockheed Vega	Amelia Earhart	Arrived from Saint John, N.B., May 20, 1932, and departed that same evening. 14 hours 54 minutes later she landed at Culmore, Northern Ireland. She was the first woman to fly the Atlantic solo. She was also the first woman to cross the Atlantic by air, when, on June 17, 1928 (with Wilmer Stutz, Pilot, and Louis Gordon, Mechanic) she flew from Trepassey Bay, Newfoundland to Burry Point, Wales, in the Tri Motor Fokker F. VII Seaplane, "Friendship", in 20 hours 40 minutes.
Lockheed Vega "Century of Progress"	Jimmy Mattern Bennett Griffin	Arrived from New York on July 5, 1932 on an around the world flight. They departed that evening for Berlin which they reached non-stop, 18 hours minutes later. They were forced down in Siberia and abandoned the flight.
Stinson SM-1, Detroiter "Green Mountain Boy"	Clyde Lee John Bochkon	Arrived from Bayer, Vermont, on August 24, 1932, after a forced landing the previous evening at Burgeo, Newfoundland. On August 25 they departed for Oslo and were lost at sea.
Bellanca CH 300 Pacemaker "City of Warsaw"	Halger Hoiris Benjamin Adamowitz Joseph Adamowitz	Arrived from New York on June 28, 1934. Hoiris, who had flown the Atlantic from Harbour Grace June 24, 1931, left the "City of Warsaw" at Harbour Grace. On June 29, the aircraft, with Benjamin Adamowitz at the controls, took off and landed at St. Andre in North France the next day. They eventually reached Warsaw, Poland.
Vultee V-1A "Lady Peace"	Henry T (Dick) Merrill, Pilot. Henry Richman	Arrived at Harbour Grace September 18, 1936, after a forced landing at Musgrave harbour, Newfoundland, due to fuel shortage. The aircraft had left England September 14, 1936 bound for New York. They left Harbour Grace on September 24 for New York.
Bellanca 28-70 Flash "Miss Dorothy"	J.A. Mollison	Arrived from New York on October 28, 1936. He departed for London on October 29 and landed at Croydon Airport, making a record crossing of 9 hours 15 mintues coast to coast. Mollison was the last of pioneering Trans-Atlantic flights to take off from Harbour Grace Airport. The aircraft was originally called, "The Irish Swoop" and had been entered in the England to Australia air race in 1934.

Sources

1. W.E. Parsons, Curator, Harbour Grace Museum.
2. F.H. Ellis, *Canada's Flying Heritage* (Toronto: University of Toronto Press, 1961), p. 265 and following.
3. Bill Parsons with Bill Bowman, *The Challenge of the Atlantic*, Robinson Blackmore Book Publishers, Nfld., 1983.
4. G.A. Fuller, J.A. Griffin, K.M. Molson, *125 Years of Canadian Aeroautics*, The Canadian Aviation Historical Society, 1983.
5. Charles Dixon, *Conquest of the Atlantic by Air*, Sampson Low & Co., London, 1931.
6. F.H. Ellis and E. Ellis, *Atlantic Air Conquest*, The Ryerson Press, Toronto, 1963.
7. T.M. McGrath, Scrapbook.

APPENDIX 22
Memorandum on the Trans-Canada Airway
(Public Archives Canada, MG 30 E243, Vol. 9)

Ottawa, Ont.,
June 17th, 1937

1. Purpose

(a) To provide modern, fast transport between the main centres of commerce and industry in Canada and through it to facilitate closer political and social relations throughout the Dominion.

(b) To safeguard Canada's favourable position on the world's airway system. The most direct airways between North America and Europe and Asia are through Canadian territory. It is essential that this traffic should be directed into Canadian channels and without the trans-Canada airway to facilitate distribution from Canadian bases of this important world traffic, the system would not be efficient.

II. History

The first trans-Canada trial flight was made September 20th, 1920, organized by the Air Board - Halifax-Winnipeg by flying boat, Winnipeg-Vancouver by landplane.

During the first years of post-war development, the energy and funds available were diverted to developing flying in the northern parts of the country, where there was a lack of transportation. Inter-city services were at that time impractical, owing to the lack of funds and the lack of proper equipment.

1926: At the Imperial Conference the Canadian Government agreed to participate in the airship scheme. (This decision was made without consulting the Air Service, whose unanimous opinion was that the development of domestic communications within Canada should have preference and that any funds available should be diverted to this object with a view to creating a trans-Canada system.)

1927-28: The expansion of the airway system in the United States and the threatened invasion of the principal centres of industry and commerce in Canada to make their traffic tributary to American transcontinental lines led the Government to decide that construction of the trans-Canada airway, as conditions and funds permitted, was advisable. Surveys were started in the Prairie Provinces.

1929: Construction continued in the Prairie Provinces, with the installation of lighted intermediate fields at approximately 30 mile intervals from Winnipeg - Calgary - Edmonton.

1930: Night service from Winnipeg to Edmonton inaugurated March 2nd, with stops at Regina, Moose Jaw, Medicine Hat and Calgary.

1931: Five radio beam stations were installed at Forrest, Regina, Maple Creek, Lethbridge and Red Deer.

The original route was changed to include Lethbridge as the survey of the route through the Rocky Mountains indicated that the southern pass would be the most efficient. The airway from Medicine Hat to Lethbridge and thence to Calgary was constructed. A feeder line to Saskatoon and North Battleford was also constructed and lighted between Moose Jaw and Saskatoon.

1932: On March 31st operation of the airway was temporarily suspended owing to the necessity for economy. Permission was given, however, to continue airway surveys through the mountains and in northern Ontario.

1933: The necessity for finding work for single, homeless men led the Government to establish labour projects and the clearing of certain aerodromes on the trans-Canada airway, of which the land purchase cost was little and the labour cost was high, was approved, and camps were organized in northern Ontario and British Columbia for this purpose.

1935: Construction of the trans-Canada airway had been continued since the fall of 1933 by relief labour. This was quite satisfactory insofar as clearing and stumping operations in forest areas were concerned but proved slow and inefficient where grading operations were necessary.

Permission was given for the purchase of a limited amount of equipment to increase the efficiency of the operations and enable faster progress to be made.

1936: On June 30th the relief labour camps were closed and the Civil Aviation Branch assumed responsibility for construction, retaining the best engineers foremen and administrative staff from the labour projects. Construction was continued on a basis of mechanical equipment, utilizing that available to advantage and hiring the minimum amount of labour necessary to operate it efficiently.

1937: Construction has been continued on this basis and by supplementing the Department's forces with contract work so as to complete the preliminary development of all intermediate aerodromes by August 1st, 1937.

Work is proceeding on the installation of additional radio range beacons in the mountains and the modernizing of those stations on the prairie system installed in 1931 and 1932. When this work is complete it will be continued in northern Ontario.

The prairie system laid in 1928 and 1929 is being revised. The spacing between the aerodrome is being increased to 60 miles; the lighting equipment will be revised and reinstalled to bring it up to present day standards.

New lighting equipment is being purchased for installation on certain aerodromes on which construction is well advanced in northern Ontario.

III. Airport Construction

Assistance is being given to municipalities on the trans-Canada airway to enable them to improve and extend their aerodromes. Agreements with Vancouver, Lethbridge, Regina, Winnipeg, Toronto and Hamilton have been reached, and others negotiated with Calgary, Edmonton, and other cities. Under these agreements the Government grants one-third of past expenditures made by the municipalities, excluding buildings, and the same proportion for any new investment made by the municipalities on their airports, exclusive of buildings.

Number of Municipal airports on the route.......17

Cities are asked to provide a minimum, for present use, of three graded runways, each 3000' long by 300' wide, two of which shall be hard surfaced, capable of extension to 5000' long by 500' wide, with provision for zoning and lighting.

IV. Intermediate Aerodromes

Minimum requirements - 3000' x 300'; where possible three runways of these dimensions, though in some cases, two have been found sufficient for preliminary development and, in the mountain valleys, one strip 3000' by 500' is sufficient. The average spacing of aerodromes is approximately 40 miles, from coast to coast, wider in level, open country and closer in the mountains and northern Ontario.

Number of intermediate aerodromes now under construction or completed...................70

V. Radio

Number of Radio Range Beacons.....................21

Number of two-way communication stations.......6

(Further communication stations may be installed by the operating company.)

VI. Lighting

All city aerodromes will be lighted in accordance with standard North American practice, with:-

(a) Airport rotating beacon;

(b) Boundary lighting system, with approach and obstruction lights, as necessary;

(c) Flood light.

Intermediate aerodromes will be on the same basis, except that no flood lighting is necessary.

VII. Meteorology

A complete meteorological service is being organized. Forecasting stations will be established at Vancouver, Lethbridge, Regina, Winnipeg, Kapuskasing, Toronto, Montréal and Moncton. Weather observations will be made at all points on the airway and at many stations off the line to give the necessary weather information. This will be communicated by teletype to all principal observing and forecasting stations. Weather reports will be conveyed to pilots in flight by two-way radio communication.

VIII. Operation Schedule

It is proposed that the official mail service shall be flown during the hours of darkness, except that portion of the route crossing the Rocky Mountains, which will not be flown at night until further experience is gained. This calls for mails to leave Toronto and Montréal after the close of the business day, approximately eight o'clock, for delivery by noon next day in Vancouver. On the eastbound trip, mails will leave Vancouver at two p.m. and arrive in Toronto and Montréal early forenoon next day.

This calls for a cruising speed under all conditions of approximately 165 miles an hour.

IX. Operations

The trans-Canada airway will be operated by a corporation specially created by an Act of Parliament, the Trans-Canada Air Lines Corporation. This is now being organized.

Orders have been placed for three Lockheed "Electra" 10A's for delivery this fall and four Lockheed "Electra" 14A's for delivery in the spring of 1938. (Two aircraft of a similar type may be taken over from Canadian Airways to augment this fleet and to operate the Seattle - Vancouver service.)

Trial flights may be expected to commence within the next three months, depending on progress in the organization of the operating company.

X. Cost

The cost of the airway to date is as follows:-

1928-30	$ 650,000.	
Construction under		
Unemployment Relief	$3,672,376.	
1936-37	- 734,240.	
		$5,056,616.
Voted 1937-38	- 1,676,355.	
Anticipated further		
requirements 1938-39	-	
	1,500,000.	
		3,176,355.
		$8,232,971.

APPENDIX 23

Letter from the Controller of Civil Aviation regarding the Unemployment Relief Scheme and the Trans-Canada Airway
(Public Archives Canada, MG30 E243, Vol. 2)
409-1-2
June 8th, 1933

L.J. Burpee, Esq.,
International Joint Commission,
Victoria Building,
Ottawa, Ont.
My dear Burpee:

With reference to your questions re the unemployment relief scheme, based on your conversation with the Chief of the General Staff on Monday, I have much pleasure in sending the following information:-

The original scheme, authorized by Order-in-Council P.C. 2248, dated October 8th, 1932, authorized the organization of work camps for single, homeless men. The specific works mentioned were the construction of intermediate aerodromes, as necessary, on the trans-Canada airway and repairs to the citadels at Halifax and Québec. The Department agreed to house, feed, clothe, transport, give medical attention and undertake the organization of the work generally. The men are recruited through the Government Employment Service throughout the country.

The original scheme has been greatly extended and now includes work on air stations and military property, such as barrack sites, rifle ranges and training grounds. Large camps have been formed at Ottawa, Trenton, Camp Borden and Lac du Bonnet Air Stations, and at the military training grounds, barrack sites and rifle ranges at Val Cartier, Long Branch (Toronto) Dundurn, Saskatchewan, Petawawa, and Cranbrook, B.C. Work is rapidly proceeding on clearing, drainage, road making, simple building construction, reforestation, and other similar work where large numbers of men may be employed without great expenditures on material.

The object of the Department is to keep the overhead cost as low as possible and no project which does not involve a large proportion of manual labour is considered. The projects are organized in groups under a Superintendent, who is paid an allowance of $100.00 a month. The camp is under a foreman, who is paid $80.00 a month and the work is organized under him, as necessary, by gang bosses. Men for these three categories are chosen in cooperation with the Unemployment Committee of the Engineering Institute of Canada, so that their unemployed members may have the first opportunity of obtaining work and, at the same time, the Department can obtain men really qualified to supervise their operations.

The work is paid for out of the general appropriation for unemployment relief. There is no particular amount fixed for this appropriation. Each project or group of projects is authorized separately and a stated appropriation is made for it, depending on the number of men to be employed, the cost of housing and maintaining the men, materials and tools required, etc. The maximum cost authorized per man per day is $1.00.

You have the latest map which shows the projects now in hand and the numbers of men employed. This shows the total number as roughly 8000, of whom about 10% are employed on the trans-Canada airway.

During the winter months it was only possible to consider projects which involved the clearing of bush. This limited the number of sites on which action could be taken to advantage but, since spring has come, allowing grading and other like operations, the number of aerodrome projects has rapidly increased and still continues to do so. By another month or six weeks it is hoped that every aerodrome requiring work of this nature will be in hand.

You enquire as to why there are few sites in Alberta and Saskatchewan. The Prairie section of the trans-Canada airway was completed in 1929 and 1930, so that there was no aerodrome work required. Other projects are now being organized, however, as fast as possible in these Provinces and an arrangement has recently been arrived at with the Government of British Columbia whereby the Dominion Government takes over the operation of all similar camps in the Province. These works include a large amount of highway construction.

Men are put to work, as far as possible, in the locality in which they normally live, though in northern Ontario and other remote districts a certain proportion of the men are taken from the cities. The unemployed men come from all walks of life, through the majority of them are manual labourers. Tradesmen of all kinds are found in the ranks - carpenters, shoemakers, barbers, tailors, etc. So far as possible each man is given work in accordance with his previous experience.

The cost of feeding the men varies, of course, with the districts. In camps near cities this is lower than in districts where the transportation charges are higher.

The whole cost of the project is charged against one vote but this Department has met its own headquarters administration cost and, in addition, the cost of surveys, engineering, accounting, and it has supplied hand tools, clothing and other materials in so far as the surplus stocks of the Department permit. Our contribution has, therefore, been a very material one. The whole object has been to reduce the overhead to the very smallest possible limits and to confine the expenditure on relief works as far as possible to actual payments for shelter, food and allowances to those employed.

Transportation for the men is supplied by a military warrant.

Feeding of the men is based on the army rations. I enclose sample menus so that you may see exactly the kind of food supplied.

You ask how the cost of this scheme compares with men under the Dole. Unfortunately, the relief funds of the municipalities made little, if any, provision for single, homeless men. Their relief schemes are mostly for men with families and house holders in their municipalities. The cost of relief varies so greatly that it is very difficult to answer this question. What is certain is that no regular provision was made for this class of men before this Department and the Labour Department undertook the organization of this work and that work of direct value to national development only is being undertaken. The Government is receiving a very considerable return for any expenditures made while, at the same time, giving every able bodied man a chance to earn his own livelihood.

There have been sporadic instances of trouble in the camps, as was to be expected, but considering the magnitude of the operations there has been surprisingly little. There is no compulsion, however, about the scheme. Men join up of their own free will and are permitted to leave if they are not satisfied with the conditions. The trouble makers are promptly ejected. The Frontier College is encouraged to conduct its work in all camps and classes of instruction are continually being organized on a wider basis.

Every effort is made to cater to the recreational needs of the employees. As you are probably aware, there have been assaults-at-arms at Rockcliffe throughout the winter. Soft ball, soccer, ice hockey, log sawing competitions, quoits, and many other games are organized. Reading matter and games are provided and the men are encouraged to organize their own amusements. A fund has been raised privately for comforts and many generous donations have been received. Recently the National Council of Women and the I.O.D.E. have undertaken to raise $15,000 and organize a comforts fund.

I trust the above will give you a good idea of the scope and nature of the work, its organization and progress. If there are any more questions you wish answered, please do not hesitate to let me know.

Yours truly,
J.A. Wilson,
Controller of Civil Aviation.

APPENDIX 24

Memorandum regarding Air Traffic Control to the Chief of Air Services fromthe Controller of Civil Aviation
(Public Archives Canada, MG30 E243, Vol. 9)

Ottawa, Ont., Sept. 29th, 1938

Subject: Air Traffic Control   5206-16
Chief of Air Services

1. The problem of air traffic control is acute in the immediate vicinity of the airports at:-
   Vancouver
   Edmonton
   Winnipeg
   Montréal
   It may also become acute in the near future at Toronto, Malton.

2. The experience of the last six months shows that some form of traffic regulation and control is necessary at major airports. Hardly a week passes but some incident is reported showing the necessity, in the interests of safety, of a proper control system.

3. The matter has been carefully studied and recommendations as to the additional equipment and form of organization necessary will be found in a memorandum dated July 20th, folio 197, file 5206-16.

4. A new licence has been instituted authorizing the holder to act in the capacity of Airport Traffic Control Officer and the qualifications for the position have been defined.

5. It is recommended:-
   (a) that a licensed Airport Traffic Control Officer be appointed at St. Hubert Airport and that the airport management at Vancouver, Edmonton and Winnipeg be requested to take similar action. If they cannot arrange for this, the Department should assume the responsibility.
   (b) that the necessary signal lamp should be installed at each airport. Estimated cost - $200.00.

(c) that radio equipment for this purpose should be installed and put in operation. The type of set is as follows:-
A low-powered 15-30 Watt 278 Kc. voice transmitter and sufficient receivers to monitor 3105-6210, 3212-5 and all other frequencies assigned to commercial aircraft. - $1300.00.

6. A staff of four men would be required to give a 24-hour service, but at present congestion is only acute at certain periods of the day and not more than two Control Officers should be necessary at any one airport, though as number of schedule grows, the number of Control Officers will have to be increased.

J.A. Wilson,
Controller of Civil Aviation.

APPENDIX 25

Radio Broadcast by the Minister of National Defence, March 1934, Dealing with the Development of Civil Aviation in Canada

(The following is an extract from a radio broadcast by the Honourable D.M. Sutherland, Minister of National Defence, in March 1934, dealing with development of Civil Aviation in Canada and particularly the Trans-Canada Airway. This extract deals only with the transatlantic air route. It is from the Public Archives of Canada, MG30 E243, Vol. 17.)

From a domestic point of view, therefore, the construction and operation of the Trans-Canada airway, as soon as financial conditions permit, would appear to be vital to the preservation, in Canadian hands, of such valuable high speed traffic across our country. Moreover, the Trans-Canada airway cannot be considered solely as a domestic problem. It is an integral part of a world wide system of fast communication and transportation. The shortest routes from the North American continent to both Europe and Asia lie through Canadian territory. The Trans-Atlantic and Trans-Pacific airways of the future are, therefore, of vital importance to us. These routes, together with the Trans-Canada airway, are the three great links still awaiting organization in the world airway system.

The North Atlantic trade route is perhaps the most important in the world. It joins the greatest centres of industry in the old and new worlds, the one lying in north western Europe, including the British Isles, and the other between the Basin of the Great Lakes and the St. Lawrence River and the northern Atlantic coast of the United States. Here, if anywhere, will be found traffic of sufficient value and quantity and with the need for high speed to justify the establishment of commercial air lines. Its eastern and western terminals lie in the British Commonwealth and from the earliest days of aviation the Canadian Government has watched its development with growing interest.

The first regular air mail service operated by the Canadian Government was from Rimouski to Montréal. This service was instituted in 1927 to hasten incoming and outgoing Trans-Atlantic mails. It was the first step towards Trans-Atlantic flying. A further step was taken in 1932, during the Imperial Economic Conference, when the Rimouski service was extended to Belle Isle and operated successfully for some weeks. By this extension, 1/3 of the total journey from Montréal to London was made by air and a 4 day mail service from London to Montréal was given. Recent re-examination of the possibilities of this route indicates the practicability of a 3 1/2 day mail service from London to Montréal. These combined air-streamer services are important steps towards the final solution of a Trans-Atlantic air service of immense potentialities to Canada.

The Pacific crossing is not of the same urgency or importance as the Atlantic crossing and has not received the same attention. Unsettled conditions in the Far East have made practical proposals for its development impossible but the extension of European air lines to the Far East will greatly affect important Canadian lines of communication and will, before many years pass, force this route into prominence for the protection of Canadian and American interests in Trans-Pacific commerce. The most efficient route lies through Canada and our interests in it must be safeguarded.

——————

History repeats itself and, just as our transcontinental railways serve as links in a system reaching across the Atlantic and Pacific through the steamship services and making connections to all parts of the world, so will the Trans-Canada airway, when completed, make connections, not only with the airways in the United States but with the world system of airways which is being built up on all continents. Improved means of transportation and communication have, from the very earliest days, been the pre-occupation of successive Canadian Governments, with the result that today, in our railways, in our steamship services on the Atlantic and Pacific; in our telegraph and telephone systems; in our radio; we hold a position and reputation for high standards of service which is unsurpassed. These services have been pioneered by Canadians. The first Trans-Atlantic steamship crossing was made by a Canadian ship; the telephone was invented in Brantford, Ontario; Canada was the first country to organize her coastal wireless in aid of marine navigation. Experience has shown that we can count on Canadians to duplicate this leadership in the air. The first British subject to fly an aeroplane was a Canadian, and the first aeroplane to fly within the Empire was flown by a Canadian in Canada.

When the Trans-Canada airway is completed, it will bring about a revolution comparable in our generation to that achieved by the Fathers of Confederation in the building of the Intercolonial and Canadian Pacific Railways. Improved communications made possible the Confederation of the scattered British colonies into the Dominion, as we know it. By air, within a few years, Vancouver will be as near Montréal as Toronto now is, Halifax will be no further in time from Toronto than Windsor now is. Winnipeg will be eight hours or less distant from Toronto, Ottawa and Montréal. Many of our present day difficulties arise from the separation of our different communities. Air transport will bridge the distances and bring all parts of the Dominion into closer relation by means of fast, comfortable and relatively cheap communication.

APPENDIX 26
Memorandum to the Deputy Minister from the Controller of Civil Aviation regarding Airway Development Maritime Provinces to Montréal
(Public Archives Canada, MG 30 E243, Vol. 10

November 27th, 1931
Airway Development
Maritime Provinces - Montréal
D.M.

1. When the appropriations for the coming fiscal year are under consideration, it is strongly urged that special study be given to the continuance of airway construction and the air mail service in the Maritime Provinces and thence to Montréal. These services not only provide improved internal communications but are the initial steps in the development of the western terminals of the world's most important airway.

2. The air operations of the past two years by

French, German and United States interests, with the support of their Governments, foreshadow coming developments and are evidence that the great powers of the world are alive to the important position our Atlantic Coast hold in relation to the trans-Atlantic route of the future.

3. A considered policy in regard to Canada's part in the development of this airway is urgently necessary. A decision in regard to this need not involve any large expenditures in the near future but it will define the objective towards which the Department should aim and all work undertaken in the region may then be fitted into the general plan.

4. The importance of a connection between Montréal, Halifax and St. John was early recognized and during the winter season of navigation of 1927-28 an experimental service was operated by the R.C.A.F. In spite of the total lack of ground facilities the results proved that, given adequate aerodromes, housing facilities for aircraft, communications and weather services, this service could be successfully operated. During the winter of 1929-30 a contract was let by the Post Office Department for the conveyance of mails to and from ocean steamers between Halifax and Montréal. The satisfactory results obtained led to this service being made a daily connection as far as Moncton, which was continued with constantly increasing efficiency until June, 1931, when it was cancelled in the interest of economy.

5. The position of the North Atlantic crossing in the commerce of the world is recognized by all trading nations. It had been studied in pre-war days by both British and American interests and in August, 1914, when wabroke out, preparations were actually under way for a trans-Atlantic flight by a flying boat, under the command of Lieutenant John Porte, R.N.,

from Newfoundland to Ireland. The first of the great succession of pioneer flights to every part of the world which have been made since the Armistice were the crossing of the North Atlantic, by Alcock and Brown, in an aeroplane, and the return flight by H.M. Airship R.34, during the summer of 1919. United States Naval Flying Boats also made the flight via Newfoundland and the Azores the same year and several other attempts were made. Interest in trans-Atlantic flying lapsed for some years but was revived again when Lindbergh made a flight in May, 1927, and since then the route has been chosen by a great majority of trans-Atlantic fliers, many of whom have stopped in the Maritime Provinces en route. These pioneer flights had no commercial significance but they foreshadowed coming developments.

6. The first commercial attempt to shorten the north Atlantic passage by the help of aircraft was the catapulting of seaplanes from the French liners off Halifax during the summer of 1930. These efforts were repeated during the past summer by similar flights from the North German Lloyd liners "Bremen" and "Europa" by the Deutsche Lufthansa.

   The mail was actually delivered in New York on one of these flights in three days and seventeen hours, beating the record by fully 24 hours.

7. Had the consequence of the cancelling of the Montréal - Moncton air mail service been realized in June, it is probable that more mature consideration would have been given before the decision was made. It was not then known that the United States were interested in the immediate development of the northern route. During the fall of 1930, they had endeavoured to arrange, in cooperation with British and French interests, and had offered a large subsidy for a trans-Atlantic

crossing from Northfolk, Va., via Bermuda, the Azores and Portugal. These negotiations had failed but this was not then acknowledged. The United States then turned their attention to the northern route and as soon as the Canadian Government cancelled the Maritime Province Services they stepped into the breach.

8. Mr. Glover, Assistant Postmaster General, in charge of air mail operations, visited Ottawa on behalf of Pan-American Airways Inc., and a contract was immediately let by his Department to it for a daily service from Boston, Portland, St. John and Halifax, with the option of extending this to Sydney and St. John's, Newfoundland. The service commenced on August 1st and continued until September 30th. The period of the contract is for 10 years and a subsidy of $2.00 per mile flown is paid for the service. It is let subject to the concurrence of the Canadian Government.

9. Had any Canadian mail service been in operation in the Maritime Provinces these proposals would have been met by counter proposals from Canadian interests for an exchange of traffic with the proposed American service at some point convenient to the border. The Canada Government would also have been in a position to represent to Washington that the proposed contract with Pan-American Airways was, in effect, subsidizing an American company to operate in competition, in Canada, with Canadian operators. It may be stated, with confidence, that had there been any Canadian service, this contract would not have been let but that such an arrangement would have been made with Mr. Glover's cooperation.

10. The cities of St. John and Halifax have spent $190,000 and $225,000 respectively on their airports and are naturally most anxious to see

these used. With the withdrawal of the Canadian service they welcomed the advent of Pan-American Airways, whose organization is of a very high type. They use only the finest class of aircraft and their operating personnel are a particularly fine class of men. In the circumstances, it was almost impossible to oppose the proposals of Pan-American Airways to run a service to St. John and Halifax, as there was no alternative to offer. Pan-American Airways immediately asked for the right to construct their own wireless for inter-communication. This was refused on the ground that the service was only a temporary one and little inconvenience would be caused as, even if permission were granted, the stations could not be put in operation for some weeks. The reason underlying this refusal was undoubtedly the desire of the Canadian Government to prevent Pan-American Airways from establishing a vested interest through a large investment on the ground.

11. Pan-American Airways have stated their intention of running this service for five months, beginning June 1st, 1932. Whether they propose to extend it farther eastward to Sydney and St. John's, Nfld., this year is not known. It would be surprising, however, to find that this was not their intention. Pan-American Airways will, undoubtedly, extend their service as far as possible, as every mile flown undoubtedly means a handsome profit to them owing to the substantial subsidy of $2.00 a mile paid to them. Pan-American Airways will undoubtedly renew their requests to be allowed to install their own ground facilities in the way of wireless, or other communication services, to increase the efficiency of the route.

12. Proposals for the establishment of radio stations on the route will probably be made by a Canadian company formed for that purpose, with the financial backing of Pan-American Airways. It will be difficult to refuse any reasonable request for the establishment of aids to air navigation in the Maritime Provinces, as they are recognized as essential to the safe conduct of air transport services such as they intend to operate. The Government will be faced with the alternative of having to furnish these itself if it wishes to maintain full control or permit them to be established by a subsidiary of Pan-American Airways.

13. It must be evident that if Canada wishes to establish these important air lines through Canadian interests, it will be necessary to act in the immediate future. In spite of the events of last summer it is felt that it is not too late to intervene. If, during the coming Spring, the Canadian connection from Montréal to St. John, Moncton and Halifax is re-established and an offer made to exchange traffic with Pan-American Airways at some convenient point adjacent to the Canadian border, before any further expense is undertaken by them, the prospects of arriving at an agreement satisfactory to both parties are considered favourable. Last summer's operations were considered experimental and no great expenditures were involved. If the service is continued next year for five months this will not be the case and the vested interest Pan-American Airways in the route will be considerable.

14. Another important phase requires consideration. The permission granted to Pan-American Airways to operate in Canada did not give them the right to carry mail or passengers between Canadian points. This prohibition is in conformity with the international agreement covering flying arrived at by the two countries. The people of Halifax and St. John are only human and wish to travel and send mails by it. The train service between the two points involves a round about and tedious journey, whereas the flight, in fine weather, is a remarkably quick and pleasant one. The subsidy paid by the United States Government to Pan-American Airways enable low rates to be charged, comparable with the railway fares. The Boards of Trade of both cities have already made representations protesting against being debarred from its use and it is certain that this pressure on the Government will be continued and intensified.

15. If no Canadian service is offered, it will be difficult to continue to refuse permission to the people of the Maritime Provinces, who wish to travel by air, even if in foreign aircraft. If Pan-American Airways are given permission to participate in domestic traffic in Canada the principle that only Canadian registered aircraft may carry on commercial operations wholly within Canada will be infringed and a precedent will be set for the operation of similar services elsewhere. Many proposals have been received in recent years looking towards this end. For instance, Canadian Colonial Airways Limited, now operating into St. Hubert daily from New York, wish to be allowed to extend their service to Québec and Ottawa. The North Western Airways are anxious to extend their service from Chicago to Minneapolis into Winnipeg. Various American companies have at different times proposed to operate a triangular service on the Pacific Coast, Seattle, Vancouver and Victoria, but as two of the points are in Canada it has been reserved for a Canadian company to operate. Proposals have also been made for the extension of the American air mail service through Canada to Alaska. It will thus be seen that the problem has wide implications and is not purely a local matter.

16. The connection by air between Montréal and the Maritime Provinces and the operation of air services in these Provinces are important in their own merits and without considering the international problem involved. The following comparisons are of interest and show the saving of time.

Destination	Miles	Train Time	Air Time
Montréal-St. John	481	15.00	4.50
Montréal-Moncton	501	24.50	5.00
Montréal-Charlottetown	578	26.00	5.45
Montréal-Truro	586	29.25	5.50
Montréal-Halifax	637	31.25	6.25
Montréal-New Glasgow	621	36.00	6.20
Montréal-Sydney	744	44.40	7.30
Moncton-St.John	90	2.50	.55
Moncton-Charlottetown	110	6.35	.45
Moncton-New Glasgow	123	6.35	1.15
Moncton-Sydney	246	15.15	2.30
Halifax-New Glasgow	86	2.35	.55
Halifax-Sydney	211	12.35	2.05
Halicax-St.John	156	9.40	1.30

Note:

The time by air is calculated on the air route miles, not the direct line of flight between the cities. In fine weather, the direct route may be taken on many of these flights, with a still greater saving of time.

17. The people in the Maritime Provinces are rapidly becoming airminded. This is proved by the establishment of airports in the principal cities and towns. There has been a remarkable change in the situation during the past two years and it is safe to say no part of the Dominion is more interested today in the extension of the Canadian air mail routes. The whole situation should receive most earnest consideration as a matter of national mo-

ment and having a vital bearing on our future.

18. The efforts made by this Department and the Post Office Department since 1927 to develop our airways have centered on the realization that the intercontinental airways leading from North America to Europe and Asia should pass over Canada. If Canada is prepared to play her part in this development her interests in the future airways of the world will be safe guarded. No passive policy will suffice, however, we must be prepared to keep pace with world progress. When fully established in the course of years there is no doubt that these airways will be used by aircraft of all nationalities and that an increased stream of valuable passenger, freight and mail traffic will move by air. If Canada participates in the development, Canadian terminals for this important traffic can be secured. It is significant that today all over the world, bullion and interest bearing documents move by air as the safest and quickest way. If Montréal can secure the terminal of the trans-Atlantic service, rather than New York, it may have a great bearing on our future financial position in the world.

J.A. Wilson
Controller of Civil Aviation.

APPENDIX 27

Press Notice issued by the Government of Canada on meeting with the Government of Newfoundland regarding the Conference of Transatlantic Air Services
(Public Archives Canada, MG 30 E243, Vol. 7)

Ottawa, Ont.,
November 6th, 1933
The Government of Canada shares the satisfaction expressed by the Prime Minster of New-

foundland over the results achieved at the Conference on trans-Atlantic air services held at his invitation in St. John's, Newfoundland, last July.

The agreements reached at the St. John's Conference are the direct outcome of the recommendations of a committee which met in Ottawa at the time of the Economic Conference in August, 1932, at the invitation of the Canadian Government. At that time, representatives of Great Britain, the Irish Free State, Newfoundland and Canada met to discuss the problem of trans-Atlantic air services in which they were all directly interested, and it was agreed that they should mutually cooperate by the frank interchange of full information and should work together, as conditions necessitated, in any development which might be found expedient.

At the Conference in St. John's in July last, important interests from the United States of America were also represented and a definite and concrete agreement was made with the consent of all parties for continued cooperation. Subject to ratification by the legislature of Newfoundland, certain rights in their territory for the construction and operation of air bases and air navigation facilities were granted to British interests. Under the agreement Canada may participate in the development and Pan American Airways, representing the interest of the United States, may be given the right to fly over any route established. The control of the bases and air navigation facilities will, however, remain exclusively British.

Important plans are now under consideration to take advantage of the privileges which have been arranged and it is hoped that the resources of all may be brought into friendly cooperation and destructive competition avoided.

The Government of Canada has made no commitment in respect to the operation of a trans-Atlantic service by any other route and any rumours to this effect are without foundation.

The day has not yet arrived when the Atlantic ocean may be flown with any regularity by commercial aircraft and until the aircraft and facilities for this are available the practical course, while fully safeguarding Canada's interests on all possible routes, is to improve communications between Montréal and the Atlantic seaboard, where connections may be made with the present steamer services which will greatly expedite the dispatch of mails to and from Europe by Canadian routes. Such practical developments will represent a step towards the eventual solution of the problem of trans-Atlantic flying and the experience gained in their operation will also help materially.

APPENDIX 28
Dominions Office Dispatch regarding plans for Transatlantic Air Service
(Public Archives Canada, MG 30 E243, Vol. 8)

Downing Street,
August 9th, 1935

NO. 320
CONFIDENTIAL
THE SECRETARY OF STATE
FOR EXTERNAL AFFAIRS,
CANADA.
Sir:

His Majesty's Government in the United Kingdom have been giving prolonged consideration to the problem of establishing an air service for the carriage of mails and passengers by heavier than air aircraft across the North Atlantic between England and Canada and the United States at the earliest possible date. They are now in a position to inform His Majesty's Government in Canada of the results of their preliminary enquiry, and to seek their assistance and cooperation in the organization of the necessary plans.

2. A careful review has been made of the various technical methods which are at present available, or are capable of being immediately developed, for operating the service (aerodromes, catapulting devices, refuelling in the air, composite aircraft, etc.), and the provisional conclusion has been reached that, while progress with these alternative methods which in some cases offer practical possibilities for the future must be watched and encouraged, plans for trans-Atlantic flying must for the time being be based on the use of flying boats. It is however proposed, as mentioned in paragraph 6 below, that an experiment should also be made with landplanes.

3. In view of the technical aspects of the problem, it is thought that attention must be concentrated on two routes, namely, the direct route via Ireland and Newfoundland and the southern route via the Azores and Bermuda.

Apart from other considerations, it is recognized that the former route has the great advantage that it could be linked direct to the trans-Canada route, but on the information at present available there is some doubt whether it could be maintained for more than perhaps six months in the year, at any rate during the early stages of the service in view of the adverse weather, ice formation and the state of the harbours in winter in Newfoundland. The southern route is generally favoured with better weather but it is considerably longer, and difficulties may be encountered in negotiating landing rights in the Azores.

It is not possible at present to indicate the precise extent to which one or other of these routes may be used. The decision must necessarily be influenced by the results of preliminary experimental flights and by meteorological and wireless investigations.

4. Questions connected with the design and construction of aircraft suitable for the trans-Atlantic service have been under detailed consideration by an Air Ministry Committee, and special steps are being taken to expedite the completion of two civil flying boats fitted with special tanks so as to afford adequate range. It is hoped that these two boats will be completed in the spring of 1936 so as to enable training and experimental flights to be carried out in the summer of that year. A suitable flying boat will also be made available by the Royal Air Force for preliminary training of personnel.

5. The Air Ministry Committee are also considering the design of a larger and more powerful flying boat, a number of which it is hoped may be ready in 1937 for the purpose of inaugurating a regular mail and passenger service. All steps possible will be taken to expedite the delivery of these boats.

6. Although as already stated it is thought here that at the present stage of aeronautical progress flying boats afford the best prospect for the successful development of trans-Atlantic air communications, it is proposed, in addition, to construct two experimental long-distance land planes in order to test out this alternative method of transportation, and it is hoped that they will be ready for service early in 1937.

7. In order that the necessary ground organization may be put in hand without delay, a preliminary survey is being immediately undertaken by Air Ministry experts to locate suitable bases in Newfoundland for use by both flying boats and land planes.

8. It is also thought necessary to take further steps, in consultation with His Majesty's Government in Canada, for collecting meteorological data in Newfoundland concerning viability and upper winds.

It is hoped that it will be possible also to arrange for the establishment of a meteorological forecasting station in Newfoundland by 1937, in readiness for the regular service. It is clearly desirable that arrangements should be made without delay for the necessary preliminary training of the staff for these stations and for the study to commence at once of the meteorological conditions of the whole route.

Discussions are proceeding with a view to the establishment of a meteorological station in Ireland (probably in the Irish Free State) for the service, and the question of the necessary re-organization and expansion of the Bermuda meteorological station is also receiving attention.

Canadian co-operation in the organization of the aforementioned facilities would, of course, be very welcome and it is also proposed that the opportunity should be taken of the forthcoming conference of Empire meteorologists in London to discuss the scientific problems involved in providing an adequate meteorological organization for the service.

9. The question of the provision of the necessary wireless facilities for the service is being closely studied.

The erection of suitable wireless stations in Newfoundland and in Ireland (probably in the Irish Free State) is clearly desirable. An expansion of the Bermuda wireless service is about to be undertaken in connection with the proposed Bermuda/New York air service to be inaugurated in the summer of 1936, and it should not be difficult to equip the station there suitably for the purpose of the larger service.

In the meantime research into the problems of short-wave wireless direction-finding is being prosecuted with energy, and in due course it is proposed to install experimental equipment of this kind at Bermuda for practical tests with aircraft in regular service as soon as the Bermuda/New York service has been established.

10. Apart from the problems involved in the actual establishment of the service, the question of the arrangements in regard to the mail to be entrusted to it will require close consideration by the authorities concerned. There will obviously be no prospect of the service being able, in 1937 or immediately afterwards, to carry the whole mail. It will probably be necessary in the beginning to impose a surcharge for air mails carried between the United Kingdom and Canada, and it may be possible to supplement this mail with other surcharged mails between the United States and the United Kingdom (and the Continent of Europe).

11. His Majesty's Government in the United Kingdom are anxious to discuss all aspects of the problem with His Majesty's Government in Canada with a view to agreeing upon the details of operating and financial co-operation between the two Governments in the organization of a through service between this country and Canada. Discussion will, of course, also be desirable with the Government of the United States with regard to the United States aspect of the problem. His Majesty's Government in the United Kingdom would accordingly propose that senior representatives of the Air Ministry and of the General Post Office should visit North America in the autumn of this year for the purpose of such discussion with the Canadian and United States Governments at as early a date as may be convenient to His Majesty's Government in Canada. As regards the United States aspect of the matter, it would appear expedient that the visit should be made as soon as possible as apart, from other considerations, it is understood that some conversations have been proceeding between the United States and the French Governments and it is obviously desirable to reach agreement with the United States Government before these conversations have proceeded too far.

It should be added that preliminary discussions with regard to co-operation also on the part of the Irish Free State authorities have been commenced, and there is reason to hope that such co-operation will be forthcoming in this service.

12. As regards the actual operation of the service, His Majesty's Government in the United Kingdom feel it essential to entrust so very important an undertaking to a company of tried experience and proved technical efficiency, and therefore they contemplate, so far as this country is concerned, entrusting to Imperial Airways Limited (or to an organization formed in association with that Company for the special purpose) the development of the service on terms and conditions which will be for future negotiation and discussion. For this reason it will probably be found convenient that a representative of Imperial Airways Limited should accompany the Government representatives on their visit to North American this autumn.

Co-operation between Imperial Airways Limited and Pan-American Airways Incorporated for the operation of a trans-Atlantic service to and from the United States on both the routes mentioned in paragraph 3 above has been envisaged by both companies for some time past and close liaison has been maintained between them, although no actual commitments have so far been entered into. This association appears to offer valuable prospects for securing for any service operated by Imperial Airways (or an associated organization) a satisfactory share of the United States mail and passenger traffic. The exact nature of the arrangements between the two Companies is obviously a matter requiring the most careful consideration and discussion by all concerned.

I have the honour to be,
Sir,
Your most obedient,
humble servant.
(signed) J.H. Thomas

APPENDIX 29
Technical Discussions on Transatlantic Air Services
(Public Archives Canada, MG 30 E243, Vol. 15)

Ottawa, November - 1935
Operating and Technical Sub-committee

Communications and Bases Section

1. Messrs. I. McClure, C.P. Edwards and J.A. Wilson met at 10:00 A.M. on November 25th to consider existing facilities in Canada and Newfoundland and the requirements for the experimental stage.

Radio

2. Radio communications were discussed with Mr. Woods Humphery. It was agreed that the present facilities were adequate for the experimental period, with the addition of a "comprehensive" station at Botwood, Newfoundland, which would be supplied and operated by the United Kingdom under arrangement with the Newfoundland authorities.

Base Facilities

3. It was agreed, Mr. Woods Humphery concurring, that the only essential installations at the bases at Botwood and Montréal were adequate moorings. Drawings and specifications would be supplied by the United Kingdom for those required at Montréal so that they might be provided by Canadian authorities. The moorings at Botwood would be supplied by the United Kingdom under arrangement with the Newfoundland authorities. Motor boat tenders would also be required at these bases. It was considered that the tender now available at the Fairchild Company's seaplane base would be adequate for the experimental period. Mr. Woods Humphery stated that if the Canadian Government wished the flying boat to visit other cities in Canada, such as Ottawa and Toronto, this could be arranged. Provision would, in that case, be necessary for mooring and tenders.

Canadian Base

4. Mr. A.D. McLean discussed seaplane bases in detail with Mr. Woods Humphery and Mr. McClure. Charts of the landing areas at Montréal, Ottawa and Toronto were examined and found to provide suitable areas. Mr. McClure has also visited St. Hubert and seen the landing areas at Montréal and Ottawa.

Communications Section

1. With the addition of one comprehensive long wave, short wave and direction finding radio station to be established by the United Kingdom authorities at Botwood, Nfld., the radio communication facilities now established and operated by Canada in Newfoundland and along the route to Montréal are regarded as adequate to provide first class communication with the plane during the test flights.

2. It may be necessary to place an extra operator on one or two of the stations during the actual flight period, in order to provide uninterrupted radio watch, and it may also be necessary to arrange for a station for "homing" purposes at Québec. This, however, can be done without involving any capital expenditure.

3. Subject to further discussions with the officers of the Air Ministry, the communication set-up contemplates the plane establishing communication on short wave with Botwood, Nfld., immediately after leaving Ireland. Botwood, in turn, will maintain communication on short wave with the airport at Montréal and with Ottawa.

4. The plane when approaching within five or six hundred miles of Newfoundland can secure accurate bearings from the Marine direction finding stations at Belle Isle and Cape Race and when approaching Botwood, Nfld., should be able to make use of the direction finding station at St. Paul for cross bearings.

5. On leaving Botwood, the plane will maintain constant communication with the short wave station at the airport in Montréal.

6. In addition, the chain of marine "aid to navigation" coast stations along the Gulf, approximately 200 miles apart, will give the plane local communication, and if she is equipped with a direction finder, she can make good use of the marine automatic radio beacon system which is operated along the St. Lawrence waterway.

7. Should the plane be fitted with a "homing device", arrangements can be made for existing stations at certain strategical points to give this service.

8. It is suggested that the Air Ministry or Imperial Airways Officer-in-Charge of radio for the experimental flights, might, with advantage, visit Canada, prior to the first flight, to discuss all the details of the communication

set-up in order that there may be complete coordination in this reference.

APPENDIX 30
Conditions of the United Kingdom Permit to
Pan American Airways to operate
Transatlantic Service
(Newfoundland Archives 570/35)

Pan American Airways is granted permission to fly into, through and away from the United Kingdom, Newfoundland and Bermuda, for the purpose of conducting a civil air transport service for the carriage of passengers, goods and mail between the United States and the United Kingdom via Newfoundland or Bermuda, and other countries, for a period of fifteen years from the first day of May, 1936, under the following conditions:

(a) That the number of round trips by Pan American Airways shall not exceed two per week, unless additional services are authorized by the Governments concerned.

(b) That the service terminates in the United Kingdom at a customs airport serving London and used by Imperial Airways, or a company in which Imperial Airways has a controlling interest, as the terminal for their reciprocal transatlantic service, at which terminal Pan American Airways may land for the purpose inter alia of picking up and discharging passengers, goods and mail.

(c) That Pan American Airways conforms to all air navigation regulations laid down by the authorities at ports in the United Kingdom and, to the extent and when applicable, in Newfoundland and Bermuda, and to all applicable regulations and statutes in force in the United Kingdom, Newfoundland and Bermuda.

(d) That Pan American Airways conforms to the airworthiness requirements specified by the United States Government for a United States international air service.

(e) That Pan American Airways agrees to carry, and carries, if tendered by the Postal Administrations of the United Kingdom (and the Irish Free State when the service is operated through the Irish Free State) up to 50% (but in no event more than Imperial Airways carries) of the total of the westbound trans-Atlantic surcharged air mail (including closed pouch mail) as is tendered by the Postal Administrations of the United Kingdom (and the Irish Free State when the service is operated through the Irish Free State), within a limit of capacity of 800 lbs., per flight, or such greater weight as may be mutually agreed; and further provided that when operating the service via the Irish Free State and Newfoundland, Pan American Airways may not accept westbound trans-Atlantic mails other than those tendered by the United Kingdom and the Irish Free State Governments.

The foregoing agreements of Pan American in paragraph (e) are subject:

1. To Imperial Airways agreeing to carry reciprocally, and carrying, if tendered by the United States Postal Administration, up to 50% (but in no event more than Pan American Airways carries) of the total eastbound transatlantic surcharged air mail of the United States, including closed pouch mail, other than closed pouch mails of Canada, Newfoundland and Bermuda, and British Colonies in the Caribbean area including the Bahamas, British Honduras, Jamaica, Trinidad, the Windward and Leeward Islands, Barbados and British Guiana, (hereinafter termed British closed pouch mails) within a limit of capacity of 800 lbs. per flight, or

such greater weight as may be mutually agreed.

The above reciprocal services shall be performed by Imperial Airways and Pan American Airways under bilateral arrangements made between Imperial Airways and Pan American Airways.)

2. To the Governments of Canada, Newfoundland and Bermuda agreeing to tender and tendering to Pan American Airways approximately 50% of all eastbound Canadian, Newfoundland and Bermuda trans-Atlantic surcharged air mails, at carriage rates to be mutually agreed upon.

3. To the Governments concerned agreeing to tender and tendering to Pan American Airways at the United States terminus of the trans-Atlantic route approximately 50% of the eastbound trans-Atlantic British closed pouch mails referred to in paragraph (e) above, at carriage rates to be mutually agreed upon.

(f) That Pan American Airways may carry passengers, goods and mail between any of the territories traversed, except local traffic between the United Kingdom and the Irish Free State, and that Pan American Airways may land, for the purpose of inter alia or picking up and discharging passengers, goods and mail, at designated ports of call in Newfoundland or Bermuda, as the case may be, being the same ports of call used by Imperial Airways Ltd., or a company in which Imperial Airways Ltd., has a controlling interest, for its reciprocal trans-Atlantic service.

(g) That Imperial Airways, or a company in which Imperial Airways has a controlling interest, is authorized concurrently by the United States Government for a similar period of fifteen years to conduct a similar reciprocal civil air transport service of the same frequency of two round trips per week for the carriage of passengers goods and mails between any of the territories traversed on the route between the United Kingdom and the United States, using as the Western Terminal of the transatlantic route a customs port serving New York City and any other ports of call in the United States used by Pan American Airways for their reciprocal trans-Atlantic service.

(h) That if the above reciprocal rights to be accorded to Imperial Airways or a company in which Imperial Airways has a controlling interest, by the United States Government lapse, the above rights granted to Pan American Airways by the Governments of the United Kingdom, Newfoundland and Bermuda will lapse simultaneously.

(i) Notwithstanding that this permit is valid for a period of fifteen years, the rights and privileges afforded herein to Pan American Airways shall not be available unless and until Imperial Airways, or a company in which Imperial Airways holds a controlling interest, shall operate its reciprocal scheduled trans-Atlantic service.

APPENDIX 31
Department of Transport Transatlant Air Service Permit to Pan American Airways
(Public Archives Canada, MG30 E243, Vol. 8)
NO. 30272

DEPARTMENT OF TRANSPORT PERMIT
From: MINISTER OF TRANSPORT
To: PAN AMERICAN AIRWAYS COMPANY

.

Date of Authorizing   PC284
   Order in Council ....February 10th, 1937.
Date of Permit ....March 5th, 1937.

Description: To fly into, through and away from the Dominion of Canada on a trans-Atlantic air transport service.
Beginning of Term .... May 1st, 1936.
End of Term .... April 30th, 1951.
Departmental Reference
       File No.   6416 (Civil Aviation)

PERMIT
From the Minister of Transport of the Dominion of Canada
To the Pan American Airways Company
TO FLY INTO, THROUGH AND AWAY FROM
THE DOMINION OF CANADA
ON A
TRANS-ATLANTIC AIR TRANSPORT SERVICE
ISSUED UNDER AUTHORITY OF ORDER-IN-COUNCIL
P.C. 284, DATED 10th OF FEBRUARY, 1937.

COPY
DEPARTMENT OF TRANSPORT
CANADA
Pan American Airways Company is granted permission to fly into, through and away from the Dominion of Canada, for the purpose of conducting a civil air transport service for the carriage of passengers, goods and mail, between the United States and the United Kingdom, via Newfoundland and other countries, for a period of fifteen years from the first day of May 1936, under the following conditions:-

(a) That the number of round trips by Pan American Airways Company shall not exceed two per week, unless additional services are authorized by the Government concerned.

(b) That the said service via Newfoundland shall call at a suitable port in Canadian territory designated by the Government of Canada, such as shall neither reduce the efficiency,

regularity and reliability of this service, nor unduly increase the cost, or at Montréal (preference being given to the latter, operating conditions and other factors being equal), with authority to pick up and discharge passengers, cargo and mail to or from points on the route outside of the Dominion of Canada.

(c) That Pan American Airways Company conforms to all air navigation regulations laid down by the authorities at the Port of call in the Dominion of Canada, and to all applicable regulations and statutes in force in the Dominion of Canada.

(d) That Pan American Airways Company conforms to the airworthiness requirements specified by the United States Government for a United States international air service.

(e) That notwithstanding that this permit is valid for a period of fifteen years, the rights and privileges afforded herein shall not be available unless and until the Government of the United Kingdom issues a permit to Pan American Airways Company to operate a civil air transport service across the North Atlantic Ocean between the United Kingdom and the United States via Newfoundland, and this permit shall lapse if and when the said permit from the Government of the United Kingdom lapses.

Dated at the City of Ottawa, in the Province of Ontario and Dominion of Canada, this fifth day of March, One Thousand Nine Hundred and thirty seven.

                    C.D. Howe
                Minister of Transport
            for the Dominion of Canada.

SEAL

APPENDIX 32
List of Department of Transport Officials Responsible for the British Commonwealth Air Training Plan Aerodrome Program

J.A. Wilson	Director of Civil Aviation
A.D. McLean	Superintendent of Airways of the Civil Aviation Division. He was in charge of the detailed execution of all work undertaken by Department of Transport for the Plan. He had a great deal of experience in aviation, having been a pilot in the First World War, and made the original aerodrome selections for the Trans-Canada Airway in the prairie provinces during 1929 and 1930. Later, McLean was responsible for the airport planning and construction on the Trans-Canada Airway elsewhere in Canada.

The selection of the airport sites and their survey was the responsibility of the District Airway Inspectors:

W.S. Lawson	Western District - British Columbia and Alberta
J.R. Robertson	Central District - Saskatchewan and Manitoba
S.S. Foley	Ontario District
S. Graham and E. Hickson	Québec and Maritime Provinces

Engineering and Construction

G.L. McGee	As Chief Airway Engineer, he was responsible for development and expansion of existing aerodromes brought into the BCATP. This was to ensure continuity of work on the Trans-Canada Airway.
F.C. Jewett	He had just finished the construction of the Newfoundland Airport (Gander), one of the largest in the world", and was placed in charge of a new organization formed to design and build the new aerodromes required for the BCATP.
A.B. Holland	He was Jewett's assistant, and formerly assistant Chief Engineer in Airways Section.

The field work came under the existing District Airway Engineers, most of whom had had long experience in such work under Department of Transport:

F. Proctor	British Columbia
A.L. Somerville	Alberta
T. Chillcott	Saskatchewan
E.F. Cooke	Manitoba
G.W. Smith	Souther Ontario
A.B. Flintoff	Eastern Ontario
O.L. Colborne	Québec
A.S. Donald	Maritime provinces

Source:

J.A. Wilson, "Aerodrome Construction for the British Commonwealth Air Training Plan 1940" *Development of Aviation in Canada* 1879-1948, (Ottawa: King's Printer) pp. 28 and 29.

APPENDIX 33
List of British Commonwealth Air Training Plan Schools and Aerodromes

Elementary Flying Training Schools

1. Malton, Ontario
2. Fort William, Ontario
3. London, Ontario
4. Windsor Mills, Québec
5. Lethbridge - High River, Alberta
6. Prince Albert, Saskatchewan
7. Windsor, Ontario
8. Vancouver, British Columbia
9. St. Catharines, Ontario
10. Hamilton - Pendleton, Ontario
11. Cap de la Madeleine, Québec
12. Goderich, Ontario
13. St. Eugene, Ontario
14. Portage la Prairie, Manitoba
15. Regina, Saskatchewan
16. Edmonton, Alberta
17. Stanley, Nova Scotia
18. Boundary Bay, B.C.
19. Virden, Manitoba
20. Oshawa, Ontario
21. Chatham, New Brunswick
22. Québec City, Québec
23. Davidson, Saskatchewan
24. Abbotsford, British Columbia
31. De Winton, Alberta
32. Bowden, Alberta
33. Caron, Saskatchewan
34. Assiniboia, Saskatchewan
35. Neepawa, Manitoba
36. Pearce, Alberta
38. Davison, Saskatchewan

Service Flying Training Schools

1. Camp Borden, Ontario
2. Ottawa, Ontario
3. Calgary, Alberta
4. Saskatoon, Saskatchewan
5. Brantford, Ontario
6. Dunnville, Ontario
7. MacLeod, Alberta
8. Moncton, New Brunswick
9. Summerside, Prince Edward Island
10. Dauphin, Manitoba
11. Yorkton, Saskatchewan
12. Brandon, Manitoba
13. St. Hubert, Québec
14. Aylmer, Ontario

15	Claresholm, Albert	
16	Hagerville, Ontario	
17	Souris, Manitoba	
18	Gimli, Manitoba	
19	Vulcan, Alberta	
31	Kingston, Ontario	
32	Moose Jaw, Saskatchewan	
33.	Carberry, Manitoba	
34	Medicine Hat, Alberta	
35	North Battleford, Saskatchewan	
36	Penhold, Alberta	
37	Calgary, Alberta	
38	Estevan, Saskatchewan	
39	Swift Current, Sawkatchewan	
41	Weyburn, Saskatchewan	

Bombing & Gunnery Schools

1   Jarvis, Ontario
2   Mossbank, Saskatchewan
3   MacDonald, Manitoba
4   Fingal, Ontario
5   Dafoe, Saskatchewan
6   Mountain View, Ontario
7   Paulson, Manitoba
8   Lethbridge, Alberta
9   Mont Joil, Québec
10   Mount Pleasant, Prince Edward Island
31   Picton, Ontario

Air Observers Schools

1   Malton, Ontario
2   Edmonton, Alberta
3   Regina, Saskatchewan - Pearce, Alberta
4   London, Ontario
5   Winnipeg, Manitoba
6   Prince Albert, Saskatchewan
7   Portage la Prairie, Manitoba
8   Québec City, Québec
9   St. Johns, Québec
10   Chatham, New Brunswick - Davidson, Saskatchewan

Air Navigation Schools

1   Trenton, Ontario - Rivers, Manitoba
2   Pennfield Ridge, New Brunswick
    Charlottetown, Prince Edward Island
3   Estevan, Saskatchewan
4   Swift Current, Saskatchewan
31   Port Alberta, Ontario
32   Charlottetown, Prince Edward Island
33   Hamilton, Ontario
    Mount Hope, Ontario

Flying Instructors Schools

1   Trenton, Ontario
2   Vulcan - Pearce, Alberta
3   Amprior, Ontario

Instrument Flying School

1   Mohawk, Ontario

Naval Gunners School

1   Yarthmouth, Nowa Scotia

Central Flying School

1   Trenton, Ontario

General Reconnaissance School

1   Summerside, Prince Edward Island
31   Charlottetown, Prince Edward Island

Operational Training Units

1   Saguenay, Québec
3   Patricia Bay, British Columbia (also 32)
5   Boundary Bay, British Columnia,
6   Comox, British Columbia (also 32)

7	Debert, Nova Scotia (also 31)	
8	Greenwood, Nova Scotia (also 36)	
34	Pennfield Ridge, New Brunswick	

Source

W.R. Constable, Directorate of History, Department of National Defence, Ottawa, May 20, 1980.

Note:
(a) Numbers over 30 indicate RAF operated schools in BCATP.
(b) In 1940 the RAF training organization in the U.K. was about the size of the BCATP. After the fall of France, most of the RAF schools were moved to Canada, a total of twenty-six. The RAF schools became part of the BCATP, and six of the RAF EFTS were operated by Canadian Flying Clubs. (Source: F.J. Hatch,"The British Commonwealth Air Training Plan", *CAHS Journal*, Vol. 19, No. 4, Winter1981.)

APPENDIX 34
Subsidised Airports—1989

Airports owned by Transport Canada, operated by others and subsidised:

Campbell River	Hamilton
Charlo	Havre Saint-Pierre
Charlevoix	Kelowna
Chevery	Lourdes-de-Blanc Sablon
Cranbrook	Lynn Lake
Dauphin	Natashquan
Dawson Creek	Peace River
Dryden	Rouyn-Noranda
Flin Flon	Sudbury

Gaspé	Thompson	Dawson City	Ross River
Gillam			Faro
			Teslin

Airports owned and operated by others, and subsidised:

Brandon	Norway House
Chatham	Pembroke
Churchill Falls	Powell River
Fort Chipewyan	Prince Albert
Fort Frances	Rainbow Lake
Grand Forks	Toronto Island
Moosonee	

Subsidised Arctic Airports operated by the Government of Northwest Territories:

Aklavik	Igloolik
Broughton Island	Lac la Martre
Cape Dorset	Lake Harbour
Chesterfield Inlet	Pangnirtung
Clyde River	Paulatuk
Coppermine	Pelly Bay
Eskimo Point	Pond Inlet
Fort Franklin	Rae/Edzo
Fort Good Home	Rae lakes
Fort Liard	Rankin Inlet
Fort McPherson	Repulse bay
Fort Norman	Sachs Harbour
Fort Providence	Sanikiluzaq
Fort Resolution	Snowdrift
Gjoa Haven	Spence Bay
Grise Fiord	Whale Cove
Holman Island	Wrigley

Subsidised Arctic Sites operated by the Government of Yukon:

Beaver Creek	Haines Junction
Burwash	Mayo
Carmacks	Old Crow

Source:

Airports Group, Transport Canada

BIBLIOGRAPHY

Allen, Peter. *The 91 Before Lindberg Airlife.* England: 1984.

Alcock, John and A.W. Brown. *Our Transatlantic Flight.* London: William Kimber, 1969.

Airports in Canada and Newfoundland. Washington: U.S. Printing Office, 1930.

Bain, D.M. *Canadian Pacific Air Lines: Its History and Aircraft.* Calgary: Kisharn Publications, 1987.

Beaty, David. *The Water Jump: The Story of Transatlantic Flight.* New York: Harper & Row, 1976.

Biermann, Helmar. "Millidgeville—the Dream of a Great Airport". Atlantic Advocate, September, 1980.

Chajkowsky, W.E. *The Royal Flying Corps—den to Texas to Beamsville.* Ontario: The Boston Mills Press, 1979.

Department of Transport. *Annual Report, 1937.* Ottawa: Transport Canada, 1937.

"Directory of Canadian Airports", Canadian Aviation, December, 1937.

Dixon, Charles. *Conquest of the Atlantic by Air.* London: Sampson Low & Co., 1931.

Douglas, W.A.B. *The Creation of a National Air Force: the Official History of the Royal Canadian Air Force.* Ottawa: University of Toronto Press in cooperation with the Department of National Defence and the Canadian Government Publishing Centre, 1986.

Daley, Robert. *An American Saga—Juan Trippe and His Pan Am Empire.* New York: Random House, 1980.

Dzinban, Stanley W. *United States Army in World War II: Military Relations between United States and Canada 1939-1949.* Washington: Office of the Chief of Military History, Department of the Army, 1959.

"Documents on Relations between Canada and Newfoundland". Ottawa: Department of External Affairs, 1974.

Ellis, Frank H. *Canadian Flying Heritage.* Toronto: University of Toronto Press, 1954.

Ellis, Frank H. *In Canadian Skies: 50 Years of Adventure and Progress..* Toronto: The Ryerson Press, 1959.

Ellis, Frank H., and E. Ellis. *Atlantic Air Conquest.* Toronto: The Ryerson Press.

Fuller, G.A., J.A. Griffin, K.M. Molson. *125 Years of Canadian Aeronautics: A Cronology 1840-1965.* Willowdale: The Canadian Aviation HIstorical Society, 1983.

Greenway, K.R. "To the Top of the World by Airstrip". *CAHS Journal*, Fall, 1980, Willowdale.

Hatch, F.J. "Ship to Shore: Airmail Service of the 1920s". *Canadian Geographic*, Aug/Sept., 1978.

Hatch, F.J. *Aerodrome of Democracy - Canada and the British Commonwealth Air Training Plan 1939-1945.* Ottawa: Department of National Defence, Directorate of History Monograph Series No. 1, 1983.

Hatch, F.j. "The British Commonwealth Air Training Plan", *CAHS Journal*, Winter 1981, Willowdale.

Highways in the Air—The Story of British Airways. London: British Airways, 1979.

Halliday, Hugh. "Beamsville Story", *CAHS Journal*, Fall, 1969, Willowdale.

Higham, Robin. *British Air Routes, 1918-1939.* London, G.J. Foulia & Co. Ltd., 1960.

Higham, Robin and John Stroud. *Annals of British and Commonwealth Air Transport.* London: Putnam, 1962.

Griffin, J. and S. Kostenuk. *RCAF Squadrons and Aircraft.* Toronto: Samuel, Stevens, Hakkert & Co., 1977.

Long, C.D. "Toronto Airport before Malton", *CAHS Journal,* Winter, 1965, Willowdale.

Main, J.R.K. *Voyageurs of the Air—A History of Civil Aviation in Canada 1958-1967.* Ottawa: Department of Transport, Queen's Printer, 1967.

McArthur, Dr. Neil. *Airport and Community Report.* Ottawa: Transport Canada, 1965.

McDonough, Kenneth. *AtlanticWings1919-1939.* England: Model Aeronautical Press Ltd., 1966.

Milberry, Larry. *Aviation in Canada.* Toronto: McGraw-Hill Ryerson Ltd., 1979.

Molson, K.M. *Pioneering in Canadian Air Transport.* Winnipeg: James Richardson & Sons Ltd., 1978.

Molson, K.M., and H.A. Taylor, *Canadian Aircraft since 1909.* Stittsville: Canada Wings, 1982.

Myles, Eugenie Louise. *Airborne from Edmonton.* Toronto: The Ryerson Press, 1959.

Parsons, Bill with Bill Bowman. *The Challenge of the Atlantic.* Newfoundland: Robinson-Blackmare Book Publishers, 1983.

Powell, Air Commander Griffith, RAF. *Per Ardua ad Astra—A Story of the Atlantic Ferry.* Montréal: No. 45 Group, RAF, The Herald press Ltd., 1945.

Reports of the Air Board for 1920 to 1922. Ottawa: King's Printer.

Roberts, Leslie. *Canada's War in the Air.* Montréal: Alvah Beatty, 1943.

Rowe, Geoff. "Early Flying in Ottawa", *CAHS Journal,* Spring, 1969, Willowdale.

Scott-Chard, *T.E. 60 Years of British Airways Aircraft.* London: British Airways, 1979.

Stroud, John. *Airports of the World.* London: Putnam, 1980.

Sullivan, Lt. Alan. *Aviation in Canada 1917-18.* Toronto: Rous & Mann Ltd., 1919.

Sutherland, Alice Gibson. *Canada's Air Pioneers.* Toronto: McGraw-Hill Ryerson Ltd., 1978.

The Magnificent Distances—Early Aviation in British Columbia 1910-1940. (The Sound Heritage Series). Edited by Derek Reimer. Victoria: The Province of British Columbia, 1980.

Wilson, J.A. "Development of Aviation in Canada 1879-1948". Ottawa: Department of Transport, 1948.

Wise, S.F. *Canadian Armies in the First World War.* Toronto: University of Toronto Press, 1980.

INDEX

PHOTO CREDITS

The following abbreviations are used:

ACA	Air Canada Archives
CFPU	Canadian Forces Photo Unit
CGPC	Canadian Government Photo Centre
CIAA	Canadian Airlines International Archives
DND	Department of National Defence
GA	Glenbow Archives, Calgary
MA	Manitoba Archives
McG	T.M. McGarth
NAM	National Aviation Museum
NAPL	National Air Photo Library (Energy & Resources Canada)
NFB	National Film Board
NLM	Northern Life Museum, Fort Smith
NM	Newfoundland Museum
NRC	National Aeronautical Establishment
PAA	Provincial Archives of Alberta
PAC	Public Archives Canada
PANL	Public Archives of Newfoundland and Labrador
TC	Transport Canada
THCA	Toronto Harbour Commission Archives
VPL	Vancouver Public Library

Photo #	Source	Negative #
1	NAM	7113
2	CFPU	AH 416
3	PAC (Kelly.V)	PA - 122520
4	US Library of Congress	
5	PAC	PA - 61493
6	PAC	PA - 61488
7	CFPU	RE 19537-A
8	PAC (T.A.Lawrence)	PA - 114525
9	PAC	PA - 22776
10	PAC	PA - 22806
11	PAC	PA - 22835

Photo #	Source	Negative #
12	PAC (W.Gilbert Collection)	C 60443
13	CFPU	RE 14912
14	NAM	11563
15	PAC	PA 119432
16	CFPU	RE 15362
17	PAC (Stedman Collection)	PA 121884
18	PAC (Stedman Collection)	PA 121883
19	PAC (Stedman Collection)	PA 121880
20	NAM	1908
21	NAPL	A 4591-16
22	NAM	1901
23	PAC (Stedman Collection)	PA 121926
24	NAM	
25	NAM	4239
26	PAC (Stuart Graham Collection)	PA 89145
27	DND	RE 14901
28	via G.S. Pavornave& K.M. Molson	
29	CFPU	AH-322-1
30	PAC	PA 117836
31	McLeod via R.H. Crone	
32	PAC	PA 61997
33	via K.M. Molson	
34	PAC	
35	de Havilland Aircraft of Canada via F.W. Hotson	DHC 690
36	C.D. Long	
37	Walter Henry	
38	de Havilland Aircraft of Canada via F.W. Hotson	
39	W.F. Shaylor via F.W. Hotson	
40	via K.M. Molson	
41	PAC	PA 67202
42	NAPL	A-4591-10
43	R.T. Parsons	

Photo #	Source	Negative #	Photo #	Source	Negative #	Photo #	Source	Negative #
44	R.T. Parsons		78	George Wotton, Charlottetown		110	TC	
45	R.T. Parsons		79	McG		111	TC	
46	PAC	PA 127539	80	via Airport Manager		112	via TC	
	(W.E. Parsons Collection)		81	via Airport Manager		113	via TC	
47	CFPU	PMR 74-956	82	TC		114	PAA	A103/18
48	CFPU	PMR 74-957	83	PAC	C-57746	115	PAC	PA 126608
49	CFPU	PMR 74-962		(W.R. May Collection,			(Transport Canada Collection -	
50	CFPU	REA-260196		Photo by Bryon - May Co.)			Photo by RCAF)	
51	PAC	PA 125898	84	PAC	C-57589	116	NAPL	RA 16-14
	(J.A. Wilson Collection)			(W.R. May Collection)			via K.M. Molson	
52	PAC	PA 61568	85	PAC	PA 117865	117	PAC	C-61597
53	PAN L			(Johnson and Small)		118	TC	
54	PANL		86	PAA	A 11662	119	McG	
55	DND	PMR 74-961	87	NAM	B-1032	120	NFB	
56	PAC	PA 120774	88	PAA	BL-424/1	121	McG	
	(W.S. May Collection)		89	PAC	PA-126604	122	Airport Manager, Kelowna	
57	CFPU	PMR 74-884		(Transport Canada Collection)		123	Airport Mangaer, Kelowna	
58	CFPU	PMR 74-954	90	TC		124	TC	
59	PAC	PA 61570	91	PAC	PA-126599	125	PAC	C-38182
60	CFPU	PMR 74-955		(Transport Canada Collection -		126	TC	
61	TC			Photo - Bland, Edmonton Bulletin)		127	via Don McClure	
62	DND	PL 78069	92	TC		128	via Don McClure	
63	GA	N-16-625	93	NLM		129	via Don McClure	
64	GA	NA-3890-13	94	NLM (Photo - Father Laferte)		130	ACA	BB-1060-1
	(Miss Nora MacKie)		95	CAIA		131	CFPU	REA-160112
65	PAC	C-43001	96	PAA	PA 176/4	132	PAC	PA 126603
66	PAC	C-43967	97	TC			(Transport Canada Collection	
	(C. Beeching Collection)		98	F.F. Smeaton, Gander			Photo - Markow)	
67	NAPL	A-3507-29	99	via McG		133	TC	
68	NAPL	A-5737-68C	100	via McG		134	TC	
69	HYDE, Calgary Airport		101	via McG		135	TC	
70	HYDE, Calgary Airport		102	McG		136	PAC	C-24125
71	ACA	No. 6994	103	DND	PMR 74-973	137	ACA	
	(George Hunter Photo)		104	Photo by Air Commodore Griffith		138	ACA	
72	HYDE, Calgary Airport			Powell RAF - via T.M. McGrath		139	TC	
73	McG		105	NM		140	Robert Stuart	
74	PAC	PA-61985	106	PAC	C53112	141	PAC	59985
75	via K.M. Molson		107	Rex Tilley via T.M. McGrath		142	H. Hands via K.M. Molson	
76	NAM		108	TC		143	PAC	C-22735
77	PAC	PA 126628	109	CFPU	REA 25397	144	PAC	PA-125898
							(J.A. Wilson Collection)	

Photo #	Source	Negative #	Photo #	Source	Negative #	Photo #	Source	Negative #
145	Ottawa"Evening Citizen"		177	PAC	PA-61662	211	PAC	PA 126611
146	NRC		178	Saskatoon Star Phoenix			(Transport Canada Collection	
147	NFB (Ted Rand)			Photo S-	SPB3414-1		Photo - RCAF)	
148	TC		179	TC		212	Copyright - The Windsor Star	
149	TC		180	Copyright - Sault Star Photo		213	Copyright - The Windsor Star	
150	PAC	PA-70847	181	via Airport Manager		214	TC	
151	CFPU	REA-160-2	182	via Airport Manager		215	MA	N-1720
152	TC		183	via Airport Manager			(Foote Collection 120)	
153	R.McCombie via R.H. Crone		184	TC		216	via TC, Winnipeg	
154	PAC	PA-1199775	185	J.A. Smith Collection		217	Northwest Airways photo	
	(NFBCollection)			via K.M. Molson		218	via TC Winnipeg	
155	McG		186	PAC	PA-126607	219	TC	Slide 941-43
156	TC			(Transport Canada Collection		220	MA	
157	PAC	C-81888		Photo RCAF)			(Barbara Johnstone Collection)	
	(Romeo Vachon Collection)		187	TC		221	TC	
158	via J.P. Audaney and K.M. Molson		188	CGPC		222	TC	
159	TC		189	THCA		223	TC	
160	PAC	C-61658	190	THCA	PC 15/3/188			
161	PAC	PA 59962	191	THCA	PC 15/3/625			
162	via K.M. Molson		192	CGPC				
163	PAC	PA 119890	193	TC				
	(J.A. Wilson Collection-		194	TC				
	Photo by Goodyear Tire & Rubber Co.)		195	THCA	PC 1/1/9193			
164	CFPU	RE-20825-6	196	via C. Leavens and K.M. Molson				
165	via K.M. Molson		197	McG				
166	PAC	PA 117691	198	McG				
	(J.H. Tudhope Collection)		199	TC				
167	PAC	C-30884	200	via T.C. Vancouver				
168	PAC	PA-89142	201	VPL	3387-B			
	(S.Graham Collection)		202	PAC	PA-125900			
169	J.F. Sears via K.M. Molson			(J.A. Wilson Collection)				
170	TC		203	TC				
171	TC		204	VPL	41254			
172	PAC	PA-126612	205	TC				
	(Transport Canada Collection		206	via Airport Manger				
	Photo - RCAF)		207	CIAA				
173	TC		208	CIAA				
174	TC		209	McG				
175	via R.H. Crone		210	McG				
176	NAPL	A2229-70						

Printed in Canada